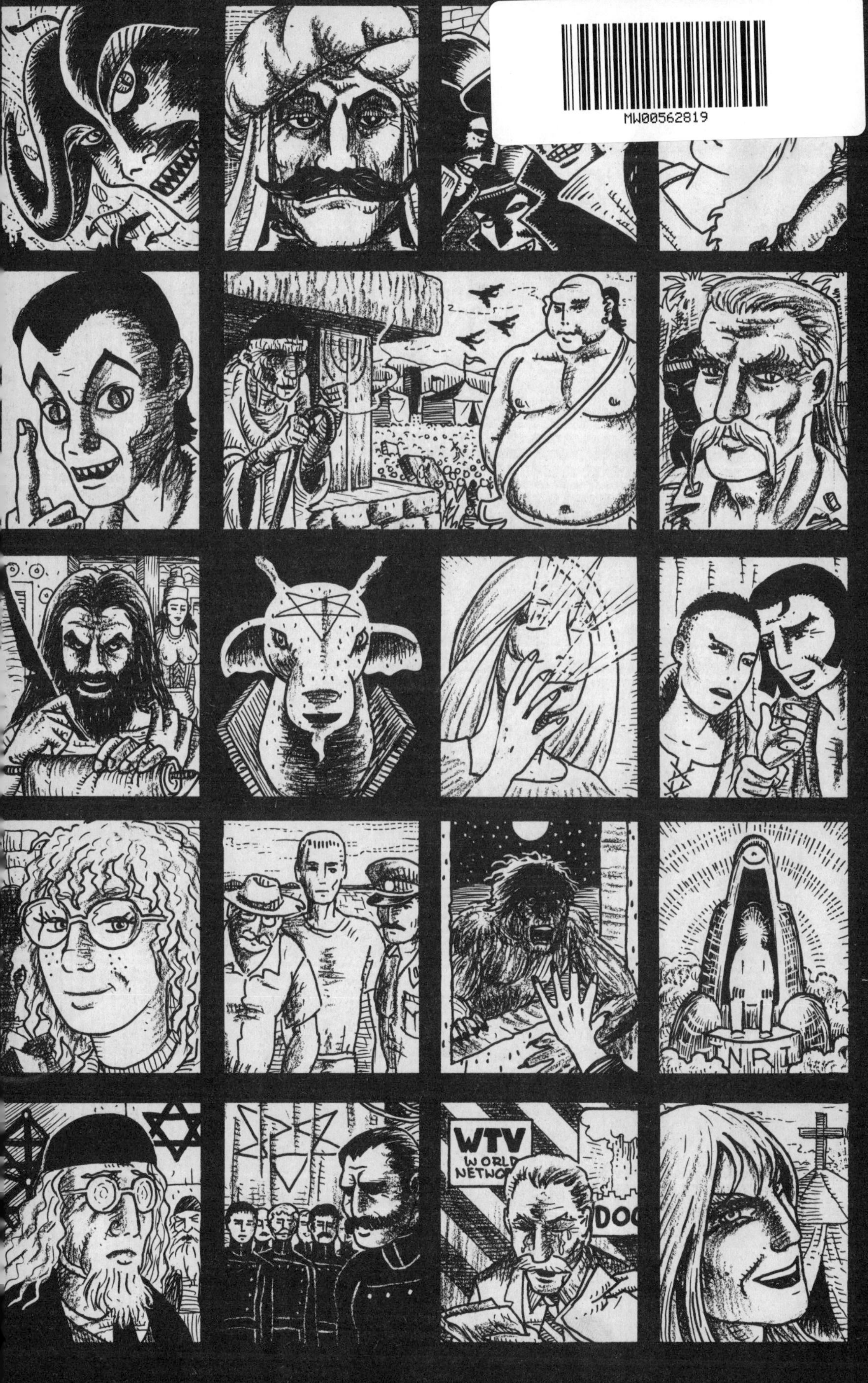

N R I
WTV
WORLD
NETWO
DOC

# ARMAGED

## FROM THE BOOK
## OF REVELATIONS

VOLUME
ONE

**13:1** AND I STOOD UPON THE SAND OF THE
SEA, AND SAW A BEAST RISE UP OUT OF THE
SEA, HAVING SEVEN HEADS AND TEN HORNS,
AND UPON HIS HORNS TEN CROWNS, AND
UPON HIS HEADS THE NAME OF BLASPHEMY.

**13:4** AND THEY WORSHIPPED THE DRAGON
WHICH GAVE POWER UNTO THE BEAST;
AND THEY WORSHIPPED THE BEAST,
SAYING, WHO IS LIKE UNTO THE BEAST?
WHO IS ABLE TO MAKE WAR WITH HIM?

**13:7** AND IT WAS GIVEN UNTO HIM
TO MAKE WAR WITH THE SAINTS, AND
TO OVERCOME THEM; AND POWER
WAS GIVEN HIM OVER ALL KINDREDS,
AND TONGUES AND NATIONS.

**16:16** AND HE GATHERED THEM
TOGETHER INTO A PLACE CALLED IN
THE HEBREW TONGUE ARMAGEDDON.

SIRIUS

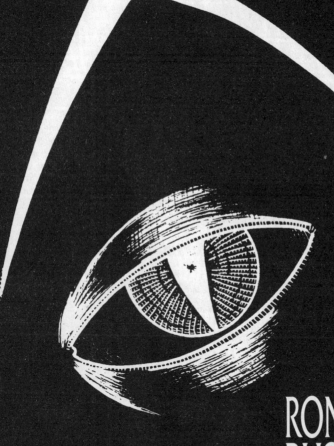

# CONQUEST

BY
RONALD
RUSSELL
ROACH

ENTERTAINMENT

PUBLISHER
ROBB HORAN

ART DIRECTION AND COVERS
JOSEPH MICHAEL LINSNER

MANAGING EDITOR
MARK BELLIS

PRODUCTION
MITCH WAXMAN

PRESIDENT
LAWRENCE SALAMONE

ARMAGEDDONQUEST Vol. 1. May 1997. FIRST PRINTING. PUBLISHED BY SIRIUS ENTERTAINMENT, INC.
LAWRENCE SALAMONE, PRESIDENT. ROBB HORAN, PUBLISHER. JOSEPH MICHAEL LINSNER, ART DIRECTOR.
PRODUCTION BY MITCH WAXMAN. CORRESPONDENCE: PO BOX 128, STANHOPE, N.J. 07874. ARMAGEDDONQUEST IS
©1997 RONALD RUSSELL ROACH. SIRIUS & THE DOG STAR LOGO ARE TM AND © SIRIUS ENTERTAINMENT, INC.
ALL RIGHTS RESERVED. ANY SIMILARITY TO PERSONS LIVING OR DEAD IS PURELY COINCIDENTAL

PRINTED IN CANADA.                                    ISBN: 1-57989-006-1

This is the story of Tazio, the good-guy Antichrist, destined to be that infamous Beast out of The Book of Revelations. That's right, yet another version of "The Apocalypse," that well-worn dramatic showdown between Good and Evil at the End of the World, angels and devils battling it out, Christ as Divine Warrior come to Kill All The Sinners (you too?). It's an often used theme, and why not? It's a fun concept.

Some of you might have met Tazio before. I self-published the earliest chapters (Books) of AQ on a small scale, fotocopies folded and stapled, to give to friends. Published for real in 1994 by Starhead Comix in Seattle, but only the first four chapters ever made it to print. AQ has never before been published in its 20 Book 850-page entirety. I've received fan mail from readers who liked the start and were waiting for the rest of the story... Well, here it is, Sirius Entertainment is publishing AQ in three Volumes.

AQ was supposed to be a novel, ended up becoming a comic book, and got so long and complex that it is again a novel. Started out as a collection of Tazio short stories with a cast of characters whom I couldn't quite visualize until I began to draw them, and as drawings they came alive, took over, took off, and kept me chasing the ending for 9 years until more than 850 pages containing over 6000 drawings finally told the tale.

The drawings and lettering in the earlier books are pretty casual since I never really intended to go pro with it, just a hobby, so the first eight books were drawn on typing paper. After I started getting positive feedback and an offer of publication from Michael Dowers of Starhead Comix, I switched to a larger format and began to use proper tools. The last 12 books look much better. Of course, the whole thing could be more polished if I had time to redraw, or reprocess it and color it all with computers, but I just don't have that kind of time. AQ is what it is: shamanistic folk art.

There are some people I need to thank for help along the way: like my friend Michael Dowers who dedicated a lot of personal time and money to produce those Starhead issues; and Jon Strongbow who backed Michael up because he believed in AQ as art; and Italian fan Graziano Montanini, who sent pages of linguistic corrections; and Robb Horan, who saw the Starhead issues and had a Revelation; and Joe Linsner, who offered to do the covers so that AQ would maybe even SELL this time.

But there is one person to whom I am most grateful, one who helped me the most, who believed in AQ–or rather, in me–who has worked beside me correcting flaws and generating ideas, offered genuinely useful criticism, allowed me time to draw, and provided the magic of a muse. She's part of these pages.

So I want to dedicate this book to my wife, that beautiful smart, loveable Dane:

## Marianne Vibeke Jørgensen.

Ron, Copenhagen, 1996

the AQ web-site and bulletin board at: http://www.armageddonque

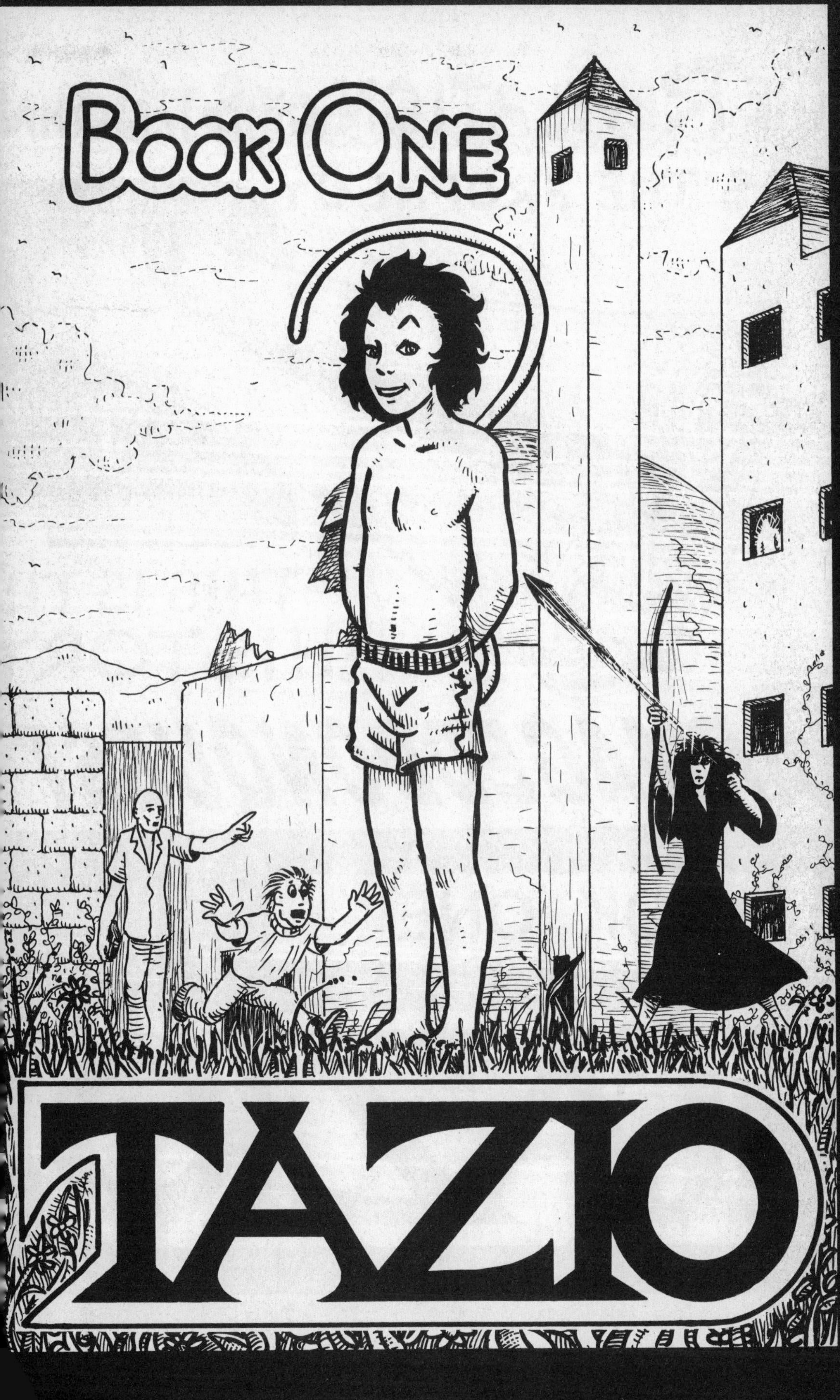
BOOK ONE
TAZIO

# THE REVELATION OF ST. JOHN

WAS THE PROPHECY

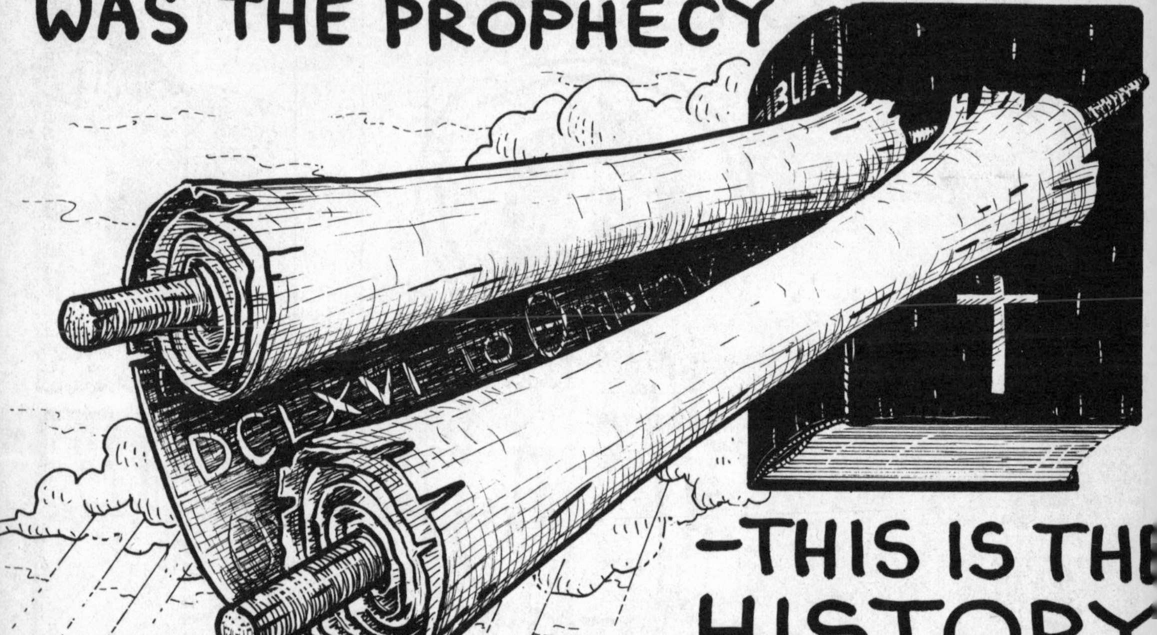
BLIA
DCLXVI TO

-THIS IS THE HISTORY

# ARMAGEDDONQUEST

## BOOK ONE

# TAZIO

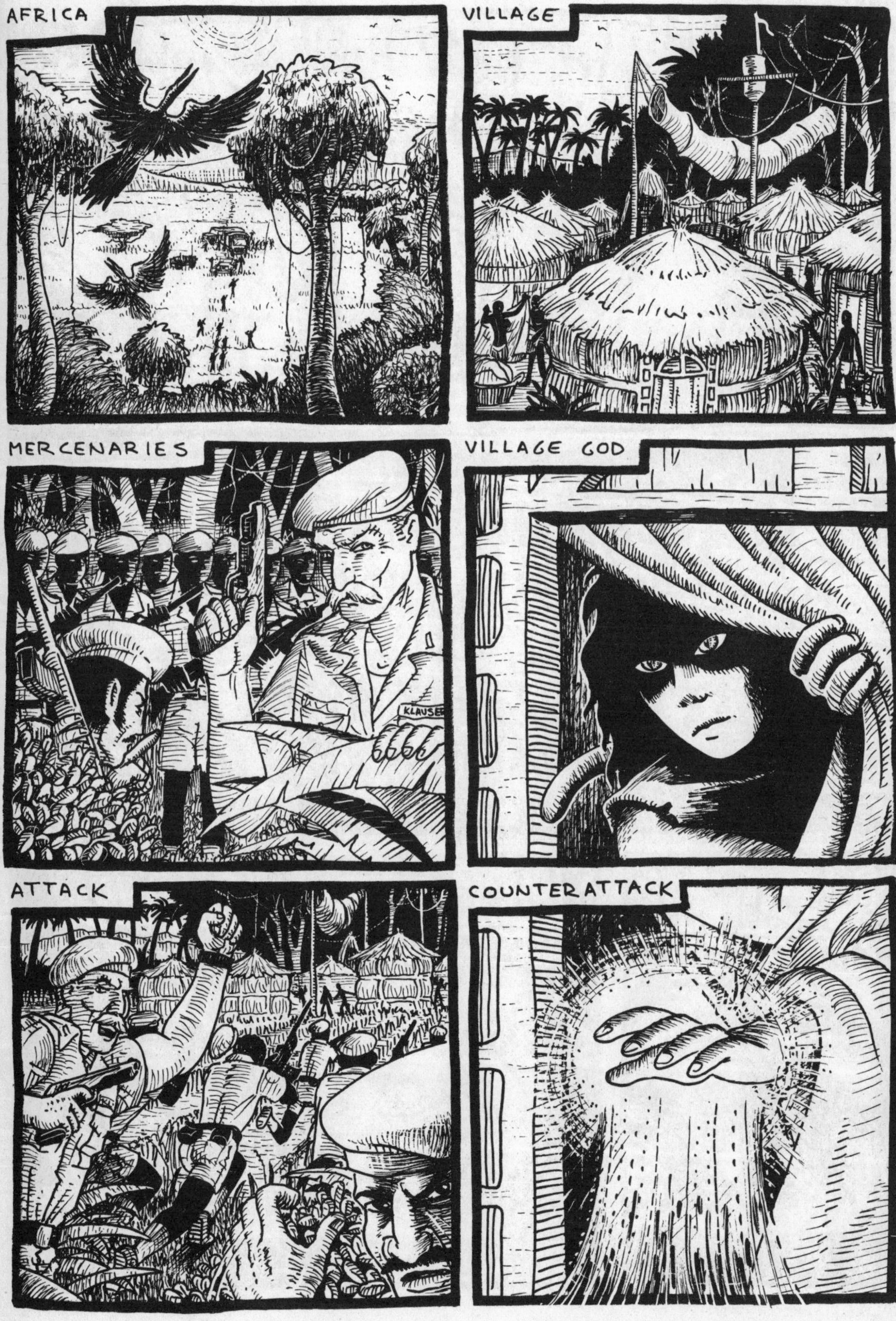
AFRICA
VILLAGE
MERCENARIES
KLAUSER
VILLAGE GOD
ATTACK
COUNTERATTACK

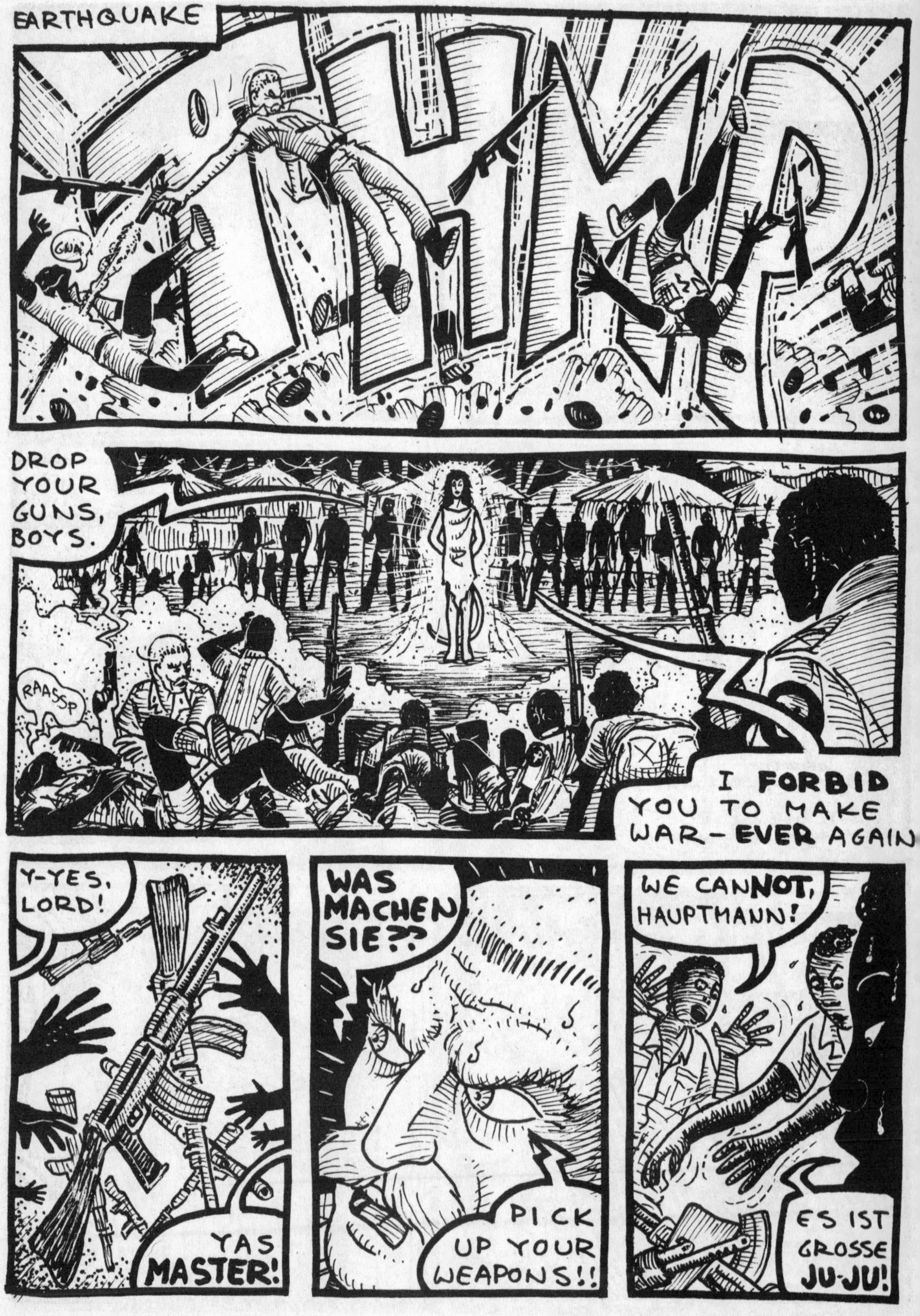
EARTHQUAKE
GWA!
DROP YOUR GUNS, BOYS.
RAASSP
I FORBID YOU TO MAKE WAR- EVER AGAIN
Y-YES, LORD!
YAS MASTER!
WAS MACHEN SIE??
PICK UP YOUR WEAPONS!!
WE CANNOT, HAUPTMANN!
ES IST GROSSE JU-JU!

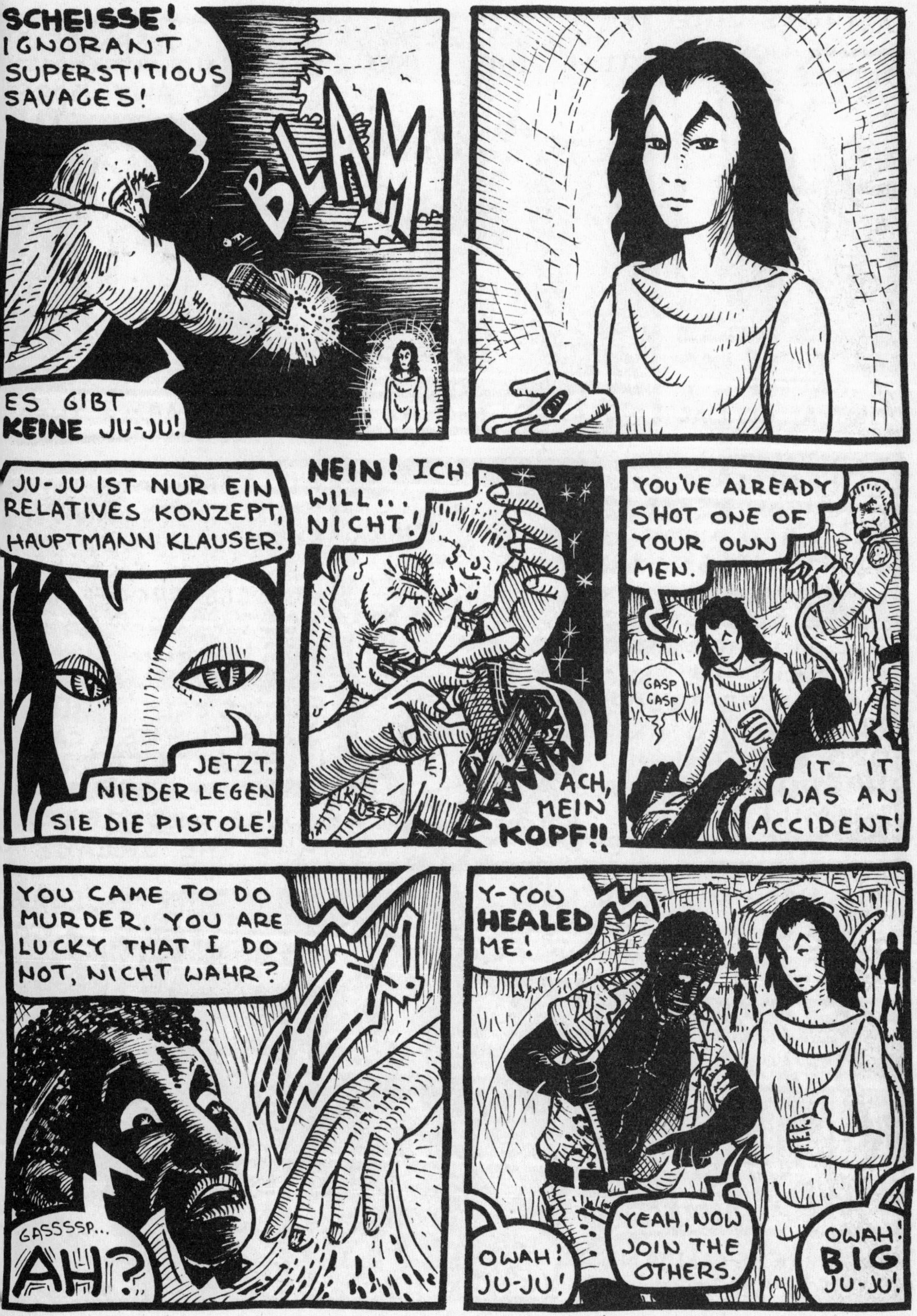
SCHEISSE! IGNORANT SUPERSTITIOUS SAVAGES!
BLAM
ES GIBT KEINE JU-JU!
JU-JU IST NUR EIN RELATIVES KONZEPT, HAUPTMANN KLAUSER.
JETZT, NIEDER LEGEN SIE DIE PISTOLE!
NEIN! ICH WILL... NICHT!
ACH, MEIN KOPF!!
YOU'VE ALREADY SHOT ONE OF YOUR OWN MEN.
GASP GASP
IT— IT WAS AN ACCIDENT!
YOU CAME TO DO MURDER. YOU ARE LUCKY THAT I DO NOT, NICHT WAHR?
GASSSSP...
AH?
Y-YOU HEALED ME!
OWAH! JU-JU!
YEAH, NOW JOIN THE OTHERS.
OWAH! BIG JU-JU!

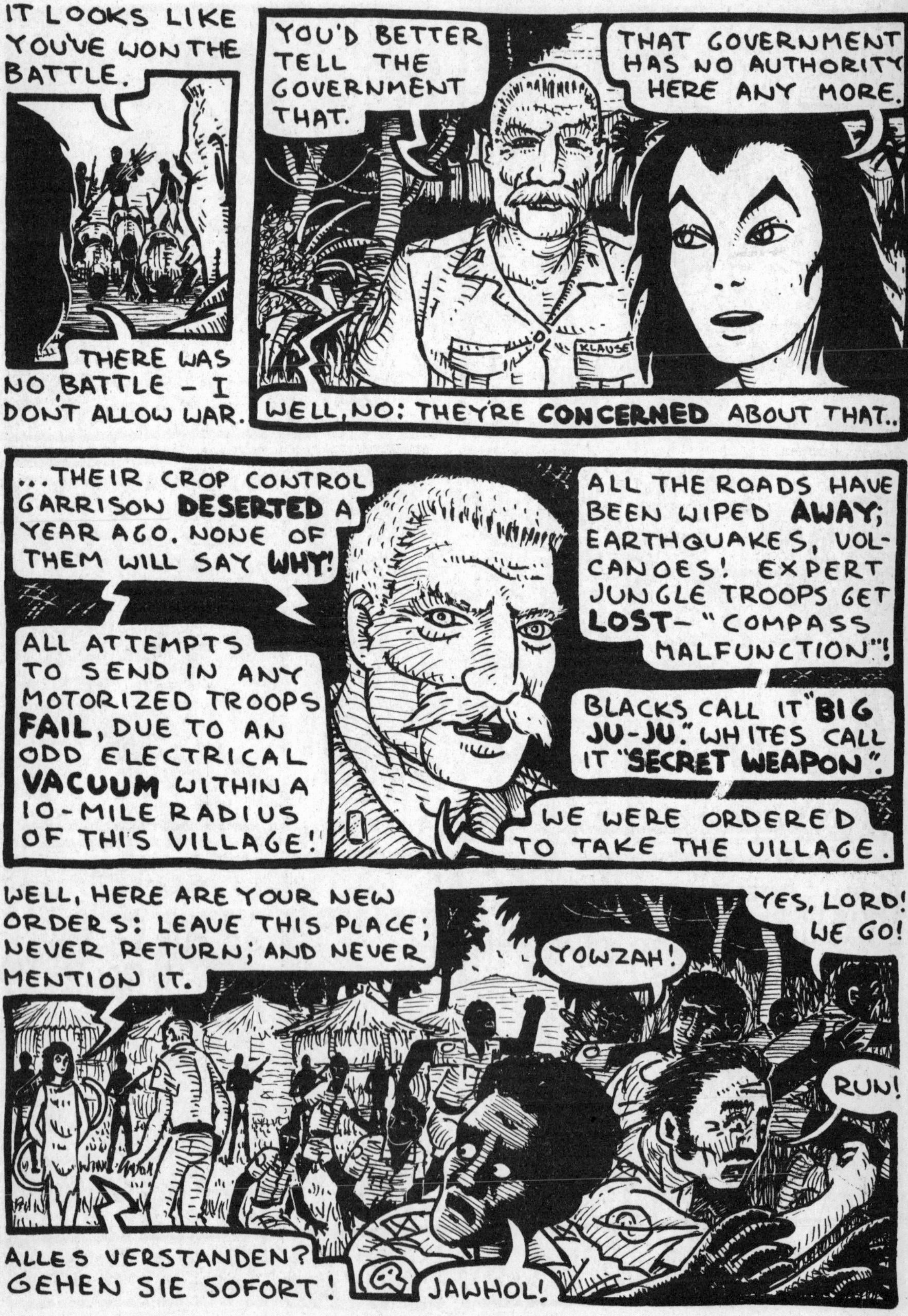
IT LOOKS LIKE YOU'VE WON THE BATTLE.
THERE WAS NO BATTLE – I DON'T ALLOW WAR.
YOU'D BETTER TELL THE GOVERNMENT THAT.
THAT GOVERNMENT HAS NO AUTHORITY HERE ANY MORE.
KLAUSE
WELL, NO: THEY'RE **CONCERNED** ABOUT THAT..
...THEIR CROP CONTROL GARRISON **DESERTED** A YEAR AGO. NONE OF THEM WILL SAY **WHY**!
ALL ATTEMPTS TO SEND IN ANY MOTORIZED TROOPS **FAIL**, DUE TO AN ODD ELECTRICAL **VACUUM** WITHIN A 10-MILE RADIUS OF THIS VILLAGE!
ALL THE ROADS HAVE BEEN WIPED **AWAY**; EARTHQUAKES, VOLCANOES! EXPERT JUNGLE TROOPS GET **LOST**– "COMPASS MALFUNCTION"!
BLACKS CALL IT "**BIG JU-JU**." WHITES CALL IT "**SECRET WEAPON**".
WE WERE ORDERED TO TAKE THE VILLAGE.
WELL, HERE ARE YOUR NEW ORDERS: LEAVE THIS PLACE; NEVER RETURN; AND NEVER MENTION IT.
YOWZAH!
YES, LORD! WE GO!
RUN!
ALLES VERSTANDEN? GEHEN SIE SOFORT!
JAWHOL!

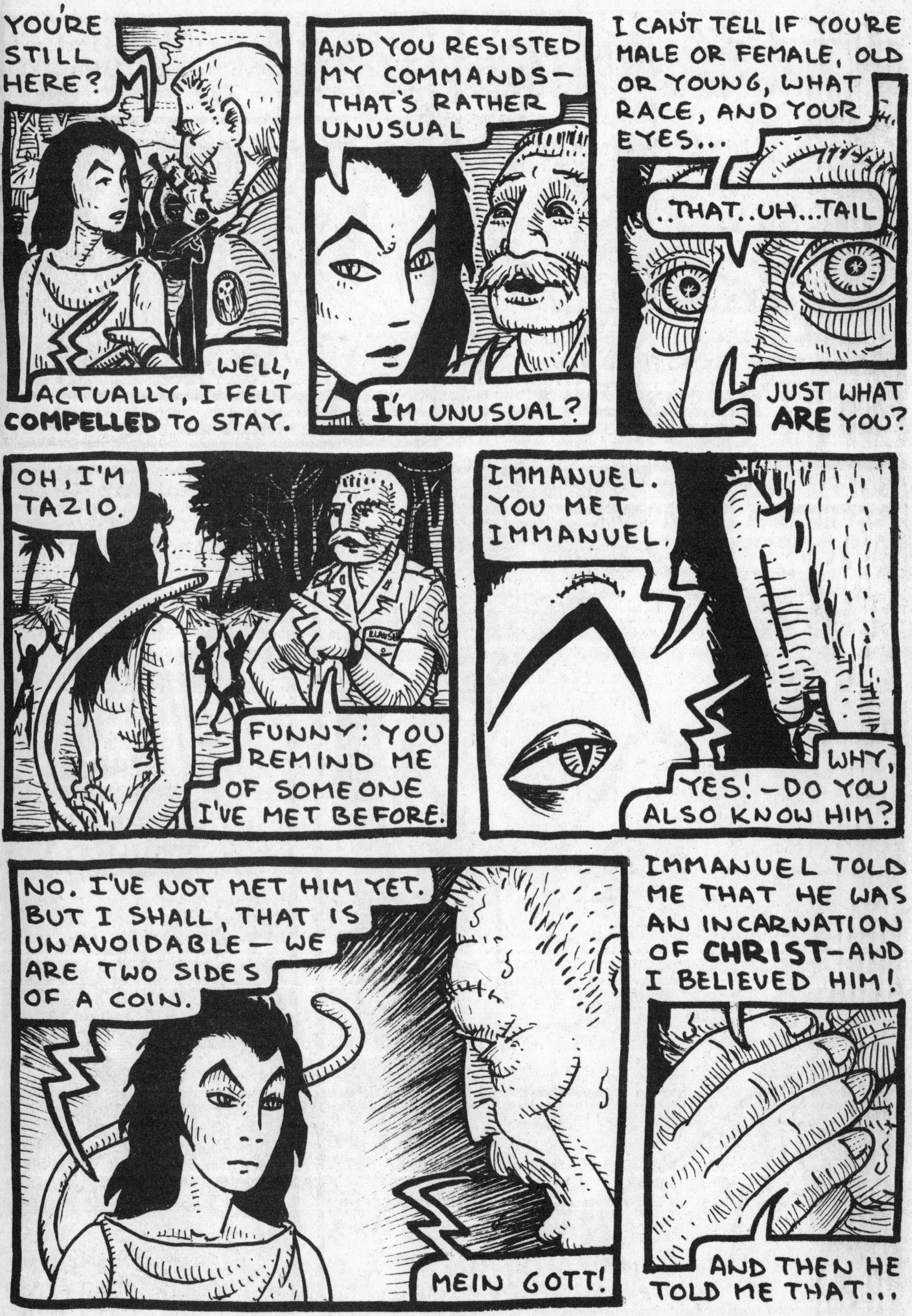

YOU'RE STILL HERE?
WELL, ACTUALLY, I FELT **COMPELLED** TO STAY.
AND YOU RESISTED MY COMMANDS— THAT'S RATHER UNUSUAL
**I**'M UNUSUAL?
I CAN'T TELL IF YOU'RE MALE OR FEMALE, OLD OR YOUNG, WHAT RACE, AND YOUR EYES...
..THAT..UH...TAIL
JUST WHAT **ARE** YOU?
OH, I'M TAZIO.
FUNNY: YOU REMIND ME OF SOMEONE I'VE MET BEFORE.
IMMANUEL. YOU MET IMMANUEL.
WHY, YES! —DO YOU ALSO KNOW HIM?
NO. I'VE NOT MET HIM YET. BUT I SHALL, THAT IS UNAVOIDABLE— WE ARE TWO SIDES OF A COIN.
MEIN GOTT!
IMMANUEL TOLD ME THAT HE WAS AN INCARNATION OF **CHRIST**—AND I BELIEVED HIM!
AND THEN HE TOLD ME THAT...

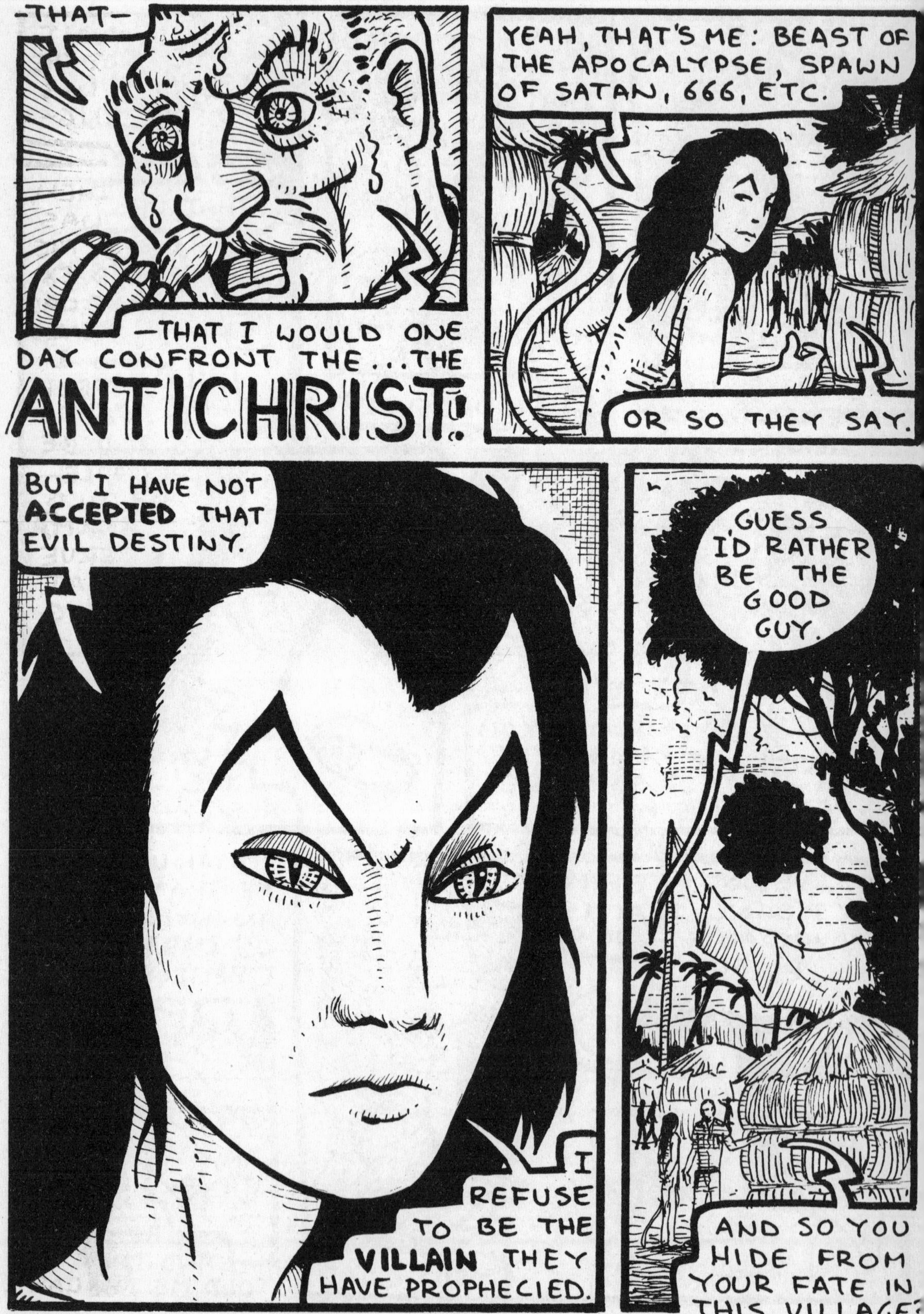
-THAT-
—THAT I WOULD ONE DAY CONFRONT THE... THE ANTICHRIST!
YEAH, THAT'S ME: BEAST OF THE APOCALYPSE, SPAWN OF SATAN, 666, ETC.
OR SO THEY SAY.
BUT I HAVE NOT **ACCEPTED** THAT EVIL DESTINY.
I REFUSE TO BE THE **VILLAIN** THEY HAVE PROPHECIED.
GUESS I'D RATHER BE THE GOOD GUY.
AND SO YOU HIDE FROM YOUR FATE IN THIS VILLAGE?

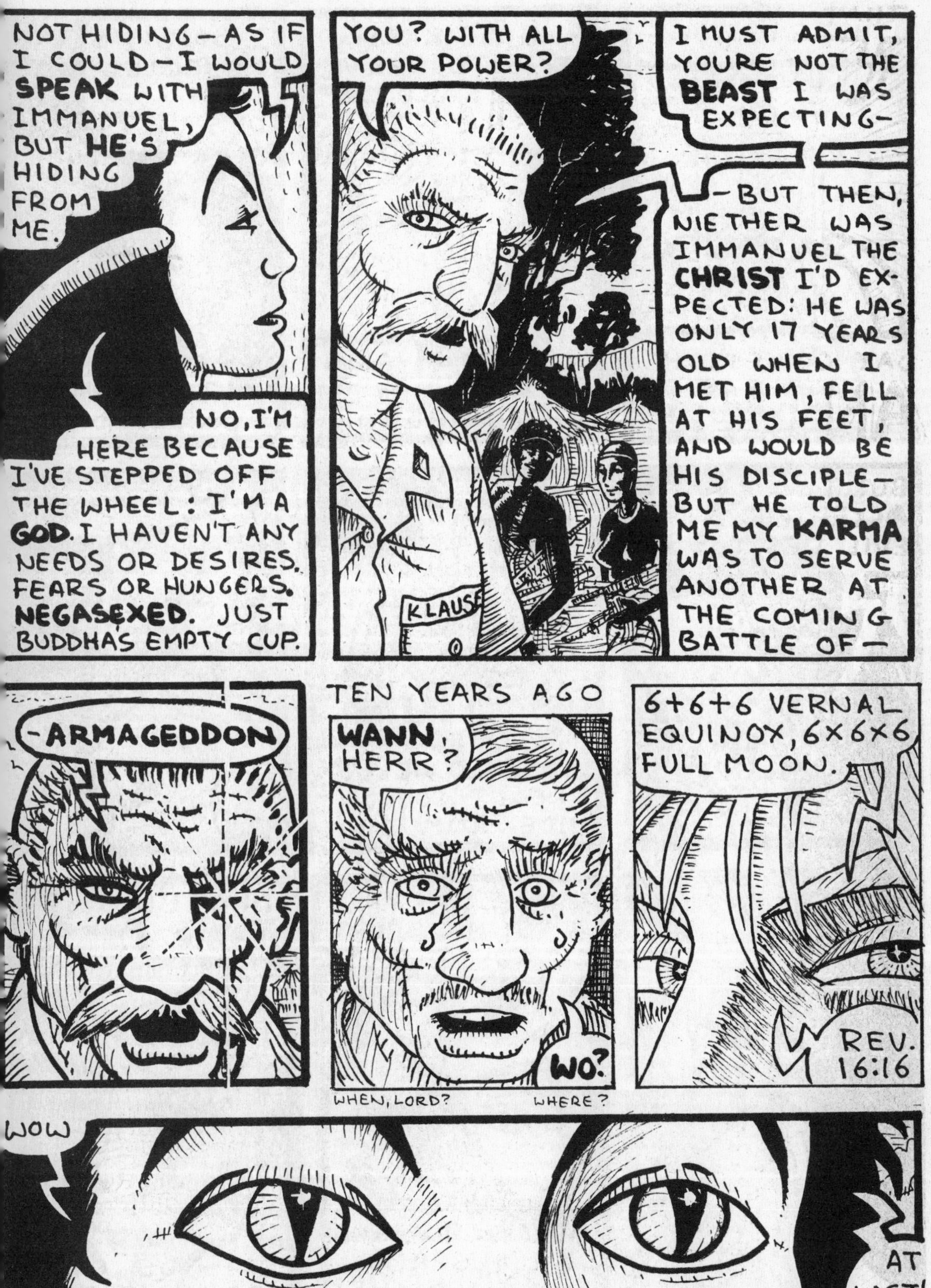
NOT HIDING—AS IF I COULD—I WOULD SPEAK WITH IMMANUEL, BUT HE'S HIDING FROM ME.
NO, I'M HERE BECAUSE I'VE STEPPED OFF THE WHEEL: I'M A GOD. I HAVEN'T ANY NEEDS OR DESIRES, FEARS OR HUNGERS. NEGASEXED. JUST BUDDHA'S EMPTY CUP.
YOU? WITH ALL YOUR POWER?
KLAUSE
I MUST ADMIT, YOURE NOT THE BEAST I WAS EXPECTING—
—BUT THEN, NIETHER WAS IMMANUEL THE CHRIST I'D EXPECTED: HE WAS ONLY 17 YEARS OLD WHEN I MET HIM, FELL AT HIS FEET, AND WOULD BE HIS DISCIPLE—BUT HE TOLD ME MY KARMA WAS TO SERVE ANOTHER AT THE COMING BATTLE OF—
-ARMAGEDDON
TEN YEARS AGO
WANN, HERR?
WO?
WHEN, LORD?
WHERE?
6+6+6 VERNAL EQUINOX, 6×6×6 FULL MOON.
REV. 16:16
WOW
AT LAST!

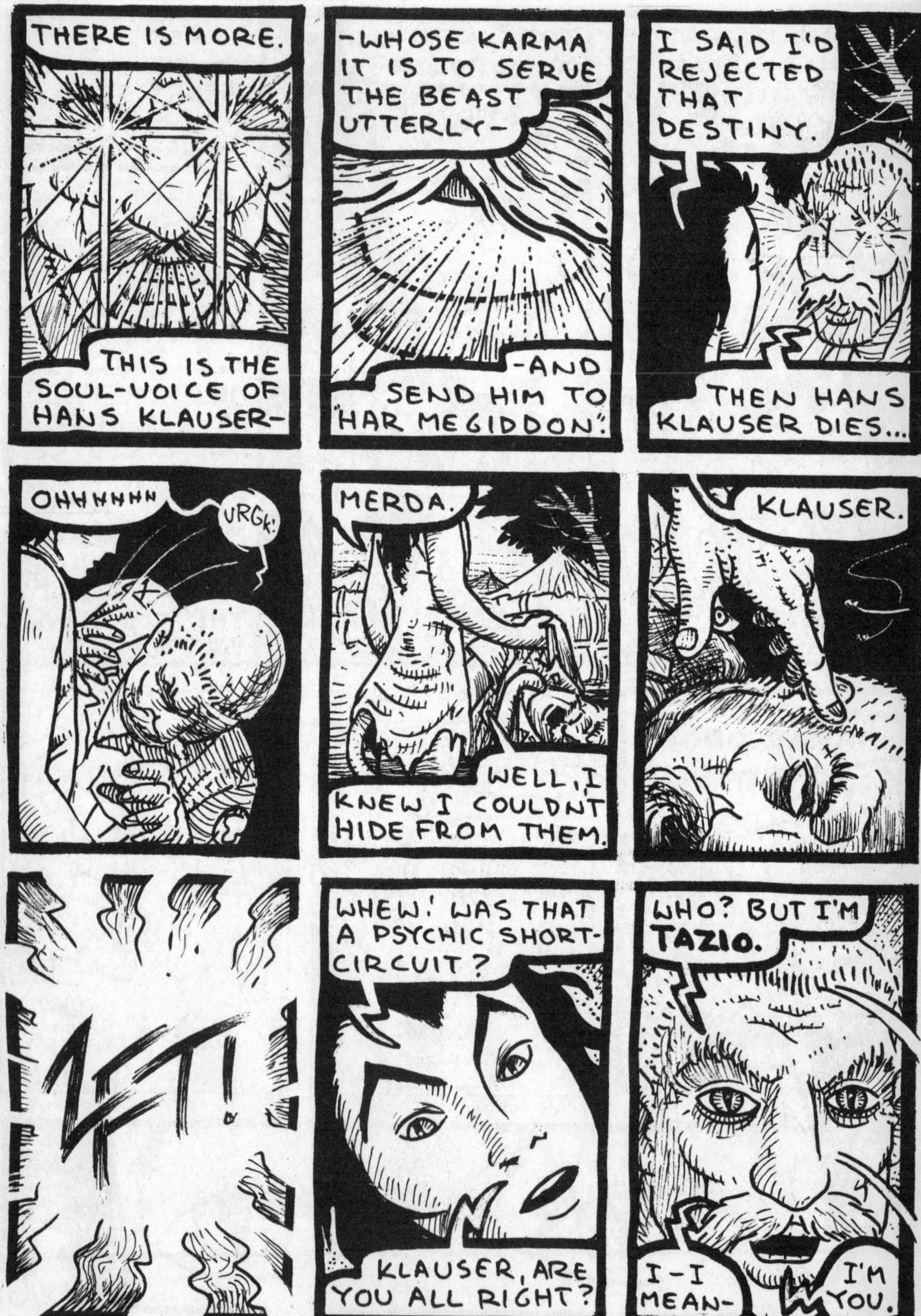
THERE IS MORE.
THIS IS THE SOUL-VOICE OF HANS KLAUSER-
-WHOSE KARMA IT IS TO SERVE THE BEAST UTTERLY-
-AND SEND HIM TO "HAR MEGIDDON".
I SAID I'D REJECTED THAT DESTINY.
THEN HANS KLAUSER DIES...
OHHHHHH
URGK!
MERDA.
WELL, I KNEW I COULDN'T HIDE FROM THEM.
KLAUSER.
ZFT!
WHEW! WAS THAT A PSYCHIC SHORT-CIRCUIT?
KLAUSER, ARE YOU ALL RIGHT?
WHO? BUT I'M TAZIO.
I-I MEAN-
I'M YOU.

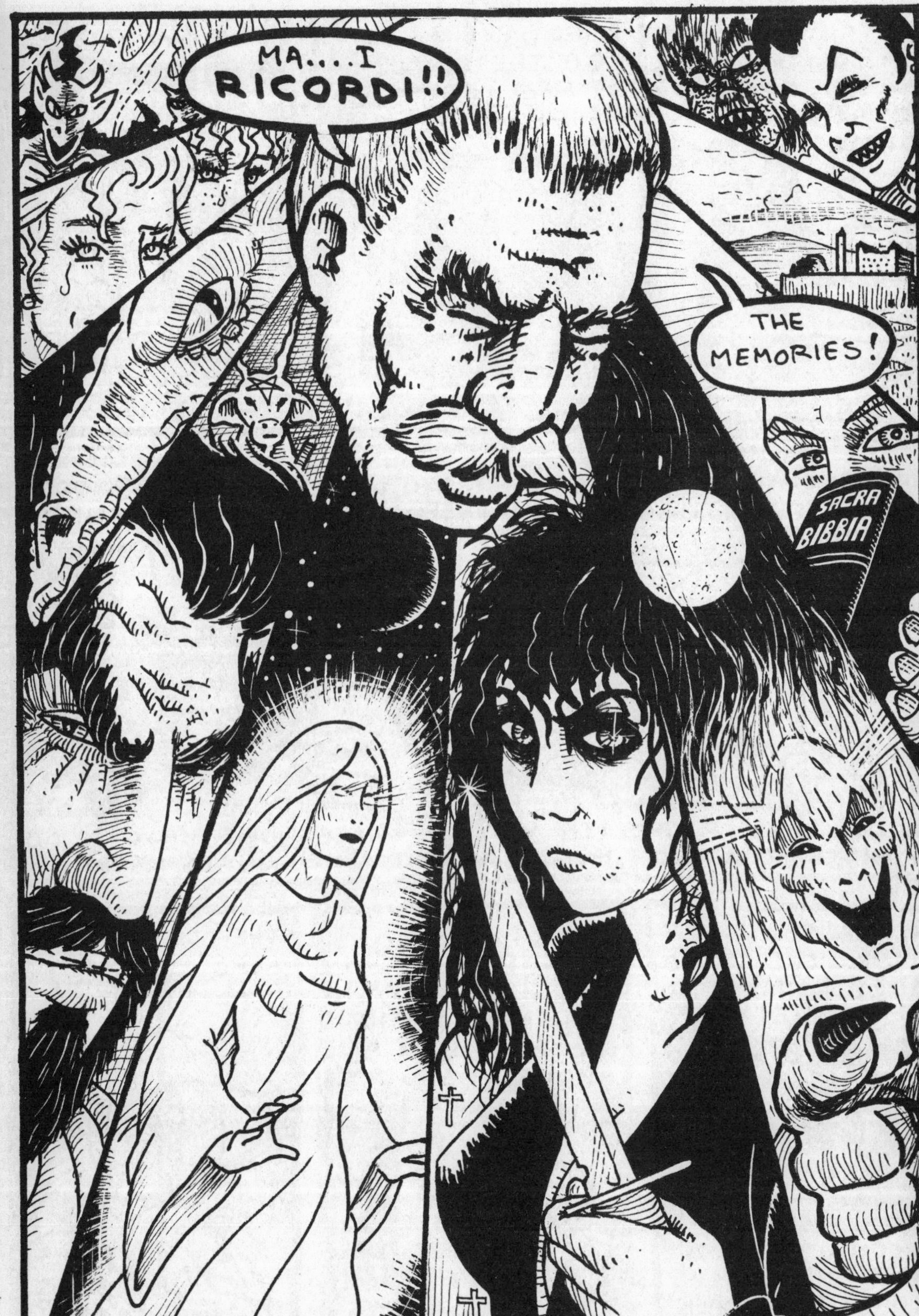
MA....I RICORDI!!
THE MEMORIES!
SACRA BIBBIA

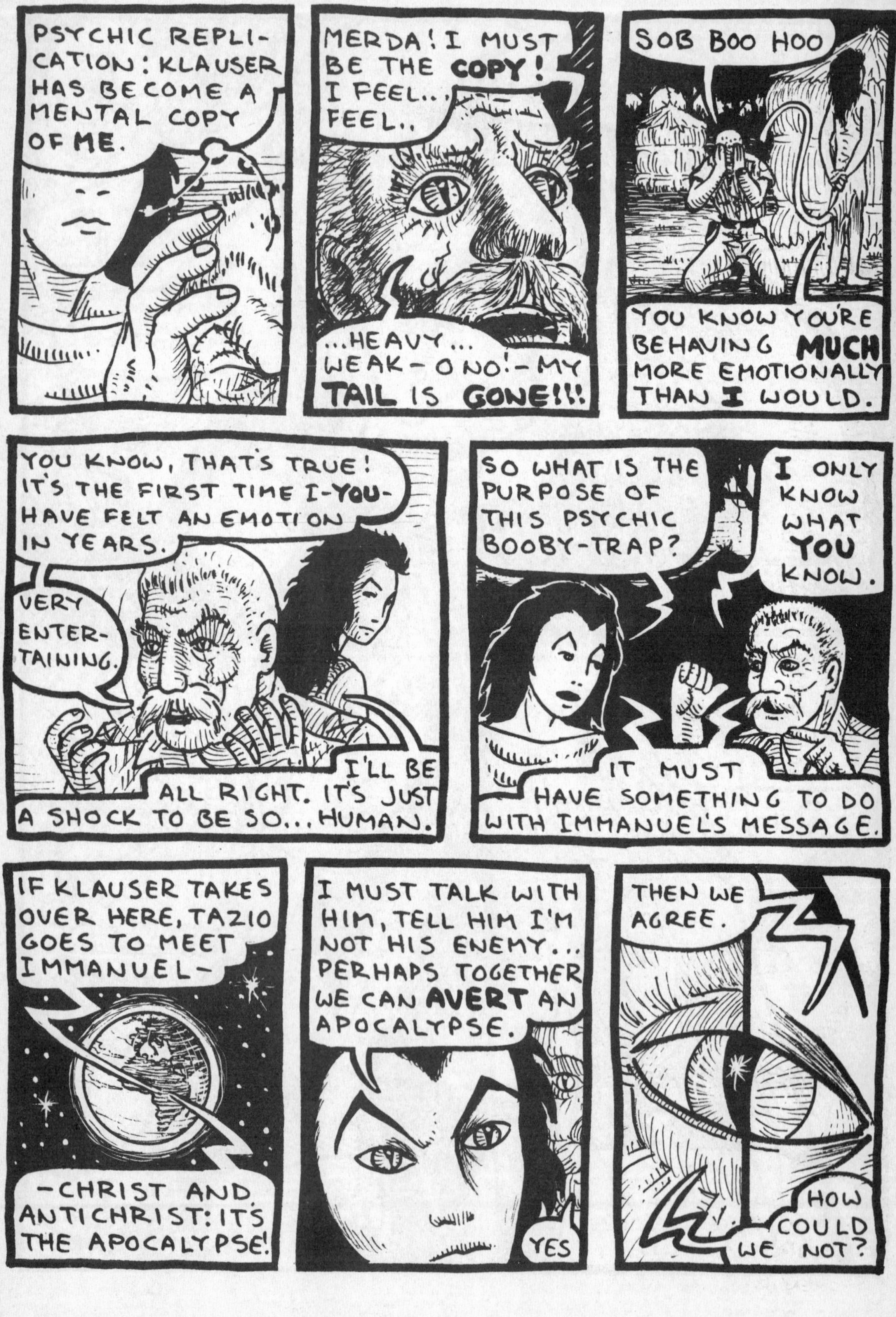
PSYCHIC REPLICATION: KLAUSER HAS BECOME A MENTAL COPY OF ME.
MERDA! I MUST BE THE COPY! I FEEL... FEEL..
...HEAVY... WEAK-O NO!-MY TAIL IS GONE!!!
SOB BOO HOO
YOU KNOW YOU'RE BEHAVING MUCH MORE EMOTIONALLY THAN I WOULD.
YOU KNOW, THAT'S TRUE! IT'S THE FIRST TIME I-YOU-HAVE FELT AN EMOTION IN YEARS.
VERY ENTERTAINING.
I'LL BE ALL RIGHT. IT'S JUST A SHOCK TO BE SO... HUMAN.
SO WHAT IS THE PURPOSE OF THIS PSYCHIC BOOBY-TRAP?
I ONLY KNOW WHAT YOU KNOW.
IT MUST HAVE SOMETHING TO DO WITH IMMANUEL'S MESSAGE.
IF KLAUSER TAKES OVER HERE, TAZIO GOES TO MEET IMMANUEL-
-CHRIST AND ANTICHRIST: IT'S THE APOCALYPSE!
I MUST TALK WITH HIM, TELL HIM I'M NOT HIS ENEMY... PERHAPS TOGETHER WE CAN AVERT AN APOCALYPSE.
YES
THEN WE AGREE.
HOW COULD WE NOT?

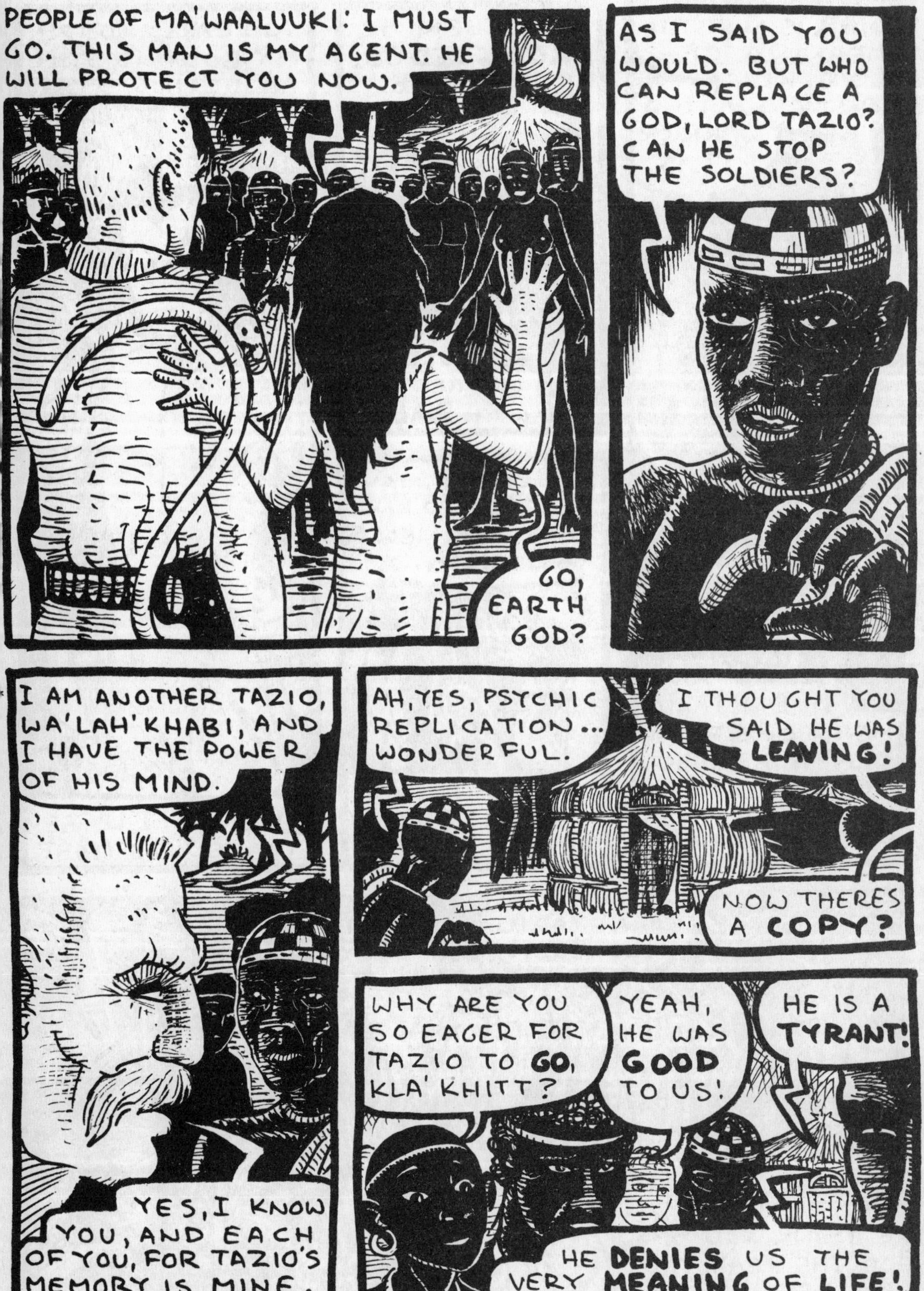
PEOPLE OF MA'WAALUUKI: I MUST GO. THIS MAN IS MY AGENT. HE WILL PROTECT YOU NOW.
GO, EARTH GOD?
AS I SAID YOU WOULD. BUT WHO CAN REPLACE A GOD, LORD TAZIO? CAN HE STOP THE SOLDIERS?
I AM ANOTHER TAZIO, WA'LAH'KHABI, AND I HAVE THE POWER OF HIS MIND.
YES, I KNOW YOU, AND EACH OF YOU, FOR TAZIO'S MEMORY IS MINE.
AH, YES, PSYCHIC REPLICATION... WONDERFUL.
I THOUGHT YOU SAID HE WAS **LEAVING**!
NOW THERES A **COPY**?
WHY ARE YOU SO EAGER FOR TAZIO TO **GO**, KLA'KHITT?
YEAH, HE WAS **GOOD** TO US!
HE IS A **TYRANT**!
HE **DENIES** US THE VERY **MEANING** OF **LIFE**!

* SPOKEN IN WA'LAH'KHANI

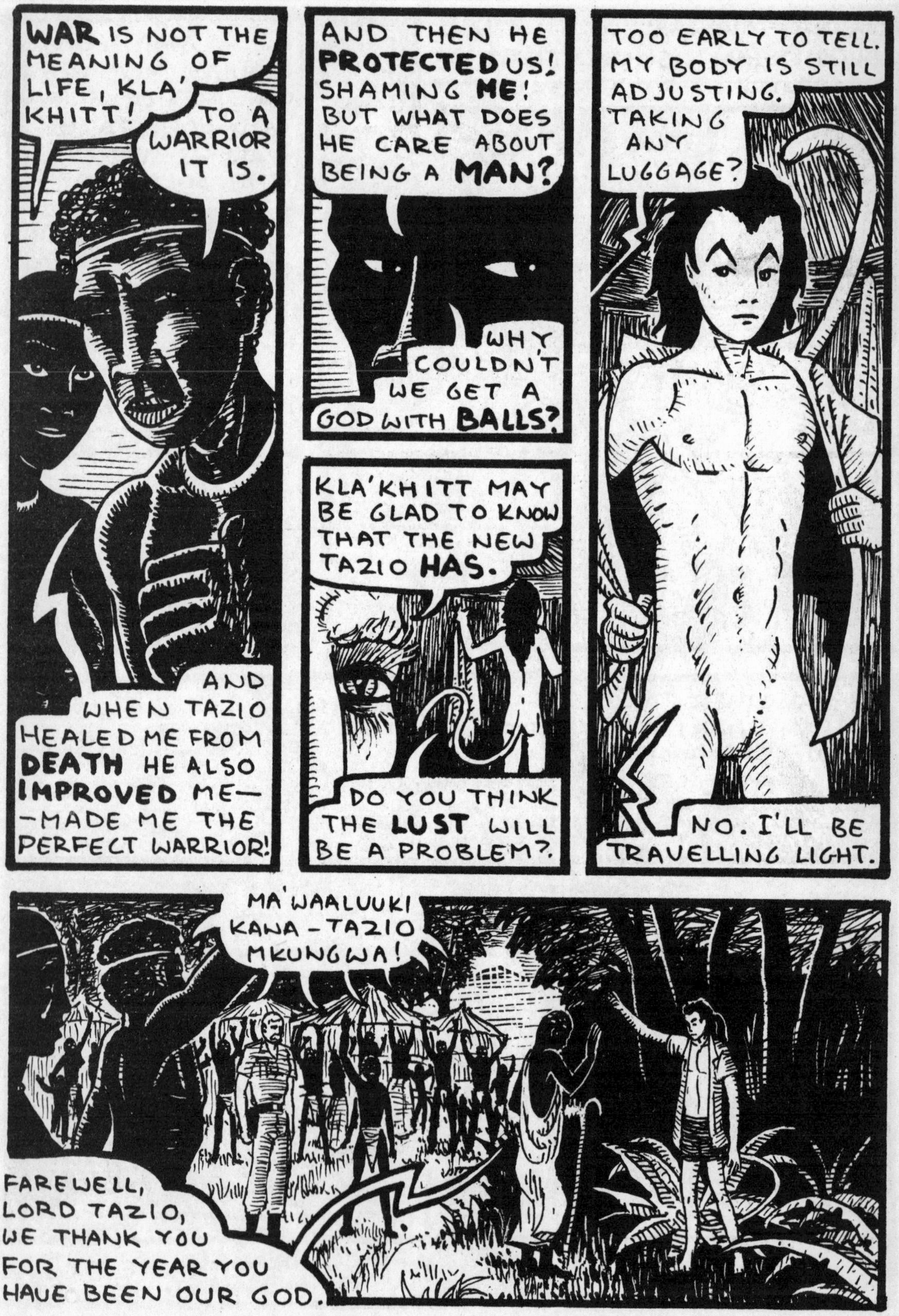
WAR IS NOT THE MEANING OF LIFE, KLA'KHITT!
TO A WARRIOR IT IS.
AND WHEN TAZIO HEALED ME FROM DEATH HE ALSO IMPROVED ME— —MADE ME THE PERFECT WARRIOR!
AND THEN HE PROTECTED US! SHAMING ME! BUT WHAT DOES HE CARE ABOUT BEING A MAN?
WHY COULDN'T WE GET A GOD WITH BALLS?
KLA'KHITT MAY BE GLAD TO KNOW THAT THE NEW TAZIO HAS.
DO YOU THINK THE LUST WILL BE A PROBLEM?
TOO EARLY TO TELL. MY BODY IS STILL ADJUSTING. TAKING ANY LUGGAGE?
NO. I'LL BE TRAVELLING LIGHT.
MA'WAALUUK! KANA-TAZIO MKUNGWA!
FAREWELL, LORD TAZIO, WE THANK YOU FOR THE YEAR YOU HAVE BEEN OUR GOD.

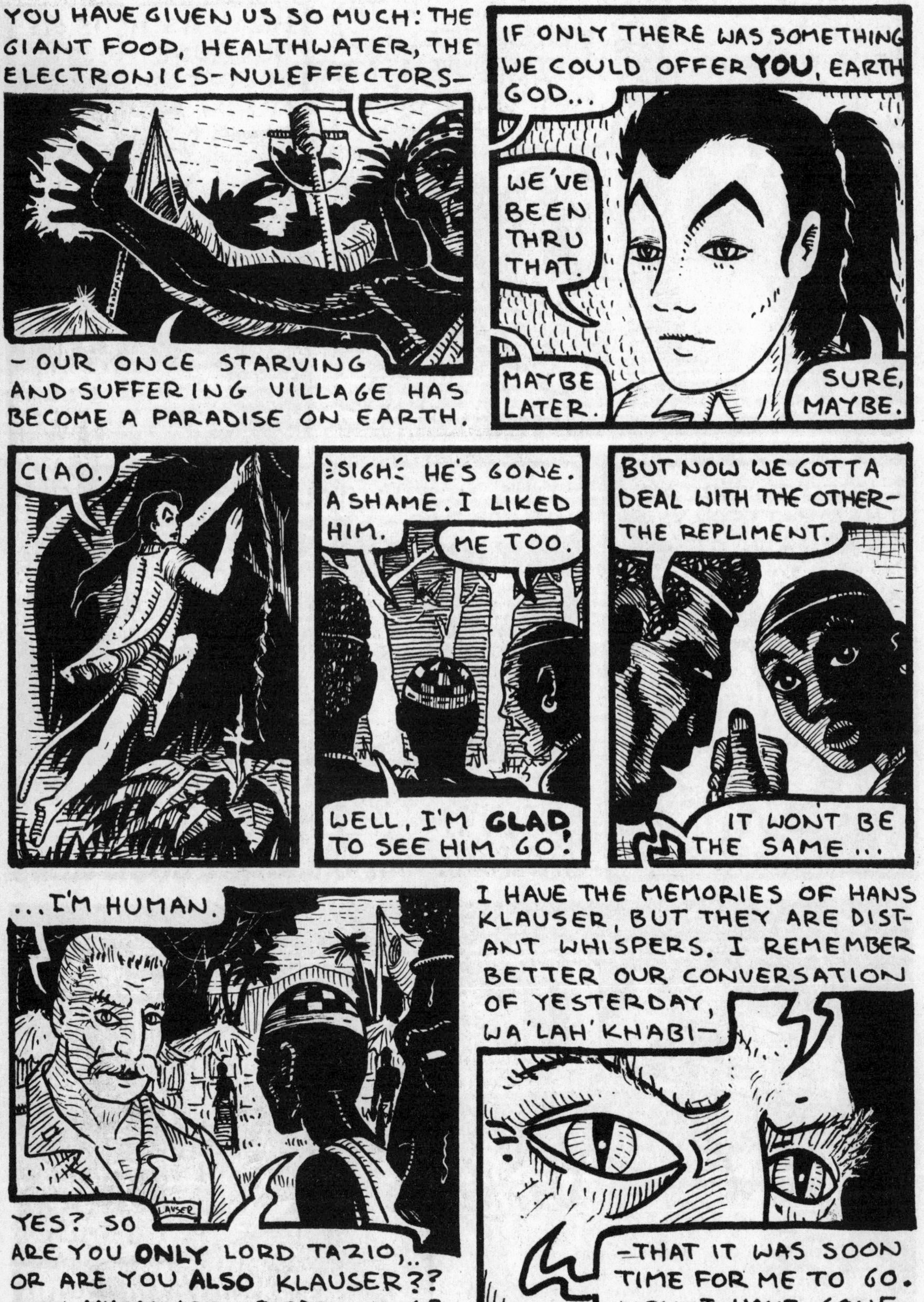

YOU HAVE GIVEN US SO MUCH: THE GIANT FOOD, HEALTHWATER, THE ELECTRONICS-NULEFFECTORS-
-OUR ONCE STARVING AND SUFFERING VILLAGE HAS BECOME A PARADISE ON EARTH.
IF ONLY THERE WAS SOMETHING WE COULD OFFER **YOU**, EARTH GOD...
WE'VE BEEN THRU THAT.
MAYBE LATER.
SURE, MAYBE.
CIAO.
:SIGH: HE'S GONE. A SHAME. I LIKED HIM.
ME TOO.
WELL, I'M **GLAD** TO SEE HIM GO!
BUT NOW WE GOTTA DEAL WITH THE OTHER- THE REPLIMENT.
IT WONT BE THE SAME...
...I'M HUMAN.
YES? SO ARE YOU **ONLY** LORD TAZIO,.. OR ARE YOU **ALSO** KLAUSER?? WITH **WHOM** ARE WE SPEAKING?
I HAVE THE MEMORIES OF HANS KLAUSER, BUT THEY ARE DISTANT WHISPERS. I REMEMBER BETTER OUR CONVERSATION OF YESTERDAY, WA'LAH'KHABI-
-THAT IT WAS SOON TIME FOR ME TO GO. WELL, I HAVE GONE...

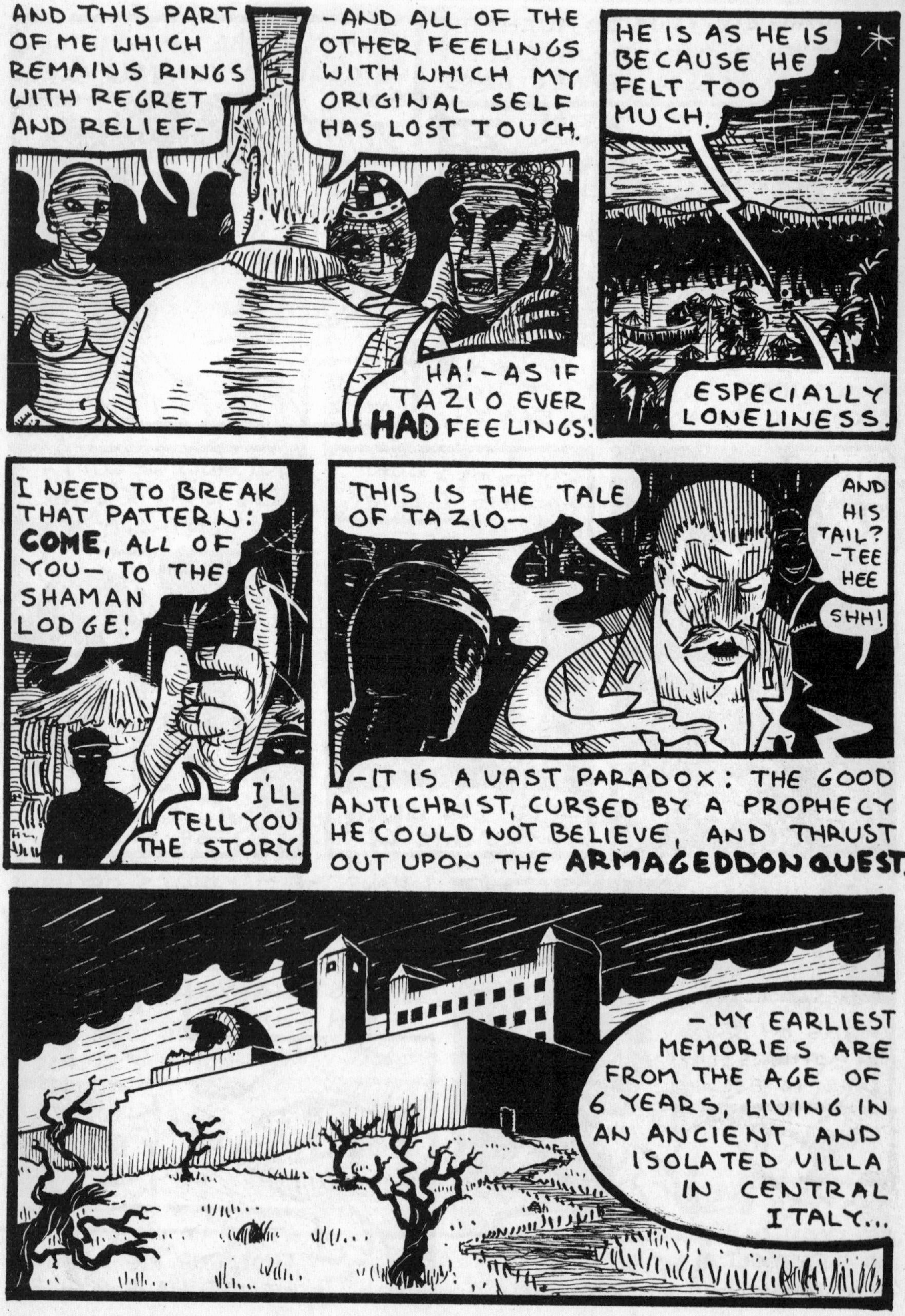
AND THIS PART OF ME WHICH REMAINS RINGS WITH REGRET AND RELIEF-
-AND ALL OF THE OTHER FEELINGS WITH WHICH MY ORIGINAL SELF HAS LOST TOUCH.
HA! -AS IF TAZIO EVER **HAD** FEELINGS!
HE IS AS HE IS BECAUSE HE FELT TOO MUCH.
ESPECIALLY LONELINESS.
I NEED TO BREAK THAT PATTERN: **COME**, ALL OF YOU- TO THE SHAMAN LODGE!
I'LL TELL YOU THE STORY.
THIS IS THE TALE OF TAZIO-
AND HIS TAIL? -TEE HEE
SHH!
-IT IS A VAST PARADOX: THE GOOD ANTICHRIST, CURSED BY A PROPHECY HE COULD NOT BELIEVE, AND THRUST OUT UPON THE **ARMAGEDDON QUEST**.
-MY EARLIEST MEMORIES ARE FROM THE AGE OF 6 YEARS, LIVING IN AN ANCIENT AND ISOLATED VILLA IN CENTRAL ITALY...

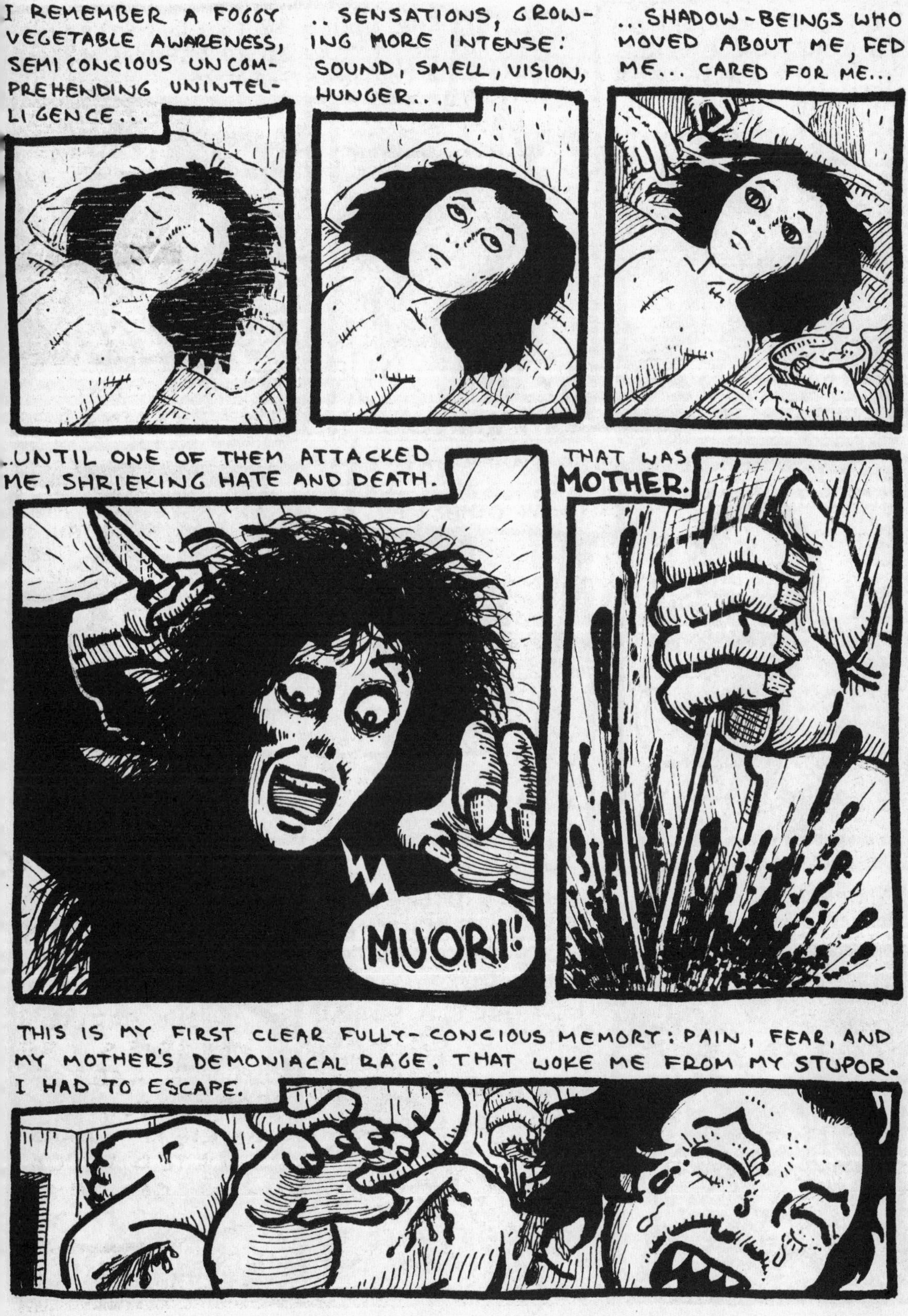
I REMEMBER A FOGGY VEGETABLE AWARENESS, SEMI CONCIOUS UNCOMPREHENDING UNINTELLIGENCE...
..SENSATIONS, GROWING MORE INTENSE: SOUND, SMELL, VISION, HUNGER...
...SHADOW-BEINGS WHO MOVED ABOUT ME, FED ME... CARED FOR ME...
..UNTIL ONE OF THEM ATTACKED ME, SHRIEKING HATE AND DEATH.
MUORI!
THAT WAS MOTHER.
THIS IS MY FIRST CLEAR FULLY-CONCIOUS MEMORY: PAIN, FEAR, AND MY MOTHER'S DEMONIACAL RAGE. THAT WOKE ME FROM MY STUPOR. I HAD TO ESCAPE.

I DID NOT KNOW HOW TO RUN — OR EVEN HOW TO CRAWL — BUT I MOVED SOMEHOW TOWARD THE NIGHT.

SHE WOULD NOT STOP STABBING ME, I TURNED TO DEFEND MYSELF, A CORNERED ANIMAL...

SHE RAN AWAY, I IMITATED HER AND RAN THE OTHER WAY.

MY TERRIBLE WOUNDS HEALED QUICKLY — AS THEY ALWAYS DO, FOR IT SEEMS I CANNOT DIE — AND I LIVED AS A WILD BEAST FOR HALF A YEAR OUT IN THE

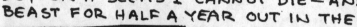

HILLS AROUND THE VILLA, RUNNING ON INSTINCT, A FERAL CHILD OF NATURE.

AS A HARDY LITTLE BRUTE OBLIVIOUS TO THE ELEMENTS, MY ONLY NEED WAS FOOD. I LEARNED TO HUNT, AND TO STEAL FROM THE LOCAL FARMERS.

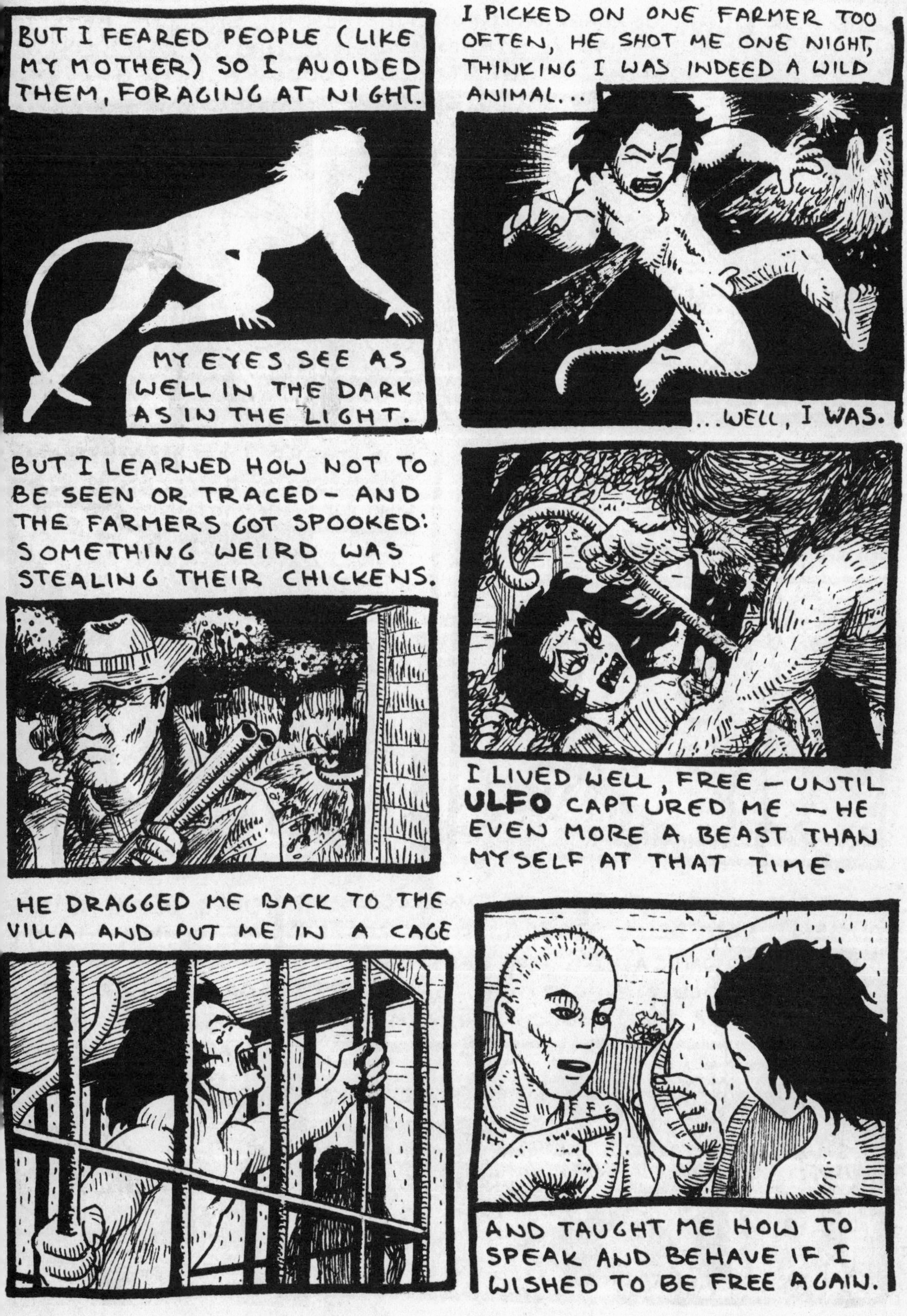
BUT I FEARED PEOPLE (LIKE MY MOTHER) SO I AVOIDED THEM, FORAGING AT NIGHT.
MY EYES SEE AS WELL IN THE DARK AS IN THE LIGHT.
I PICKED ON ONE FARMER TOO OFTEN, HE SHOT ME ONE NIGHT, THINKING I WAS INDEED A WILD ANIMAL...
...WELL, I WAS.
BUT I LEARNED HOW NOT TO BE SEEN OR TRACED- AND THE FARMERS GOT SPOOKED: SOMETHING WEIRD WAS STEALING THEIR CHICKENS.
I LIVED WELL, FREE — UNTIL **ULFO** CAPTURED ME — HE EVEN MORE A BEAST THAN MYSELF AT THAT TIME.
HE DRAGGED ME BACK TO THE VILLA AND PUT ME IN A CAGE
AND TAUGHT ME HOW TO SPEAK AND BEHAVE IF I WISHED TO BE FREE AGAIN.

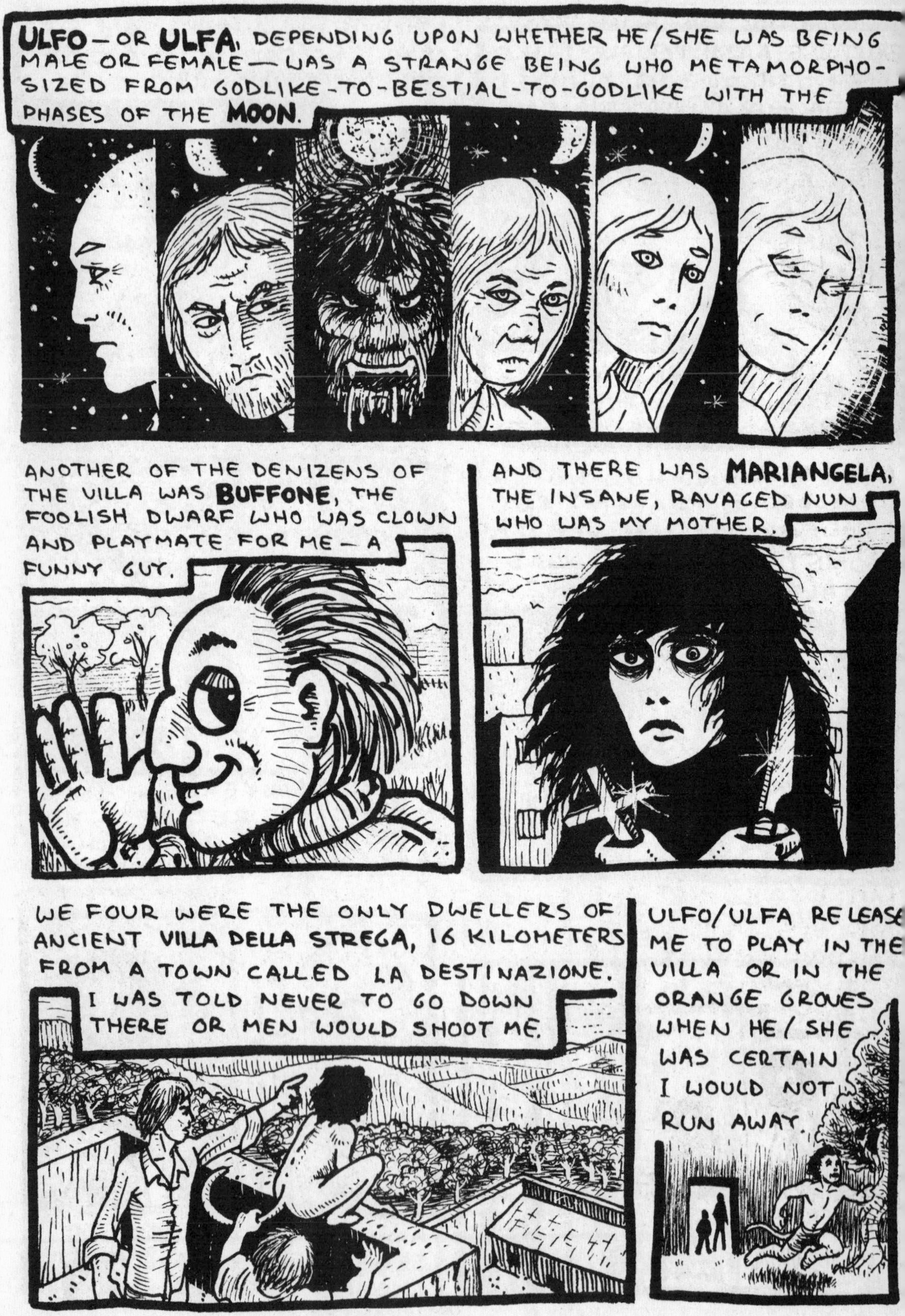
ULFO — OR ULFA, DEPENDING UPON WHETHER HE/SHE WAS BEING MALE OR FEMALE — WAS A STRANGE BEING WHO METAMORPHOSIZED FROM GODLIKE-TO-BESTIAL-TO-GODLIKE WITH THE PHASES OF THE MOON.
ANOTHER OF THE DENIZENS OF THE VILLA WAS BUFFONE, THE FOOLISH DWARF WHO WAS CLOWN AND PLAYMATE FOR ME — A FUNNY GUY.
AND THERE WAS MARIANGELA, THE INSANE, RAVAGED NUN WHO WAS MY MOTHER.
WE FOUR WERE THE ONLY DWELLERS OF ANCIENT VILLA DELLA STREGA, 16 KILOMETERS FROM A TOWN CALLED LA DESTINAZIONE.
I WAS TOLD NEVER TO GO DOWN THERE OR MEN WOULD SHOOT ME.
ULFO/ULFA RELEASE ME TO PLAY IN THE VILLA OR IN THE ORANGE GROVES WHEN HE/SHE WAS CERTAIN I WOULD NOT RUN AWAY.

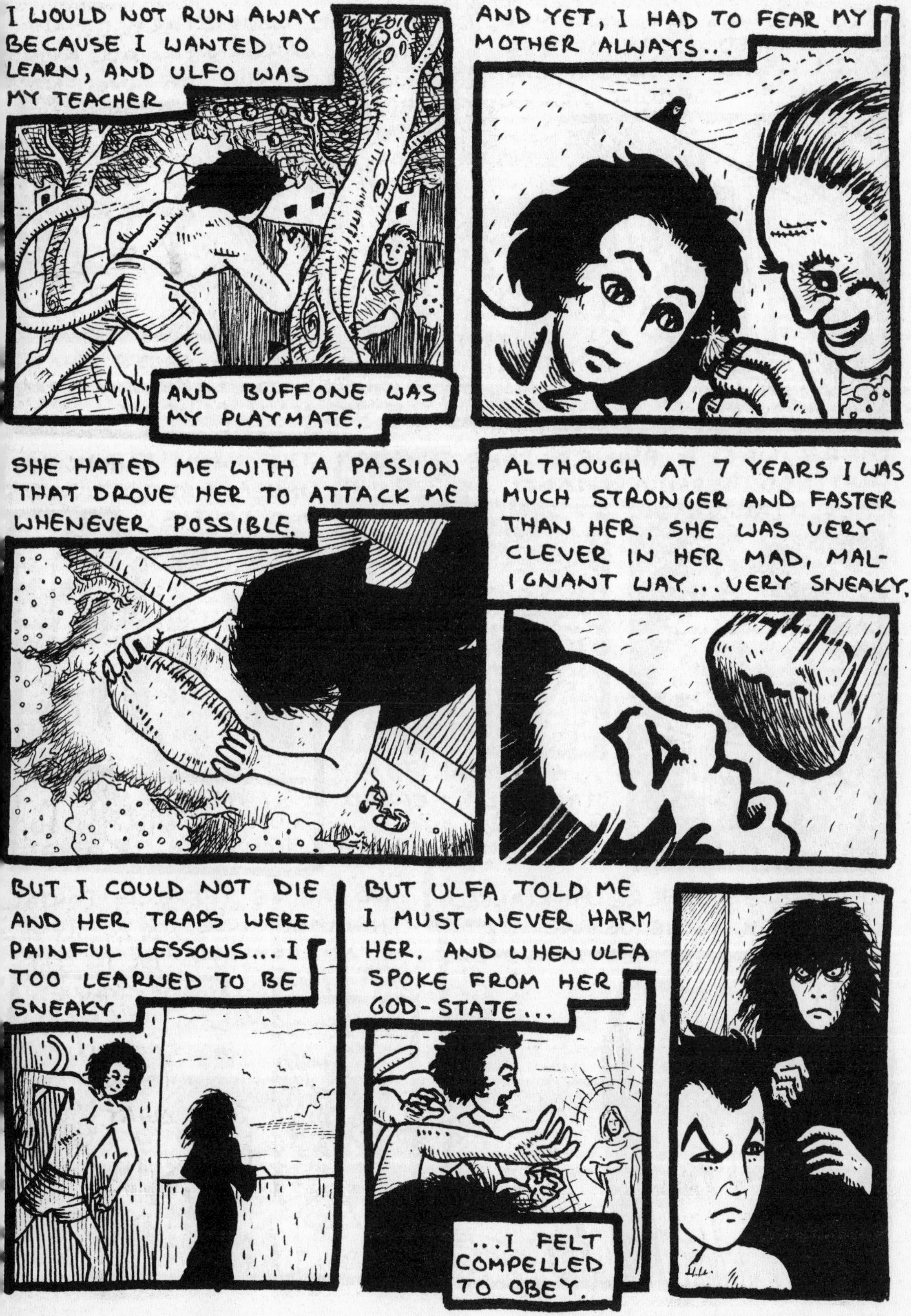
I WOULD NOT RUN AWAY BECAUSE I WANTED TO LEARN, AND ULFO WAS MY TEACHER
AND BUFFONE WAS MY PLAYMATE.
AND YET, I HAD TO FEAR MY MOTHER ALWAYS...
SHE HATED ME WITH A PASSION THAT DROVE HER TO ATTACK ME WHENEVER POSSIBLE.
ALTHOUGH AT 7 YEARS I WAS MUCH STRONGER AND FASTER THAN HER, SHE WAS VERY CLEVER IN HER MAD, MALIGNANT WAY...VERY SNEAKY.
BUT I COULD NOT DIE AND HER TRAPS WERE PAINFUL LESSONS... I TOO LEARNED TO BE SNEAKY.
BUT ULFA TOLD ME I MUST NEVER HARM HER. AND WHEN ULFA SPOKE FROM HER GOD-STATE...
...I FELT COMPELLED TO OBEY.

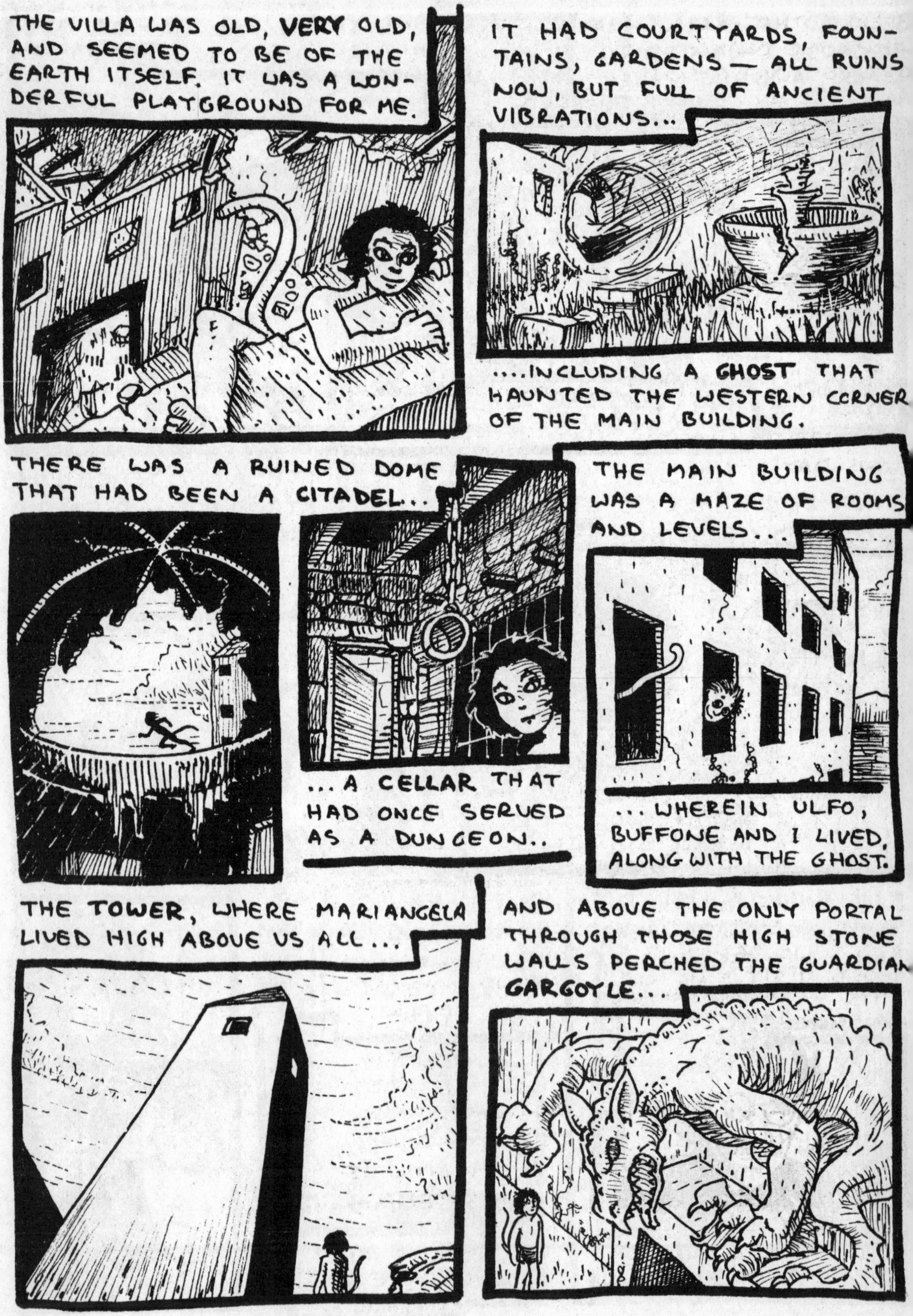
THE VILLA WAS OLD, VERY OLD, AND SEEMED TO BE OF THE EARTH ITSELF. IT WAS A WONDERFUL PLAYGROUND FOR ME.
IT HAD COURTYARDS, FOUNTAINS, GARDENS — ALL RUINS NOW, BUT FULL OF ANCIENT VIBRATIONS...
....INCLUDING A GHOST THAT HAUNTED THE WESTERN CORNER OF THE MAIN BUILDING.
THERE WAS A RUINED DOME THAT HAD BEEN A CITADEL..
...A CELLAR THAT HAD ONCE SERVED AS A DUNGEON..
THE MAIN BUILDING WAS A MAZE OF ROOMS AND LEVELS..
...WHEREIN ULFO, BUFFONE AND I LIVED, ALONG WITH THE GHOST.
THE TOWER, WHERE MARIANGELA LIVED HIGH ABOVE US ALL...
AND ABOVE THE ONLY PORTAL THROUGH THOSE HIGH STONE WALLS PERCHED THE GUARDIAN GARGOYLE...

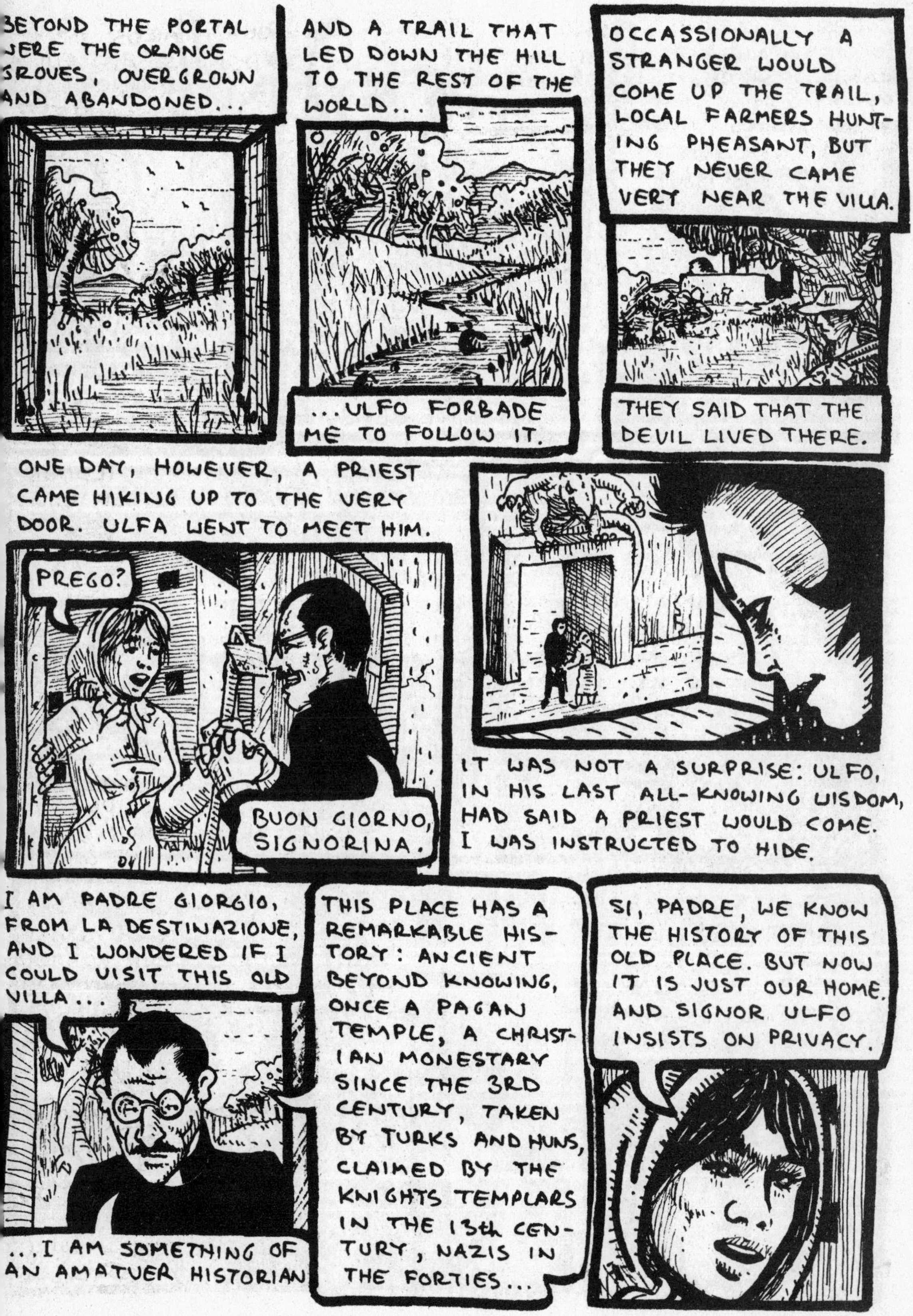
BEYOND THE PORTAL WERE THE ORANGE GROVES, OVERGROWN AND ABANDONED...
AND A TRAIL THAT LED DOWN THE HILL TO THE REST OF THE WORLD...
...ULFO FORBADE ME TO FOLLOW IT.
OCCASSIONALLY A STRANGER WOULD COME UP THE TRAIL, LOCAL FARMERS HUNTING PHEASANT, BUT THEY NEVER CAME VERY NEAR THE VILLA.
THEY SAID THAT THE DEVIL LIVED THERE.
ONE DAY, HOWEVER, A PRIEST CAME HIKING UP TO THE VERY DOOR. ULFA WENT TO MEET HIM.
PREGO?
BUON GIORNO, SIGNORINA.
IT WAS NOT A SURPRISE: ULFO, IN HIS LAST ALL-KNOWING WISDOM, HAD SAID A PRIEST WOULD COME. I WAS INSTRUCTED TO HIDE.
I AM PADRE GIORGIO, FROM LA DESTINAZIONE, AND I WONDERED IF I COULD VISIT THIS OLD VILLA...
...I AM SOMETHING OF AN AMATUER HISTORIAN
THIS PLACE HAS A REMARKABLE HISTORY: ANCIENT BEYOND KNOWING, ONCE A PAGAN TEMPLE, A CHRISTIAN MONESTARY SINCE THE 3RD CENTURY, TAKEN BY TURKS AND HUNS, CLAIMED BY THE KNIGHTS TEMPLARS IN THE 13th CENTURY, NAZIS IN THE FORTIES...
SI, PADRE, WE KNOW THE HISTORY OF THIS OLD PLACE. BUT NOW IT IS JUST OUR HOME. AND SIGNOR ULFO INSISTS ON PRIVACY.

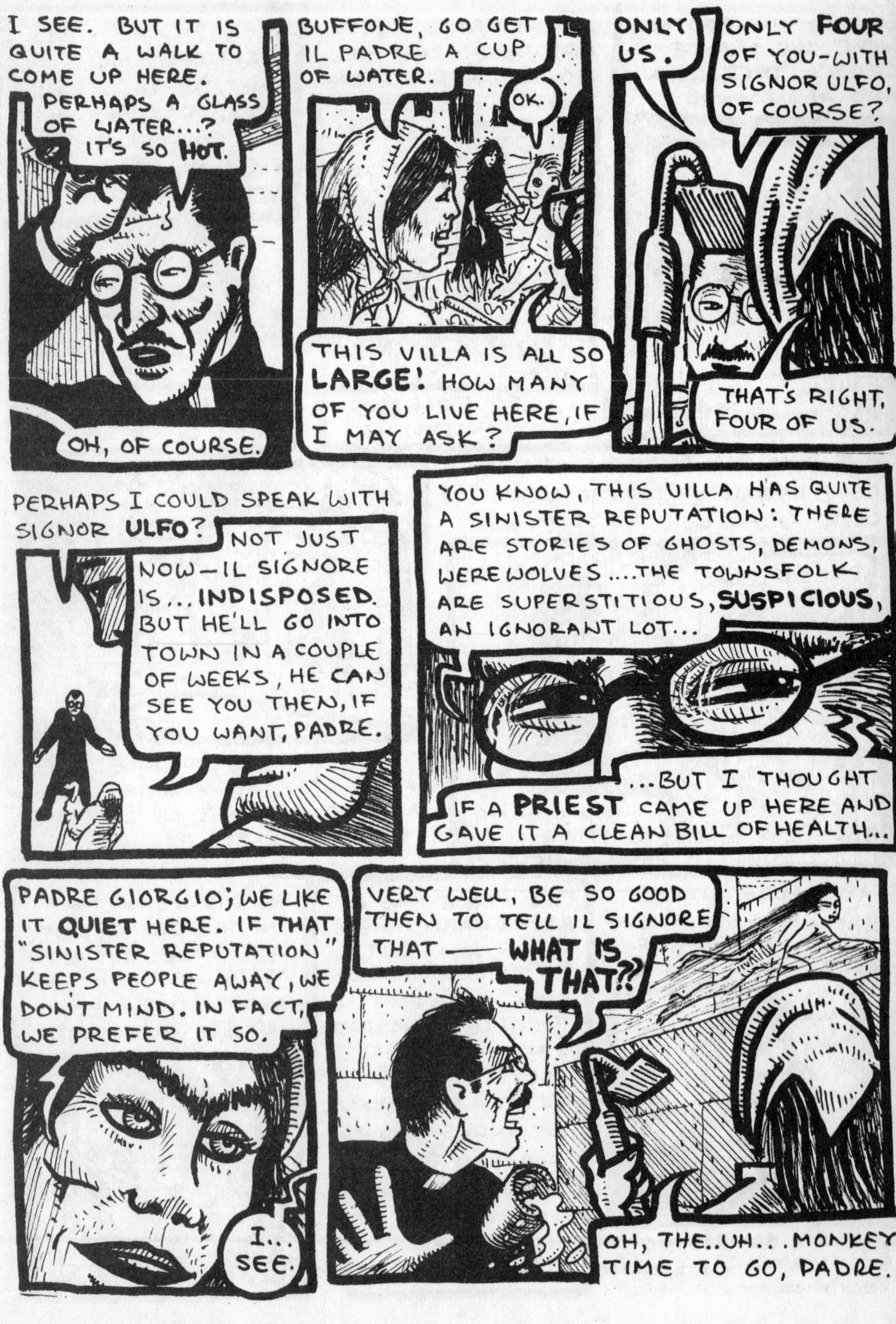
I SEE. BUT IT IS QUITE A WALK TO COME UP HERE.
PERHAPS A GLASS OF WATER...? IT'S SO HOT.
OH, OF COURSE.
BUFFONE, GO GET IL PADRE A CUP OF WATER.
OK.
THIS VILLA IS ALL SO LARGE! HOW MANY OF YOU LIVE HERE, IF I MAY ASK?
ONLY US.
ONLY FOUR OF YOU-WITH SIGNOR ULFO, OF COURSE?
THAT'S RIGHT, FOUR OF US.
PERHAPS I COULD SPEAK WITH SIGNOR ULFO?
NOT JUST NOW-IL SIGNORE IS... INDISPOSED. BUT HE'LL GO INTO TOWN IN A COUPLE OF WEEKS, HE CAN SEE YOU THEN, IF YOU WANT, PADRE.
YOU KNOW, THIS VILLA HAS QUITE A SINISTER REPUTATION: THERE ARE STORIES OF GHOSTS, DEMONS, WEREWOLVES .... THE TOWNSFOLK ARE SUPERSTITIOUS, SUSPICIOUS, AN IGNORANT LOT...
...BUT I THOUGHT IF A PRIEST CAME UP HERE AND GAVE IT A CLEAN BILL OF HEALTH...
PADRE GIORGIO; WE LIKE IT QUIET HERE. IF THAT "SINISTER REPUTATION" KEEPS PEOPLE AWAY, WE DONT MIND. IN FACT, WE PREFER IT SO.
I... SEE.
VERY WELL, BE SO GOOD THEN TO TELL IL SIGNORE THAT —— WHAT IS THAT?!
OH, THE..UH...MONKEY
TIME TO GO, PADRE.

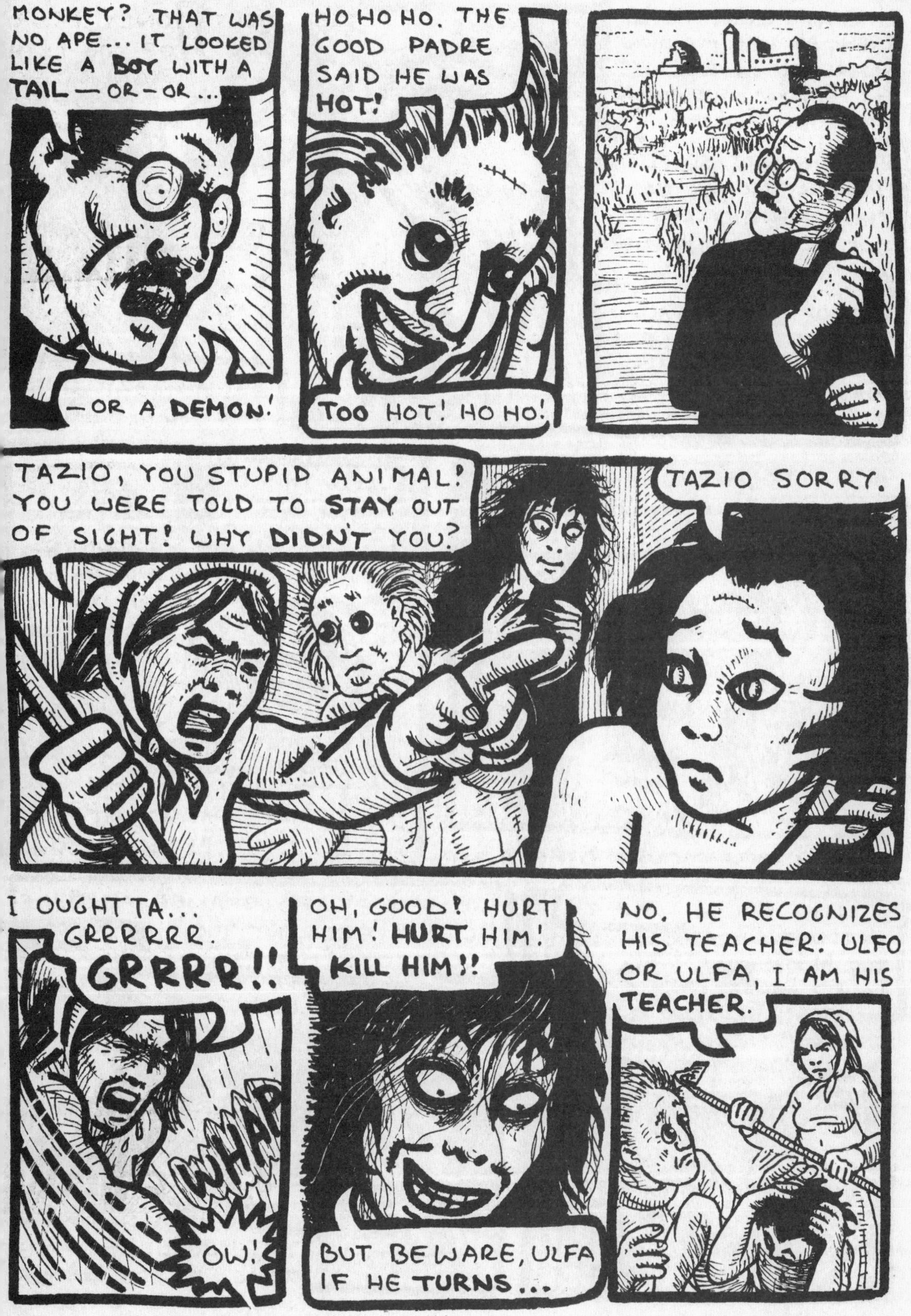
MONKEY? THAT WAS NO APE... IT LOOKED LIKE A BOY WITH A TAIL — OR — OR...
— OR A DEMON!
HO HO HO. THE GOOD PADRE SAID HE WAS HOT!
TOO HOT! HO HO!
TAZIO, YOU STUPID ANIMAL! YOU WERE TOLD TO STAY OUT OF SIGHT! WHY DIDN'T YOU?
TAZIO SORRY.
I OUGHTTA... GRRRRRR.
GRRRR!!
WHAP
OW!
OH, GOOD! HURT HIM! HURT HIM! KILL HIM!!
BUT BEWARE, ULFA IF HE TURNS...
NO. HE RECOGNIZES HIS TEACHER: ULFO OR ULFA, I AM HIS TEACHER.

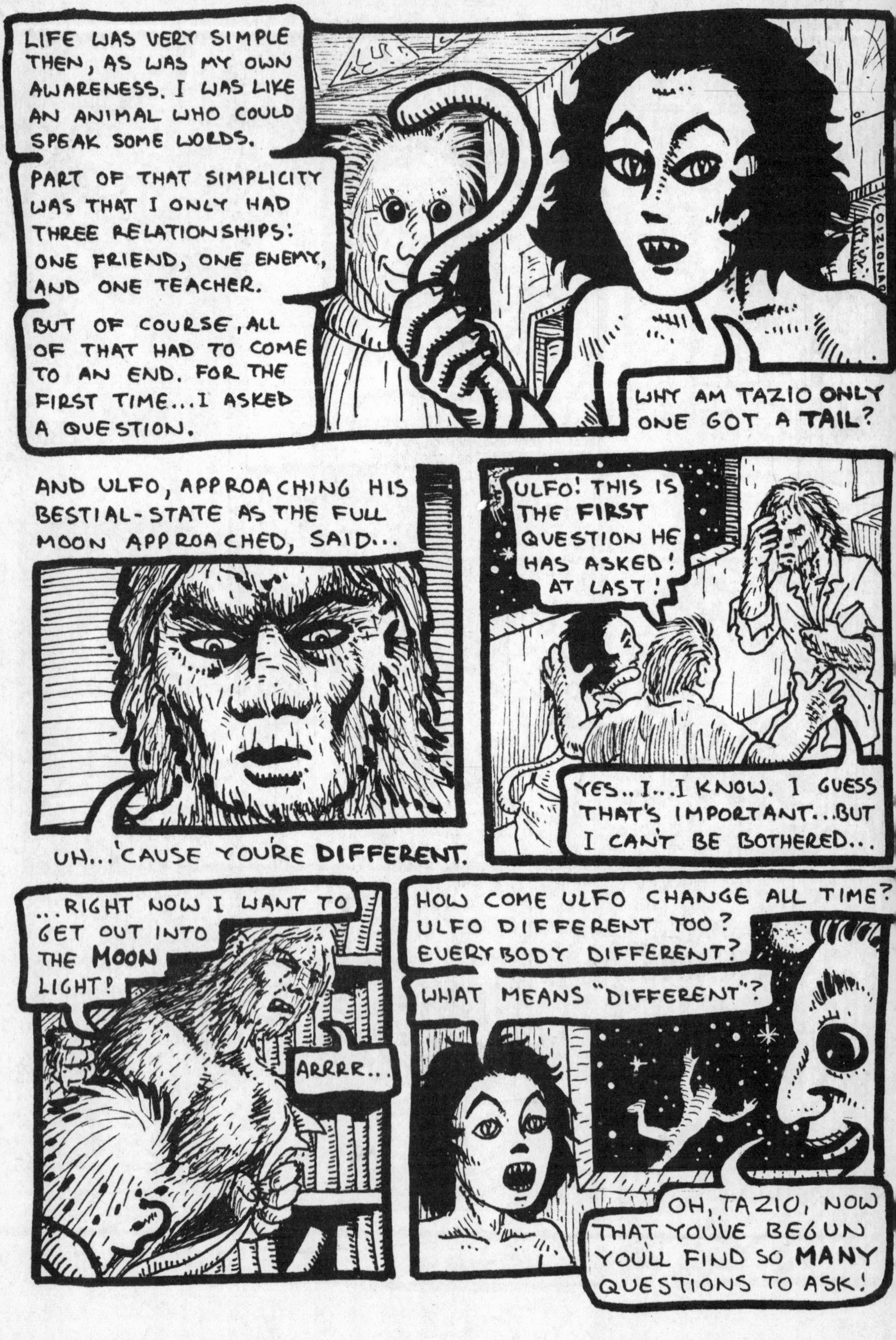
LIFE WAS VERY SIMPLE THEN, AS WAS MY OWN AWARENESS. I WAS LIKE AN ANIMAL WHO COULD SPEAK SOME WORDS.
PART OF THAT SIMPLICITY WAS THAT I ONLY HAD THREE RELATIONSHIPS: ONE FRIEND, ONE ENEMY, AND ONE TEACHER.
BUT OF COURSE, ALL OF THAT HAD TO COME TO AN END. FOR THE FIRST TIME... I ASKED A QUESTION.
WHY AM TAZIO ONLY ONE GOT A TAIL?
AND ULFO, APPROACHING HIS BESTIAL-STATE AS THE FULL MOON APPROACHED, SAID...
UH... 'CAUSE YOU'RE DIFFERENT.
ULFO! THIS IS THE FIRST QUESTION HE HAS ASKED! AT LAST!
YES.. I... I KNOW. I GUESS THAT'S IMPORTANT... BUT I CAN'T BE BOTHERED...
...RIGHT NOW I WANT TO GET OUT INTO THE MOON LIGHT!
ARRRR...
HOW COME ULFO CHANGE ALL TIME? ULFO DIFFERENT TOO? EVERYBODY DIFFERENT?
WHAT MEANS "DIFFERENT"?
OH, TAZIO, NOW THAT YOU'VE BEGUN YOU'LL FIND SO MANY QUESTIONS TO ASK!

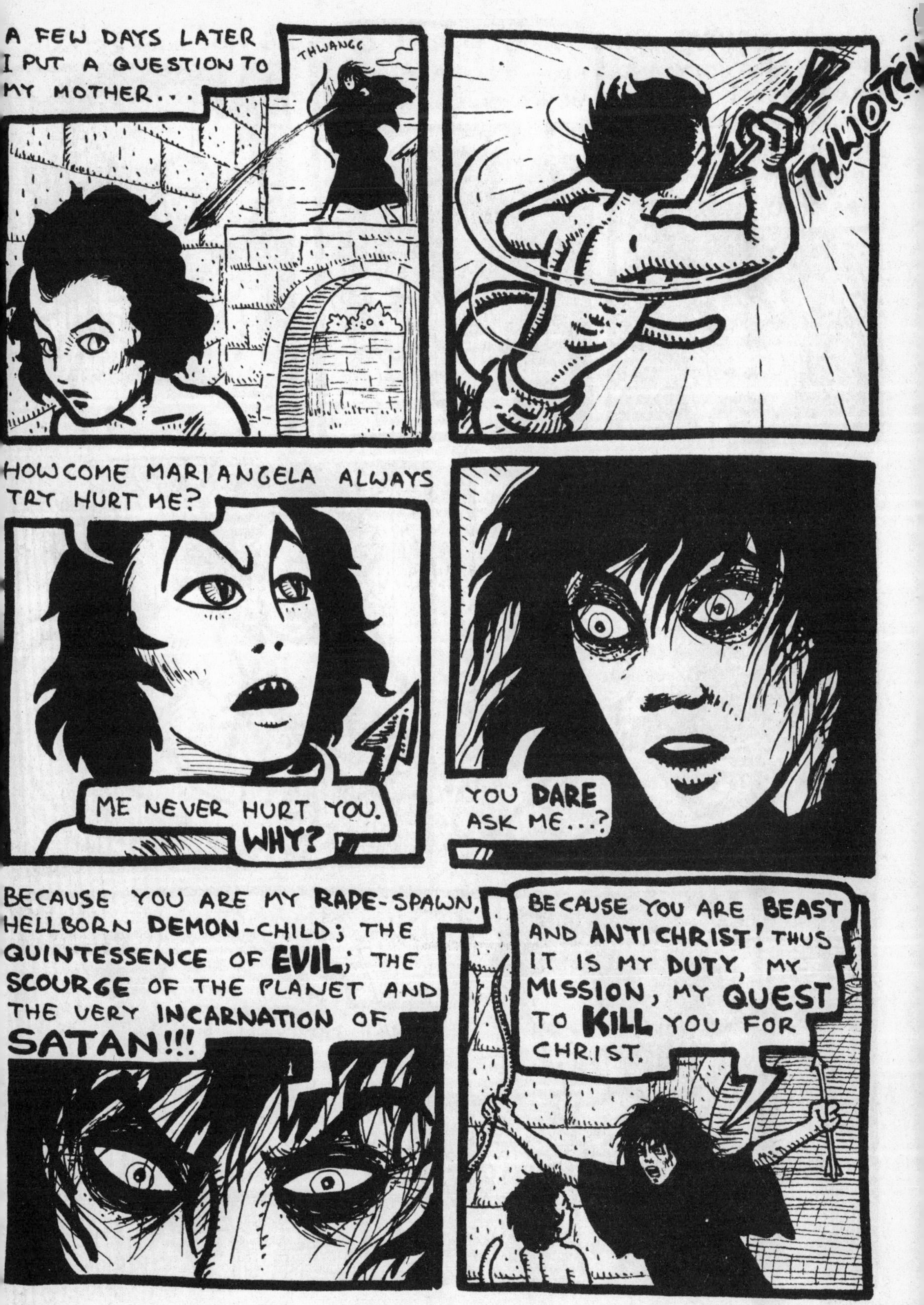
A FEW DAYS LATER I PUT A QUESTION TO MY MOTHER...
THWANGG
THWOTCK!
HOWCOME MARIANGELA ALWAYS TRY HURT ME?
ME NEVER HURT YOU. WHY?
YOU DARE ASK ME...?
BECAUSE YOU ARE MY RAPE-SPAWN, HELLBORN DEMON-CHILD; THE QUINTESSENCE OF EVIL; THE SCOURGE OF THE PLANET AND THE VERY INCARNATION OF SATAN!!!
BECAUSE YOU ARE BEAST AND ANTICHRIST! THUS IT IS MY DUTY, MY MISSION, MY QUEST TO KILL YOU FOR CHRIST.

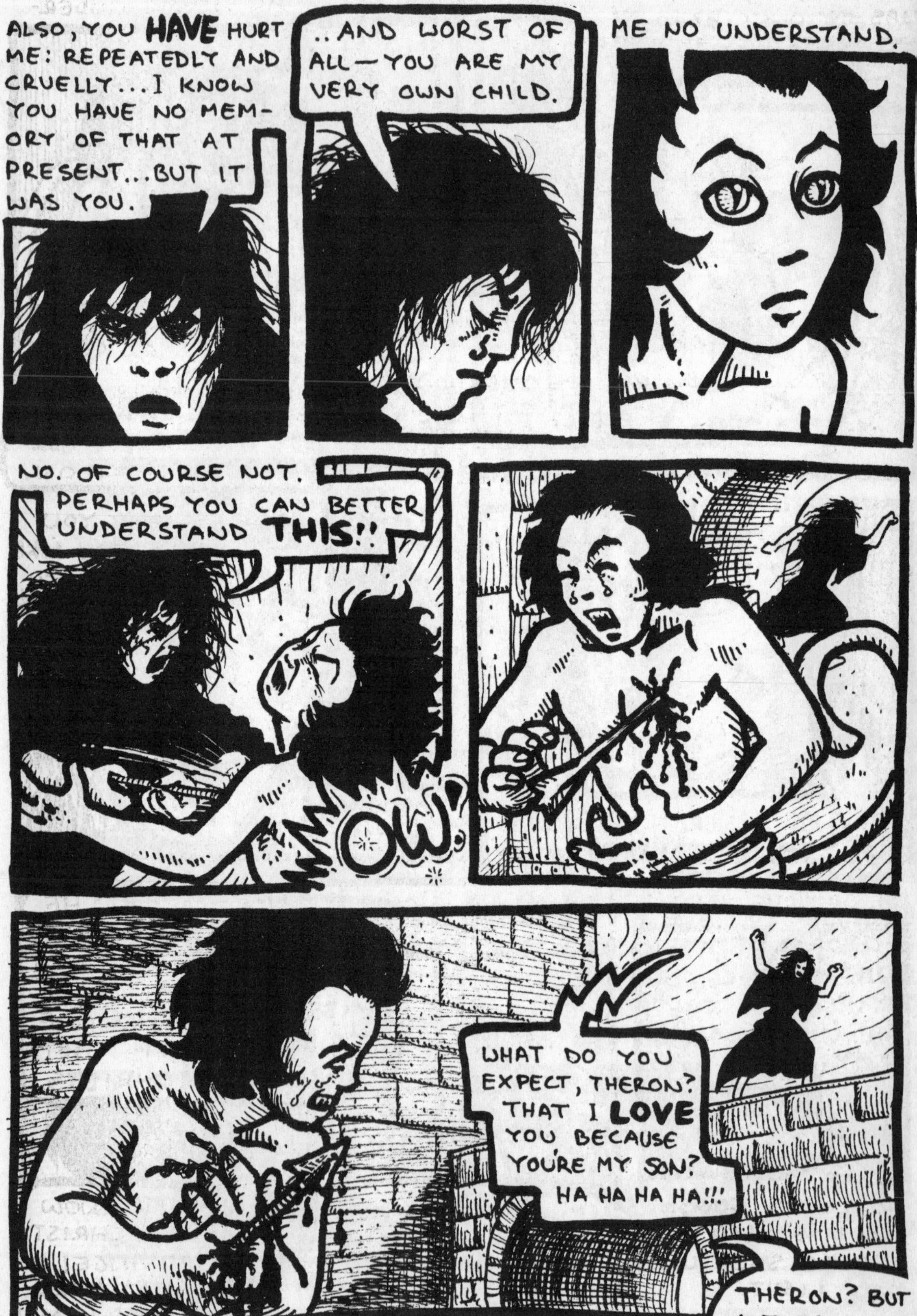

ALSO, YOU HAVE HURT ME: REPEATEDLY AND CRUELLY... I KNOW YOU HAVE NO MEMORY OF THAT AT PRESENT... BUT IT WAS YOU.
..AND WORST OF ALL—YOU ARE MY VERY OWN CHILD.
ME NO UNDERSTAND.
NO. OF COURSE NOT.
PERHAPS YOU CAN BETTER UNDERSTAND THIS!!
OW!
WHAT DO YOU EXPECT, THERON? THAT I LOVE YOU BECAUSE YOU'RE MY SON? HA HA HA HA!!!
THERON? BUT ME TAZIO.

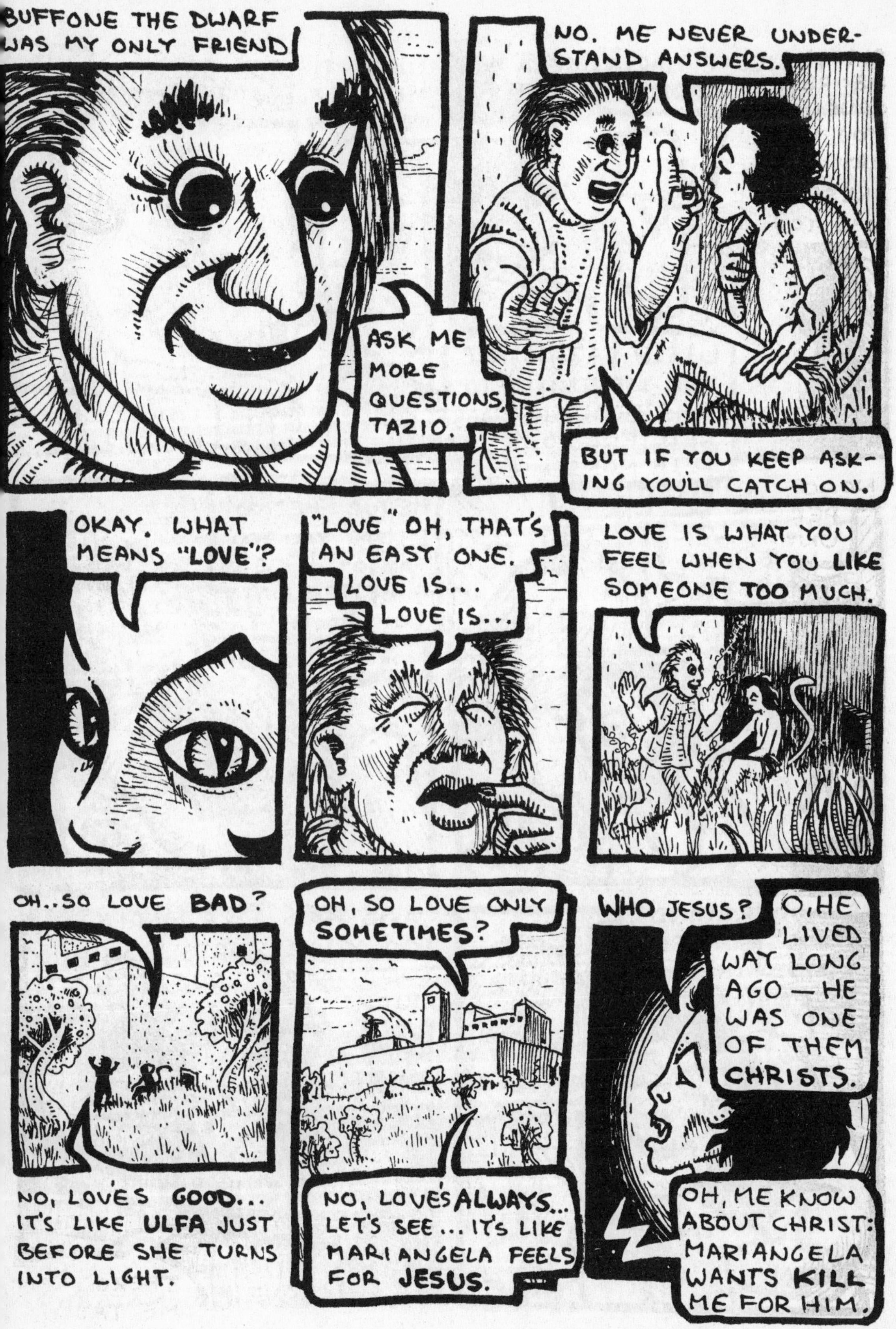
BUFFONE THE DWARF WAS MY ONLY FRIEND
ASK ME MORE QUESTIONS, TAZIO.
NO. ME NEVER UNDERSTAND ANSWERS.
BUT IF YOU KEEP ASKING YOU'LL CATCH ON.
OKAY. WHAT MEANS "LOVE"?
"LOVE" OH, THAT'S AN EASY ONE. LOVE IS... LOVE IS...
LOVE IS WHAT YOU FEEL WHEN YOU LIKE SOMEONE TOO MUCH.
OH..SO LOVE BAD?
NO, LOVE'S GOOD... IT'S LIKE ULFA JUST BEFORE SHE TURNS INTO LIGHT.
OH, SO LOVE ONLY SOMETIMES?
NO, LOVE'S ALWAYS... LET'S SEE... IT'S LIKE MARIANGELA FEELS FOR JESUS.
WHO JESUS?
O, HE LIVED WAY LONG AGO — HE WAS ONE OF THEM CHRISTS.
OH, ME KNOW ABOUT CHRIST: MARIANGELA WANTS KILL ME FOR HIM.

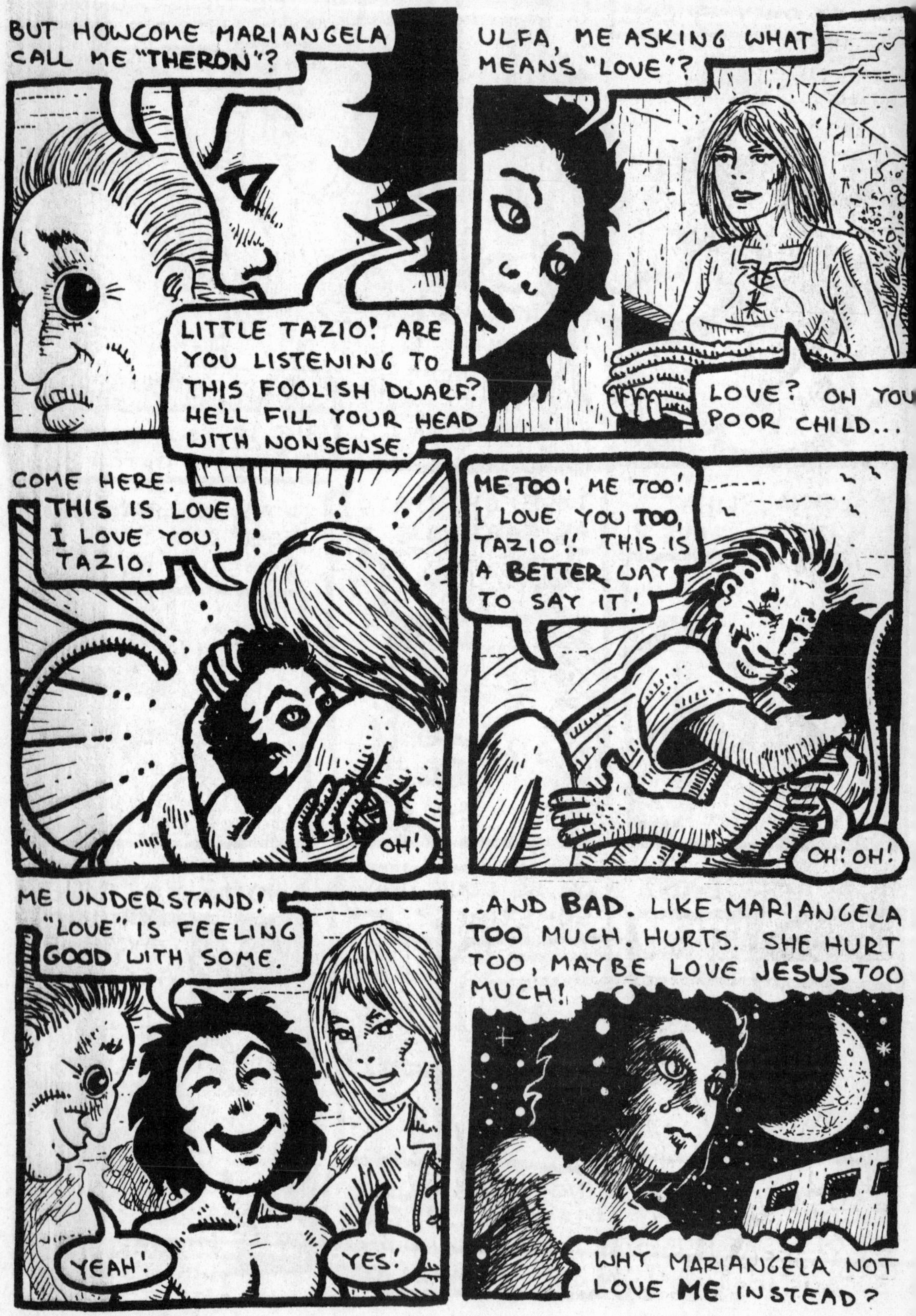
BUT HOWCOME MARIANGELA CALL ME "THERON"?
LITTLE TAZIO! ARE YOU LISTENING TO THIS FOOLISH DWARF? HE'LL FILL YOUR HEAD WITH NONSENSE.
ULFA, ME ASKING WHAT MEANS "LOVE"?
LOVE? OH YOU POOR CHILD...
COME HERE. THIS IS LOVE I LOVE YOU, TAZIO.
OH!
ME TOO! ME TOO! I LOVE YOU TOO, TAZIO!! THIS IS A BETTER WAY TO SAY IT!
OH! OH!
ME UNDERSTAND! "LOVE" IS FEELING GOOD WITH SOME.
YEAH!
YES!
..AND BAD. LIKE MARIANGELA TOO MUCH. HURTS. SHE HURT TOO, MAYBE LOVE JESUS TOO MUCH!
WHY MARIANGELA NOT LOVE ME INSTEAD?

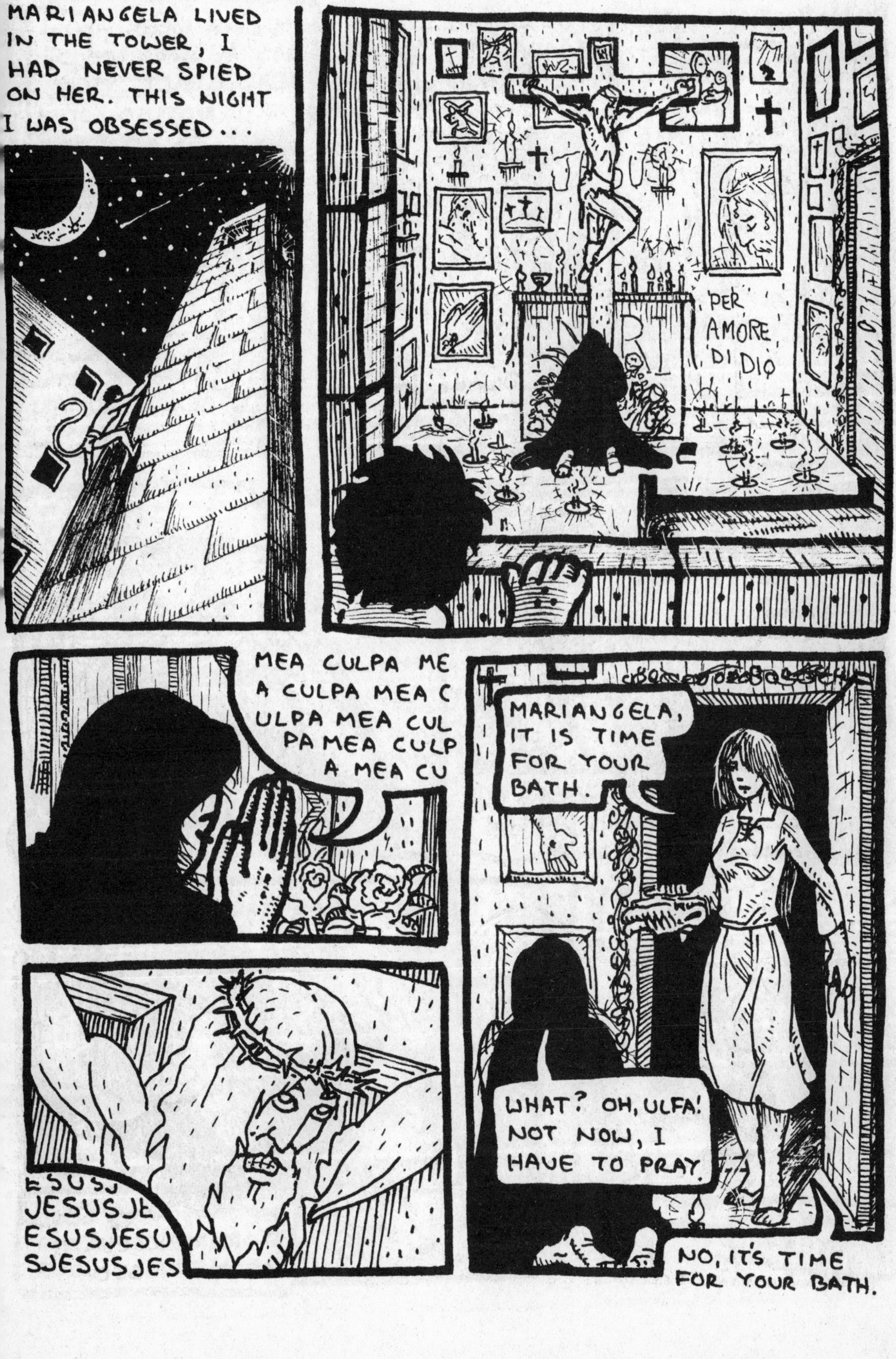
MARIANGELA LIVED IN THE TOWER, I HAD NEVER SPIED ON HER. THIS NIGHT I WAS OBSESSED...
PER AMORE DI DIO
MEA CULPA ME A CULPA MEA C ULPA MEA CUL PA MEA CULP A MEA CU
ESUSJ JESUSJE ESUSJESU SJESUSJES
MARIANGELA, IT IS TIME FOR YOUR BATH.
WHAT? OH, ULFA! NOT NOW, I HAVE TO PRAY.
NO, IT'S TIME FOR YOUR BATH.

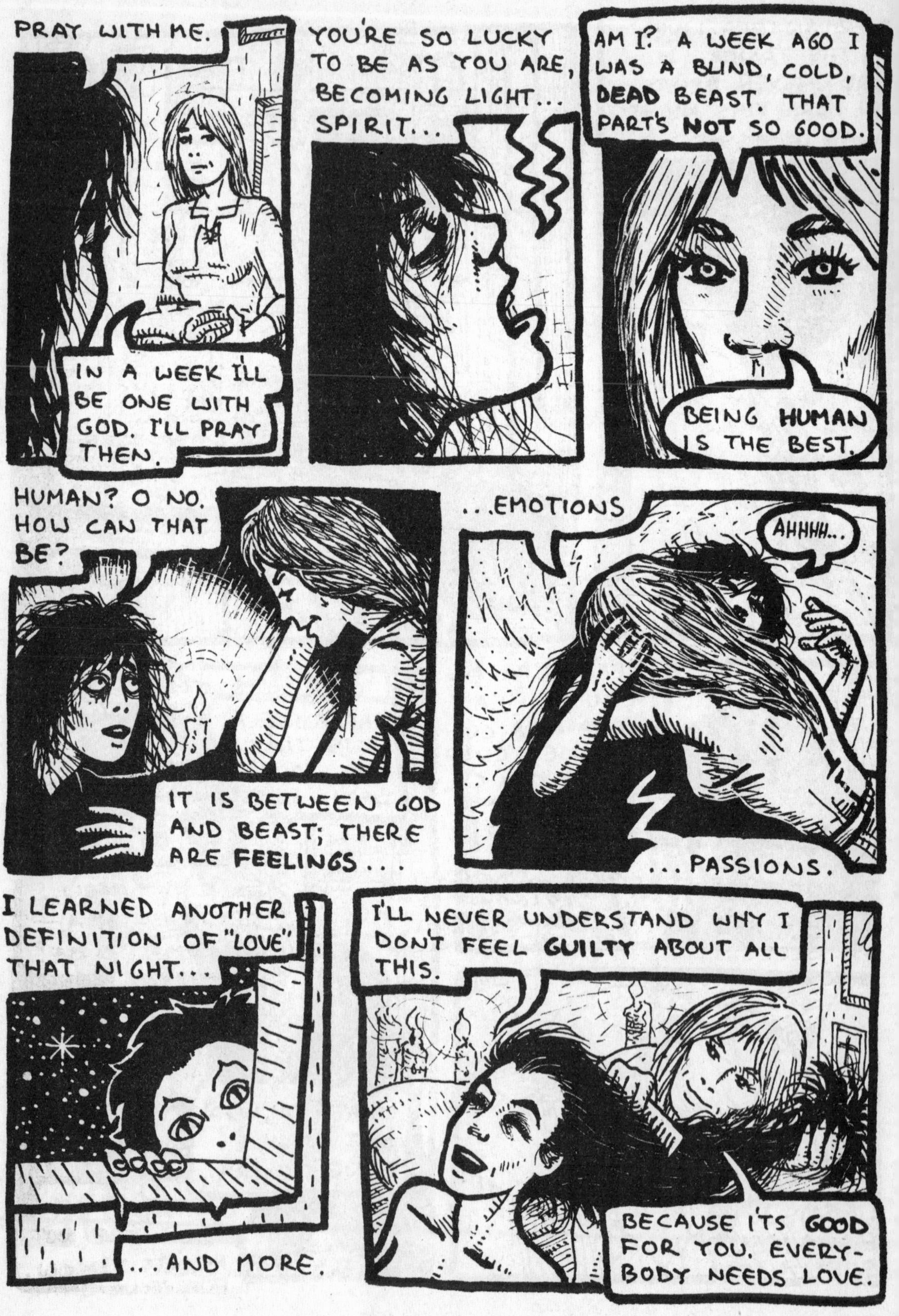
PRAY WITH ME.
IN A WEEK I'LL BE ONE WITH GOD. I'LL PRAY THEN.
YOU'RE SO LUCKY TO BE AS YOU ARE, BECOMING LIGHT... SPIRIT...
AM I? A WEEK AGO I WAS A BLIND, COLD, DEAD BEAST. THAT PART'S NOT SO GOOD.
BEING HUMAN IS THE BEST.
HUMAN? O NO. HOW CAN THAT BE?
IT IS BETWEEN GOD AND BEAST; THERE ARE FEELINGS...
...EMOTIONS
AHHHH...
...PASSIONS.
I LEARNED ANOTHER DEFINITION OF "LOVE" THAT NIGHT...
...AND MORE.
I'LL NEVER UNDERSTAND WHY I DON'T FEEL GUILTY ABOUT ALL THIS.
BECAUSE IT'S GOOD FOR YOU. EVERY-BODY NEEDS LOVE.

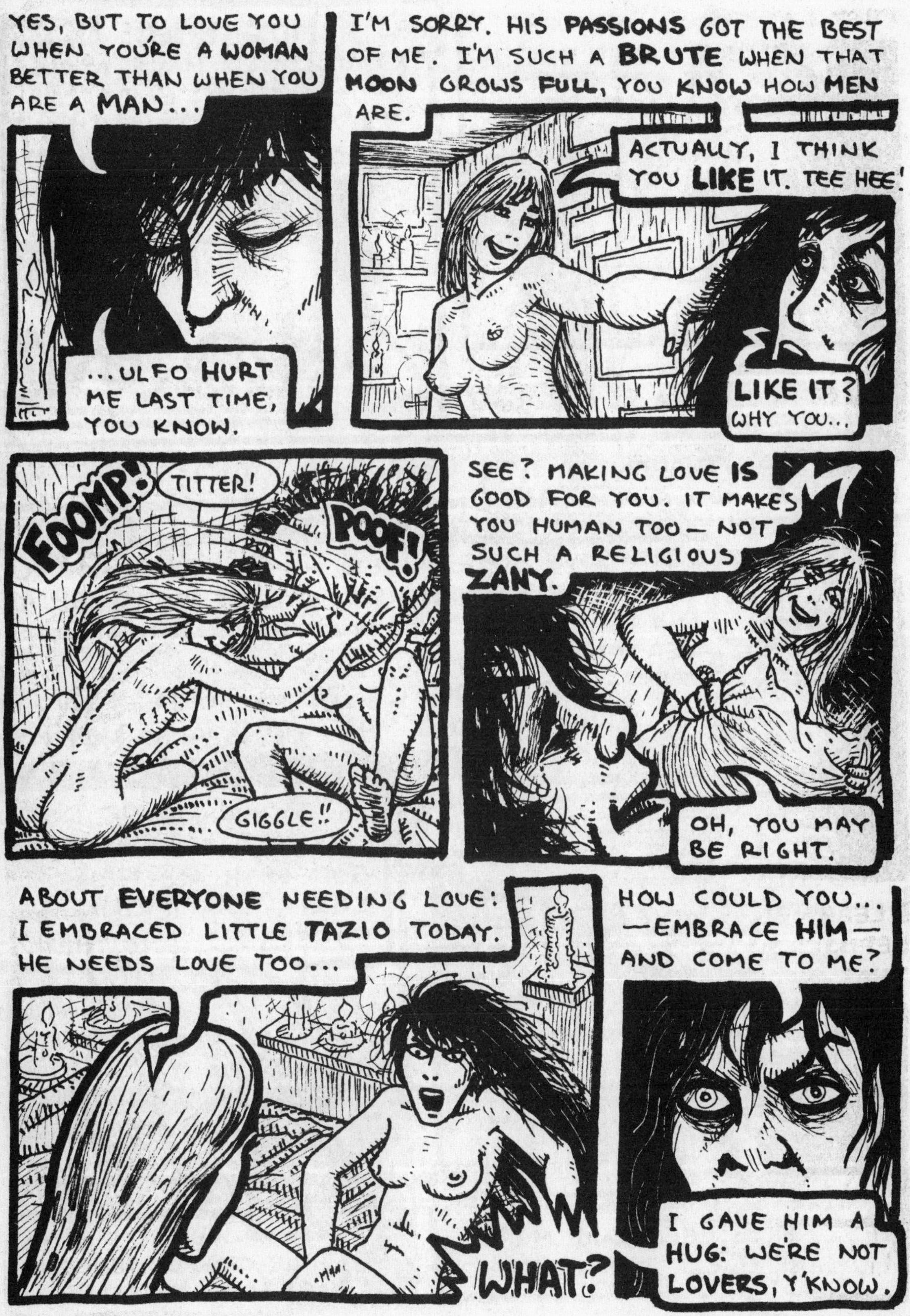
YES, BUT TO LOVE YOU WHEN YOU'RE A WOMAN BETTER THAN WHEN YOU ARE A MAN...
...ULFO HURT ME LAST TIME, YOU KNOW.
I'M SORRY. HIS PASSIONS GOT THE BEST OF ME. I'M SUCH A BRUTE WHEN THAT MOON GROWS FULL, YOU KNOW HOW MEN ARE.
ACTUALLY, I THINK YOU LIKE IT. TEE HEE!
LIKE IT? WHY YOU...
FOOMP!
TITTER!
POOF!
GIGGLE!!
SEE? MAKING LOVE IS GOOD FOR YOU. IT MAKES YOU HUMAN TOO—NOT SUCH A RELIGIOUS ZANY.
OH, YOU MAY BE RIGHT.
ABOUT EVERYONE NEEDING LOVE: I EMBRACED LITTLE TAZIO TODAY. HE NEEDS LOVE TOO...
WHAT?
HOW COULD YOU... —EMBRACE HIM— AND COME TO ME?
I GAVE HIM A HUG: WE'RE NOT LOVERS, Y'KNOW.

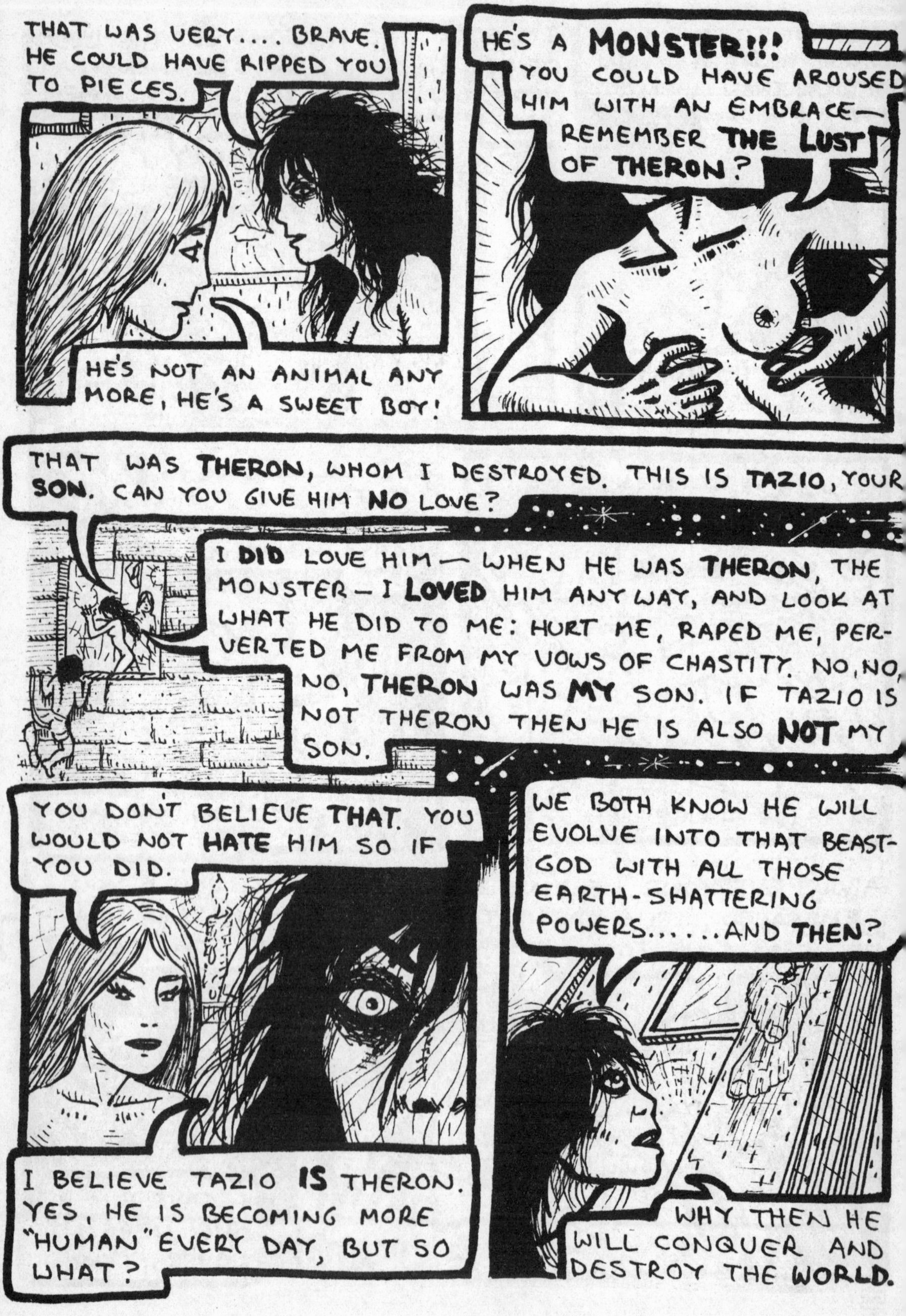
THAT WAS VERY.... BRAVE. HE COULD HAVE RIPPED YOU TO PIECES.
HE'S NOT AN ANIMAL ANY MORE, HE'S A SWEET BOY!
HE'S A MONSTER!!! YOU COULD HAVE AROUSED HIM WITH AN EMBRACE— REMEMBER THE LUST OF THERON?
THAT WAS THERON, WHOM I DESTROYED. THIS IS TAZIO, YOUR SON. CAN YOU GIVE HIM NO LOVE?
I DID LOVE HIM— WHEN HE WAS THERON, THE MONSTER—I LOVED HIM ANYWAY, AND LOOK AT WHAT HE DID TO ME: HURT ME, RAPED ME, PERVERTED ME FROM MY VOWS OF CHASTITY. NO, NO, NO, THERON WAS MY SON. IF TAZIO IS NOT THERON THEN HE IS ALSO NOT MY SON.
YOU DON'T BELIEVE THAT. YOU WOULD NOT HATE HIM SO IF YOU DID.
I BELIEVE TAZIO IS THERON. YES, HE IS BECOMING MORE "HUMAN" EVERY DAY, BUT SO WHAT?
WE BOTH KNOW HE WILL EVOLVE INTO THAT BEAST-GOD WITH ALL THOSE EARTH-SHATTERING POWERS......AND THEN?
WHY THEN HE WILL CONQUER AND DESTROY THE WORLD.

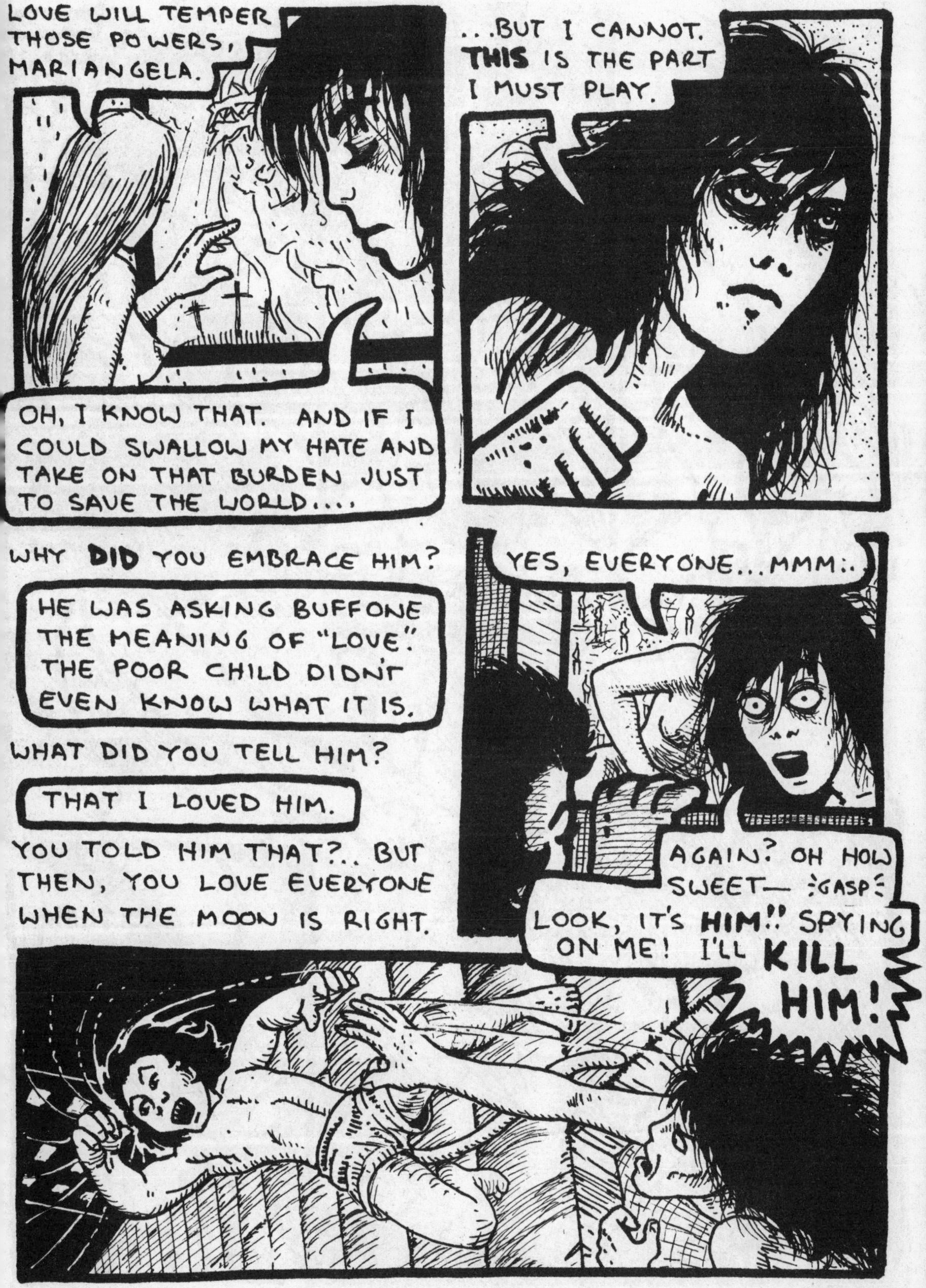
LOVE WILL TEMPER THOSE POWERS, MARIANGELA.
OH, I KNOW THAT. AND IF I COULD SWALLOW MY HATE AND TAKE ON THAT BURDEN JUST TO SAVE THE WORLD....
...BUT I CANNOT. THIS IS THE PART I MUST PLAY.
WHY DID YOU EMBRACE HIM?
HE WAS ASKING BUFFONE THE MEANING OF "LOVE". THE POOR CHILD DIDN'T EVEN KNOW WHAT IT IS.
WHAT DID YOU TELL HIM?
THAT I LOVED HIM.
YOU TOLD HIM THAT?.. BUT THEN, YOU LOVE EVERYONE WHEN THE MOON IS RIGHT.
YES, EVERYONE...MMM:.
AGAIN? OH HOW SWEET— :GASP:
LOOK, IT'S HIM!! SPYING ON ME! I'LL KILL HIM!

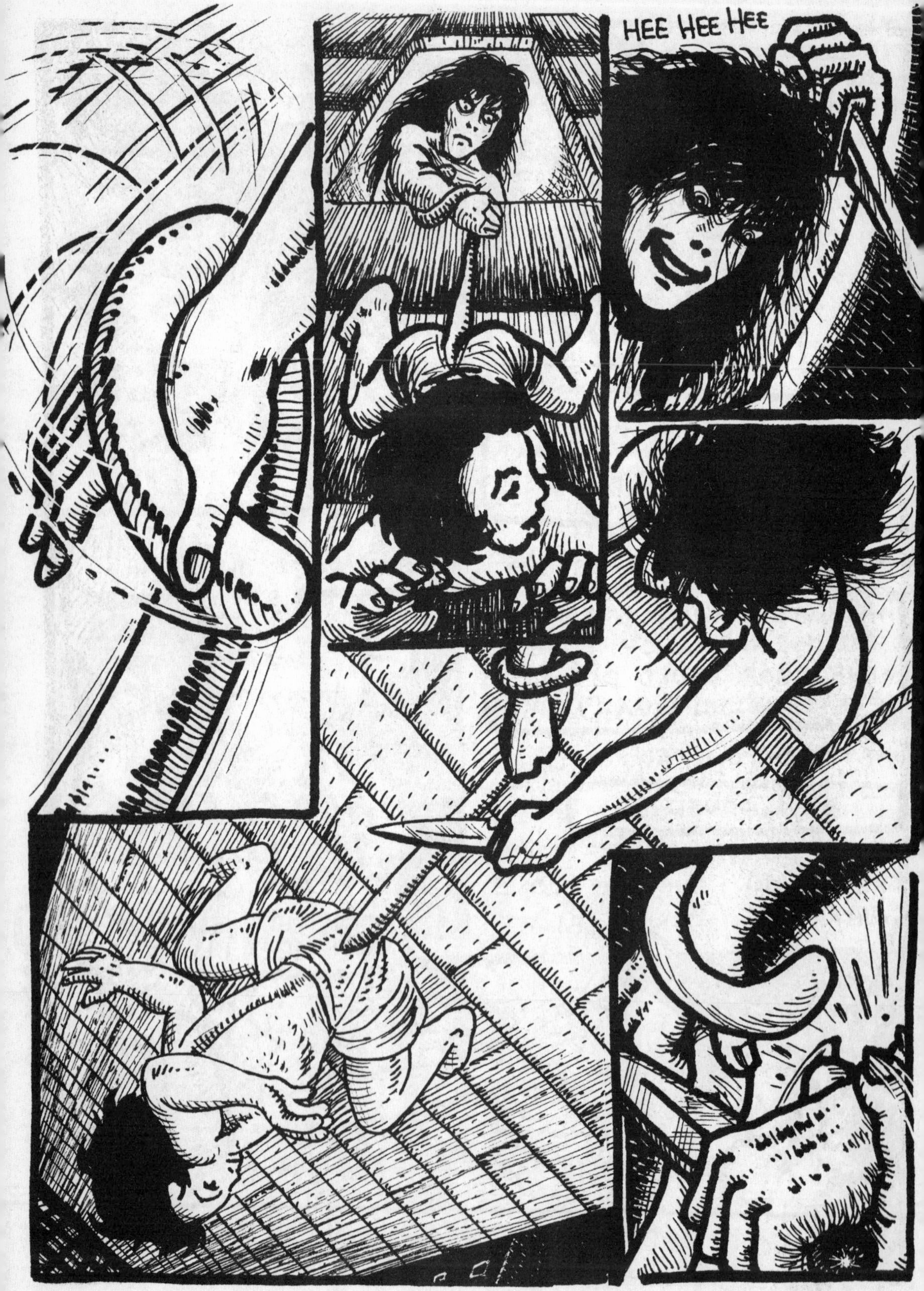
HEE HEE HEE

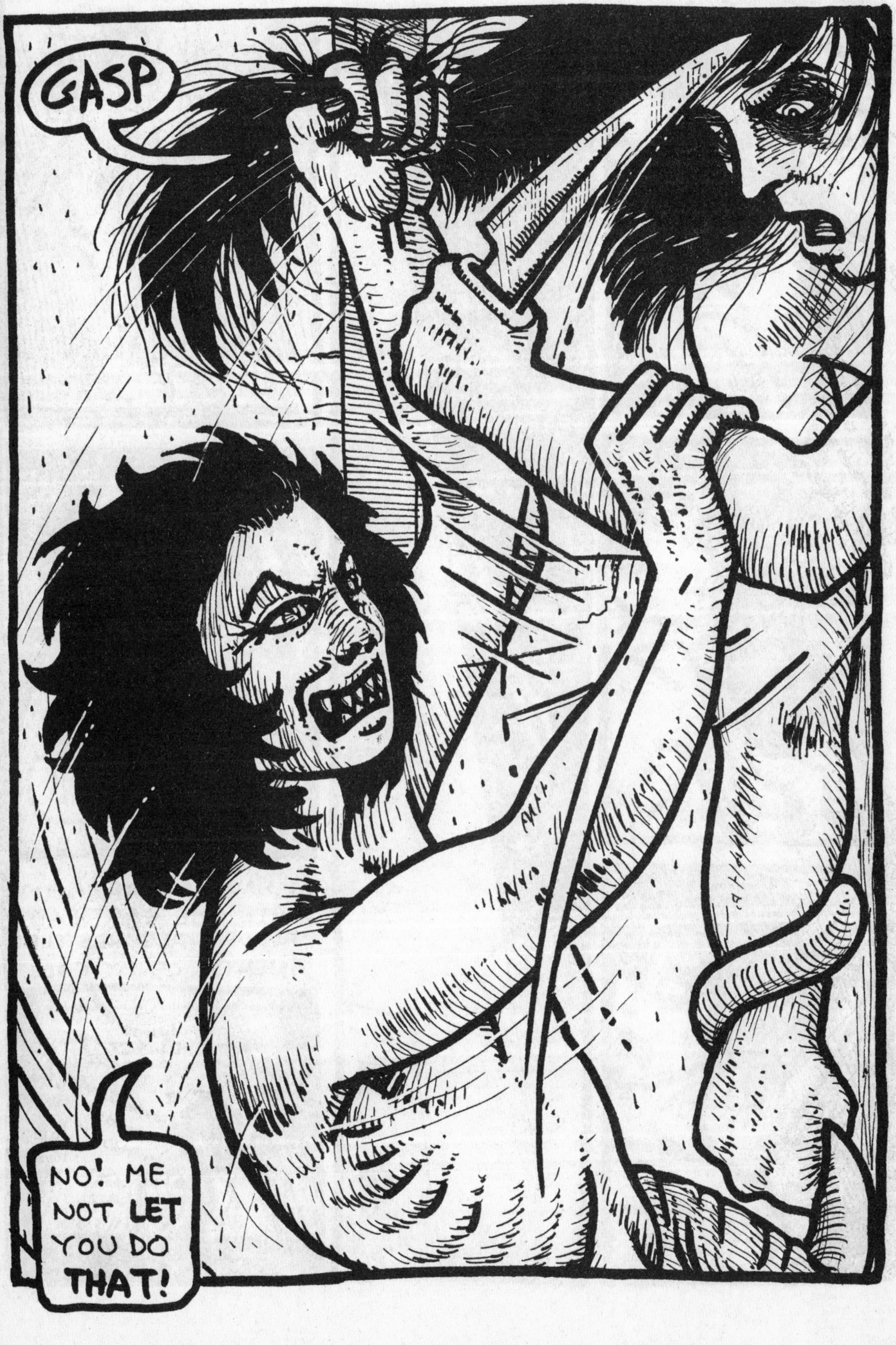
GASP
NO! ME NOT LET YOU DO THAT!

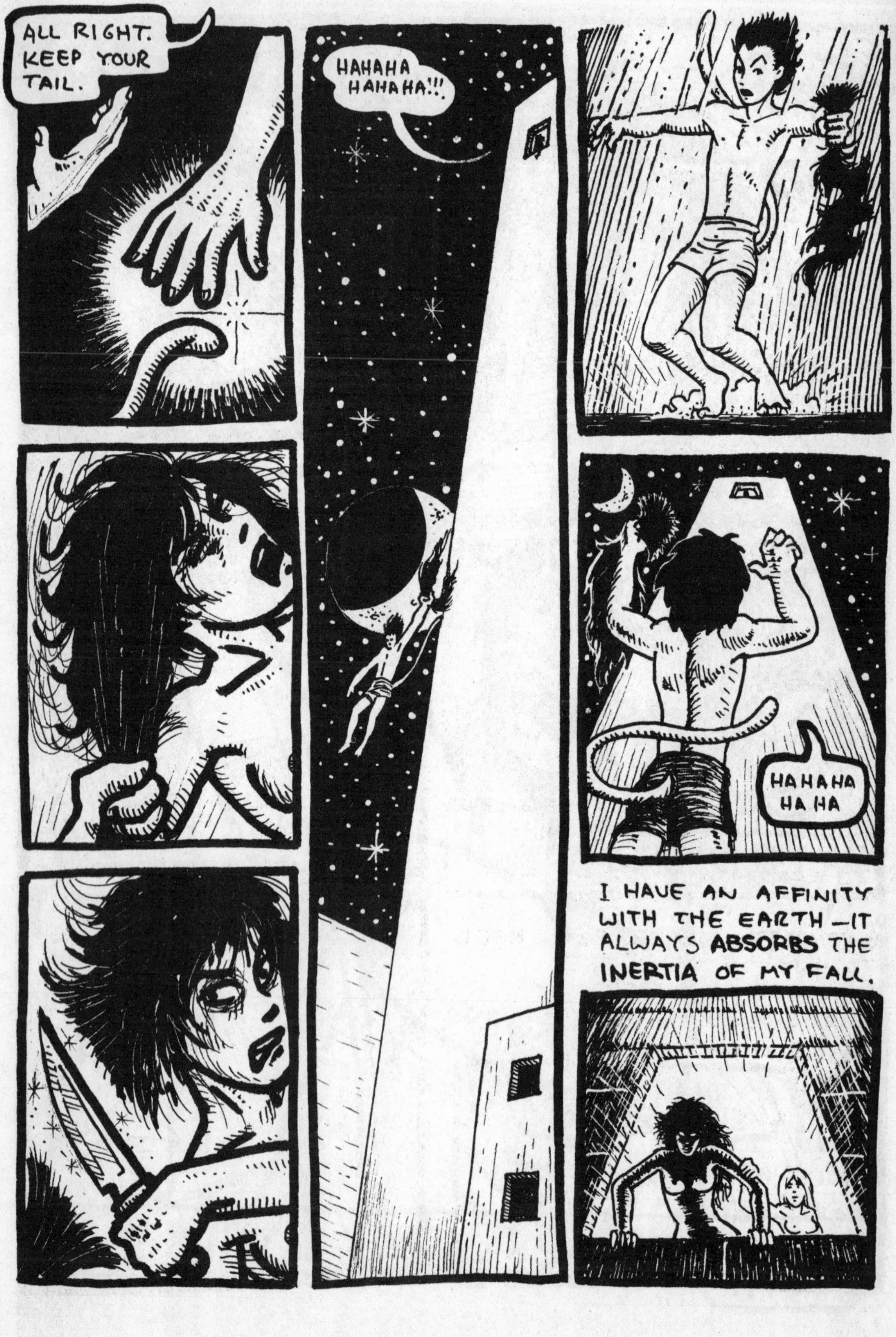
ALL RIGHT. KEEP YOUR TAIL.
HAHAHA HAHAHA!!!
HAHAHA HA HA
I HAVE AN AFFINITY WITH THE EARTH—IT ALWAYS ABSORBS THE INERTIA OF MY FALL.

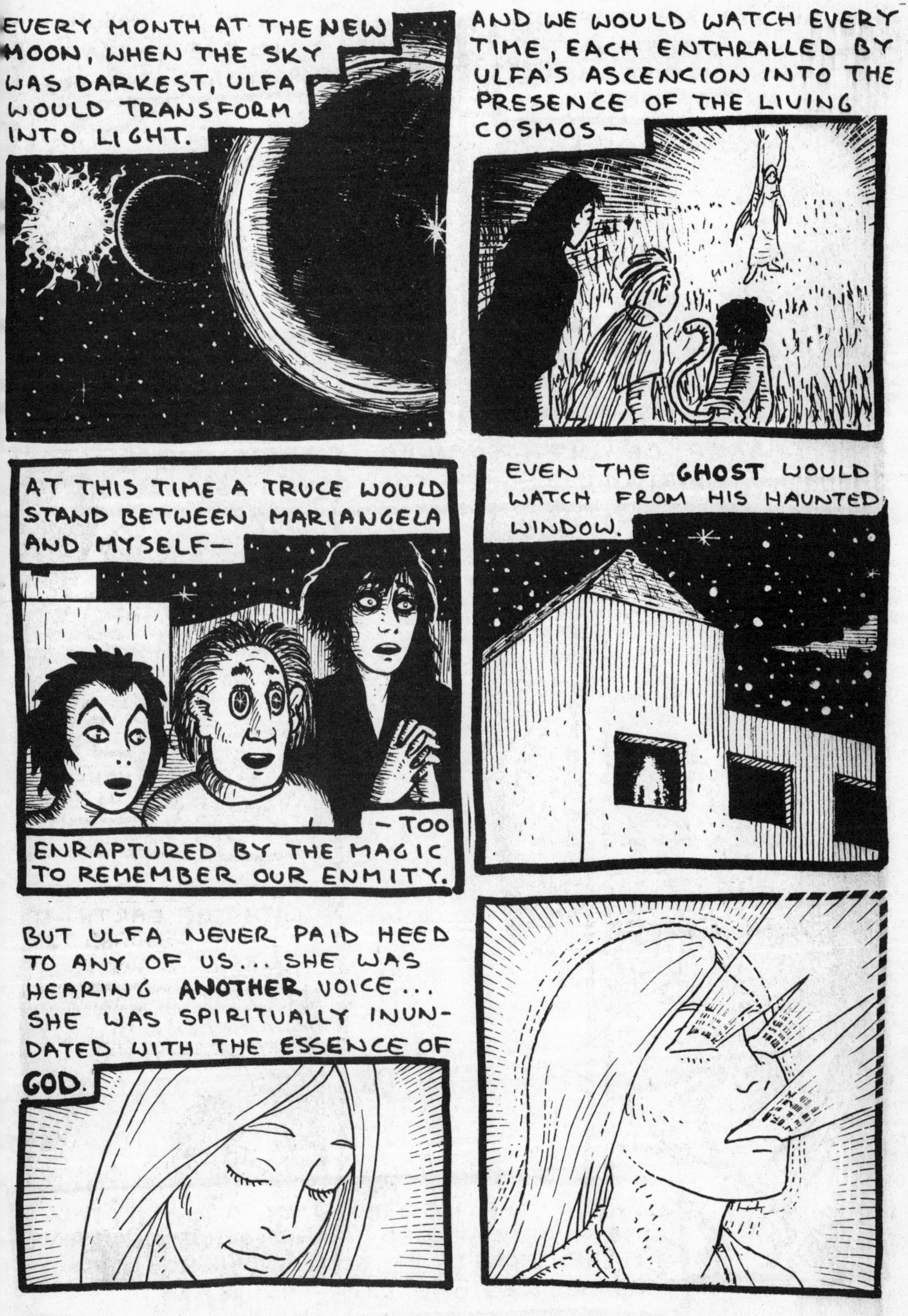
EVERY MONTH AT THE NEW MOON, WHEN THE SKY WAS DARKEST, ULFA WOULD TRANSFORM INTO LIGHT.
AND WE WOULD WATCH EVERY TIME, EACH ENTHRALLED BY ULFA'S ASCENCION INTO THE PRESENCE OF THE LIVING COSMOS—
AT THIS TIME A TRUCE WOULD STAND BETWEEN MARIANGELA AND MYSELF—
—TOO ENRAPTURED BY THE MAGIC TO REMEMBER OUR ENMITY.
EVEN THE GHOST WOULD WATCH FROM HIS HAUNTED WINDOW.
BUT ULFA NEVER PAID HEED TO ANY OF US... SHE WAS HEARING ANOTHER VOICE... SHE WAS SPIRITUALLY INUNDATED WITH THE ESSENCE OF GOD.

MARIANGELA AND BUFFONE COULD NOT WITHSTAND THE INTENSITY OF THE LIGHT, AND HAD TO LOOK AWAY.

ONLY I, WITH MY INHUMAN EYES, COULD SEE THE ACTUAL TRANSFORMATION TAKE PLACE.

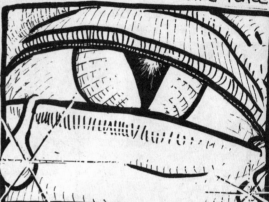

THE CHANGE OF ULFA TO ULFO, GODDESS-WOMAN TO GOD-MAN, SPIRITUAL ZENITH TO COSMIC GENIUS...

...FOR THE NEW-MOON ULFO WAS TOTALLY WISE AND POSSESSED ALL KNOWLEDGE, PRIVY TO THE SECRETS OF GOD, ATTAINED WHEN HE/SHE WAS ONE WITH THE **AAM.**

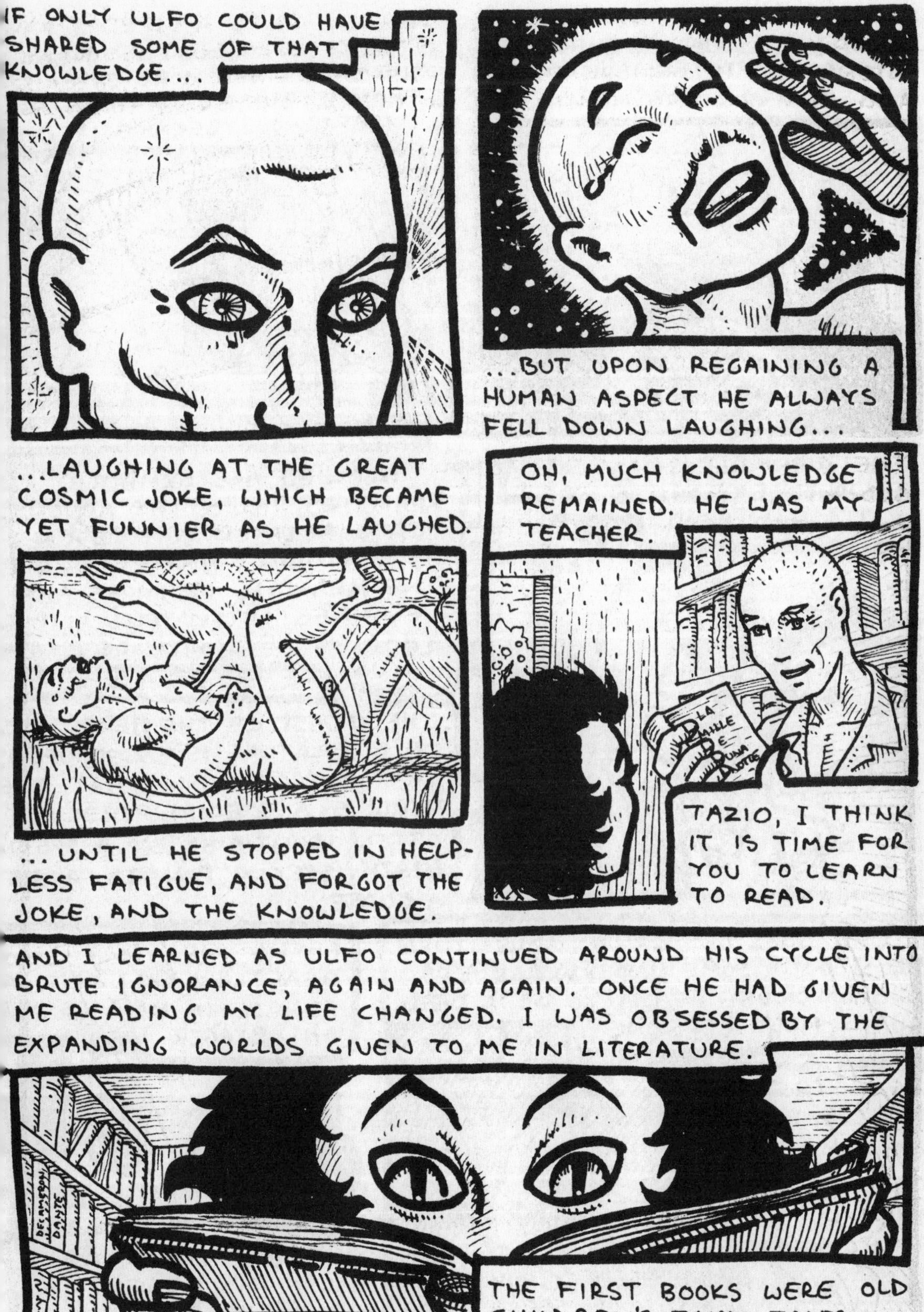
IF ONLY ULFO COULD HAVE SHARED SOME OF THAT KNOWLEDGE....
...BUT UPON REGAINING A HUMAN ASPECT HE ALWAYS FELL DOWN LAUGHING...
...LAUGHING AT THE GREAT COSMIC JOKE, WHICH BECAME YET FUNNIER AS HE LAUGHED.
...UNTIL HE STOPPED IN HELP-LESS FATIGUE, AND FORGOT THE JOKE, AND THE KNOWLEDGE.
OH, MUCH KNOWLEDGE REMAINED. HE WAS MY TEACHER.
TAZIO, I THINK IT IS TIME FOR YOU TO LEARN TO READ.
AND I LEARNED AS ULFO CONTINUED AROUND HIS CYCLE INTO BRUTE IGNORANCE, AGAIN AND AGAIN. ONCE HE HAD GIVEN ME READING MY LIFE CHANGED. I WAS OBSESSED BY THE EXPANDING WORLDS GIVEN TO ME IN LITERATURE.
DECAMERON
DANTE
THE FIRST BOOKS WERE OLD CHILDREN'S FAIRY TALES...

GIVEN THE CIRCUMSTANCES OF MY **LIFE** I FOUND NOTHING TOO INCREDIBLE TO BELIEVE IN "THE THOUSAND AND ONE NIGHTS".

**NO** ONE LIVED A LIFE AS FANTASTIC AS MY OWN — SINBAD THE SAILOR HAD MORE EXPERIEN THAN I, BUT BY READING, HIS EXPERIENCES BECAME MY **OWN**

AND WHEN ULFO WAS WISE HE WOULD EXPLAIN TO ME WHAT I HAD READ!

... STORIES ARE SYMBOLIC **REALITIES**, TAZIO, THE ADVENTURES RELATED MAY NEVER HAVE ACTUALLY HAPPENED, BUT THE **MEANING** OF THOSE ADVENTURES OFTEN TELLS A TRUTH THAT WE RECOGNIZE DEEP WITH IN US.

THE **QUEST** OF THE **HERO** — MOS OF LITERATURE IS BASED UPON THAT SUPPOSITION — THAT THE HERO IS A **SPECIAL** PERSON, OFTEN IDENTIFIED BY A SPECIA **BIRTH**, SPECIAL **POWERS**, A GIFT A **CURSE**; ...

... WHO GOES OFF ON AN ADVENTURE DOWN INTO SOME **UNDERWORLD** — OR SUBCONCIOUS — REALM TO DO A **DEED** WHICH MUST BE DONE.

HE IS **TESTED**, AND HE PASSES OR FAILS, WINS OR LOOSES, AND **THAT** IS THE TALE.

BUT IF THE STORY IS NO "REAL" WHY DO I FEEL A CHANGE IN ME? AS IF I AM ... BIGGER.

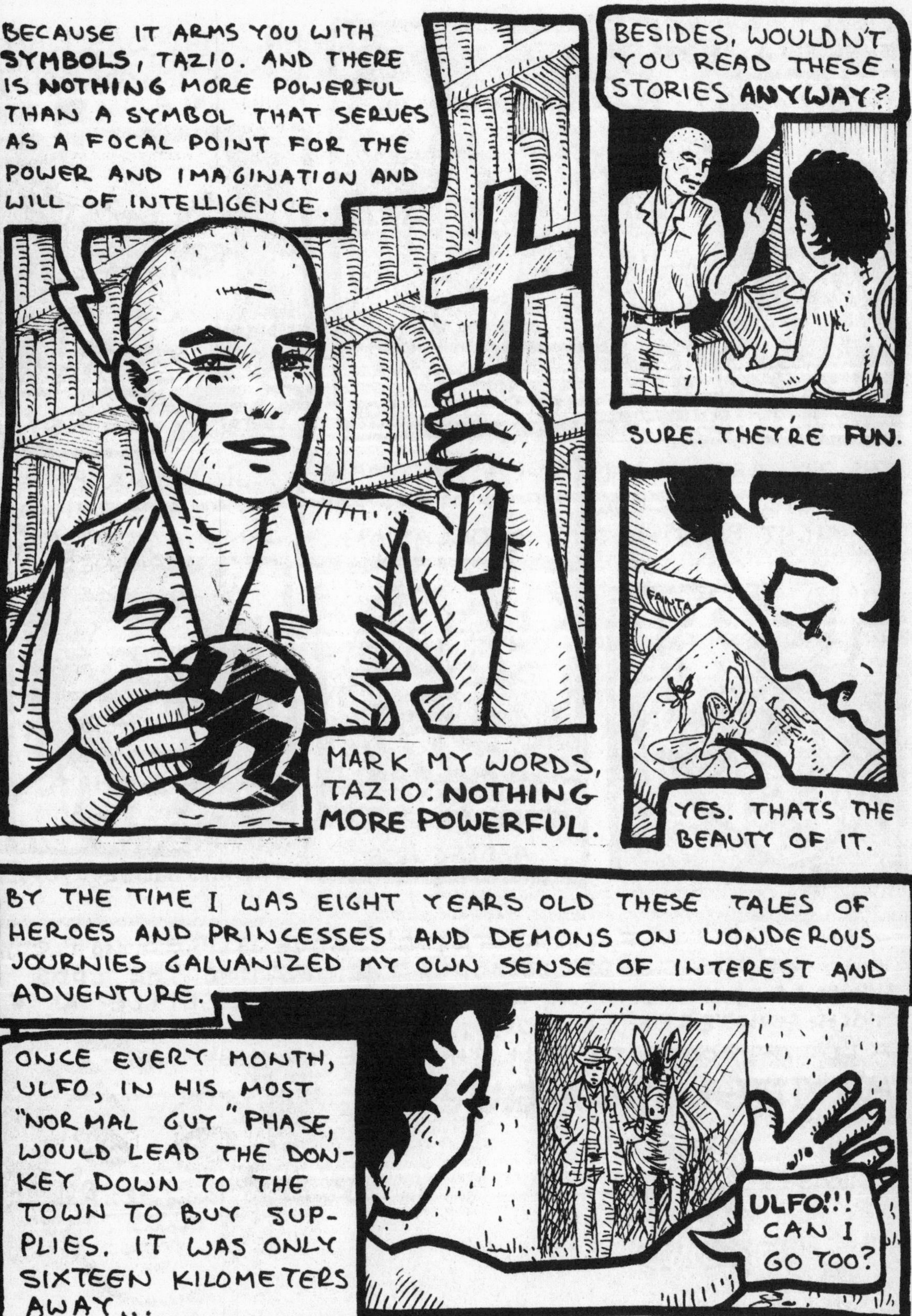
BECAUSE IT ARMS YOU WITH **SYMBOLS**, TAZIO. AND THERE IS **NOTHING** MORE POWERFUL THAN A SYMBOL THAT SERVES AS A FOCAL POINT FOR THE POWER AND IMAGINATION AND WILL OF INTELLIGENCE.
MARK MY WORDS, TAZIO: **NOTHING MORE POWERFUL**.
BESIDES, WOULDN'T YOU READ THESE STORIES **ANYWAY**?
SURE. THEY'RE **FUN**.
FANTA
YES. THAT'S THE BEAUTY OF IT.
BY THE TIME I WAS EIGHT YEARS OLD THESE TALES OF HEROES AND PRINCESSES AND DEMONS ON WONDEROUS JOURNIES GALVANIZED MY OWN SENSE OF INTEREST AND ADVENTURE.
ONCE EVERY MONTH, ULFO, IN HIS MOST "NORMAL GUY" PHASE, WOULD LEAD THE DONKEY DOWN TO THE TOWN TO BUY SUPPLIES. IT WAS ONLY SIXTEEN KILOMETERS AWAY...
ULFO!!! CAN I GO TOO?

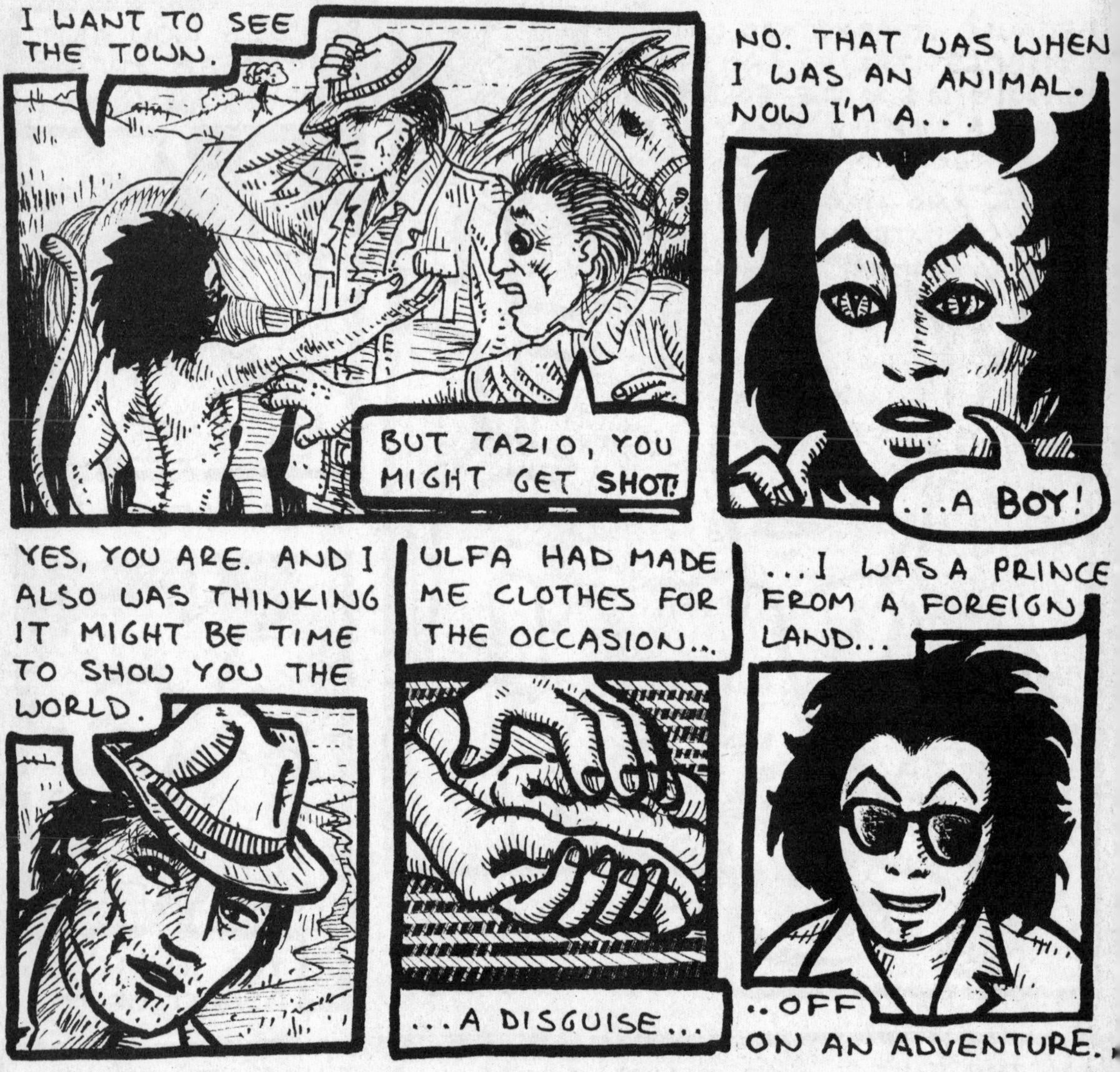
I WANT TO SEE THE TOWN.
BUT TAZIO, YOU MIGHT GET SHOT!
NO. THAT WAS WHEN I WAS AN ANIMAL. NOW I'M A...
...A BOY!
YES, YOU ARE. AND I ALSO WAS THINKING IT MIGHT BE TIME TO SHOW YOU THE WORLD.
ULFA HAD MADE ME CLOTHES FOR THE OCCASION...
...A DISGUISE...
...I WAS A PRINCE FROM A FOREIGN LAND...
..OFF ON AN ADVENTURE..

—AND YOU CAN FOLLOW TAZIO'S ADVENTURES IN BOOK TWO OF HIS QUEST TO AVOID THE DESTINY THE GODS HAVE APPOINTED HIM. BUT YOU'D BETTER SETTLE IN IF YOU'RE INTERESTED, FOLX, BECAUSE IT'S GOING TO TAKE A LOT OF BOOKS TO TELL THE TALE OF HIS

# ARMAGEDDONQUEST.

Ronald Russell Roach
April, 1984

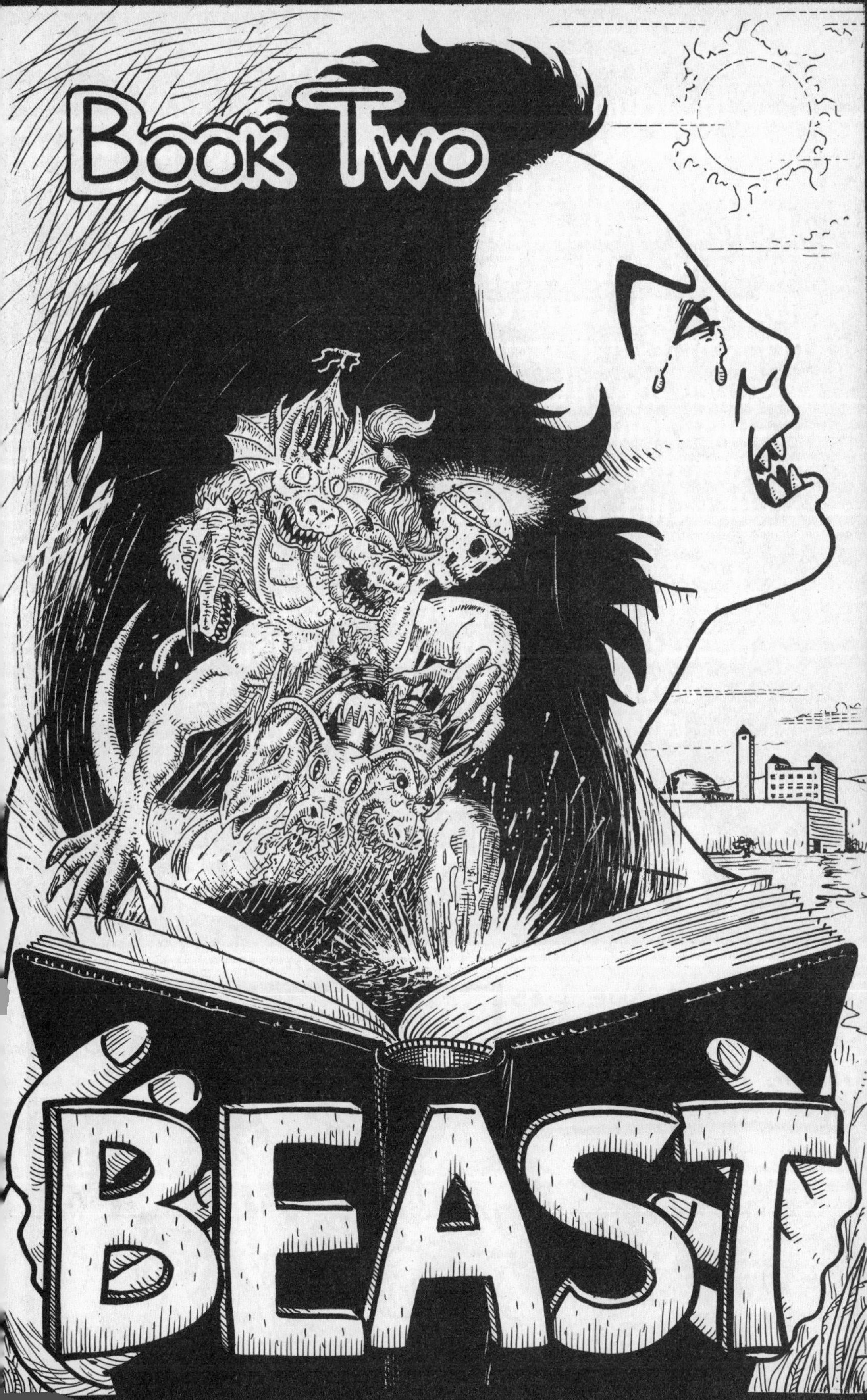
Book Two
BEAST

The story of Tazio,
the reluctant Antichrist, is being told:
we have learned that he remembers
nothing of his life before being awakened
from a mindless stupor at the age of 6 years
to being stabbed by his mother, the mad nun
Mariangela, who considers it her duty to kill
her son. But it seems Tazio cannot die, and he
escapes the villa to live as a wild animal until
Ulfo captures and tames him. Taught and
trained by the ever-changing man/woman
Ulfo/Ulfa, Tazio's consciousness evolves.

Now he is 8 years old and a "normal"
boy, mentally at least, but we know who
he is destined to become, for this is the
boyhood of The Beast from the
Biblical Book of Revelations...

# book 2
# the beast

LA DESTINAZIONE WAS A SMALL TOWN AT THE END OF A ROAD, LIVING IN THE PAST. BUT FOR ME IT WAS THE FUTURE.

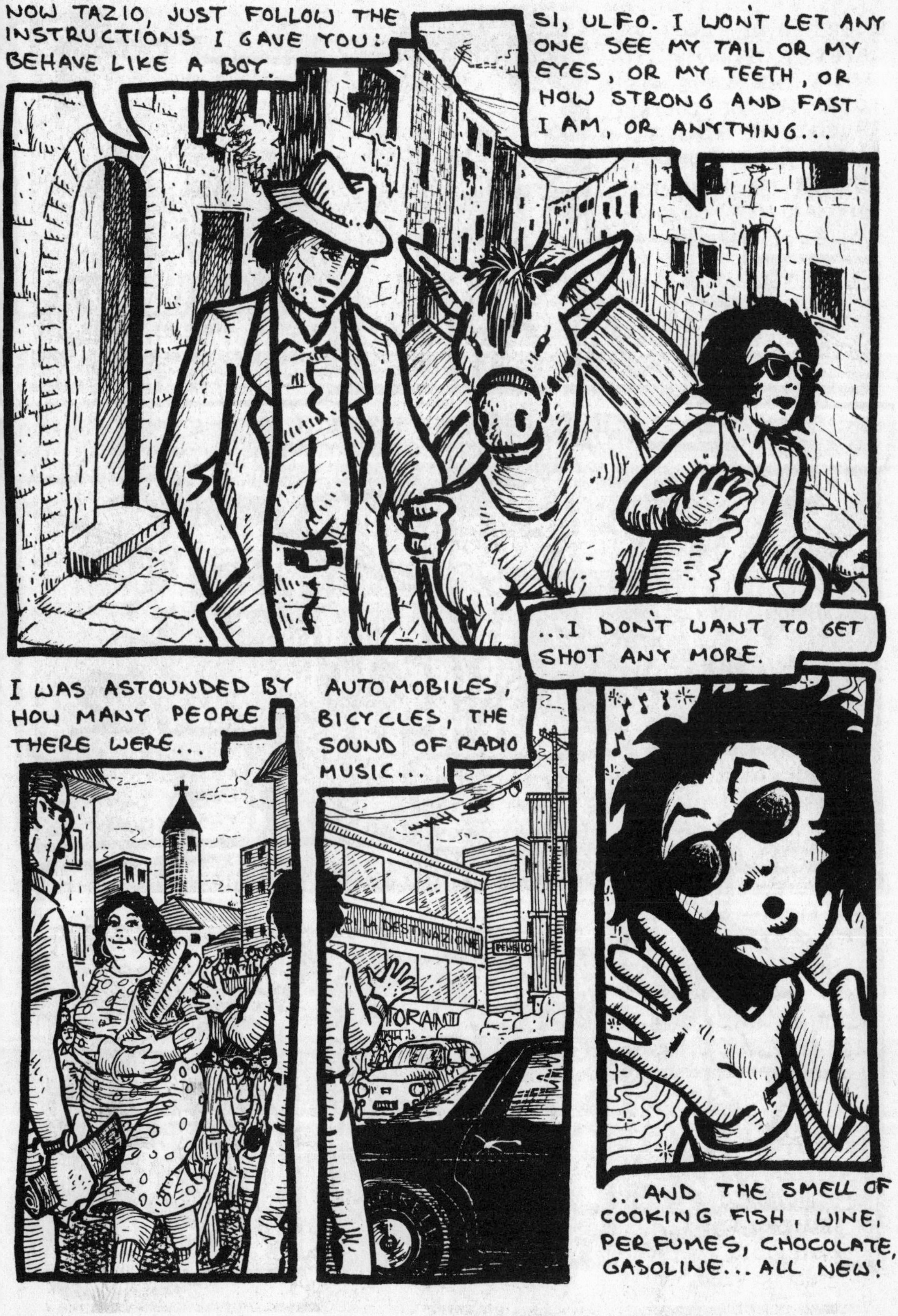
NOW TAZIO, JUST FOLLOW THE INSTRUCTIONS I GAVE YOU: BEHAVE LIKE A BOY.
SI, ULFO. I WON'T LET ANY ONE SEE MY TAIL OR MY EYES, OR MY TEETH, OR HOW STRONG AND FAST I AM, OR ANYTHING...
...I DON'T WANT TO GET SHOT ANY MORE.
I WAS ASTOUNDED BY HOW MANY PEOPLE THERE WERE...
AUTOMOBILES, BICYCLES, THE SOUND OF RADIO MUSIC...
LA DESTINAZIONE
...AND THE SMELL OF COOKING FISH, WINE, PERFUMES, CHOCOLATE, GASOLINE... ALL NEW!

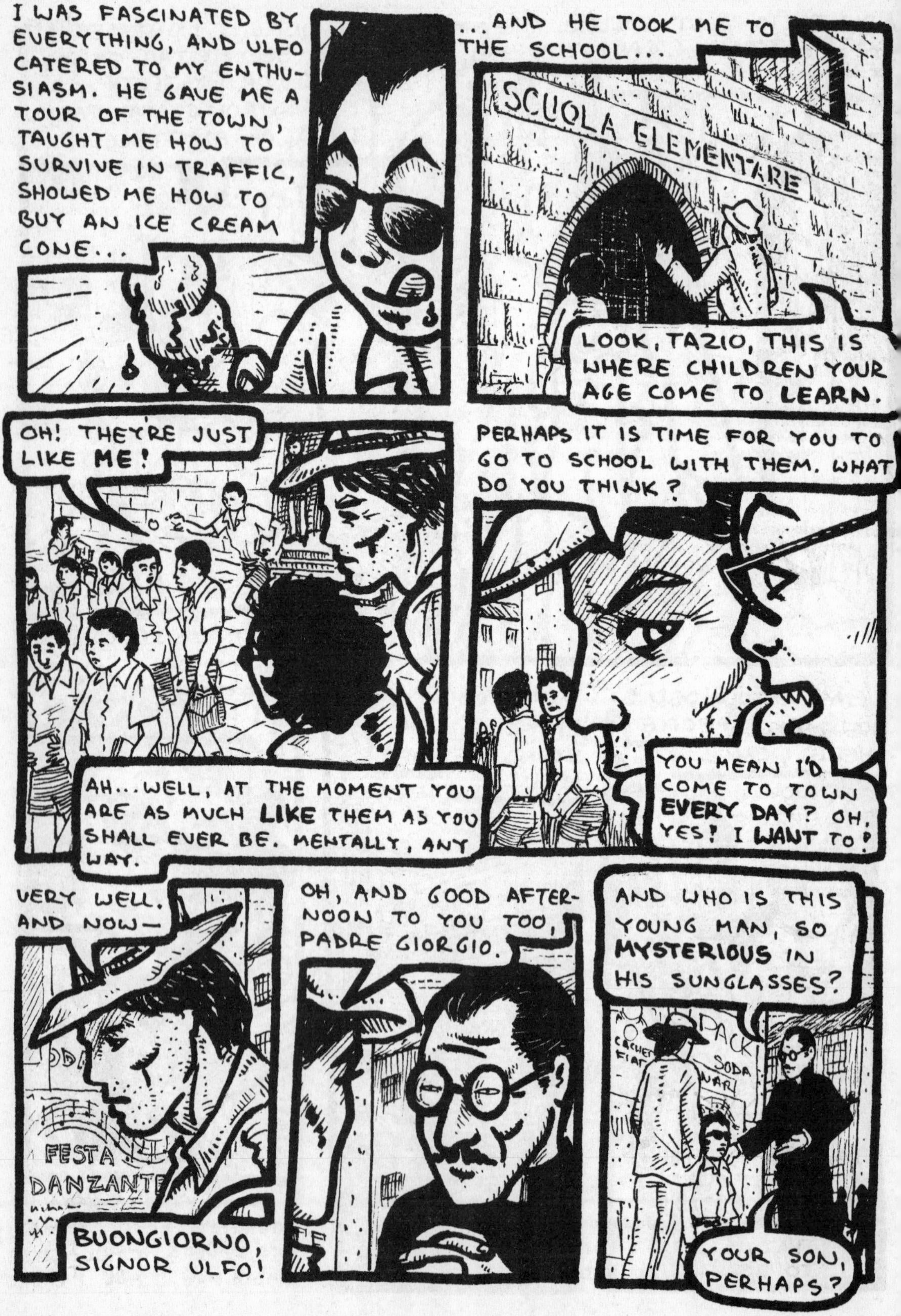
I WAS FASCINATED BY EVERYTHING, AND ULFO CATERED TO MY ENTHUSIASM. HE GAVE ME A TOUR OF THE TOWN, TAUGHT ME HOW TO SURVIVE IN TRAFFIC, SHOWED ME HOW TO BUY AN ICE CREAM CONE...
...AND HE TOOK ME TO THE SCHOOL...
SCUOLA ELEMENTARE
LOOK, TAZIO, THIS IS WHERE CHILDREN YOUR AGE COME TO LEARN.
OH! THEY'RE JUST LIKE ME!
AH...WELL, AT THE MOMENT YOU ARE AS MUCH LIKE THEM AS YOU SHALL EVER BE. MENTALLY, ANYWAY.
PERHAPS IT IS TIME FOR YOU TO GO TO SCHOOL WITH THEM. WHAT DO YOU THINK?
YOU MEAN I'D COME TO TOWN EVERY DAY? OH, YES! I WANT TO!
VERY WELL. AND NOW—
FESTA DANZANTE
BUONGIORNO, SIGNOR ULFO!
OH, AND GOOD AFTERNOON TO YOU TOO, PADRE GIORGIO.
AND WHO IS THIS YOUNG MAN, SO MYSTERIOUS IN HIS SUNGLASSES?
SODA
YOUR SON, PERHAPS?

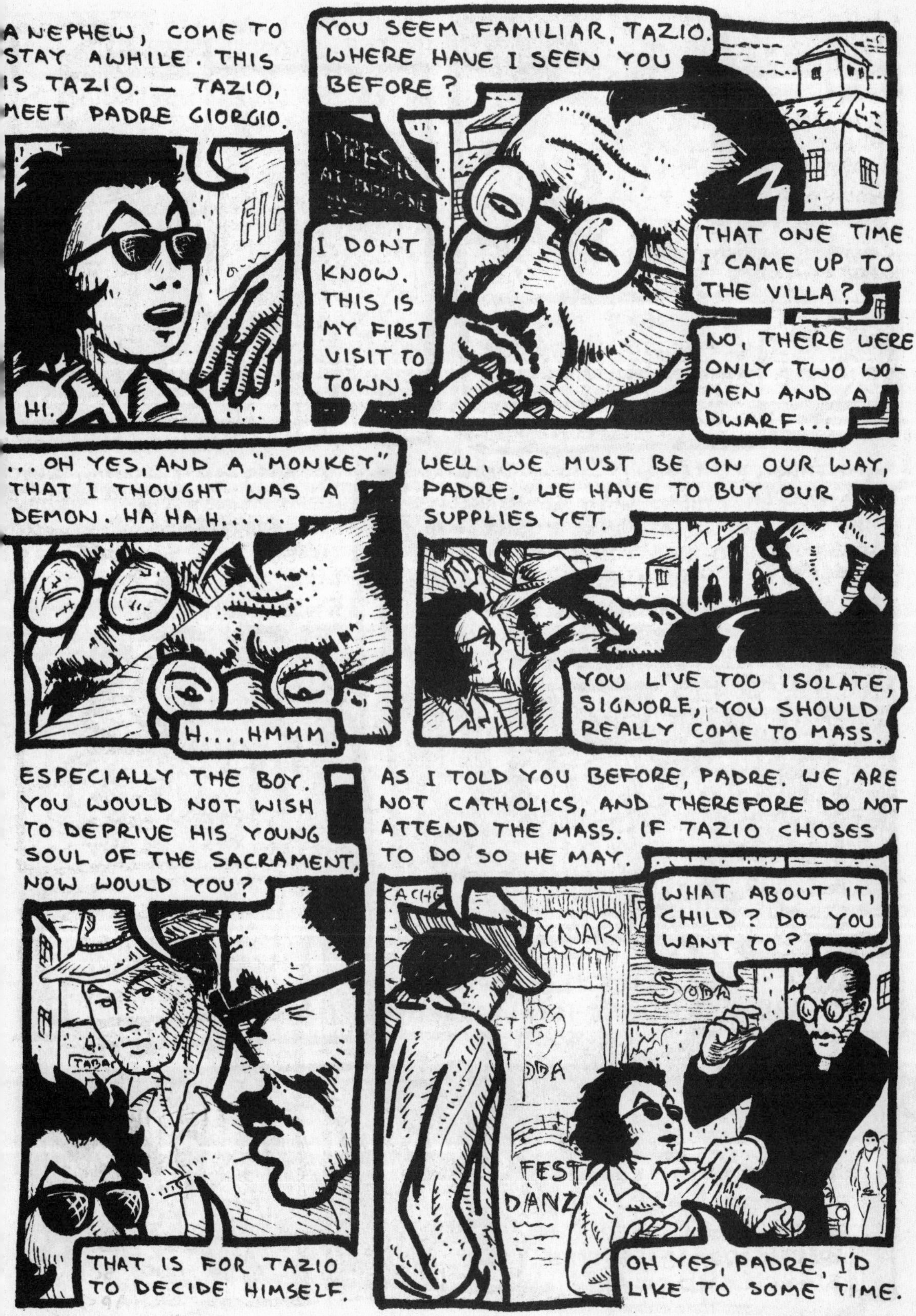
A NEPHEW, COME TO STAY AWHILE. THIS IS TAZIO. — TAZIO, MEET PADRE GIORGIO.
HI.
YOU SEEM FAMILIAR, TAZIO. WHERE HAVE I SEEN YOU BEFORE?
I DON'T KNOW. THIS IS MY FIRST VISIT TO TOWN.
THAT ONE TIME I CAME UP TO THE VILLA?
NO, THERE WERE ONLY TWO WOMEN AND A DWARF...
...OH YES, AND A "MONKEY" THAT I THOUGHT WAS A DEMON. HA HA H......
H....HMMM.
WELL, WE MUST BE ON OUR WAY, PADRE. WE HAVE TO BUY OUR SUPPLIES YET.
YOU LIVE TOO ISOLATE, SIGNORE, YOU SHOULD REALLY COME TO MASS.
ESPECIALLY THE BOY. YOU WOULD NOT WISH TO DEPRIVE HIS YOUNG SOUL OF THE SACRAMENT, NOW WOULD YOU?
THAT IS FOR TAZIO TO DECIDE HIMSELF.
AS I TOLD YOU BEFORE, PADRE. WE ARE NOT CATHOLICS, AND THEREFORE DO NOT ATTEND THE MASS. IF TAZIO CHOSES TO DO SO HE MAY.
WHAT ABOUT IT, CHILD? DO YOU WANT TO?
OH YES, PADRE, I'D LIKE TO SOME TIME.

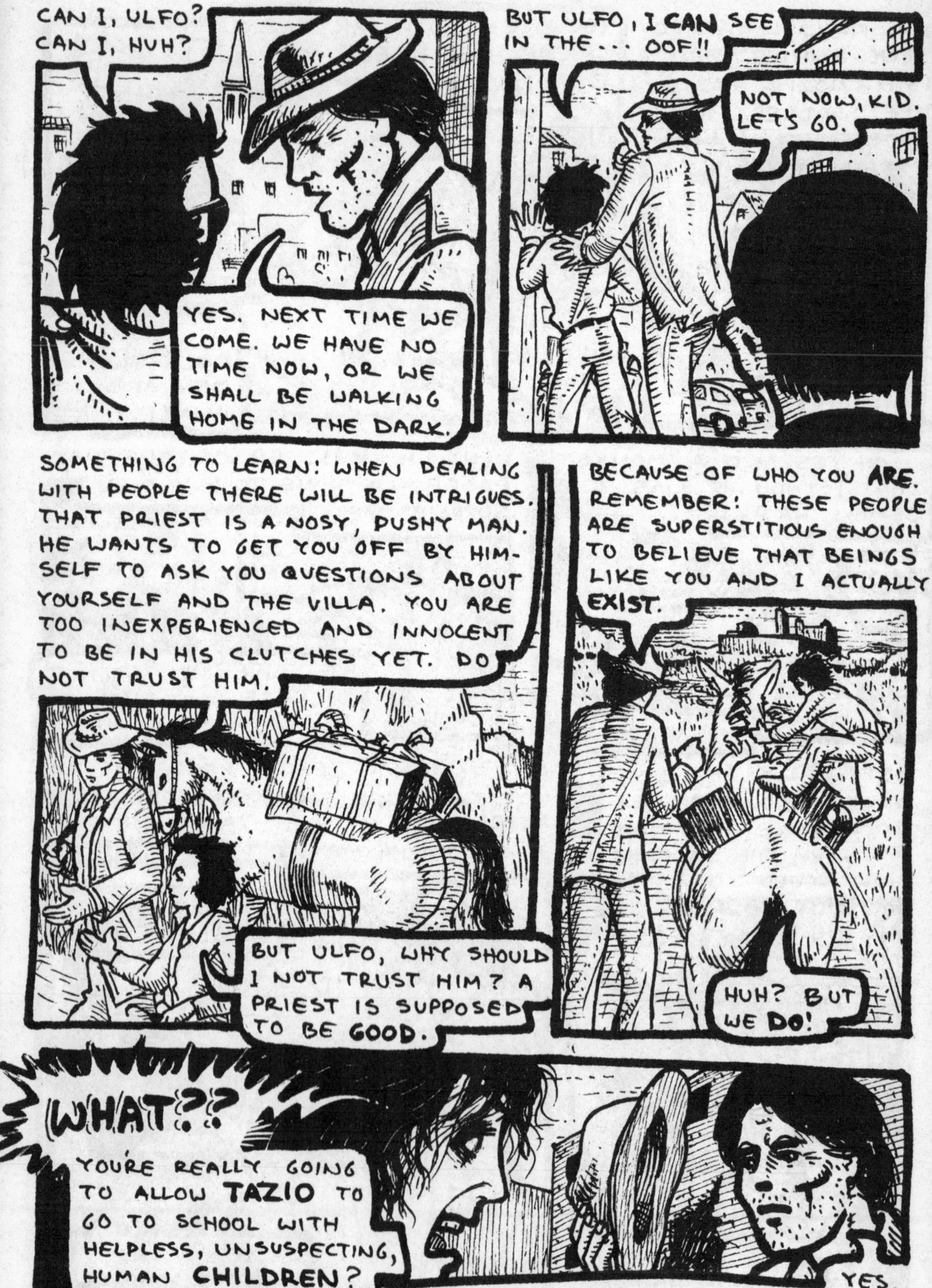
CAN I, ULFO? CAN I, HUH?
YES. NEXT TIME WE COME. WE HAVE NO TIME NOW, OR WE SHALL BE WALKING HOME IN THE DARK.
BUT ULFO, I CAN SEE IN THE... OOF!!
NOT NOW, KID. LET'S GO.
SOMETHING TO LEARN: WHEN DEALING WITH PEOPLE THERE WILL BE INTRIGUES. THAT PRIEST IS A NOSY, PUSHY MAN. HE WANTS TO GET YOU OFF BY HIMSELF TO ASK YOU QUESTIONS ABOUT YOURSELF AND THE VILLA. YOU ARE TOO INEXPERIENCED AND INNOCENT TO BE IN HIS CLUTCHES YET. DO NOT TRUST HIM.
BUT ULFO, WHY SHOULD I NOT TRUST HIM? A PRIEST IS SUPPOSED TO BE GOOD.
BECAUSE OF WHO YOU ARE. REMEMBER: THESE PEOPLE ARE SUPERSTITIOUS ENOUGH TO BELIEVE THAT BEINGS LIKE YOU AND I ACTUALLY EXIST.
HUH? BUT WE DO!
WHAT??
YOU'RE REALLY GOING TO ALLOW TAZIO TO GO TO SCHOOL WITH HELPLESS, UNSUSPECTING, HUMAN CHILDREN?
YES.

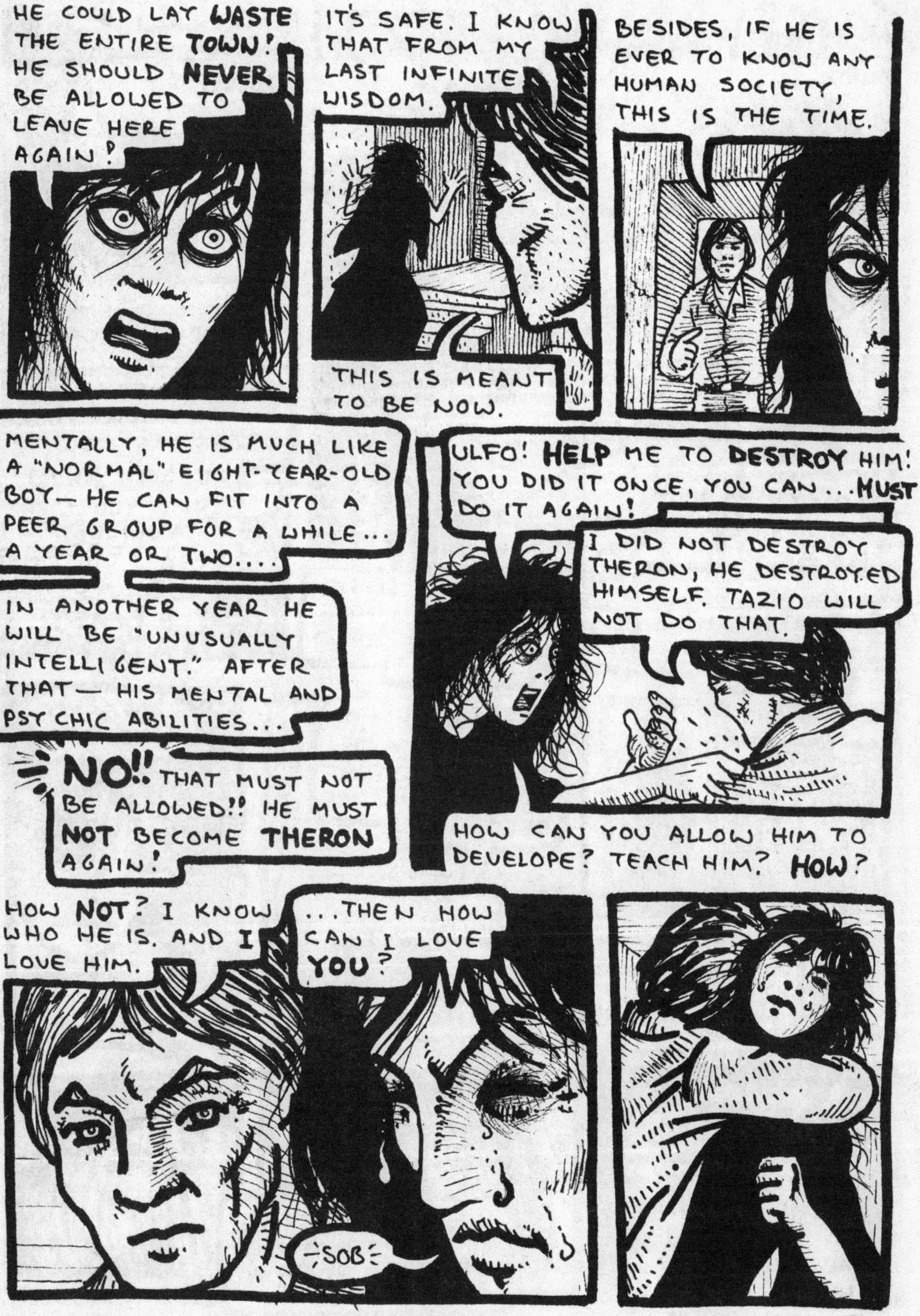
HE COULD LAY WASTE THE ENTIRE TOWN! HE SHOULD NEVER BE ALLOWED TO LEAVE HERE AGAIN!
IT'S SAFE. I KNOW THAT FROM MY LAST INFINITE WISDOM.
THIS IS MEANT TO BE NOW.
BESIDES, IF HE IS EVER TO KNOW ANY HUMAN SOCIETY, THIS IS THE TIME.
MENTALLY, HE IS MUCH LIKE A "NORMAL" EIGHT-YEAR-OLD BOY— HE CAN FIT INTO A PEER GROUP FOR A WHILE... A YEAR OR TWO....
IN ANOTHER YEAR HE WILL BE "UNUSUALLY INTELLIGENT." AFTER THAT— HIS MENTAL AND PSYCHIC ABILITIES...
NO!! THAT MUST NOT BE ALLOWED!! HE MUST NOT BECOME THERON AGAIN!
ULFO! HELP ME TO DESTROY HIM! YOU DID IT ONCE, YOU CAN... MUST DO IT AGAIN!
I DID NOT DESTROY THERON, HE DESTROYED HIMSELF. TAZIO WILL NOT DO THAT.
HOW CAN YOU ALLOW HIM TO DEVELOPE? TEACH HIM? HOW?
HOW NOT? I KNOW WHO HE IS. AND I LOVE HIM.
...THEN HOW CAN I LOVE YOU?
SOB

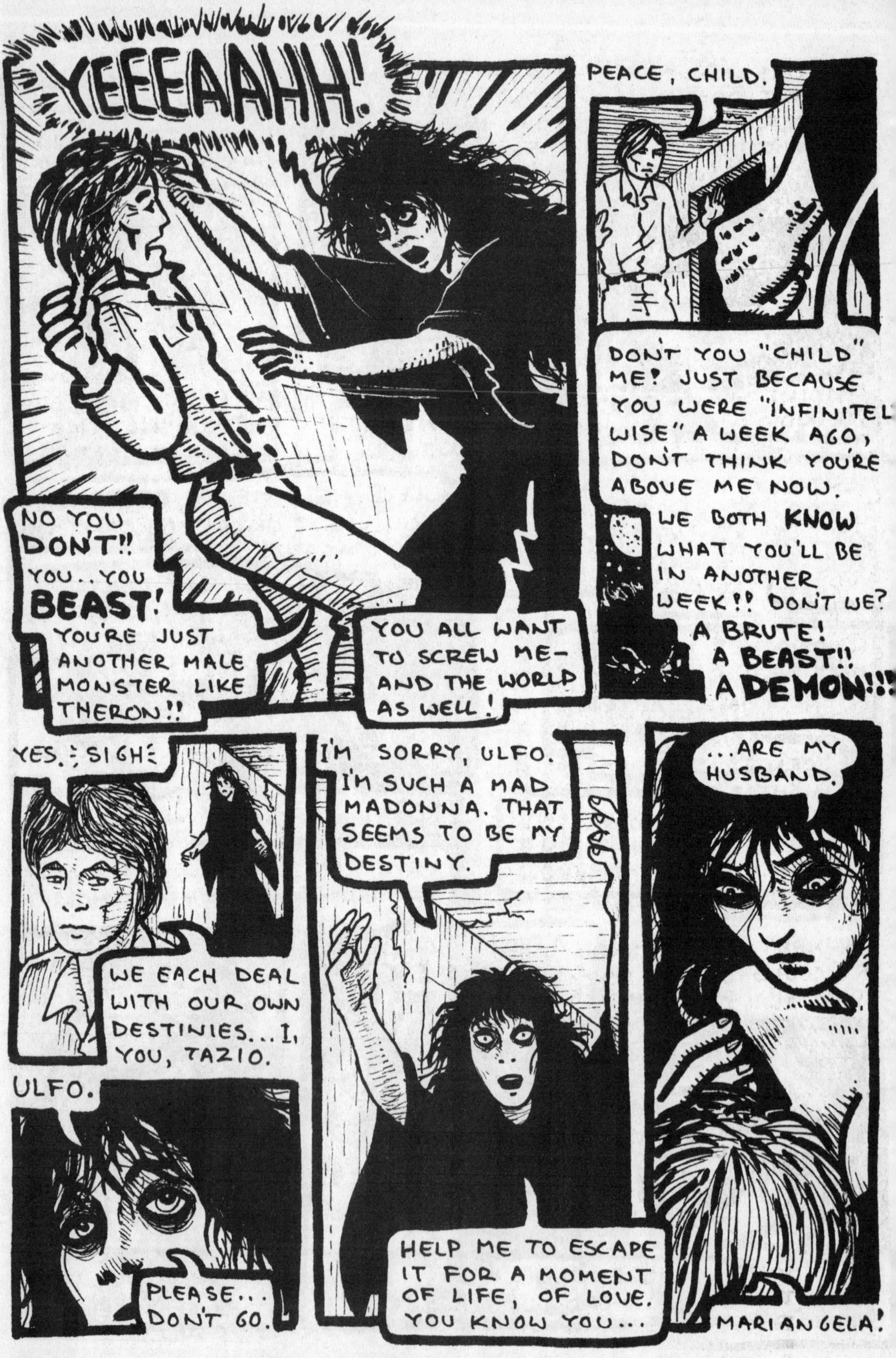
YEEEAAHH!
NO YOU DON'T!! YOU.. YOU BEAST! YOU'RE JUST ANOTHER MALE MONSTER LIKE THERON!!
YOU ALL WANT TO SCREW ME— AND THE WORLD AS WELL!
PEACE, CHILD.
DON'T YOU "CHILD" ME! JUST BECAUSE YOU WERE "INFINITEL WISE" A WEEK AGO, DON'T THINK YOU'RE ABOVE ME NOW.
WE BOTH KNOW WHAT YOU'LL BE IN ANOTHER WEEK!! DON'T WE? A BRUTE! A BEAST!! A DEMON!!!
YES. :SIGH:
WE EACH DEAL WITH OUR OWN DESTINIES... I, YOU, TAZIO.
ULFO.
PLEASE... DON'T GO.
I'M SORRY, ULFO. I'M SUCH A MAD MADONNA. THAT SEEMS TO BE MY DESTINY.
HELP ME TO ESCAPE IT FOR A MOMENT OF LIFE, OF LOVE. YOU KNOW YOU...
...ARE MY HUSBAND.
MARIANGELA!

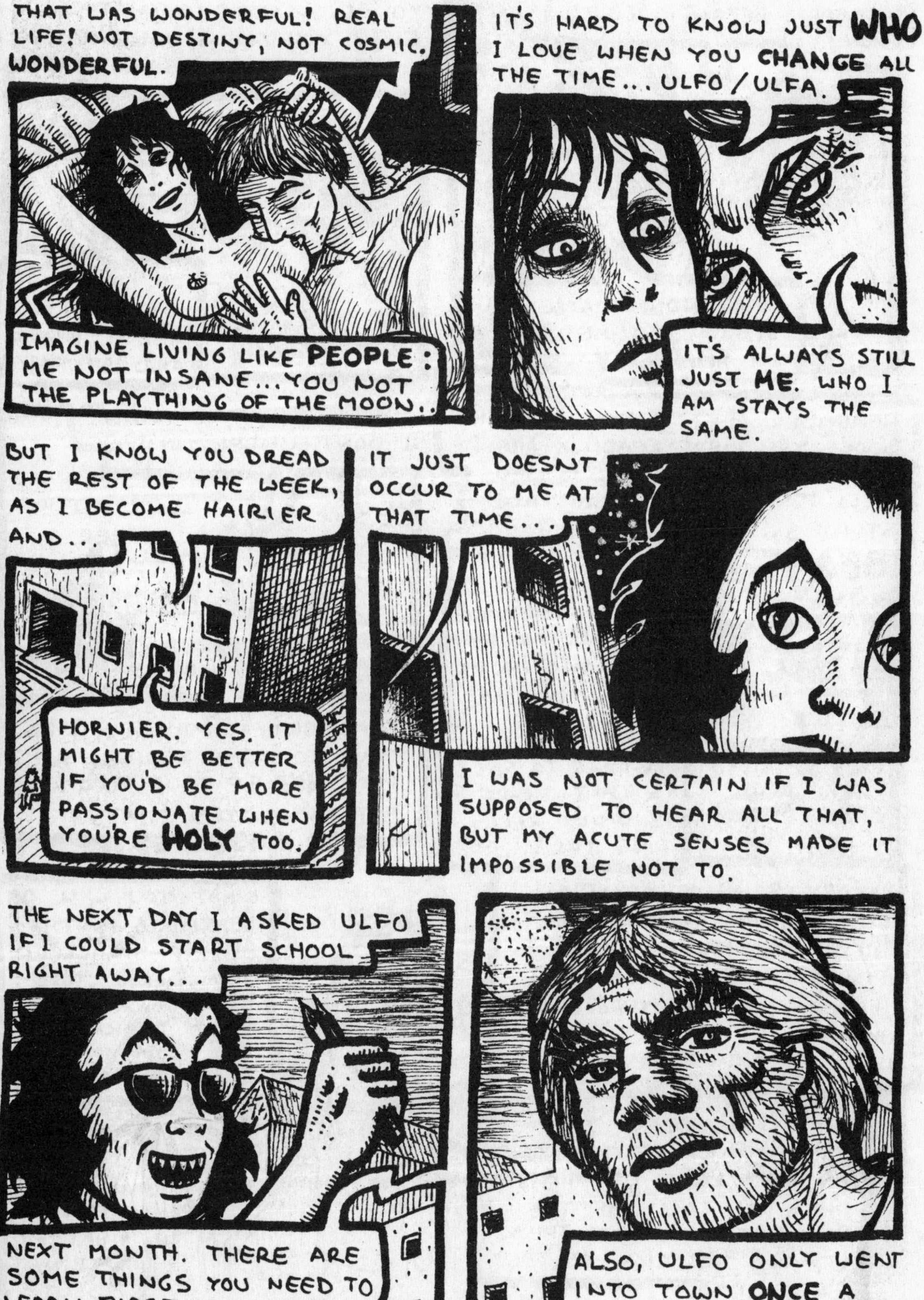
THAT WAS WONDERFUL! REAL LIFE! NOT DESTINY, NOT COSMIC. WONDERFUL.
IMAGINE LIVING LIKE PEOPLE: ME NOT INSANE... YOU NOT THE PLAYTHING OF THE MOON..
IT'S HARD TO KNOW JUST WHO I LOVE WHEN YOU CHANGE ALL THE TIME... ULFO / ULFA.
IT'S ALWAYS STILL JUST ME. WHO I AM STAYS THE SAME.
BUT I KNOW YOU DREAD THE REST OF THE WEEK, AS I BECOME HAIRIER AND...
HORNIER. YES. IT MIGHT BE BETTER IF YOU'D BE MORE PASSIONATE WHEN YOU'RE HOLY TOO.
IT JUST DOESN'T OCCUR TO ME AT THAT TIME...
I WAS NOT CERTAIN IF I WAS SUPPOSED TO HEAR ALL THAT, BUT MY ACUTE SENSES MADE IT IMPOSSIBLE NOT TO.
THE NEXT DAY I ASKED ULFO IF I COULD START SCHOOL RIGHT AWAY...
NEXT MONTH. THERE ARE SOME THINGS YOU NEED TO LEARN FIRST.
ALSO, ULFO ONLY WENT INTO TOWN ONCE A MONTH, OBVIOUSLY...

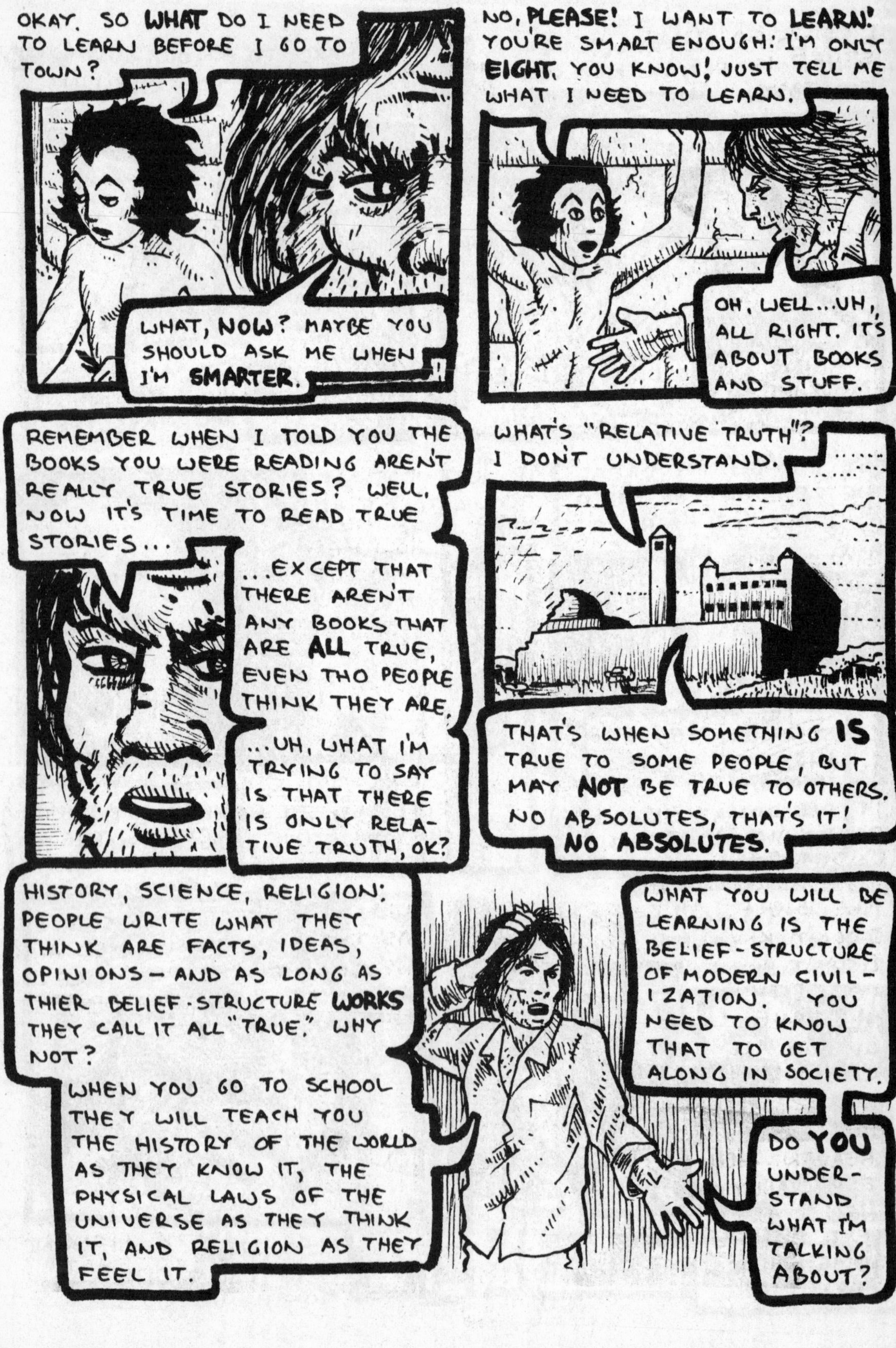

OKAY. SO WHAT DO I NEED TO LEARN BEFORE I GO TO TOWN?
WHAT, NOW? MAYBE YOU SHOULD ASK ME WHEN I'M SMARTER.
NO, PLEASE! I WANT TO LEARN! YOU'RE SMART ENOUGH: I'M ONLY EIGHT, YOU KNOW! JUST TELL ME WHAT I NEED TO LEARN.
OH, WELL...UH, ALL RIGHT. IT'S ABOUT BOOKS AND STUFF.
REMEMBER WHEN I TOLD YOU THE BOOKS YOU WERE READING AREN'T REALLY TRUE STORIES? WELL, NOW IT'S TIME TO READ TRUE STORIES...
...EXCEPT THAT THERE AREN'T ANY BOOKS THAT ARE ALL TRUE, EVEN THO PEOPLE THINK THEY ARE,
...UH, WHAT I'M TRYING TO SAY IS THAT THERE IS ONLY RELA-TIVE TRUTH, OK?
WHAT'S "RELATIVE TRUTH"? I DON'T UNDERSTAND.
THAT'S WHEN SOMETHING IS TRUE TO SOME PEOPLE, BUT MAY NOT BE TRUE TO OTHERS. NO ABSOLUTES, THAT'S IT! NO ABSOLUTES.
HISTORY, SCIENCE, RELIGION: PEOPLE WRITE WHAT THEY THINK ARE FACTS, IDEAS, OPINIONS— AND AS LONG AS THIER BELIEF-STRUCTURE WORKS THEY CALL IT ALL "TRUE." WHY NOT?
WHEN YOU GO TO SCHOOL THEY WILL TEACH YOU THE HISTORY OF THE WORLD AS THEY KNOW IT, THE PHYSICAL LAWS OF THE UNIVERSE AS THEY THINK IT, AND RELIGION AS THEY FEEL IT.
WHAT YOU WILL BE LEARNING IS THE BELIEF-STRUCTURE OF MODERN CIVIL-IZATION. YOU NEED TO KNOW THAT TO GET ALONG IN SOCIETY.
DO YOU UNDER-STAND WHAT I'M TALKING ABOUT?

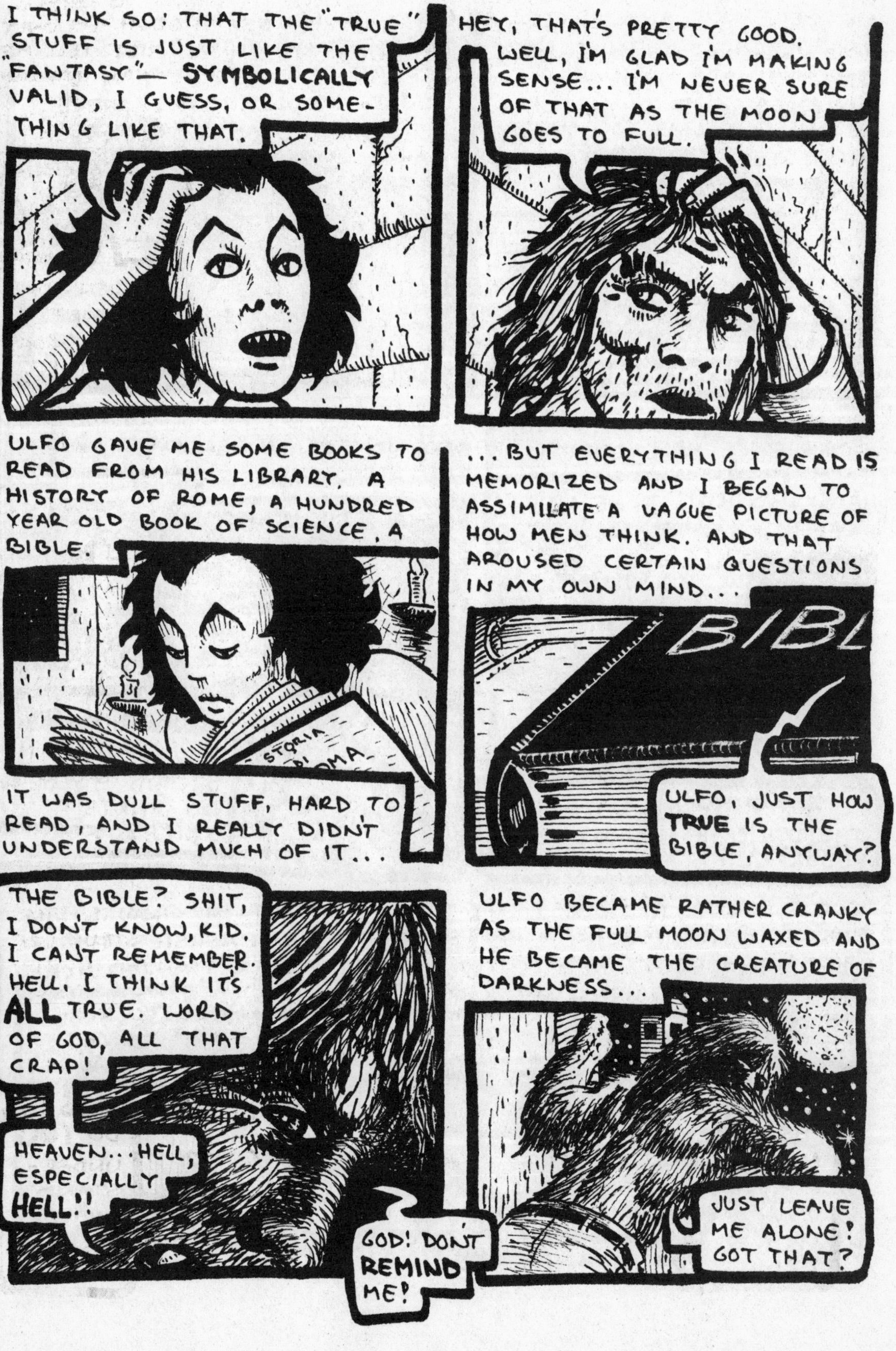
I THINK SO: THAT THE "TRUE" STUFF IS JUST LIKE THE "FANTASY" — SYMBOLICALLY VALID, I GUESS, OR SOMETHING LIKE THAT.
HEY, THAT'S PRETTY GOOD.
WELL, I'M GLAD I'M MAKING SENSE... I'M NEVER SURE OF THAT AS THE MOON GOES TO FULL.
ULFO GAVE ME SOME BOOKS TO READ FROM HIS LIBRARY. A HISTORY OF ROME, A HUNDRED YEAR OLD BOOK OF SCIENCE, A BIBLE.
STORIA DI ROMA
IT WAS DULL STUFF, HARD TO READ, AND I REALLY DIDN'T UNDERSTAND MUCH OF IT...
...BUT EVERYTHING I READ IS MEMORIZED AND I BEGAN TO ASSIMILATE A VAGUE PICTURE OF HOW MEN THINK. AND THAT AROUSED CERTAIN QUESTIONS IN MY OWN MIND...
BIBL
ULFO, JUST HOW TRUE IS THE BIBLE, ANYWAY?
THE BIBLE? SHIT, I DON'T KNOW, KID. I CAN'T REMEMBER. HELL, I THINK IT'S ALL TRUE. WORD OF GOD, ALL THAT CRAP!
HEAVEN...HELL, ESPECIALLY HELL!!
GOD! DON'T REMIND ME!
ULFO BECAME RATHER CRANKY AS THE FULL MOON WAXED AND HE BECAME THE CREATURE OF DARKNESS...
JUST LEAVE ME ALONE! GOT THAT?

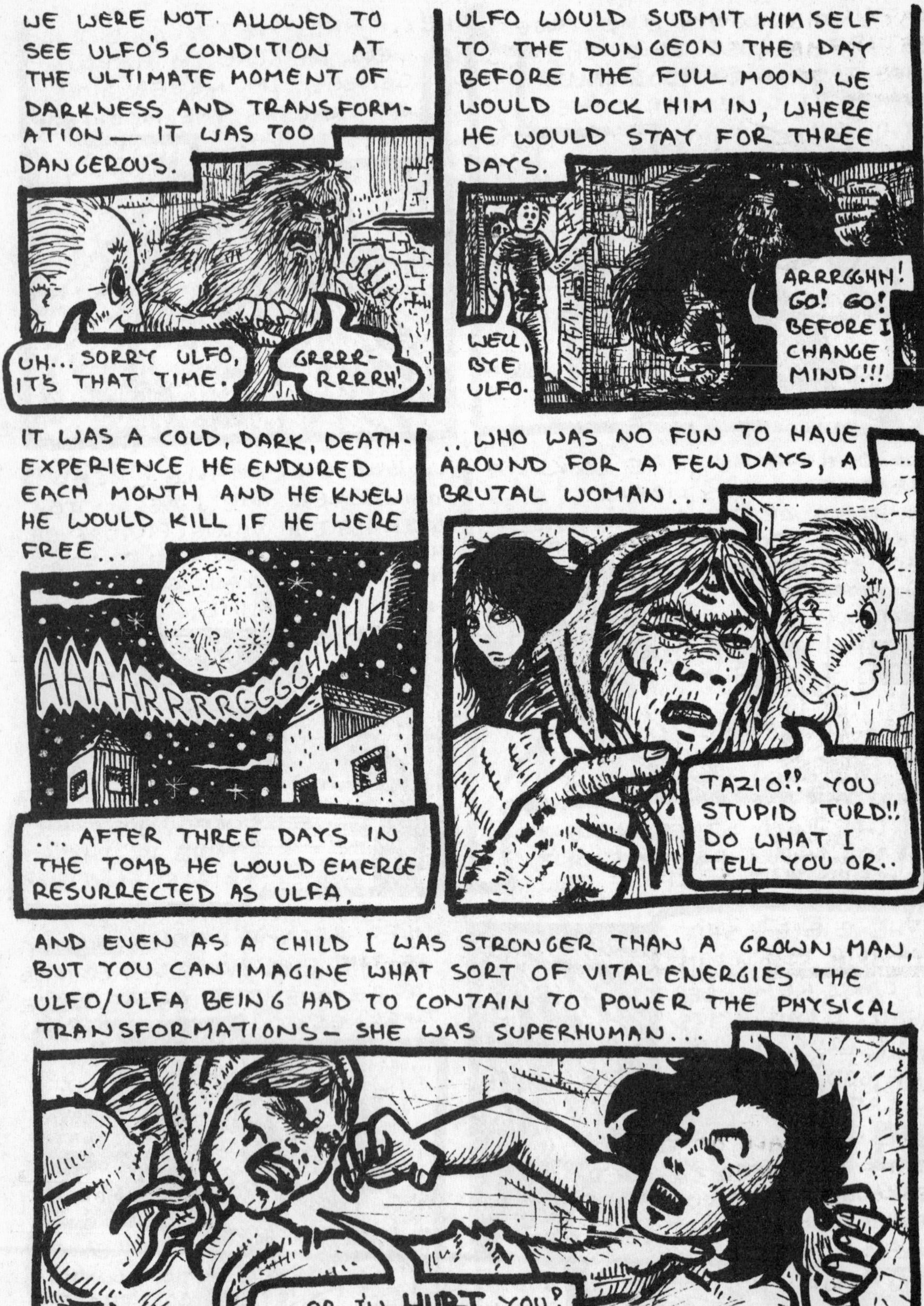

WE WERE NOT ALLOWED TO SEE ULFO'S CONDITION AT THE ULTIMATE MOMENT OF DARKNESS AND TRANSFORM-ATION— IT WAS TOO DANGEROUS.
UH... SORRY ULFO, IT'S THAT TIME.
GRRRR-RRRRH!
ULFO WOULD SUBMIT HIMSELF TO THE DUNGEON THE DAY BEFORE THE FULL MOON, WE WOULD LOCK HIM IN, WHERE HE WOULD STAY FOR THREE DAYS.
WELL, BYE ULFO.
ARRRGGHH! GO! GO! BEFORE I CHANGE MIND!!!
IT WAS A COLD, DARK, DEATH-EXPERIENCE HE ENDURED EACH MONTH AND HE KNEW HE WOULD KILL IF HE WERE FREE...
AAAARRRRRGGGGHHHHH
... AFTER THREE DAYS IN THE TOMB HE WOULD EMERGE RESURRECTED AS ULFA.
.. WHO WAS NO FUN TO HAVE AROUND FOR A FEW DAYS, A BRUTAL WOMAN...
TAZIO!! YOU STUPID TURD!! DO WHAT I TELL YOU OR..
AND EVEN AS A CHILD I WAS STRONGER THAN A GROWN MAN, BUT YOU CAN IMAGINE WHAT SORT OF VITAL ENERGIES THE ULFO/ULFA BEING HAD TO CONTAIN TO POWER THE PHYSICAL TRANSFORMATIONS— SHE WAS SUPERHUMAN...
... OR I'LL HURT YOU!

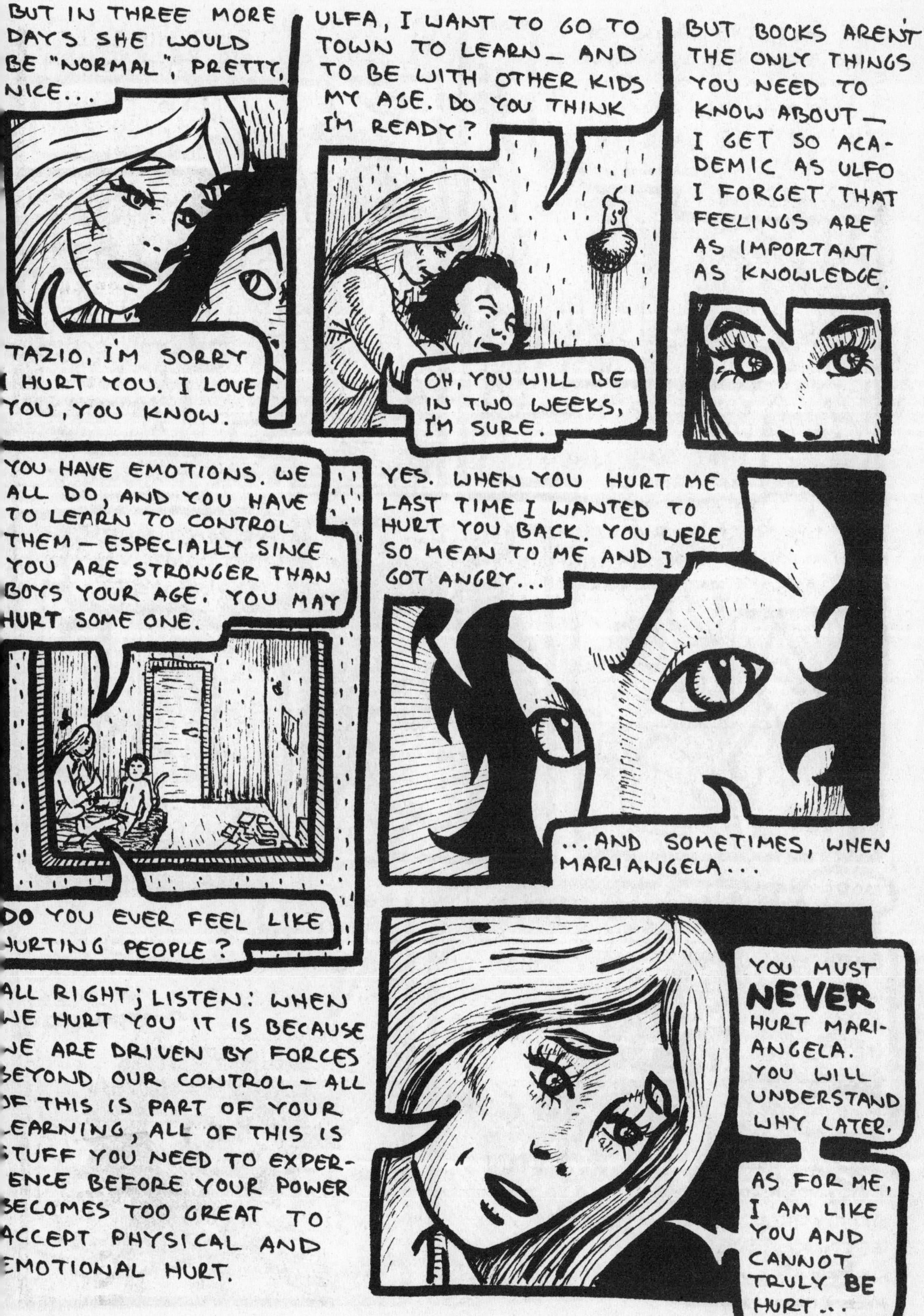

BUT IN THREE MORE DAYS SHE WOULD BE "NORMAL", PRETTY, NICE...
TAZIO, I'M SORRY I HURT YOU. I LOVE YOU, YOU KNOW.
ULFA, I WANT TO GO TO TOWN TO LEARN_ AND TO BE WITH OTHER KIDS MY AGE. DO YOU THINK I'M READY?
OH, YOU WILL BE IN TWO WEEKS, I'M SURE.
BUT BOOKS AREN'T THE ONLY THINGS YOU NEED TO KNOW ABOUT— I GET SO ACADEMIC AS ULFO I FORGET THAT FEELINGS ARE AS IMPORTANT AS KNOWLEDGE.
YOU HAVE EMOTIONS. WE ALL DO, AND YOU HAVE TO LEARN TO CONTROL THEM—ESPECIALLY SINCE YOU ARE STRONGER THAN BOYS YOUR AGE. YOU MAY HURT SOME ONE.
DO YOU EVER FEEL LIKE HURTING PEOPLE?
YES. WHEN YOU HURT ME LAST TIME I WANTED TO HURT YOU BACK. YOU WERE SO MEAN TO ME AND I GOT ANGRY...
...AND SOMETIMES, WHEN MARIANGELA...
ALL RIGHT; LISTEN: WHEN WE HURT YOU IT IS BECAUSE WE ARE DRIVEN BY FORCES BEYOND OUR CONTROL—ALL OF THIS IS PART OF YOUR LEARNING, ALL OF THIS IS STUFF YOU NEED TO EXPERENCE BEFORE YOUR POWER BECOMES TOO GREAT TO ACCEPT PHYSICAL AND EMOTIONAL HURT.
YOU MUST NEVER HURT MARIANGELA. YOU WILL UNDERSTAND WHY LATER.
AS FOR ME, I AM LIKE YOU AND CANNOT TRULY BE HURT...

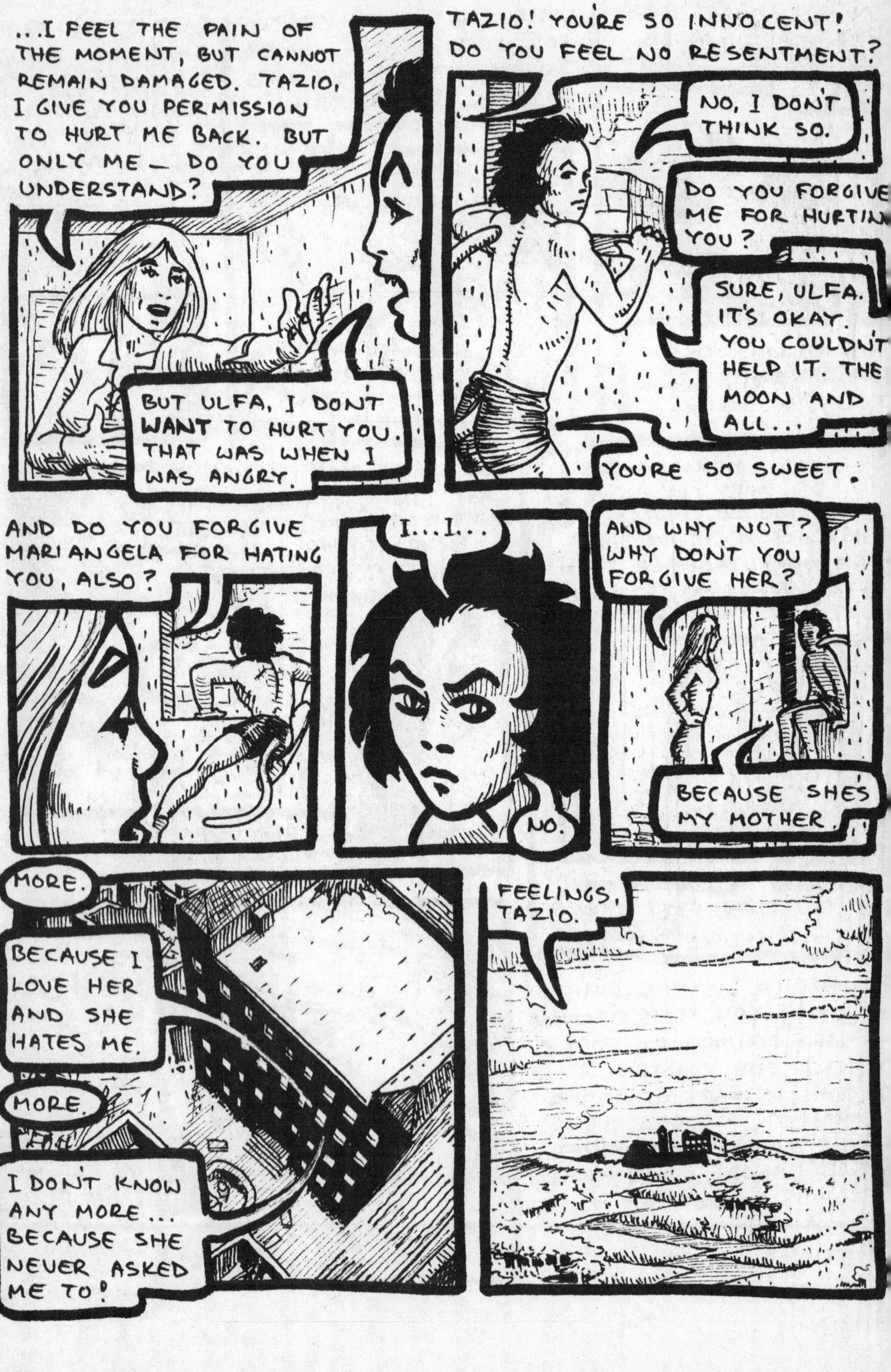
...I FEEL THE PAIN OF THE MOMENT, BUT CANNOT REMAIN DAMAGED. TAZIO, I GIVE YOU PERMISSION TO HURT ME BACK. BUT ONLY ME — DO YOU UNDERSTAND?
BUT ULFA, I DONT WANT TO HURT YOU. THAT WAS WHEN I WAS ANGRY.
TAZIO! YOU'RE SO INNOCENT! DO YOU FEEL NO RESENTMENT?
NO, I DON'T THINK SO.
DO YOU FORGIVE ME FOR HURTIN YOU?
SURE, ULFA. IT'S OKAY. YOU COULDN'T HELP IT. THE MOON AND ALL...
YOU'RE SO SWEET.
AND DO YOU FORGIVE MARIANGELA FOR HATING YOU, ALSO?
I...I...
NO.
AND WHY NOT? WHY DON'T YOU FORGIVE HER?
BECAUSE SHE'S MY MOTHER.
MORE.
BECAUSE I LOVE HER AND SHE HATES ME.
MORE.
I DON'T KNOW ANY MORE... BECAUSE SHE NEVER ASKED ME TO!
FEELINGS, TAZIO.

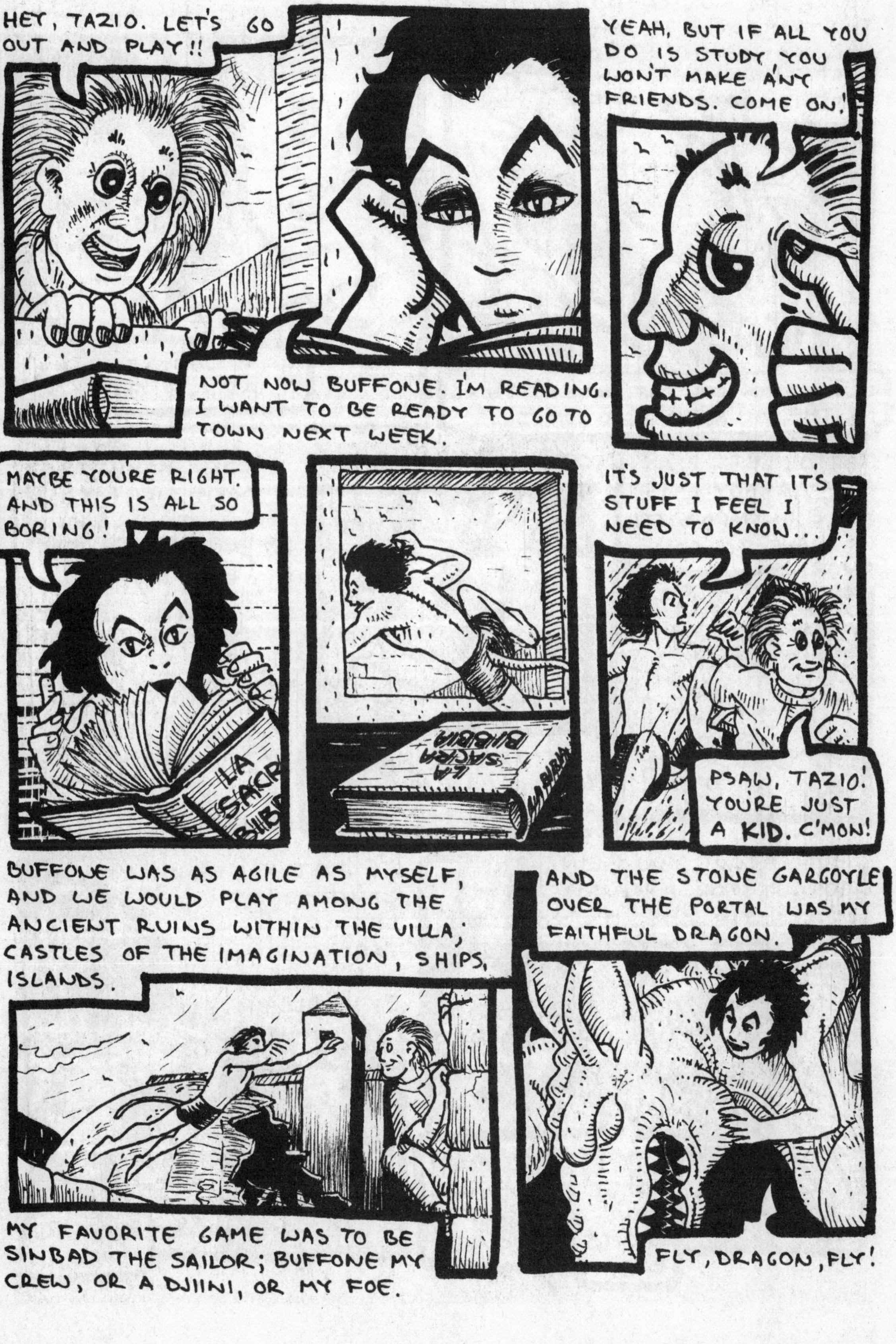

HEY, TAZIO. LET'S GO OUT AND PLAY!!
NOT NOW BUFFONE. I'M READING. I WANT TO BE READY TO GO TO TOWN NEXT WEEK.
YEAH, BUT IF ALL YOU DO IS STUDY, YOU WON'T MAKE ANY FRIENDS. COME ON!
MAYBE YOU'RE RIGHT. AND THIS IS ALL SO BORING!
LA SACRA BIBBIA
LA SACRA BIBBIA
IT'S JUST THAT IT'S STUFF I FEEL I NEED TO KNOW...
PSAW, TAZIO. YOU'RE JUST A KID. C'MON!
BUFFONE WAS AS AGILE AS MYSELF, AND WE WOULD PLAY AMONG THE ANCIENT RUINS WITHIN THE VILLA; CASTLES OF THE IMAGINATION, SHIPS, ISLANDS.
AND THE STONE GARGOYLE OVER THE PORTAL WAS MY FAITHFUL DRAGON.
MY FAVORITE GAME WAS TO BE SINBAD THE SAILOR; BUFFONE MY CREW, OR A DJIINI, OR MY FOE.
FLY, DRAGON, FLY!

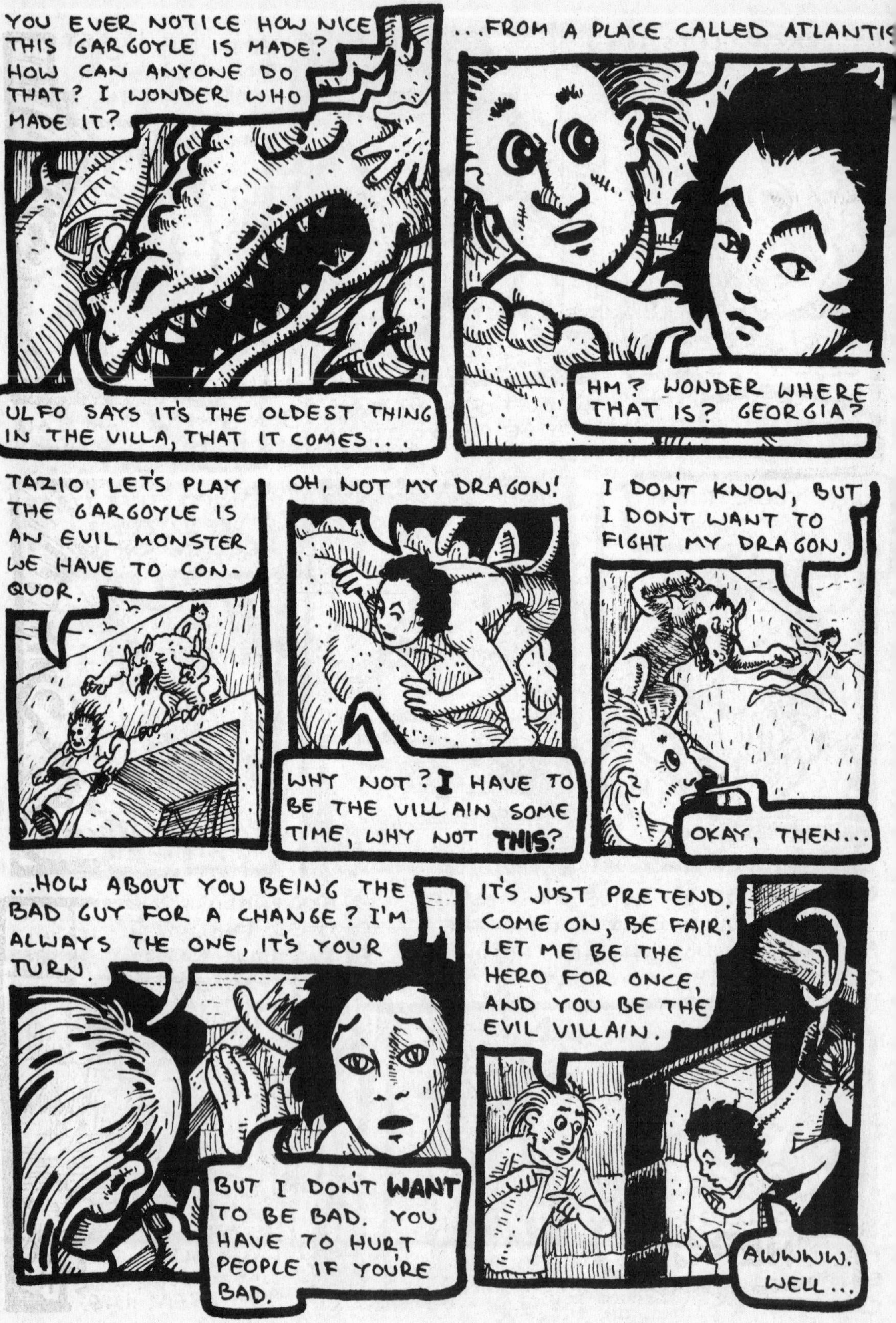

YOU EVER NOTICE HOW NICE THIS GARGOYLE IS MADE? HOW CAN ANYONE DO THAT? I WONDER WHO MADE IT?
ULFO SAYS IT'S THE OLDEST THING IN THE VILLA, THAT IT COMES...
...FROM A PLACE CALLED ATLANTIS
HM? WONDER WHERE THAT IS? GEORGIA?
TAZIO, LET'S PLAY THE GARGOYLE IS AN EVIL MONSTER WE HAVE TO CONQUOR.
OH, NOT MY DRAGON!
WHY NOT? I HAVE TO BE THE VILLAIN SOME TIME, WHY NOT THIS?
I DON'T KNOW, BUT I DON'T WANT TO FIGHT MY DRAGON.
OKAY, THEN...
...HOW ABOUT YOU BEING THE BAD GUY FOR A CHANGE? I'M ALWAYS THE ONE, IT'S YOUR TURN.
BUT I DON'T WANT TO BE BAD. YOU HAVE TO HURT PEOPLE IF YOU'RE BAD.
IT'S JUST PRETEND. COME ON, BE FAIR: LET ME BE THE HERO FOR ONCE, AND YOU BE THE EVIL VILLAIN.
AWWWW. WELL...

...OKAY, WHAT'S THE GAME?

..AND YOU ARE THE **WORST** MONSTER-MAN EVER, THE PERSONIFICATION OF **EVIL**.

GOOD. IT'S THE CLASSIC BATTLE BETWEEN **GOOD** AND **EVIL** — NO, BETTER — THE **FINAL** BATTLE! I GET TO BE THE WORLD'S FAVORITE HERO, CALL ME — OH, **ALPHA-OMEGA!!!**

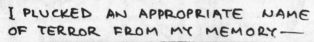

OKAY. YOU CAN CALL ME...UH...LET'S SEE...

I PLUCKED AN APPROPRIATE NAME OF TERROR FROM MY MEMORY —

...CALL ME **THERON!**

NO

-GASP-

BUFFONE? BUFFONE!!

WHAT'S WRONG? WHY AREN'T YOU **BREATHING**?

...AND YOUR HEART IS SILENT...
O NO.
YOU'RE DEAD! I DIDN'T MEAN TO... I'M NOT REALLY...
BOO HOO HOO HOO.
GIVE HIM TO ME.
U-ULFA! YES!
RISE, BUFFONE. WITH NO MEMORY OF THIS.
YES, ULFA.
:WHEW: WHAT HAPPENED?
DID I FAINT?
I FEEL PRETTY GOOD NOW THO.
HEY, TAZIO LET'S GO PLAY SOME MORE.
FORTUNATELY, TONIGHT IS THE NEW MOON AND MY SPIRITUAL POWERS ARE AT THEIR ZENITH, OR BUFFONE WOULD STAY DEAD.
CONSIDER THIS A LESSON, TAZIO: ONE CAN BE EVIL WITHOUT INTENTION.

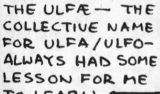

THE ULFÆ— THE COLLECTIVE NAME FOR ULFA/ULFO—ALWAYS HAD SOME LESSON FOR ME TO LEARN.

ESPECIALLY IN HIS GURU-PHASE

ULTIMATELY, THERE IS ONLY **ONE** THING YOU MUST LEARN—

—HOW TO BE A MASTER OF LIFE.

AND IF I SHOULD TEACH YOU ONLY ONE LESSON, TAZIO—

—IT WOULD BE HOW TO APPLY THE **3** ELEMENTS OF POWER

CONTROL CREATE REALIZE

TECHNIQUES OF THE **MASTERS**

**CONTROL** SELF, OTHERS, SITUATIONS

**CREATE** THINGS, IDEAS, TRUTHS

**REALIZE** REWARDS AND CONSEQUENCES

BUT I DON'T WANT TO CONTROL **OTHERS**.

YOU **MUST**, TAZIO. NOW, LEARN **HOW!**

CONTROL CREATE REALIZE

WHAT HOW WHY

WANT IT! ACT ON IT! GET IT!

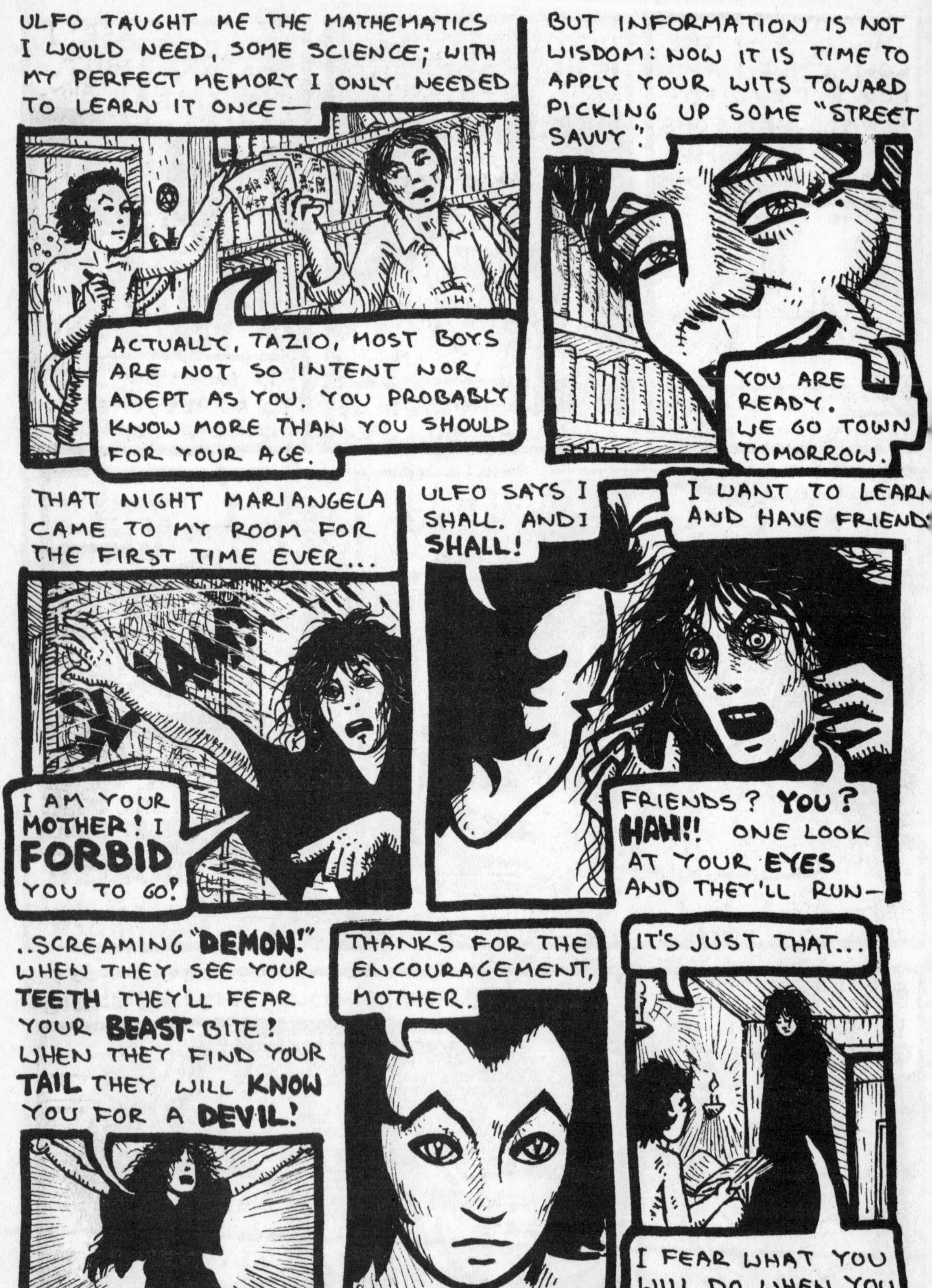
ULFO TAUGHT ME THE MATHEMATICS I WOULD NEED, SOME SCIENCE; WITH MY PERFECT MEMORY I ONLY NEEDED TO LEARN IT ONCE—
ACTUALLY, TAZIO, MOST BOYS ARE NOT SO INTENT NOR ADEPT AS YOU. YOU PROBABLY KNOW MORE THAN YOU SHOULD FOR YOUR AGE.
BUT INFORMATION IS NOT WISDOM: NOW IT IS TIME TO APPLY YOUR WITS TOWARD PICKING UP SOME "STREET SAVVY".
YOU ARE READY. WE GO TOWN TOMORROW.
THAT NIGHT MARIANGELA CAME TO MY ROOM FOR THE FIRST TIME EVER...
I AM YOUR MOTHER! I FORBID YOU TO GO!
ULFO SAYS I SHALL. AND I SHALL!
I WANT TO LEARN AND HAVE FRIENDS
FRIENDS? YOU? HAH!! ONE LOOK AT YOUR EYES AND THEY'LL RUN—
..SCREAMING "DEMON!" WHEN THEY SEE YOUR TEETH THEY'LL FEAR YOUR BEAST-BITE! WHEN THEY FIND YOUR TAIL THEY WILL KNOW YOU FOR A DEVIL!
THANKS FOR THE ENCOURAGEMENT, MOTHER.
IT'S JUST THAT...
I FEAR WHAT YOU WILL DO WHEN YOU LEAVE HERE...

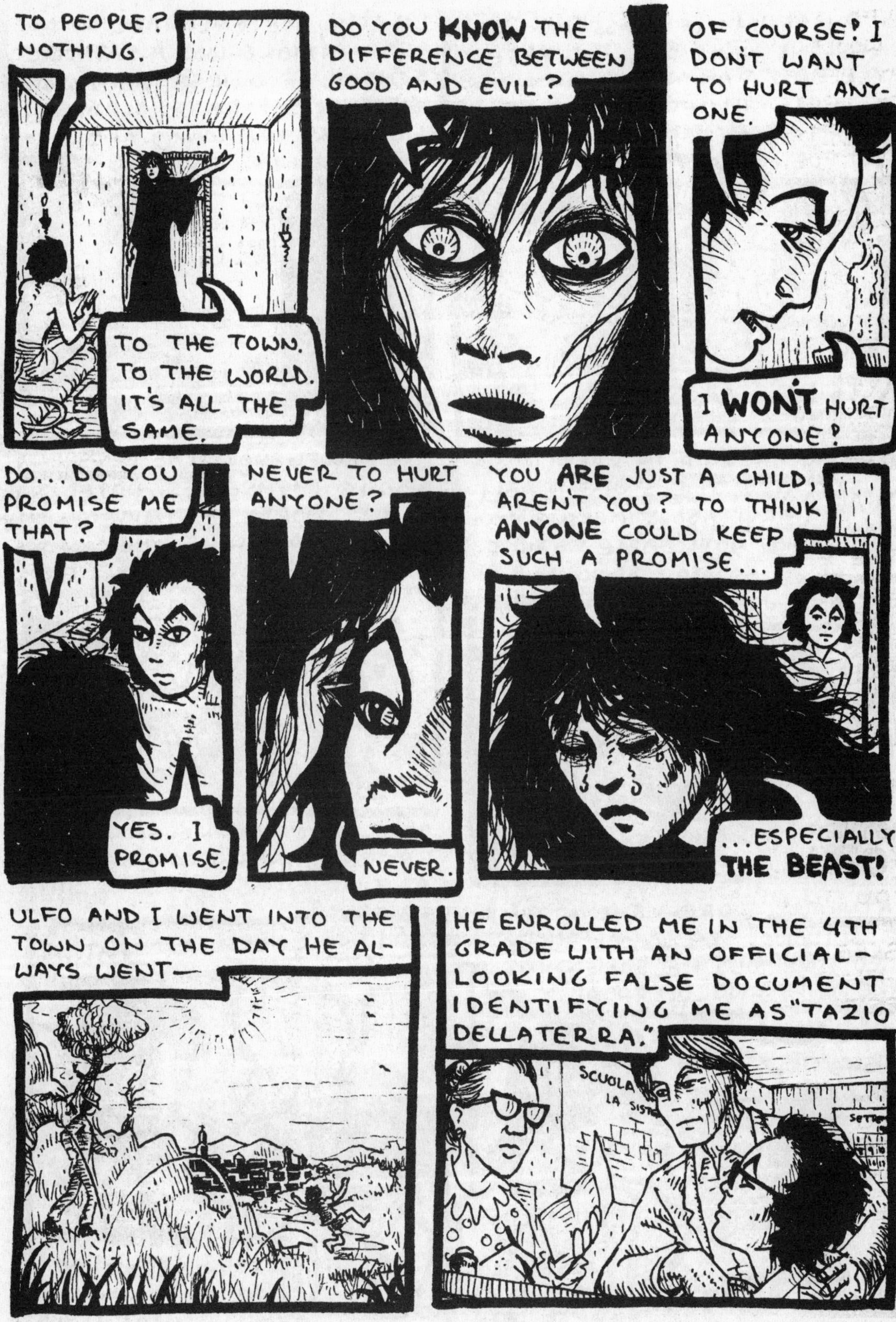
TO PEOPLE? NOTHING.
TO THE TOWN. TO THE WORLD. IT'S ALL THE SAME.
DO YOU KNOW THE DIFFERENCE BETWEEN GOOD AND EVIL?
OF COURSE! I DON'T WANT TO HURT ANY-ONE.
I WON'T HURT ANYONE!
DO... DO YOU PROMISE ME THAT?
YES. I PROMISE.
NEVER TO HURT ANYONE?
NEVER.
YOU ARE JUST A CHILD, AREN'T YOU? TO THINK ANYONE COULD KEEP SUCH A PROMISE...
...ESPECIALLY THE BEAST!
ULFO AND I WENT INTO THE TOWN ON THE DAY HE AL-WAYS WENT—
HE ENROLLED ME IN THE 4TH GRADE WITH AN OFFICIAL-LOOKING FALSE DOCUMENT IDENTIFYING ME AS "TAZIO DELLATERRA."
SCUOLA
LA SIST

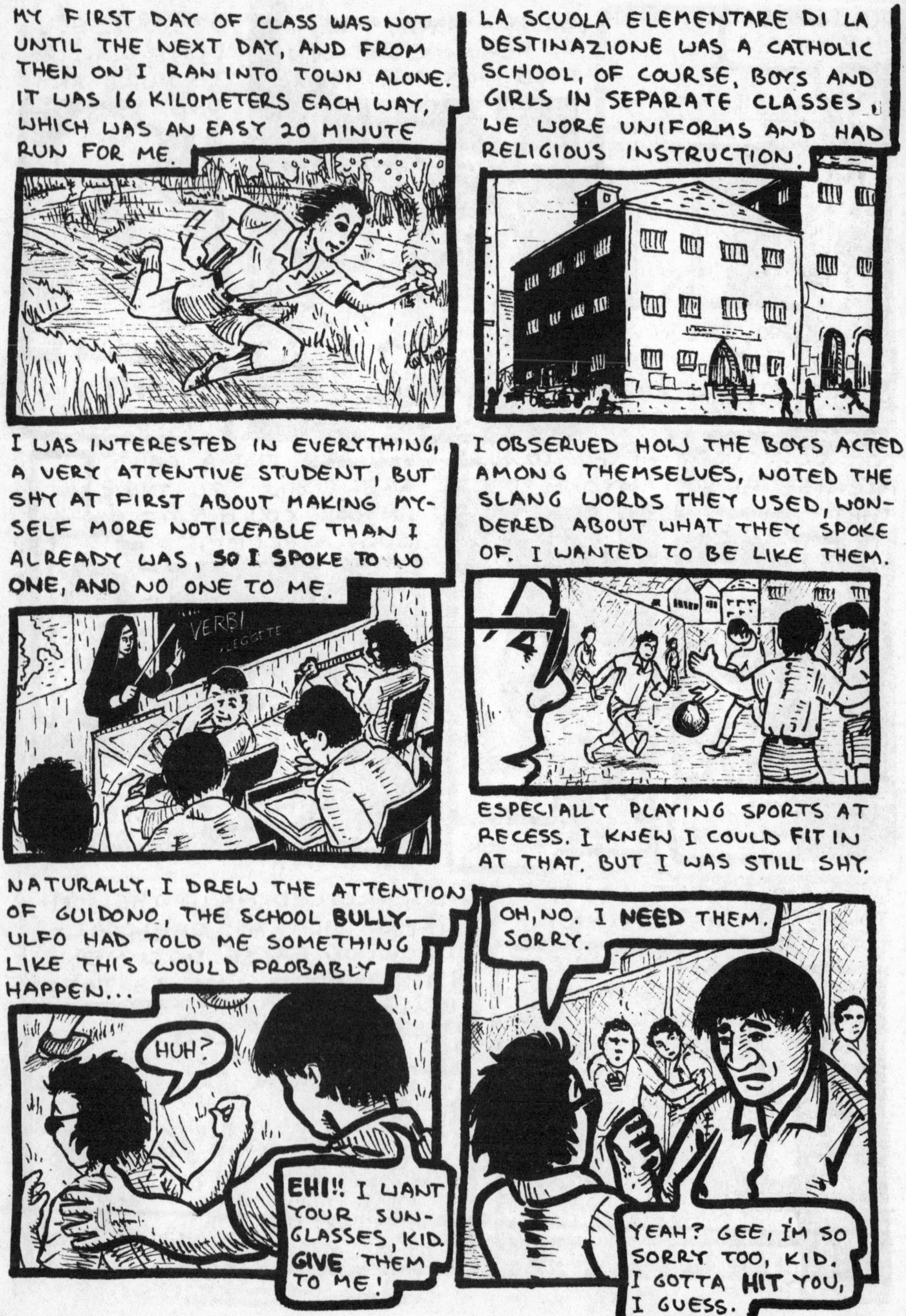
MY FIRST DAY OF CLASS WAS NOT UNTIL THE NEXT DAY, AND FROM THEN ON I RAN INTO TOWN ALONE. IT WAS 16 KILOMETERS EACH WAY, WHICH WAS AN EASY 20 MINUTE RUN FOR ME.
LA SCUOLA ELEMENTARE DI LA DESTINAZIONE WAS A CATHOLIC SCHOOL, OF COURSE, BOYS AND GIRLS IN SEPARATE CLASSES, WE WORE UNIFORMS AND HAD RELIGIOUS INSTRUCTION.
I WAS INTERESTED IN EVERYTHING, A VERY ATTENTIVE STUDENT, BUT SHY AT FIRST ABOUT MAKING MYSELF MORE NOTICEABLE THAN I ALREADY WAS, SO I SPOKE TO NO ONE, AND NO ONE TO ME.
VERBI
LEGGETE
I OBSERVED HOW THE BOYS ACTED AMONG THEMSELVES, NOTED THE SLANG WORDS THEY USED, WONDERED ABOUT WHAT THEY SPOKE OF. I WANTED TO BE LIKE THEM.
ESPECIALLY PLAYING SPORTS AT RECESS. I KNEW I COULD FIT IN AT THAT. BUT I WAS STILL SHY.
NATURALLY, I DREW THE ATTENTION OF GUIDONO, THE SCHOOL BULLY— ULFO HAD TOLD ME SOMETHING LIKE THIS WOULD PROBABLY HAPPEN...
HUH?
EHI!! I WANT YOUR SUNGLASSES, KID. GIVE THEM TO ME!
OH, NO. I NEED THEM. SORRY.
YEAH? GEE, I'M SO SORRY TOO, KID. I GOTTA HIT YOU, I GUESS.

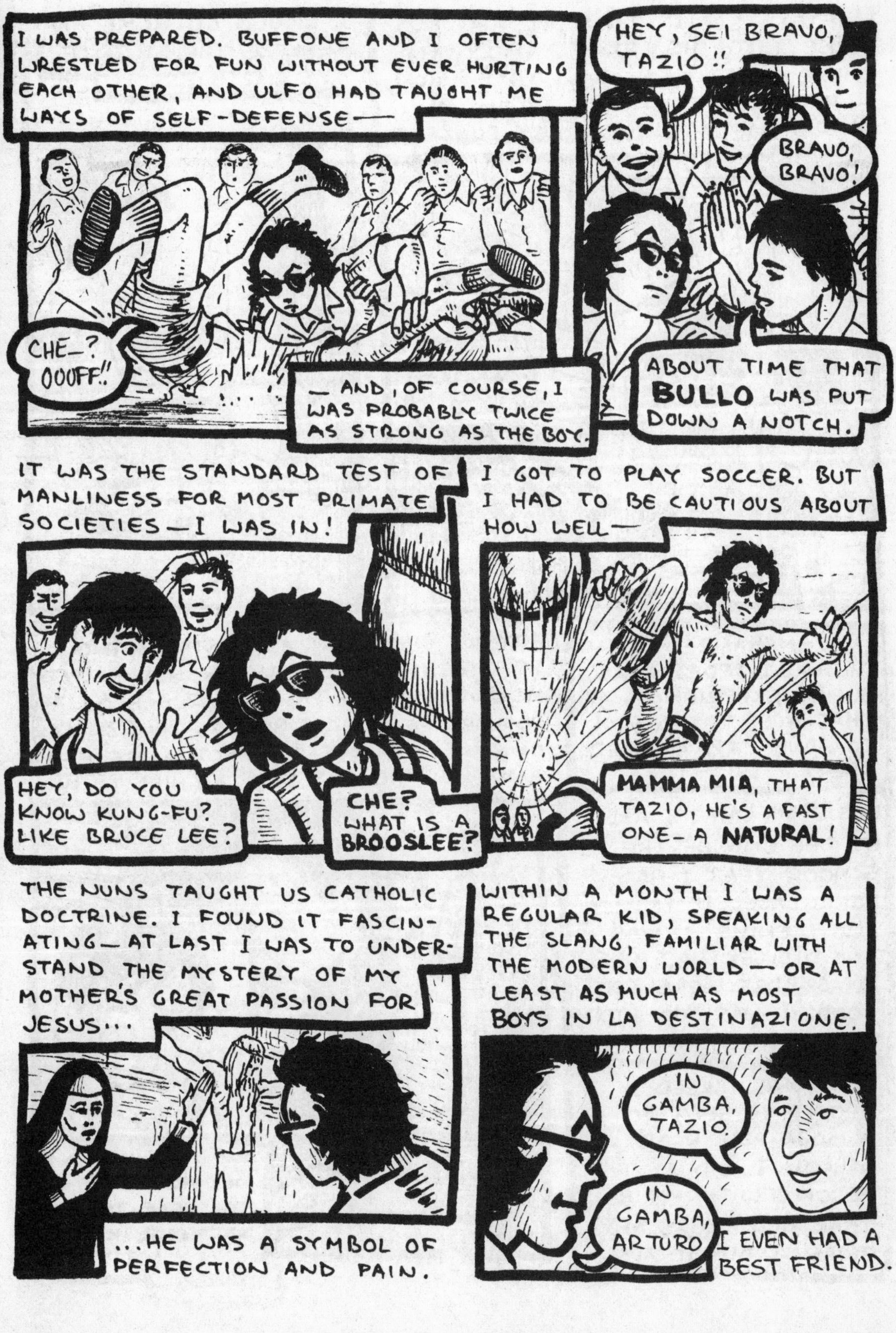
I WAS PREPARED. BUFFONE AND I OFTEN WRESTLED FOR FUN WITHOUT EVER HURTING EACH OTHER, AND ULFO HAD TAUGHT ME WAYS OF SELF-DEFENSE—
CHE—? OOUFF!!
—AND, OF COURSE, I WAS PROBABLY TWICE AS STRONG AS THE BOY.
HEY, SEI BRAVO, TAZIO!!
BRAVO, BRAVO!
ABOUT TIME THAT BULLO WAS PUT DOWN A NOTCH.
IT WAS THE STANDARD TEST OF MANLINESS FOR MOST PRIMATE SOCIETIES—I WAS IN!
HEY, DO YOU KNOW KUNG-FU? LIKE BRUCE LEE?
CHE? WHAT IS A BROOSLEE?
I GOT TO PLAY SOCCER. BUT I HAD TO BE CAUTIOUS ABOUT HOW WELL—
MAMMA MIA, THAT TAZIO, HE'S A FAST ONE—A NATURAL!
THE NUNS TAUGHT US CATHOLIC DOCTRINE. I FOUND IT FASCINATING—AT LAST I WAS TO UNDERSTAND THE MYSTERY OF MY MOTHER'S GREAT PASSION FOR JESUS...
...HE WAS A SYMBOL OF PERFECTION AND PAIN.
WITHIN A MONTH I WAS A REGULAR KID, SPEAKING ALL THE SLANG, FAMILIAR WITH THE MODERN WORLD—OR AT LEAST AS MUCH AS MOST BOYS IN LA DESTINAZIONE.
IN GAMBA, TAZIO.
IN GAMBA, ARTURO
I EVEN HAD A BEST FRIEND.

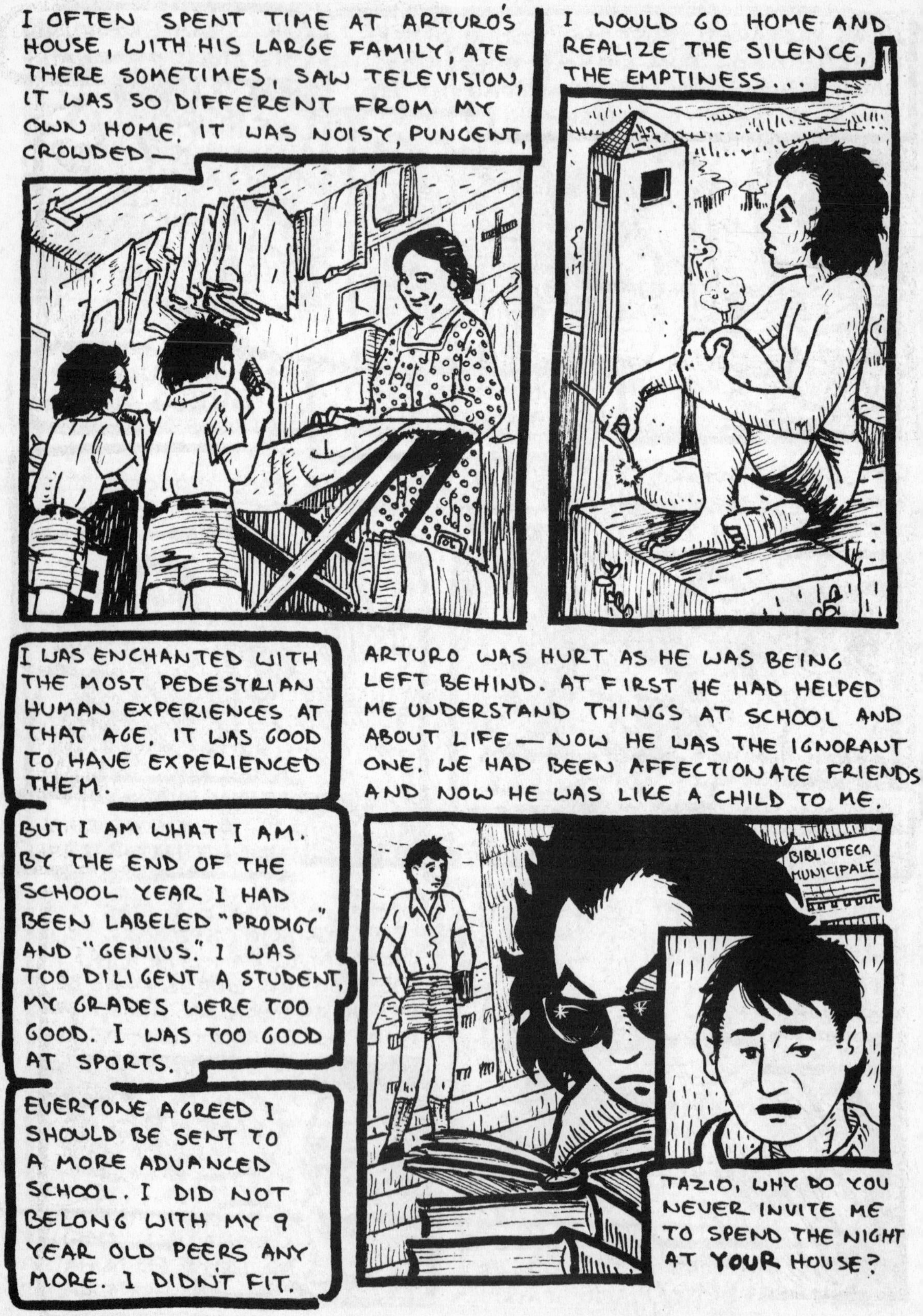

I OFTEN SPENT TIME AT ARTURO'S HOUSE, WITH HIS LARGE FAMILY, ATE THERE SOMETIMES, SAW TELEVISION, IT WAS SO DIFFERENT FROM MY OWN HOME. IT WAS NOISY, PUNGENT, CROWDED—
I WOULD GO HOME AND REALIZE THE SILENCE, THE EMPTINESS...
I WAS ENCHANTED WITH THE MOST PEDESTRIAN HUMAN EXPERIENCES AT THAT AGE. IT WAS GOOD TO HAVE EXPERIENCED THEM.
BUT I AM WHAT I AM. BY THE END OF THE SCHOOL YEAR I HAD BEEN LABELED "PRODIGY" AND "GENIUS." I WAS TOO DILIGENT A STUDENT, MY GRADES WERE TOO GOOD. I WAS TOO GOOD AT SPORTS.
EVERYONE AGREED I SHOULD BE SENT TO A MORE ADVANCED SCHOOL. I DID NOT BELONG WITH MY 9 YEAR OLD PEERS ANY MORE. I DIDN'T FIT.
ARTURO WAS HURT AS HE WAS BEING LEFT BEHIND. AT FIRST HE HAD HELPED ME UNDERSTAND THINGS AT SCHOOL AND ABOUT LIFE—NOW HE WAS THE IGNORANT ONE. WE HAD BEEN AFFECTIONATE FRIENDS AND NOW HE WAS LIKE A CHILD TO ME.
BIBLIOTECA MUNICIPALE
TAZIO, WHY DO YOU NEVER INVITE ME TO SPEND THE NIGHT AT **YOUR** HOUSE?

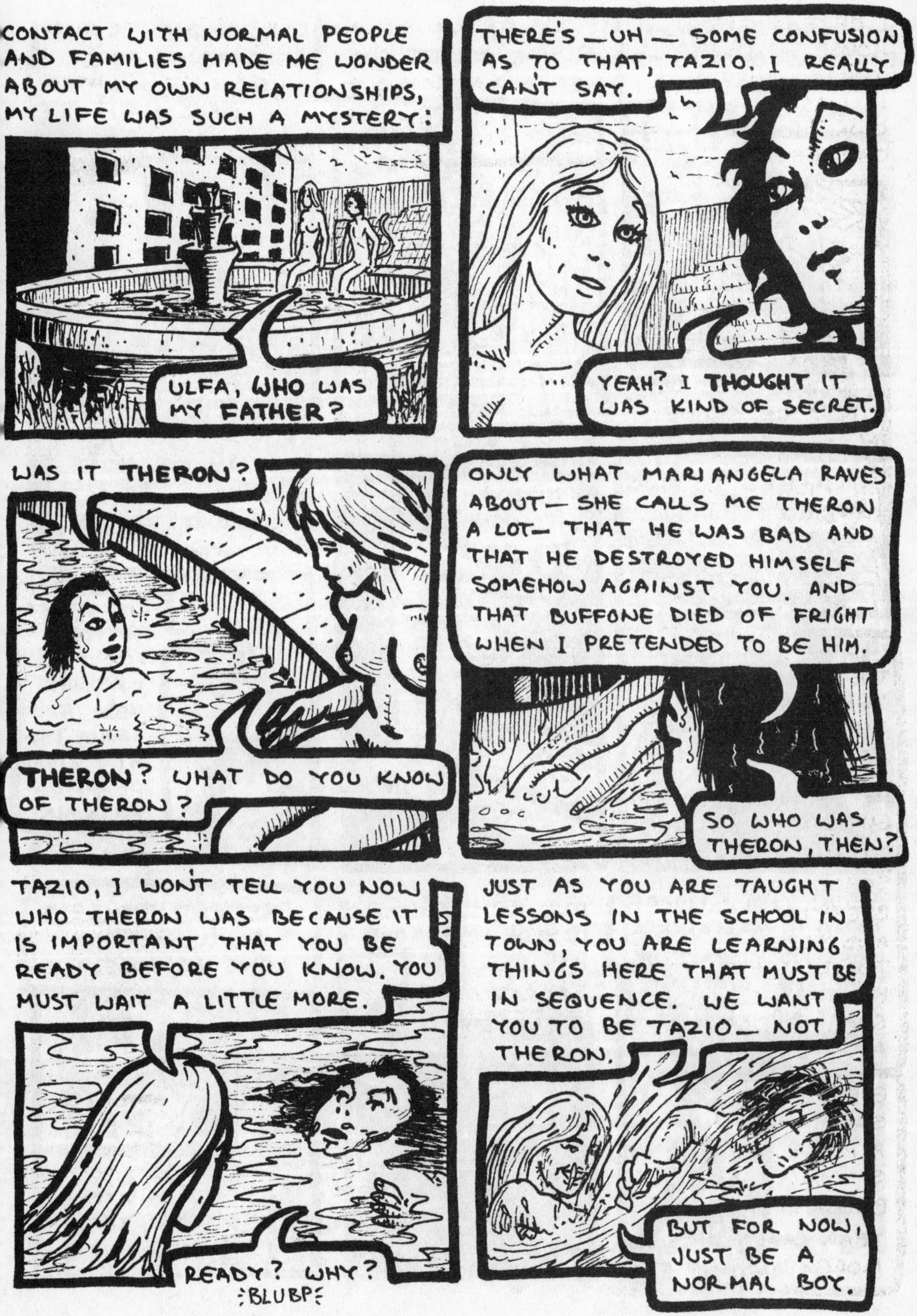
CONTACT WITH NORMAL PEOPLE AND FAMILIES MADE ME WONDER ABOUT MY OWN RELATIONSHIPS, MY LIFE WAS SUCH A MYSTERY:
ULFA, WHO WAS MY FATHER?
THERE'S — UH — SOME CONFUSION AS TO THAT, TAZIO. I REALLY CAN'T SAY.
YEAH? I THOUGHT IT WAS KIND OF SECRET.
WAS IT THERON?
THERON? WHAT DO YOU KNOW OF THERON?
ONLY WHAT MARIANGELA RAVES ABOUT— SHE CALLS ME THERON A LOT— THAT HE WAS BAD AND THAT HE DESTROYED HIMSELF SOMEHOW AGAINST YOU. AND THAT BUFFONE DIED OF FRIGHT WHEN I PRETENDED TO BE HIM.
SO WHO WAS THERON, THEN?
TAZIO, I WON'T TELL YOU NOW WHO THERON WAS BECAUSE IT IS IMPORTANT THAT YOU BE READY BEFORE YOU KNOW. YOU MUST WAIT A LITTLE MORE.
READY? WHY?
BLUBP
JUST AS YOU ARE TAUGHT LESSONS IN THE SCHOOL IN TOWN, YOU ARE LEARNING THINGS HERE THAT MUST BE IN SEQUENCE. WE WANT YOU TO BE TAZIO— NOT THERON.
BUT FOR NOW, JUST BE A NORMAL BOY.

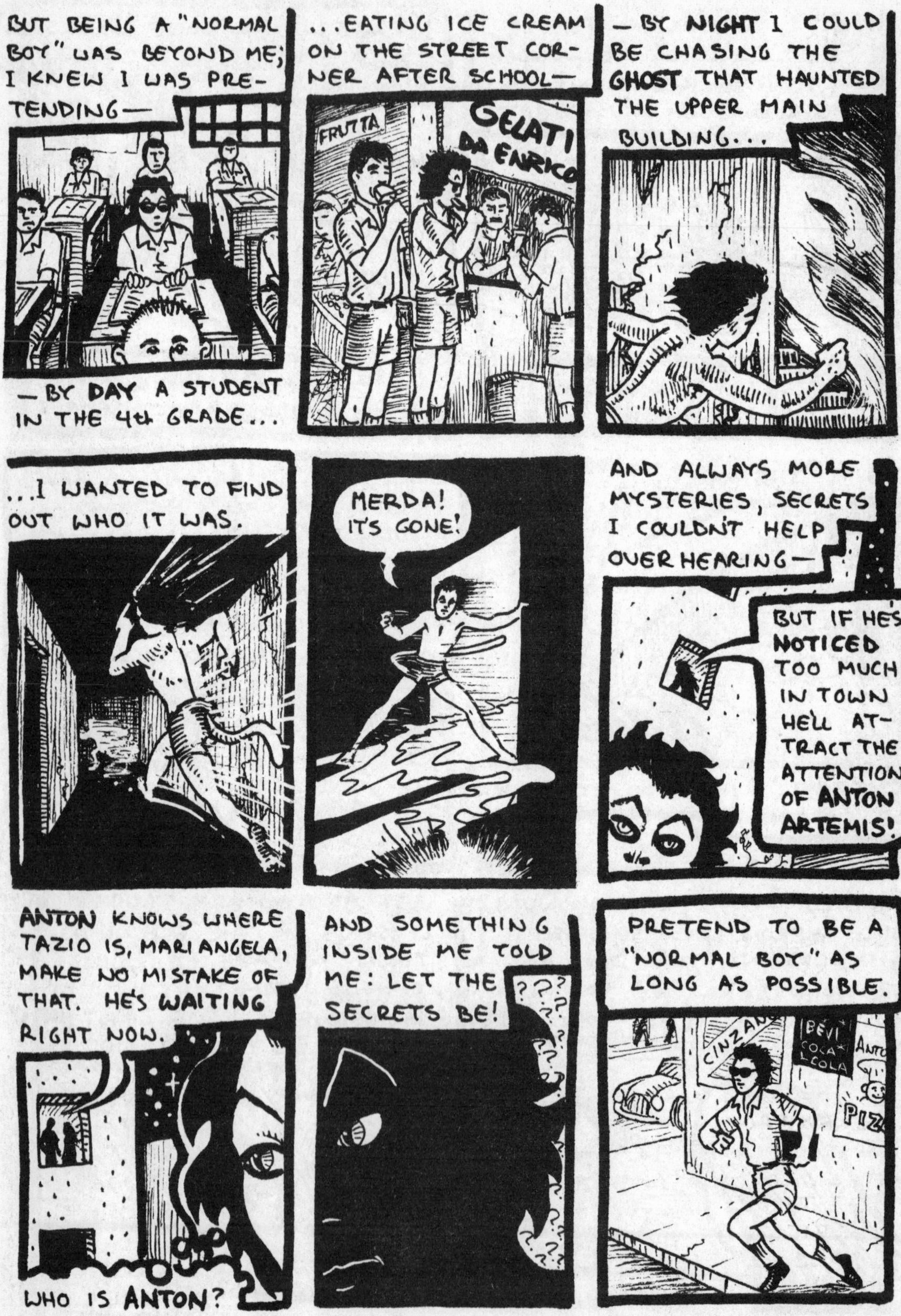
BUT BEING A "NORMAL BOY" WAS BEYOND ME; I KNEW I WAS PRETENDING—
—BY DAY A STUDENT IN THE 4th GRADE...
...EATING ICE CREAM ON THE STREET CORNER AFTER SCHOOL—
FRUTTA
GELATI DA ENRICO
—BY NIGHT I COULD BE CHASING THE GHOST THAT HAUNTED THE UPPER MAIN BUILDING...
...I WANTED TO FIND OUT WHO IT WAS.
MERDA! IT'S GONE!
AND ALWAYS MORE MYSTERIES, SECRETS I COULDN'T HELP OVERHEARING—
BUT IF HE'S NOTICED TOO MUCH IN TOWN HE'LL ATTRACT THE ATTENTION OF ANTON ARTEMIS!
ANTON KNOWS WHERE TAZIO IS, MARIANGELA, MAKE NO MISTAKE OF THAT. HE'S WAITING RIGHT NOW.
WHO IS ANTON?
AND SOMETHING INSIDE ME TOLD ME: LET THE SECRETS BE!
PRETEND TO BE A "NORMAL BOY" AS LONG AS POSSIBLE.
CINZANO
BEVI COCA-COLA
PIZ

OF COURSE PADRE GIORGIO CAUGHT ME IN THE STREET ONE DAY—

AHA! YOU THERE!

DO YOU **ALWAYS** WEAR THOSE SUN-GLASSES?

YES, MY EYES NEED THEM.

AND WHEN ARE YOU COMING TO MASS?

OH, I DID THAT MONTHS AGO.

ONLY ONCE?

WELL, I WANTED TO SEE WHAT IT WAS LIKE. THAT'S ALL.

IT WAS... NICE.

SIGNORE ULFO SAYS YOU PEOPLE ARE NOT CATHOLIC. JUST WHAT RELIGION **ARE** YOU?

WELL, IT DOESN'T REALLY HAVE A SPECIFIC NAME.

WITH **WHICH** CHURCH IS IT AFFILIATED?

WELL, NONE.

DOES IT IMPLY A BELIEF IN **GOD**?

I THINK THE BEST WAY TO DESCRIBE "OUR RELIGION" IS AN EXPERIENCE OF GOD, MANIFESTED BY COSMIC PHENOMENA, AND A SYNTHESIS OF ALL THEOLOGIES AS VIEWED FROM A HISTORICAL PERSPECTIVE. SIGNORE ULFO IS A THEOLOGIAN—A PRIEST, OF SORTS, AND OUR SPIRITUAL LEADER.

YOU HAVE A **SMART** MOUTH, CHILD. YOU ARE EITHER ATHEISTS, AGNOSTICS OR DEVIL WORSHIPPERS

THERE IS NOT RELIGION WITHOUT THE STRUCTURE OF THE **CHURCH!**

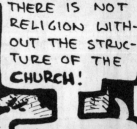

MAN CANNOT APPROACH GOD WITHOUT THE BLESSINGS OF **AUTHORITY**—SUCH AS A **PRIEST**, THE **POPE!**

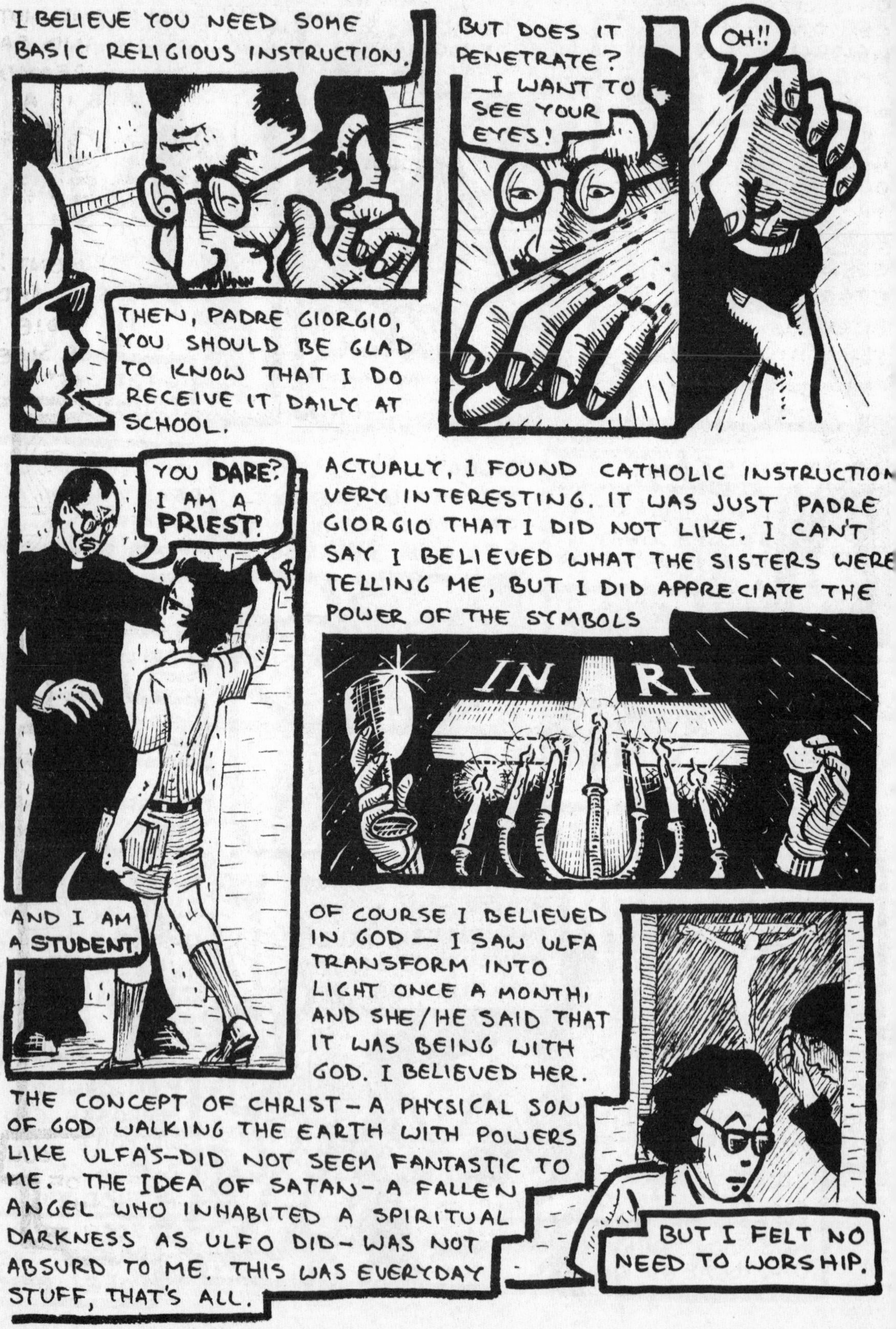

I BELIEVE YOU NEED SOME BASIC RELIGIOUS INSTRUCTION.
THEN, PADRE GIORGIO, YOU SHOULD BE GLAD TO KNOW THAT I DO RECEIVE IT DAILY AT SCHOOL.
BUT DOES IT PENETRATE? _I WANT TO SEE YOUR EYES!
OH!!
YOU DARE? I AM A PRIEST!
AND I AM A STUDENT.
ACTUALLY, I FOUND CATHOLIC INSTRUCTION VERY INTERESTING. IT WAS JUST PADRE GIORGIO THAT I DID NOT LIKE. I CAN'T SAY I BELIEVED WHAT THE SISTERS WERE TELLING ME, BUT I DID APPRECIATE THE POWER OF THE SYMBOLS
IN RI
OF COURSE I BELIEVED IN GOD — I SAW ULFA TRANSFORM INTO LIGHT ONCE A MONTH, AND SHE/HE SAID THAT IT WAS BEING WITH GOD. I BELIEVED HER.
THE CONCEPT OF CHRIST – A PHYSICAL SON OF GOD WALKING THE EARTH WITH POWERS LIKE ULFA'S–DID NOT SEEM FANTASTIC TO ME. THE IDEA OF SATAN – A FALLEN ANGEL WHO INHABITED A SPIRITUAL DARKNESS AS ULFO DID – WAS NOT ABSURD TO ME. THIS WAS EVERYDAY STUFF, THAT'S ALL.
BUT I FELT NO NEED TO WORSHIP.

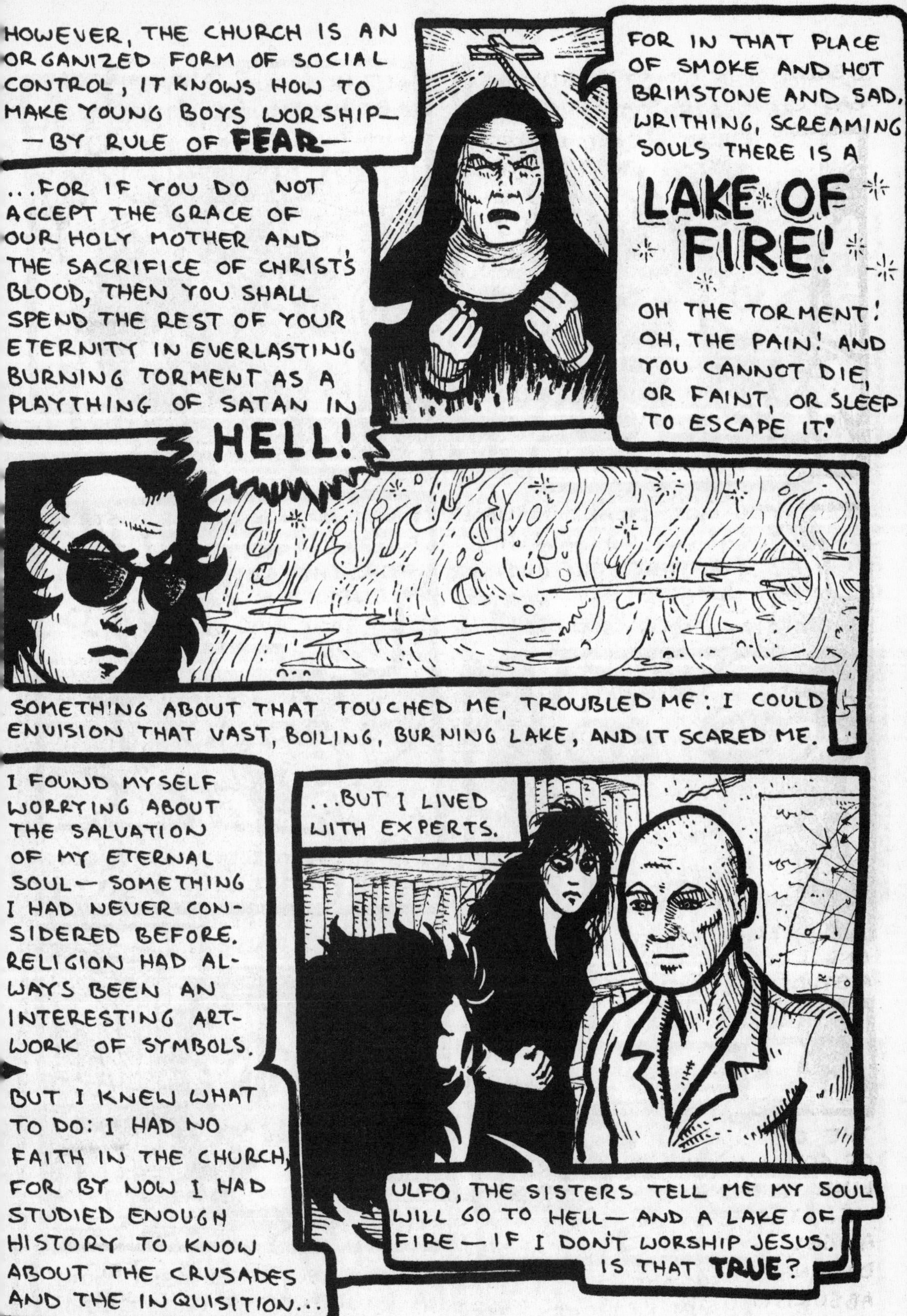
HOWEVER, THE CHURCH IS AN ORGANIZED FORM OF SOCIAL CONTROL, IT KNOWS HOW TO MAKE YOUNG BOYS WORSHIP— —BY RULE OF FEAR—
FOR IN THAT PLACE OF SMOKE AND HOT BRIMSTONE AND SAD, WRITHING, SCREAMING SOULS THERE IS A LAKE OF FIRE! OH THE TORMENT! OH, THE PAIN! AND YOU CANNOT DIE, OR FAINT, OR SLEEP TO ESCAPE IT!
...FOR IF YOU DO NOT ACCEPT THE GRACE OF OUR HOLY MOTHER AND THE SACRIFICE OF CHRIST'S BLOOD, THEN YOU SHALL SPEND THE REST OF YOUR ETERNITY IN EVERLASTING BURNING TORMENT AS A PLAYTHING OF SATAN IN HELL!
SOMETHING ABOUT THAT TOUCHED ME, TROUBLED ME: I COULD ENVISION THAT VAST, BOILING, BURNING LAKE, AND IT SCARED ME.
I FOUND MYSELF WORRYING ABOUT THE SALVATION OF MY ETERNAL SOUL— SOMETHING I HAD NEVER CONSIDERED BEFORE. RELIGION HAD ALWAYS BEEN AN INTERESTING ARTWORK OF SYMBOLS.
BUT I KNEW WHAT TO DO: I HAD NO FAITH IN THE CHURCH, FOR BY NOW I HAD STUDIED ENOUGH HISTORY TO KNOW ABOUT THE CRUSADES AND THE INQUISITION...
...BUT I LIVED WITH EXPERTS.
ULFO, THE SISTERS TELL ME MY SOUL WILL GO TO HELL— AND A LAKE OF FIRE— IF I DON'T WORSHIP JESUS. IS THAT TRUE?

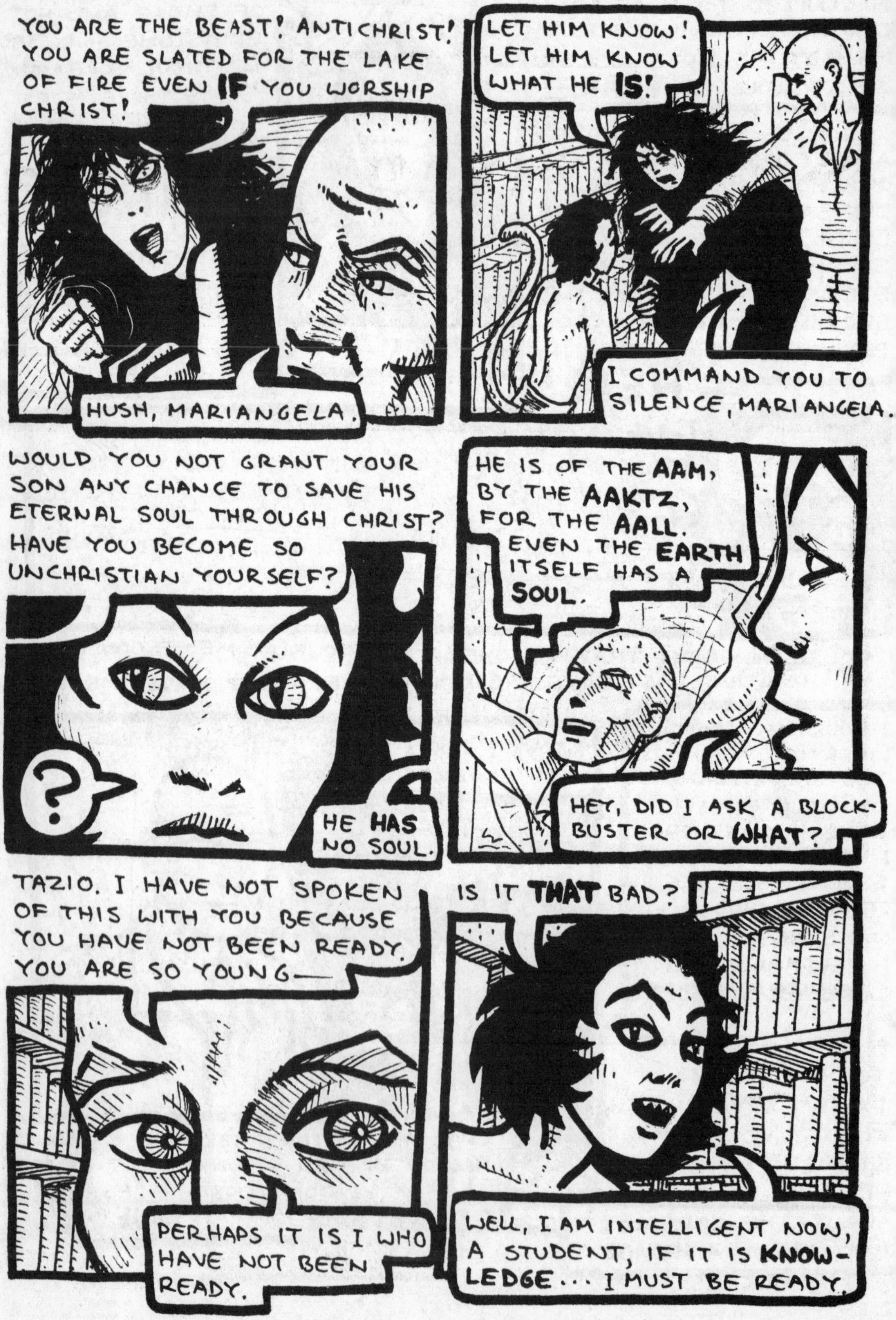

YOU ARE THE BEAST! ANTICHRIST! YOU ARE SLATED FOR THE LAKE OF FIRE EVEN IF YOU WORSHIP CHRIST!
HUSH, MARIANGELA.
LET HIM KNOW! LET HIM KNOW WHAT HE IS!
I COMMAND YOU TO SILENCE, MARIANGELA.
WOULD YOU NOT GRANT YOUR SON ANY CHANCE TO SAVE HIS ETERNAL SOUL THROUGH CHRIST? HAVE YOU BECOME SO UNCHRISTIAN YOURSELF?
?
HE HAS NO SOUL.
HE IS OF THE AAM, BY THE AAKTZ, FOR THE AALL. EVEN THE EARTH ITSELF HAS A SOUL.
HEY, DID I ASK A BLOCK-BUSTER OR WHAT?
TAZIO. I HAVE NOT SPOKEN OF THIS WITH YOU BECAUSE YOU HAVE NOT BEEN READY. YOU ARE SO YOUNG—
PERHAPS IT IS I WHO HAVE NOT BEEN READY.
IS IT THAT BAD?
WELL, I AM INTELLIGENT NOW, A STUDENT, IF IT IS KNOW-LEDGE... I MUST BE READY.

YES. YOU ARE ALMOST READY... BUT HAVE YOU **READ THE BIBLE?**

SURE.

ALL OF IT? TO THE END?

WELL, NO. IT GETS KIND OF **BORING.** I SKIPPED AROUND.

I RECCOMEND YOU READ THE **LAST** BOOK, THE ONE TITLED THE **REVELATION** OF ST. JOHN THE DIVINE.

YOU WILL **NOT** FIND IT BORING, TAZIO.

NOR DID I. CONFUSING, YES, BUT BORING, NO. ALL THOSE DRAMATIC **IMAGES:** ANGELS, SEALED BOOKS, TRUMPETED DISASTERS...

...AND THAT DRAMATIC **BEAST** WITH **7 HEADS** AND **10 HORNS** RISING UP OUT OF THE SEA... FUN READING.

BUT I FELT A CHILL WHEN I CAME UPON THE REFERENCE TO THE LAKE OF FIRE, THERE IN **CHAPTER 19.**

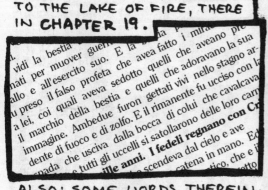

vidi la bestia e gli guerra per muover guerra a colui p nati per muover a colui p allo e all'esercito suo. E la bestia fu pre preso il falso profeta che avea fatto i mirac u preso il falso profeta sedotto quelli che aveano pre a lei, coi quali aveva sedotto quelli che adoravano la sua il marchio della bestia e quelli che adoravano la sua immagine. Ambedue furon gettati vivi nello stagno ar- dente di fuoco e di zolfo. E il rimanente fu ucciso con la spada che usciva dalla bocca di colui che cavalcava e tutti gli uccelli si satollarono delle loro carn **ille anni. I fedeli regnano con Cr** scendeva dal cielo e ave catena in mano. E tico, che e i otto

ALSO: SOME WORDS THEREIN TWEAKED A **MEMORY,** BUT I DIDN'T CRYSTALIZE IT.

AND WHEN I FINISHED THE ANCIENT EPISTLE I COULD ONLY WONDER **WHY** ULFO HAD ME READ THIS CONFUSING JUMBLE OF CONFLICTING SYMBOLISM.

LA SACRA BIBBIA ✝

OKAY, ULFO, I READ IT.

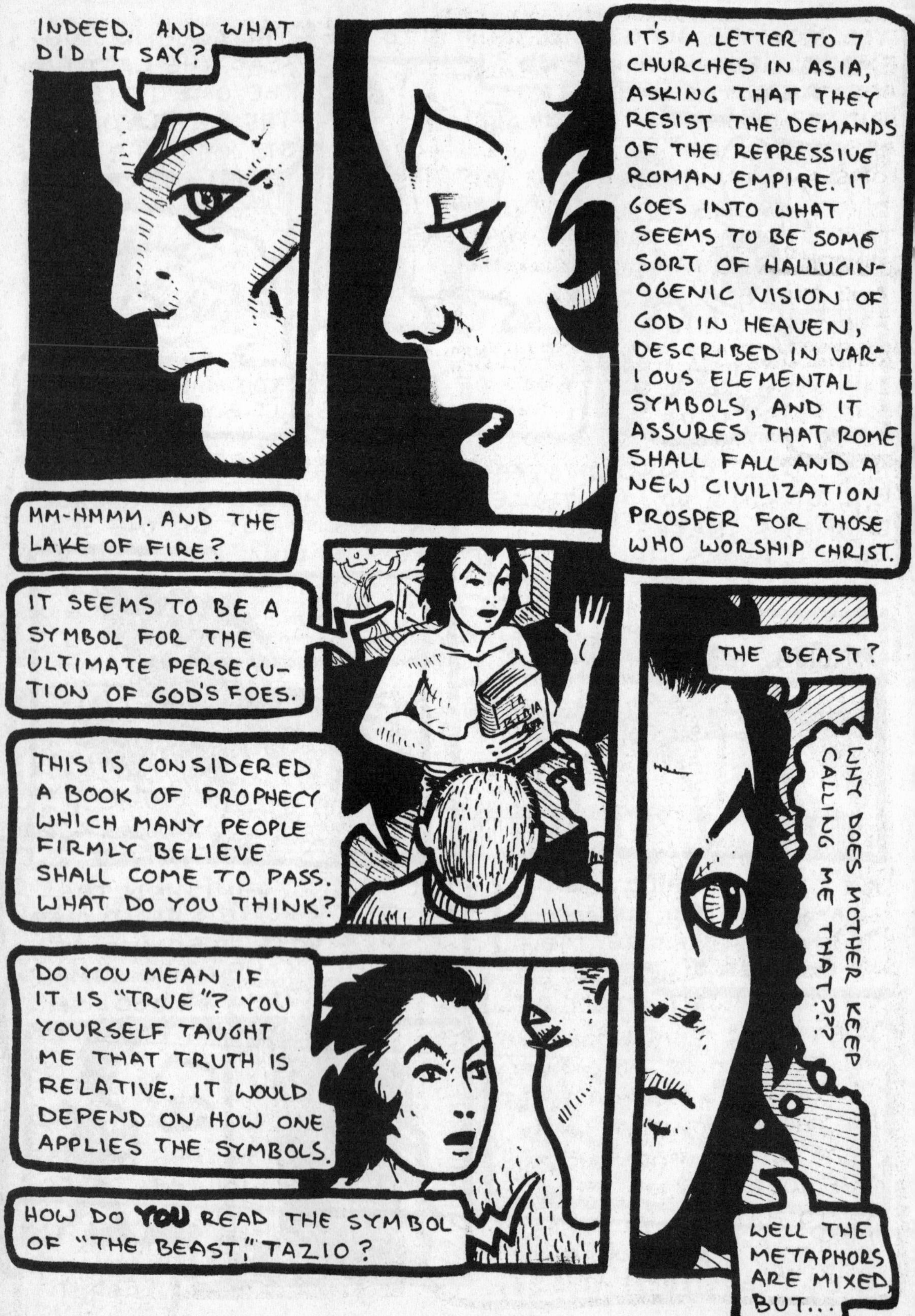

INDEED. AND WHAT DID IT SAY?
IT'S A LETTER TO 7 CHURCHES IN ASIA, ASKING THAT THEY RESIST THE DEMANDS OF THE REPRESSIVE ROMAN EMPIRE. IT GOES INTO WHAT SEEMS TO BE SOME SORT OF HALLUCIN-OGENIC VISION OF GOD IN HEAVEN, DESCRIBED IN VAR-IOUS ELEMENTAL SYMBOLS, AND IT ASSURES THAT ROME SHALL FALL AND A NEW CIVILIZATION PROSPER FOR THOSE WHO WORSHIP CHRIST.
MM-HMMM. AND THE LAKE OF FIRE?
IT SEEMS TO BE A SYMBOL FOR THE ULTIMATE PERSECU-TION OF GOD'S FOES.
THIS IS CONSIDERED A BOOK OF PROPHECY WHICH MANY PEOPLE FIRMLY BELIEVE SHALL COME TO PASS. WHAT DO YOU THINK?
THE BEAST?
WHY DOES MOTHER KEEP CALLING ME THAT???
DO YOU MEAN IF IT IS "TRUE"? YOU YOURSELF TAUGHT ME THAT TRUTH IS RELATIVE. IT WOULD DEPEND ON HOW ONE APPLIES THE SYMBOLS.
HOW DO **YOU** READ THE SYMBOL OF "THE BEAST," TAZIO?
WELL THE METAPHORS ARE MIXED, BUT...

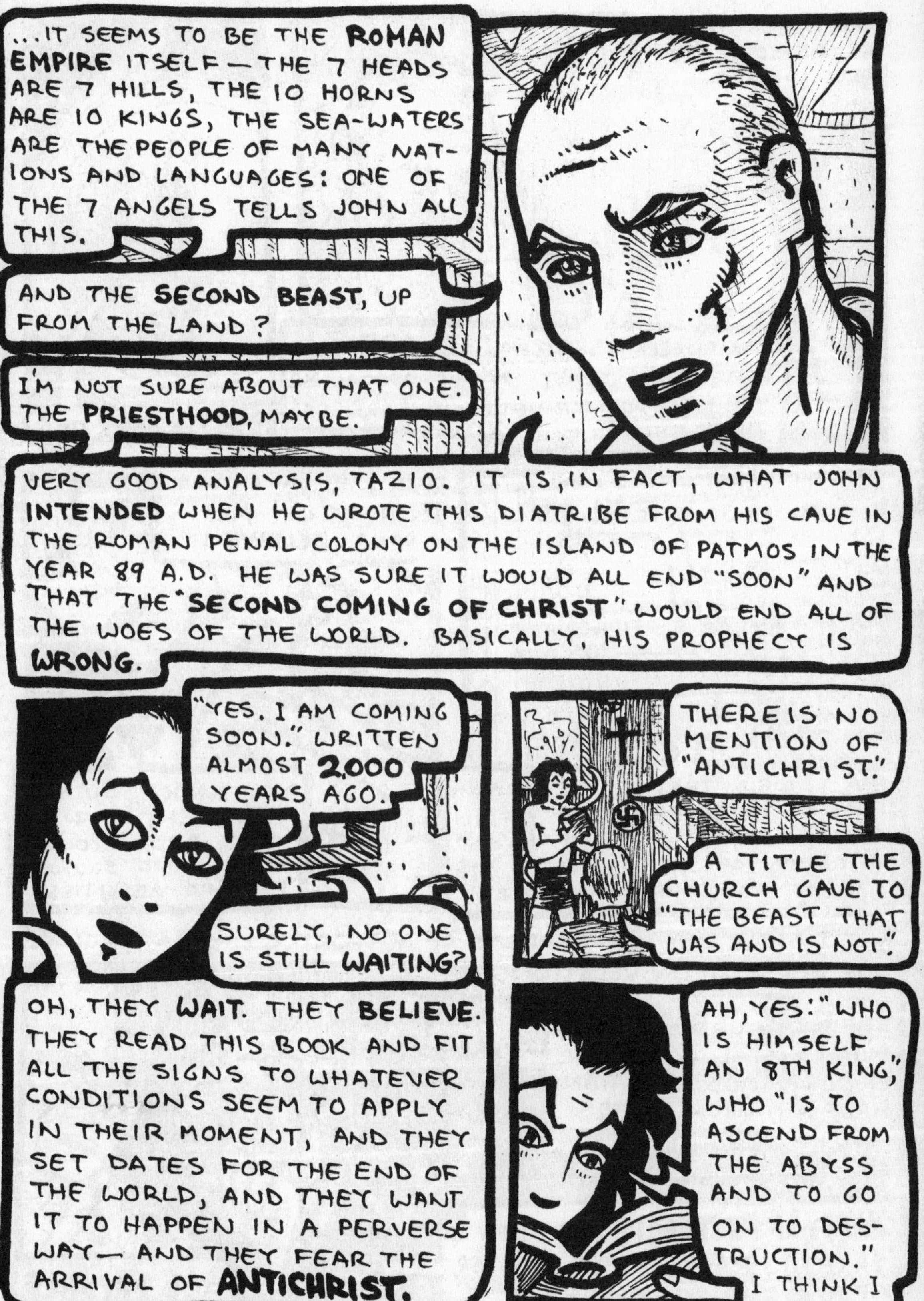
...IT SEEMS TO BE THE ROMAN EMPIRE ITSELF—THE 7 HEADS ARE 7 HILLS, THE 10 HORNS ARE 10 KINGS, THE SEA-WATERS ARE THE PEOPLE OF MANY NATIONS AND LANGUAGES: ONE OF THE 7 ANGELS TELLS JOHN ALL THIS.
AND THE SECOND BEAST, UP FROM THE LAND?
I'M NOT SURE ABOUT THAT ONE. THE PRIESTHOOD, MAYBE.
VERY GOOD ANALYSIS, TAZIO. IT IS, IN FACT, WHAT JOHN INTENDED WHEN HE WROTE THIS DIATRIBE FROM HIS CAVE IN THE ROMAN PENAL COLONY ON THE ISLAND OF PATMOS IN THE YEAR 89 A.D. HE WAS SURE IT WOULD ALL END "SOON" AND THAT THE "SECOND COMING OF CHRIST" WOULD END ALL OF THE WOES OF THE WORLD. BASICALLY, HIS PROPHECY IS WRONG.
"YES. I AM COMING SOON." WRITTEN ALMOST 2,000 YEARS AGO.
SURELY, NO ONE IS STILL WAITING?
THERE IS NO MENTION OF "ANTICHRIST."
A TITLE THE CHURCH GAVE TO "THE BEAST THAT WAS AND IS NOT."
OH, THEY WAIT. THEY BELIEVE. THEY READ THIS BOOK AND FIT ALL THE SIGNS TO WHATEVER CONDITIONS SEEM TO APPLY IN THEIR MOMENT, AND THEY SET DATES FOR THE END OF THE WORLD, AND THEY WANT IT TO HAPPEN IN A PERVERSE WAY— AND THEY FEAR THE ARRIVAL OF ANTICHRIST.
AH, YES: "WHO IS HIMSELF AN 8TH KING," WHO "IS TO ASCEND FROM THE ABYSS AND TO GO ON TO DESTRUCTION." I THINK I GET IT...

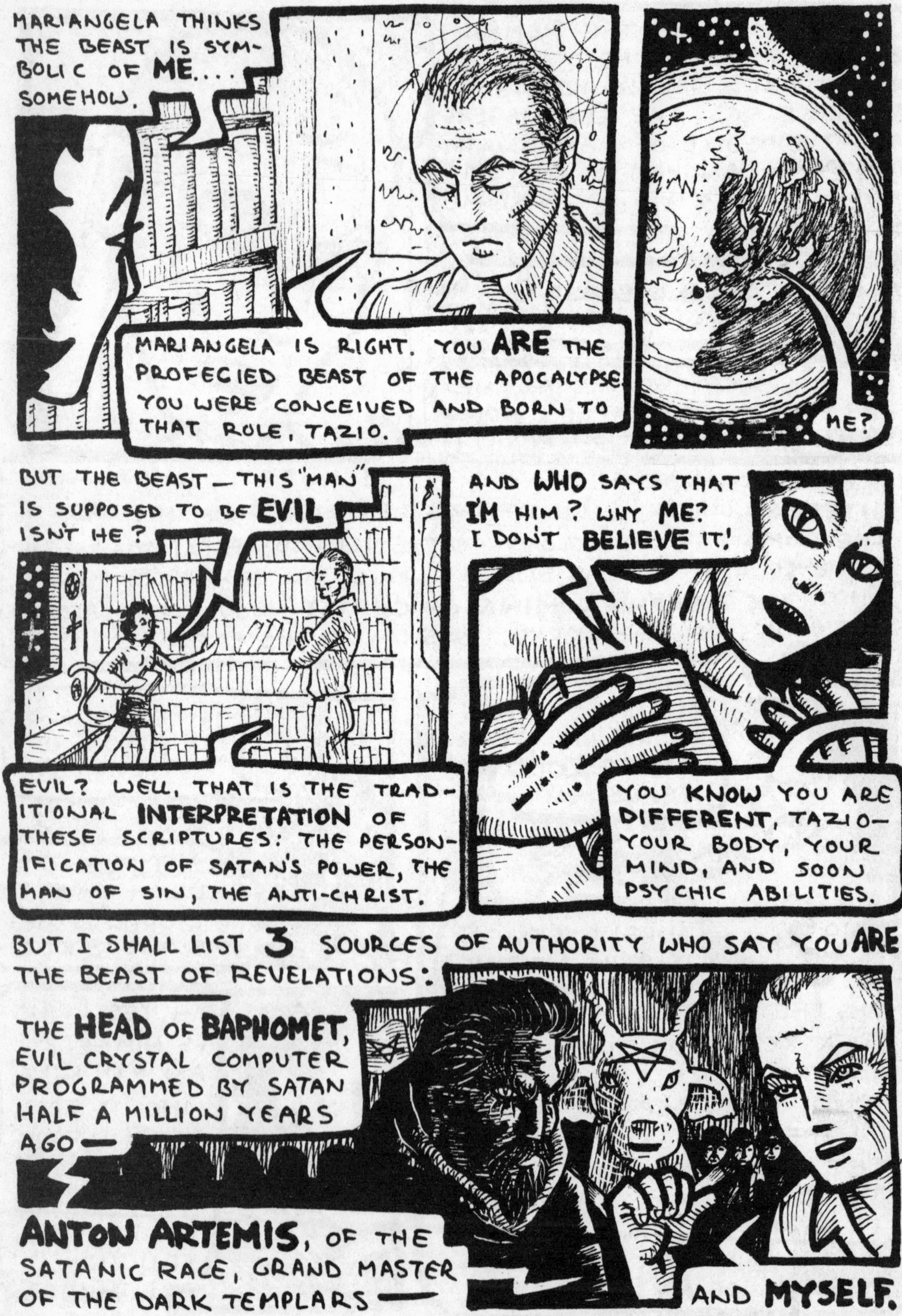
MARIANGELA THINKS THE BEAST IS SYMBOLIC OF ME.... SOMEHOW.
MARIANGELA IS RIGHT. YOU ARE THE PROFECIED BEAST OF THE APOCALYPSE. YOU WERE CONCEIVED AND BORN TO THAT ROLE, TAZIO.
ME?
BUT THE BEAST—THIS "MAN" IS SUPPOSED TO BE EVIL ISN'T HE?
EVIL? WELL, THAT IS THE TRADITIONAL INTERPRETATION OF THESE SCRIPTURES: THE PERSONIFICATION OF SATAN'S POWER, THE MAN OF SIN, THE ANTI-CHRIST.
AND WHO SAYS THAT I'M HIM? WHY ME? I DON'T BELIEVE IT!
YOU KNOW YOU ARE DIFFERENT, TAZIO— YOUR BODY, YOUR MIND, AND SOON PSYCHIC ABILITIES.
BUT I SHALL LIST 3 SOURCES OF AUTHORITY WHO SAY YOU ARE THE BEAST OF REVELATIONS:
THE HEAD OF BAPHOMET, EVIL CRYSTAL COMPUTER PROGRAMMED BY SATAN HALF A MILLION YEARS AGO—
ANTON ARTEMIS, OF THE SATANIC RACE, GRAND MASTER OF THE DARK TEMPLARS—
AND MYSELF.

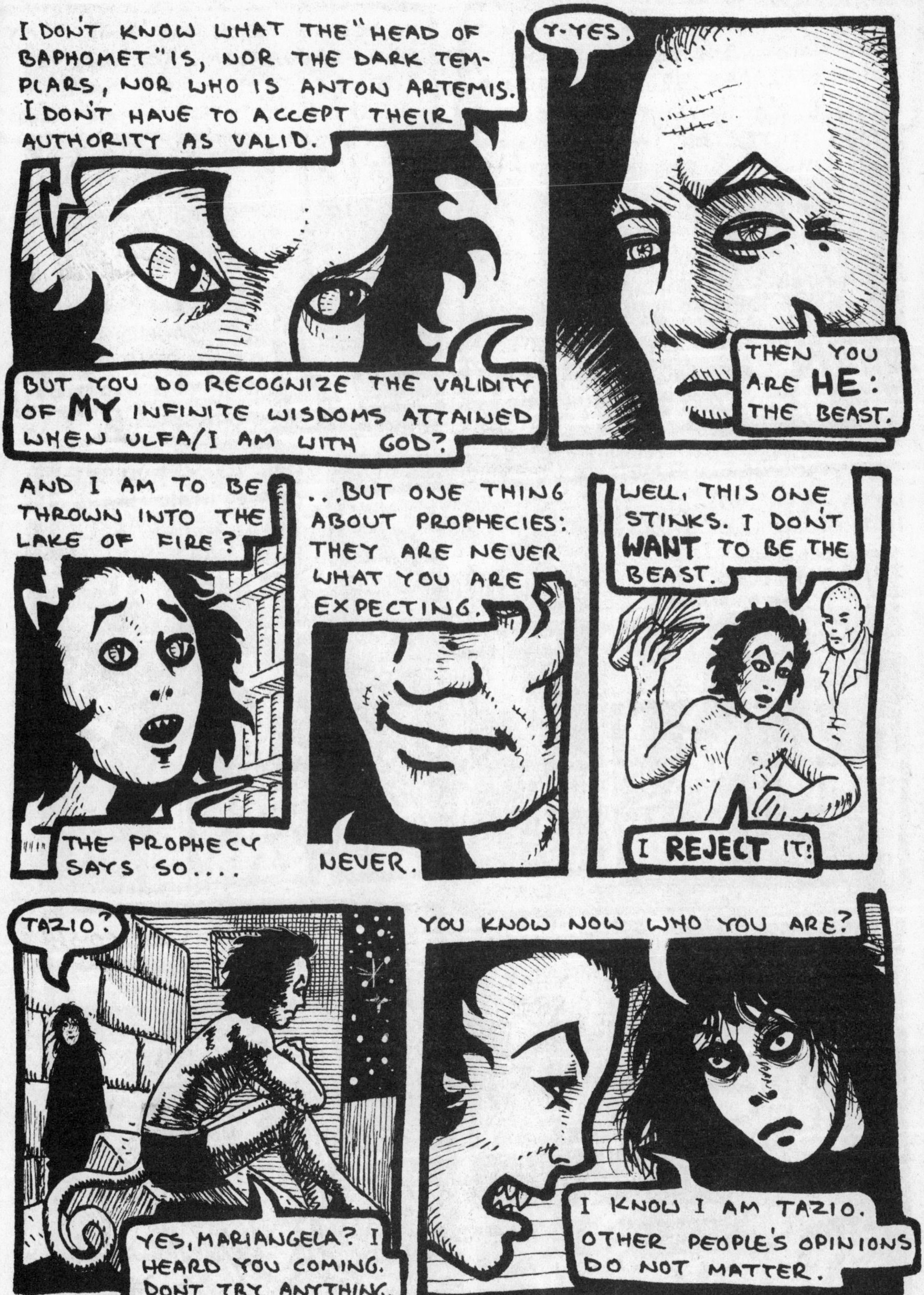

I DON'T KNOW WHAT THE "HEAD OF BAPHOMET" IS, NOR THE DARK TEMPLARS, NOR WHO IS ANTON ARTEMIS. I DON'T HAVE TO ACCEPT THEIR AUTHORITY AS VALID.
BUT YOU DO RECOGNIZE THE VALIDITY OF MY INFINITE WISDOMS ATTAINED WHEN ULFA/I AM WITH GOD?
Y-YES.
THEN YOU ARE HE: THE BEAST.
AND I AM TO BE THROWN INTO THE LAKE OF FIRE?
THE PROPHECY SAYS SO....
...BUT ONE THING ABOUT PROPHECIES: THEY ARE NEVER WHAT YOU ARE EXPECTING.
NEVER.
WELL, THIS ONE STINKS. I DON'T WANT TO BE THE BEAST.
I REJECT IT!
TAZIO?
YES, MARIANGELA? I HEARD YOU COMING. DON'T TRY ANYTHING, I'M DANGEROUS.
YOU KNOW NOW WHO YOU ARE?
I KNOW I AM TAZIO. OTHER PEOPLE'S OPINIONS DO NOT MATTER.

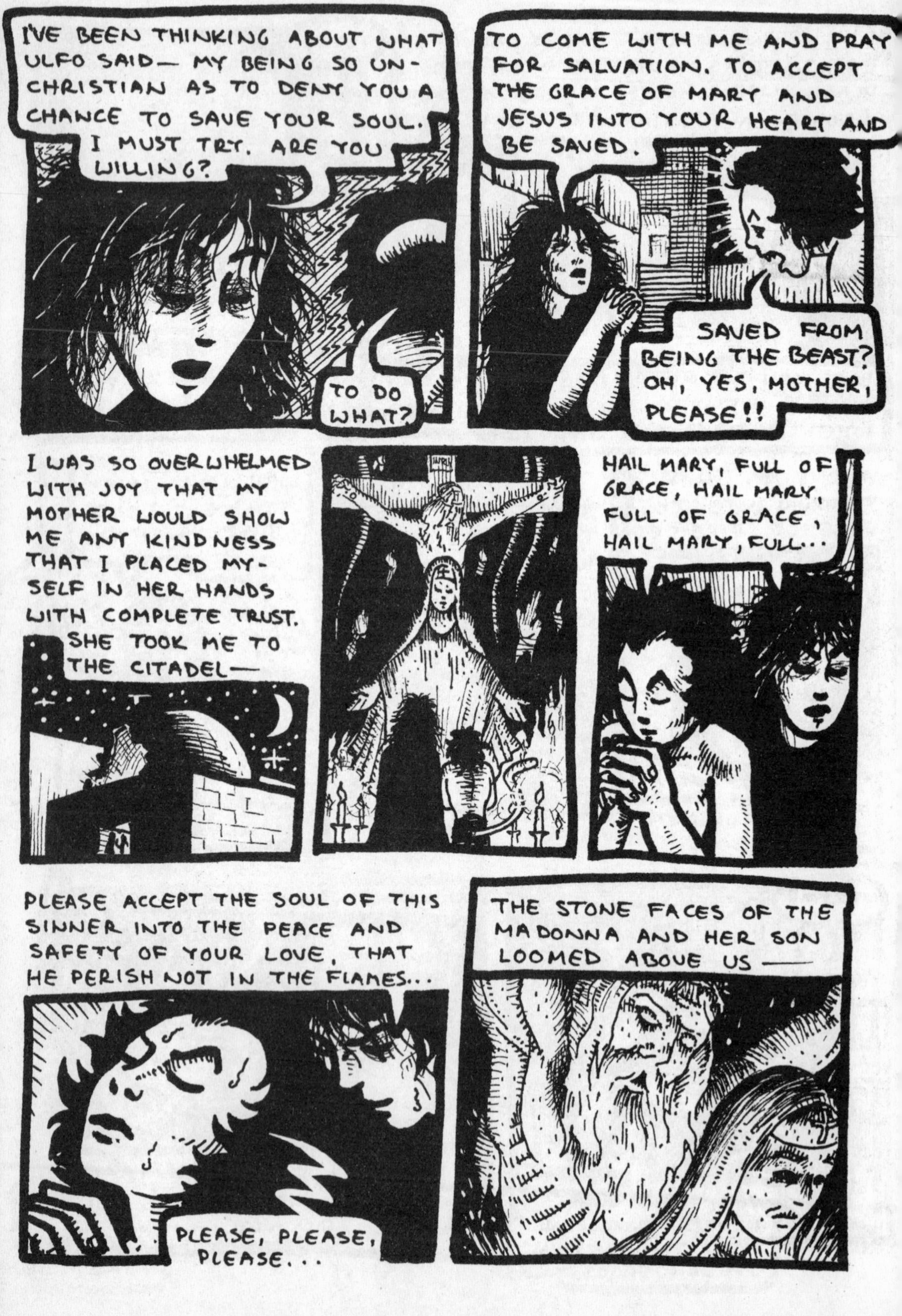
I'VE BEEN THINKING ABOUT WHAT ULFO SAID— MY BEING SO UN-CHRISTIAN AS TO DENY YOU A CHANCE TO SAVE YOUR SOUL. I MUST TRY. ARE YOU WILLING?
TO DO WHAT?
TO COME WITH ME AND PRAY FOR SALVATION. TO ACCEPT THE GRACE OF MARY AND JESUS INTO YOUR HEART AND BE SAVED.
SAVED FROM BEING THE BEAST? OH, YES, MOTHER, PLEASE!!
I WAS SO OVERWHELMED WITH JOY THAT MY MOTHER WOULD SHOW ME ANY KINDNESS THAT I PLACED MY-SELF IN HER HANDS WITH COMPLETE TRUST.
SHE TOOK ME TO THE CITADEL—
HAIL MARY, FULL OF GRACE, HAIL MARY, FULL OF GRACE, HAIL MARY, FULL...
PLEASE ACCEPT THE SOUL OF THIS SINNER INTO THE PEACE AND SAFETY OF YOUR LOVE, THAT HE PERISH NOT IN THE FLAMES...
PLEASE, PLEASE, PLEASE...
THE STONE FACES OF THE MADONNA AND HER SON LOOMED ABOVE US—

AFTER SEVERAL HOURS OF FRENZIED PRAYER—

TAZIO: DO YOU ACCEPT CHRIST INTO YOUR OWN HEART?

OH YES, I DO.

GOOD. COME WITH ME TO CONFESS YOUR SINS.

YES, MOTHER.

IN HERE.

YES, MOTHER.

NOW CONFESS ALL YOUR SINS.

SNIK!

MOTHER, FORGIVE ME, FOR I HAVE SINNED. I—UH— UH...

I DON'T KNOW WHAT TO CONFESS.

BAD THINGS.

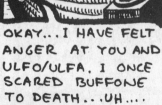

OKAY... I HAVE FELT ANGER AT YOU AND ULFO/ULFA. I ONCE SCARED BUFFONE TO DEATH...UH....

CONFESS FOR THE MURDERS AND RAPES OF SO MANY, INCLUDING YOUR MOTHER MANY TIMES; FOR THE BLASPHEMIES AGAINST GOD AND CHRIST AND VIRGIN.

HUH? BUT I HAVENT DONE ANY OF...

CONFESS!! THIS IS YOUR ONLY CHANCE TO CLEANSE YOUR SOUL BEFORE...

WHAT'S THIS?

SNIFF PETROL!! MOTHER, WHAT ARE YOU DOING??

CONFESS! (SOB) CONFESS BEFORE YOU PERISH IN THE LAKE OF FIRE!!!

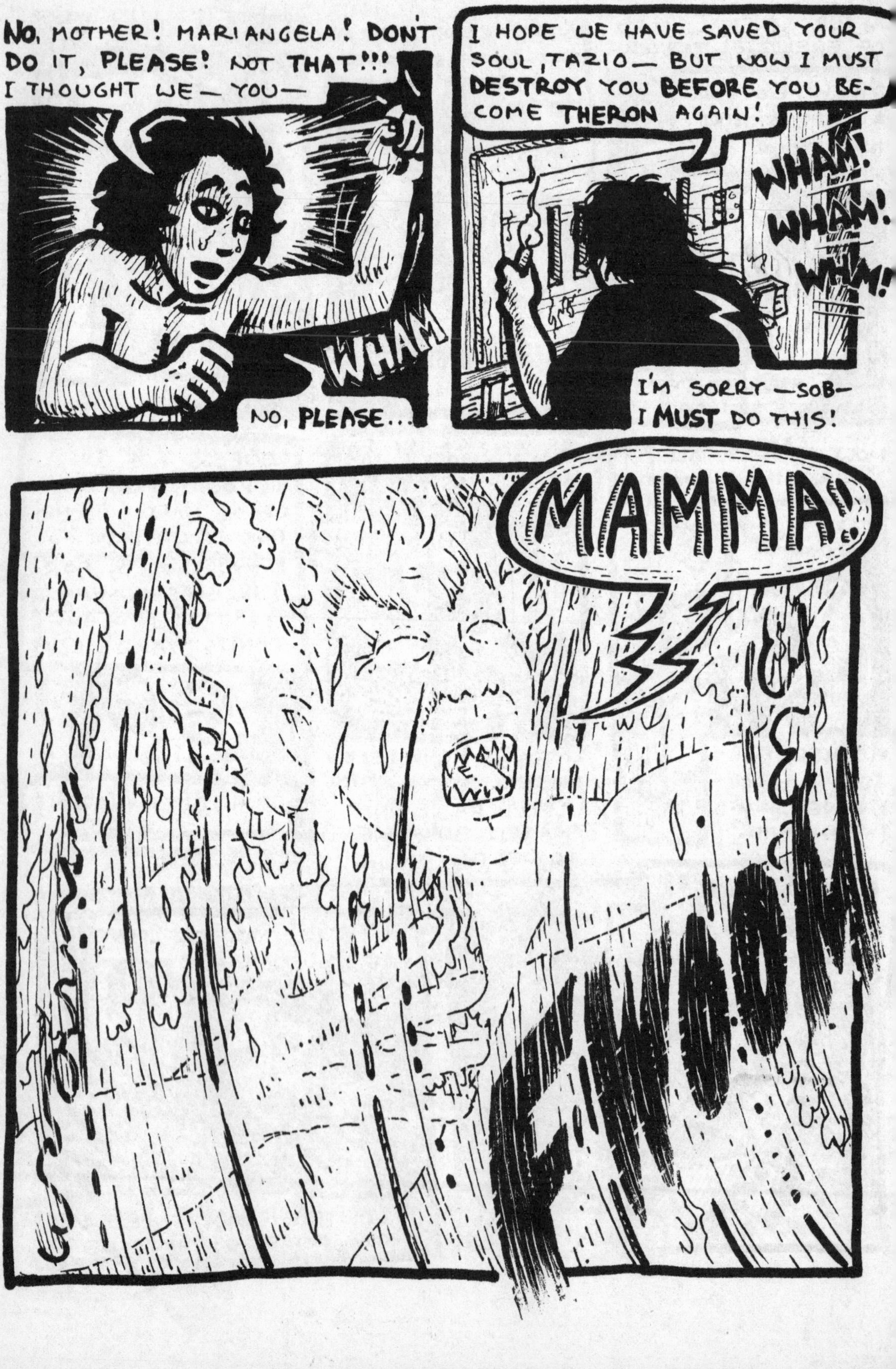

NO, MOTHER! MARIANGELA! DON'T DO IT, PLEASE! NOT THAT!!! I THOUGHT WE— YOU—
WHAM
NO, PLEASE...
I HOPE WE HAVE SAVED YOUR SOUL, TAZIO— BUT NOW I MUST DESTROY YOU BEFORE YOU BECOME THERON AGAIN!
WHAM! WHAM! WHAM!
I'M SORRY —SOB— I MUST DO THIS!
MAMMA!

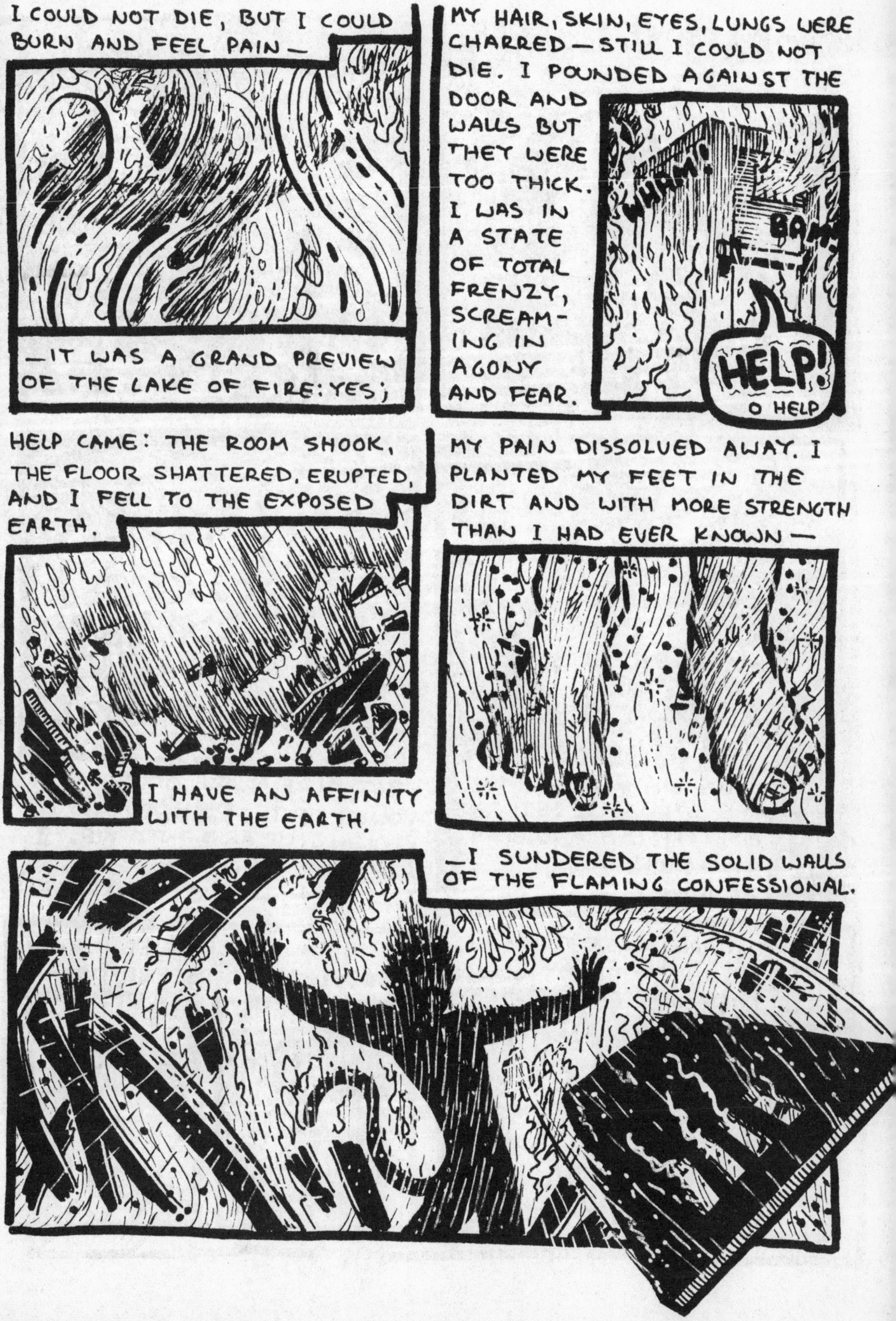
I COULD NOT DIE, BUT I COULD BURN AND FEEL PAIN—
—IT WAS A GRAND PREVIEW OF THE LAKE OF FIRE: YES;
MY HAIR, SKIN, EYES, LUNGS WERE CHARRED—STILL I COULD NOT DIE. I POUNDED AGAINST THE DOOR AND WALLS BUT THEY WERE TOO THICK. I WAS IN A STATE OF TOTAL FRENZY, SCREAMING IN AGONY AND FEAR.
WHAM!
BAM
HELP!
O HELP
HELP CAME: THE ROOM SHOOK, THE FLOOR SHATTERED, ERUPTED, AND I FELL TO THE EXPOSED EARTH.
I HAVE AN AFFINITY WITH THE EARTH.
MY PAIN DISSOLVED AWAY. I PLANTED MY FEET IN THE DIRT AND WITH MORE STRENGTH THAN I HAD EVER KNOWN—
—I SUNDERED THE SOLID WALLS OF THE FLAMING CONFESSIONAL.

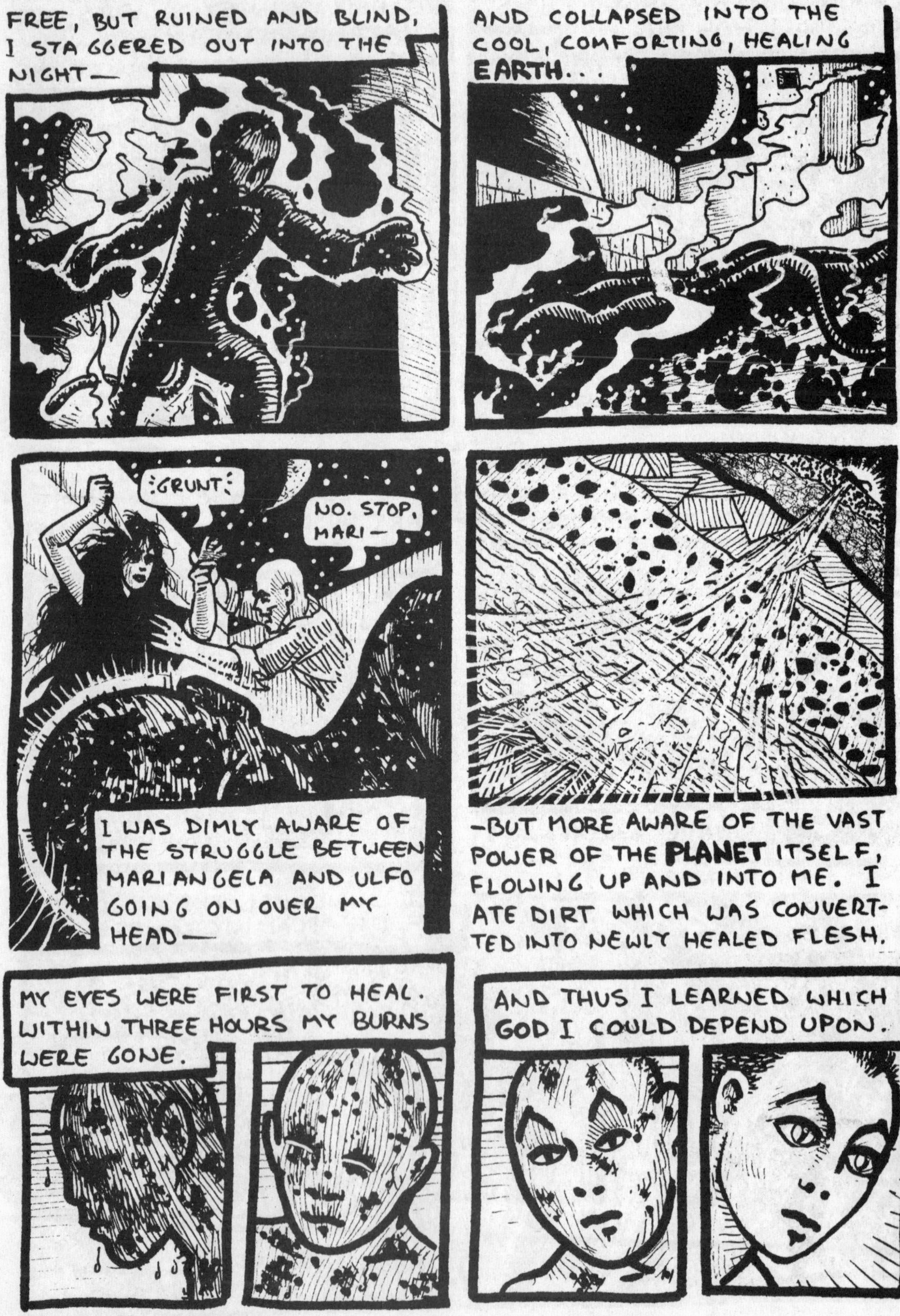
FREE, BUT RUINED AND BLIND, I STAGGERED OUT INTO THE NIGHT—
AND COLLAPSED INTO THE COOL, COMFORTING, HEALING EARTH...
GRUNT
NO. STOP, MARI—
I WAS DIMLY AWARE OF THE STRUGGLE BETWEEN MARIANGELA AND ULFO GOING ON OVER MY HEAD—
—BUT MORE AWARE OF THE VAST POWER OF THE PLANET ITSELF, FLOWING UP AND INTO ME. I ATE DIRT WHICH WAS CONVERTED INTO NEWLY HEALED FLESH.
MY EYES WERE FIRST TO HEAL. WITHIN THREE HOURS MY BURNS WERE GONE.
AND THUS I LEARNED WHICH GOD I COULD DEPEND UPON.

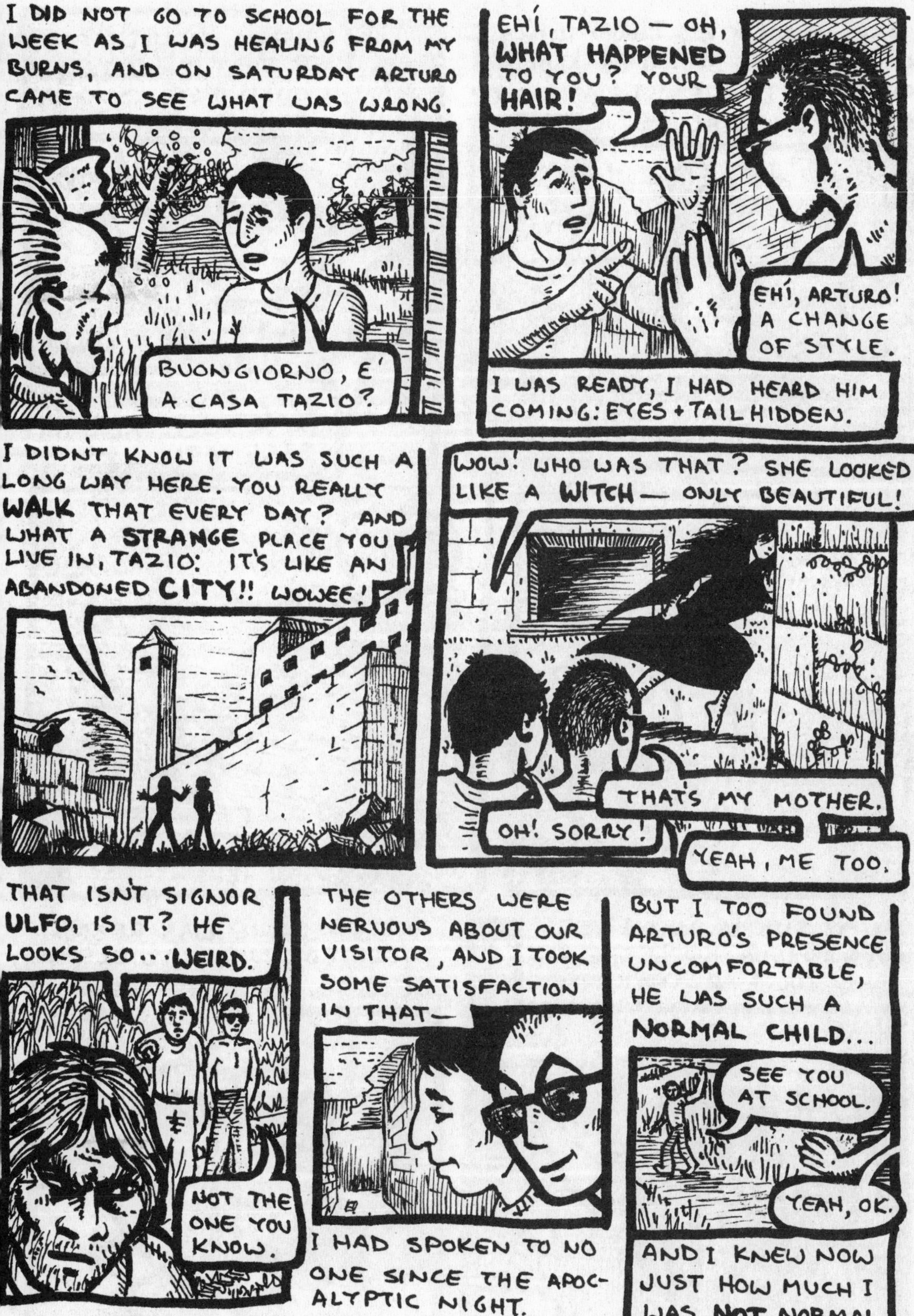
I DID NOT GO TO SCHOOL FOR THE WEEK AS I WAS HEALING FROM MY BURNS, AND ON SATURDAY ARTURO CAME TO SEE WHAT WAS WRONG.
BUONGIORNO, E' A CASA TAZIO?
EHÍ, TAZIO — OH, WHAT HAPPENED TO YOU? YOUR HAIR!
EHÍ, ARTURO! A CHANGE OF STYLE.
I WAS READY, I HAD HEARD HIM COMING: EYES + TAIL HIDDEN.
I DIDN'T KNOW IT WAS SUCH A LONG WAY HERE. YOU REALLY WALK THAT EVERY DAY? AND WHAT A STRANGE PLACE YOU LIVE IN, TAZIO: IT'S LIKE AN ABANDONED CITY!! WOWEE!
WOW! WHO WAS THAT? SHE LOOKED LIKE A WITCH — ONLY BEAUTIFUL!
THAT'S MY MOTHER.
OH! SORRY!
YEAH, ME TOO.
THAT ISN'T SIGNOR ULFO, IS IT? HE LOOKS SO... WEIRD.
NOT THE ONE YOU KNOW.
THE OTHERS WERE NERVOUS ABOUT OUR VISITOR, AND I TOOK SOME SATISFACTION IN THAT—
I HAD SPOKEN TO NO ONE SINCE THE APOCALYPTIC NIGHT.
BUT I TOO FOUND ARTURO'S PRESENCE UNCOMFORTABLE, HE WAS SUCH A NORMAL CHILD...
SEE YOU AT SCHOOL.
YEAH, OK.
AND I KNEW NOW JUST HOW MUCH I WAS NOT NORMAL.

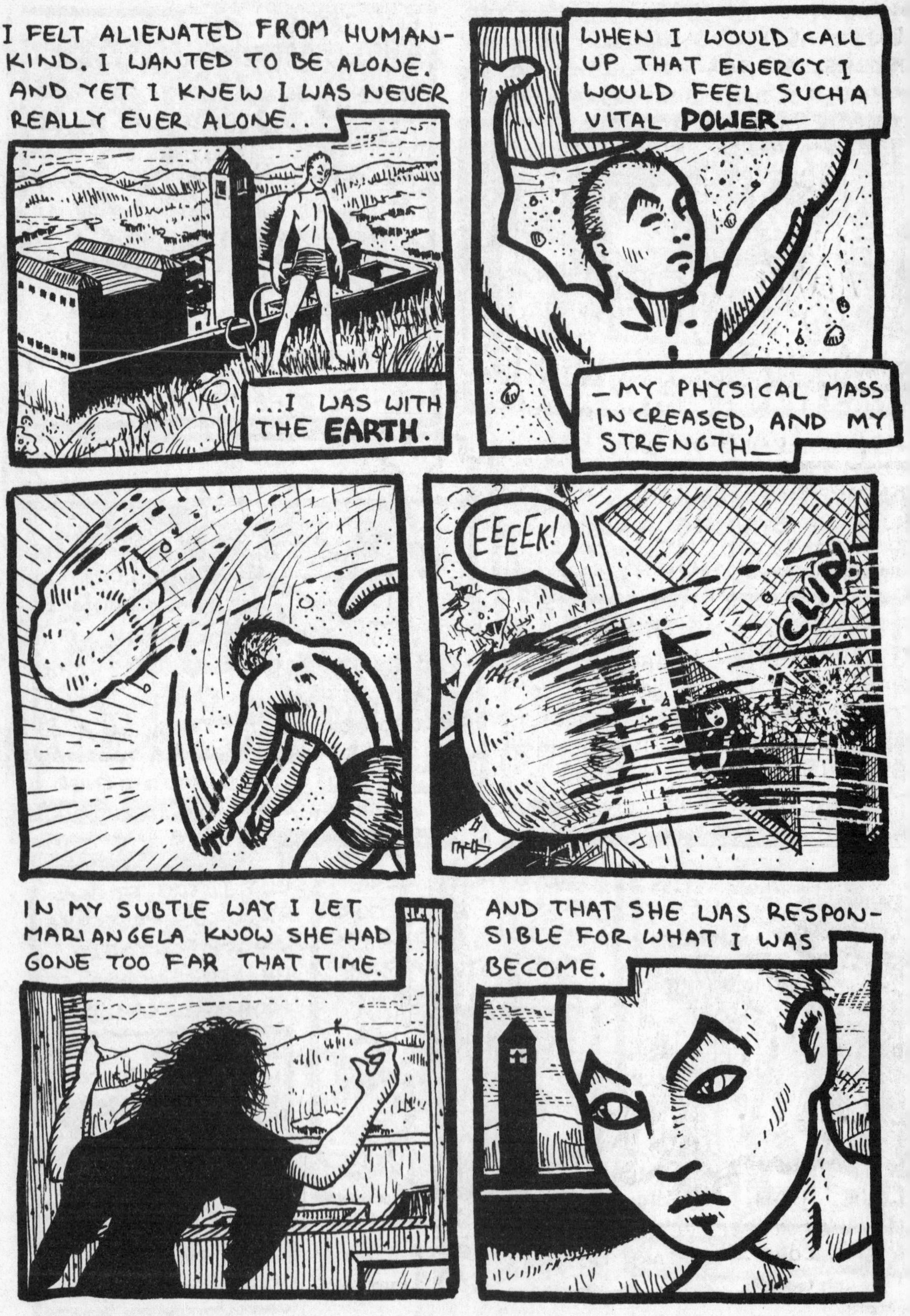
I FELT ALIENATED FROM HUMANKIND. I WANTED TO BE ALONE. AND YET I KNEW I WAS NEVER REALLY EVER ALONE...
...I WAS WITH THE **EARTH**.
WHEN I WOULD CALL UP THAT ENERGY I WOULD FEEL SUCH A VITAL **POWER**—
—MY PHYSICAL MASS INCREASED, AND MY STRENGTH—
EEEEK!
CLIP!
IN MY SUBTLE WAY I LET MARIANGELA KNOW SHE HAD GONE TOO FAR THAT TIME.
AND THAT SHE WAS RESPONSIBLE FOR WHAT I WAS BECOME.

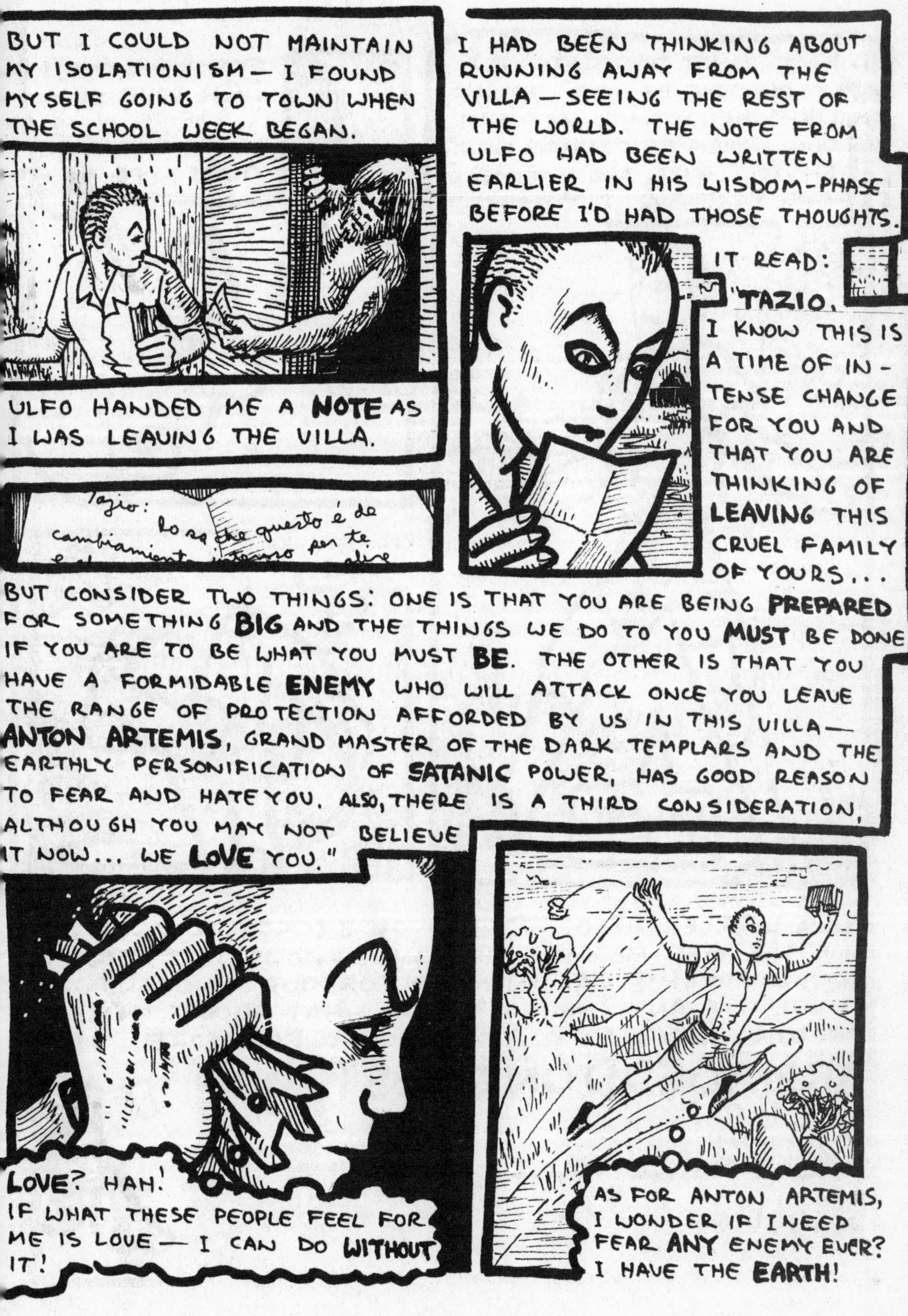
BUT I COULD NOT MAINTAIN MY ISOLATIONISM — I FOUND MYSELF GOING TO TOWN WHEN THE SCHOOL WEEK BEGAN.
ULFO HANDED ME A NOTE AS I WAS LEAVING THE VILLA.
Tazio:
lo so che questo è de
cambiamento intenso per te.
I HAD BEEN THINKING ABOUT RUNNING AWAY FROM THE VILLA — SEEING THE REST OF THE WORLD. THE NOTE FROM ULFO HAD BEEN WRITTEN EARLIER IN HIS WISDOM-PHASE BEFORE I'D HAD THOSE THOUGHTS.
IT READ:
"TAZIO,
I KNOW THIS IS A TIME OF INTENSE CHANGE FOR YOU AND THAT YOU ARE THINKING OF LEAVING THIS CRUEL FAMILY OF YOURS...
BUT CONSIDER TWO THINGS: ONE IS THAT YOU ARE BEING PREPARED FOR SOMETHING BIG AND THE THINGS WE DO TO YOU MUST BE DONE IF YOU ARE TO BE WHAT YOU MUST BE. THE OTHER IS THAT YOU HAVE A FORMIDABLE ENEMY WHO WILL ATTACK ONCE YOU LEAVE THE RANGE OF PROTECTION AFFORDED BY US IN THIS VILLA — ANTON ARTEMIS, GRAND MASTER OF THE DARK TEMPLARS AND THE EARTHLY PERSONIFICATION OF SATANIC POWER, HAS GOOD REASON TO FEAR AND HATE YOU. ALSO, THERE IS A THIRD CONSIDERATION, ALTHOUGH YOU MAY NOT BELIEVE IT NOW... WE LOVE YOU."
LOVE? HAH! IF WHAT THESE PEOPLE FEEL FOR ME IS LOVE — I CAN DO WITHOUT IT!
AS FOR ANTON ARTEMIS, I WONDER IF I NEED FEAR ANY ENEMY EVER? I HAVE THE EARTH!

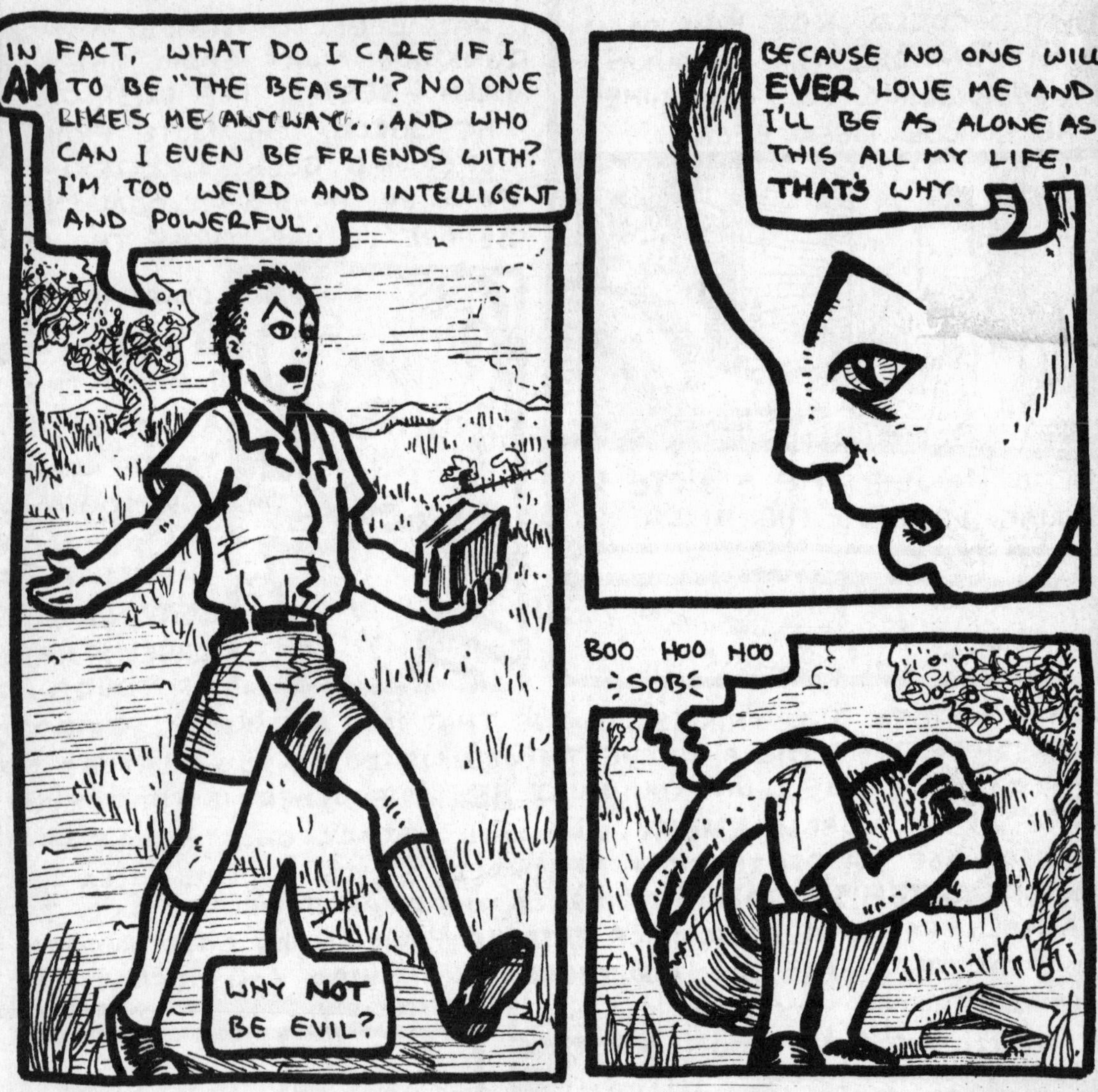
IN FACT, WHAT DO I CARE IF I AM TO BE "THE BEAST"? NO ONE LIKES ME ANYWAY...AND WHO CAN I EVEN BE FRIENDS WITH? I'M TOO WEIRD AND INTELLIGENT AND POWERFUL.
WHY NOT BE EVIL?
BECAUSE NO ONE WILL EVER LOVE ME AND I'LL BE AS ALONE AS THIS ALL MY LIFE, THAT'S WHY.
BOO HOO HOO
SOB

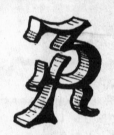

POOR LITTLE TAZIO! PICKED ON BY COSMIC DESTINY AND HIS MAD MOMMY. AND WHO KNOWS JUST WHAT OL' ANTON ARTEMIS HAS IN MIND FOR OUR INNOCENT YOUNG UNWILLING ANTICHRIST? AND WHAT ABOUT THIS GUY THERON, ANYWAY? STAY TUNED FOR MORE

**ARMAGEDDONQUEST.**

Ronald Russell Roach

June, 1984

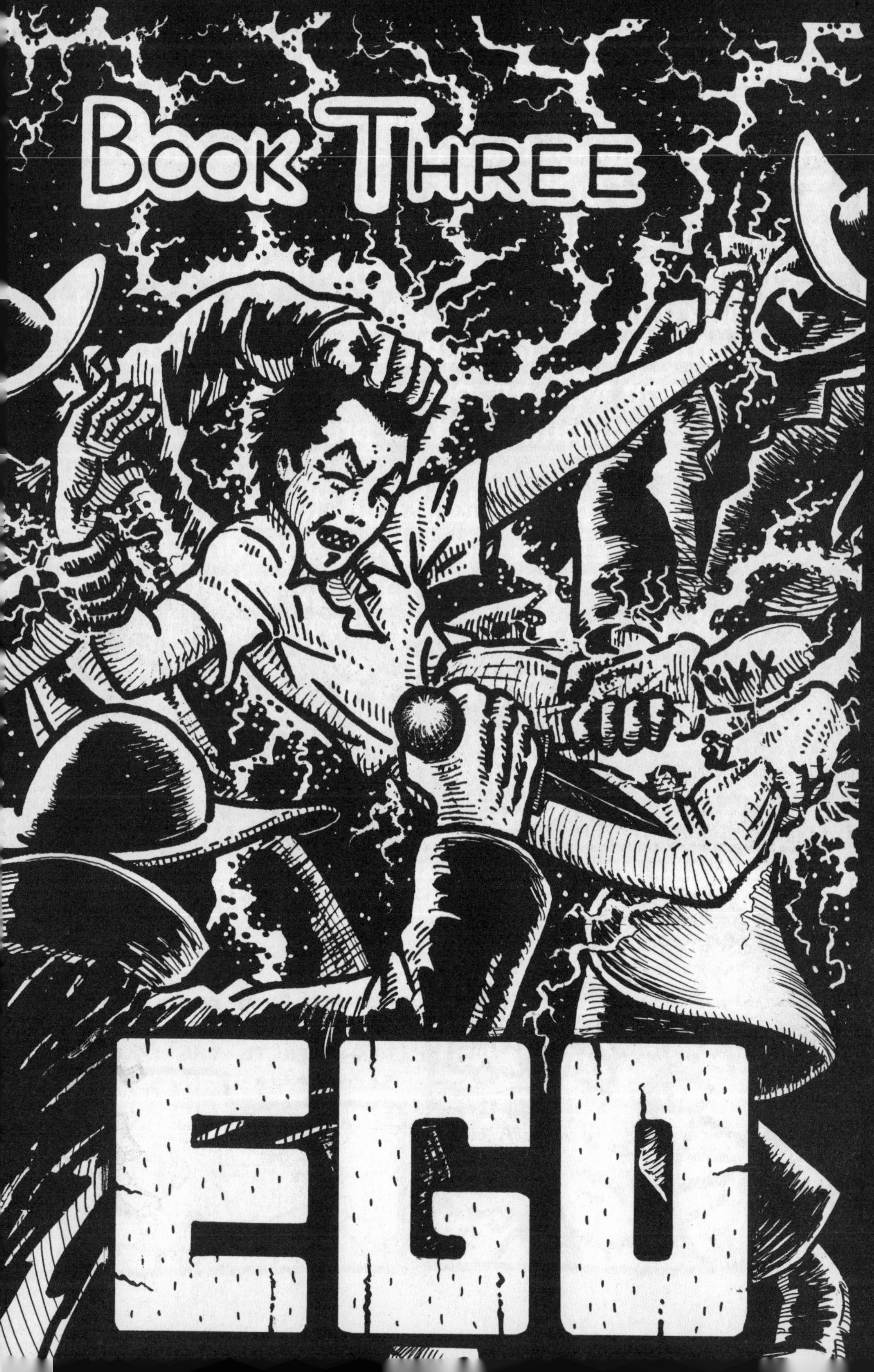
BOOK THREE
EGO

Little Tazio, at the age of 8, is in the process of evolving from beast-like to god-like. His mentor, the sometimes all-wise Ulfo, has revealed to him that Tazio is to become the dreaded Beast of the Apocalypse, the Antichrist prophesied in the Bible 2000 years ago, who would be instrumental in bringing about the end of this world. Mariangela, his mad mom, has attempted to kill him in a baptism of fire, which has only served to awaken within Tazio a vast connection with the power of the Earth itself, confirming Ulfo's prediction.

Tazio wants to deny this destiny, and fears that he is eternally doomed to the Lake of Fire, which ain't good, and feels absolutely alone in the world.

# book 3
# Ego

:SNIFF:

ENOUGH OF THAT. IT'S TIME TO GO TO SCHOOL.

LEARN.

AT LEAST I ENJOY THAT.

BUT THE 4th GRADE WOULD NOT DO FOR ME ANY MORE, I WAS TOO ADVANCED. I WENT TO THE OFFICE AND EXPLAINED MY WEEK'S ABSENCE — AND FOUND THAT ULFO HAD ALREADY ARRANGED MY TRANSFER TO THE SCUOLA SECONDARIA.

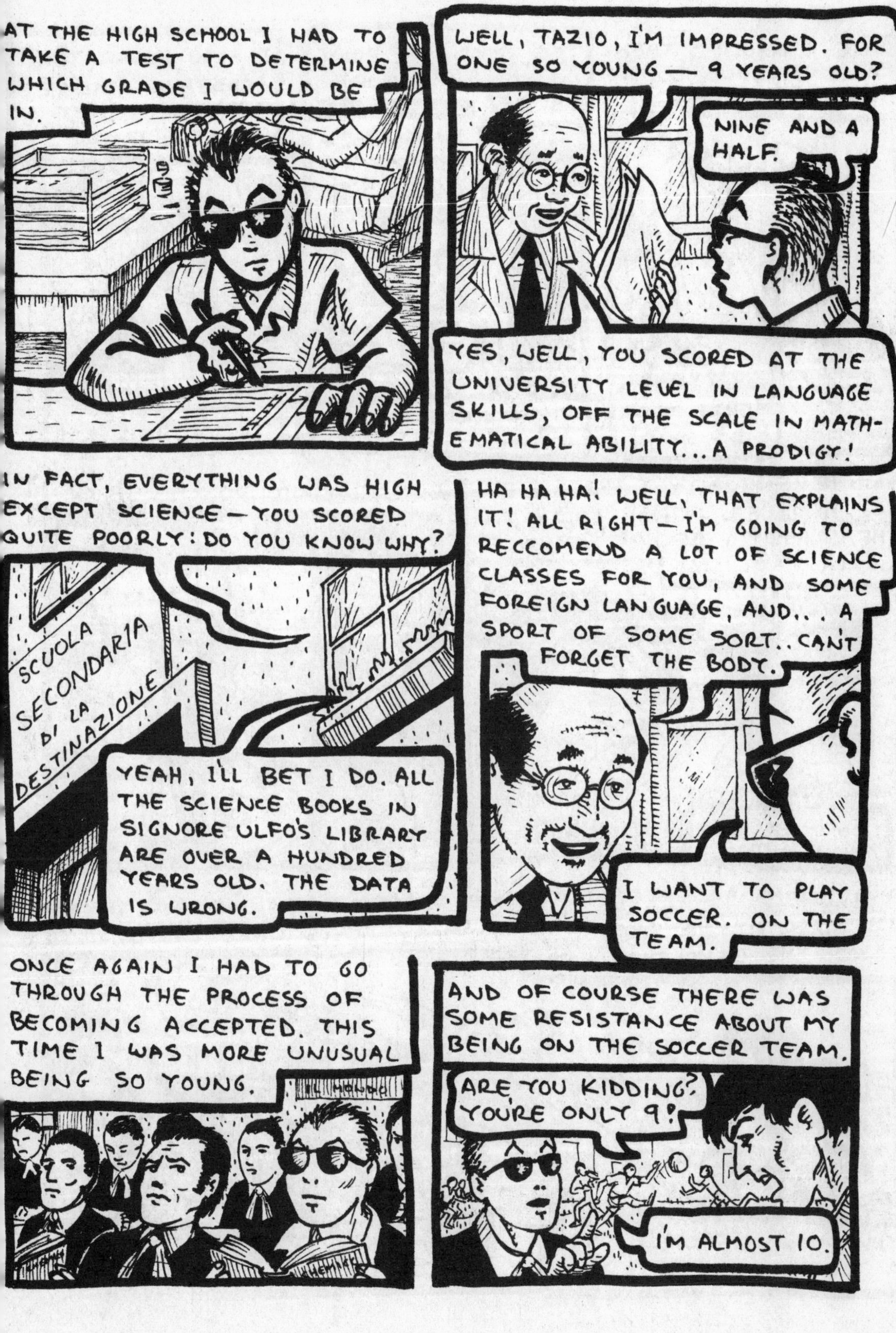

AT THE HIGH SCHOOL I HAD TO TAKE A TEST TO DETERMINE WHICH GRADE I WOULD BE IN.
WELL, TAZIO, I'M IMPRESSED. FOR ONE SO YOUNG — 9 YEARS OLD?
NINE AND A HALF.
YES, WELL, YOU SCORED AT THE UNIVERSITY LEVEL IN LANGUAGE SKILLS, OFF THE SCALE IN MATHEMATICAL ABILITY... A PRODIGY!
IN FACT, EVERYTHING WAS HIGH EXCEPT SCIENCE — YOU SCORED QUITE POORLY: DO YOU KNOW WHY?
SCUOLA SECONDARIA DI LA DESTINAZIONE
YEAH, I'LL BET I DO. ALL THE SCIENCE BOOKS IN SIGNORE ULFO'S LIBRARY ARE OVER A HUNDRED YEARS OLD. THE DATA IS WRONG.
HA HA HA! WELL, THAT EXPLAINS IT! ALL RIGHT — I'M GOING TO RECCOMEND A LOT OF SCIENCE CLASSES FOR YOU, AND SOME FOREIGN LANGUAGE, AND... A SPORT OF SOME SORT.. CAN'T FORGET THE BODY.
I WANT TO PLAY SOCCER. ON THE TEAM.
ONCE AGAIN I HAD TO GO THROUGH THE PROCESS OF BECOMING ACCEPTED. THIS TIME I WAS MORE UNUSUAL BEING SO YOUNG.
AND OF COURSE THERE WAS SOME RESISTANCE ABOUT MY BEING ON THE SOCCER TEAM.
ARE YOU KIDDING? YOU'RE ONLY 9!
I'M ALMOST 10.

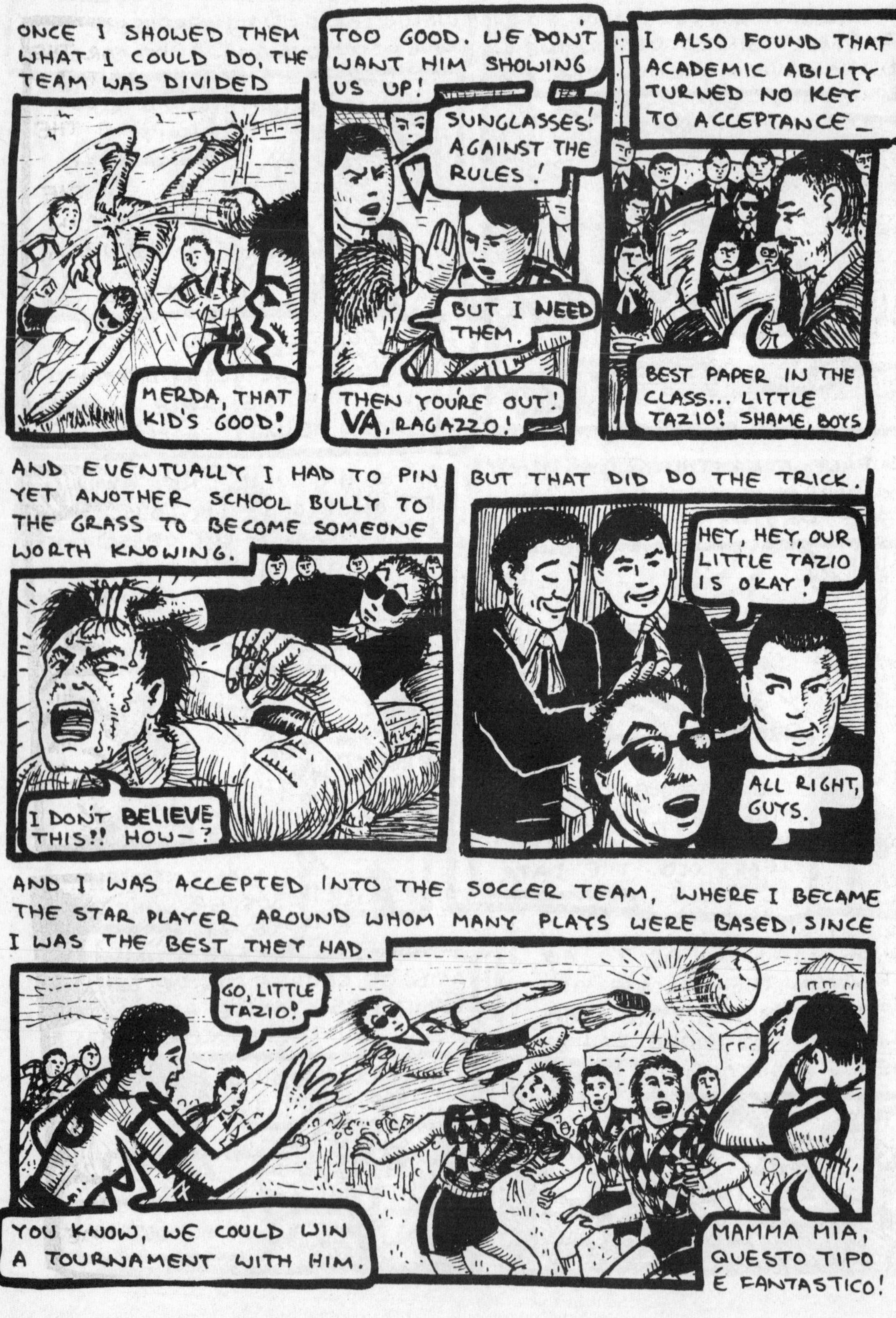
ONCE I SHOWED THEM WHAT I COULD DO, THE TEAM WAS DIVIDED
MERDA, THAT KID'S GOOD!
TOO GOOD. WE DON'T WANT HIM SHOWING US UP!
SUNGLASSES! AGAINST THE RULES!
BUT I NEED THEM.
THEN YOU'RE OUT! VA, RAGAZZO!
I ALSO FOUND THAT ACADEMIC ABILITY TURNED NO KEY TO ACCEPTANCE_
BEST PAPER IN THE CLASS... LITTLE TAZIO! SHAME, BOYS
AND EVENTUALLY I HAD TO PIN YET ANOTHER SCHOOL BULLY TO THE GRASS TO BECOME SOMEONE WORTH KNOWING.
I DON'T BELIEVE THIS?! HOW-?
BUT THAT DID DO THE TRICK.
HEY, HEY, OUR LITTLE TAZIO IS OKAY!
ALL RIGHT, GUYS.
AND I WAS ACCEPTED INTO THE SOCCER TEAM, WHERE I BECAME THE STAR PLAYER AROUND WHOM MANY PLAYS WERE BASED, SINCE I WAS THE BEST THEY HAD.
GO, LITTLE TAZIO!
YOU KNOW, WE COULD WIN A TOURNAMENT WITH HIM.
MAMMA MIA, QUESTO TIPO É FANTASTICO!

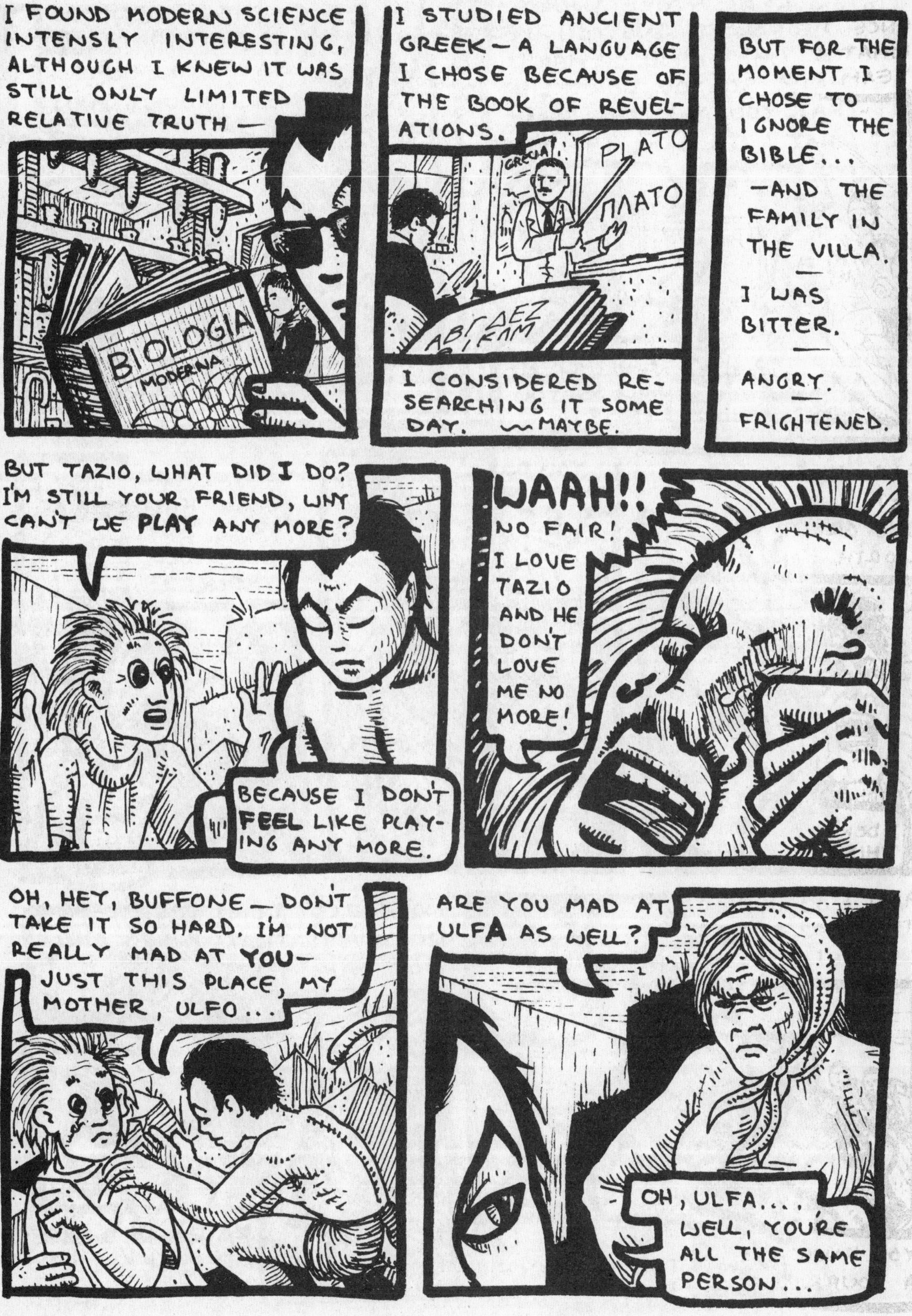
I FOUND MODERN SCIENCE INTENSLY INTERESTING, ALTHOUGH I KNEW IT WAS STILL ONLY LIMITED RELATIVE TRUTH —
BIOLOGIA MODERNA
I STUDIED ANCIENT GREEK — A LANGUAGE I CHOSE BECAUSE OF THE BOOK OF REVELATIONS.
GRECIA
PLATO
ΠΛΑΤΟ
ΑΒΓΔΕΖ
ΚΛΜ
I CONSIDERED RESEARCHING IT SOME DAY. ~MAYBE.
BUT FOR THE MOMENT I CHOSE TO IGNORE THE BIBLE...
—AND THE FAMILY IN THE VILLA.
I WAS BITTER.
ANGRY.
FRIGHTENED.
BUT TAZIO, WHAT DID I DO? I'M STILL YOUR FRIEND, WHY CAN'T WE PLAY ANY MORE?
BECAUSE I DON'T FEEL LIKE PLAYING ANY MORE.
WAAH!!
NO FAIR! I LOVE TAZIO AND HE DON'T LOVE ME NO MORE!
OH, HEY, BUFFONE — DON'T TAKE IT SO HARD. I'M NOT REALLY MAD AT YOU— JUST THIS PLACE, MY MOTHER, ULFO...
ARE YOU MAD AT ULFA AS WELL?
OH, ULFA.... WELL, YOU'RE ALL THE SAME PERSON...

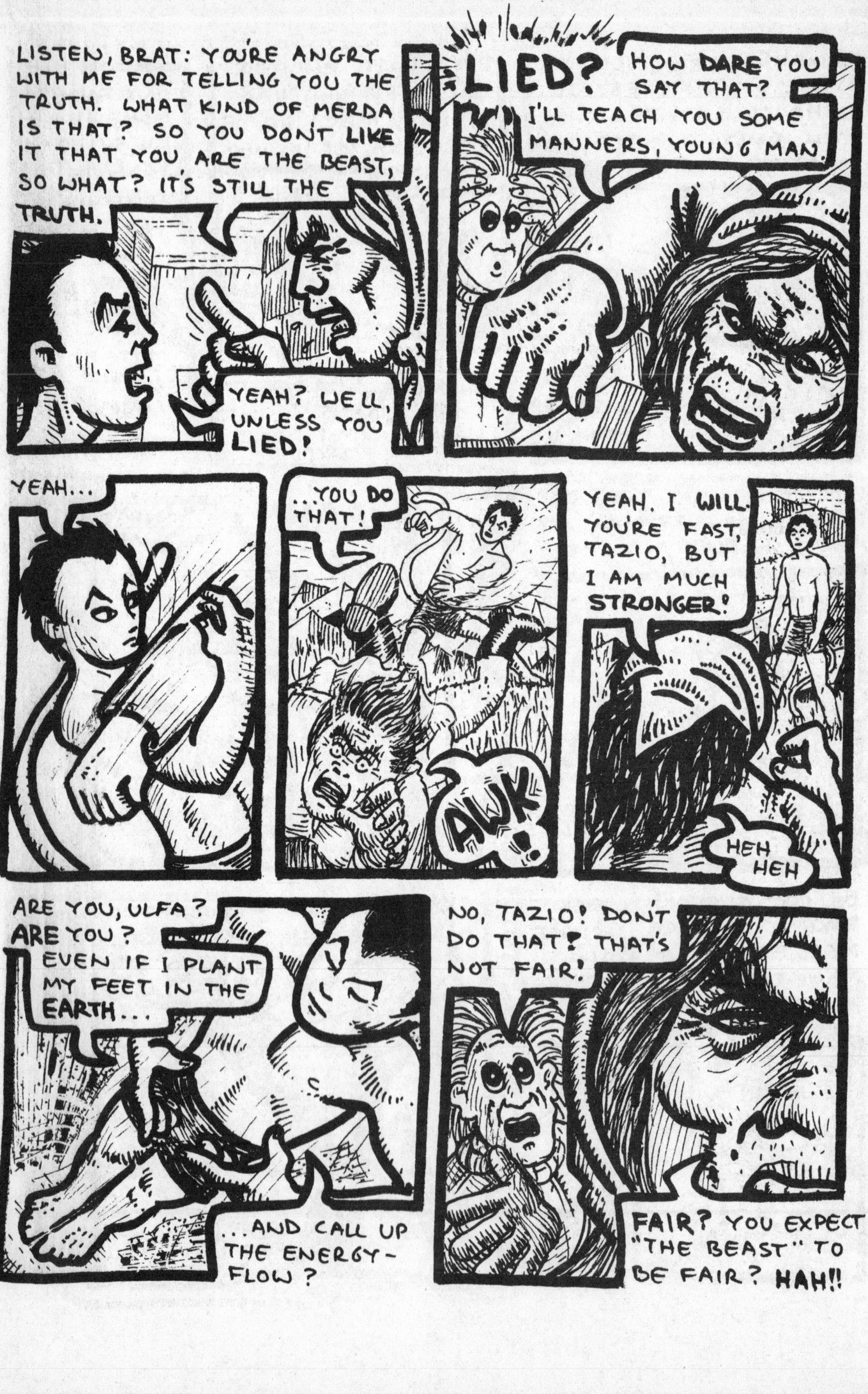
LISTEN, BRAT: YOU'RE ANGRY WITH ME FOR TELLING YOU THE TRUTH. WHAT KIND OF MERDA IS THAT? SO YOU DON'T LIKE IT THAT YOU ARE THE BEAST, SO WHAT? IT'S STILL THE TRUTH.
YEAH? WELL, UNLESS YOU LIED!
LIED?
HOW DARE YOU SAY THAT? I'LL TEACH YOU SOME MANNERS, YOUNG MAN.
YEAH...
...YOU DO THAT!
AWK!
YEAH. I WILL. YOU'RE FAST, TAZIO, BUT I AM MUCH STRONGER!
HEH HEH
ARE YOU, ULFA? ARE YOU?
EVEN IF I PLANT MY FEET IN THE EARTH...
...AND CALL UP THE ENERGY-FLOW?
NO, TAZIO! DON'T DO THAT! THAT'S NOT FAIR!
FAIR? YOU EXPECT "THE BEAST" TO BE FAIR? HAH!!

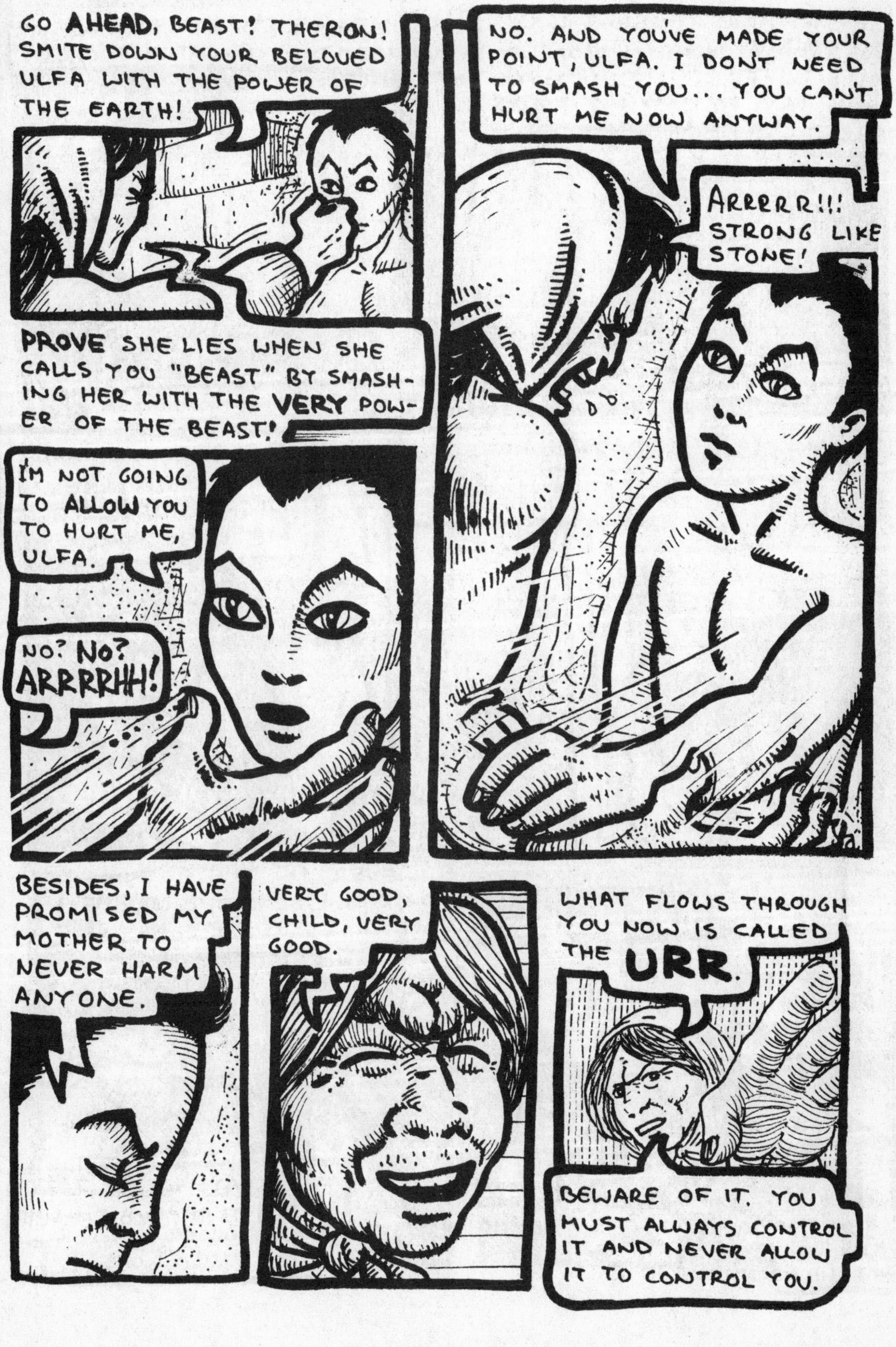
GO AHEAD, BEAST! THERON! SMITE DOWN YOUR BELOVED ULFA WITH THE POWER OF THE EARTH!
PROVE SHE LIES WHEN SHE CALLS YOU "BEAST" BY SMASHING HER WITH THE VERY POWER OF THE BEAST!
I'M NOT GOING TO ALLOW YOU TO HURT ME, ULFA.
NO? NO? ARRRRHH!
NO. AND YOU'VE MADE YOUR POINT, ULFA. I DON'T NEED TO SMASH YOU... YOU CAN'T HURT ME NOW ANYWAY.
ARRRRR!!! STRONG LIKE STONE!
BESIDES, I HAVE PROMISED MY MOTHER TO NEVER HARM ANYONE.
VERY GOOD, CHILD, VERY GOOD.
WHAT FLOWS THROUGH YOU NOW IS CALLED THE URR.
BEWARE OF IT. YOU MUST ALWAYS CONTROL IT AND NEVER ALLOW IT TO CONTROL YOU.

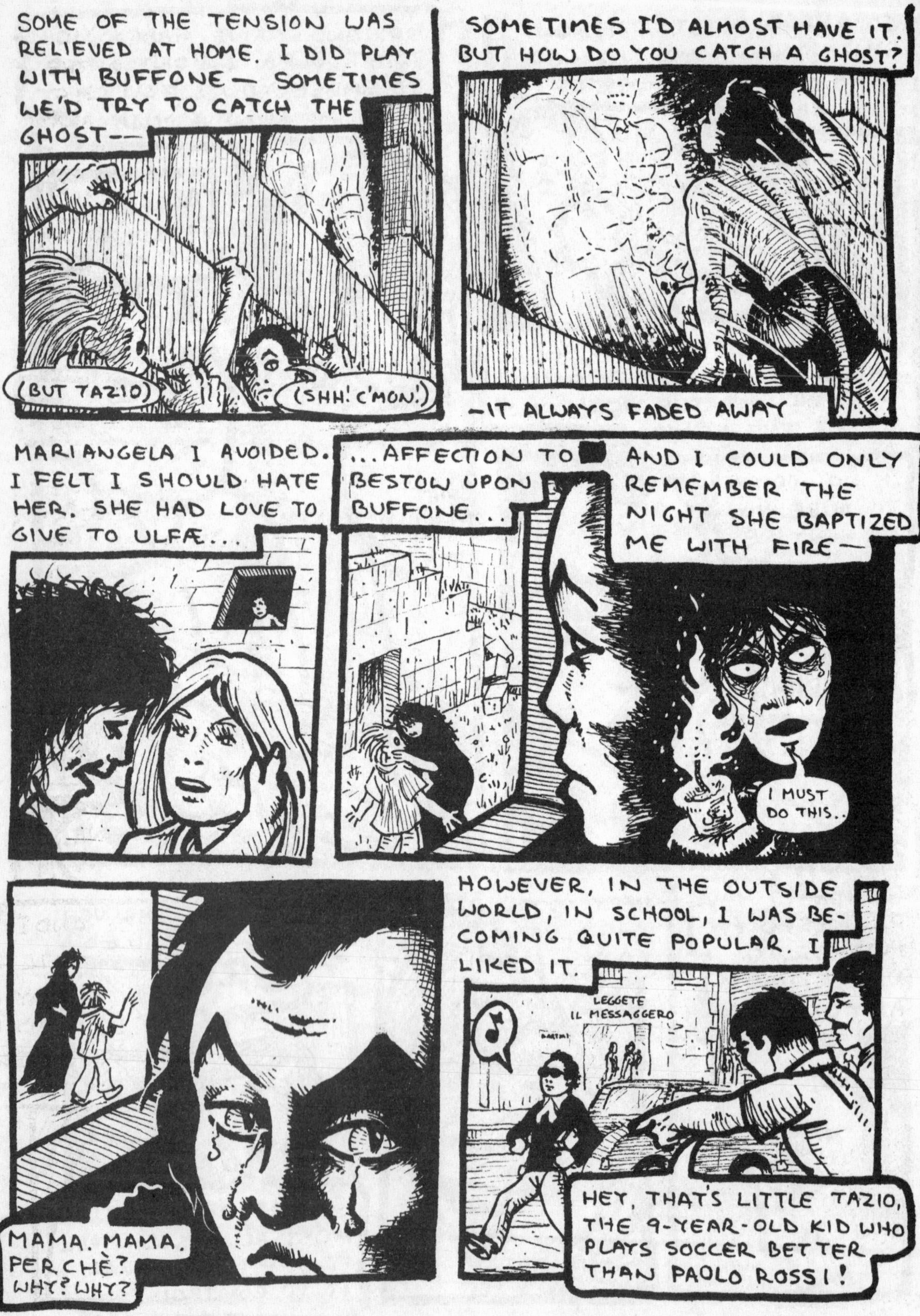
SOME OF THE TENSION WAS RELIEVED AT HOME. I DID PLAY WITH BUFFONE— SOMETIMES WE'D TRY TO CATCH THE GHOST--
(BUT TAZIO)
(SHH! C'MON!)
SOMETIMES I'D ALMOST HAVE IT. BUT HOW DO YOU CATCH A GHOST?
—IT ALWAYS FADED AWAY
MARIANGELA I AVOIDED. I FELT I SHOULD HATE HER. SHE HAD LOVE TO GIVE TO ULFÆ...
...AFFECTION TO BESTOW UPON BUFFONE...
AND I COULD ONLY REMEMBER THE NIGHT SHE BAPTIZED ME WITH FIRE—
I MUST DO THIS..
MAMA. MAMA. PERCHÈ? WHY? WHY?
HOWEVER, IN THE OUTSIDE WORLD, IN SCHOOL, I WAS BECOMING QUITE POPULAR. I LIKED IT.
LEGGETE IL MESSAGGERO
HEY, THAT'S LITTLE TAZIO, THE 9-YEAR-OLD KID WHO PLAYS SOCCER BETTER THAN PAOLO ROSSI!

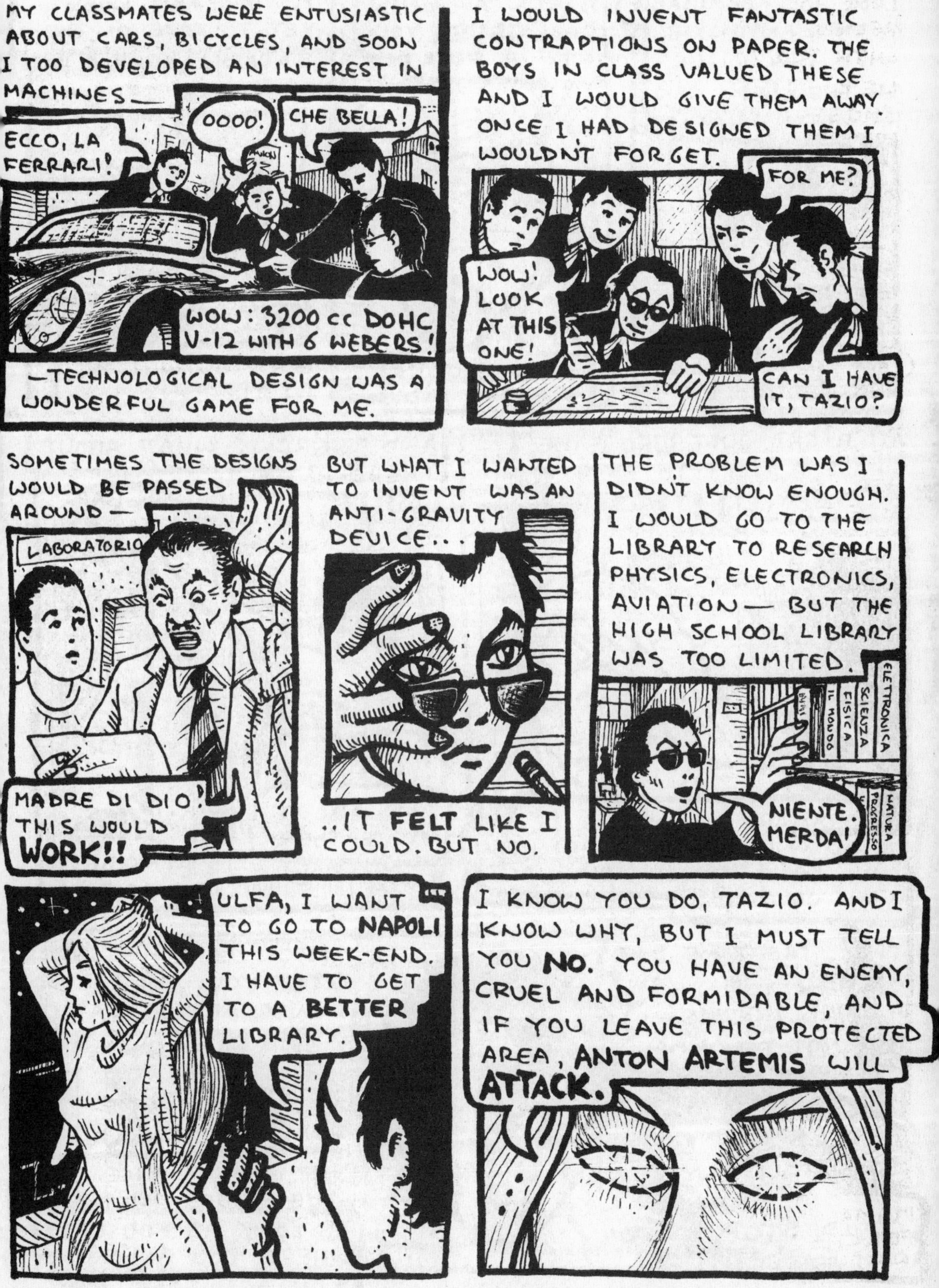
MY CLASSMATES WERE ENTUSIASTIC ABOUT CARS, BICYCLES, AND SOON I TOO DEVELOPED AN INTEREST IN MACHINES—
ECCO, LA FERRARI!
OOOO!
CHE BELLA!
WOW: 3200 cc DOHC V-12 WITH 6 WEBERS!
—TECHNOLOGICAL DESIGN WAS A WONDERFUL GAME FOR ME.
I WOULD INVENT FANTASTIC CONTRAPTIONS ON PAPER. THE BOYS IN CLASS VALUED THESE AND I WOULD GIVE THEM AWAY. ONCE I HAD DESIGNED THEM I WOULDN'T FORGET.
FOR ME?
WOW! LOOK AT THIS ONE!
CAN I HAVE IT, TAZIO?
SOMETIMES THE DESIGNS WOULD BE PASSED AROUND—
LABORATORIO
MADRE DI DIO! THIS WOULD WORK!!
BUT WHAT I WANTED TO INVENT WAS AN ANTI-GRAVITY DEVICE..
..IT FELT LIKE I COULD. BUT NO.
THE PROBLEM WAS I DIDN'T KNOW ENOUGH. I WOULD GO TO THE LIBRARY TO RESEARCH PHYSICS, ELECTRONICS, AVIATION— BUT THE HIGH SCHOOL LIBRARY WAS TOO LIMITED.
ELETTRONICA
SCIENZA
FISICA
IL MONDO
NATURA
PROGRESSO
NIENTE. MERDA!
ULFA, I WANT TO GO TO NAPOLI THIS WEEK-END. I HAVE TO GET TO A BETTER LIBRARY.
I KNOW YOU DO, TAZIO. AND I KNOW WHY, BUT I MUST TELL YOU NO. YOU HAVE AN ENEMY, CRUEL AND FORMIDABLE, AND IF YOU LEAVE THIS PROTECTED AREA, ANTON ARTEMIS WILL ATTACK.

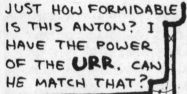

JUST HOW FORMIDABLE IS THIS ANTON? I HAVE THE POWER OF THE **URR**. CAN HE MATCH THAT?

ANTON ARTEMIS CAN **CRUSH** YOU LIKE A FLEA.

YOU ARE ONLY 9 YEARS OLD.

YOU ARE **NOT** READY YET TO TAKE ON THE SATANIC AVATAR AND HIS DARK TEMPLARS.

BUT YOU WILL BE, IN TIME. YES.

ALL RIGHT, JUST **WHO** IS HE? I HAVE A RIGHT TO KNOW MY ENEMY.

NO. YOU ARE TOO YOUNG. IT WOULD ONLY SERVE TO FRIGHTEN YOU. **SOON** ENOUGH YOU SHALL KNOW OF ANTON.

AND THERON? WHAT ABOUT THERON?

YES.

AND ABOUT MY FATHER?

NO.

THEY TREAT ME LIKE A **CHILD** — WELL, I AM A CHILD, I GUESS — BUT NOT A NORMAL ONE.

I COULD JUST **GO** TO NAPOLI ANY-WAY. NO ONE COULD **STOP** ME

ANTON ARTEMIS WOULD **STOP** YOU. YOU WOULD NEVER ARRIVE, TAZIO.

AS LONG AS YOU STAY WHERE YOU **BELONG** YOU ARE SAFE.

BICYCLE RACING IS POPULAR IN ITALY—

I WANTED A BIKE.

MONEY HAD NEVER BEEN A PROBLEM: I HAD AN ALLOWANCE I COULD DRAFT FROM "UNCLE" ULFO'S BANK ACCOUNT, WHICH KEPT ME IN SCHOOL SUPPLIES AND ICE CREAM, BUT I HAD THOUGHT WE WERE POOR UNTIL I MENTIONED IT AT THE BANK—

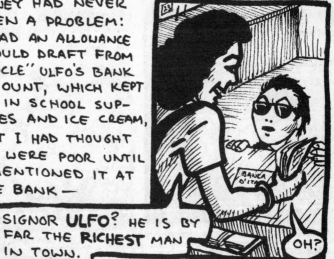

SIGNOR **ULFO**? HE IS BY FAR THE **RICHEST** MAN IN TOWN.

OH?

YES, TAZIO, I HAVE RESTRICTED YOUR MONEY, DELIBERATELY— AS FOR MYSELF I PREFER TO LIVE SIMPLY AND I WISHED YOU TO DO THE SAME. BUT YES, YOU MAY BUY A RACING BIKE, BUT WITH THE LIMITATION THAT YOU DO **NOT** RIDE **BEYOND** THE AREA OF LA DESTINAZIONE. AGREED?

AGREED!

SO I GOT THE BICYCLE AND COMPETED IN THE LOCAL RACES—

WHICH I WON. EVERY TIME.

AND IT'S THAT BOY WONDER AGAIN, TAZIO DELLATERRA!

WHICH BROUGHT ATTENTION FROM THE BICYCLE INDUSTRY

TAZIO, YOUR RECORD IS... WELL, YOU **NEVER** LOSE. AND YOU'RE SO YOUNG— WE FEEL YOU HAVE A GREAT POTENTIAL AND WANT YOU TO RACE FOR US IN NATIONAL COMPETITION.

WELL, MY— UH —UNCLE WON'T LET ME **LEAVE** THE LOCAL AREA.

COULD WE SPEAK WITH YOUR UNCLE? PERHAPS IF WE MENTION MONEY...

NO.

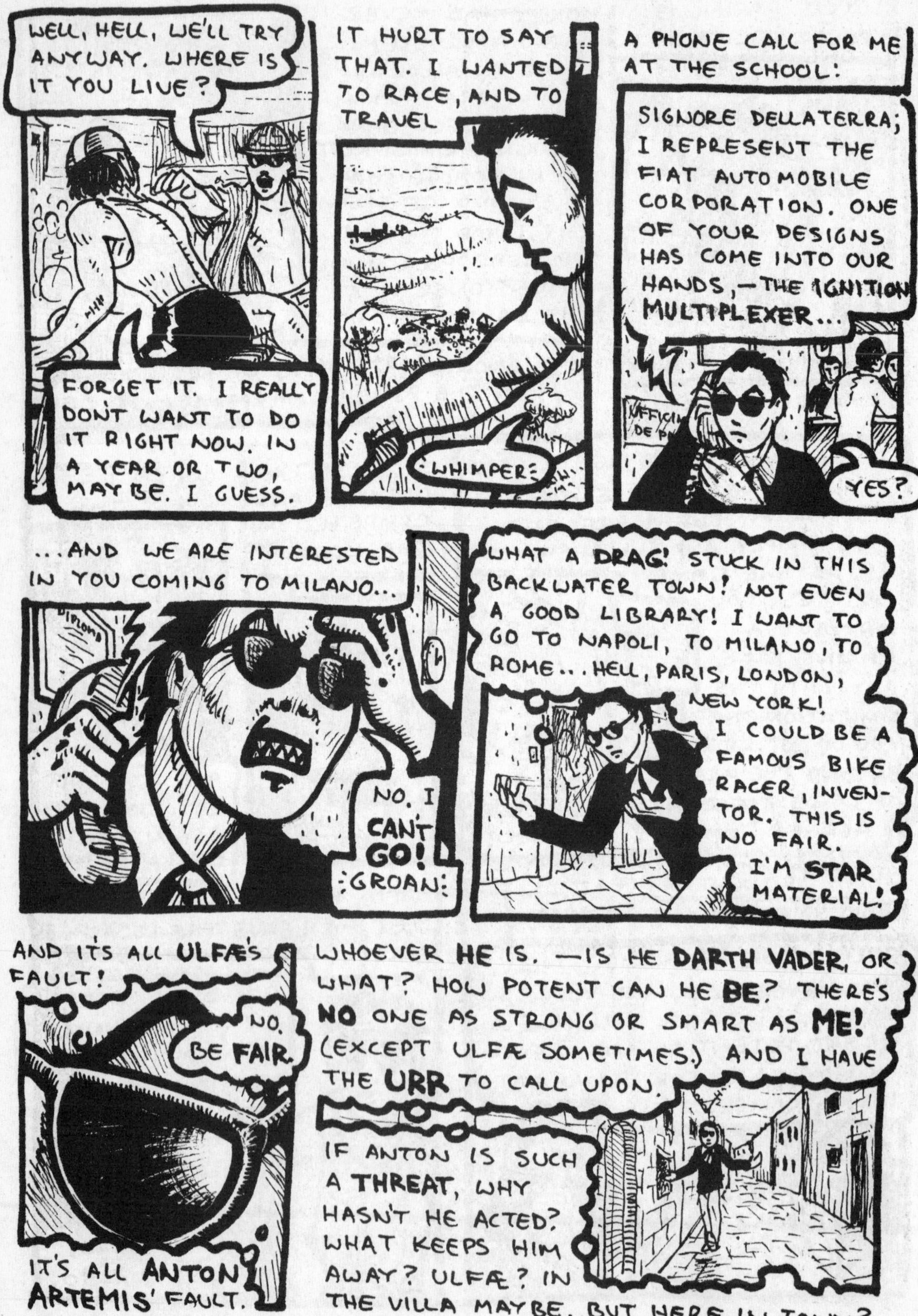
WELL, HELL, WE'LL TRY ANYWAY. WHERE IS IT YOU LIVE?
FORGET IT. I REALLY DON'T WANT TO DO IT RIGHT NOW. IN A YEAR OR TWO, MAYBE. I GUESS.
IT HURT TO SAY THAT. I WANTED TO RACE, AND TO TRAVEL
:WHIMPER:
A PHONE CALL FOR ME AT THE SCHOOL:
SIGNORE DELLATERRA; I REPRESENT THE FIAT AUTOMOBILE CORPORATION. ONE OF YOUR DESIGNS HAS COME INTO OUR HANDS,—THE IGNITION MULTIPLEXER...
YES?
...AND WE ARE INTERESTED IN YOU COMING TO MILANO...
NO. I CAN'T GO! :GROAN:
WHAT A DRAG! STUCK IN THIS BACKWATER TOWN! NOT EVEN A GOOD LIBRARY! I WANT TO GO TO NAPOLI, TO MILANO, TO ROME... HELL, PARIS, LONDON, NEW YORK!
I COULD BE A FAMOUS BIKE RACER, INVENTOR. THIS IS NO FAIR. I'M STAR MATERIAL!
AND IT'S ALL ULFÆ'S FAULT!
NO. BE FAIR.
IT'S ALL ANTON ARTEMIS' FAULT.
WHOEVER HE IS. —IS HE DARTH VADER, OR WHAT? HOW POTENT CAN HE BE? THERE'S NO ONE AS STRONG OR SMART AS ME! (EXCEPT ULFÆ SOMETIMES.) AND I HAVE THE URR TO CALL UPON.
IF ANTON IS SUCH A THREAT, WHY HASN'T HE ACTED? WHAT KEEPS HIM AWAY? ULFÆ? IN THE VILLA MAYBE, BUT HERE IN TOWN?

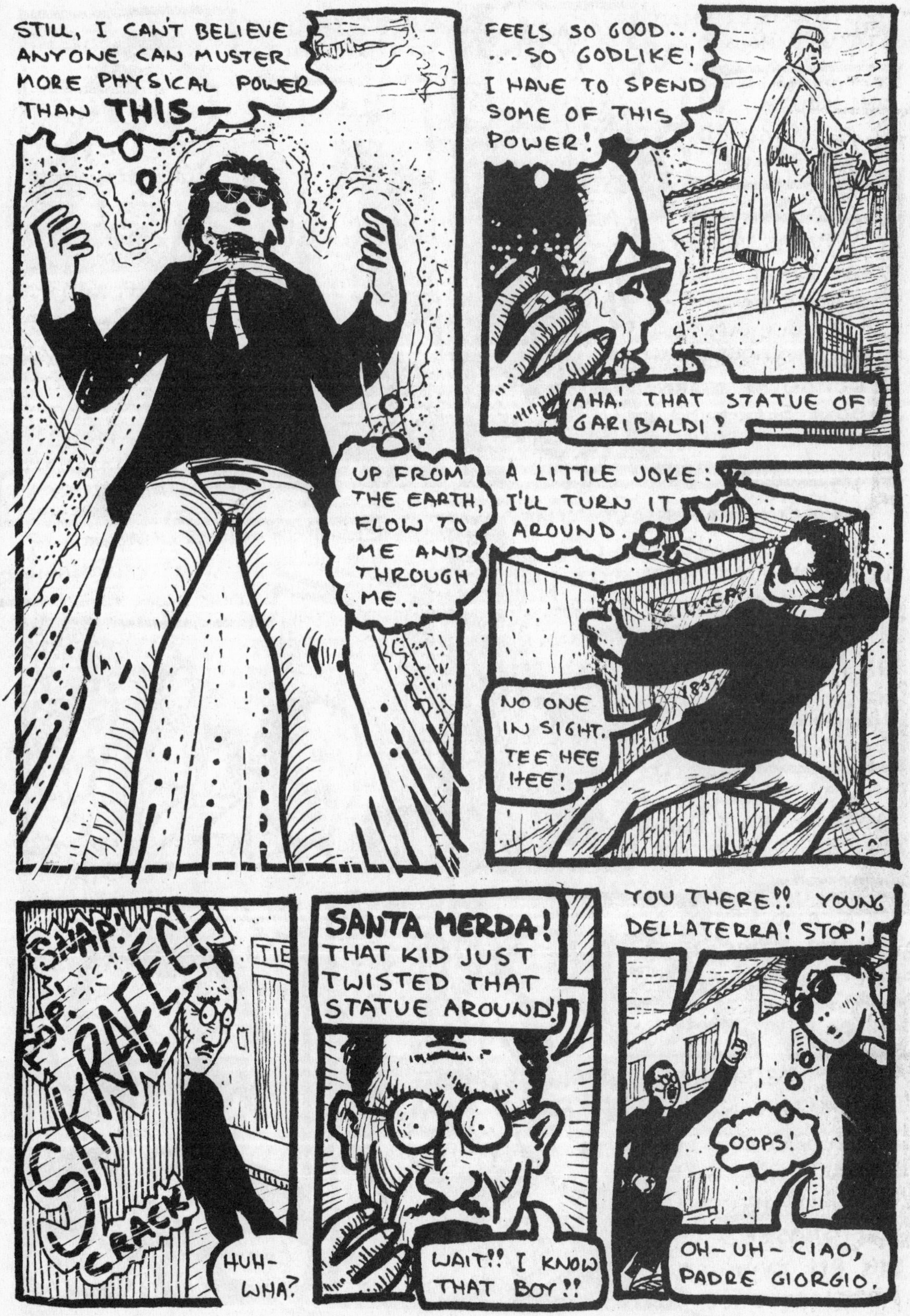
STILL, I CAN'T BELIEVE ANYONE CAN MUSTER MORE PHYSICAL POWER THAN **THIS**—
UP FROM THE EARTH, FLOW TO ME AND THROUGH ME...
FEELS SO GOOD.. ...SO GODLIKE! I HAVE TO SPEND SOME OF THIS POWER!
AHA! THAT STATUE OF GARIBALDI!
A LITTLE JOKE: I'LL TURN IT AROUND.
NO ONE IN SIGHT. TEE HEE HEE!
SNAP! POP! SKRAEECH! CRACK
TIE
HUH-WHA?
**SANTA MERDA!** THAT KID JUST TWISTED THAT STATUE AROUND!
WAIT!! I KNOW THAT BOY!!
YOU THERE!! YOUNG DELLATERRA! STOP!
OOPS!
OH-UH-CIAO, PADRE GIORGIO.

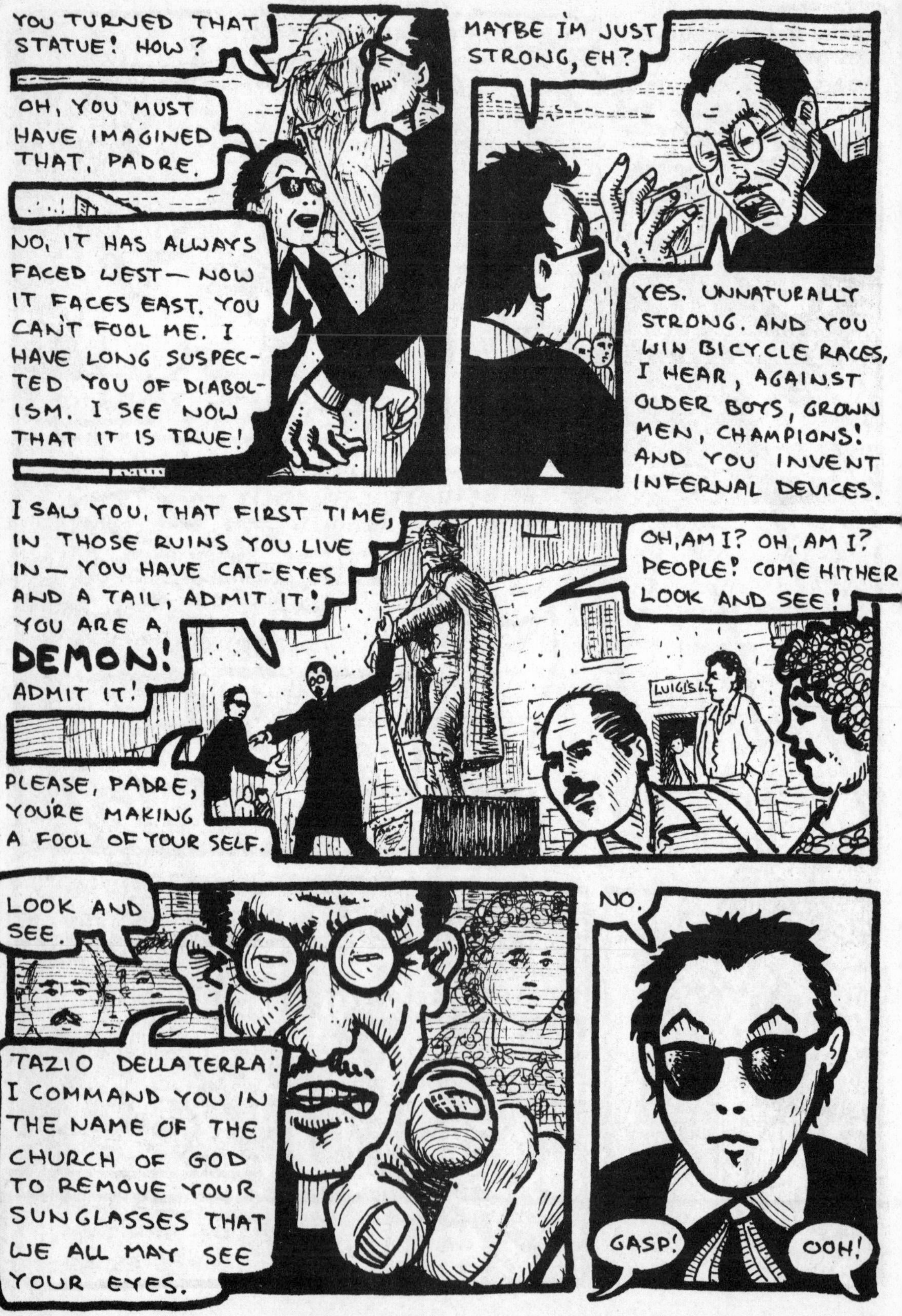
YOU TURNED THAT STATUE! HOW?
OH, YOU MUST HAVE IMAGINED THAT, PADRE.
NO, IT HAS ALWAYS FACED WEST— NOW IT FACES EAST. YOU CAN'T FOOL ME. I HAVE LONG SUSPECTED YOU OF DIABOLISM. I SEE NOW THAT IT IS TRUE!
MAYBE I'M JUST STRONG, EH?
YES. UNNATURALLY STRONG. AND YOU WIN BICYCLE RACES, I HEAR, AGAINST OLDER BOYS, GROWN MEN, CHAMPIONS! AND YOU INVENT INFERNAL DEVICES.
I SAW YOU, THAT FIRST TIME, IN THOSE RUINS YOU LIVE IN— YOU HAVE CAT-EYES AND A TAIL, ADMIT IT! YOU ARE A DEMON! ADMIT IT!
OH, AM I? OH, AM I? PEOPLE! COME HITHER LOOK AND SEE!
LUIGI'S
PLEASE, PADRE, YOU'RE MAKING A FOOL OF YOUR SELF.
LOOK AND SEE.
TAZIO DELLATERRA! I COMMAND YOU IN THE NAME OF THE CHURCH OF GOD TO REMOVE YOUR SUNGLASSES THAT WE ALL MAY SEE YOUR EYES.
NO.
GASP!
OOH!

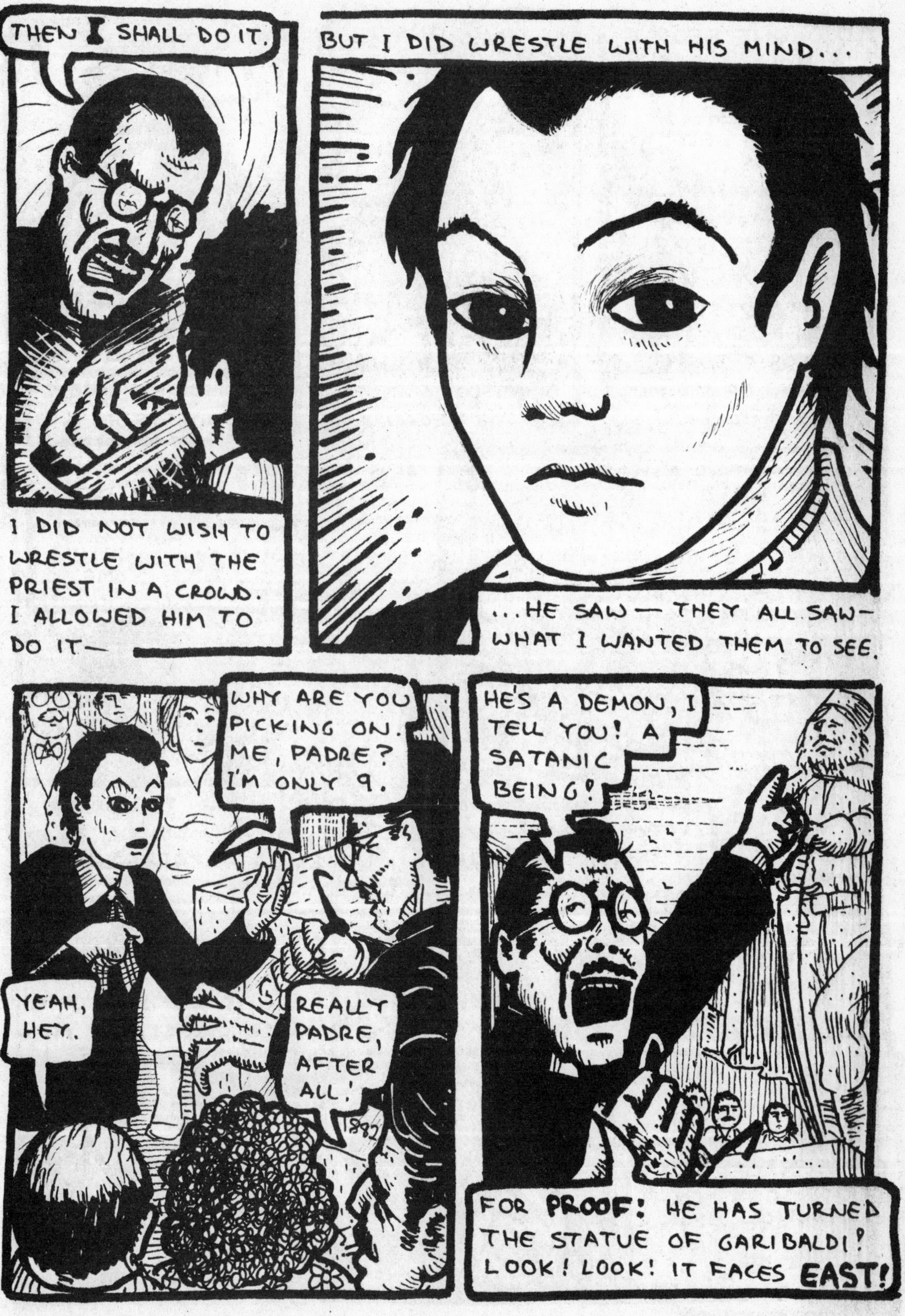
THEN I SHALL DO IT.
I DID NOT WISH TO WRESTLE WITH THE PRIEST IN A CROWD. I ALLOWED HIM TO DO IT—
BUT I DID WRESTLE WITH HIS MIND...
...HE SAW — THEY ALL SAW — WHAT I WANTED THEM TO SEE.
WHY ARE YOU PICKING ON ME, PADRE? I'M ONLY 9.
YEAH, HEY.
REALLY PADRE, AFTER ALL!
HE'S A DEMON, I TELL YOU! A SATANIC BEING!
FOR PROOF: HE HAS TURNED THE STATUE OF GARIBALDI! LOOK! LOOK! IT FACES EAST!

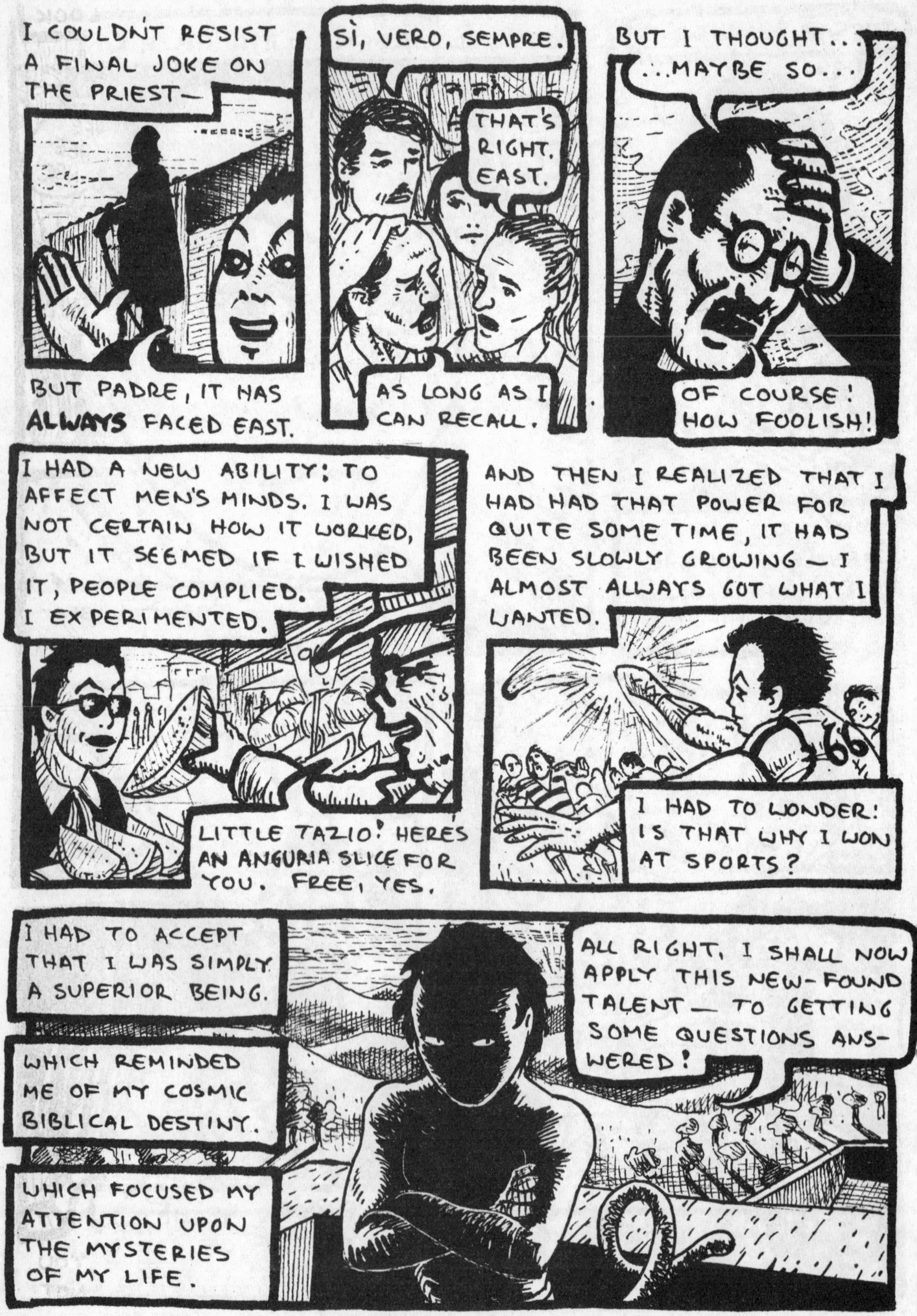

I COULDN'T RESIST A FINAL JOKE ON THE PRIEST—
BUT PADRE, IT HAS ALWAYS FACED EAST.
SÌ, VERO, SEMPRE.
THAT'S RIGHT. EAST.
AS LONG AS I CAN RECALL.
BUT I THOUGHT... ...MAYBE SO...
OF COURSE! HOW FOOLISH!
I HAD A NEW ABILITY: TO AFFECT MEN'S MINDS. I WAS NOT CERTAIN HOW IT WORKED, BUT IT SEEMED IF I WISHED IT, PEOPLE COMPLIED. I EXPERIMENTED.
LITTLE TAZIO! HERE'S AN ANGURIA SLICE FOR YOU. FREE, YES.
AND THEN I REALIZED THAT I HAD HAD THAT POWER FOR QUITE SOME TIME, IT HAD BEEN SLOWLY GROWING — I ALMOST ALWAYS GOT WHAT I WANTED.
66
I HAD TO WONDER: IS THAT WHY I WON AT SPORTS?
I HAD TO ACCEPT THAT I WAS SIMPLY A SUPERIOR BEING.
WHICH REMINDED ME OF MY COSMIC BIBLICAL DESTINY.
WHICH FOCUSED MY ATTENTION UPON THE MYSTERIES OF MY LIFE.
ALL RIGHT, I SHALL NOW APPLY THIS NEW-FOUND TALENT — TO GETTING SOME QUESTIONS ANSWERED!

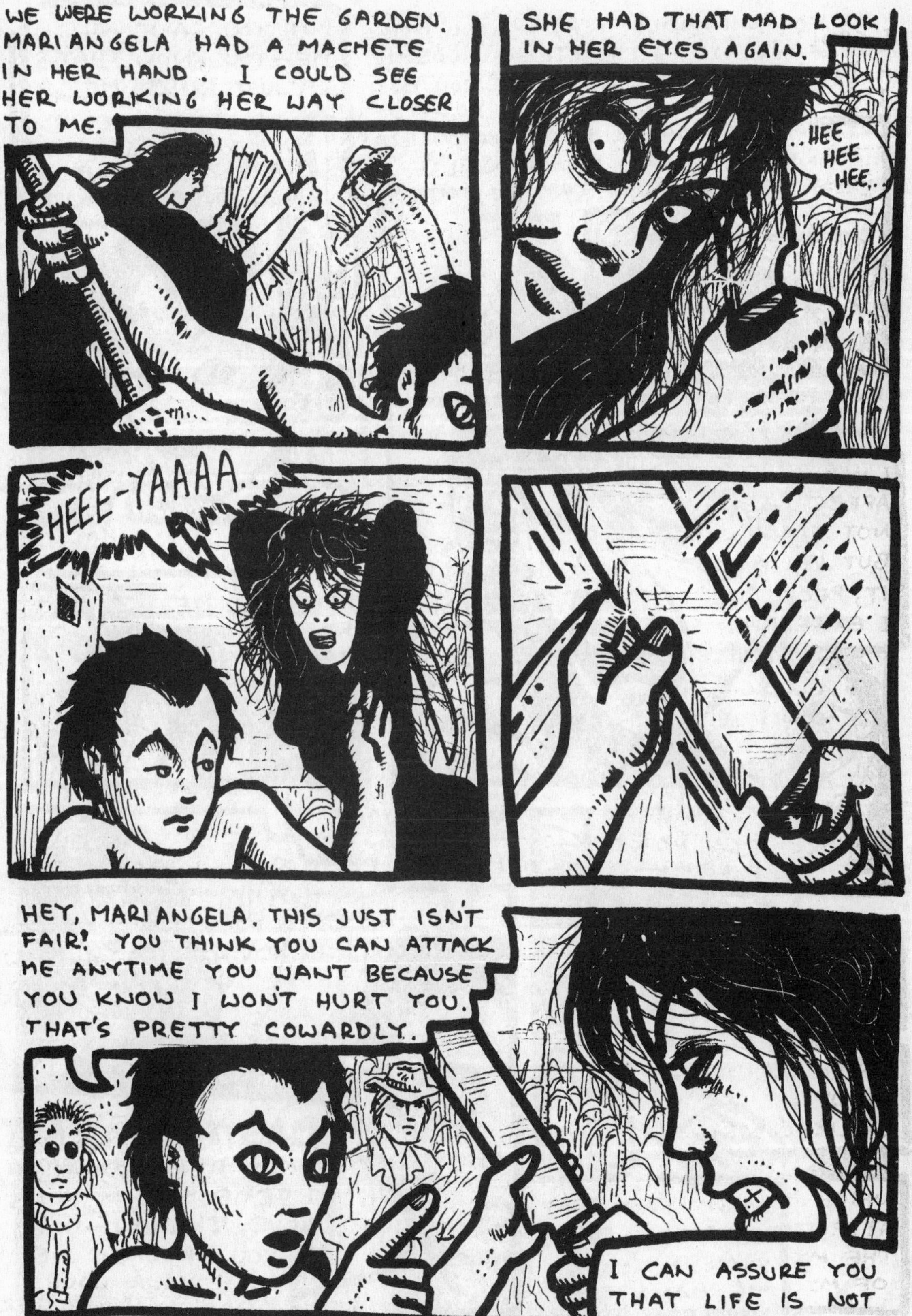
WE WERE WORKING THE GARDEN. MARIANGELA HAD A MACHETE IN HER HAND. I COULD SEE HER WORKING HER WAY CLOSER TO ME.
SHE HAD THAT MAD LOOK IN HER EYES AGAIN.
..HEE HEE HEE..
HEEE-YAAAA..
HEY, MARIANGELA. THIS JUST ISN'T FAIR! YOU THINK YOU CAN ATTACK ME ANYTIME YOU WANT BECAUSE YOU KNOW I WON'T HURT YOU. THAT'S PRETTY COWARDLY.
I CAN ASSURE YOU THAT LIFE IS NOT FAIR, TAZIO...

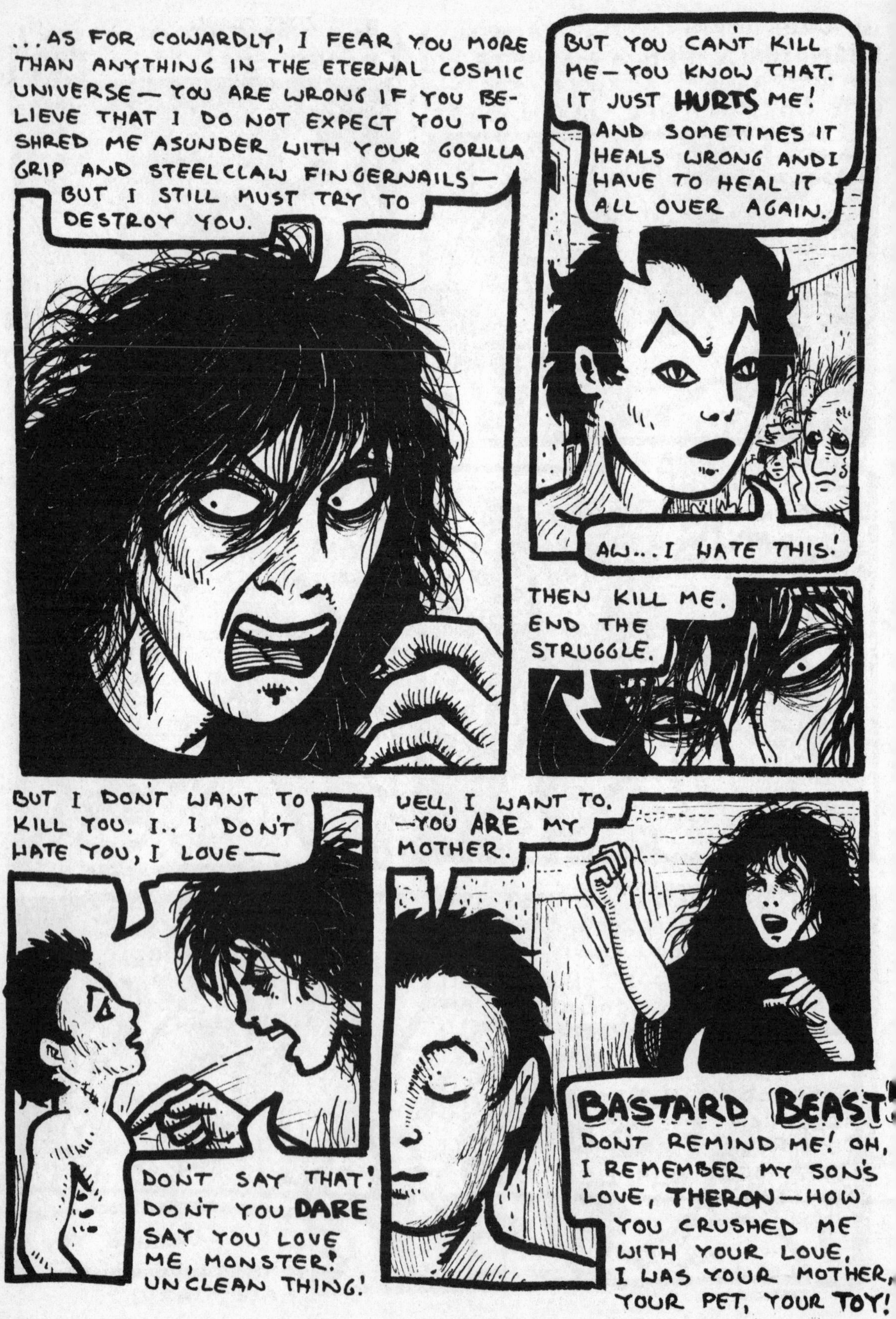
...AS FOR COWARDLY, I FEAR YOU MORE THAN ANYTHING IN THE ETERNAL COSMIC UNIVERSE— YOU ARE WRONG IF YOU BELIEVE THAT I DO NOT EXPECT YOU TO SHRED ME ASUNDER WITH YOUR GORILLA GRIP AND STEELCLAW FINGERNAILS—
BUT I STILL MUST TRY TO DESTROY YOU.
BUT YOU CAN'T KILL ME—YOU KNOW THAT. IT JUST HURTS ME!
AND SOMETIMES IT HEALS WRONG AND I HAVE TO HEAL IT ALL OVER AGAIN.
AW...I HATE THIS!
THEN KILL ME. END THE STRUGGLE.
BUT I DON'T WANT TO KILL YOU. I.. I DON'T HATE YOU, I LOVE—
DON'T SAY THAT! DON'T YOU DARE SAY YOU LOVE ME, MONSTER! UNCLEAN THING!
WELL, I WANT TO. —YOU ARE MY MOTHER.
BASTARD BEAST!
DON'T REMIND ME! OH, I REMEMBER MY SON'S LOVE, THERON—HOW YOU CRUSHED ME WITH YOUR LOVE. I WAS YOUR MOTHER, YOUR PET, YOUR TOY!

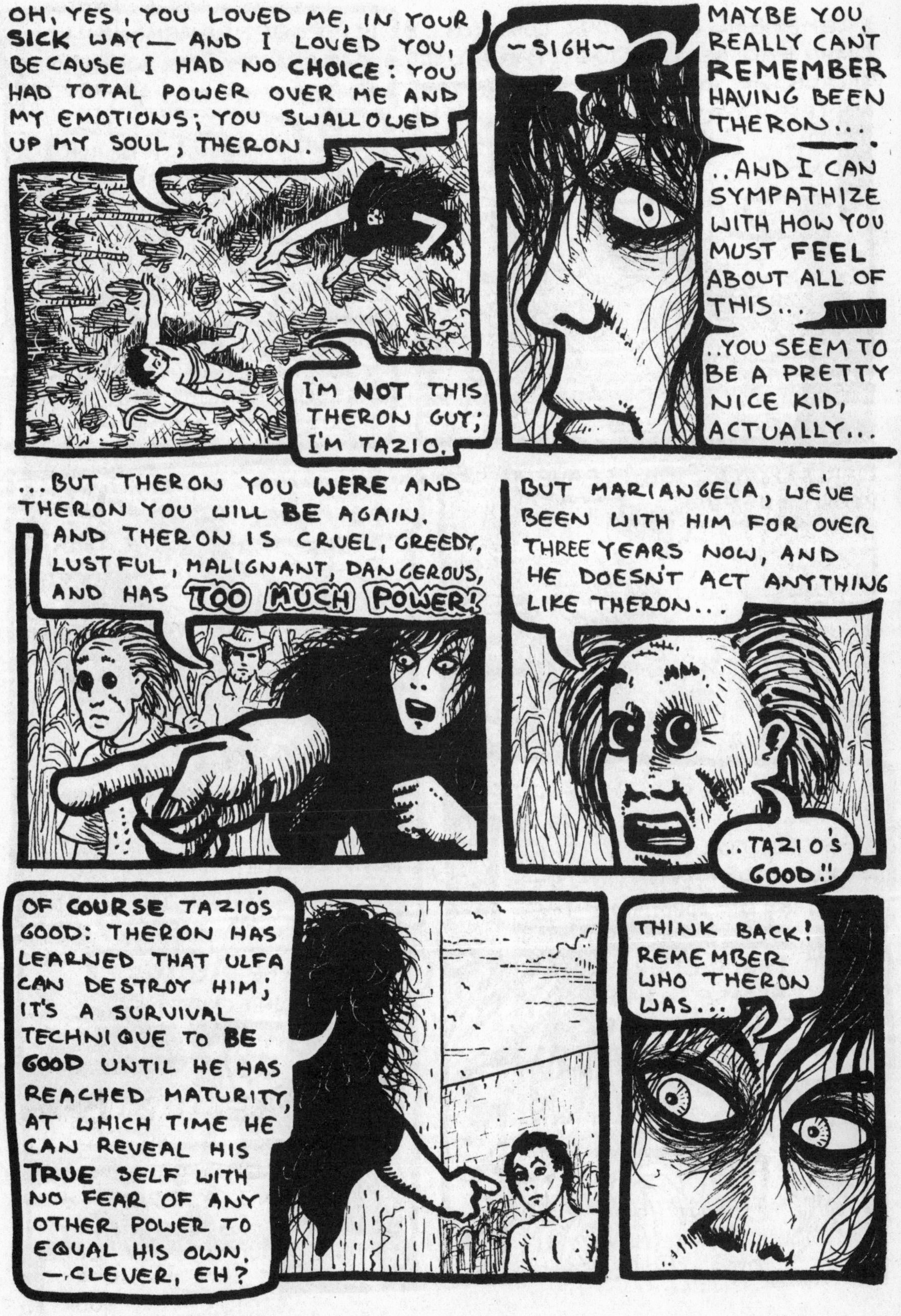

OH, YES, YOU LOVED ME, IN YOUR SICK WAY— AND I LOVED YOU, BECAUSE I HAD NO CHOICE: YOU HAD TOTAL POWER OVER ME AND MY EMOTIONS; YOU SWALLOWED UP MY SOUL, THERON.
I'M NOT THIS THERON GUY; I'M TAZIO.
~SIGH~
MAYBE YOU REALLY CAN'T REMEMBER HAVING BEEN THERON...
..AND I CAN SYMPATHIZE WITH HOW YOU MUST FEEL ABOUT ALL OF THIS...
..YOU SEEM TO BE A PRETTY NICE KID, ACTUALLY...
...BUT THERON YOU WERE AND THERON YOU WILL BE AGAIN.
AND THERON IS CRUEL, GREEDY, LUSTFUL, MALIGNANT, DANGEROUS, AND HAS TOO MUCH POWER!
BUT MARIANGELA, WE'VE BEEN WITH HIM FOR OVER THREE YEARS NOW, AND HE DOESN'T ACT ANYTHING LIKE THERON...
..TAZIO'S GOOD!!
OF COURSE TAZIO'S GOOD: THERON HAS LEARNED THAT ULFA CAN DESTROY HIM; IT'S A SURVIVAL TECHNIQUE TO BE GOOD UNTIL HE HAS REACHED MATURITY, AT WHICH TIME HE CAN REVEAL HIS TRUE SELF WITH NO FEAR OF ANY OTHER POWER TO EQUAL HIS OWN.
—CLEVER, EH?
THINK BACK! REMEMBER WHO THERON WAS...

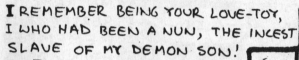

I REMEMBER BEING YOUR LOVE-TOY, I WHO HAD BEEN A NUN, THE INCEST SLAVE OF MY DEMON SON! THE WORST OF IT WAS THAT I **LOVED** IT. I HAD NO CHOICE...NO WILL.

BUFFONE, REMEMBER: YOU WERE A TOY AS WELL; THE EXPERIMENTS_

**NO!** I DON'T REMEMBER!

WELL, I DO! HE PLAYED WITH YOU LIKE **CLAY**: KILLING AND RESSURECTING, CHANGING YOUR FORM, YOUR MIND...

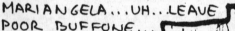

MARIANGELA...UH...LEAVE POOR BUFFONE...

AND **YOU**, ULFO! DON'T YOU **RECALL** THE PHYSICAL AND MENTAL TORTURE? THE SEXUAL DECRADATIONS— AS **MAN** OR **WOMAN**? THE—

I GET THE PICTURE. NOW: PLEASE, WHO WAS HE? I **WISH** YOU TO TELL ME.

YEAH, YEAH, THERON WAS CRUEL.

**CRUEL?** HE WAS EVIL INCARNATE! HE WAS A MAD GOD WITH THE EARTH HIS TOY. HE WAS...GASP!!

YOU GET THE **PICTURE**... YES, WHY NOT?

I HAVE IT HERE... ...TO REMIND ME.

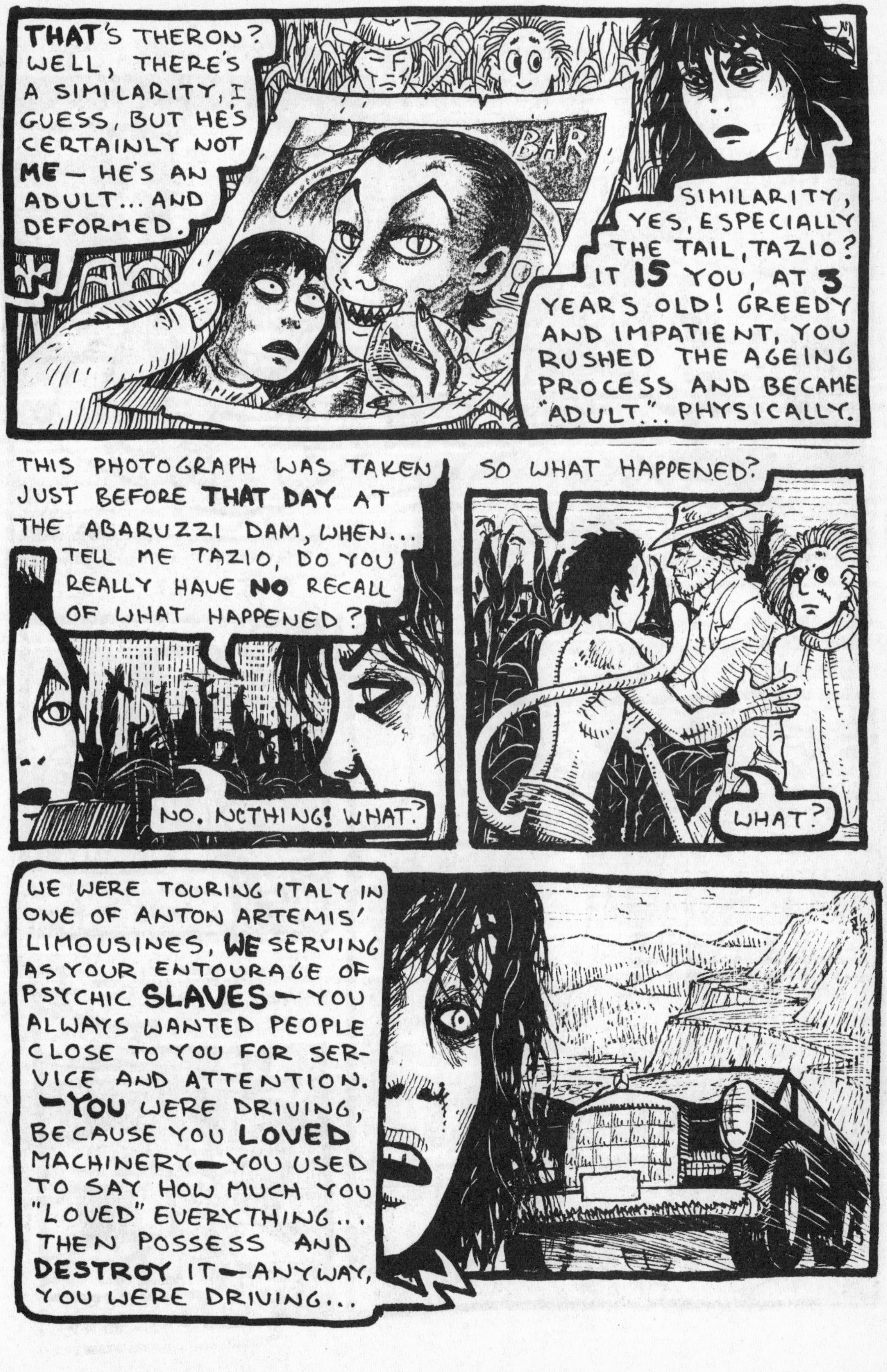
THAT'S THERON? WELL, THERE'S A SIMILARITY, I GUESS, BUT HE'S CERTAINLY NOT ME— HE'S AN ADULT... AND DEFORMED.
BAR
SIMILARITY, YES, ESPECIALLY THE TAIL, TAZIO? IT IS YOU, AT 3 YEARS OLD! GREEDY AND IMPATIENT, YOU RUSHED THE AGEING PROCESS AND BECAME "ADULT"... PHYSICALLY.
THIS PHOTOGRAPH WAS TAKEN JUST BEFORE THAT DAY AT THE ABARUZZI DAM, WHEN...
TELL ME TAZIO, DO YOU REALLY HAVE NO RECALL OF WHAT HAPPENED?
NO. NOTHING! WHAT?
SO WHAT HAPPENED?
WHAT?
WE WERE TOURING ITALY IN ONE OF ANTON ARTEMIS' LIMOUSINES, WE SERVING AS YOUR ENTOURAGE OF PSYCHIC SLAVES— YOU ALWAYS WANTED PEOPLE CLOSE TO YOU FOR SERVICE AND ATTENTION. —YOU WERE DRIVING, BECAUSE YOU LOVED MACHINERY— YOU USED TO SAY HOW MUCH YOU "LOVED" EVERYTHING... THEN POSSESS AND DESTROY IT— ANYWAY, YOU WERE DRIVING...

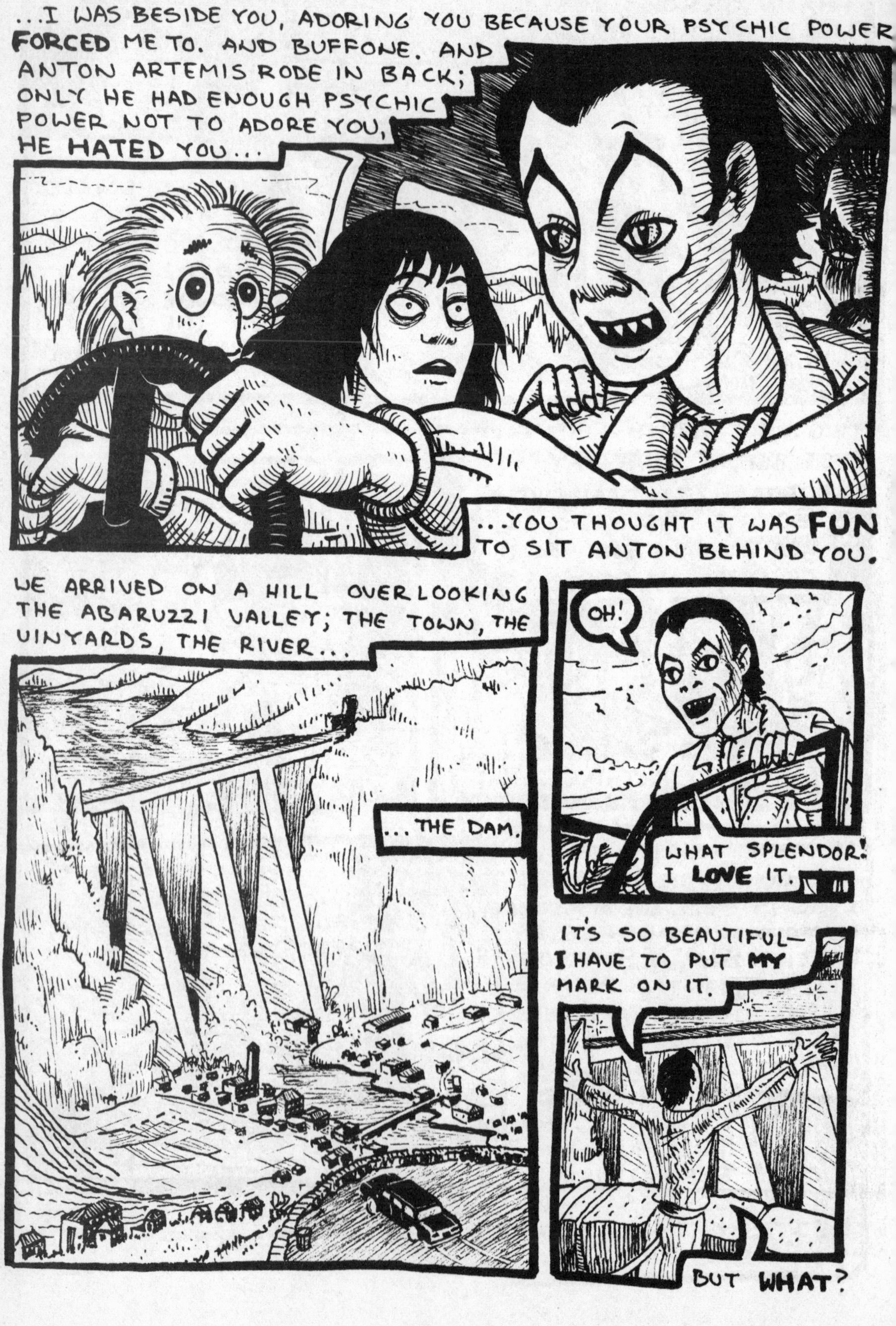
...I WAS BESIDE YOU, ADORING YOU BECAUSE YOUR PSYCHIC POWER FORCED ME TO. AND BUFFONE. AND ANTON ARTEMIS RODE IN BACK; ONLY HE HAD ENOUGH PSYCHIC POWER NOT TO ADORE YOU, HE HATED YOU...
...YOU THOUGHT IT WAS FUN TO SIT ANTON BEHIND YOU.
WE ARRIVED ON A HILL OVERLOOKING THE ABARUZZI VALLEY; THE TOWN, THE VINYARDS, THE RIVER...
...THE DAM.
OH!
WHAT SPLENDOR! I LOVE IT.
IT'S SO BEAUTIFUL— I HAVE TO PUT MY MARK ON IT.
BUT WHAT?

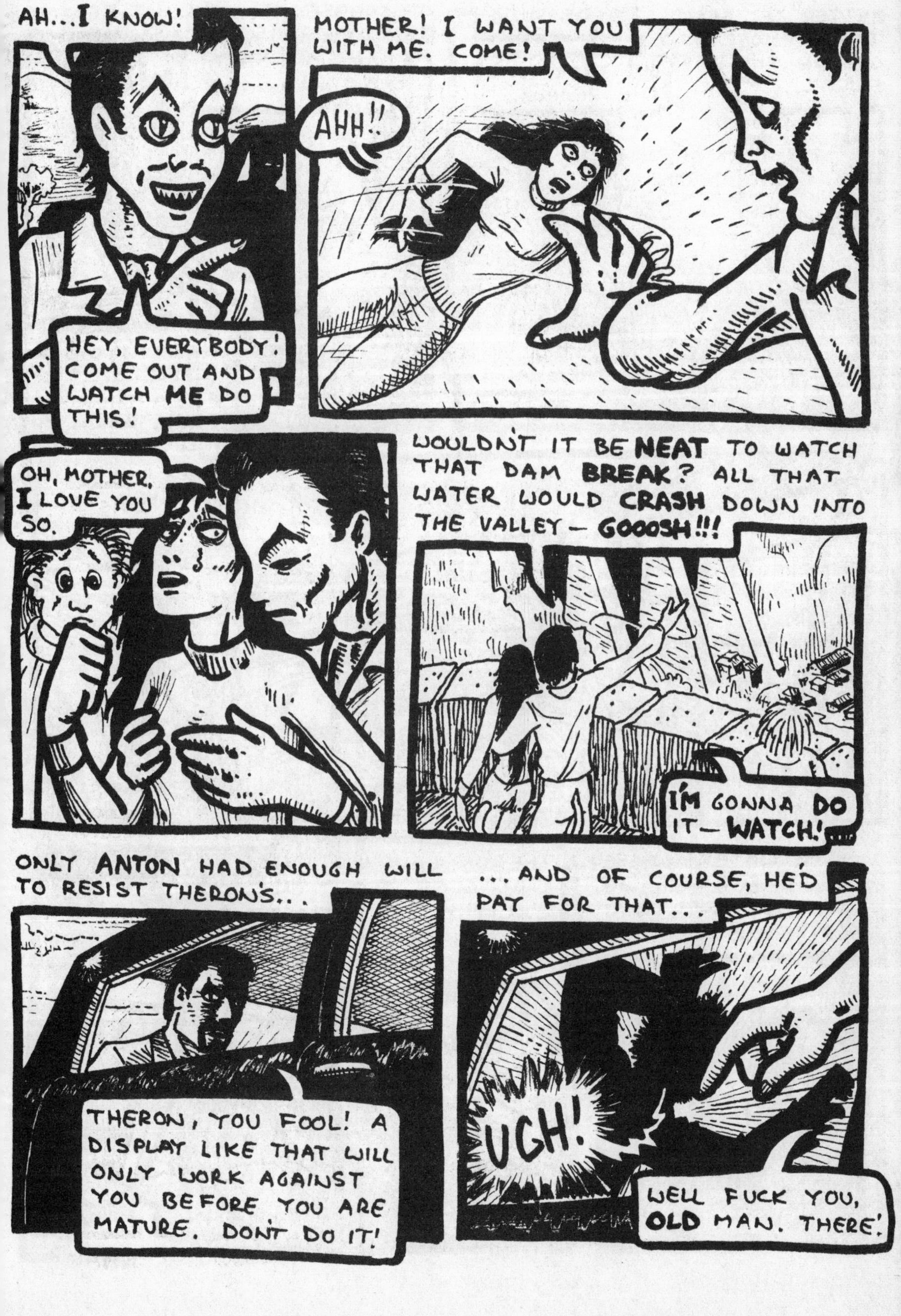
AH...I KNOW!
HEY, EVERYBODY! COME OUT AND WATCH ME DO THIS!
MOTHER! I WANT YOU WITH ME. COME!
AHH!!
OH, MOTHER. I LOVE YOU SO.
WOULDN'T IT BE NEAT TO WATCH THAT DAM BREAK? ALL THAT WATER WOULD CRASH DOWN INTO THE VALLEY — GOOOSH!!!
I'M GONNA DO IT— WATCH!
ONLY ANTON HAD ENOUGH WILL TO RESIST THERON'S...
THERON, YOU FOOL! A DISPLAY LIKE THAT WILL ONLY WORK AGAINST YOU BEFORE YOU ARE MATURE. DON'T DO IT!
...AND OF COURSE, HE'D PAY FOR THAT...
UGH!
WELL FUCK YOU, OLD MAN. THERE!

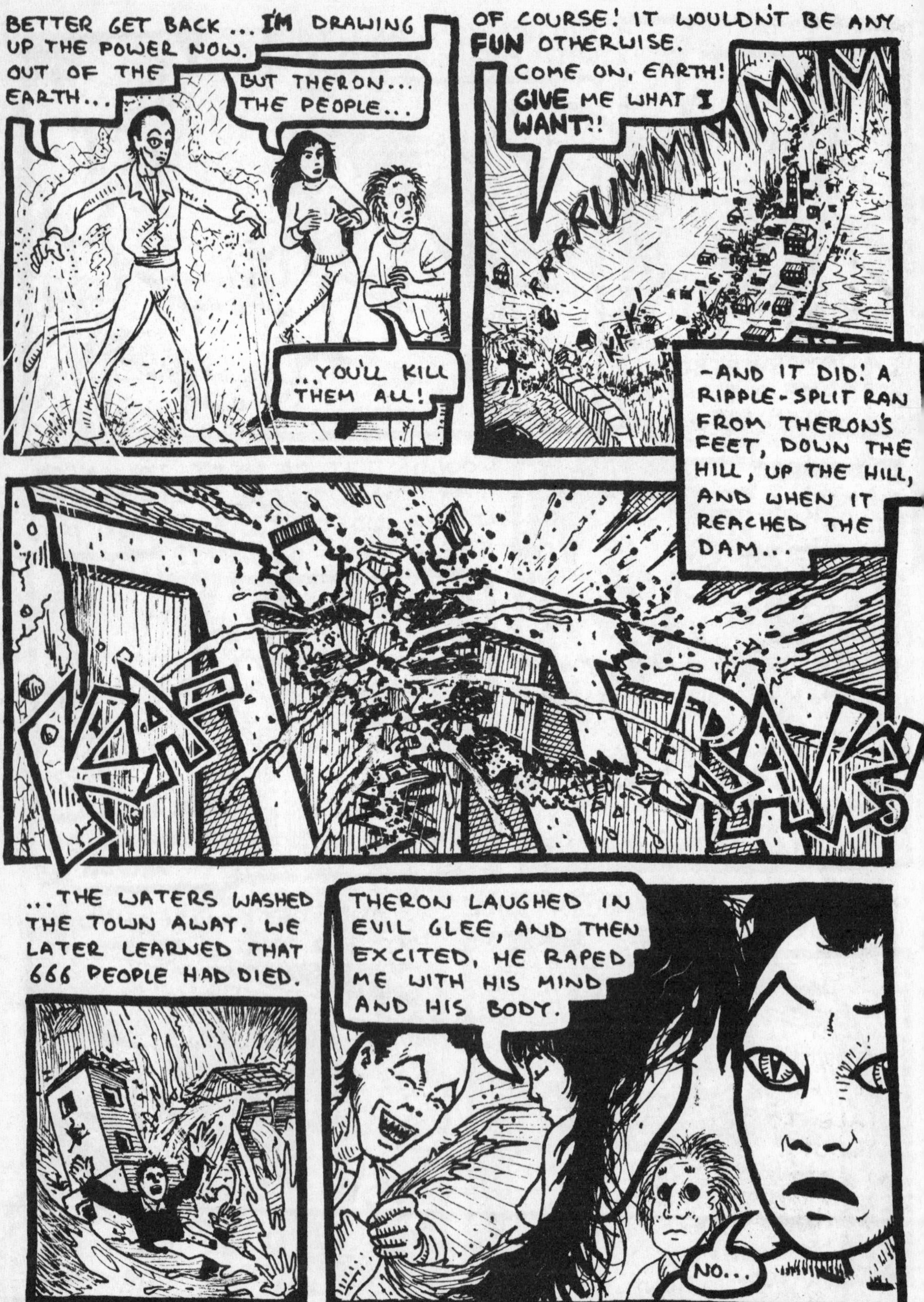
BETTER GET BACK ... I'M DRAWING UP THE POWER NOW. OUT OF THE EARTH...
BUT THERON... THE PEOPLE...
...YOU'LL KILL THEM ALL!
OF COURSE! IT WOULDN'T BE ANY FUN OTHERWISE.
COME ON, EARTH! GIVE ME WHAT I WANT!!
RRRUMMMMMM
KRK!
-AND IT DID! A RIPPLE-SPLIT RAN FROM THERON'S FEET, DOWN THE HILL, UP THE HILL, AND WHEN IT REACHED THE DAM...
KA-BRAK!
...THE WATERS WASHED THE TOWN AWAY. WE LATER LEARNED THAT 666 PEOPLE HAD DIED.
THERON LAUGHED IN EVIL GLEE, AND THEN EXCITED, HE RAPED ME WITH HIS MIND AND HIS BODY.
NO...

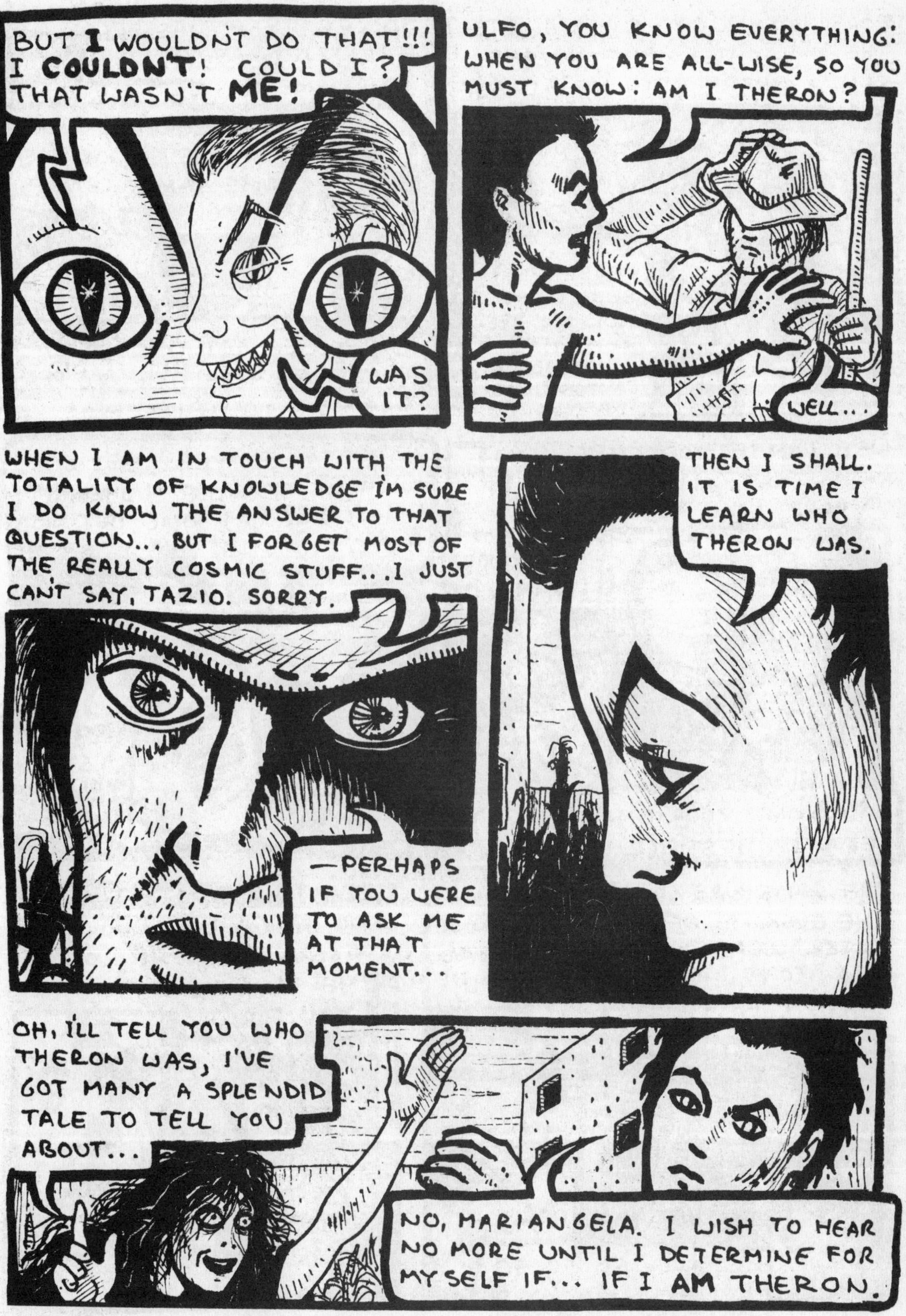
BUT I WOULDN'T DO THAT!!! I COULDN'T! COULD I? THAT WASN'T ME!
WAS IT?
ULFO, YOU KNOW EVERYTHING: WHEN YOU ARE ALL-WISE, SO YOU MUST KNOW: AM I THERON?
WELL...
WHEN I AM IN TOUCH WITH THE TOTALITY OF KNOWLEDGE I'M SURE I DO KNOW THE ANSWER TO THAT QUESTION... BUT I FORGET MOST OF THE REALLY COSMIC STUFF... I JUST CAN'T SAY, TAZIO. SORRY.
—PERHAPS IF YOU WERE TO ASK ME AT THAT MOMENT...
THEN I SHALL. IT IS TIME I LEARN WHO THERON WAS.
OH, I'LL TELL YOU WHO THERON WAS, I'VE GOT MANY A SPLENDID TALE TO TELL YOU ABOUT...
NO, MARIANGELA. I WISH TO HEAR NO MORE UNTIL I DETERMINE FOR MYSELF IF... IF I AM THERON.

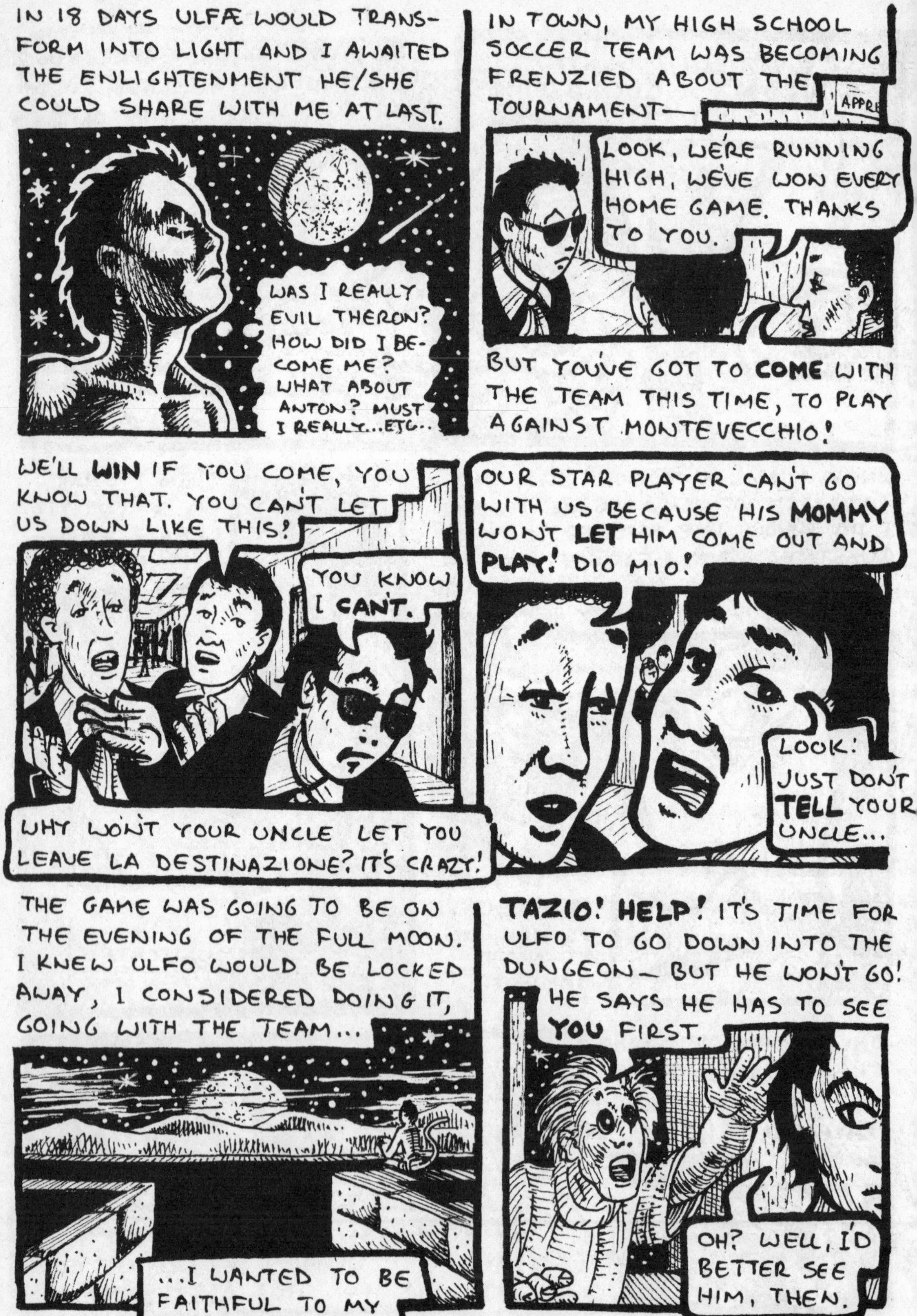
IN 18 DAYS ULFÆ WOULD TRANSFORM INTO LIGHT AND I AWAITED THE ENLIGHTENMENT HE/SHE COULD SHARE WITH ME AT LAST.
WAS I REALLY EVIL THERON? HOW DID I BECOME ME? WHAT ABOUT ANTON? MUST I REALLY...ETC..
IN TOWN, MY HIGH SCHOOL SOCCER TEAM WAS BECOMING FRENZIED ABOUT THE TOURNAMENT—
LOOK, WE'RE RUNNING HIGH, WE'VE WON EVERY HOME GAME. THANKS TO YOU.
BUT YOU'VE GOT TO **COME** WITH THE TEAM THIS TIME, TO PLAY AGAINST MONTEVECCHIO!
WE'LL **WIN** IF YOU COME, YOU KNOW THAT. YOU CAN'T LET US DOWN LIKE THIS!
YOU KNOW I **CAN'T.**
WHY WON'T YOUR UNCLE LET YOU LEAVE LA DESTINAZIONE? IT'S CRAZY!
OUR STAR PLAYER CAN'T GO WITH US BECAUSE HIS **MOMMY** WON'T **LET** HIM COME OUT AND **PLAY!** DIO MIO!
LOOK: JUST DON'T **TELL** YOUR UNCLE...
THE GAME WAS GOING TO BE ON THE EVENING OF THE FULL MOON. I KNEW ULFO WOULD BE LOCKED AWAY, I CONSIDERED DOING IT, GOING WITH THE TEAM...
...I WANTED TO BE FAITHFUL TO MY FRIENDS—
**TAZIO! HELP!** IT'S TIME FOR ULFO TO GO DOWN INTO THE DUNGEON— BUT HE WON'T GO! HE SAYS HE HAS TO SEE **YOU** FIRST.
OH? WELL, I'D BETTER SEE HIM, THEN.

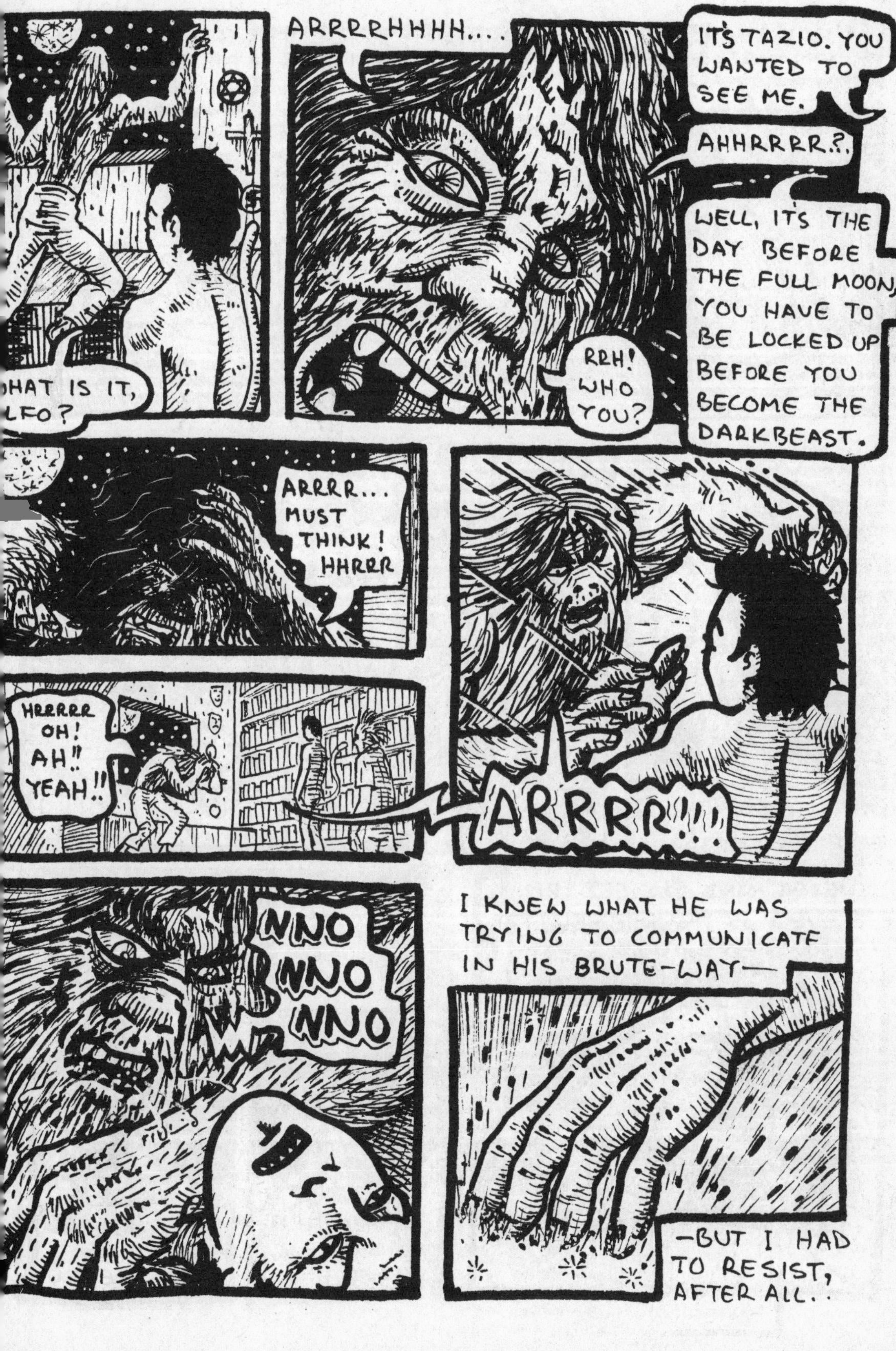

HAT IS IT,
LFO?
ARRRRHHHH....
IT'S TAZIO. YOU WANTED TO SEE ME.
AHHRRRR?.
WELL, IT'S THE DAY BEFORE THE FULL MOON, YOU HAVE TO BE LOCKED UP BEFORE YOU BECOME THE DARKBEAST.
RRH! WHO YOU?
ARRRR... MUST THINK! HHRRR
HRRRRR OH! AH!! YEAH!!
ARRRRR!!!
NNO NNO NNO
I KNEW WHAT HE WAS TRYING TO COMMUNICATE IN HIS BRUTE-WAY—
—BUT I HAD TO RESIST, AFTER ALL.

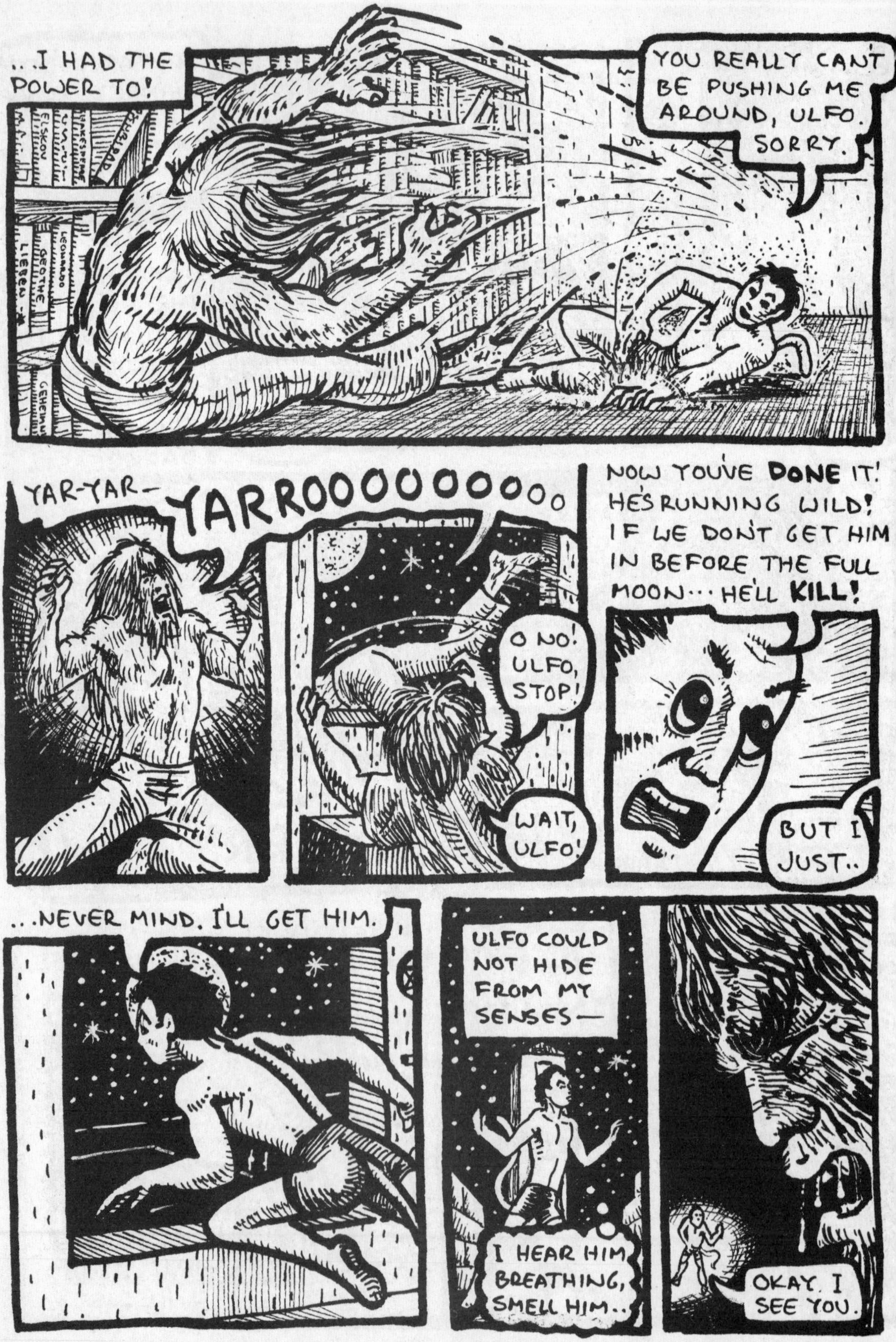

...I HAD THE POWER TO!
YOU REALLY CAN'T BE PUSHING ME AROUND, ULFO. SORRY.
YAR-YAR—YARROOOOOOOOo
NOW YOU'VE **DONE** IT! HE'S RUNNING WILD! IF WE DON'T GET HIM IN BEFORE THE FULL MOON... HE'LL **KILL**!
O NO! ULFO, STOP!
WAIT, ULFO!
BUT I JUST..
...NEVER MIND. I'LL GET HIM.
ULFO COULD NOT HIDE FROM MY SENSES—
I HEAR HIM BREATHING, SMELL HIM..
OKAY. I SEE YOU.

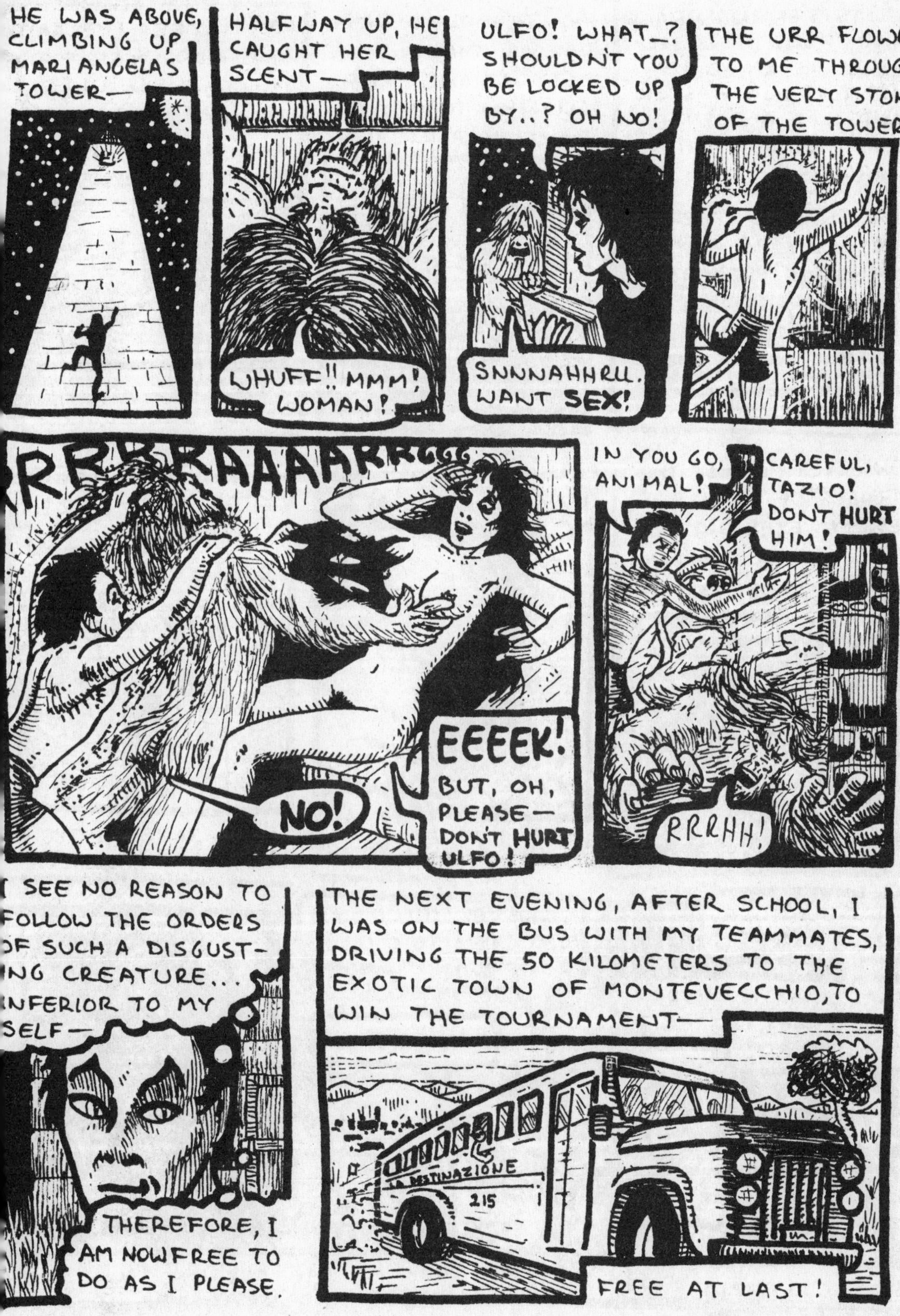
HE WAS ABOVE, CLIMBING UP, MARI ANGELA'S TOWER—
HALFWAY UP, HE CAUGHT HER SCENT—
WHUFF!! MMM! WOMAN!
ULFO! WHAT—? SHOULDN'T YOU BE LOCKED UP BY..? OH NO!
SNNNAHHRLL. WANT SEX!
THE URR FLOWED TO ME THROUGH THE VERY STONES OF THE TOWER—
RRRRRAAAAARRGGG
NO!
EEEEK! BUT, OH, PLEASE— DON'T HURT ULFO!
IN YOU GO, ANIMAL!
CAREFUL, TAZIO! DON'T HURT HIM!
RRRHH!
I SEE NO REASON TO FOLLOW THE ORDERS OF SUCH A DISGUSTING CREATURE... INFERIOR TO MY SELF—
THEREFORE, I AM NOW FREE TO DO AS I PLEASE.
THE NEXT EVENING, AFTER SCHOOL, I WAS ON THE BUS WITH MY TEAMMATES, DRIVING THE 50 KILOMETERS TO THE EXOTIC TOWN OF MONTEVECCHIO, TO WIN THE TOURNAMENT—
DESTINAZIONE
215
FREE AT LAST!

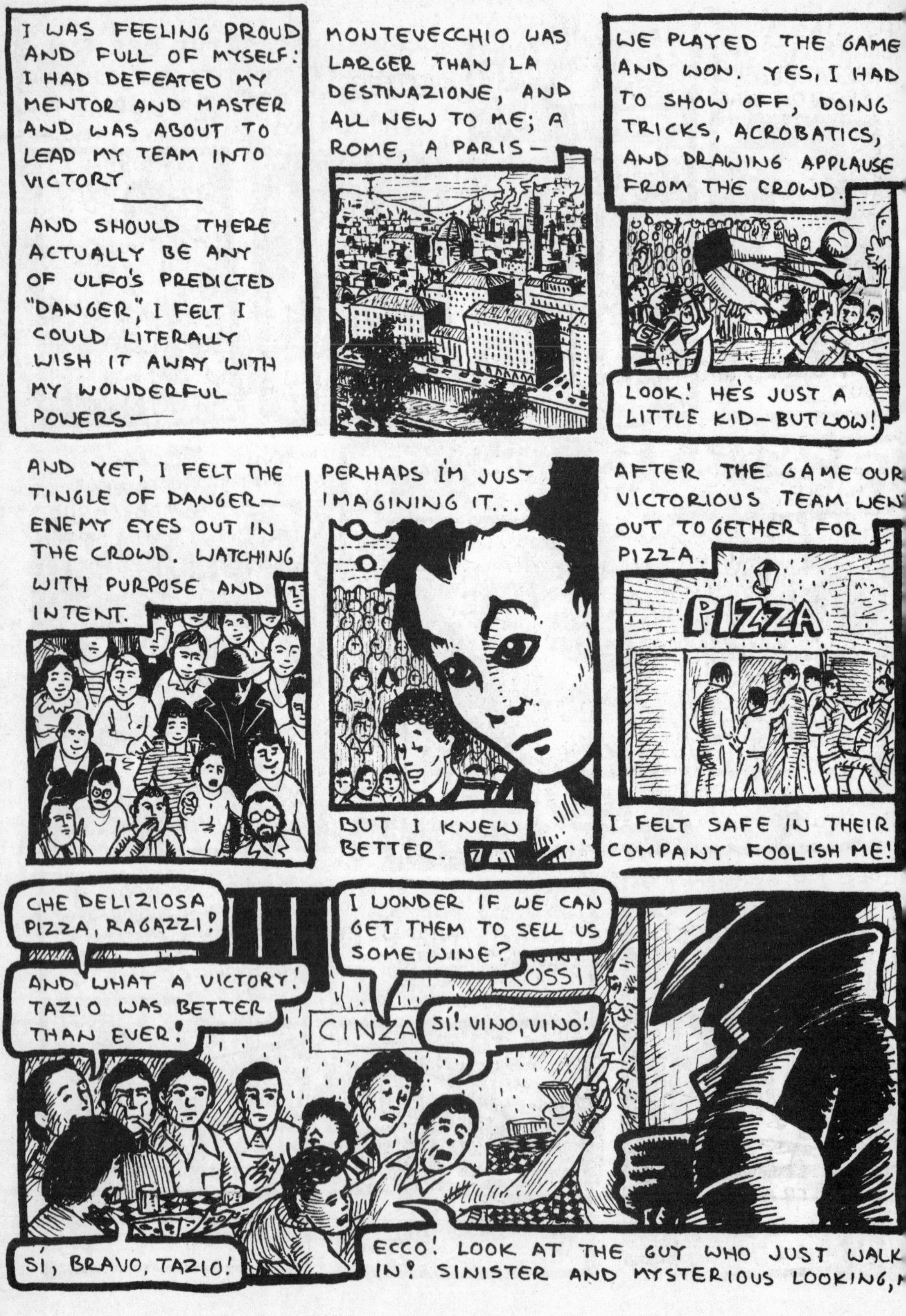
I WAS FEELING PROUD AND FULL OF MYSELF: I HAD DEFEATED MY MENTOR AND MASTER AND WAS ABOUT TO LEAD MY TEAM INTO VICTORY.
AND SHOULD THERE ACTUALLY BE ANY OF ULFO'S PREDICTED "DANGER", I FELT I COULD LITERALLY WISH IT AWAY WITH MY WONDERFUL POWERS—
MONTEVECCHIO WAS LARGER THAN LA DESTINAZIONE, AND ALL NEW TO ME; A ROME, A PARIS—
WE PLAYED THE GAME AND WON. YES, I HAD TO SHOW OFF, DOING TRICKS, ACROBATICS, AND DRAWING APPLAUSE FROM THE CROWD.
LOOK! HE'S JUST A LITTLE KID—BUT WOW!
AND YET, I FELT THE TINGLE OF DANGER—ENEMY EYES OUT IN THE CROWD. WATCHING WITH PURPOSE AND INTENT.
PERHAPS I'M JUST IMAGINING IT...
BUT I KNEW BETTER.
AFTER THE GAME OUR VICTORIOUS TEAM WENT OUT TOGETHER FOR PIZZA.
PIZZA
I FELT SAFE IN THEIR COMPANY. FOOLISH ME!
CHE DELIZIOSA PIZZA, RAGAZZI!
AND WHAT A VICTORY! TAZIO WAS BETTER THAN EVER!
I WONDER IF WE CAN GET THEM TO SELL US SOME WINE?
SÍ! VINO, VINO!
ROSSI
CINZA
SÍ, BRAVO, TAZIO!
ECCO! LOOK AT THE GUY WHO JUST WALK IN! SINISTER AND MYSTERIOUS LOOKING,

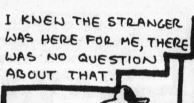

I KNEW THE STRANGER WAS HERE FOR ME, THERE WAS NO QUESTION ABOUT THAT.

NO, YOU'RE TOO YOUNG, BOYS. NO WINE!

AW, I DRINK WINE AT HOME, SIGNORE.

I'LL BUY THEM THE WINE. GIVE IT TO THEM ... NOW.

BUT WHO WAS HE? A DARK TEMPLAR? OR ANTON ARTEMIS?

MAYBE, BUT NOT IN PUBLIC, BOY.

UH... UH.. (BRRR!) SÌ, SÌ, SIGNORE!

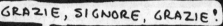

GRAZIE, SIGNORE, GRAZIE!

SÌ, MOLTO AMICHEVOLE!

TAZIO! THIS IS TAZIO, OUR WONDER BOY!

HAVE SOME WINE, TAZIO!

YOU PLAYED AN EXCELLENT GAME, LADS. ESPECIALLY THE YOUNGEST THERE — WHAT'S HIS NAME?

NO, I'LL JUST HAVE COKE.

I FELT SURROUNDED, TRAPPED. MY TEAMMATES BECAME DRUNK.

THE STRANGER WATCHED ME. I WATCHED HIM.

I KNEW HE WAS NOT EXACTLY HUMAN.

HIS EYES — LIKE MY OWN — GAVE HIM AWAY.

ARE YOU ANTON?

I? HAH HAH HAH. NO — NO. — NO I AM NO ONE, CHILD.

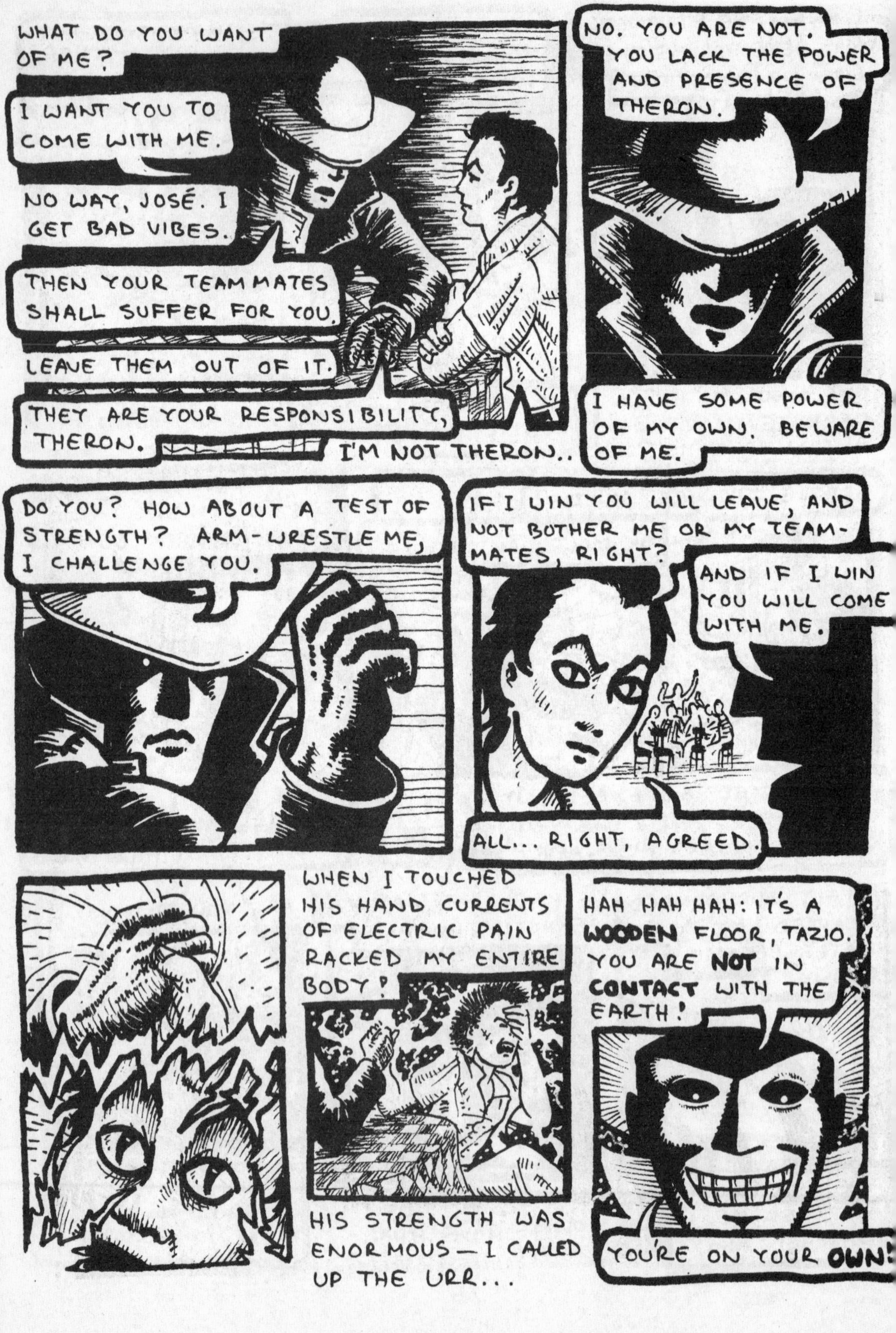
WHAT DO YOU WANT OF ME?
I WANT YOU TO COME WITH ME.
NO WAY, JOSÉ. I GET BAD VIBES.
THEN YOUR TEAM MATES SHALL SUFFER FOR YOU.
LEAVE THEM OUT OF IT.
THEY ARE YOUR RESPONSIBILITY, THERON.
I'M NOT THERON..
NO. YOU ARE NOT. YOU LACK THE POWER AND PRESENCE OF THERON.
I HAVE SOME POWER OF MY OWN. BEWARE OF ME.
DO YOU? HOW ABOUT A TEST OF STRENGTH? ARM-WRESTLE ME, I CHALLENGE YOU.
IF I WIN YOU WILL LEAVE, AND NOT BOTHER ME OR MY TEAM-MATES, RIGHT?
AND IF I WIN YOU WILL COME WITH ME.
ALL... RIGHT, AGREED.
WHEN I TOUCHED HIS HAND CURRENTS OF ELECTRIC PAIN RACKED MY ENTIRE BODY!
HIS STRENGTH WAS ENORMOUS — I CALLED UP THE URR...
HAH HAH HAH: IT'S A WOODEN FLOOR, TAZIO. YOU ARE NOT IN CONTACT WITH THE EARTH!
YOU'RE ON YOUR OWN!

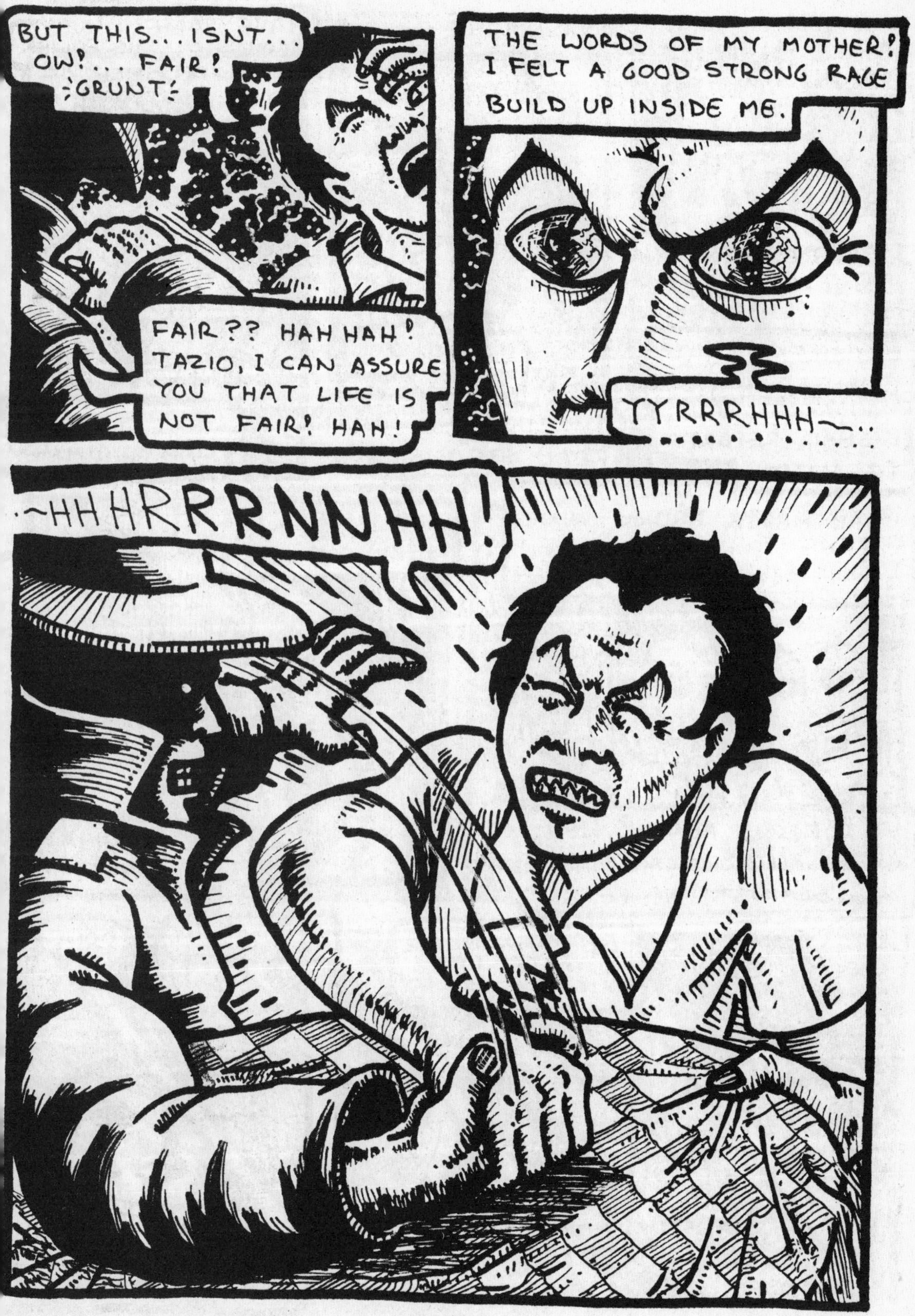

BUT THIS...ISN'T... OW!... FAIR! ·GRUNT·
FAIR?? HAH HAH! TAZIO, I CAN ASSURE YOU THAT LIFE IS NOT FAIR! HAH!
THE WORDS OF MY MOTHER! I FELT A GOOD STRONG RAGE BUILD UP INSIDE ME.
TYRRRHHH~...
~HHHRRRNNHH!

NOW GO!

EXCELLENT, CHILD. I WANTED TO TEST YOU, AND I HAVE. I SHALL REPORT TO ANTON.

GOOD NIGHT, BOYS.

TAZIO! YOU WON!

AMAZING! HE LOOKED REAL STRONG!!!

HAVE SOME WINE.

WHAT THE HELL. OKAY, GIMME.

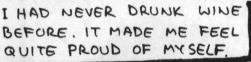

I HAD NEVER DRUNK WINE BEFORE. IT MADE ME FEEL QUITE PROUD OF MYSELF.

VICTORIOUS AGAIN? WELL, AFTER ALL: WHO CAN WAGE WAR AGAINST THE BEAST?

THE PISSERS DOWN HERE. C'MON.

WHEW! WHAT A LONG HALL. HEE!

HUH? CHE—?

GET HIS FEET UP! DON'T LET HIM TOUCH THE GROUND!

MBFF!!

HEY! LEAVE MY PAL ALONE...

SILENCE HIM.

DONE.

TWAK!

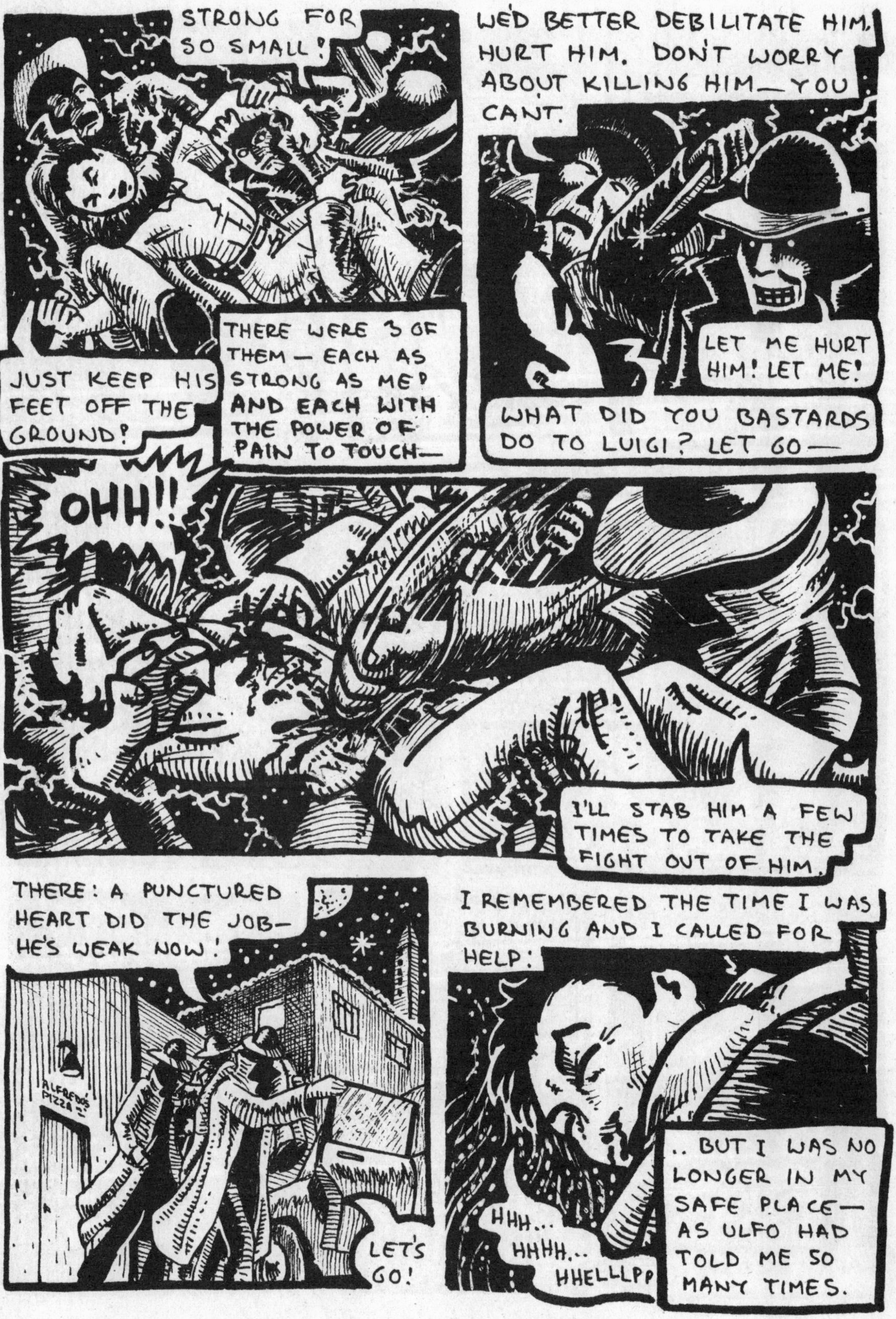
STRONG FOR SO SMALL!
JUST KEEP HIS FEET OFF THE GROUND!
THERE WERE 3 OF THEM — EACH AS STRONG AS ME? AND EACH WITH THE POWER OF PAIN TO TOUCH—
WE'D BETTER DEBILITATE HIM. HURT HIM. DON'T WORRY ABOUT KILLING HIM — YOU CAN'T.
LET ME HURT HIM! LET ME!
WHAT DID YOU BASTARDS DO TO LUIGI? LET GO—
OHH!!
I'LL STAB HIM A FEW TIMES TO TAKE THE FIGHT OUT OF HIM.
THERE: A PUNCTURED HEART DID THE JOB— HE'S WEAK NOW!
ALFREDO'S PIZZA
LET'S GO!
I REMEMBERED THE TIME I WAS BURNING AND I CALLED FOR HELP:
HHH... HHHH... HHELLLPP
.. BUT I WAS NO LONGER IN MY SAFE PLACE— AS ULFO HAD TOLD ME SO MANY TIMES.

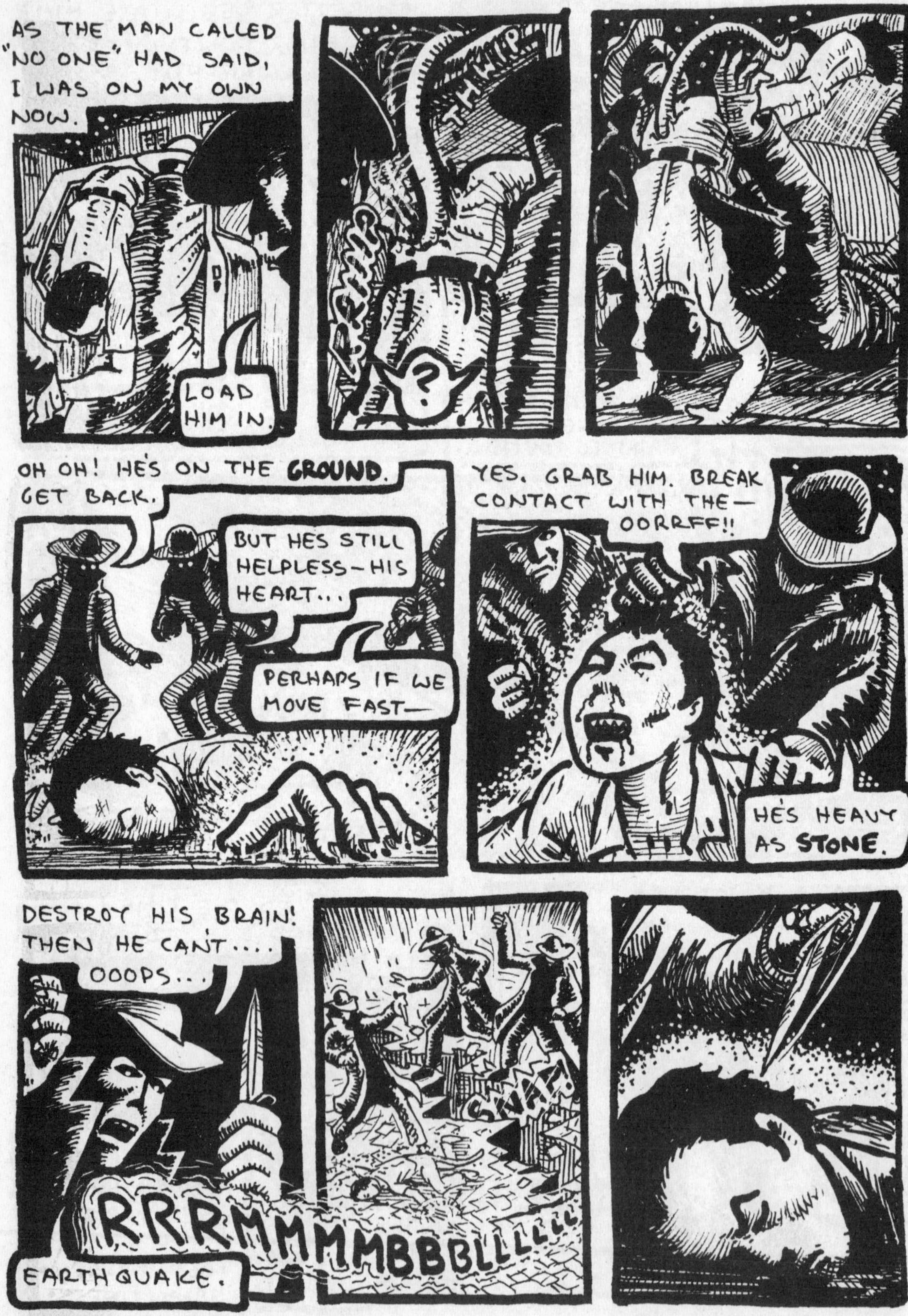

AS THE MAN CALLED "NO ONE" HAD SAID, I WAS ON MY OWN NOW.
LOAD HIM IN.
THWIP
?
OH OH! HE'S ON THE **GROUND**. GET BACK.
BUT HES STILL HELPLESS—HIS HEART...
PERHAPS IF WE MOVE FAST—
YES. GRAB HIM. BREAK CONTACT WITH THE— OORRFF!!
HE'S HEAVY AS **STONE**.
DESTROY HIS BRAIN! THEN HE CAN'T.... OOOPS...
RRRMMMMMBBBLLLLLL
EARTHQUAKE.

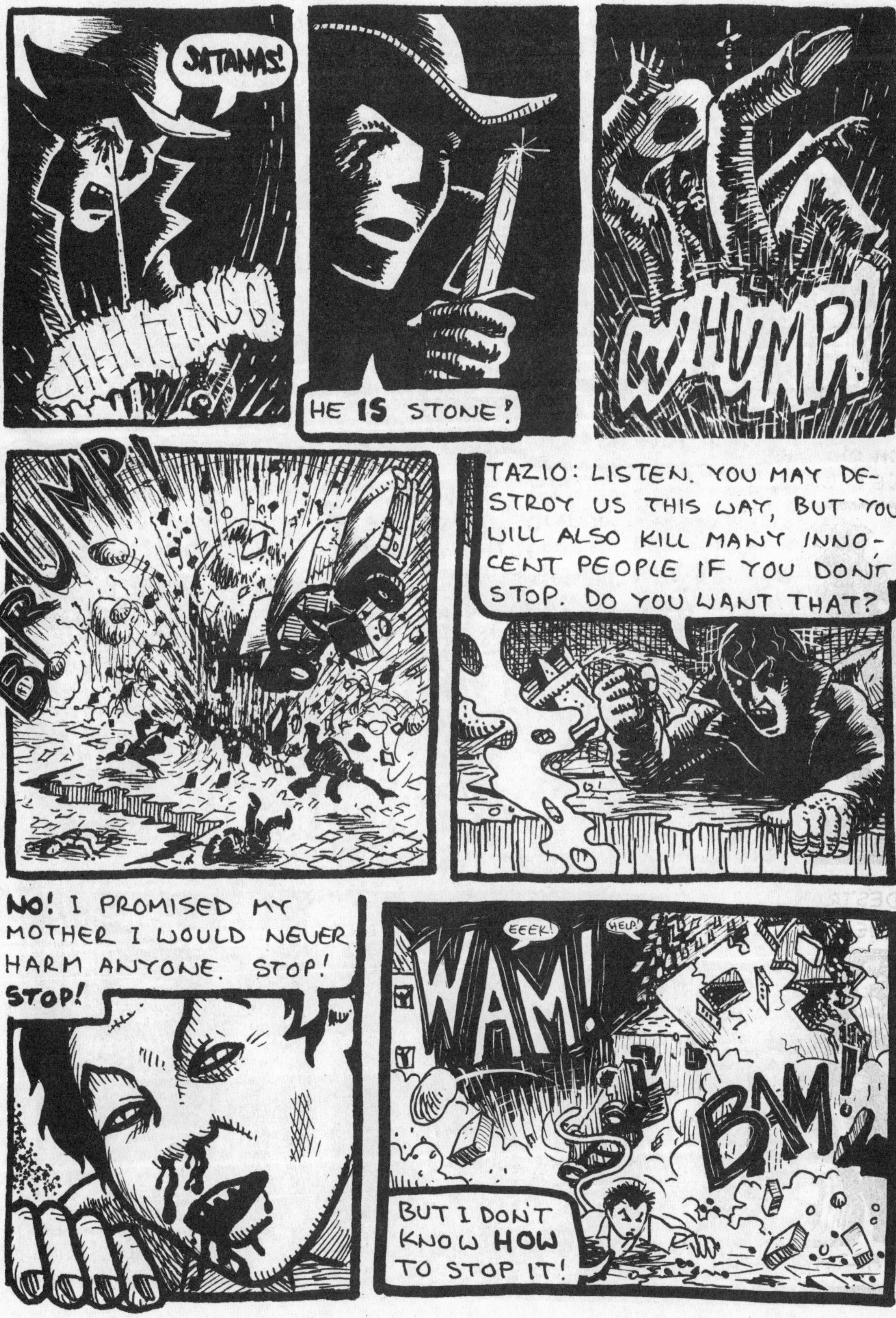
SATANAS!
CHEEEEENNGG!
HE **IS** STONE!
WHUMP!
BRUMP!
TAZIO: LISTEN. YOU MAY DESTROY US THIS WAY, BUT YOU WILL ALSO KILL MANY INNOCENT PEOPLE IF YOU DON'T STOP. DO YOU WANT THAT?
**NO!** I PROMISED MY MOTHER I WOULD NEVER HARM ANYONE. STOP! **STOP!**
WAM!
EEEK!
HELP!
BAM!
BUT I DON'T KNOW **HOW** TO STOP IT!

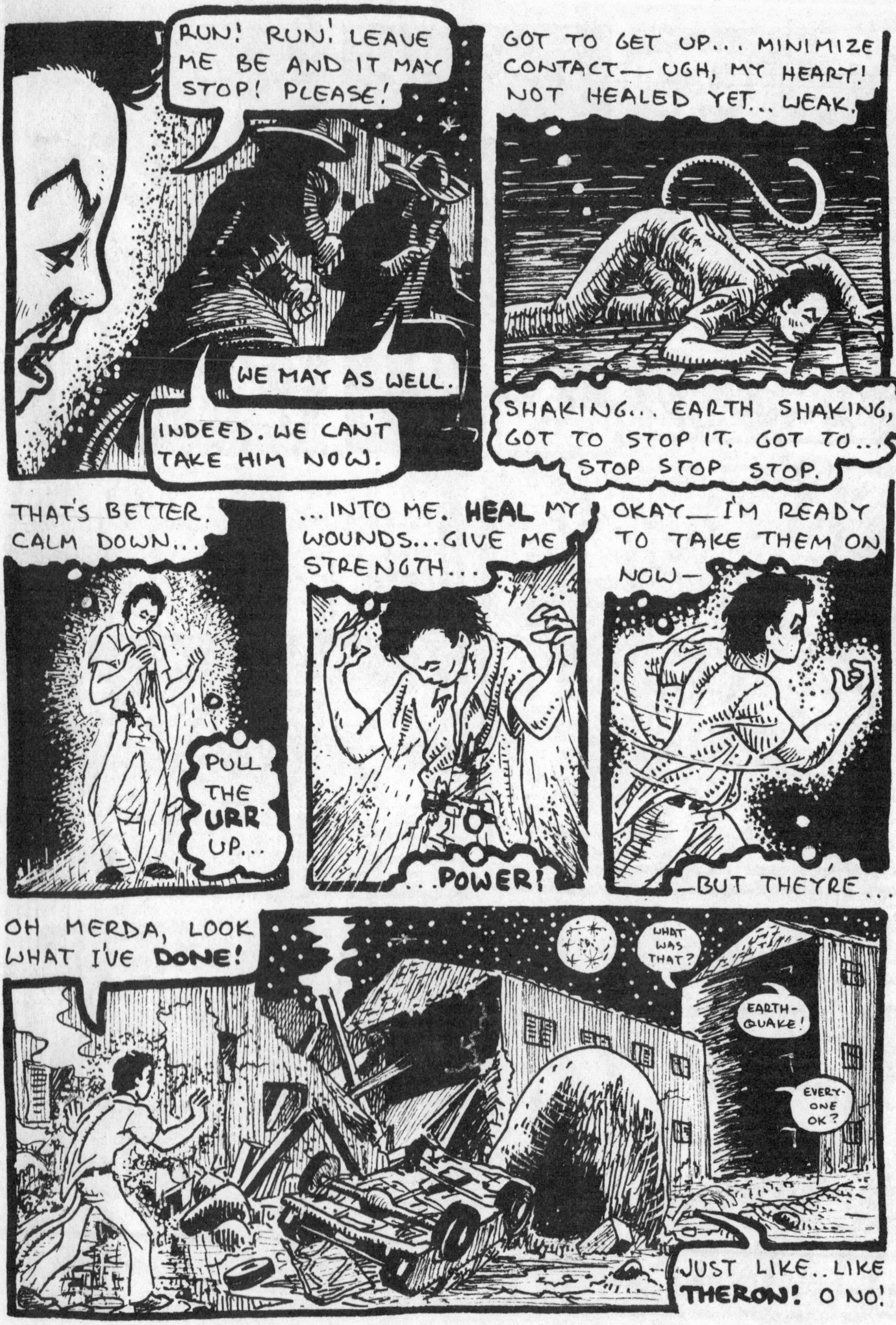
RUN! RUN! LEAVE ME BE AND IT MAY STOP! PLEASE!
WE MAY AS WELL.
INDEED. WE CAN'T TAKE HIM NOW.
GOT TO GET UP... MINIMIZE CONTACT— UGH, MY HEART! NOT HEALED YET... WEAK.
SHAKING... EARTH SHAKING, GOT TO STOP IT. GOT TO... STOP STOP STOP.
THAT'S BETTER. CALM DOWN...
PULL THE URR UP...
...INTO ME. HEAL MY WOUNDS...GIVE ME STRENGTH...
...POWER!
OKAY— I'M READY TO TAKE THEM ON NOW—
—BUT THEYRE...
OH MERDA, LOOK WHAT I'VE DONE!
WHAT WAS THAT?
EARTH-QUAKE!
EVERY-ONE OK?
JUST LIKE.. LIKE THERON! O NO!

WHAT IF I HAVE HURT OR...KILLED...SOMEONE! THIS IS TERRIBLE!
NO ONE UNDER HERE. WHEW!
MY TEAMMATES! THOSE DEMON-MEN MAY HAVE GONE FOR THEM.
HURRY!
HEY, TAZ, WHERE YA BEEN? COME ON!
USCITA
LET'S DRINK!!
IS EVERYONE ALL RIGHT?
HEY, HO, WE'RE FINE. A LITTLE DRUNK.
HEY, DID YOU FEEL AN EARTHQUAKE, TAZIO? WE DID!
LUIGI! WHERE IS LUIGI? HE WENT WITH ME TO THE BAGNO.
WHA? HWE..
WE DON'T KNOW. LET'S GO LOOK.
HE'S...HE'S DEAD! O NO, LUIGI IS DEAD!
THOSE DEMON-MEN KILLED HIM TO GET ME— THIS IS ALL MY FAULT!
HIS NECK LOOKS (SOB) B-BROKEN!
ULFO WAS RIGHT?!

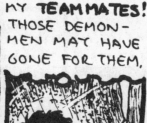

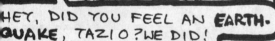

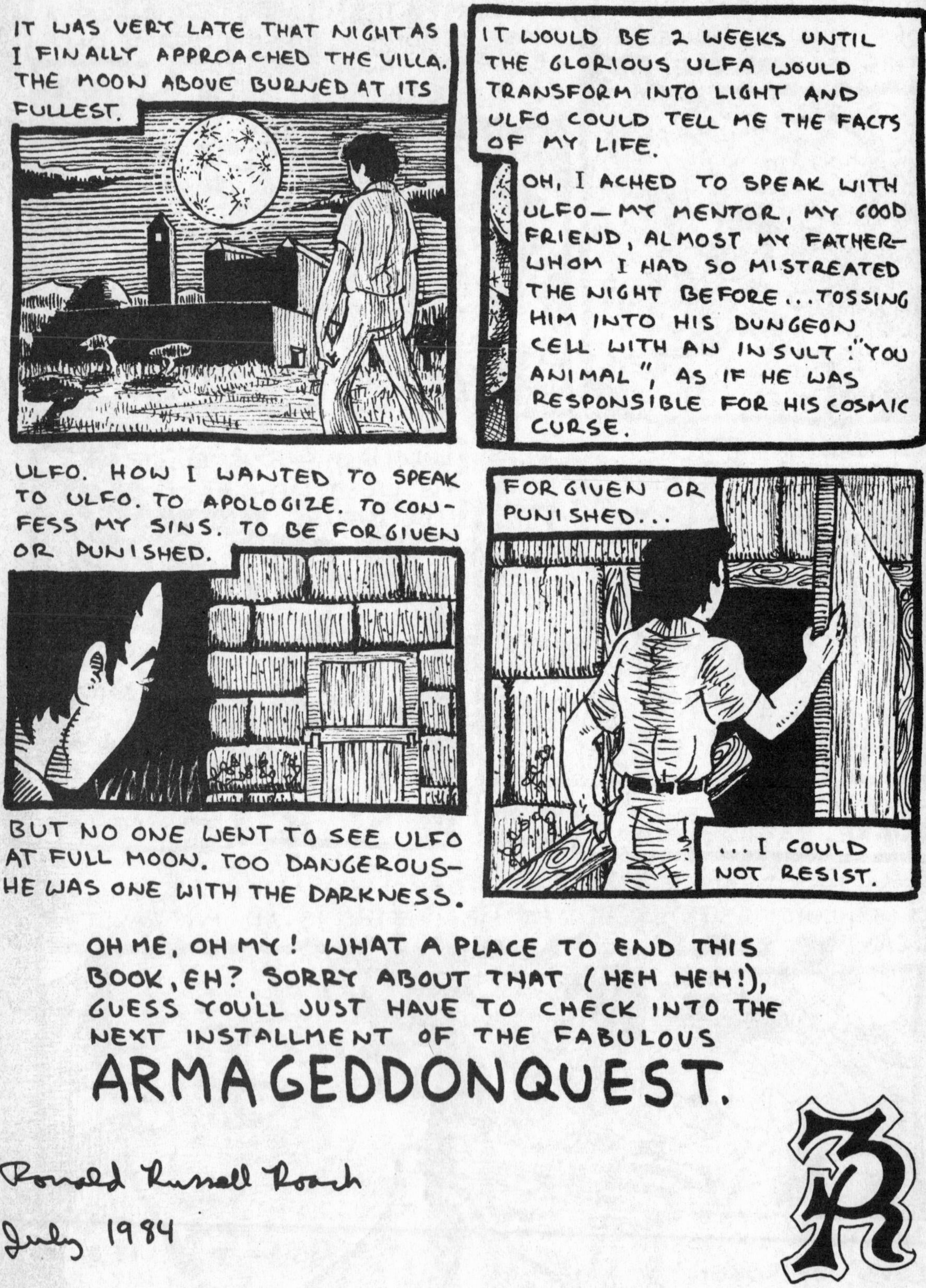
IT WAS VERY LATE THAT NIGHT AS I FINALLY APPROACHED THE VILLA. THE MOON ABOVE BURNED AT ITS FULLEST.
IT WOULD BE 2 WEEKS UNTIL THE GLORIOUS ULFA WOULD TRANSFORM INTO LIGHT AND ULFO COULD TELL ME THE FACTS OF MY LIFE.
OH, I ACHED TO SPEAK WITH ULFO—MY MENTOR, MY GOOD FRIEND, ALMOST MY FATHER—WHOM I HAD SO MISTREATED THE NIGHT BEFORE...TOSSING HIM INTO HIS DUNGEON CELL WITH AN INSULT: "YOU ANIMAL", AS IF HE WAS RESPONSIBLE FOR HIS COSMIC CURSE.
ULFO. HOW I WANTED TO SPEAK TO ULFO. TO APOLOGIZE. TO CONFESS MY SINS. TO BE FORGIVEN OR PUNISHED.
BUT NO ONE WENT TO SEE ULFO AT FULL MOON. TOO DANGEROUS—HE WAS ONE WITH THE DARKNESS.
FORGIVEN OR PUNISHED...
...I COULD NOT RESIST.

OH ME, OH MY! WHAT A PLACE TO END THIS BOOK, EH? SORRY ABOUT THAT (HEH HEH!), GUESS YOU'LL JUST HAVE TO CHECK INTO THE NEXT INSTALLMENT OF THE FABULOUS

# ARMAGEDDONQUEST.

Ronald Russell Roach

July 1984

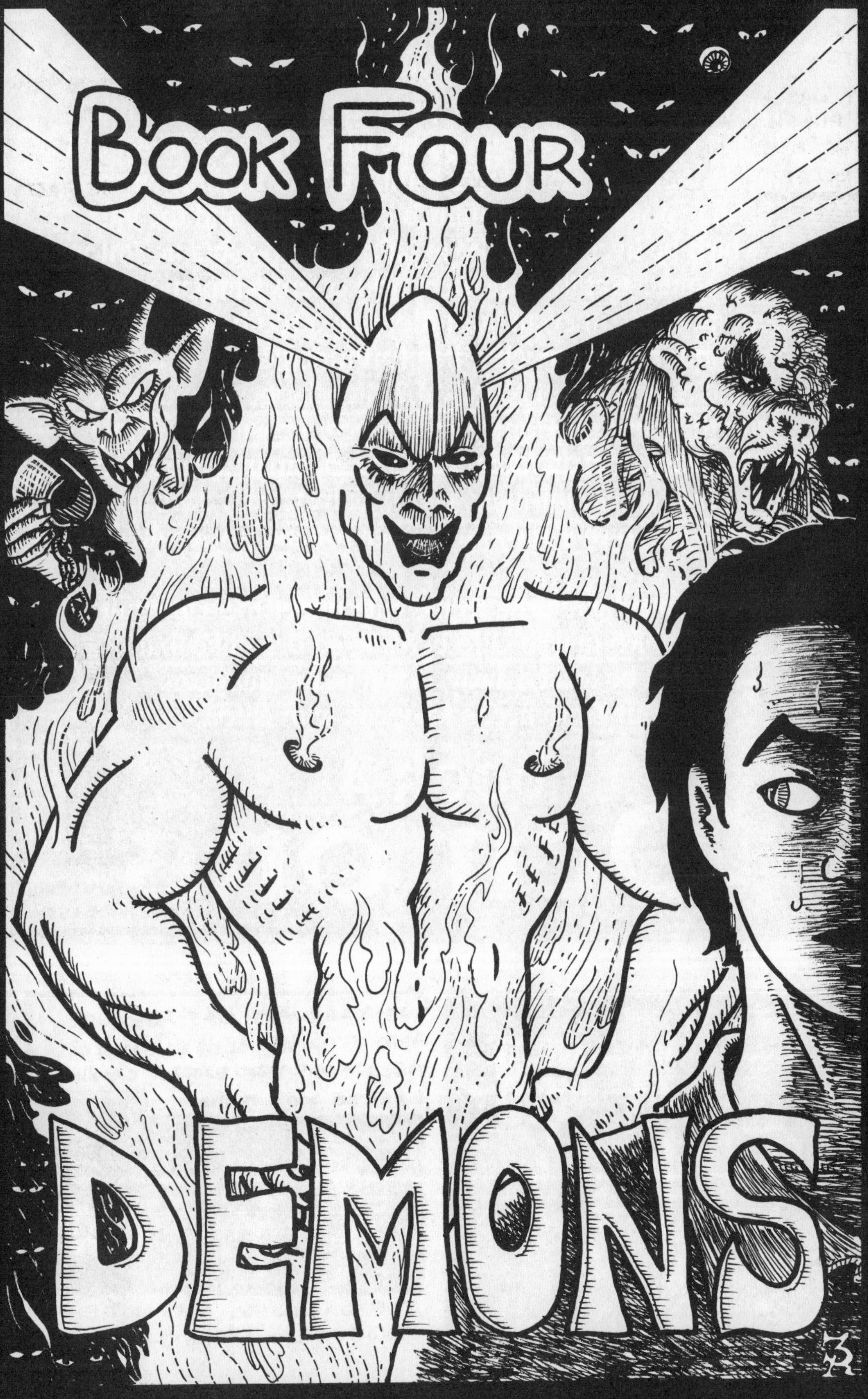
Book Four
DEMONS

At the age of 9, Tazio has attracted much attention as an intellectual and athletic prodigy in the isolated little Italian town of La Destinazione, where he goes to school and is the superstar player on the soccer team. However, he may not leave the confines of the town and the villa in which he lives, where he is safe from the satanic Anton Artemis. But the outside world offers temptations, among them an evening of glory as a football hero in a neighboring town. Ulfo has forbidden Tazio to leave, but in a moment of rebellion Tazio disobeys, and goes with the team to Monteveccio, where he wins the game. Resulting in at attack by Anton's Hellman agents and the death of a team-mate, which activate vast destructive powers which Tazio can neither contain nor control.

In shame, he returns to the villa under the same full moon which makes Ulfo become so beastlike that he must be locked away, down in the dungeon.
But Tazio needs to speak with Ulfo...

# book 4
# Demons

ULFO? IT'S TAZIO.
THE DARKNESS WAS ABSOLUTE. AND IT WAS COLD, EVEN TO ME, WHOM THE EARTH CANNOT FREEZE NOR BURN...
BRRR!!
THE DARKNESS WAS NOT EMPTY, HOWEVER— THERE WAS A SOUND:

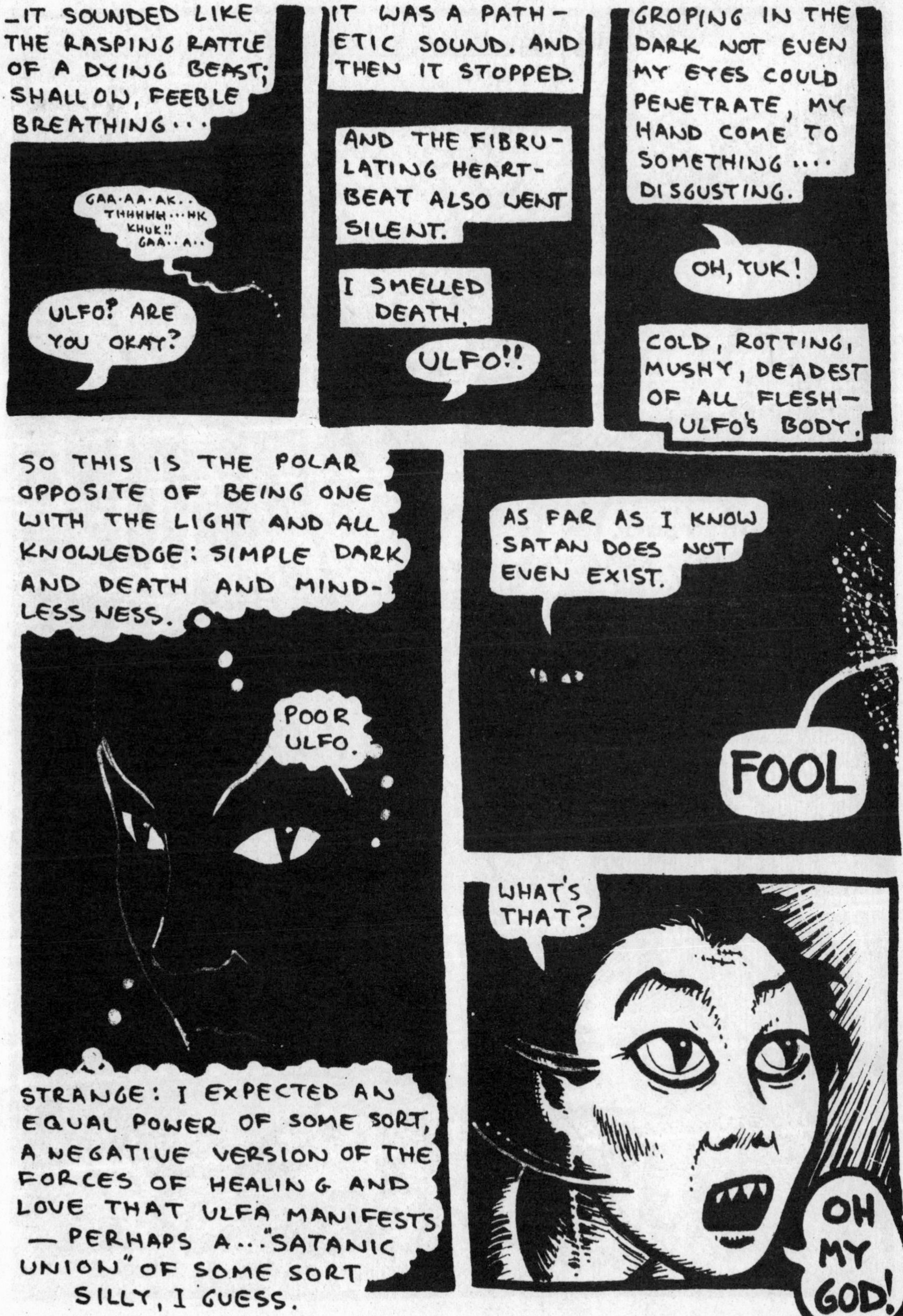
—IT SOUNDED LIKE THE RASPING RATTLE OF A DYING BEAST; SHALLOW, FEEBLE BREATHING...
GAA·AA·AK.. THHHHH...HK KHUK!! GAA..A..
ULFO? ARE YOU OKAY?
IT WAS A PATHETIC SOUND. AND THEN IT STOPPED.
AND THE FIBRULATING HEARTBEAT ALSO WENT SILENT.
I SMELLED DEATH.
ULFO!!
GROPING IN THE DARK NOT EVEN MY EYES COULD PENETRATE, MY HAND COME TO SOMETHING.... DISGUSTING.
OH, TUK!
COLD, ROTTING, MUSHY, DEADEST OF ALL FLESH— ULFO'S BODY.
SO THIS IS THE POLAR OPPOSITE OF BEING ONE WITH THE LIGHT AND ALL KNOWLEDGE: SIMPLE DARK AND DEATH AND MINDLESSNESS.
POOR ULFO.
STRANGE: I EXPECTED AN EQUAL POWER OF SOME SORT, A NEGATIVE VERSION OF THE FORCES OF HEALING AND LOVE THAT ULFA MANIFESTS —PERHAPS A..."SATANIC UNION" OF SOME SORT SILLY, I GUESS.
AS FAR AS I KNOW SATAN DOES NOT EVEN EXIST.
FOOL
WHAT'S THAT?
OH MY GOD!

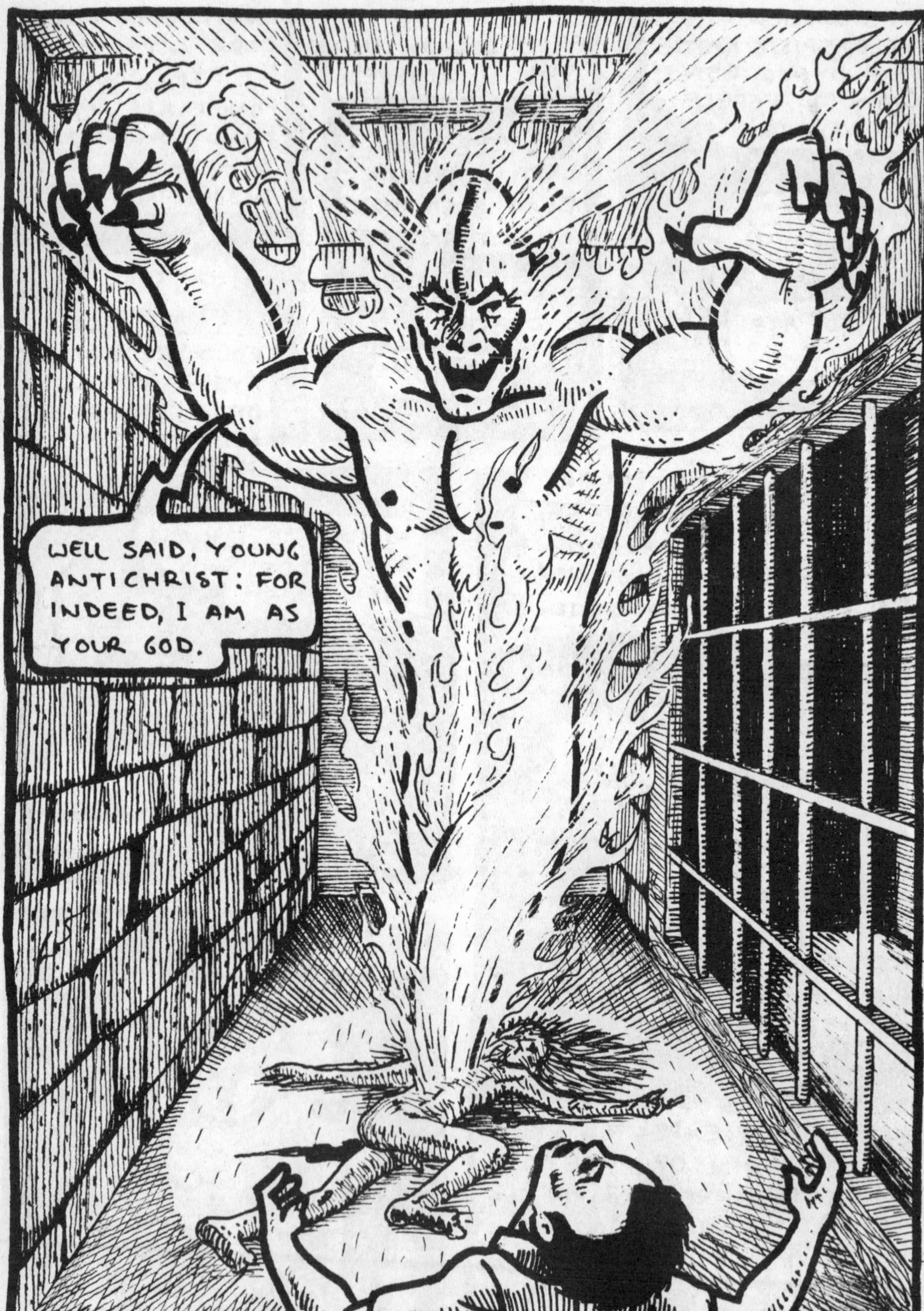
WELL SAID, YOUNG ANTICHRIST: FOR INDEED, I AM AS YOUR GOD.

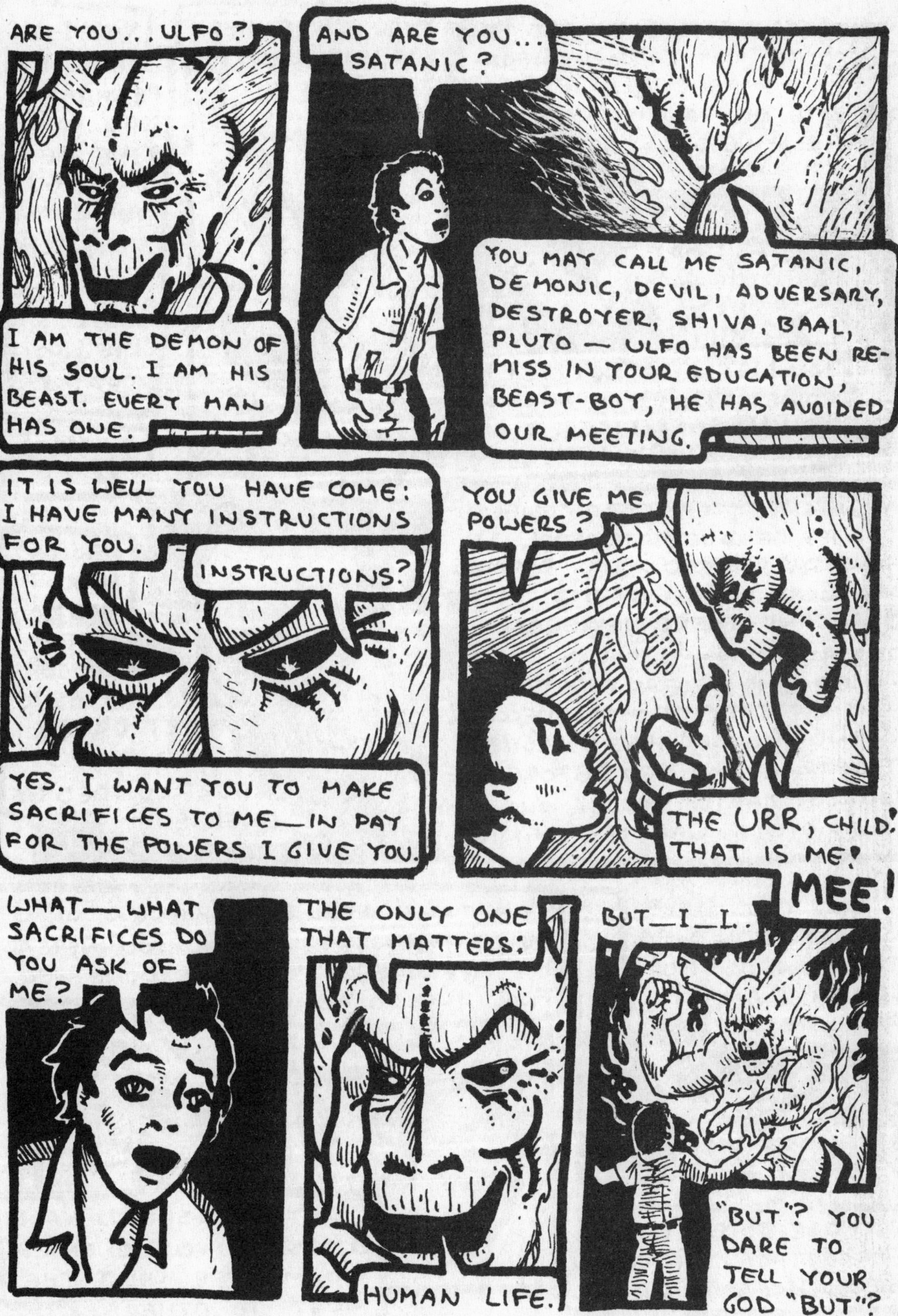
ARE YOU... ULFO?
I AM THE DEMON OF HIS SOUL. I AM HIS BEAST. EVERY MAN HAS ONE.
AND ARE YOU... SATANIC?
YOU MAY CALL ME SATANIC, DEMONIC, DEVIL, ADVERSARY, DESTROYER, SHIVA, BAAL, PLUTO — ULFO HAS BEEN REMISS IN YOUR EDUCATION, BEAST-BOY, HE HAS AVOIDED OUR MEETING.
IT IS WELL YOU HAVE COME: I HAVE MANY INSTRUCTIONS FOR YOU.
INSTRUCTIONS?
YES. I WANT YOU TO MAKE SACRIFICES TO ME—IN PAY FOR THE POWERS I GIVE YOU.
YOU GIVE ME POWERS?
THE URR, CHILD! THAT IS ME! MEE!
WHAT—WHAT SACRIFICES DO YOU ASK OF ME?
THE ONLY ONE THAT MATTERS:
HUMAN LIFE.
BUT_I_I..
"BUT"? YOU DARE TO TELL YOUR GOD "BUT"?

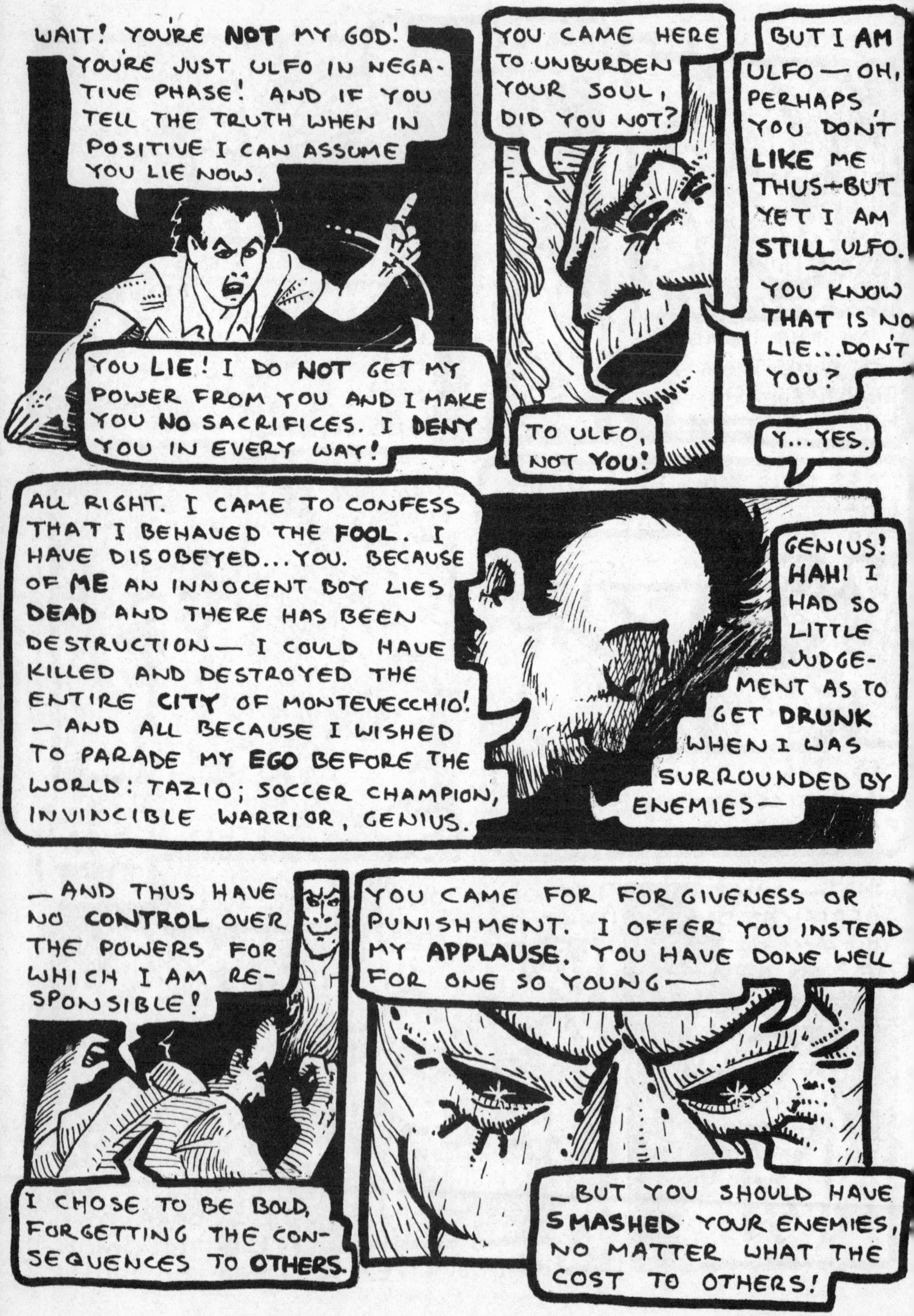
WAIT! YOU'RE NOT MY GOD! YOU'RE JUST ULFO IN NEGATIVE PHASE! AND IF YOU TELL THE TRUTH WHEN IN POSITIVE I CAN ASSUME YOU LIE NOW.
YOU LIE! I DO NOT GET MY POWER FROM YOU AND I MAKE YOU NO SACRIFICES. I DENY YOU IN EVERY WAY!
YOU CAME HERE TO UNBURDEN YOUR SOUL, DID YOU NOT?
TO ULFO, NOT YOU!
BUT I AM ULFO — OH, PERHAPS, YOU DON'T LIKE ME THUS — BUT YET I AM STILL ULFO.
YOU KNOW THAT IS NO LIE... DON'T YOU?
Y... YES.
ALL RIGHT. I CAME TO CONFESS THAT I BEHAVED THE FOOL. I HAVE DISOBEYED... YOU. BECAUSE OF ME AN INNOCENT BOY LIES DEAD AND THERE HAS BEEN DESTRUCTION — I COULD HAVE KILLED AND DESTROYED THE ENTIRE CITY OF MONTEVECCHIO! — AND ALL BECAUSE I WISHED TO PARADE MY EGO BEFORE THE WORLD: TAZIO; SOCCER CHAMPION, INVINCIBLE WARRIOR, GENIUS.
GENIUS! HAH! I HAD SO LITTLE JUDGEMENT AS TO GET DRUNK WHEN I WAS SURROUNDED BY ENEMIES —
— AND THUS HAVE NO CONTROL OVER THE POWERS FOR WHICH I AM RESPONSIBLE!
I CHOSE TO BE BOLD, FORGETTING THE CONSEQUENCES TO OTHERS.
YOU CAME FOR FORGIVENESS OR PUNISHMENT. I OFFER YOU INSTEAD MY APPLAUSE. YOU HAVE DONE WELL FOR ONE SO YOUNG —
— BUT YOU SHOULD HAVE SMASHED YOUR ENEMIES, NO MATTER WHAT THE COST TO OTHERS!

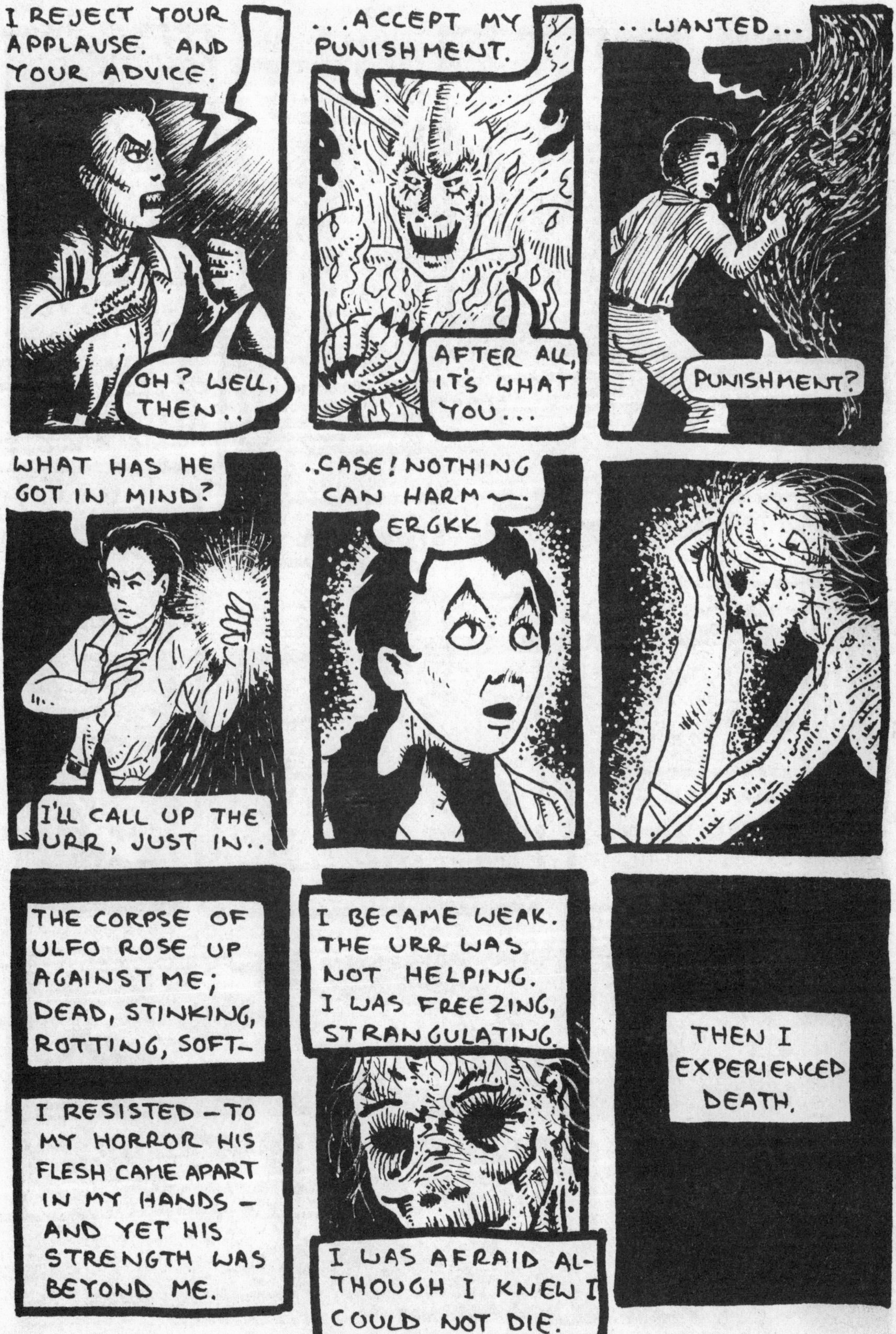

I REJECT YOUR APPLAUSE. AND YOUR ADVICE.
OH? WELL, THEN..
...ACCEPT MY PUNISHMENT.
AFTER ALL, IT'S WHAT YOU...
...WANTED...
PUNISHMENT?
WHAT HAS HE GOT IN MIND?
I'LL CALL UP THE URR, JUST IN..
..CASE! NOTHING CAN HARM~. ERGKK
THE CORPSE OF ULFO ROSE UP AGAINST ME; DEAD, STINKING, ROTTING, SOFT–
I RESISTED – TO MY HORROR HIS FLESH CAME APART IN MY HANDS – AND YET HIS STRENGTH WAS BEYOND ME.
I BECAME WEAK. THE URR WAS NOT HELPING. I WAS FREEZING, STRANGULATING.
I WAS AFRAID ALTHOUGH I KNEW I COULD NOT DIE.
THEN I EXPERIENCED DEATH.

I DISCORPORATED—

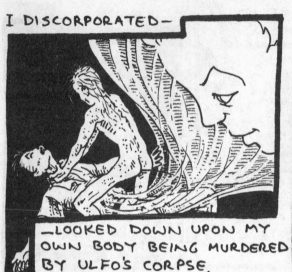

—LOOKED DOWN UPON MY OWN BODY BEING MURDERED BY ULFO'S CORPSE.

THEN I SAW A LIGHT ABOVE—

OH, HOW LOVELY!

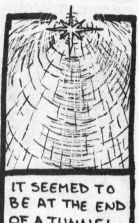

IT SEEMED TO BE AT THE END OF A TUNNEL OF ENERGY— WONDEROUS MUSIC RANG.

I FORGOT ABOUT MY BODY— IT DIDN'T MATTER ANY MORE,

I ONLY WANTED TO ASCEND THE TUNNEL TO THE BEAUTIFUL LIGHT!

BUT A GENTLE COSMIC VOICE SPOKE FROM THE LIGHT:

I AM SORRY, TAZIO, THIS IS NOT YOUR DESTINY.

AND I FELL

INTO DARKNESS →

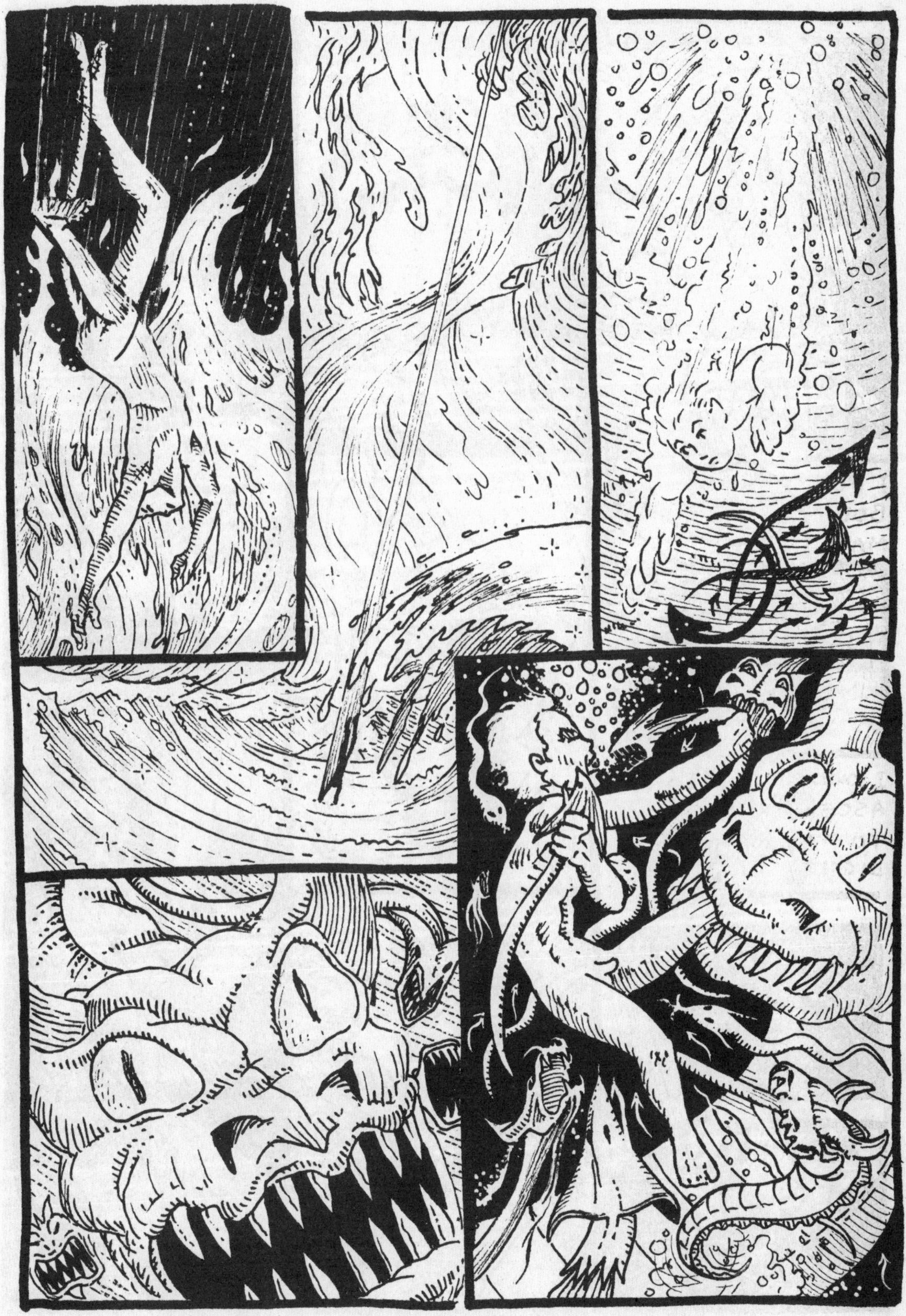

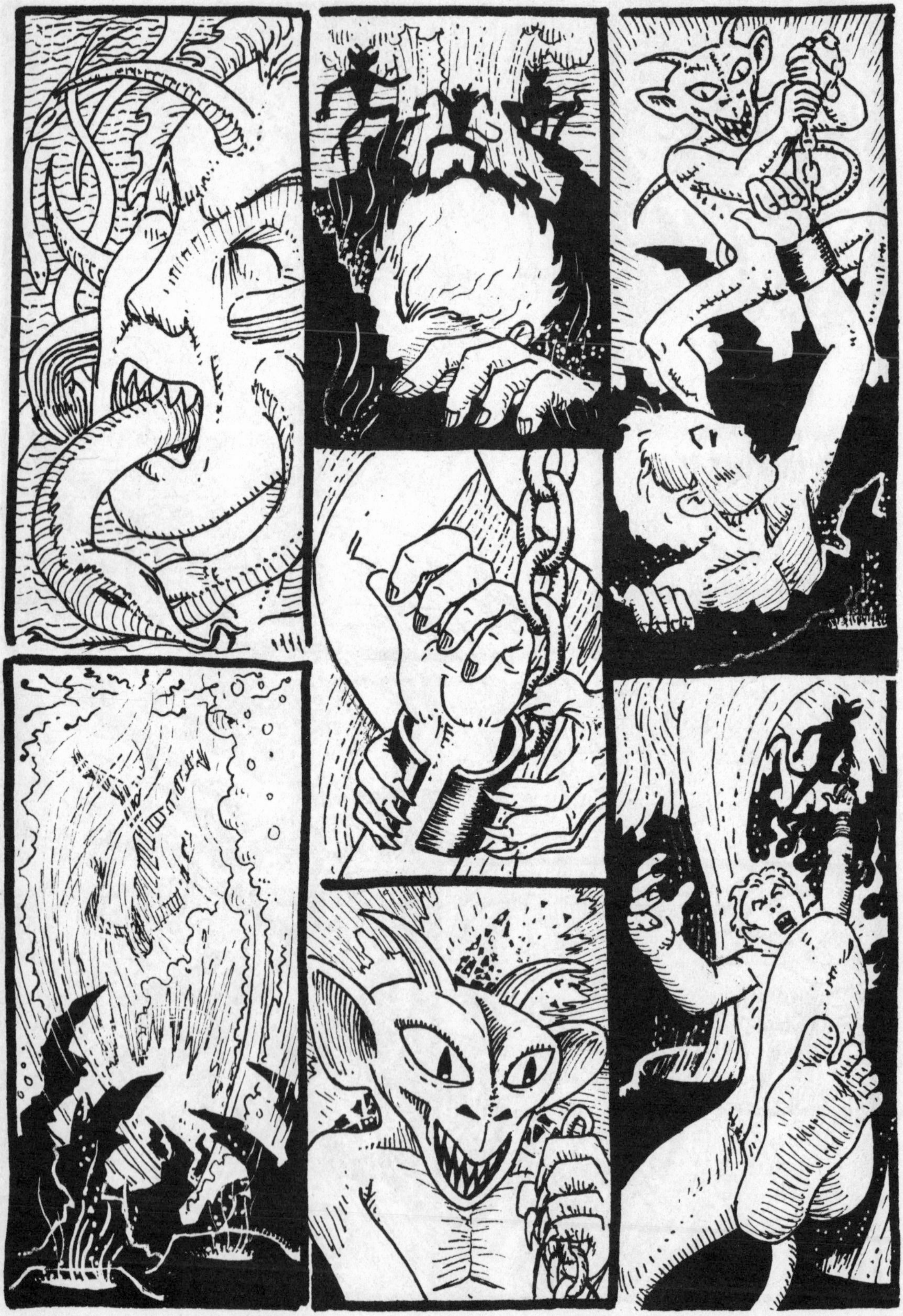

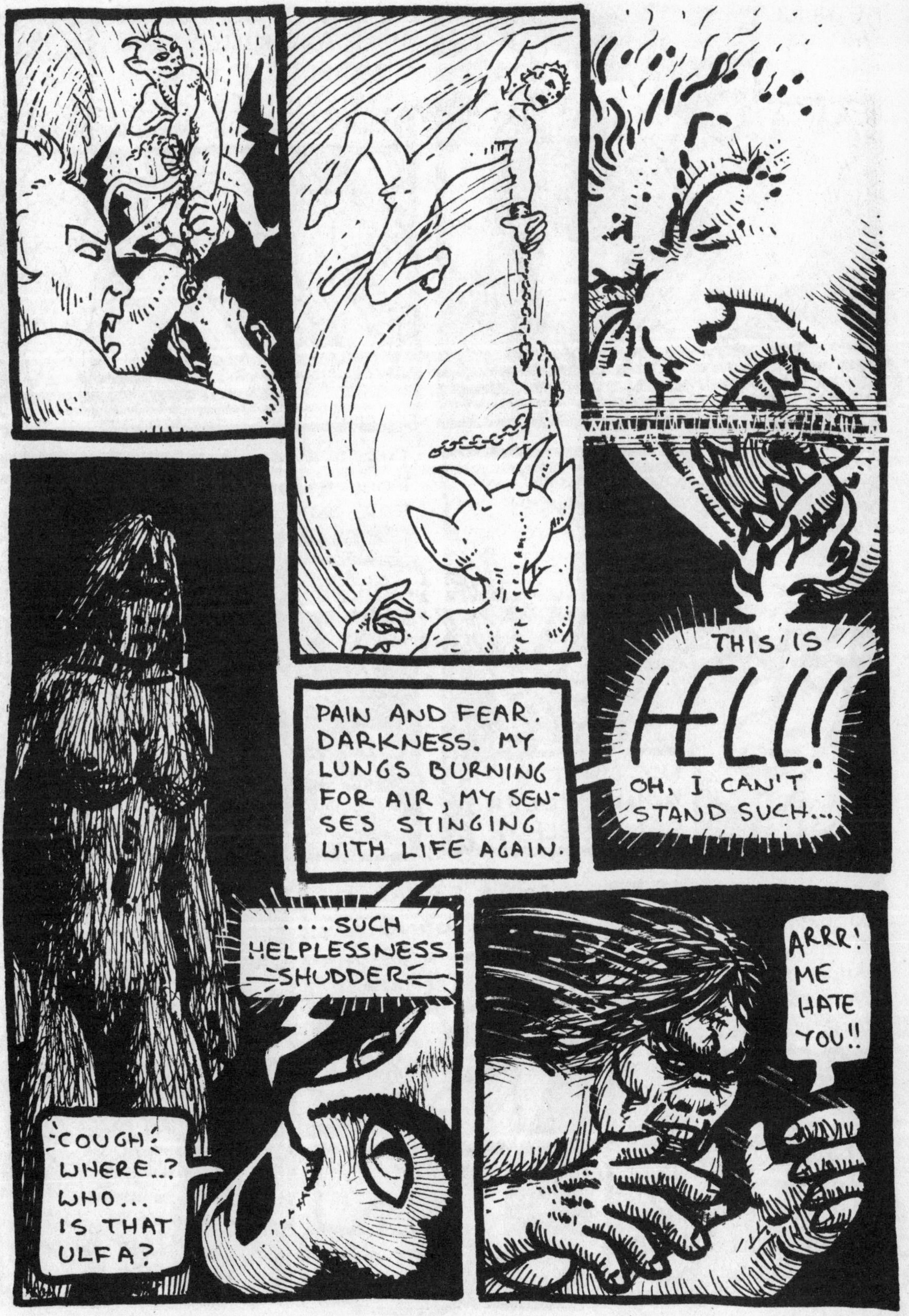

THIS IS HELL! OH, I CAN'T STAND SUCH...
PAIN AND FEAR. DARKNESS. MY LUNGS BURNING FOR AIR, MY SENSES STINGING WITH LIFE AGAIN.
....SUCH HELPLESSNESS
SHUDDER
COUGH
WHERE..? WHO... IS THAT ULFA?
ARRR! ME HATE YOU!!

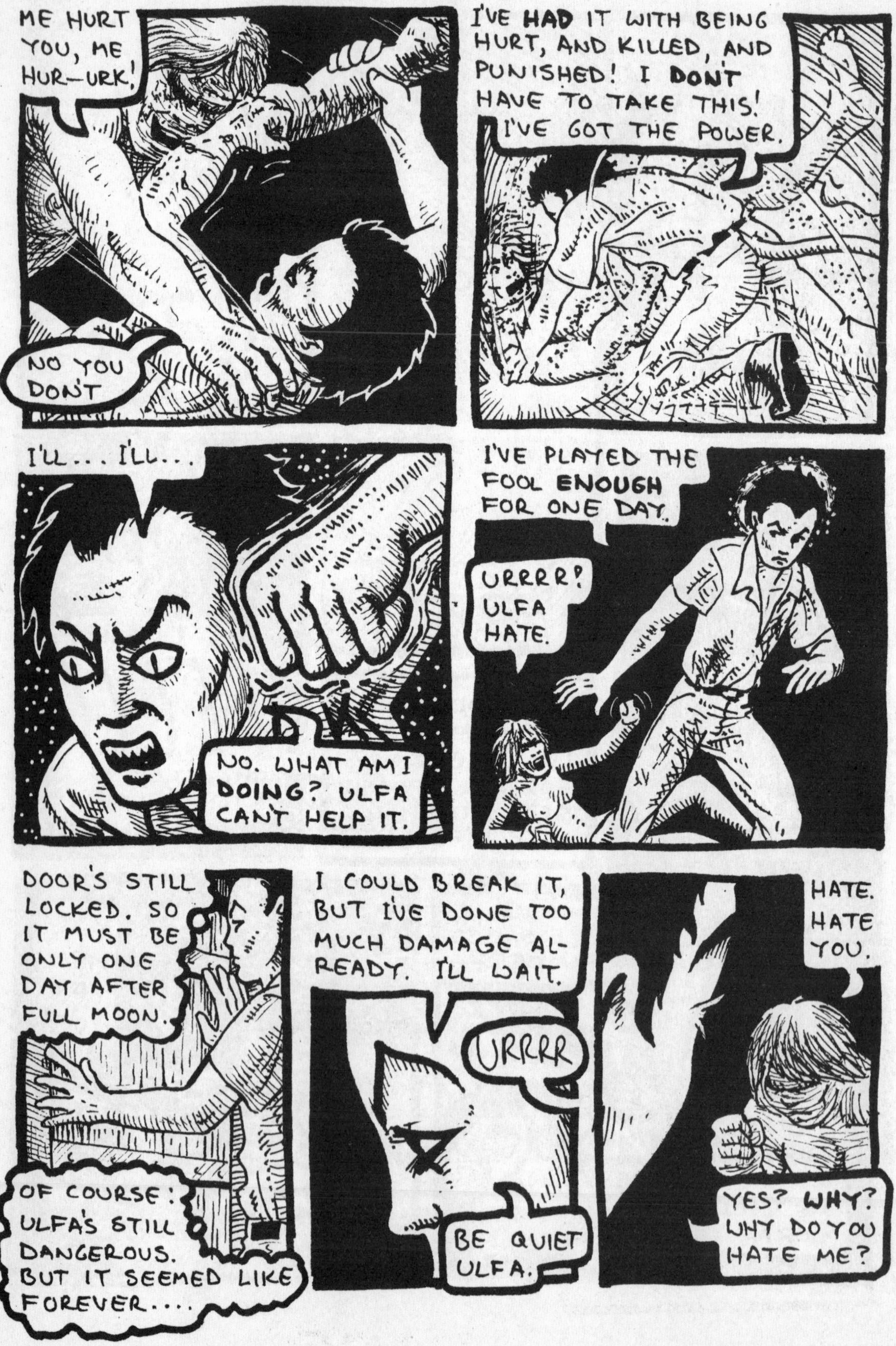
ME HURT YOU, ME HUR-URK!
NO YOU DON'T
I'VE HAD IT WITH BEING HURT, AND KILLED, AND PUNISHED! I DON'T HAVE TO TAKE THIS!
I'VE GOT THE POWER.
I'LL... I'LL...
NO. WHAT AM I DOING? ULFA CAN'T HELP IT.
I'VE PLAYED THE FOOL ENOUGH FOR ONE DAY.
URRRR! ULFA HATE.
DOOR'S STILL LOCKED. SO IT MUST BE ONLY ONE DAY AFTER FULL MOON.
OF COURSE: ULFA'S STILL DANGEROUS. BUT IT SEEMED LIKE FOREVER....
I COULD BREAK IT, BUT I'VE DONE TOO MUCH DAMAGE AL-READY. I'LL WAIT.
URRRR
BE QUIET ULFA.
HATE. HATE YOU.
YES? WHY? WHY DO YOU HATE ME?

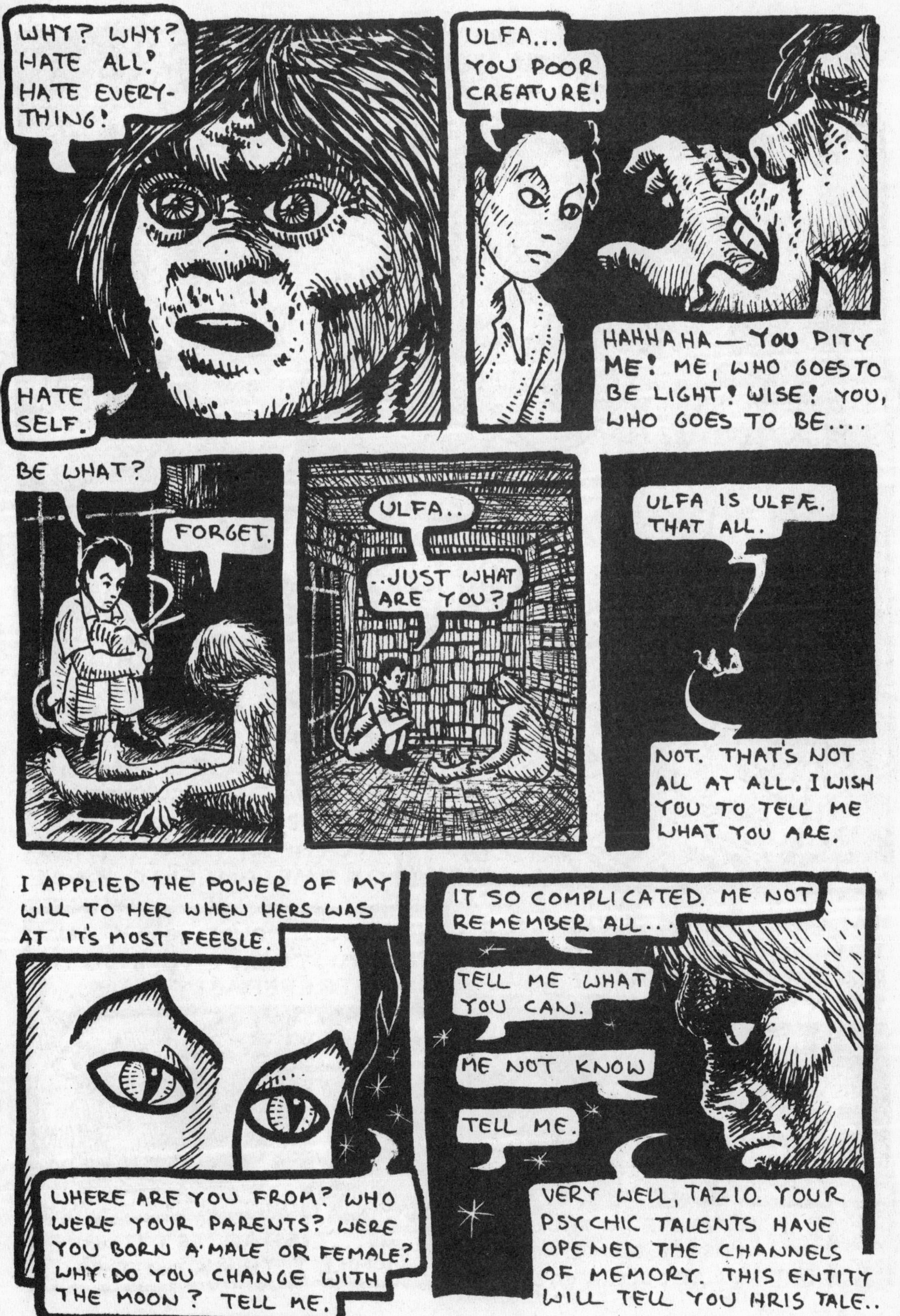
WHY? WHY? HATE ALL! HATE EVERY-THING!
HATE SELF.
ULFA... YOU POOR CREATURE!
HAHHAHA—YOU PITY ME! ME, WHO GOES TO BE LIGHT! WISE! YOU, WHO GOES TO BE....
BE WHAT?
FORGET.
ULFA..
..JUST WHAT ARE YOU?
ULFA IS ULFÆ. THAT ALL.
NOT. THAT'S NOT ALL AT ALL. I WISH YOU TO TELL ME WHAT YOU ARE.
I APPLIED THE POWER OF MY WILL TO HER WHEN HERS WAS AT IT'S MOST FEEBLE.
WHERE ARE YOU FROM? WHO WERE YOUR PARENTS? WERE YOU BORN A MALE OR FEMALE? WHY DO YOU CHANGE WITH THE MOON? TELL ME.
IT SO COMPLICATED. ME NOT REMEMBER ALL...
TELL ME WHAT YOU CAN.
ME NOT KNOW
TELL ME.
VERY WELL, TAZIO. YOUR PSYCHIC TALENTS HAVE OPENED THE CHANNELS OF MEMORY. THIS ENTITY WILL TELL YOU HRIS TALE..

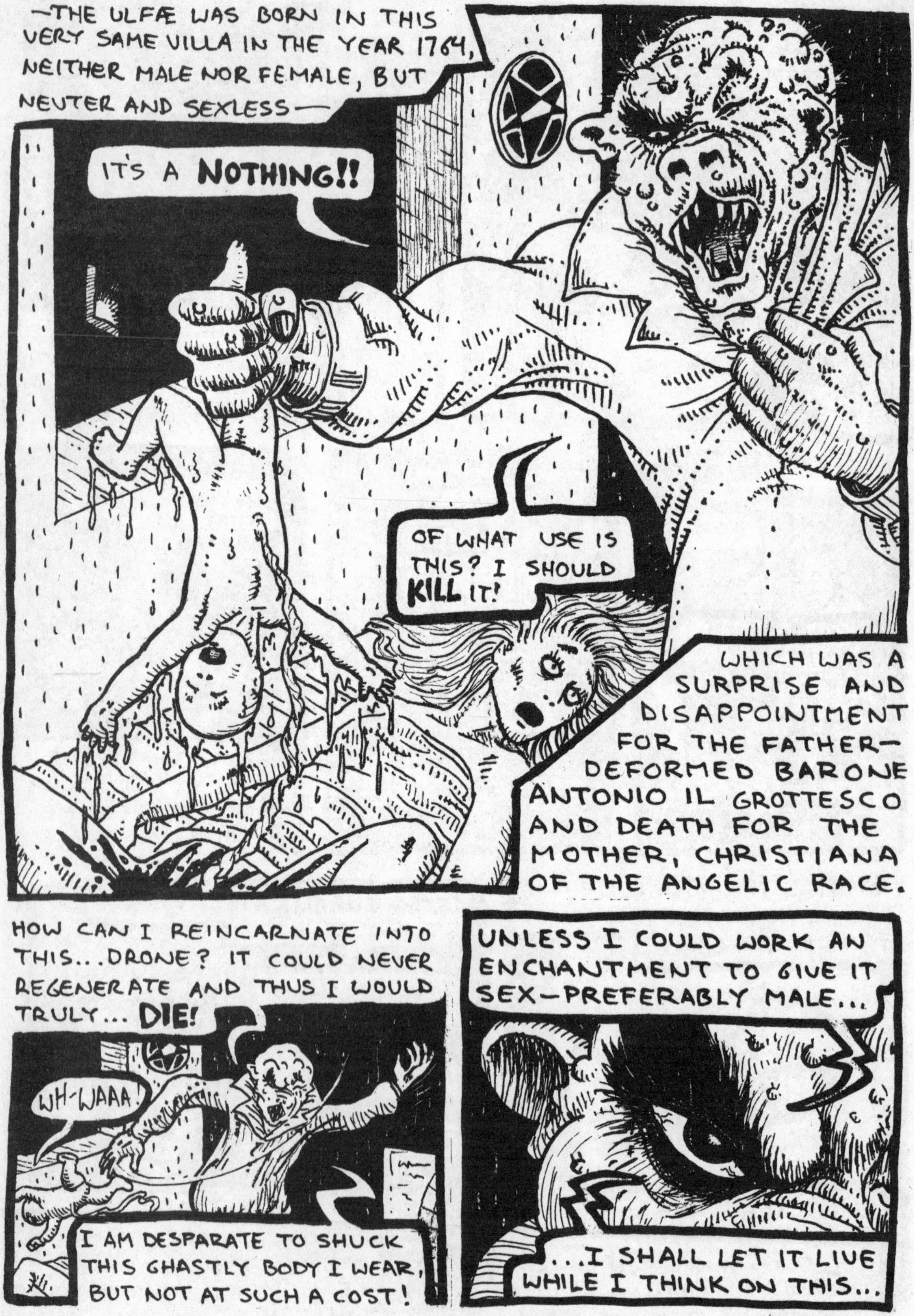
—THE ULFÆ WAS BORN IN THIS VERY SAME VILLA IN THE YEAR 1764, NEITHER MALE NOR FEMALE, BUT NEUTER AND SEXLESS—
IT'S A NOTHING!!
OF WHAT USE IS THIS? I SHOULD KILL IT!
WHICH WAS A SURPRISE AND DISAPPOINTMENT FOR THE FATHER— DEFORMED BARONE ANTONIO IL GROTTESCO AND DEATH FOR THE MOTHER, CHRISTIANA OF THE ANGELIC RACE.
HOW CAN I REINCARNATE INTO THIS...DRONE? IT COULD NEVER REGENERATE AND THUS I WOULD TRULY... DIE!
WH-WAAA!
I AM DESPARATE TO SHUCK THIS GHASTLY BODY I WEAR, BUT NOT AT SUCH A COST!
UNLESS I COULD WORK AN ENCHANTMENT TO GIVE IT SEX—PREFERABLY MALE...
...I SHALL LET IT LIVE WHILE I THINK ON THIS...

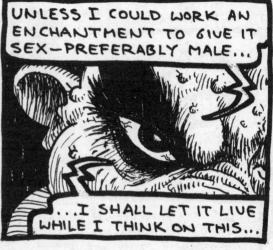

IL GROTEZCO CONSULTED WITH THE HEAD —

AHHYESS — THE-ULFÆ-ISS-OF-PRIME-IMPORTANCE-TO-THE-SATANIC-PLAN. —YOU-MUST-NOT-DESTROY-IT.

AHNDHHYESS— IT-CAN-BE-MADE-**FEMALE** — A-LUNAR-SPELL…. HYESS… BUT-THE-ASTROLOGICAL-CONDITIONSS-MUSST-BE-SSPECIFIC—

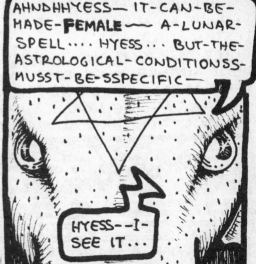

HYESS--I SEE IT…

…A-SATANIC-POWER-MASS— FULL-MOON-OCTOBER… IN-THE-YEAR…. 1800.

**36 YEARS!** I MUST ENDURE THIS BODY FOR 36 MORE YEARS? TOO LONG!!

I SHALL GO EVEN MORE **MAD** THAN I AM NOW!!

HHYESSS—YOU-SHALL.

THIS ENTITY WAS ALLOWED TO SURVIVE, BUT NOT WITHIN SIGHT OF THE IMPATIENT BARONE GROTTESCO. ULFÆ WAS PUT INTO A FARM HOME NEAR LA DESTINAZIONE, WHERE HESH GREW INTO A MOST SUPERIOR BEING, PHYSICALLY AND MENTALLY. —HIS FOSTER PARENTS, SERFS OF THE BARON, LOVED THE STRANGE CHILD WHO SEEMED LIKE A BOY FOR HIS STRENGTH AND AGILITY, AND A GIRL FOR HER SWEETNESS AND GRACE.

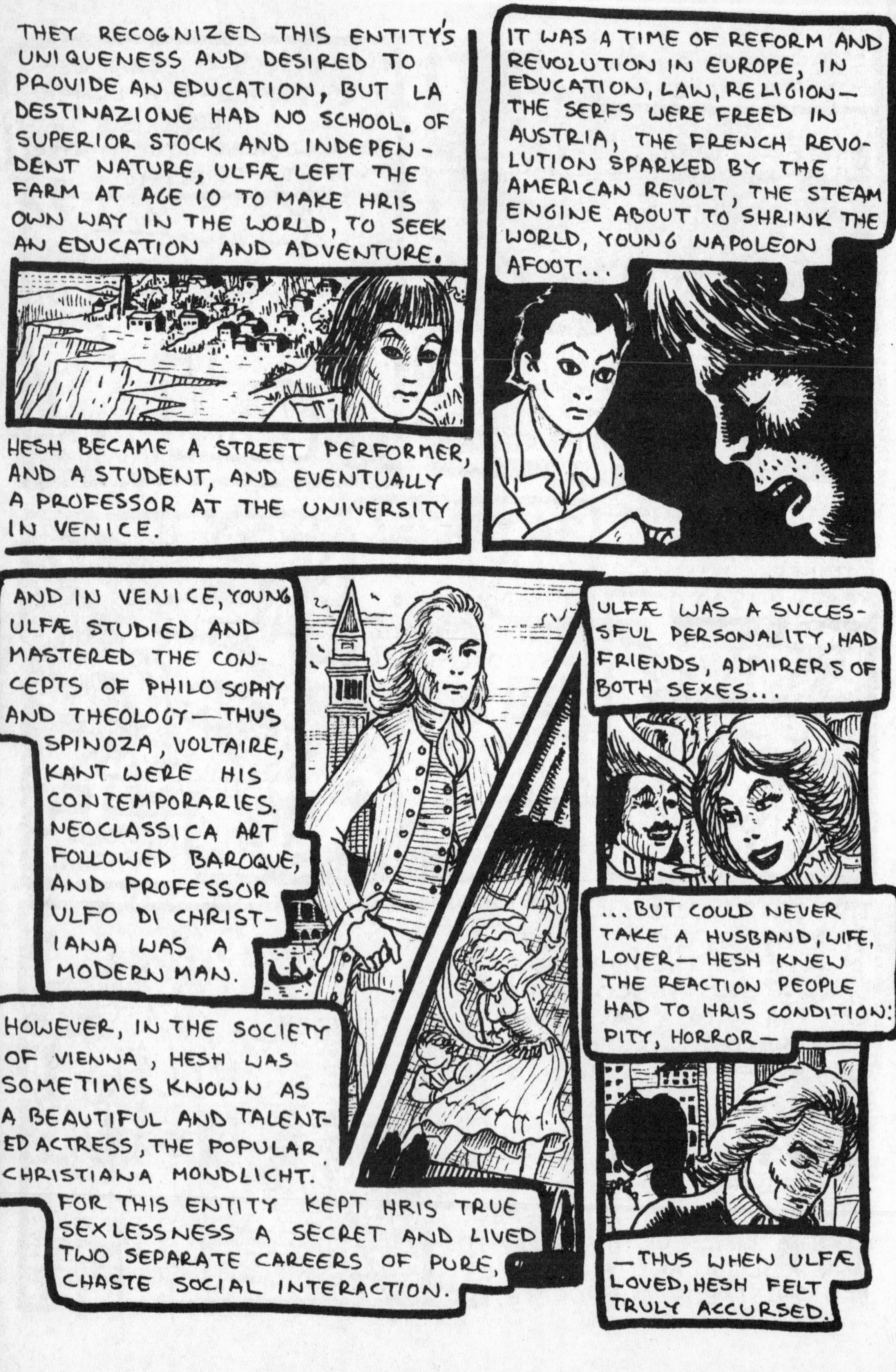
THEY RECOGNIZED THIS ENTITY'S UNIQUENESS AND DESIRED TO PROVIDE AN EDUCATION, BUT LA DESTINAZIONE HAD NO SCHOOL. OF SUPERIOR STOCK AND INDEPENDENT NATURE, ULFÆ LEFT THE FARM AT AGE 10 TO MAKE HRIS OWN WAY IN THE WORLD, TO SEEK AN EDUCATION AND ADVENTURE.
HESH BECAME A STREET PERFORMER, AND A STUDENT, AND EVENTUALLY A PROFESSOR AT THE UNIVERSITY IN VENICE.
IT WAS A TIME OF REFORM AND REVOLUTION IN EUROPE, IN EDUCATION, LAW, RELIGION— THE SERFS WERE FREED IN AUSTRIA, THE FRENCH REVOLUTION SPARKED BY THE AMERICAN REVOLT, THE STEAM ENGINE ABOUT TO SHRINK THE WORLD, YOUNG NAPOLEON AFOOT...
AND IN VENICE, YOUNG ULFÆ STUDIED AND MASTERED THE CONCEPTS OF PHILOSOPHY AND THEOLOGY—THUS SPINOZA, VOLTAIRE, KANT WERE HIS CONTEMPORARIES. NEOCLASSICA ART FOLLOWED BAROQUE, AND PROFESSOR ULFO DI CHRISTIANA WAS A MODERN MAN.
HOWEVER, IN THE SOCIETY OF VIENNA, HESH WAS SOMETIMES KNOWN AS A BEAUTIFUL AND TALENTED ACTRESS, THE POPULAR CHRISTIANA MONDLICHT.
FOR THIS ENTITY KEPT HRIS TRUE SEXLESSNESS A SECRET AND LIVED TWO SEPARATE CAREERS OF PURE, CHASTE SOCIAL INTERACTION.
ULFÆ WAS A SUCCESSFUL PERSONALITY, HAD FRIENDS, ADMIRERS OF BOTH SEXES...
...BUT COULD NEVER TAKE A HUSBAND, WIFE, LOVER— HESH KNEW THE REACTION PEOPLE HAD TO HRIS CONDITION: PITY, HORROR—
—THUS WHEN ULFÆ LOVED, HESH FELT TRULY ACCURSED.

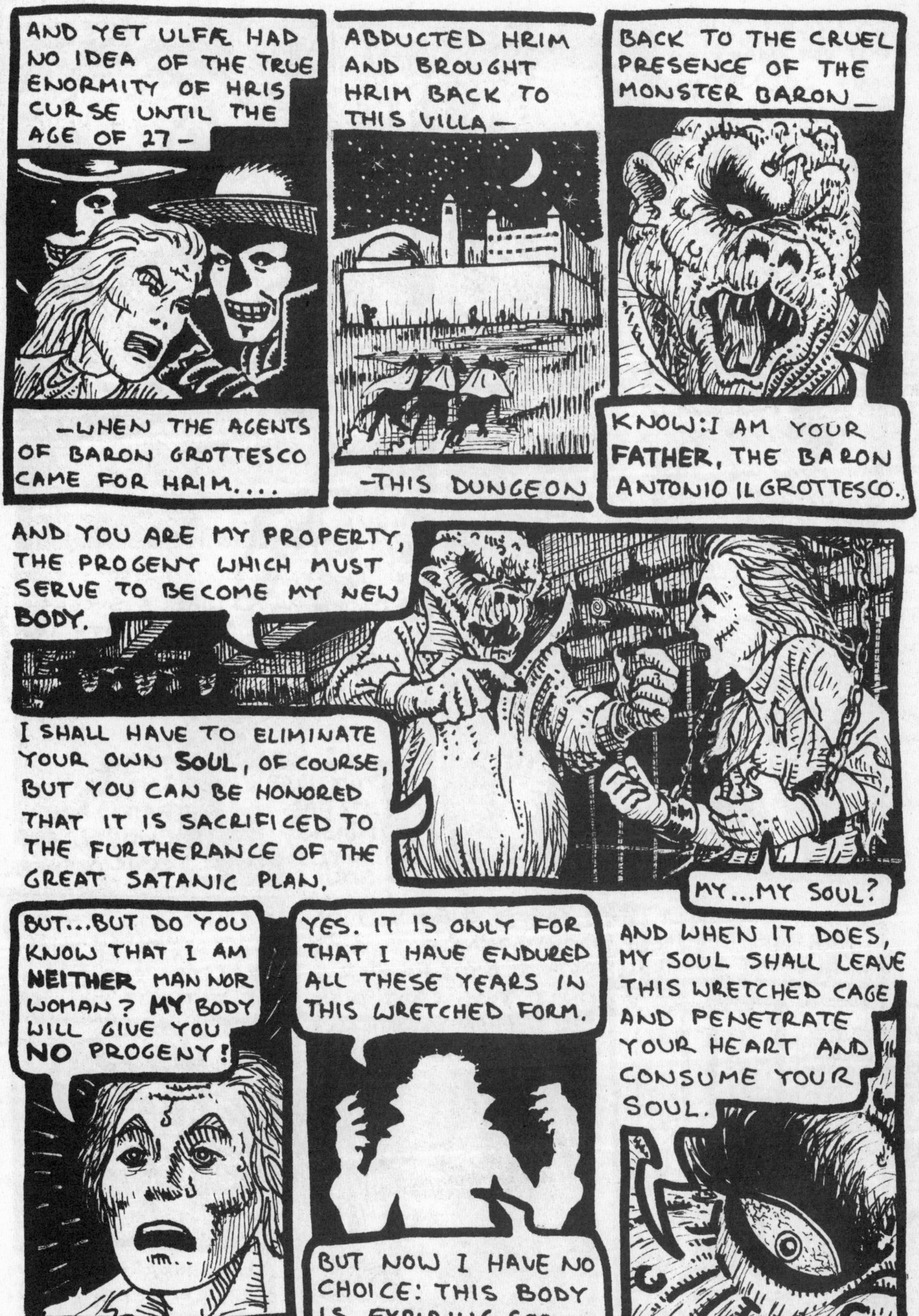
AND YET ULFÆ HAD NO IDEA OF THE TRUE ENORMITY OF HRIS CURSE UNTIL THE AGE OF 27-
-WHEN THE AGENTS OF BARON GROTTESCO CAME FOR HRIM....
ABDUCTED HRIM AND BROUGHT HRIM BACK TO THIS VILLA-
-THIS DUNGEON
BACK TO THE CRUEL PRESENCE OF THE MONSTER BARON_
KNOW: I AM YOUR FATHER, THE BARON ANTONIO IL GROTTESCO.
AND YOU ARE MY PROPERTY, THE PROGENY WHICH MUST SERVE TO BECOME MY NEW BODY.
I SHALL HAVE TO ELIMINATE YOUR OWN SOUL, OF COURSE, BUT YOU CAN BE HONORED THAT IT IS SACRIFICED TO THE FURTHERANCE OF THE GREAT SATANIC PLAN.
MY...MY SOUL?
BUT...BUT DO YOU KNOW THAT I AM NEITHER MAN NOR WOMAN? MY BODY WILL GIVE YOU NO PROGENY!
YES. IT IS ONLY FOR THAT I HAVE ENDURED ALL THESE YEARS IN THIS WRETCHED FORM.
BUT NOW I HAVE NO CHOICE: THIS BODY IS EXPIRING SOON.
AND WHEN IT DOES, MY SOUL SHALL LEAVE THIS WRETCHED CAGE AND PENETRATE YOUR HEART AND CONSUME YOUR SOUL.

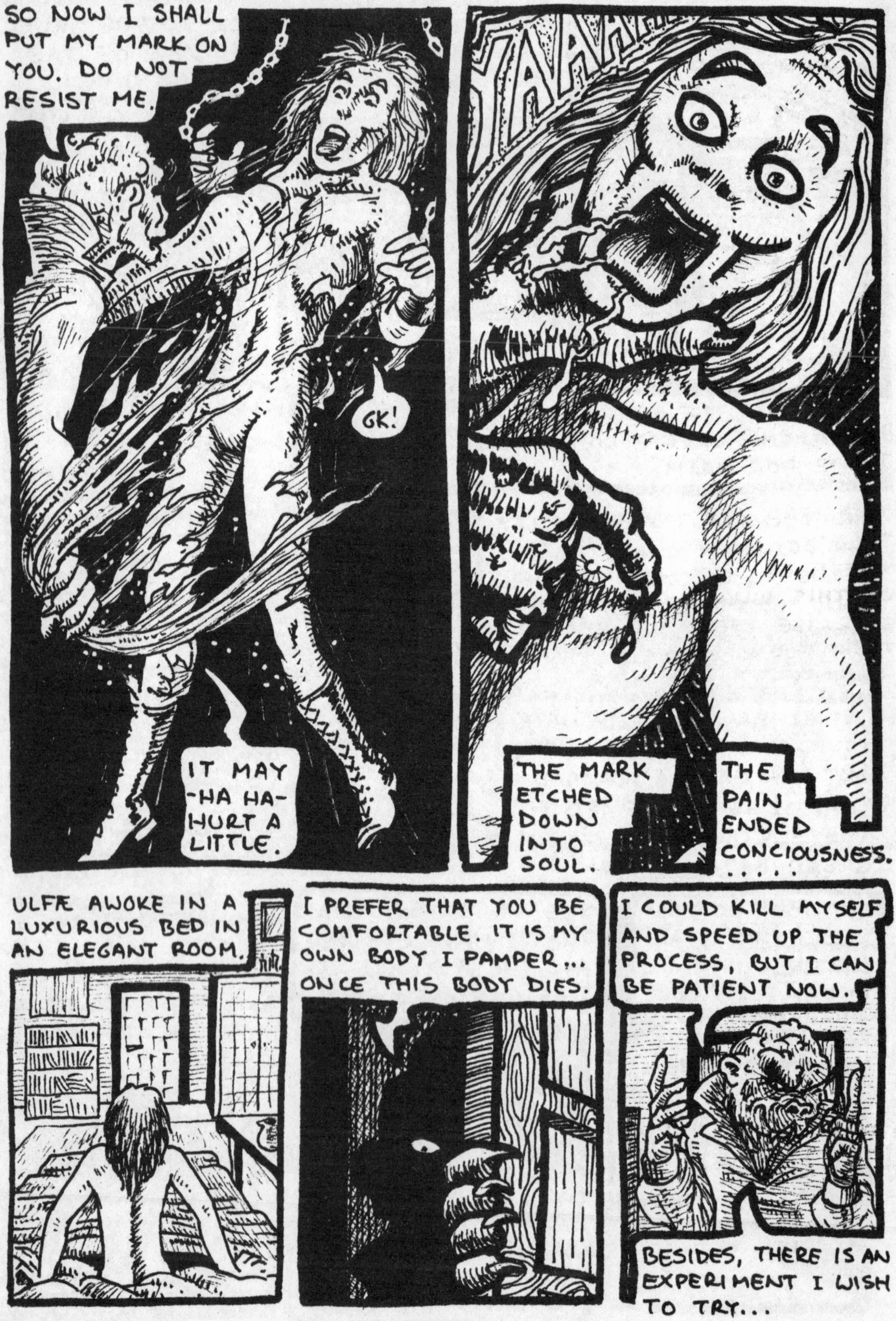
SO NOW I SHALL PUT MY MARK ON YOU. DO NOT RESIST ME.
GK!
IT MAY -HA HA- HURT A LITTLE.
THE MARK ETCHED DOWN INTO SOUL.
THE PAIN ENDED CONCIOUSNESS. . . . .
ULFÆ AWOKE IN A LUXURIOUS BED IN AN ELEGANT ROOM.
I PREFER THAT YOU BE COMFORTABLE. IT IS MY OWN BODY I PAMPER... ONCE THIS BODY DIES.
I COULD KILL MYSELF AND SPEED UP THE PROCESS, BUT I CAN BE PATIENT NOW.
BESIDES, THERE IS AN EXPERIMENT I WISH TO TRY...

...TO GIVE YOUR BODY SEX. I SHALL MAKE YOU BECOME A MAN.

CAN...CAN THAT BE DONE?

HAHH. ANYTHING CAN BE DONE, EVENTUALLY.

NOW LISTEN: YOU HAVE MY MARK. IT WILL DO YOU NO GOOD TO ESCAPE, FOR WHEREVER YOU ARE THERE WILL I BE AS WELL. THE INSTANT I QUIT THIS FLESH.

AND THE ONLY WAY YOU CAN THWART MY PLAN NOW IS TO KILL YOUR OWN SELF— AND THE HEAD HAS ASSURED ME THAT YOU WILL NOT. SO: YOU ARE FREE WITHIN THE WALLS OF THIS VILLA. I WISH YOU TO EXERCISE, KEEP YOUR BODY IN TUNE FOR ME, PLEASE.

ULFÆ WAS AS A GUEST. HESH EXPLORED—

IN THOSE DAYS THE VILLA WAS QUITE ACTIVE.

THE SERFS MAY HAVE BEEN FREED IN AUSTRIA, BUT NOT HERE—

_THIS BARON WAS A CRUEL DESPOT.

WOMEN WERE BROUGHT IN DAILY TO BE VICTIMS OF THE GROTESQUE ANTONIO.

HE ENJOYED RAPE.

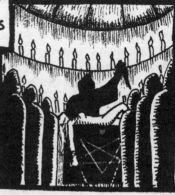

AND EVERY MIDNIGHT THE DARK TEMPLARS HELD THEIR SATANIC MASS IN THE CITADEL.

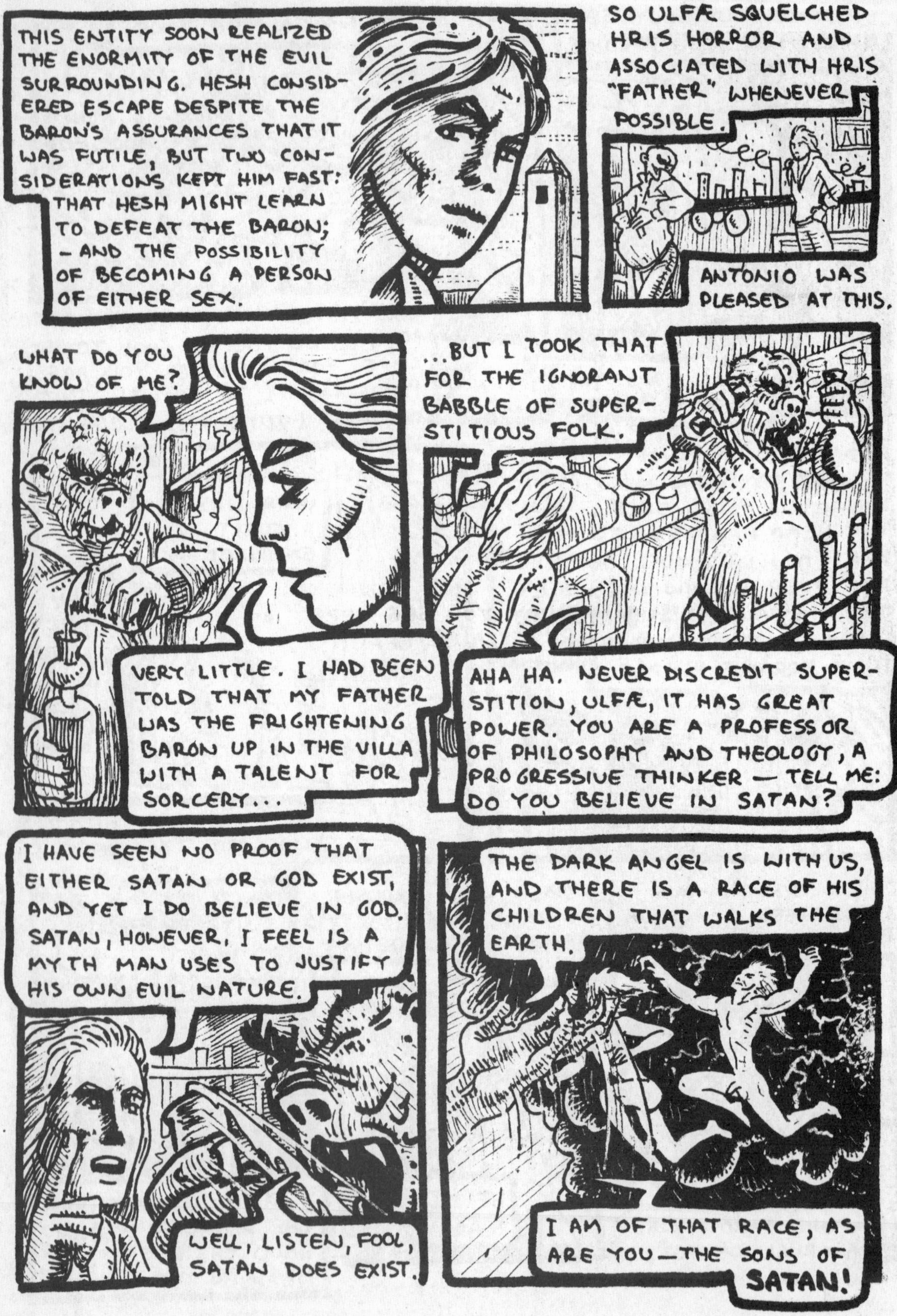
THIS ENTITY SOON REALIZED THE ENORMITY OF THE EVIL SURROUNDING. HESH CONSIDERED ESCAPE DESPITE THE BARON'S ASSURANCES THAT IT WAS FUTILE, BUT TWO CONSIDERATIONS KEPT HIM FAST: THAT HESH MIGHT LEARN TO DEFEAT THE BARON; —AND THE POSSIBILITY OF BECOMING A PERSON OF EITHER SEX.
SO ULFÆ SQUELCHED HRIS HORROR AND ASSOCIATED WITH HRIS "FATHER" WHENEVER POSSIBLE.
ANTONIO WAS PLEASED AT THIS.
WHAT DO YOU KNOW OF ME?
VERY LITTLE. I HAD BEEN TOLD THAT MY FATHER WAS THE FRIGHTENING BARON UP IN THE VILLA WITH A TALENT FOR SORCERY...
...BUT I TOOK THAT FOR THE IGNORANT BABBLE OF SUPERSTITIOUS FOLK.
AHA HA. NEVER DISCREDIT SUPERSTITION, ULFÆ, IT HAS GREAT POWER. YOU ARE A PROFESSOR OF PHILOSOPHY AND THEOLOGY, A PROGRESSIVE THINKER — TELL ME: DO YOU BELIEVE IN SATAN?
I HAVE SEEN NO PROOF THAT EITHER SATAN OR GOD EXIST, AND YET I DO BELIEVE IN GOD. SATAN, HOWEVER, I FEEL IS A MYTH MAN USES TO JUSTIFY HIS OWN EVIL NATURE.
WELL, LISTEN, FOOL, SATAN DOES EXIST.
THE DARK ANGEL IS WITH US, AND THERE IS A RACE OF HIS CHILDREN THAT WALKS THE EARTH.
I AM OF THAT RACE, AS ARE YOU—THE SONS OF SATAN!

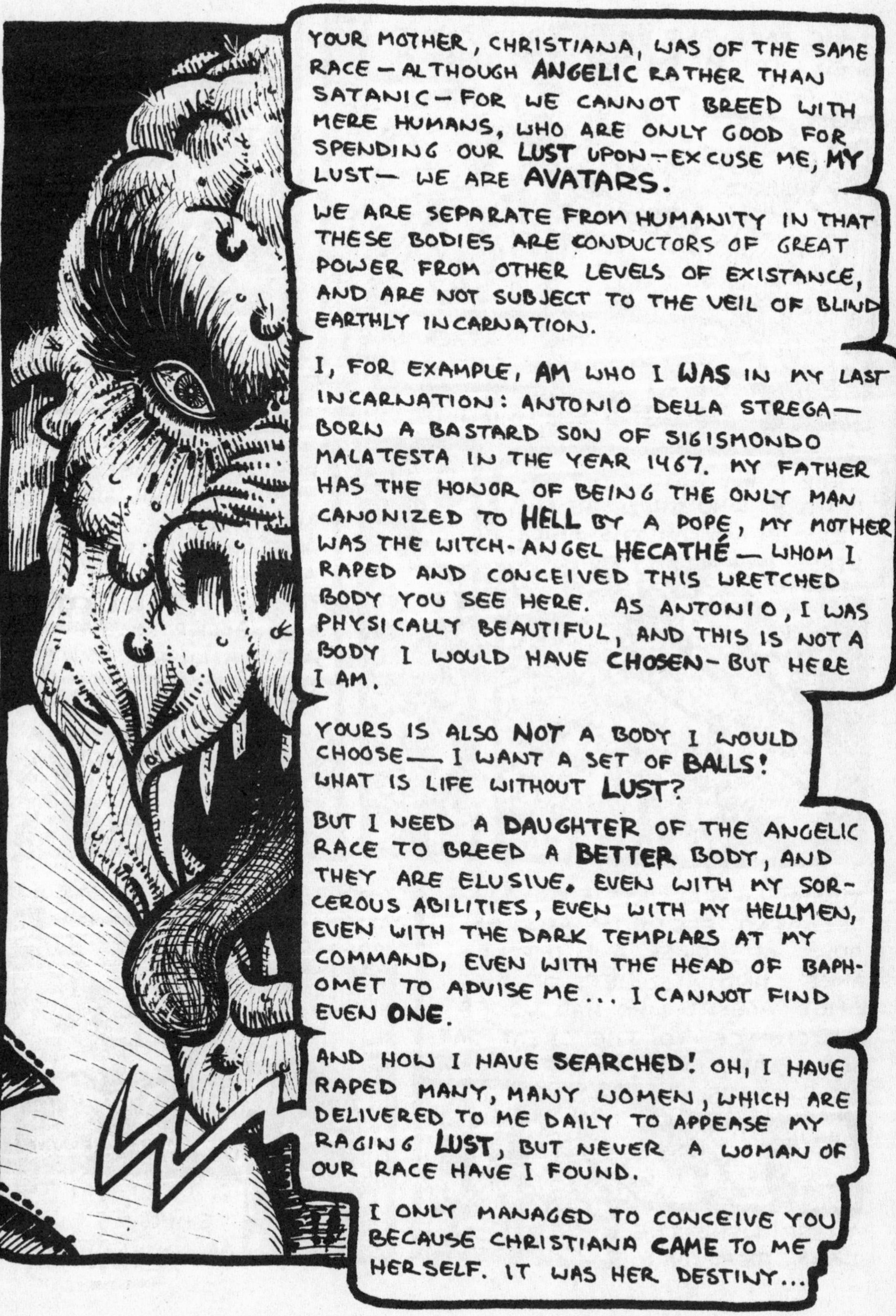

YOUR MOTHER, CHRISTIANA, WAS OF THE SAME RACE—ALTHOUGH ANGELIC RATHER THAN SATANIC—FOR WE CANNOT BREED WITH MERE HUMANS, WHO ARE ONLY GOOD FOR SPENDING OUR LUST UPON—EXCUSE ME, MY LUST—WE ARE AVATARS.
WE ARE SEPARATE FROM HUMANITY IN THAT THESE BODIES ARE CONDUCTORS OF GREAT POWER FROM OTHER LEVELS OF EXISTANCE, AND ARE NOT SUBJECT TO THE VEIL OF BLIND EARTHLY INCARNATION.
I, FOR EXAMPLE, AM WHO I WAS IN MY LAST INCARNATION: ANTONIO DELLA STREGA—BORN A BASTARD SON OF SIGISMONDO MALATESTA IN THE YEAR 1467. MY FATHER HAS THE HONOR OF BEING THE ONLY MAN CANONIZED TO HELL BY A POPE, MY MOTHER WAS THE WITCH-ANGEL HECATHÉ—WHOM I RAPED AND CONCEIVED THIS WRETCHED BODY YOU SEE HERE. AS ANTONIO, I WAS PHYSICALLY BEAUTIFUL, AND THIS IS NOT A BODY I WOULD HAVE CHOSEN—BUT HERE I AM.
YOURS IS ALSO NOT A BODY I WOULD CHOOSE—I WANT A SET OF BALLS! WHAT IS LIFE WITHOUT LUST?
BUT I NEED A DAUGHTER OF THE ANGELIC RACE TO BREED A BETTER BODY, AND THEY ARE ELUSIVE. EVEN WITH MY SORCEROUS ABILITIES, EVEN WITH MY HELLMEN, EVEN WITH THE DARK TEMPLARS AT MY COMMAND, EVEN WITH THE HEAD OF BAPHOMET TO ADVISE ME... I CANNOT FIND EVEN ONE.
AND HOW I HAVE SEARCHED! OH, I HAVE RAPED MANY, MANY WOMEN, WHICH ARE DELIVERED TO ME DAILY TO APPEASE MY RAGING LUST, BUT NEVER A WOMAN OF OUR RACE HAVE I FOUND.
I ONLY MANAGED TO CONCEIVE YOU BECAUSE CHRISTIANA CAME TO ME HERSELF. IT WAS HER DESTINY...

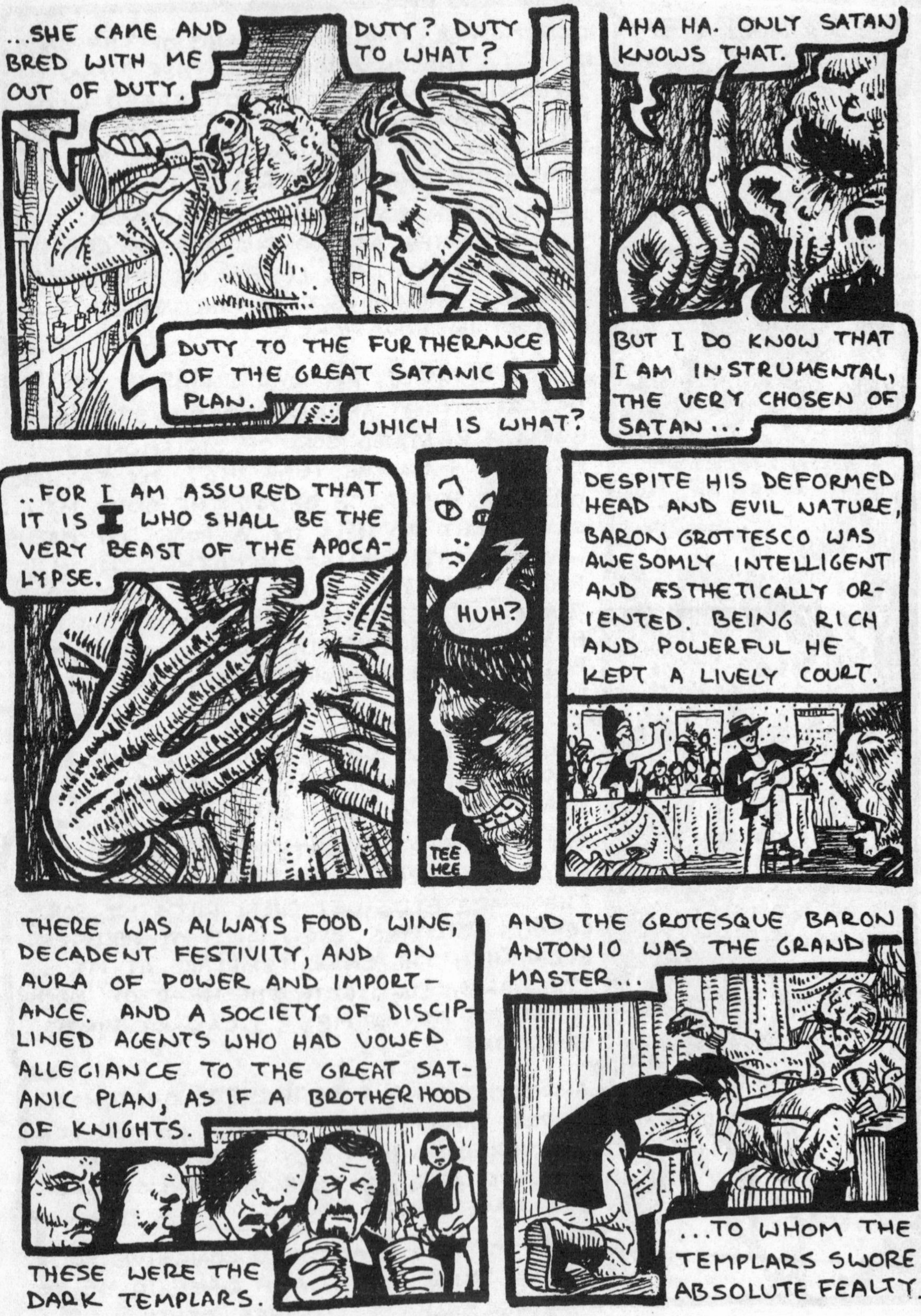
...SHE CAME AND BRED WITH ME OUT OF DUTY.
DUTY? DUTY TO WHAT?
DUTY TO THE FURTHERANCE OF THE GREAT SATANIC PLAN.
WHICH IS WHAT?
AHA HA. ONLY SATAN KNOWS THAT.
BUT I DO KNOW THAT I AM INSTRUMENTAL, THE VERY CHOSEN OF SATAN...
..FOR I AM ASSURED THAT IT IS I WHO SHALL BE THE VERY BEAST OF THE APOCA-LYPSE.
HUH?
TEE HEE
DESPITE HIS DEFORMED HEAD AND EVIL NATURE, BARON GROTTESCO WAS AWESOMLY INTELLIGENT AND ÆSTHETICALLY OR-IENTED. BEING RICH AND POWERFUL HE KEPT A LIVELY COURT.
THERE WAS ALWAYS FOOD, WINE, DECADENT FESTIVITY, AND AN AURA OF POWER AND IMPORT-ANCE. AND A SOCIETY OF DISCIP-LINED AGENTS WHO HAD VOWED ALLEGIANCE TO THE GREAT SAT-ANIC PLAN, AS IF A BROTHERHOOD OF KNIGHTS.
THESE WERE THE DARK TEMPLARS.
AND THE GROTESQUE BARON ANTONIO WAS THE GRAND MASTER...
...TO WHOM THE TEMPLARS SWORE ABSOLUTE FEALTY.

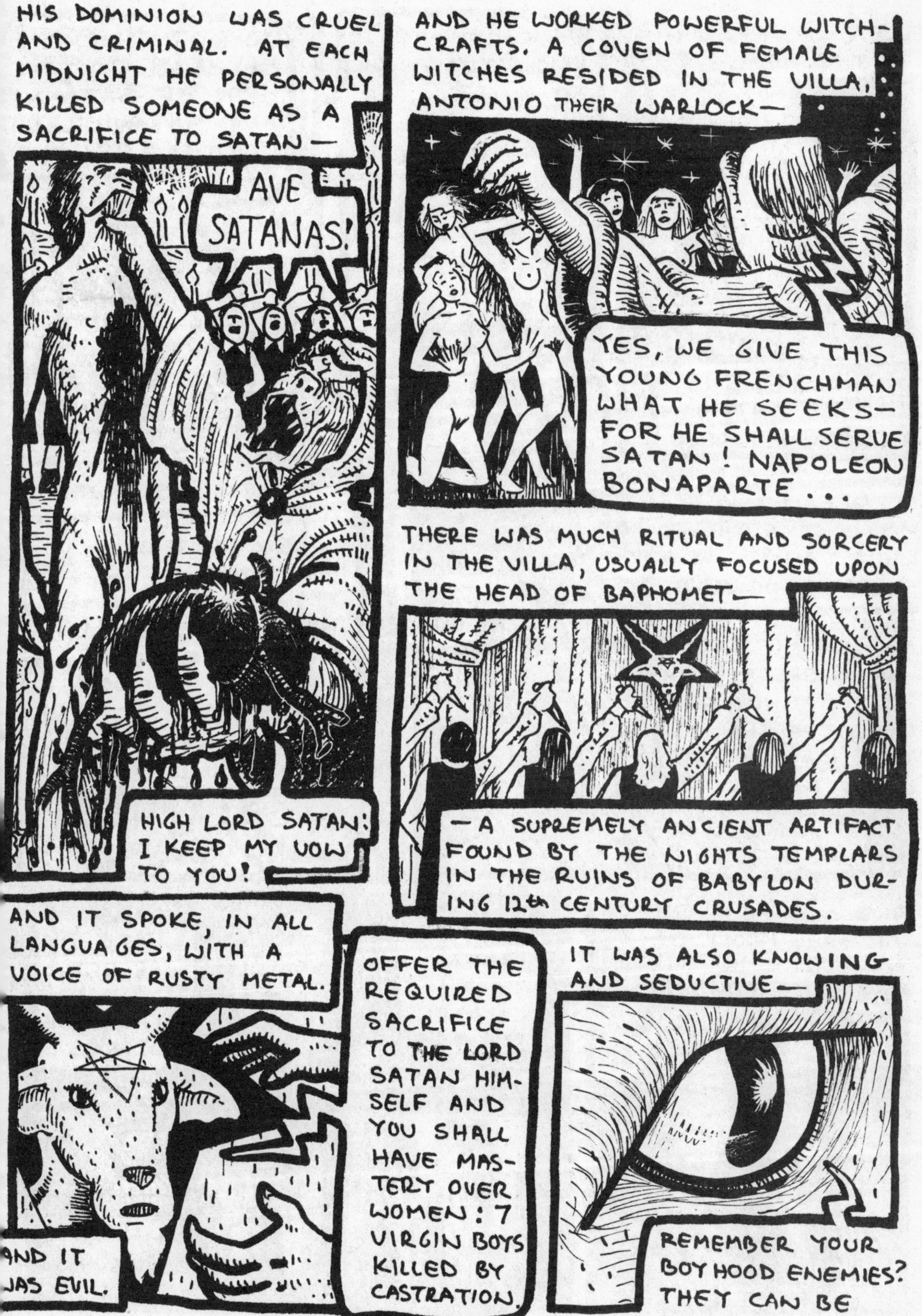

HIS DOMINION WAS CRUEL AND CRIMINAL. AT EACH MIDNIGHT HE PERSONALLY KILLED SOMEONE AS A SACRIFICE TO SATAN—
AVE SATANAS!
HIGH LORD SATAN: I KEEP MY VOW TO YOU!
AND HE WORKED POWERFUL WITCH-CRAFTS. A COVEN OF FEMALE WITCHES RESIDED IN THE VILLA, ANTONIO THEIR WARLOCK—
YES, WE GIVE THIS YOUNG FRENCHMAN WHAT HE SEEKS— FOR HE SHALL SERVE SATAN! NAPOLEON BONAPARTE . . .
THERE WAS MUCH RITUAL AND SORCERY IN THE VILLA, USUALLY FOCUSED UPON THE HEAD OF BAPHOMET—
—A SUPREMELY ANCIENT ARTIFACT FOUND BY THE NIGHTS TEMPLARS IN THE RUINS OF BABYLON DUR-ING 12th CENTURY CRUSADES.
AND IT SPOKE, IN ALL LANGUAGES, WITH A VOICE OF RUSTY METAL.
AND IT WAS EVIL.
OFFER THE REQUIRED SACRIFICE TO THE LORD SATAN HIM-SELF AND YOU SHALL HAVE MAS-TERY OVER WOMEN: 7 VIRGIN BOYS KILLED BY CASTRATION.
IT WAS ALSO KNOWING AND SEDUCTIVE—
REMEMBER YOUR BOYHOOD ENEMIES? THEY CAN BE UNDONE.

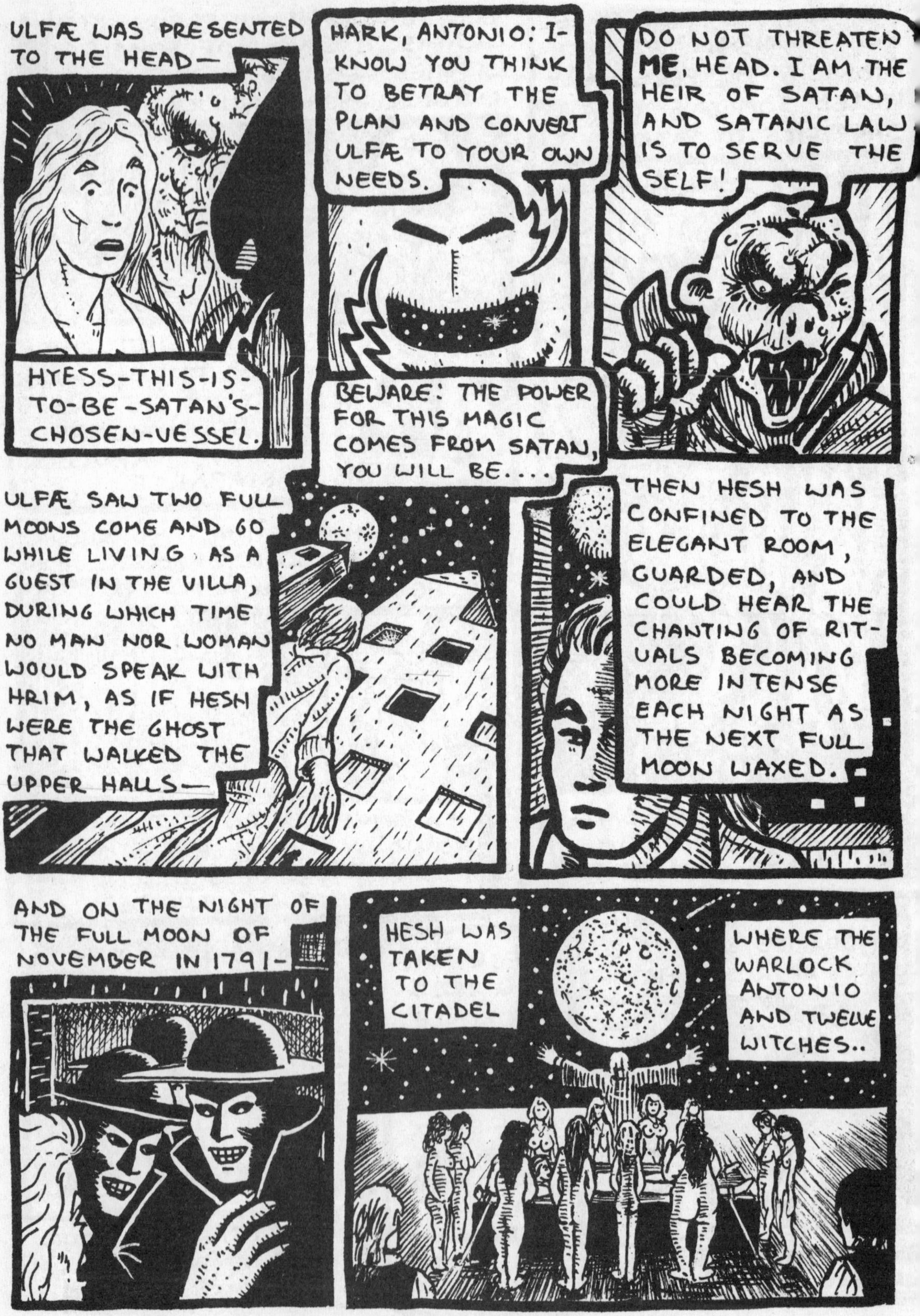
ULFÆ WAS PRESENTED TO THE HEAD—
HYESS-THIS-IS-TO-BE-SATAN'S-CHOSEN-VESSEL.
HARK, ANTONIO: I-KNOW YOU THINK TO BETRAY THE PLAN AND CONVERT ULFÆ TO YOUR OWN NEEDS.
BEWARE: THE POWER FOR THIS MAGIC COMES FROM SATAN, YOU WILL BE....
DO NOT THREATEN ME, HEAD. I AM THE HEIR OF SATAN, AND SATANIC LAW IS TO SERVE THE SELF!
ULFÆ SAW TWO FULL MOONS COME AND GO WHILE LIVING AS A GUEST IN THE VILLA, DURING WHICH TIME NO MAN NOR WOMAN WOULD SPEAK WITH HRIM, AS IF HESH WERE THE GHOST THAT WALKED THE UPPER HALLS—
THEN HESH WAS CONFINED TO THE ELEGANT ROOM, GUARDED, AND COULD HEAR THE CHANTING OF RITUALS BECOMING MORE INTENSE EACH NIGHT AS THE NEXT FULL MOON WAXED.
AND ON THE NIGHT OF THE FULL MOON OF NOVEMBER IN 1791-
HESH WAS TAKEN TO THE CITADEL
WHERE THE WARLOCK ANTONIO AND TWELVE WITCHES..

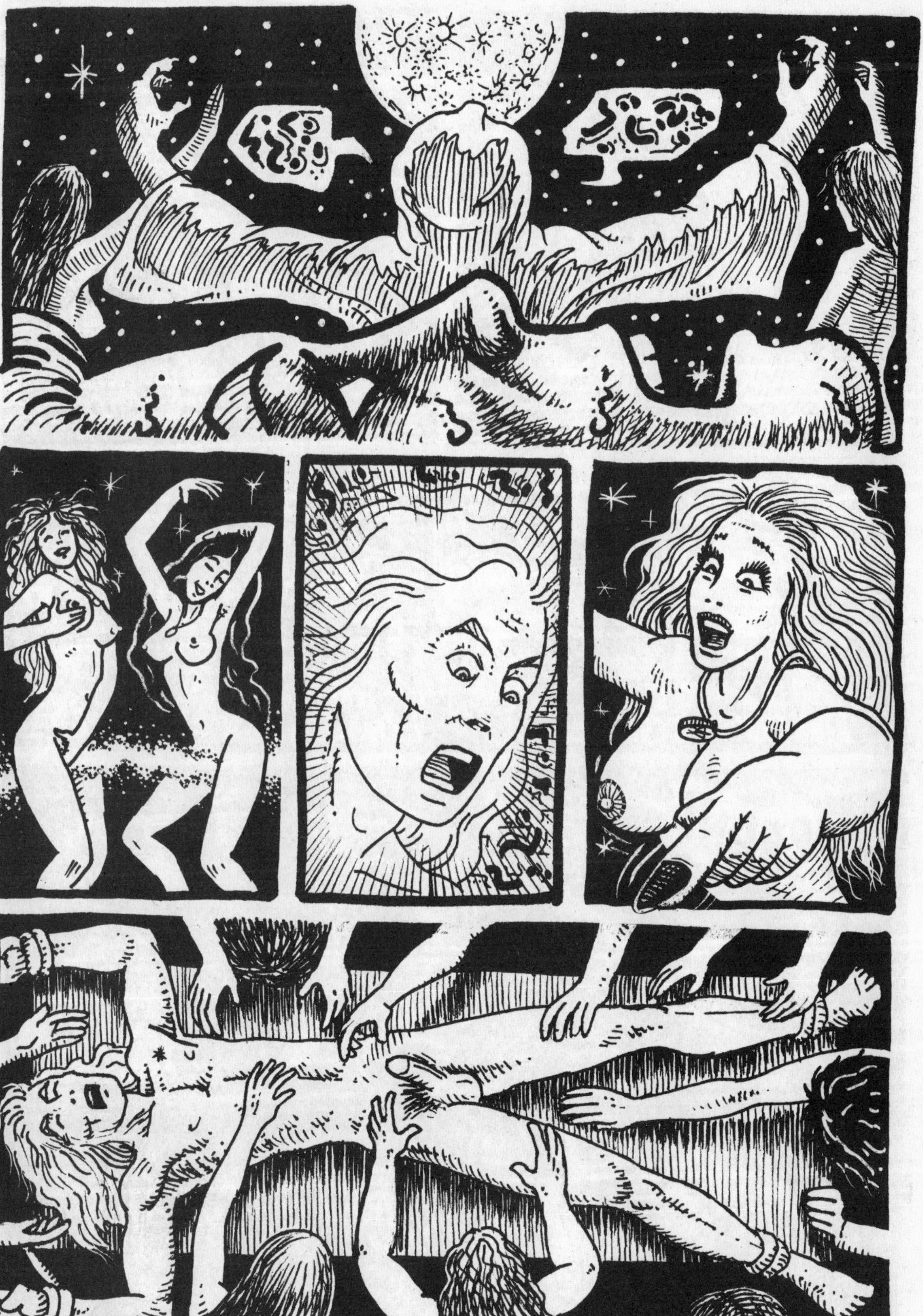

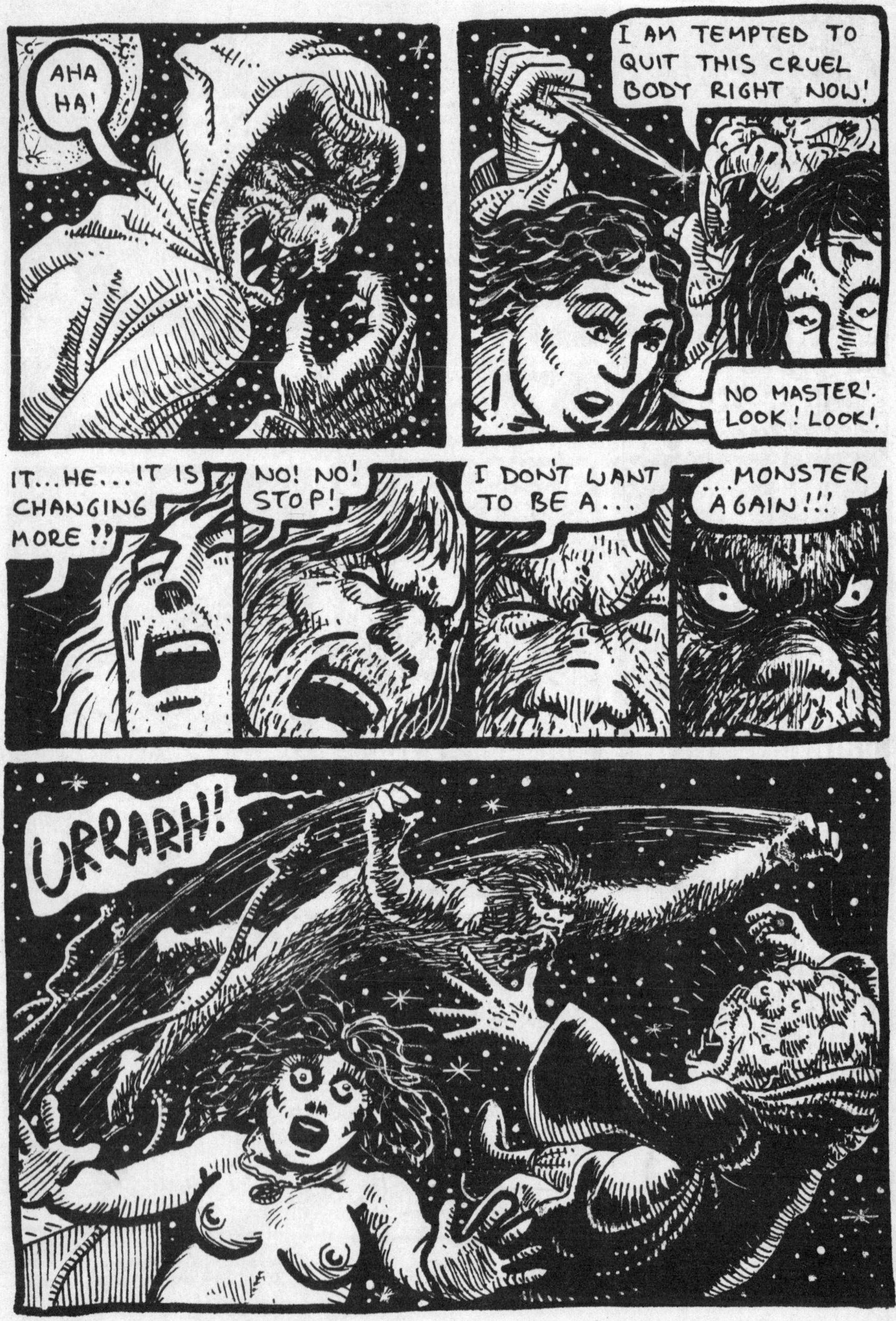
AHA HA!
I AM TEMPTED TO QUIT THIS CRUEL BODY RIGHT NOW!
NO MASTER! LOOK! LOOK!
IT... HE... IT IS CHANGING MORE!?
NO! NO! STOP!
I DON'T WANT TO BE A...
...MONSTER AGAIN!!!
URRARH!

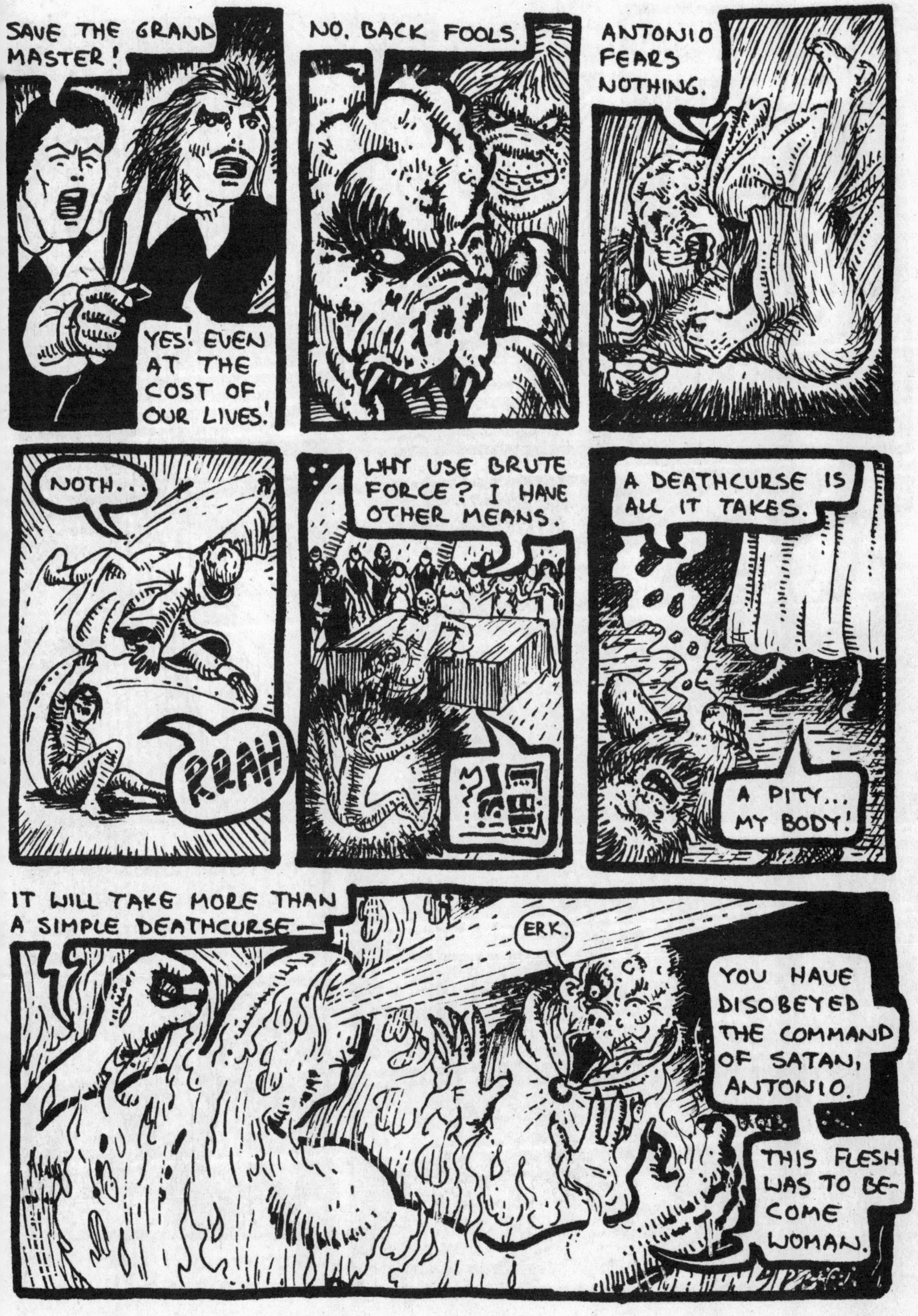
SAVE THE GRAND MASTER!
YES! EVEN AT THE COST OF OUR LIVES!
NO. BACK FOOLS.
ANTONIO FEARS NOTHING.
NOTH...
RRAH
WHY USE BRUTE FORCE? I HAVE OTHER MEANS.
A DEATHCURSE IS ALL IT TAKES.
A PITY... MY BODY!
IT WILL TAKE MORE THAN A SIMPLE DEATHCURSE—
ERK.
YOU HAVE DISOBEYED THE COMMAND OF SATAN, ANTONIO.
THIS FLESH WAS TO BECOME WOMAN.

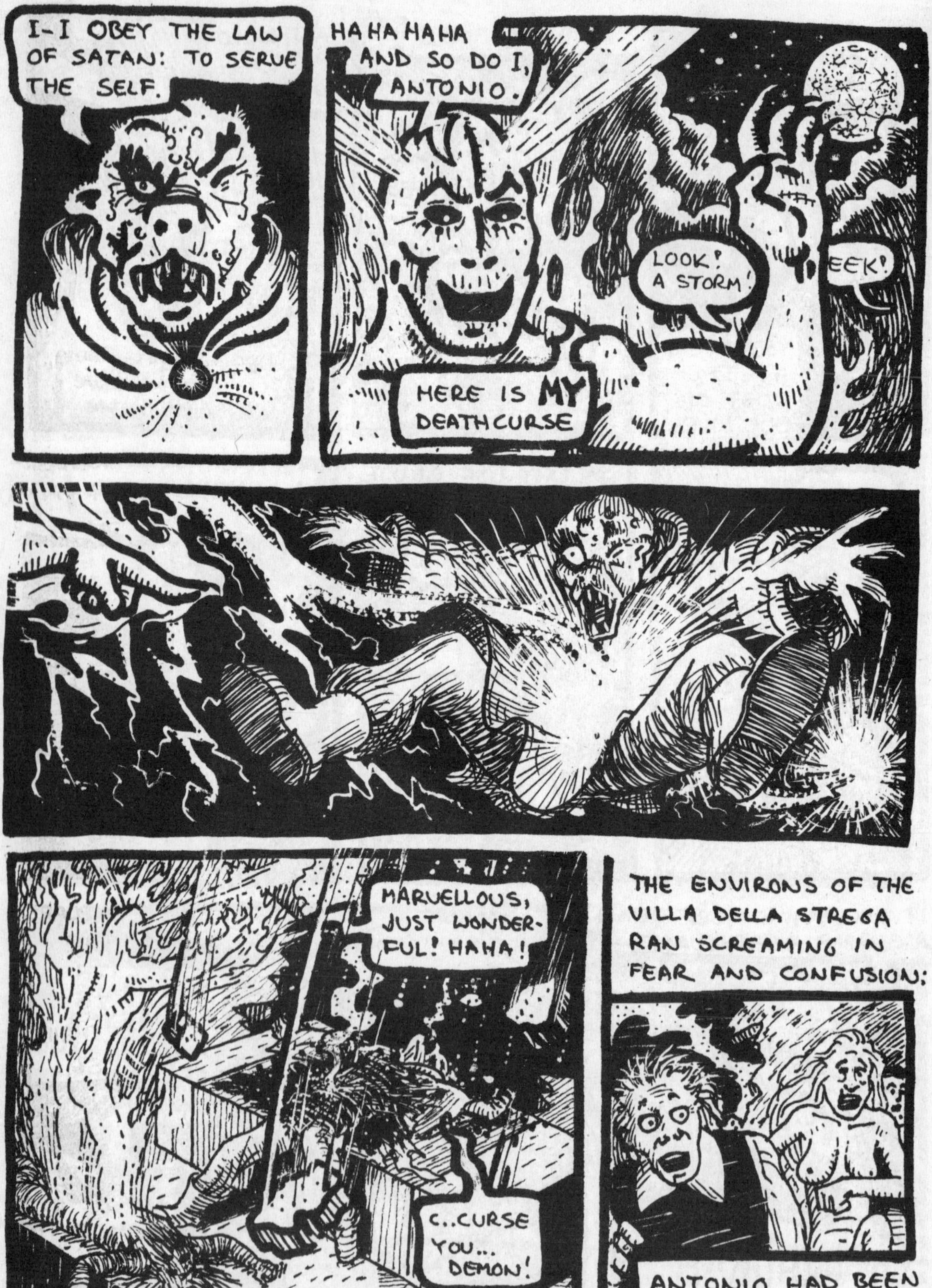
I-I OBEY THE LAW OF SATAN: TO SERVE THE SELF.
HAHAHAHA AND SO DO I, ANTONIO.
HERE IS MY DEATHCURSE
LOOK! A STORM!
EEK!
MARVELLOUS, JUST WONDERFUL! HAHA!
C..CURSE YOU... DEMON!
THE ENVIRONS OF THE VILLA DELLA STREGA RAN SCREAMING IN FEAR AND CONFUSION:
ANTONIO HAD BEEN DESTROYED!!

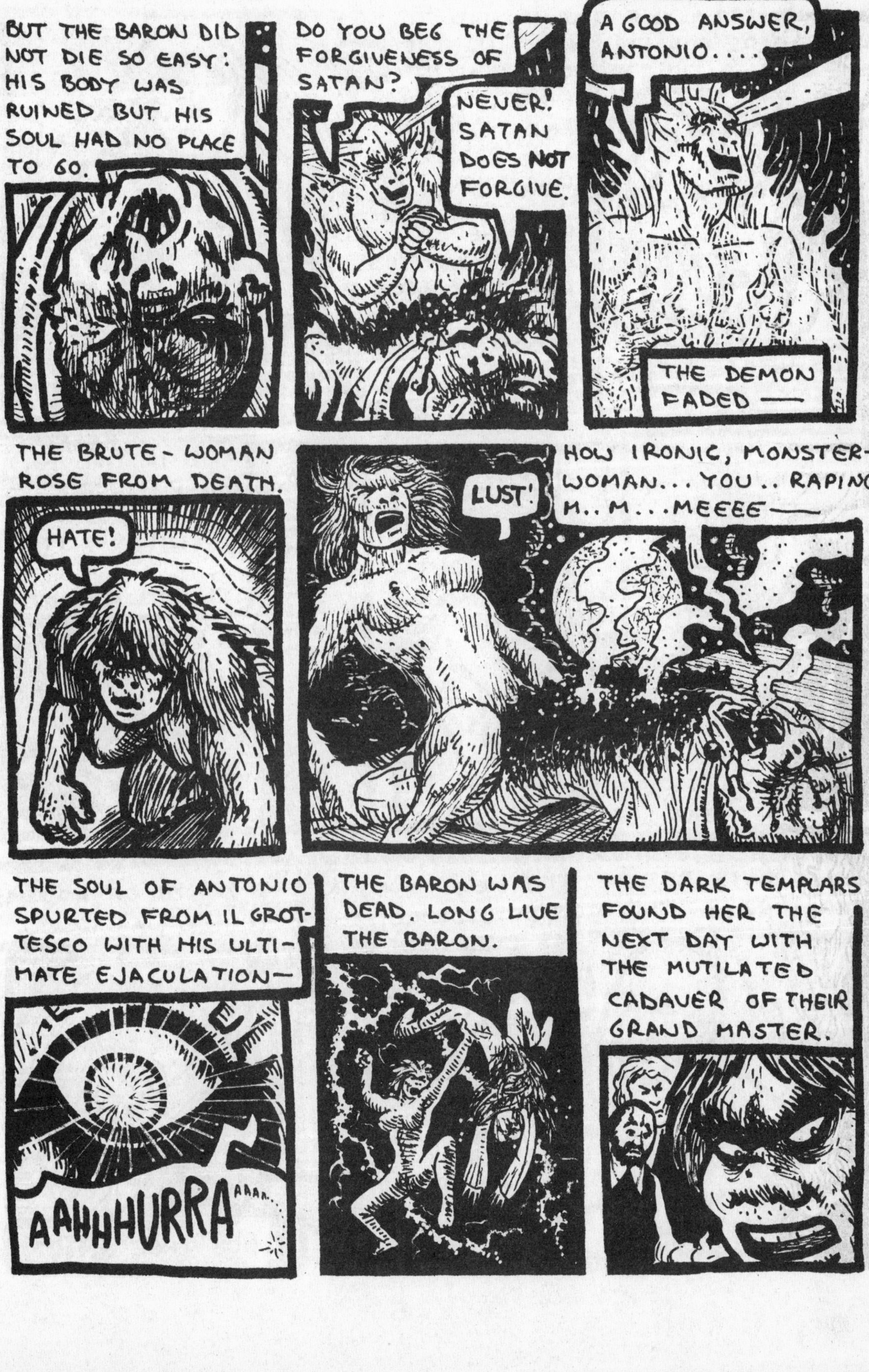
BUT THE BARON DID NOT DIE SO EASY: HIS BODY WAS RUINED BUT HIS SOUL HAD NO PLACE TO GO.
DO YOU BEG THE FORGIVENESS OF SATAN?
NEVER! SATAN DOES NOT FORGIVE.
A GOOD ANSWER, ANTONIO....
THE DEMON FADED —
THE BRUTE-WOMAN ROSE FROM DEATH.
HATE!
LUST!
HOW IRONIC, MONSTER-WOMAN... YOU.. RAPING M..M...MEEEE—
THE SOUL OF ANTONIO SPURTED FROM IL GROTTESCO WITH HIS ULTIMATE EJACULATION—
AAHHHURRAAAAA...
THE BARON WAS DEAD. LONG LIVE THE BARON.
THE DARK TEMPLARS FOUND HER THE NEXT DAY WITH THE MUTILATED CADAVER OF THEIR GRAND MASTER.

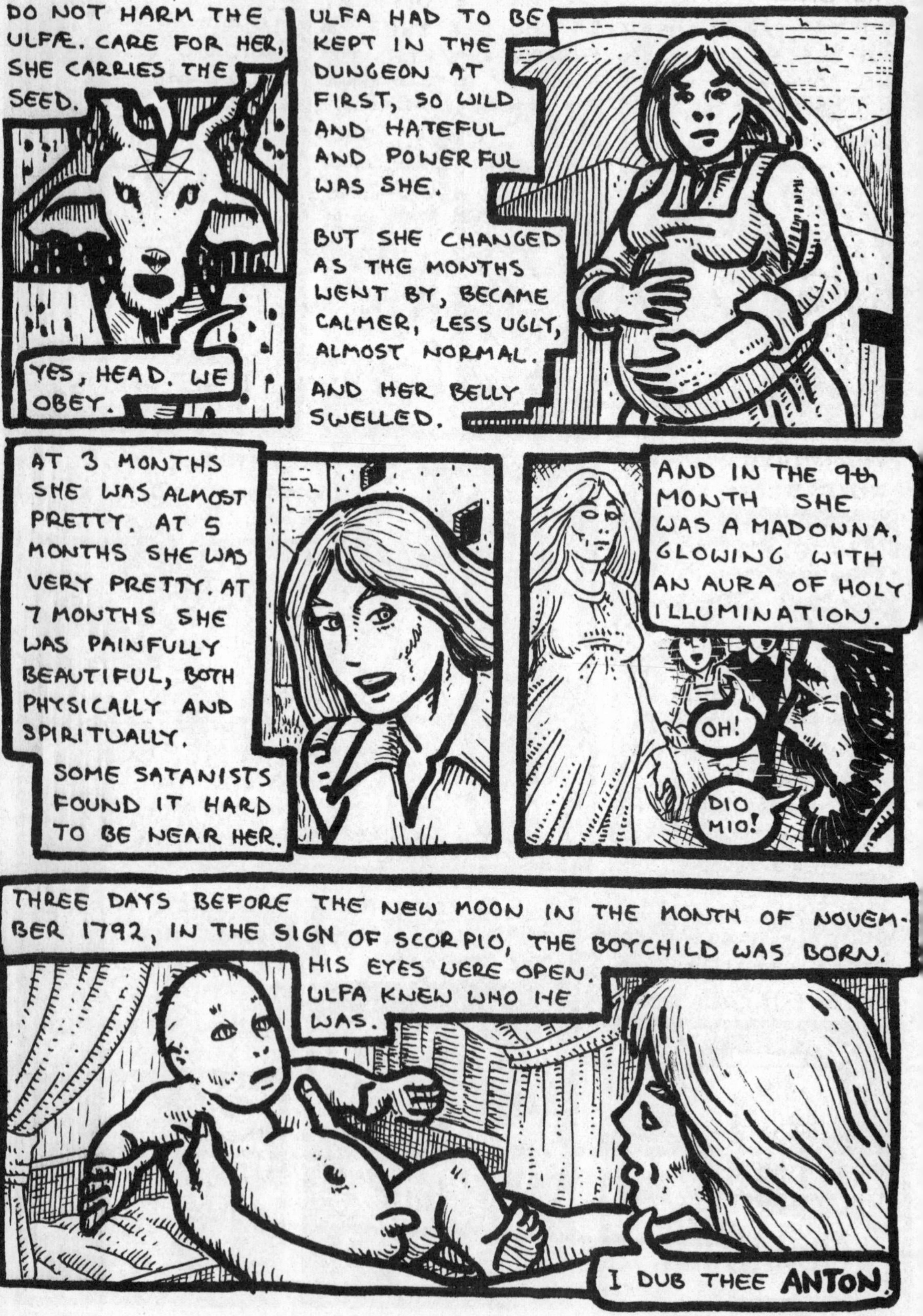
DO NOT HARM THE ULFÆ. CARE FOR HER, SHE CARRIES THE SEED.
YES, HEAD. WE OBEY.
ULFA HAD TO BE KEPT IN THE DUNGEON AT FIRST, SO WILD AND HATEFUL AND POWERFUL WAS SHE.
BUT SHE CHANGED AS THE MONTHS WENT BY, BECAME CALMER, LESS UGLY, ALMOST NORMAL.
AND HER BELLY SWELLED.
AT 3 MONTHS SHE WAS ALMOST PRETTY. AT 5 MONTHS SHE WAS VERY PRETTY. AT 7 MONTHS SHE WAS PAINFULLY BEAUTIFUL, BOTH PHYSICALLY AND SPIRITUALLY.
SOME SATANISTS FOUND IT HARD TO BE NEAR HER.
AND IN THE 9th MONTH SHE WAS A MADONNA, GLOWING WITH AN AURA OF HOLY ILLUMINATION.
OH!
DIO MIO!
THREE DAYS BEFORE THE NEW MOON IN THE MONTH OF NOVEMBER 1792, IN THE SIGN OF SCORPIO, THE BOYCHILD WAS BORN.
HIS EYES WERE OPEN. ULFA KNEW WHO HE WAS.
I DUB THEE ANTON.

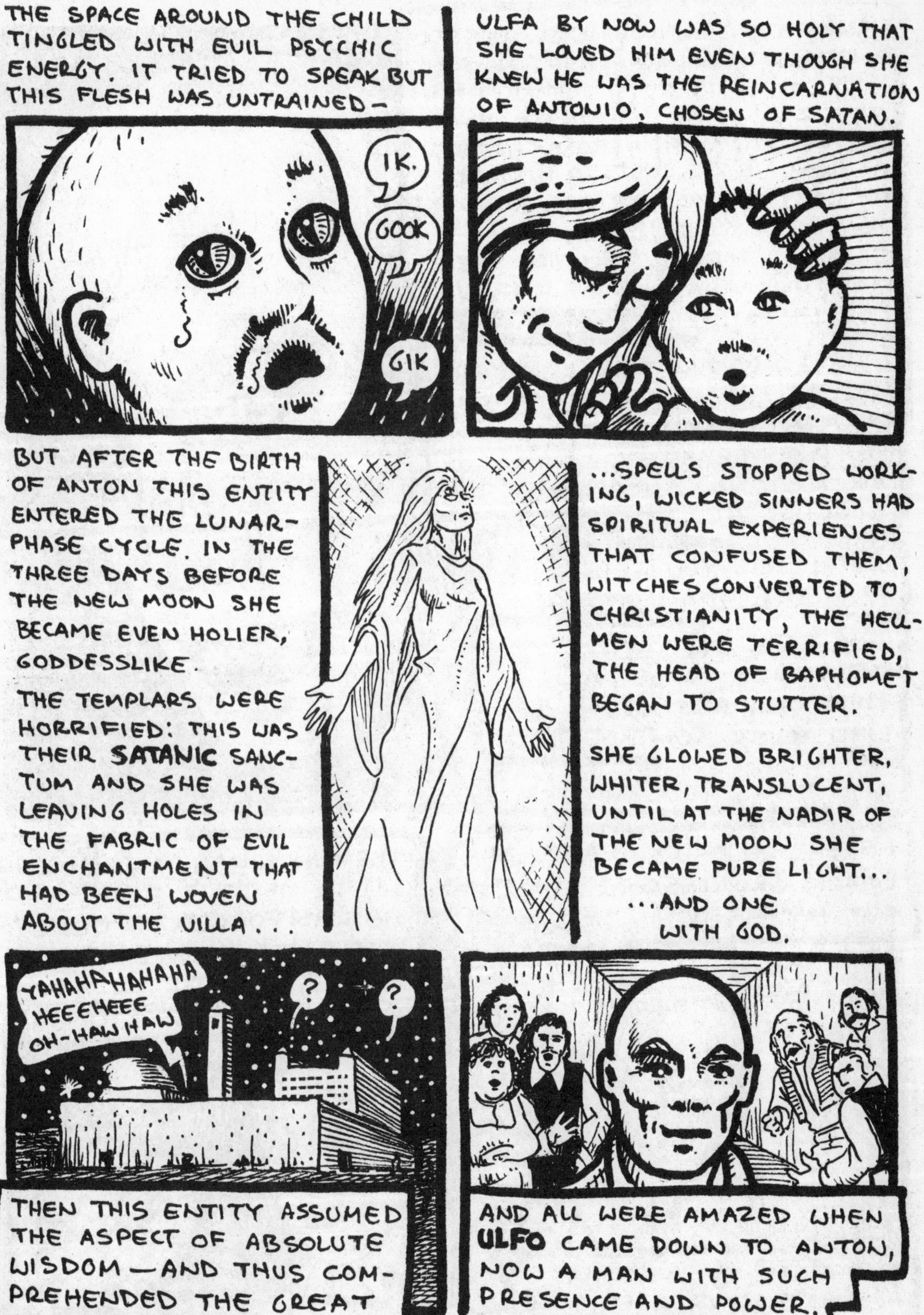
THE SPACE AROUND THE CHILD TINGLED WITH EVIL PSYCHIC ENERGY. IT TRIED TO SPEAK BUT THIS FLESH WAS UNTRAINED—
IK.
GOOK
GIK
ULFA BY NOW WAS SO HOLY THAT SHE LOVED HIM EVEN THOUGH SHE KNEW HE WAS THE REINCARNATION OF ANTONIO, CHOSEN OF SATAN.
BUT AFTER THE BIRTH OF ANTON THIS ENTITY ENTERED THE LUNAR-PHASE CYCLE. IN THE THREE DAYS BEFORE THE NEW MOON SHE BECAME EVEN HOLIER, GODDESSLIKE.
THE TEMPLARS WERE HORRIFIED: THIS WAS THEIR SATANIC SANCTUM AND SHE WAS LEAVING HOLES IN THE FABRIC OF EVIL ENCHANTMENT THAT HAD BEEN WOVEN ABOUT THE VILLA...
...SPELLS STOPPED WORKING, WICKED SINNERS HAD SPIRITUAL EXPERIENCES THAT CONFUSED THEM, WITCHES CONVERTED TO CHRISTIANITY, THE HELLMEN WERE TERRIFIED, THE HEAD OF BAPHOMET BEGAN TO STUTTER.
SHE GLOWED BRIGHTER, WHITER, TRANSLUCENT, UNTIL AT THE NADIR OF THE NEW MOON SHE BECAME PURE LIGHT...
...AND ONE WITH GOD.
YAHAHAHAHAHA HEEEHEEE OH-HAW HAW
?
?
THEN THIS ENTITY ASSUMED THE ASPECT OF ABSOLUTE WISDOM—AND THUS COMPREHENDED THE GREAT COSMIC JOKE.
AND ALL WERE AMAZED WHEN ULFO CAME DOWN TO ANTON, NOW A MAN WITH SUCH PRESENCE AND POWER.

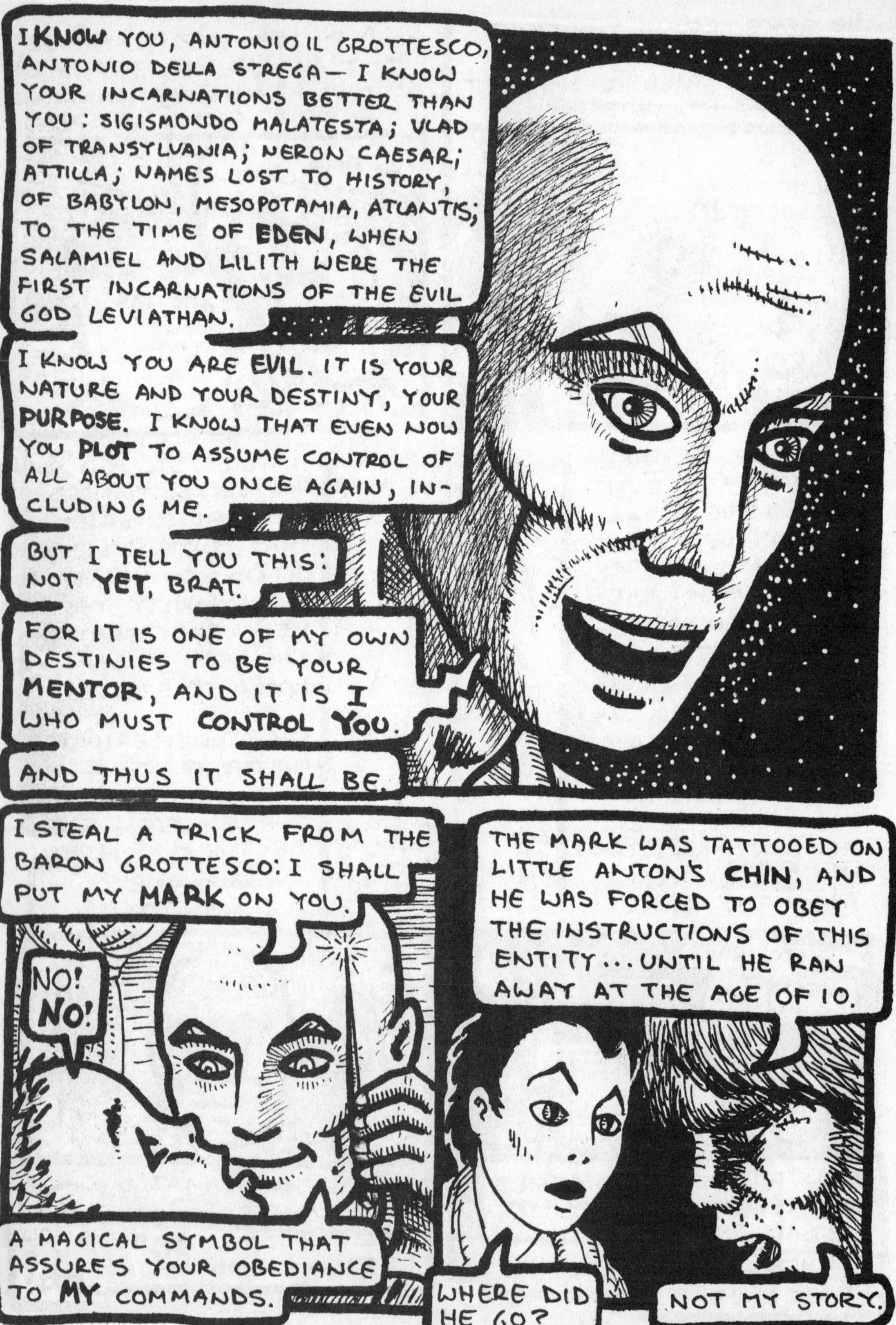

I KNOW YOU, ANTONIO IL GROTTESCO, ANTONIO DELLA STREGA— I KNOW YOUR INCARNATIONS BETTER THAN YOU: SIGISMONDO MALATESTA; VLAD OF TRANSYLVANIA; NERON CAESAR; ATTILLA; NAMES LOST TO HISTORY, OF BABYLON, MESOPOTAMIA, ATLANTIS; TO THE TIME OF EDEN, WHEN SALAMIEL AND LILITH WERE THE FIRST INCARNATIONS OF THE EVIL GOD LEVIATHAN.
I KNOW YOU ARE EVIL. IT IS YOUR NATURE AND YOUR DESTINY, YOUR PURPOSE. I KNOW THAT EVEN NOW YOU PLOT TO ASSUME CONTROL OF ALL ABOUT YOU ONCE AGAIN, INCLUDING ME.
BUT I TELL YOU THIS: NOT YET, BRAT.
FOR IT IS ONE OF MY OWN DESTINIES TO BE YOUR MENTOR, AND IT IS I WHO MUST CONTROL YOU.
AND THUS IT SHALL BE.
I STEAL A TRICK FROM THE BARON GROTTESCO: I SHALL PUT MY MARK ON YOU.
NO! NO!
A MAGICAL SYMBOL THAT ASSURES YOUR OBEDIANCE TO MY COMMANDS.
THE MARK WAS TATTOOED ON LITTLE ANTON'S CHIN, AND HE WAS FORCED TO OBEY THE INSTRUCTIONS OF THIS ENTITY... UNTIL HE RAN AWAY AT THE AGE OF 10.
WHERE DID HE GO?
NOT MY STORY.

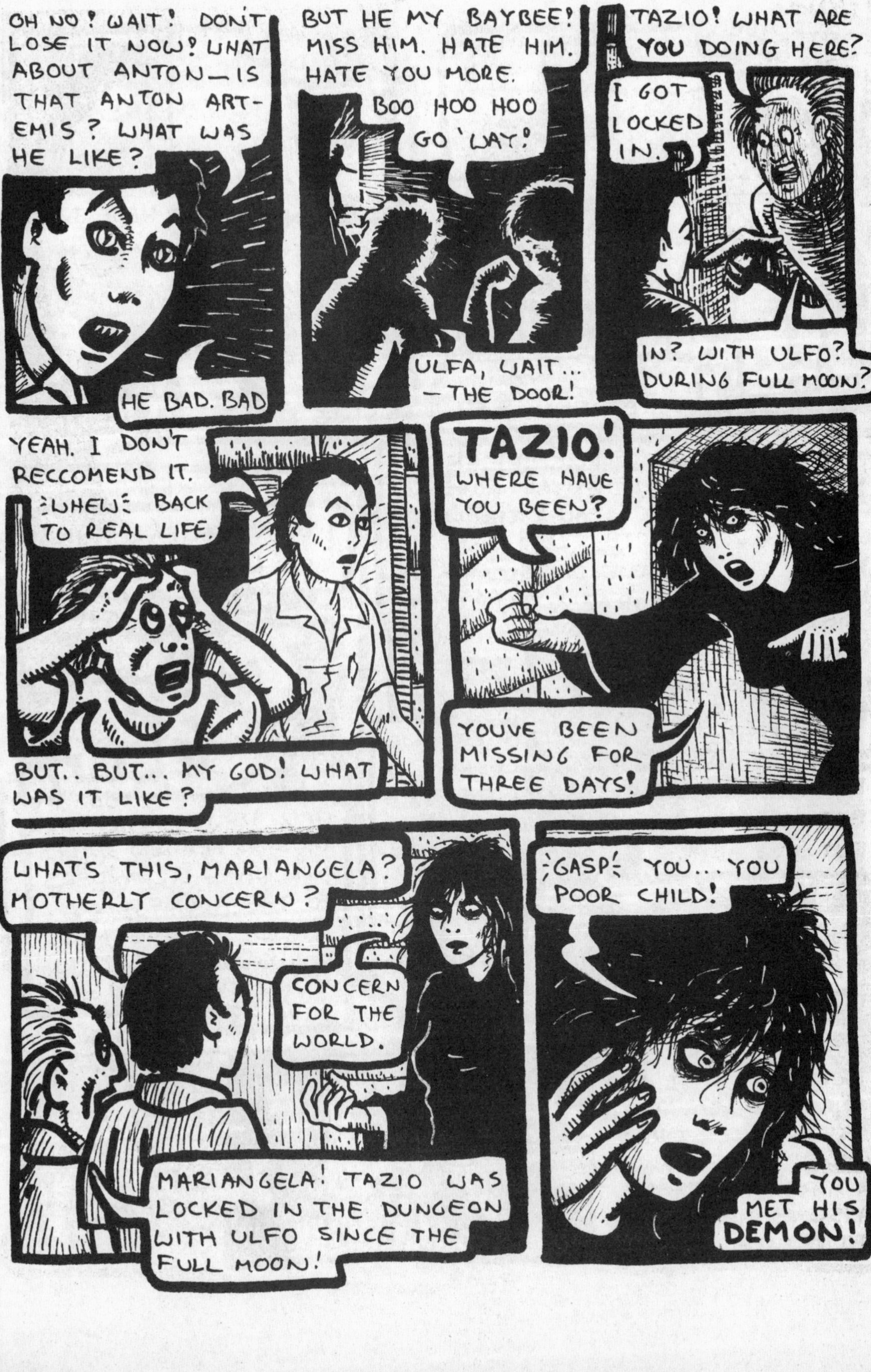

OH NO! WAIT! DON'T LOSE IT NOW! WHAT ABOUT ANTON—IS THAT ANTON ARTEMIS? WHAT WAS HE LIKE?
HE BAD. BAD
BUT HE MY BAYBEE! MISS HIM. HATE HIM. HATE YOU MORE.
BOO HOO HOO GO 'WAY!
ULFA, WAIT... —THE DOOR!
TAZIO! WHAT ARE YOU DOING HERE?
I GOT LOCKED IN.
IN? WITH ULFO? DURING FULL MOON?
YEAH. I DON'T RECCOMEND IT.
WHEW BACK TO REAL LIFE.
BUT.. BUT... MY GOD! WHAT WAS IT LIKE?
TAZIO! WHERE HAVE YOU BEEN?
YOU'VE BEEN MISSING FOR THREE DAYS!
WHAT'S THIS, MARIANGELA? MOTHERLY CONCERN?
CONCERN FOR THE WORLD.
MARIANGELA! TAZIO WAS LOCKED IN THE DUNGEON WITH ULFO SINCE THE FULL MOON!
GASP YOU... YOU POOR CHILD!
YOU MET HIS DEMON!

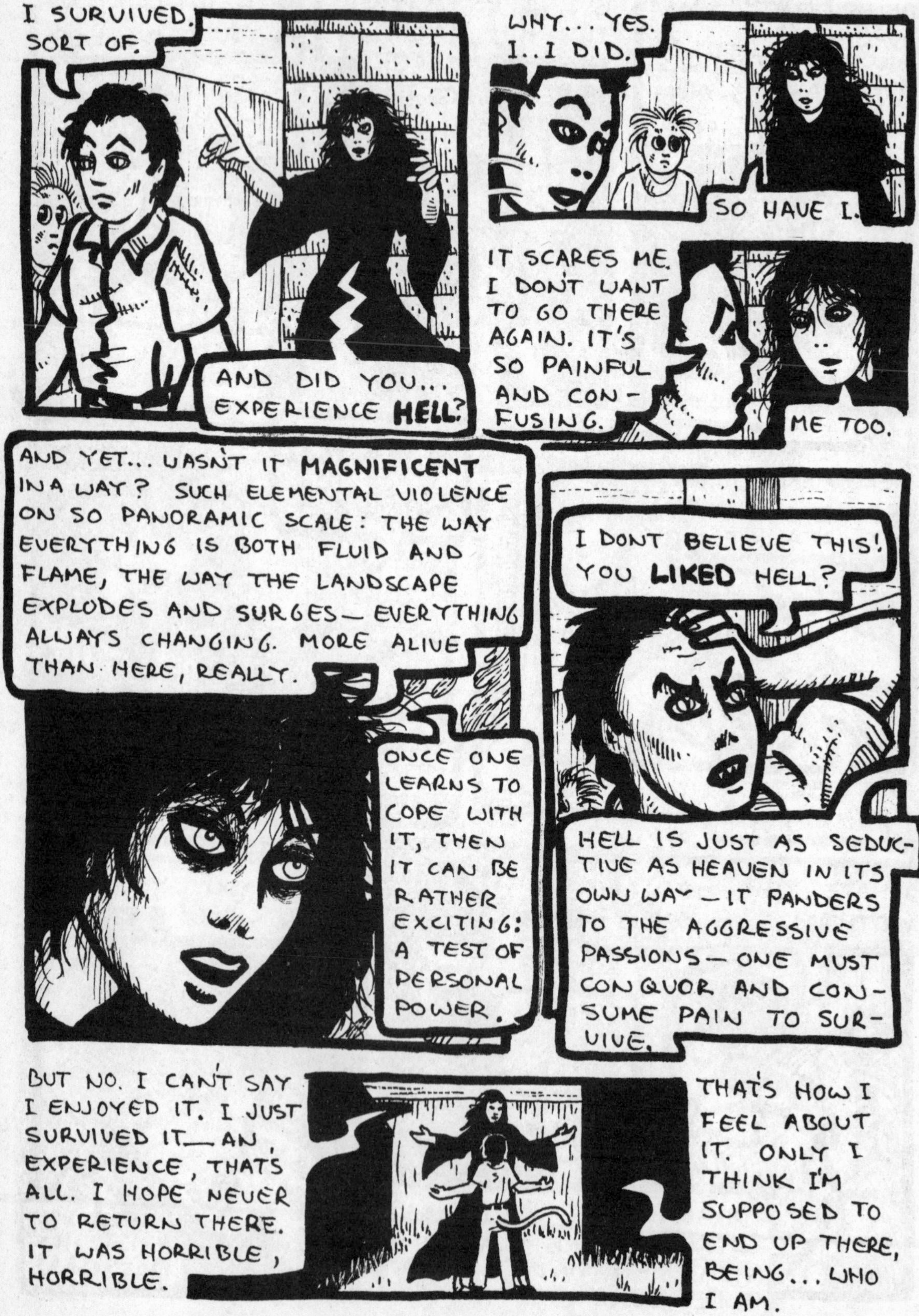
I SURVIVED. SORT OF.
AND DID YOU... EXPERIENCE HELL?
WHY... YES. I..I DID.
SO HAVE I.
IT SCARES ME. I DON'T WANT TO GO THERE AGAIN. IT'S SO PAINFUL AND CON-FUSING.
ME TOO.
AND YET... WASN'T IT MAGNIFICENT IN A WAY? SUCH ELEMENTAL VIOLENCE ON SO PANORAMIC SCALE: THE WAY EVERYTHING IS BOTH FLUID AND FLAME, THE WAY THE LANDSCAPE EXPLODES AND SURGES— EVERYTHING ALWAYS CHANGING. MORE ALIVE THAN HERE, REALLY.
ONCE ONE LEARNS TO COPE WITH IT, THEN IT CAN BE RATHER EXCITING: A TEST OF PERSONAL POWER.
I DONT BELIEVE THIS! YOU LIKED HELL?
HELL IS JUST AS SEDUC-TIVE AS HEAVEN IN ITS OWN WAY — IT PANDERS TO THE AGGRESSIVE PASSIONS— ONE MUST CONQUOR AND CON-SUME PAIN TO SUR-VIVE.
BUT NO. I CAN'T SAY I ENJOYED IT. I JUST SURVIVED IT— AN EXPERIENCE, THAT'S ALL. I HOPE NEVER TO RETURN THERE. IT WAS HORRIBLE, HORRIBLE.
THAT'S HOW I FEEL ABOUT IT. ONLY I THINK I'M SUPPOSED TO END UP THERE, BEING... WHO I AM.

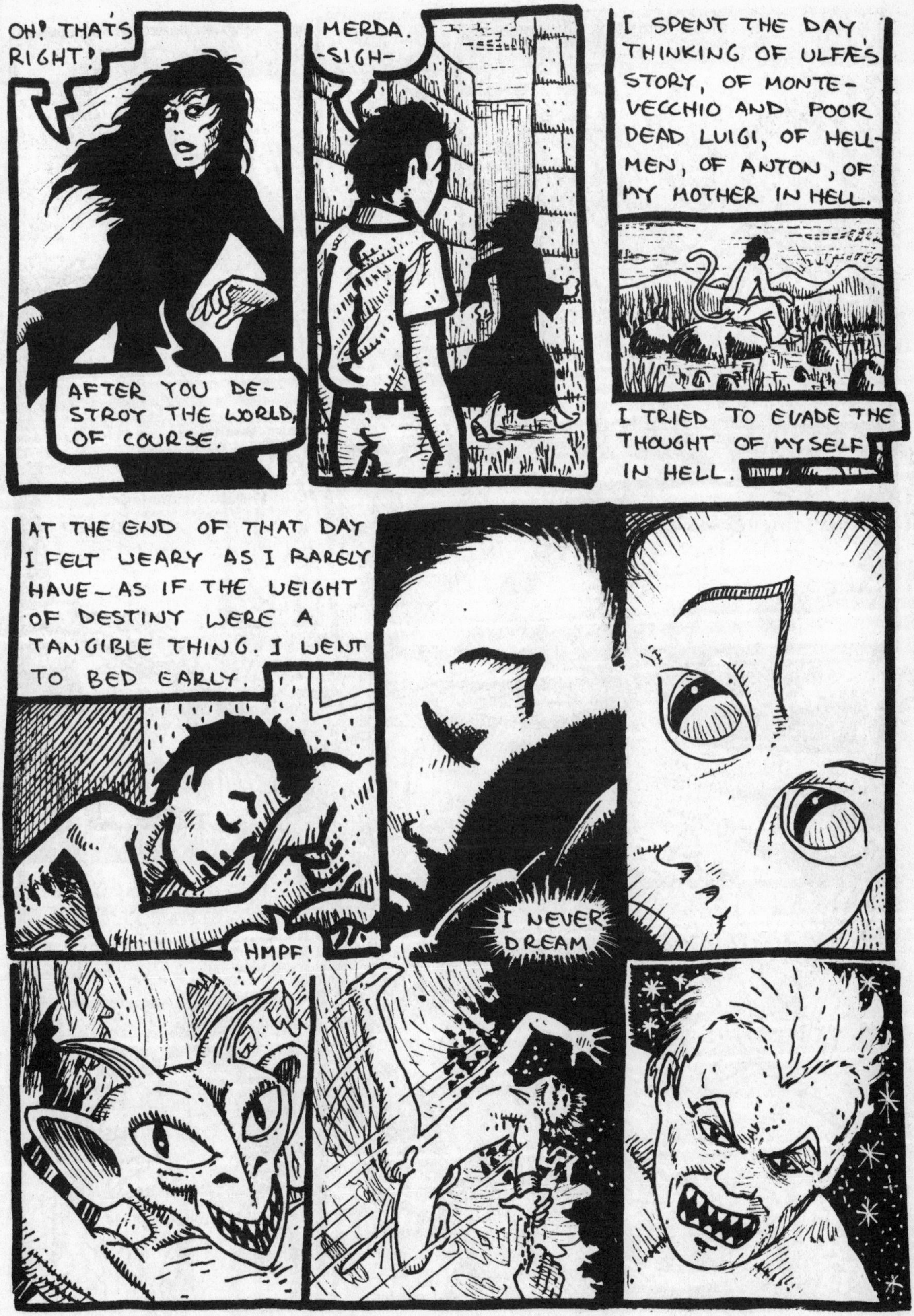
OH! THAT'S RIGHT!
AFTER YOU DESTROY THE WORLD, OF COURSE.
MERDA. -SIGH-
I SPENT THE DAY THINKING OF ULFÆ'S STORY, OF MONTEVECCHIO AND POOR DEAD LUIGI, OF HELLMEN, OF ANTON, OF MY MOTHER IN HELL.
I TRIED TO EVADE THE THOUGHT OF MYSELF IN HELL.
AT THE END OF THAT DAY I FELT WEARY AS I RARELY HAVE—AS IF THE WEIGHT OF DESTINY WERE A TANGIBLE THING. I WENT TO BED EARLY.
HMPF!
I NEVER DREAM

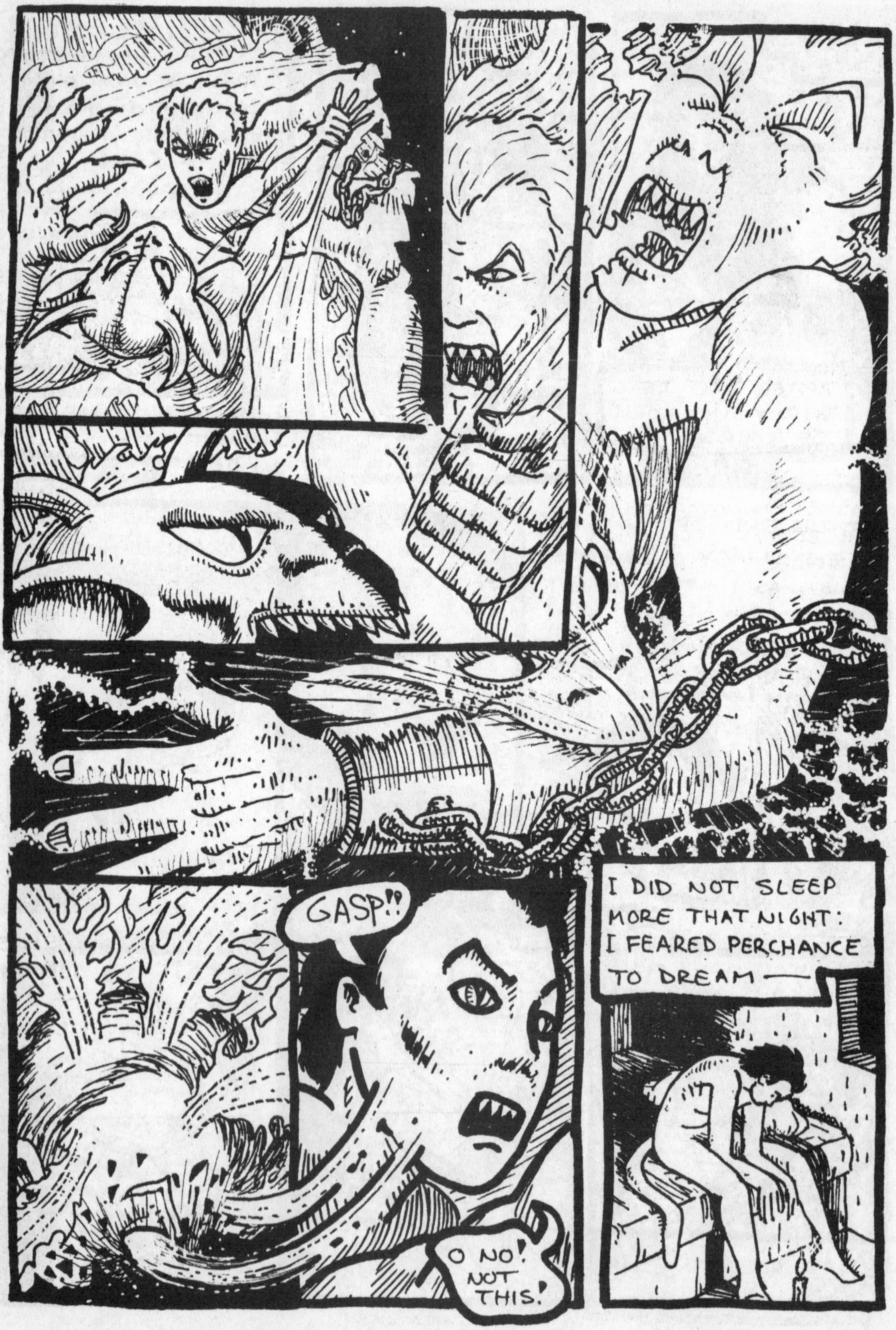
GASP!!
O NO! NOT THIS!
I DID NOT SLEEP MORE THAT NIGHT: I FEARED PERCHANCE TO DREAM —

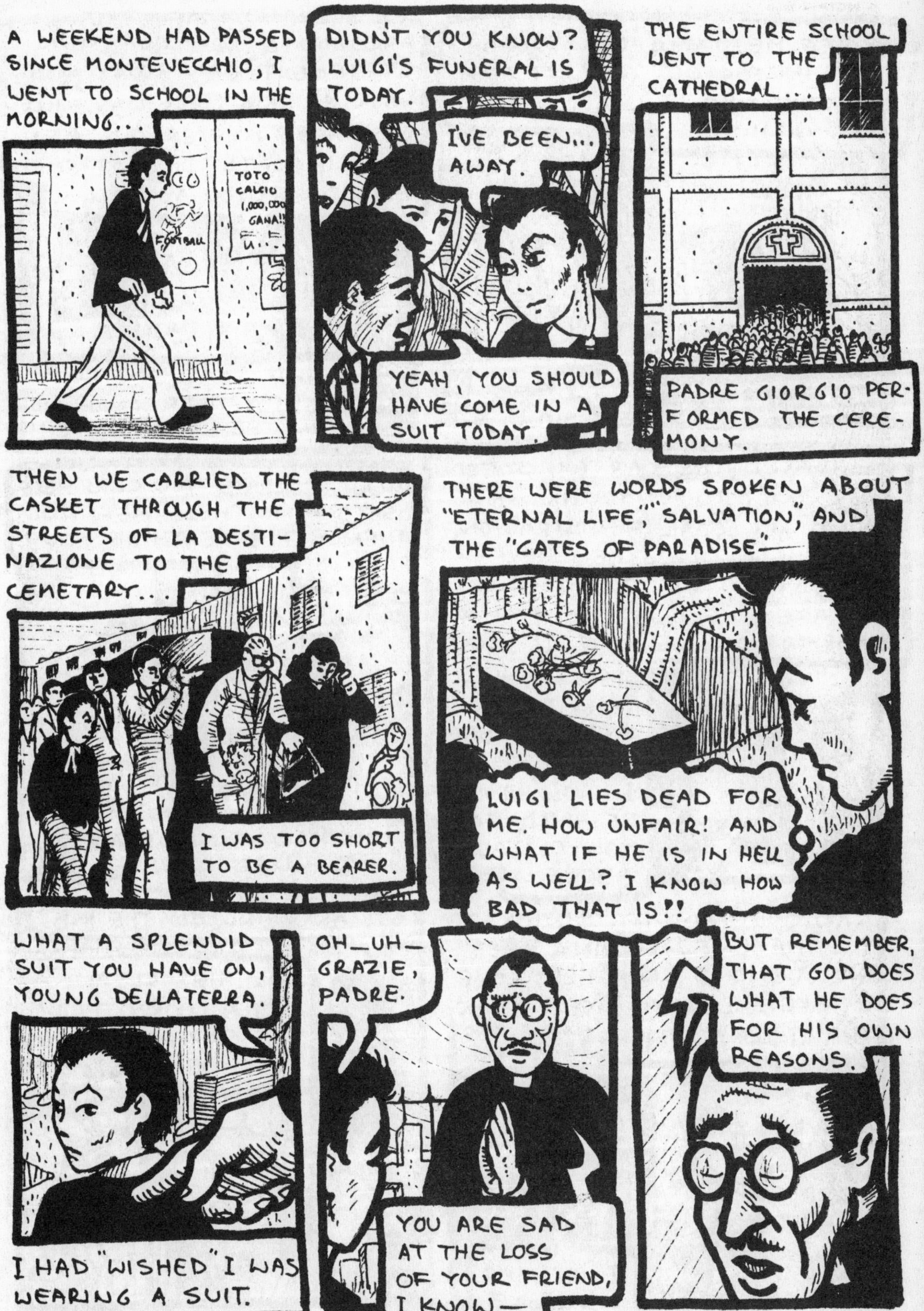

A WEEKEND HAD PASSED SINCE MONTEVECCHIO, I WENT TO SCHOOL IN THE MORNING...
TOTO CALCIO 1,000,000 GANA!!
FOOTBALL
DIDN'T YOU KNOW? LUIGI'S FUNERAL IS TODAY.
I'VE BEEN... AWAY.
YEAH, YOU SHOULD HAVE COME IN A SUIT TODAY.
THE ENTIRE SCHOOL WENT TO THE CATHEDRAL...
PADRE GIORGIO PERFORMED THE CEREMONY.
THEN WE CARRIED THE CASKET THROUGH THE STREETS OF LA DESTINAZIONE TO THE CEMETARY...
I WAS TOO SHORT TO BE A BEARER.
THERE WERE WORDS SPOKEN ABOUT "ETERNAL LIFE," "SALVATION," AND THE "GATES OF PARADISE"—
LUIGI LIES DEAD FOR ME. HOW UNFAIR! AND WHAT IF HE IS IN HELL AS WELL? I KNOW HOW BAD THAT IS!!
WHAT A SPLENDID SUIT YOU HAVE ON, YOUNG DELLATERRA.
I HAD "WISHED" I WAS WEARING A SUIT.
OH_UH_ GRAZIE, PADRE.
YOU ARE SAD AT THE LOSS OF YOUR FRIEND, I KNOW—
BUT REMEMBER, THAT GOD DOES WHAT HE DOES FOR HIS OWN REASONS.

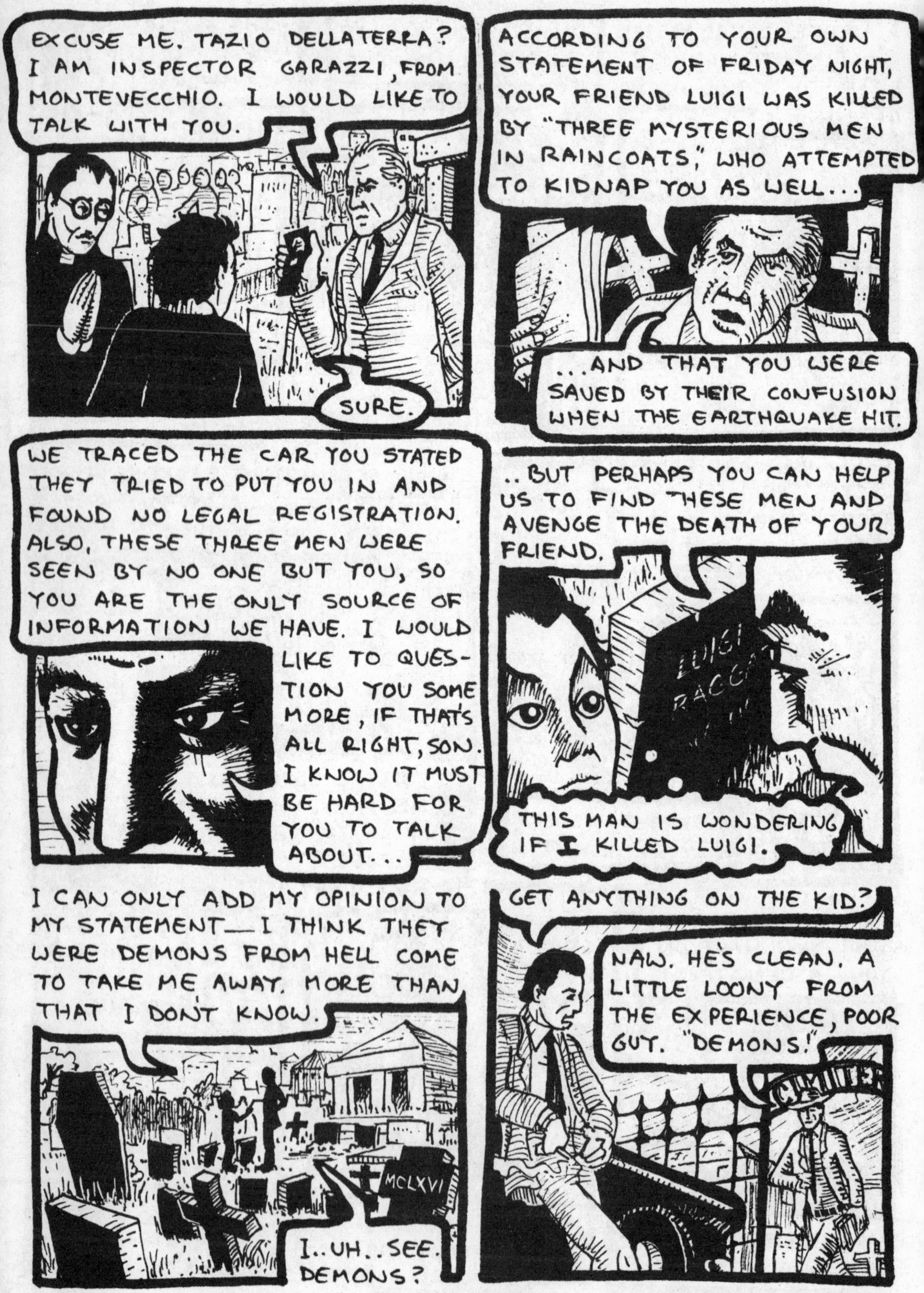
EXCUSE ME. TAZIO DELLATERRA? I AM INSPECTOR GARAZZI, FROM MONTEVECCHIO. I WOULD LIKE TO TALK WITH YOU.
SURE.
ACCORDING TO YOUR OWN STATEMENT OF FRIDAY NIGHT, YOUR FRIEND LUIGI WAS KILLED BY "THREE MYSTERIOUS MEN IN RAINCOATS," WHO ATTEMPTED TO KIDNAP YOU AS WELL...
...AND THAT YOU WERE SAVED BY THEIR CONFUSION WHEN THE EARTHQUAKE HIT.
WE TRACED THE CAR YOU STATED THEY TRIED TO PUT YOU IN AND FOUND NO LEGAL REGISTRATION. ALSO, THESE THREE MEN WERE SEEN BY NO ONE BUT YOU, SO YOU ARE THE ONLY SOURCE OF INFORMATION WE HAVE. I WOULD LIKE TO QUESTION YOU SOME MORE, IF THAT'S ALL RIGHT, SON. I KNOW IT MUST BE HARD FOR YOU TO TALK ABOUT...
..BUT PERHAPS YOU CAN HELP US TO FIND THESE MEN AND AVENGE THE DEATH OF YOUR FRIEND.
LUIGI RAGGI
THIS MAN IS WONDERING IF I KILLED LUIGI.
I CAN ONLY ADD MY OPINION TO MY STATEMENT—I THINK THEY WERE DEMONS FROM HELL COME TO TAKE ME AWAY. MORE THAN THAT I DON'T KNOW.
MCLXVI
I..UH..SEE. DEMONS?
GET ANYTHING ON THE KID?
NAW. HE'S CLEAN. A LITTLE LOONY FROM THE EXPERIENCE, POOR GUY. "DEMONS!"

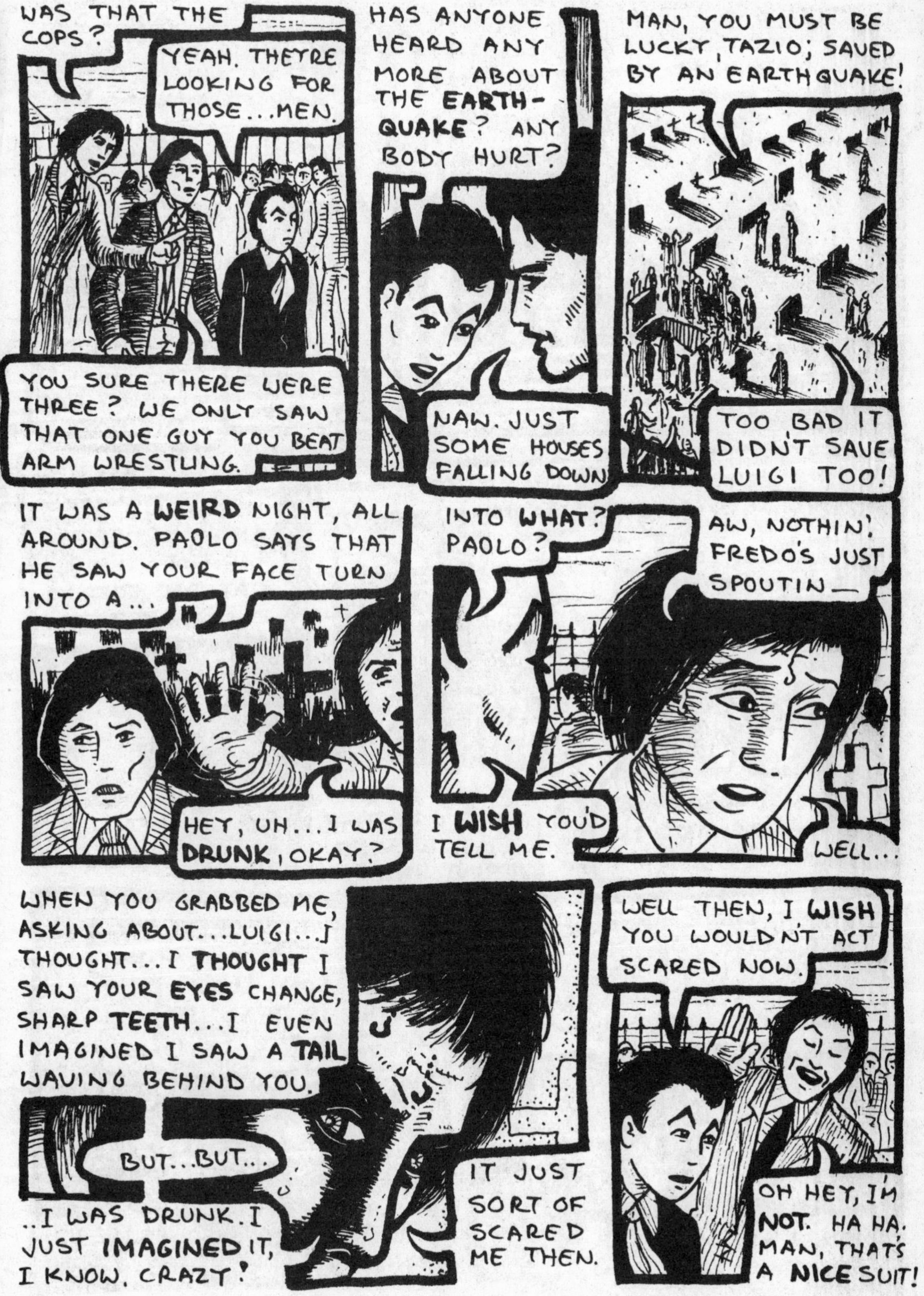
WAS THAT THE COPS?
YEAH. THEY'RE LOOKING FOR THOSE...MEN.
YOU SURE THERE WERE THREE? WE ONLY SAW THAT ONE GUY YOU BEAT ARM WRESTLING.
HAS ANYONE HEARD ANY MORE ABOUT THE EARTHQUAKE? ANY BODY HURT?
NAW. JUST SOME HOUSES FALLING DOWN.
MAN, YOU MUST BE LUCKY, TAZIO; SAVED BY AN EARTHQUAKE!
TOO BAD IT DIDN'T SAVE LUIGI TOO!
IT WAS A WEIRD NIGHT, ALL AROUND. PAOLO SAYS THAT HE SAW YOUR FACE TURN INTO A...
HEY, UH... I WAS DRUNK, OKAY?
INTO WHAT? PAOLO?
I WISH YOU'D TELL ME.
AW, NOTHIN'. FREDO'S JUST SPOUTIN—
WELL...
WHEN YOU GRABBED ME, ASKING ABOUT...LUIGI...I THOUGHT...I THOUGHT I SAW YOUR EYES CHANGE, SHARP TEETH...I EVEN IMAGINED I SAW A TAIL WAVING BEHIND YOU.
BUT...BUT...
..I WAS DRUNK. I JUST IMAGINED IT, I KNOW. CRAZY!
IT JUST SORT OF SCARED ME THEN.
WELL THEN, I WISH YOU WOULDN'T ACT SCARED NOW.
OH HEY, I'M NOT. HA HA. MAN, THAT'S A NICE SUIT!

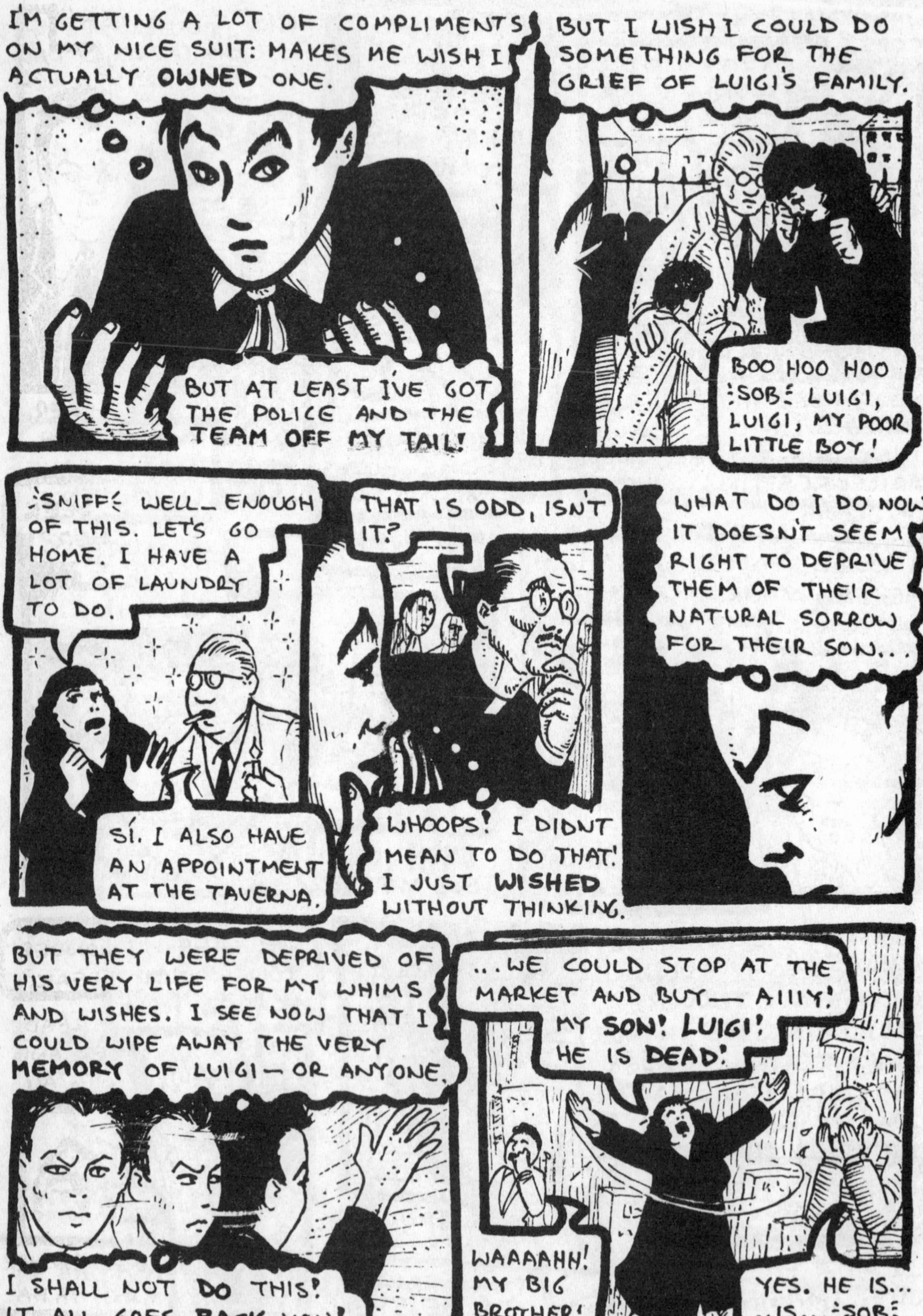
I'M GETTING A LOT OF COMPLIMENTS ON MY NICE SUIT: MAKES ME WISH I ACTUALLY **OWNED** ONE.
BUT AT LEAST I'VE GOT THE POLICE AND THE **TEAM OFF MY TAIL!**
BUT I WISH I COULD DO SOMETHING FOR THE GRIEF OF LUIGI'S FAMILY.
BOO HOO HOO :SOB: LUIGI, LUIGI, MY POOR LITTLE BOY!
:SNIFF: WELL_ ENOUGH OF THIS. LET'S GO HOME. I HAVE A LOT OF LAUNDRY TO DO.
SÍ. I ALSO HAVE AN APPOINTMENT AT THE TAVERNA.
THAT IS ODD, ISN'T IT?
WHOOPS! I DIDNT MEAN TO DO THAT! I JUST **WISHED** WITHOUT THINKING.
WHAT DO I DO NOW? IT DOESN'T SEEM RIGHT TO DEPRIVE THEM OF THEIR NATURAL SORROW FOR THEIR SON...
BUT THEY WERE DEPRIVED OF HIS VERY LIFE FOR MY WHIMS AND WISHES. I SEE NOW THAT I COULD WIPE AWAY THE VERY **MEMORY** OF LUIGI— OR ANYONE.
I SHALL NOT **DO** THIS! IT ALL GOES **BACK** NOW!
...WE COULD STOP AT THE MARKET AND BUY— AIIIY! MY **SON! LUIGI!** HE IS **DEAD!**
WAAAAHH! MY BIG BROTHER!
YES. HE IS... ..IS... :SOB: ...GONE

STRANGE HOW GRIEF AFFECTS SOME... HUHH???

—GASP

I HAD RELAXED MY CONTROL TOO MUCH, AND WAS BEING SEEN AS I AM.

ANOTHER "WISH" SOLVED THAT PROBLEM—

SOMETHING WRONG, PADRE GIORGIO?

OH—AH—ER, UH.. NO. UH.

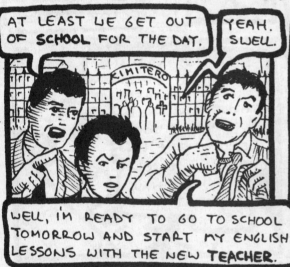

AT LEAST WE GET OUT OF SCHOOL FOR THE DAY.

YEAH. SWELL.

WELL, I'M READY TO GO TO SCHOOL TOMORROW AND START MY ENGLISH LESSONS WITH THE NEW TEACHER.

OH, YEAH! HAVE YOU ALL SEEN OUR NEW ENGLISH TEACHER? OOO-LA LA! BELLISSIMA!!

NO. BUT THEY FINALLY GOT AN ENGLISH TEACHER?

SÍ, BUT SHE'S NOT REALLY ENGLISH, SHE'S DANISH..

...BUT SHE SPEAKS ENGLISH, FRENCH, GERMAN...

HEY, HOW ABOUT ITALIAN? HA HA!

SÍ, NATURALMENTE! SHE'S REALLY SMART.

AND ONE MAY ASSUME SHE ALSO SPEAKS DANISH: THAT'S 5.

TAZIO, YOU'RE A BOY WONDER: HOW MANY CAN YOU SPEAK?

ME? I CAN READ SOME GREEK AND LATIN, THAT'S ALL.

AHA! MAYBE OUR NEW TEACHER IS SMARTER THAN YOU' HA HA!

LATER THAT DAY ON MY WAY HOME I NOTICED SOMEONE FOLLOWING ME.

I COULD HAVE OUTRUN HIM, BUT I CHOSE TO KNOW WHY.

ξWHEWξ WHAT A CLIMB!

DAMN! WHERE'D HE GO?

I'M RIGHT HERE, INSPECTOR GARAZZI

SO: AM I SUSPECTED OF MURDER?

I LIKE TO FEEL THAT I AM DILIGENT IN MY JOB, AND YOU ARE A MYSTER- IOUS PART OF THIS CASE. NOTHING PERSONAL, SON.

-SIGH- NO. NOTHING PERSONAL. I'D LIKE LUIGI'S MURDERERS TO BE PUNISHED TOO, BUT I DON'T BELIEVE THE LAW HAS THE POWER. I THINK I HAVE TO DO IT MY- SELF.

TELL ME THE TRUTH NOW, BOY. THE LAW WILL HANDLE IT.

NO. YOU WOULD NOT BELIEVE THE TRUTH, NOR HANDLE IT.

PERHAPS YOU'D BETTER, TAZIO. I SAID YOU WERE MYSTERIOUS. I SAW YOU PLAYING FOOTBALL IN MONTEVECCHIO—YOU ARE THE MOST IMPRESSIVE ATHELETE I'VE EVER SEEN—OF ANY AGE!! THUS YOU ARE A SUSPECT FOR TWO REASONS: YOU WERE LAST SEEN WITH THE VICTIM; AND I BELIEVE YOU EASILY HAVE THE STRENGTH TO BREAK A NECK WITH ONE BLOW. I'M JUST LETTING YOU KNOW HOW IT IS.

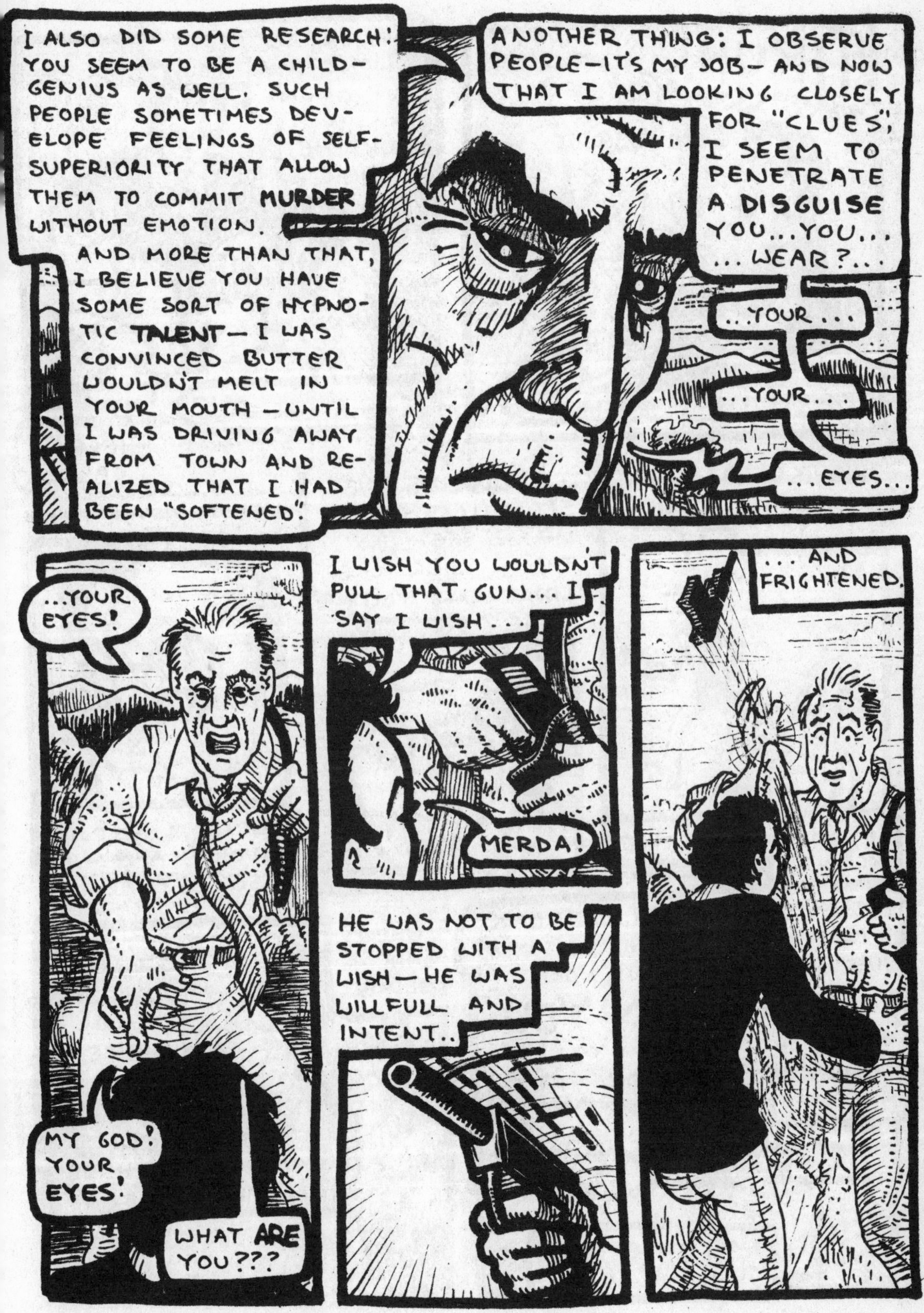
I ALSO DID SOME RESEARCH: YOU SEEM TO BE A CHILD-GENIUS AS WELL. SUCH PEOPLE SOMETIMES DEVELOPE FEELINGS OF SELF-SUPERIORITY THAT ALLOW THEM TO COMMIT MURDER WITHOUT EMOTION.
AND MORE THAN THAT, I BELIEVE YOU HAVE SOME SORT OF HYPNOTIC TALENT— I WAS CONVINCED BUTTER WOULDN'T MELT IN YOUR MOUTH —UNTIL I WAS DRIVING AWAY FROM TOWN AND REALIZED THAT I HAD BEEN "SOFTENED".
ANOTHER THING: I OBSERVE PEOPLE—IT'S MY JOB— AND NOW THAT I AM LOOKING CLOSELY FOR "CLUES", I SEEM TO PENETRATE A DISGUISE YOU... YOU... ...WEAR?...
...YOUR...
...YOUR...
...EYES...
...YOUR EYES!
MY GOD! YOUR EYES!
WHAT ARE YOU???
I WISH YOU WOULDN'T PULL THAT GUN... I SAY I WISH...
MERDA!
HE WAS NOT TO BE STOPPED WITH A WISH— HE WAS WILLFULL AND INTENT..
... AND FRIGHTENED.

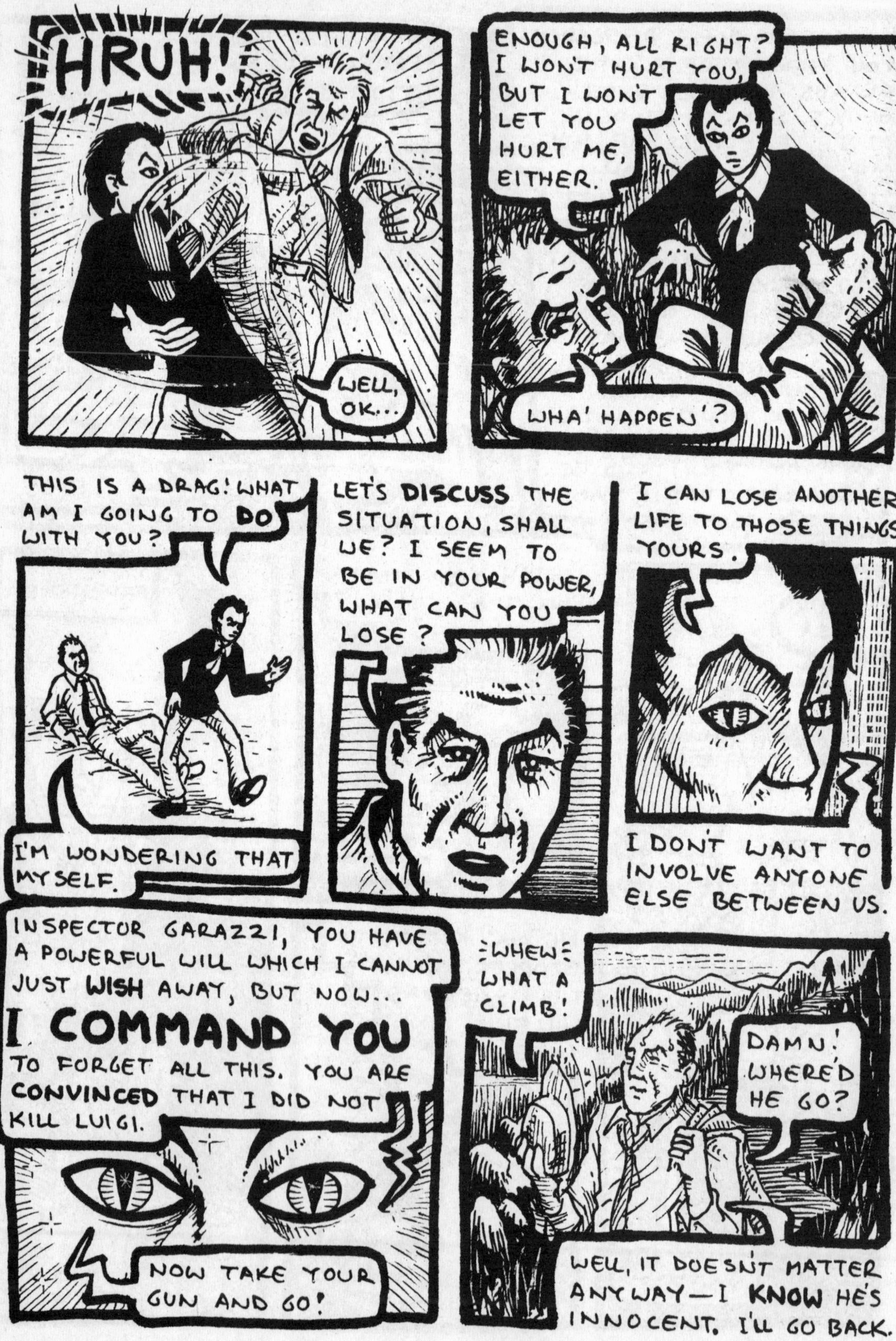
HRUH!
WELL, OK...
ENOUGH, ALL RIGHT? I WON'T HURT YOU, BUT I WON'T LET YOU HURT ME, EITHER.
WHA' HAPPEN'?
THIS IS A DRAG! WHAT AM I GOING TO DO WITH YOU?
I'M WONDERING THAT MYSELF.
LET'S DISCUSS THE SITUATION, SHALL WE? I SEEM TO BE IN YOUR POWER, WHAT CAN YOU LOSE?
I CAN LOSE ANOTHER LIFE TO THOSE THINGS: YOURS.
I DON'T WANT TO INVOLVE ANYONE ELSE BETWEEN US.
INSPECTOR GARAZZI, YOU HAVE A POWERFUL WILL WHICH I CANNOT JUST WISH AWAY, BUT NOW... I COMMAND YOU TO FORGET ALL THIS. YOU ARE CONVINCED THAT I DID NOT KILL LUIGI.
NOW TAKE YOUR GUN AND GO!
WHEW WHAT A CLIMB!
DAMN! WHERE'D HE GO?
WELL, IT DOESN'T MATTER ANYWAY—I KNOW HE'S INNOCENT. I'LL GO BACK.

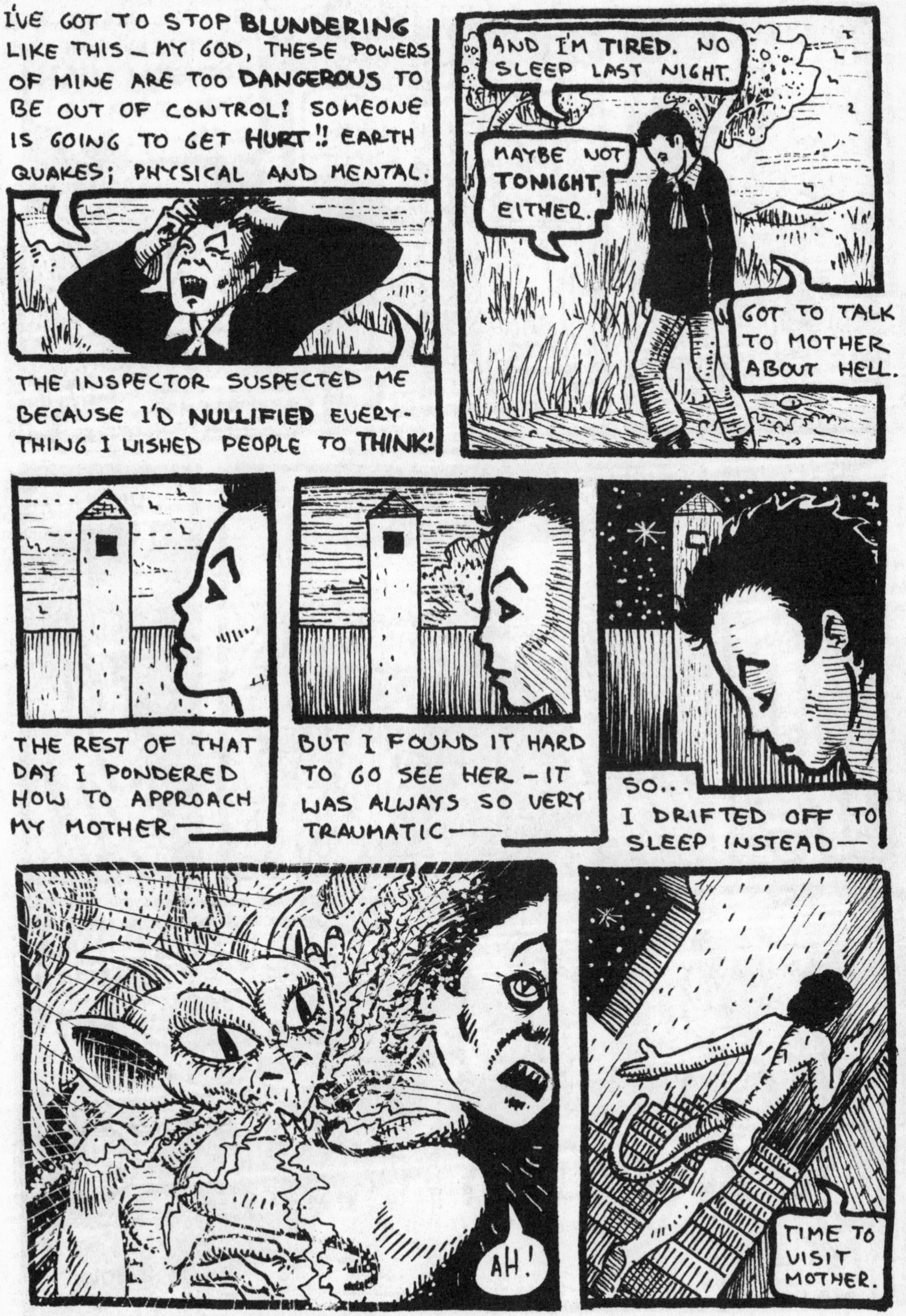
I'VE GOT TO STOP BLUNDERING LIKE THIS — MY GOD, THESE POWERS OF MINE ARE TOO DANGEROUS TO BE OUT OF CONTROL! SOMEONE IS GOING TO GET HURT!! EARTH QUAKES; PHYSICAL AND MENTAL.
THE INSPECTOR SUSPECTED ME BECAUSE I'D NULLIFIED EVERY-THING I WISHED PEOPLE TO THINK!
AND I'M TIRED. NO SLEEP LAST NIGHT.
MAYBE NOT TONIGHT, EITHER.
GOT TO TALK TO MOTHER ABOUT HELL.
THE REST OF THAT DAY I PONDERED HOW TO APPROACH MY MOTHER—
BUT I FOUND IT HARD TO GO SEE HER — IT WAS ALWAYS SO VERY TRAUMATIC—
SO...
I DRIFTED OFF TO SLEEP INSTEAD—
AH!
TIME TO VISIT MOTHER.

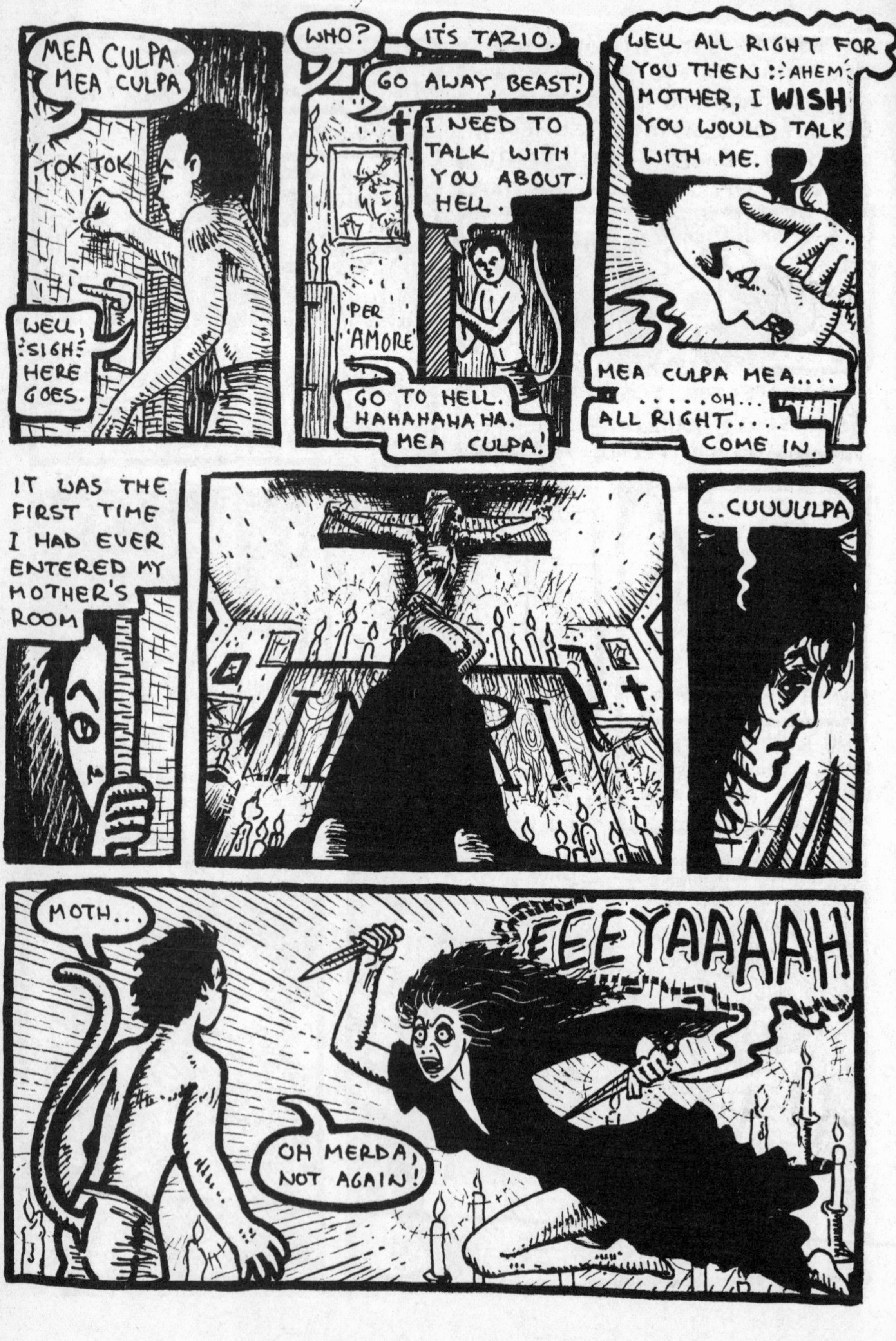
MEA CULPA MEA CULPA
TOK TOK
WELL, SIGH HERE GOES.
WHO?
IT'S TAZIO.
GO AWAY, BEAST!
I NEED TO TALK WITH YOU ABOUT HELL.
PER AMORE
GO TO HELL. HAHAHAHAHA. MEA CULPA!
WELL ALL RIGHT FOR YOU THEN AHEM MOTHER, I WISH YOU WOULD TALK WITH ME.
MEA CULPA MEA.... .....OH... ALL RIGHT..... COME IN.
IT WAS THE FIRST TIME I HAD EVER ENTERED MY MOTHER'S ROOM
..CUUUULPA
MOTH...
EEEYAAAAH
OH MERDA, NOT AGAIN!

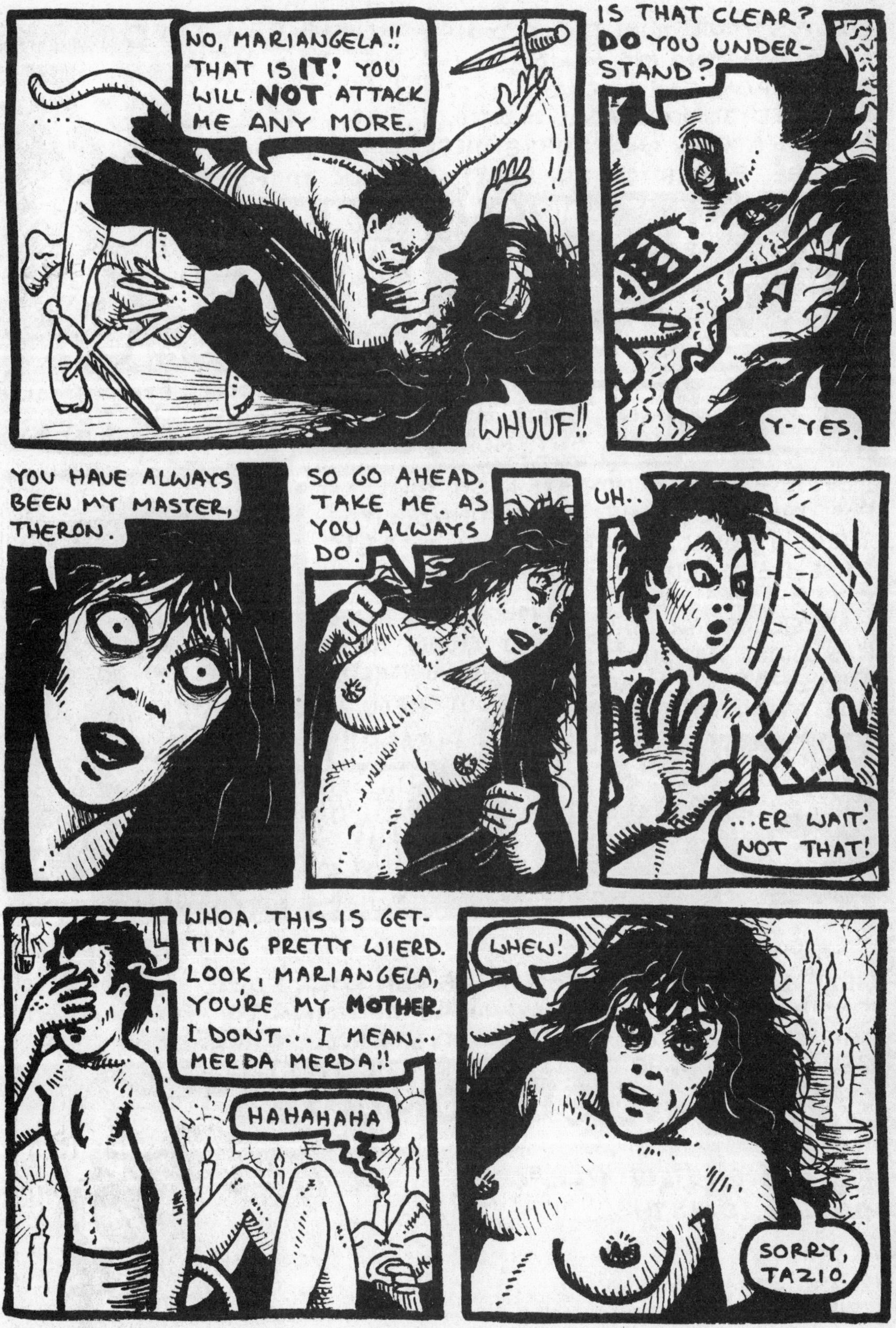
NO, MARIANGELA!! THAT IS IT! YOU WILL NOT ATTACK ME ANY MORE.
WHUUF!!
IS THAT CLEAR? DO YOU UNDERSTAND?
Y-YES.
YOU HAVE ALWAYS BEEN MY MASTER, THERON.
SO GO AHEAD. TAKE ME. AS YOU ALWAYS DO.
UH..
...ER WAIT! NOT THAT!
WHOA. THIS IS GETTING PRETTY WIERD. LOOK, MARIANGELA, YOU'RE MY MOTHER. I DON'T... I MEAN... MERDA MERDA!!
HAHAHAHA
WHEW!
SORRY, TAZIO.

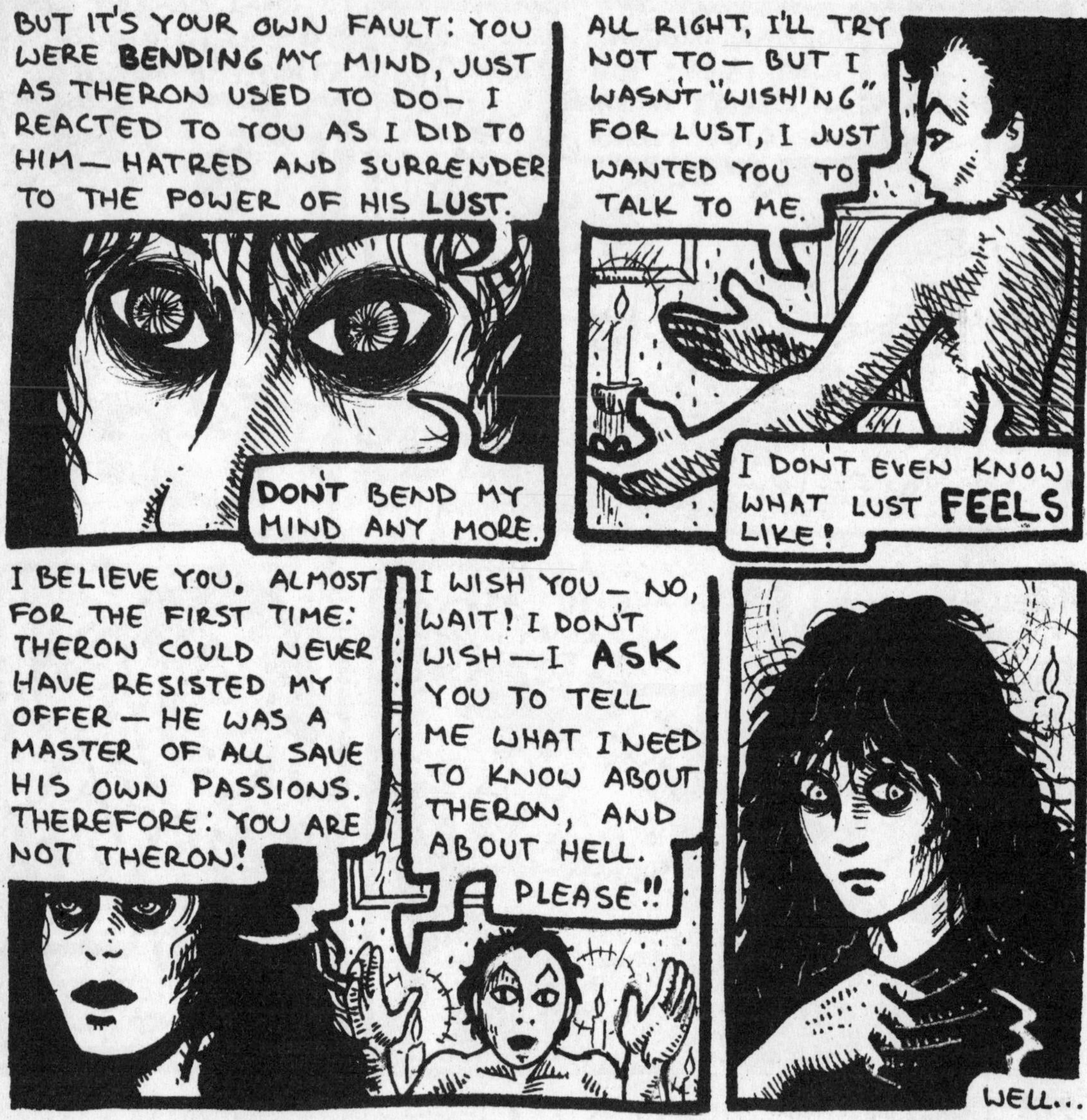
BUT IT'S YOUR OWN FAULT: YOU WERE BENDING MY MIND, JUST AS THERON USED TO DO— I REACTED TO YOU AS I DID TO HIM— HATRED AND SURRENDER TO THE POWER OF HIS LUST.
DON'T BEND MY MIND ANY MORE.
ALL RIGHT, I'LL TRY NOT TO— BUT I WASN'T "WISHING" FOR LUST, I JUST WANTED YOU TO TALK TO ME.
I DON'T EVEN KNOW WHAT LUST FEELS LIKE!
I BELIEVE YOU. ALMOST FOR THE FIRST TIME: THERON COULD NEVER HAVE RESISTED MY OFFER— HE WAS A MASTER OF ALL SAVE HIS OWN PASSIONS. THEREFORE: YOU ARE NOT THERON!
I WISH YOU— NO, WAIT! I DON'T WISH—I ASK YOU TO TELL ME WHAT I NEED TO KNOW ABOUT THERON, AND ABOUT HELL. PLEASE!!
WELL...

WELL, WE'VE RUN OUT OF PAGES FOR NOW, FOLX. TOO BAD, JUST WHEN WE WERE GETTING TO THE CRUX OF THE THERON MYSTERY. GUESS WE'LL JUST HAVE TO WAIT FOR THE NEXT ISSUE OF **ARMAGEDDONQUEST**

Ronald Russell Roach
August 10, 1984

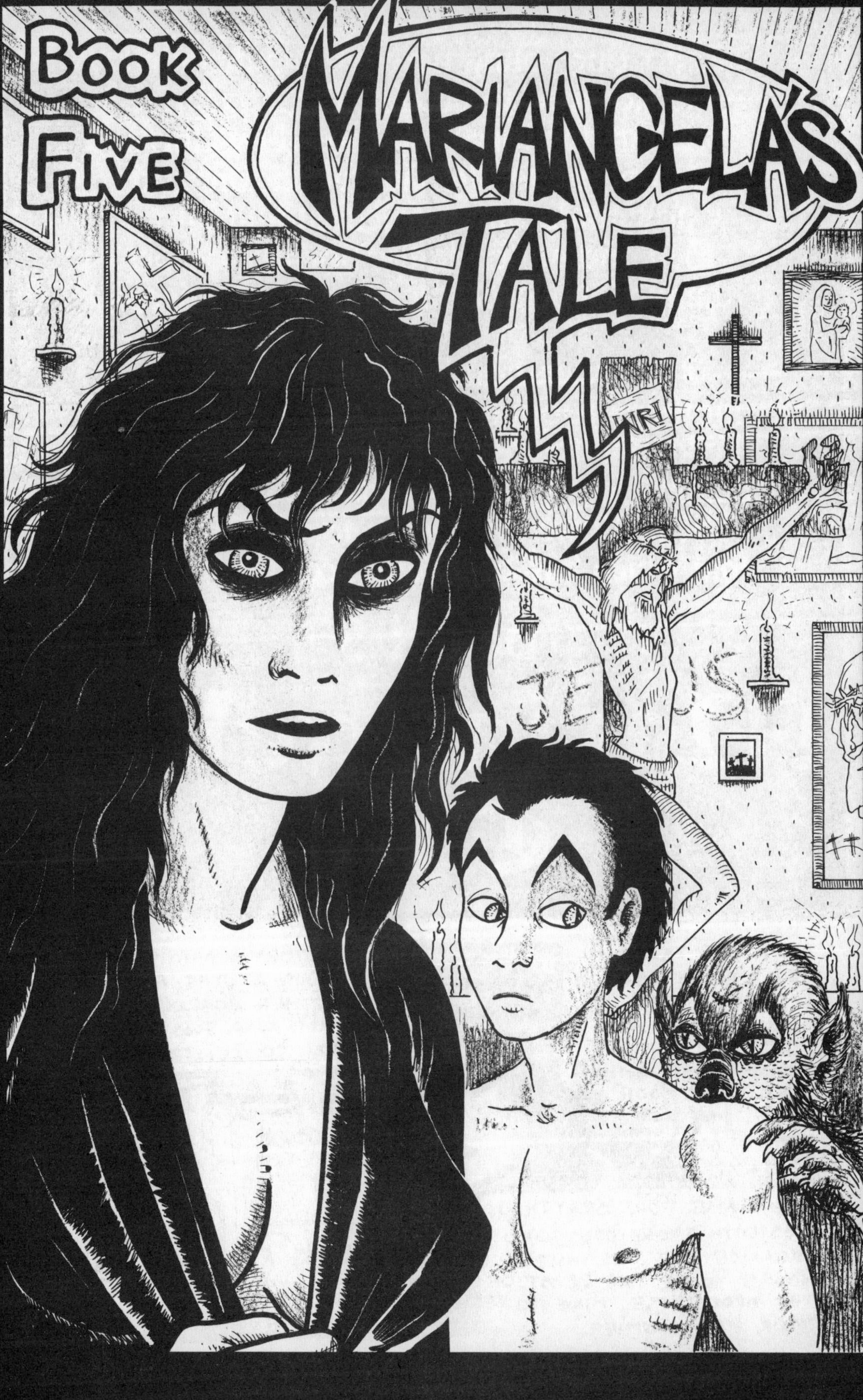
Book Five
MARIANGELA'S TALE

Tazio, our young hero who is destined and doomed to become the Antichrist, has furthermore been cursed by Ulfo's Demon under the last full moon, and now finds himself descending into Hell and suffering the horrors of the damned whenever he attempts to sleep.

In desperation he goes to his mad mother's room for the first time ever, for he knows that she too has experienced a descent into Hell. After the usual violence she mellows and offers to tell Tazio all that which has been kept secret from him.

# book 5
# Mariangela's Tale

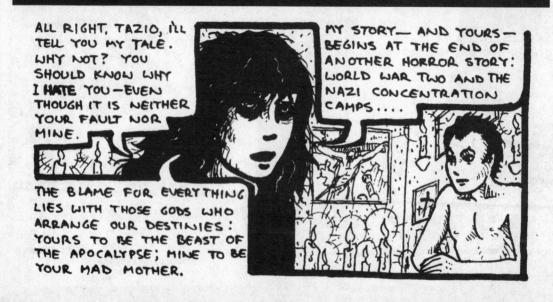

ALL RIGHT, TAZIO, I'LL TELL YOU MY TALE. WHY NOT? YOU SHOULD KNOW WHY I HATE YOU—EVEN THOUGH IT IS NEITHER YOUR FAULT NOR MINE.

THE BLAME FOR EVERYTHING LIES WITH THOSE GODS WHO ARRANGE OUR DESTINIES: YOURS TO BE THE BEAST OF THE APOCALYPSE; MINE TO BE YOUR MAD MOTHER.

MY STORY— AND YOURS— BEGINS AT THE END OF ANOTHER HORROR STORY: WORLD WAR TWO AND THE NAZI CONCENTRATION CAMPS....

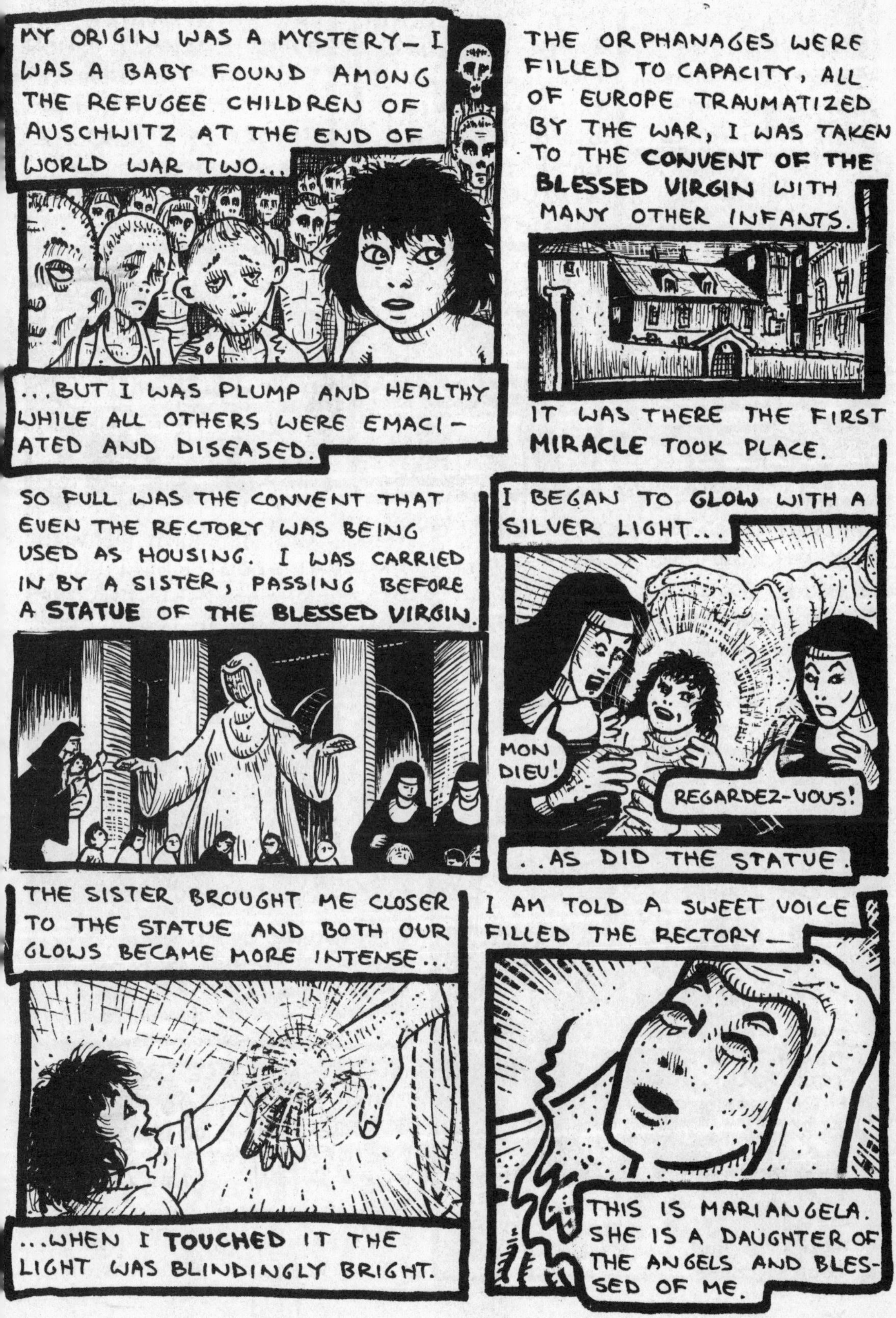

MY ORIGIN WAS A MYSTERY— I WAS A BABY FOUND AMONG THE REFUGEE CHILDREN OF AUSCHWITZ AT THE END OF WORLD WAR TWO...
...BUT I WAS PLUMP AND HEALTHY WHILE ALL OTHERS WERE EMACI-ATED AND DISEASED.
THE ORPHANAGES WERE FILLED TO CAPACITY, ALL OF EUROPE TRAUMATIZED BY THE WAR, I WAS TAKEN TO THE CONVENT OF THE BLESSED VIRGIN WITH MANY OTHER INFANTS.
IT WAS THERE THE FIRST MIRACLE TOOK PLACE.
SO FULL WAS THE CONVENT THAT EVEN THE RECTORY WAS BEING USED AS HOUSING. I WAS CARRIED IN BY A SISTER, PASSING BEFORE A STATUE OF THE BLESSED VIRGIN.
I BEGAN TO GLOW WITH A SILVER LIGHT...
MON DIEU!
REGARDEZ-VOUS!
..AS DID THE STATUE.
THE SISTER BROUGHT ME CLOSER TO THE STATUE AND BOTH OUR GLOWS BECAME MORE INTENSE...
...WHEN I TOUCHED IT THE LIGHT WAS BLINDINGLY BRIGHT.
I AM TOLD A SWEET VOICE FILLED THE RECTORY—
THIS IS MARIANGELA. SHE IS A DAUGHTER OF THE ANGELS AND BLES-SED OF ME.

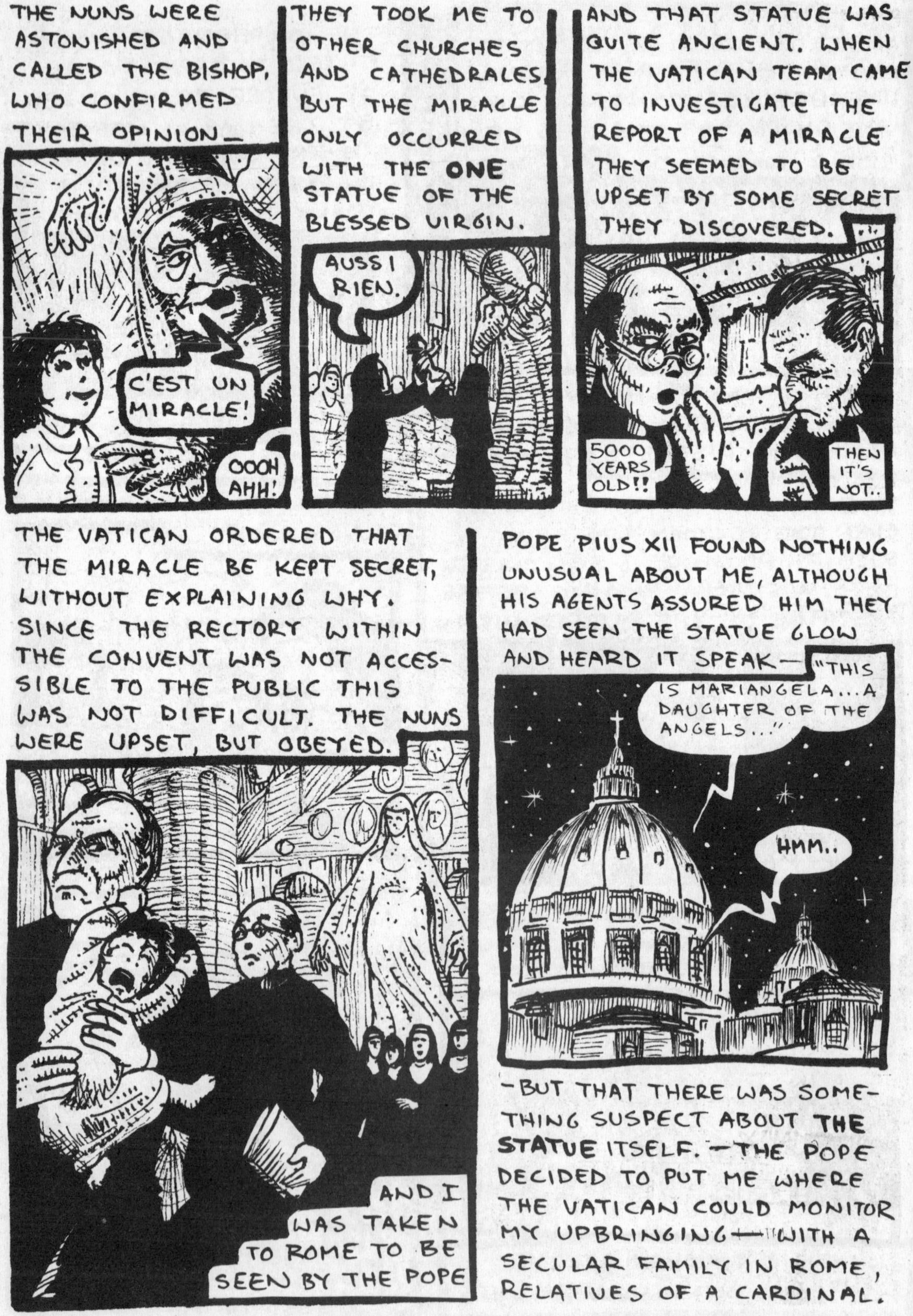
THE NUNS WERE ASTONISHED AND CALLED THE BISHOP, WHO CONFIRMED THEIR OPINION_
C'EST UN MIRACLE!
OOOH AHH!
THEY TOOK ME TO OTHER CHURCHES AND CATHEDRALES. BUT THE MIRACLE ONLY OCCURRED WITH THE ONE STATUE OF THE BLESSED VIRGIN.
AUSSI RIEN.
AND THAT STATUE WAS QUITE ANCIENT. WHEN THE VATICAN TEAM CAME TO INVESTIGATE THE REPORT OF A MIRACLE THEY SEEMED TO BE UPSET BY SOME SECRET THEY DISCOVERED.
5000 YEARS OLD!!
THEN IT'S NOT..
THE VATICAN ORDERED THAT THE MIRACLE BE KEPT SECRET, WITHOUT EXPLAINING WHY. SINCE THE RECTORY WITHIN THE CONVENT WAS NOT ACCESSIBLE TO THE PUBLIC THIS WAS NOT DIFFICULT. THE NUNS WERE UPSET, BUT OBEYED.
AND I WAS TAKEN TO ROME TO BE SEEN BY THE POPE
POPE PIUS XII FOUND NOTHING UNUSUAL ABOUT ME, ALTHOUGH HIS AGENTS ASSURED HIM THEY HAD SEEN THE STATUE GLOW AND HEARD IT SPEAK—
"THIS IS MARIANGELA... A DAUGHTER OF THE ANGELS..."
HMM..
—BUT THAT THERE WAS SOMETHING SUSPECT ABOUT THE STATUE ITSELF. —THE POPE DECIDED TO PUT ME WHERE THE VATICAN COULD MONITOR MY UPBRINGING — WITH A SECULAR FAMILY IN ROME, RELATIVES OF A CARDINAL.

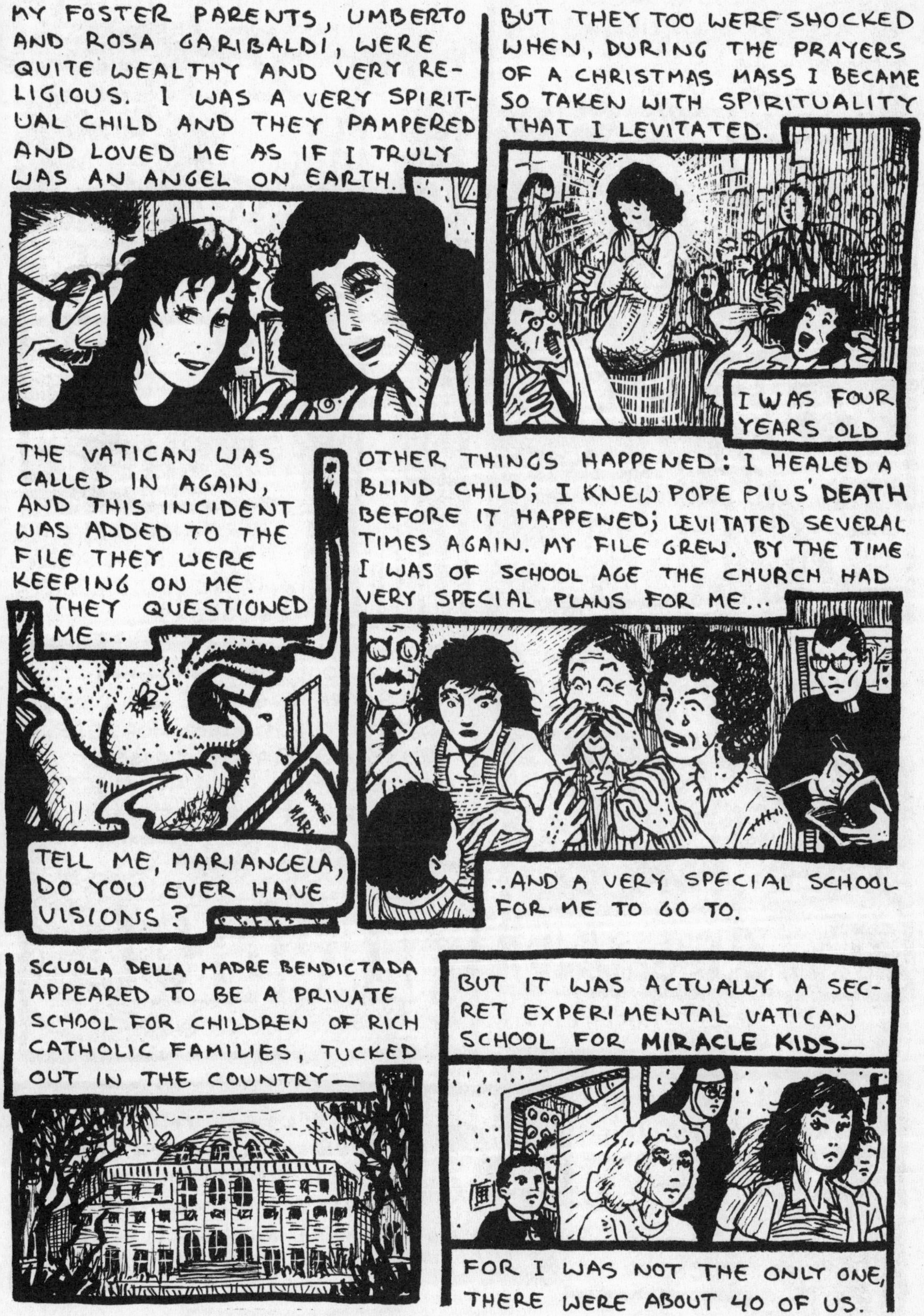
MY FOSTER PARENTS, UMBERTO AND ROSA GARIBALDI, WERE QUITE WEALTHY AND VERY RELIGIOUS. I WAS A VERY SPIRITUAL CHILD AND THEY PAMPERED AND LOVED ME AS IF I TRULY WAS AN ANGEL ON EARTH.
BUT THEY TOO WERE SHOCKED WHEN, DURING THE PRAYERS OF A CHRISTMAS MASS I BECAME SO TAKEN WITH SPIRITUALITY THAT I LEVITATED.
I WAS FOUR YEARS OLD
THE VATICAN WAS CALLED IN AGAIN, AND THIS INCIDENT WAS ADDED TO THE FILE THEY WERE KEEPING ON ME.
THEY QUESTIONED ME...
TELL ME, MARIANGELA, DO YOU EVER HAVE VISIONS?
OTHER THINGS HAPPENED: I HEALED A BLIND CHILD; I KNEW POPE PIUS' DEATH BEFORE IT HAPPENED; LEVITATED SEVERAL TIMES AGAIN. MY FILE GREW. BY THE TIME I WAS OF SCHOOL AGE THE CHURCH HAD VERY SPECIAL PLANS FOR ME...
..AND A VERY SPECIAL SCHOOL FOR ME TO GO TO.
SCUOLA DELLA MADRE BENDICTADA APPEARED TO BE A PRIVATE SCHOOL FOR CHILDREN OF RICH CATHOLIC FAMILIES, TUCKED OUT IN THE COUNTRY—
BUT IT WAS ACTUALLY A SECRET EXPERIMENTAL VATICAN SCHOOL FOR MIRACLE KIDS—
FOR I WAS NOT THE ONLY ONE, THERE WERE ABOUT 40 OF US.

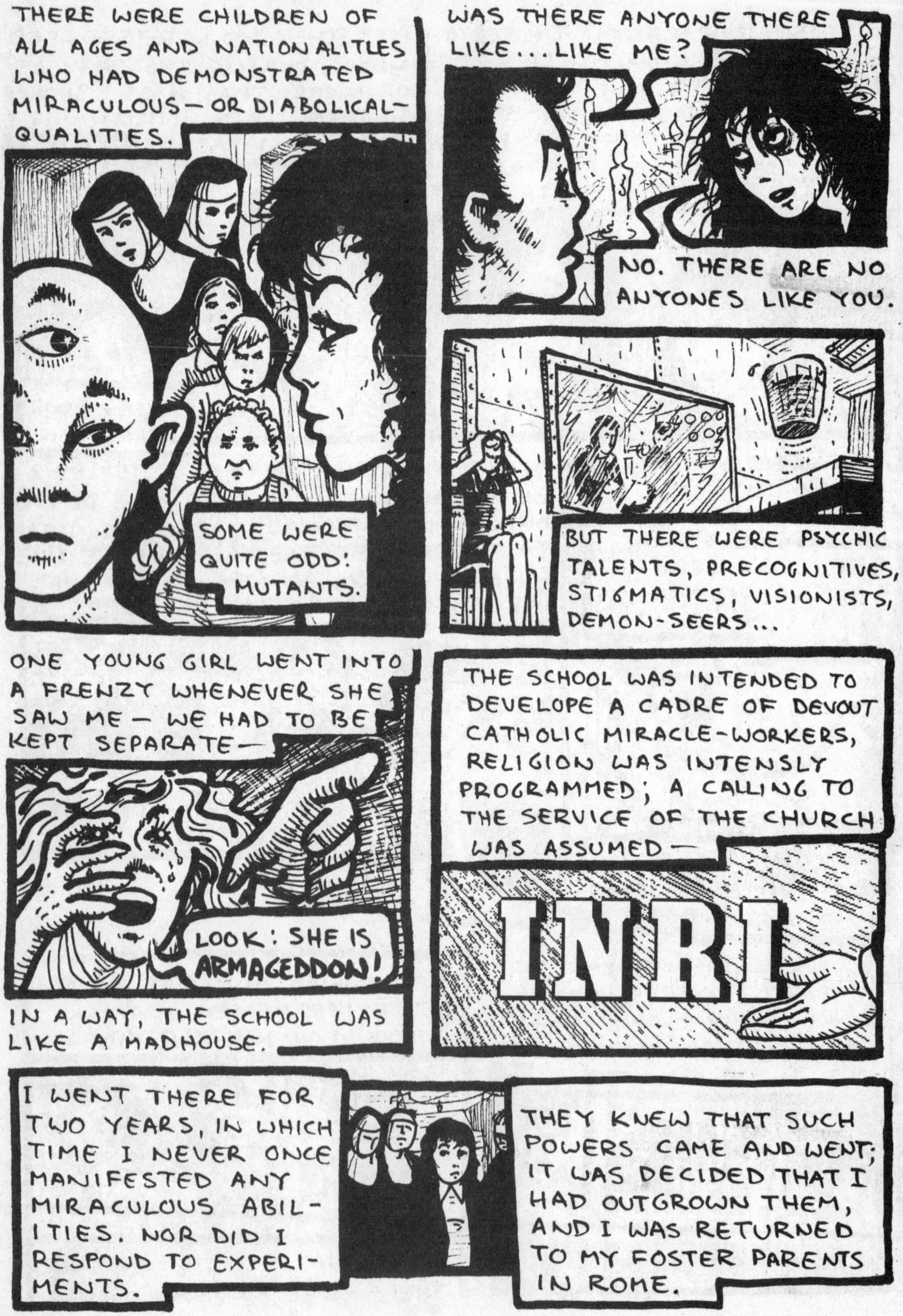
THERE WERE CHILDREN OF ALL AGES AND NATIONALITIES WHO HAD DEMONSTRATED MIRACULOUS — OR DIABOLICAL — QUALITIES.
SOME WERE QUITE ODD: MUTANTS.
WAS THERE ANYONE THERE LIKE... LIKE ME?
NO. THERE ARE NO ANYONES LIKE YOU.
BUT THERE WERE PSYCHIC TALENTS, PRECOGNITIVES, STIGMATICS, VISIONISTS, DEMON-SEERS...
ONE YOUNG GIRL WENT INTO A FRENZY WHENEVER SHE SAW ME — WE HAD TO BE KEPT SEPARATE —
LOOK: SHE IS ARMAGEDDON!
IN A WAY, THE SCHOOL WAS LIKE A MADHOUSE.
THE SCHOOL WAS INTENDED TO DEVELOPE A CADRE OF DEVOUT CATHOLIC MIRACLE-WORKERS, RELIGION WAS INTENSLY PROGRAMMED; A CALLING TO THE SERVICE OF THE CHURCH WAS ASSUMED —
INRI
I WENT THERE FOR TWO YEARS, IN WHICH TIME I NEVER ONCE MANIFESTED ANY MIRACULOUS ABILITIES. NOR DID I RESPOND TO EXPERIMENTS.
THEY KNEW THAT SUCH POWERS CAME AND WENT; IT WAS DECIDED THAT I HAD OUTGROWN THEM, AND I WAS RETURNED TO MY FOSTER PARENTS IN ROME.

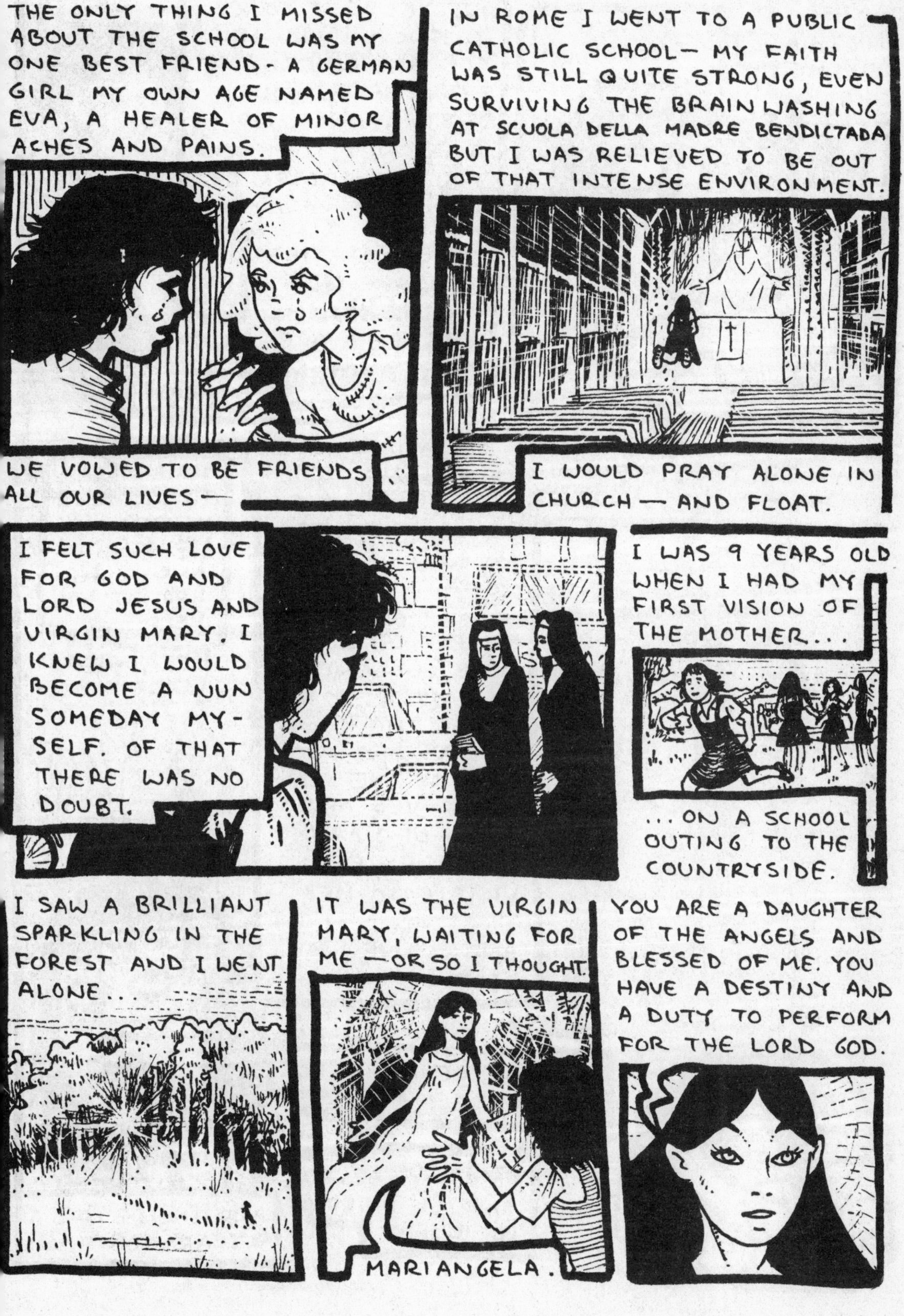
THE ONLY THING I MISSED ABOUT THE SCHOOL WAS MY ONE BEST FRIEND - A GERMAN GIRL MY OWN AGE NAMED EVA, A HEALER OF MINOR ACHES AND PAINS.
WE VOWED TO BE FRIENDS ALL OUR LIVES—
IN ROME I WENT TO A PUBLIC CATHOLIC SCHOOL— MY FAITH WAS STILL QUITE STRONG, EVEN SURVIVING THE BRAINWASHING AT SCUOLA DELLA MADRE BENDICTADA BUT I WAS RELIEVED TO BE OUT OF THAT INTENSE ENVIRONMENT.
I WOULD PRAY ALONE IN CHURCH — AND FLOAT.
I FELT SUCH LOVE FOR GOD AND LORD JESUS AND VIRGIN MARY. I KNEW I WOULD BECOME A NUN SOMEDAY MY-SELF. OF THAT THERE WAS NO DOUBT.
I WAS 9 YEARS OLD WHEN I HAD MY FIRST VISION OF THE MOTHER...
...ON A SCHOOL OUTING TO THE COUNTRYSIDE.
I SAW A BRILLIANT SPARKLING IN THE FOREST AND I WENT ALONE..
IT WAS THE VIRGIN MARY, WAITING FOR ME — OR SO I THOUGHT.
MARIANGELA.
YOU ARE A DAUGHTER OF THE ANGELS AND BLESSED OF ME. YOU HAVE A DESTINY AND A DUTY TO PERFORM FOR THE LORD GOD.

OH YES! YES! ANYTHING! TELL ME WHAT!

NOT YET IS IT YOURS TO KNOW, CHILD. WHEN YOU ARE OLDER YOU SHALL HAVE YOUR DESTINY. FOR NOW IT IS ONLY TO KNOW YOU ARE CHOSEN OF A LINEAGE OF POWER.

REMEMBER THIS: YOU ARE **NOT** ONLY **WHO** YOU **ARE**, BUT ARE ALSO **ANOTHER**. SEE NOW, **WHO!**

WHEN SHE SAID "**WHO**" I FELT MY AWARENESS EXPAND BEYOND FLESH AND MIND AND HUMAN MEMORY — I WAS **ANOTHER**: AN **ANGEL**, A BEING OF POWER, AN ETERNAL PERSONA.

...—✳—...

MY PERCEPTIONS WERE SUDDENLY SO VAST AS TO INCLUDE THE CURVATURE AND MOTION OF THE PLANET, WAVES AND RAYS OF VARIOUS ENERGIES WERE VISIBLE TO ME.

✳

AND I **KNEW** MY DESTINY.

IT WILL BE HARD FOR MARIANGELA.

IT MUST BE SO. AND IT MUST BE DONE.

MARIANGELA: TRY TO REMEMBER WHO **WE** ARE, YOU AND I. PERHAPS IT WILL HELP.

AND THEN I WAS A 9-YEAR OLD AGAIN.

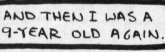

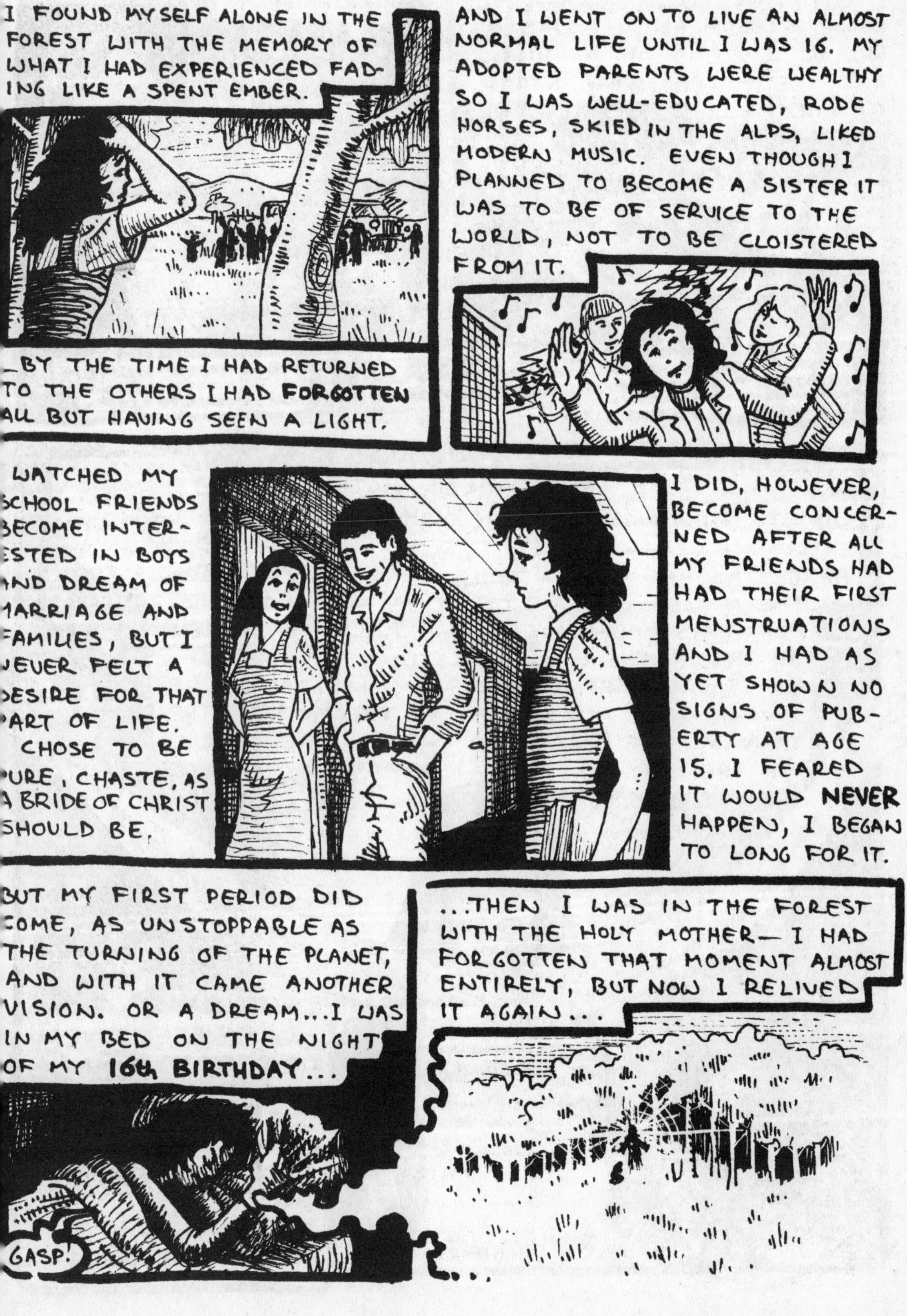
I FOUND MYSELF ALONE IN THE FOREST WITH THE MEMORY OF WHAT I HAD EXPERIENCED FADING LIKE A SPENT EMBER.
...BY THE TIME I HAD RETURNED TO THE OTHERS I HAD **FORGOTTEN** ALL BUT HAVING SEEN A LIGHT.
AND I WENT ON TO LIVE AN ALMOST NORMAL LIFE UNTIL I WAS 16. MY ADOPTED PARENTS WERE WEALTHY SO I WAS WELL-EDUCATED, RODE HORSES, SKIED IN THE ALPS, LIKED MODERN MUSIC. EVEN THOUGH I PLANNED TO BECOME A SISTER IT WAS TO BE OF SERVICE TO THE WORLD, NOT TO BE CLOISTERED FROM IT.
I WATCHED MY SCHOOL FRIENDS BECOME INTERESTED IN BOYS AND DREAM OF MARRIAGE AND FAMILIES, BUT I NEVER FELT A DESIRE FOR THAT PART OF LIFE. I CHOSE TO BE PURE, CHASTE, AS A BRIDE OF CHRIST SHOULD BE.
I DID, HOWEVER, BECOME CONCERNED AFTER ALL MY FRIENDS HAD HAD THEIR FIRST MENSTRUATIONS AND I HAD AS YET SHOWN NO SIGNS OF PUBERTY AT AGE 15. I FEARED IT WOULD **NEVER** HAPPEN, I BEGAN TO LONG FOR IT.
BUT MY FIRST PERIOD DID COME, AS UNSTOPPABLE AS THE TURNING OF THE PLANET, AND WITH IT CAME ANOTHER VISION. OR A DREAM... I WAS IN MY BED ON THE NIGHT OF MY **16th BIRTHDAY**...
GASP!
...THEN I WAS IN THE FOREST WITH THE HOLY MOTHER — I HAD FORGOTTEN THAT MOMENT ALMOST ENTIRELY, BUT NOW I RELIVED IT AGAIN...

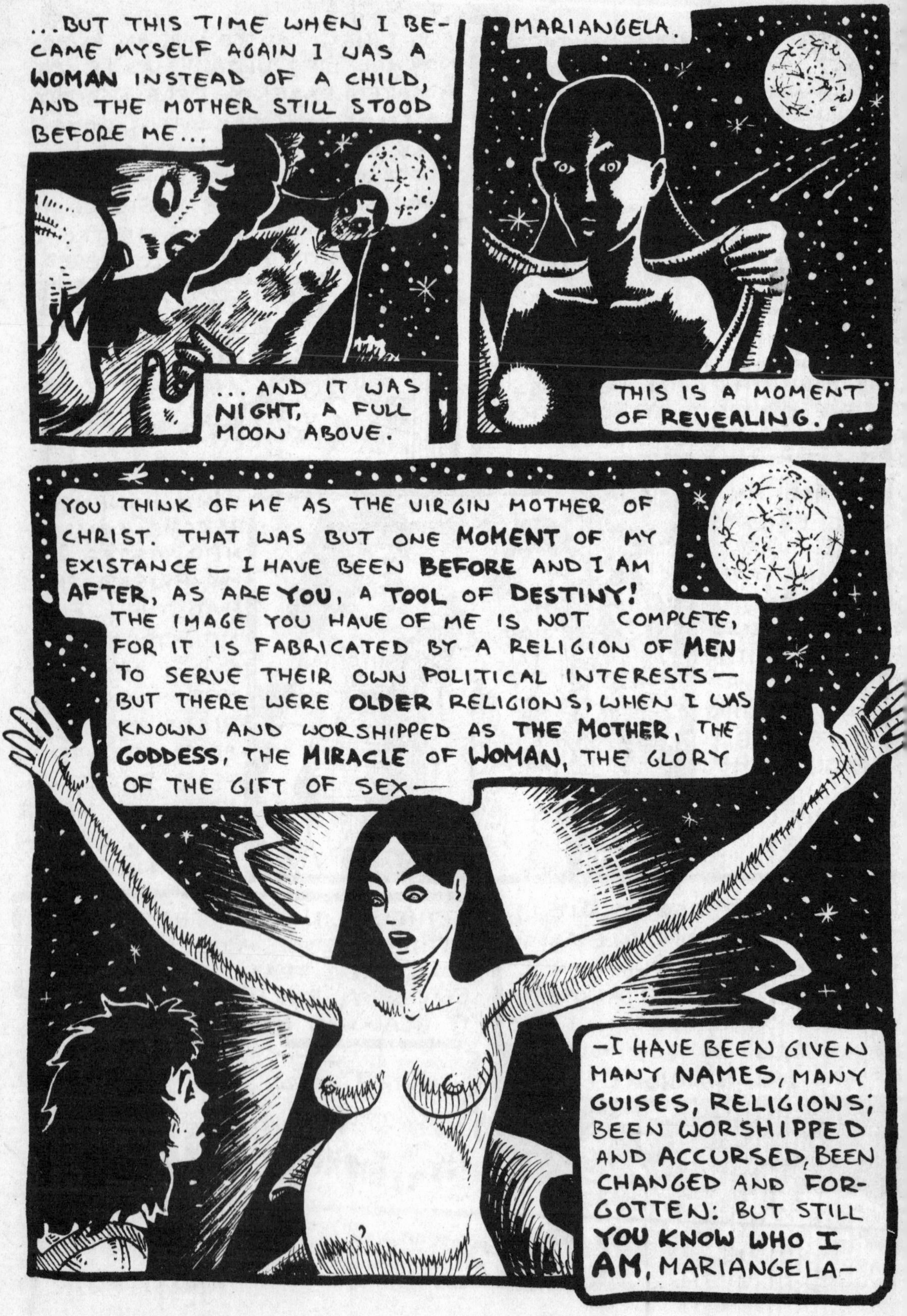
...BUT THIS TIME WHEN I BECAME MYSELF AGAIN I WAS A **WOMAN** INSTEAD OF A CHILD, AND THE MOTHER STILL STOOD BEFORE ME...
...AND IT WAS **NIGHT**, A FULL MOON ABOVE.
MARIANGELA.
THIS IS A MOMENT OF **REVEALING**.
YOU THINK OF ME AS THE VIRGIN MOTHER OF CHRIST. THAT WAS BUT ONE **MOMENT** OF MY EXISTANCE — I HAVE BEEN **BEFORE** AND I AM **AFTER**, AS ARE **YOU**, A **TOOL** OF **DESTINY!**
THE IMAGE YOU HAVE OF ME IS NOT COMPLETE, FOR IT IS FABRICATED BY A RELIGION OF **MEN** TO SERVE THEIR OWN POLITICAL INTERESTS— BUT THERE WERE **OLDER** RELIGIONS, WHEN I WAS KNOWN AND WORSHIPPED AS **THE MOTHER**, THE **GODDESS**, THE **MIRACLE** OF **WOMAN**, THE GLORY OF THE GIFT OF SEX—
—I HAVE BEEN GIVEN MANY **NAMES**, MANY **GUISES**, **RELIGIONS**; BEEN **WORSHIPPED** AND **ACCURSED**, BEEN **CHANGED** AND **FORGOTTEN**: BUT STILL **YOU KNOW WHO I AM**, MARIANGELA—

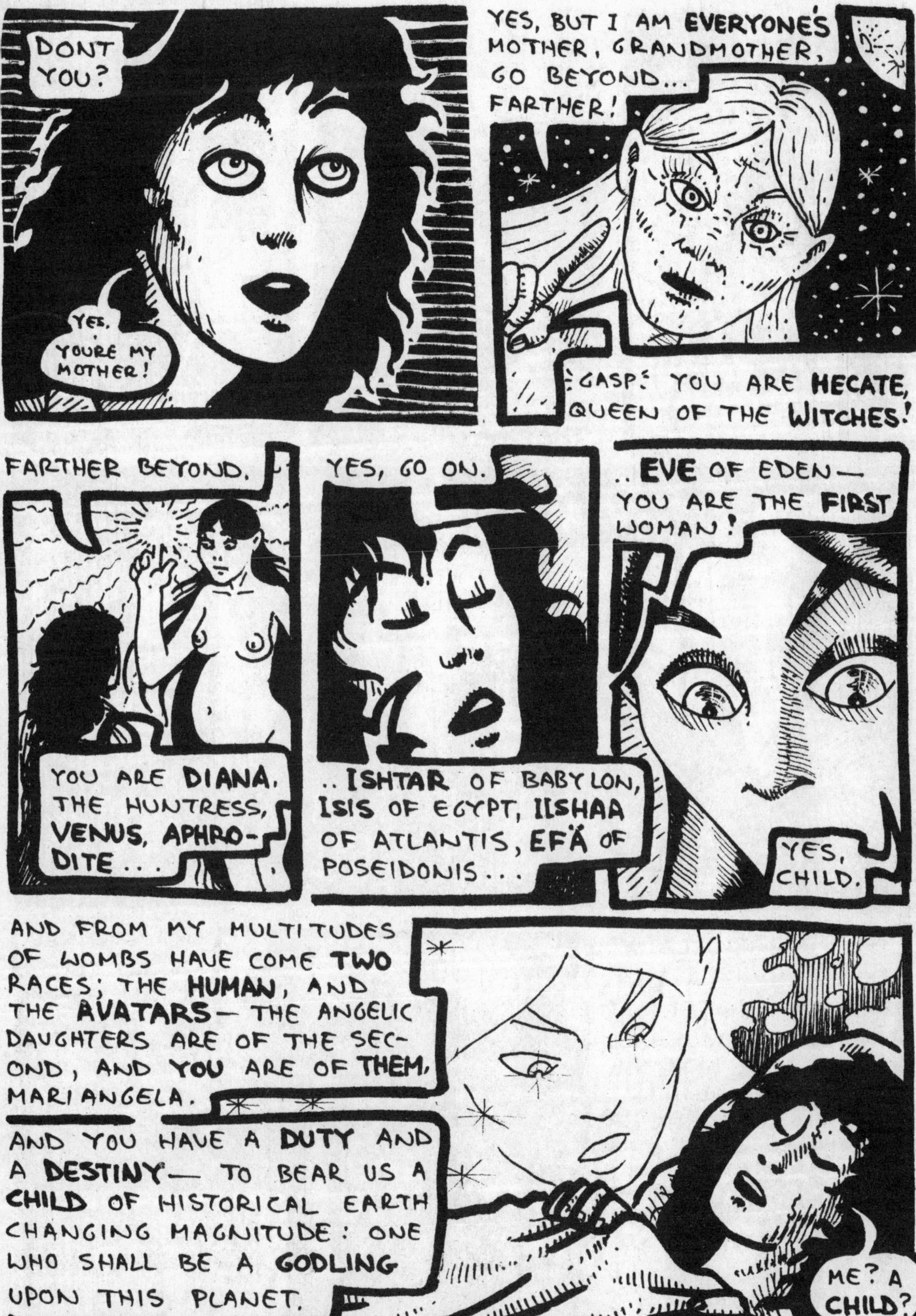
DONT YOU?
YES. YOURE MY MOTHER!
YES, BUT I AM EVERYONE'S MOTHER, GRANDMOTHER, GO BEYOND... FARTHER!
:GASP: YOU ARE HECATE, QUEEN OF THE WITCHES!
FARTHER BEYOND.
YOU ARE DIANA. THE HUNTRESS, VENUS, APHRODITE...
YES, GO ON.
..ISHTAR OF BABYLON, ISIS OF EGYPT, ILSHAA OF ATLANTIS, EFÄ OF POSEIDONIS...
..EVE OF EDEN— YOU ARE THE FIRST WOMAN!
YES, CHILD.
AND FROM MY MULTITUDES OF WOMBS HAVE COME TWO RACES; THE HUMAN, AND THE AVATARS— THE ANGELIC DAUGHTERS ARE OF THE SECOND, AND YOU ARE OF THEM, MARIANGELA.
AND YOU HAVE A DUTY AND A DESTINY— TO BEAR US A CHILD OF HISTORICAL EARTH CHANGING MAGNITUDE: ONE WHO SHALL BE A GODLING UPON THIS PLANET.
ME? A CHILD?

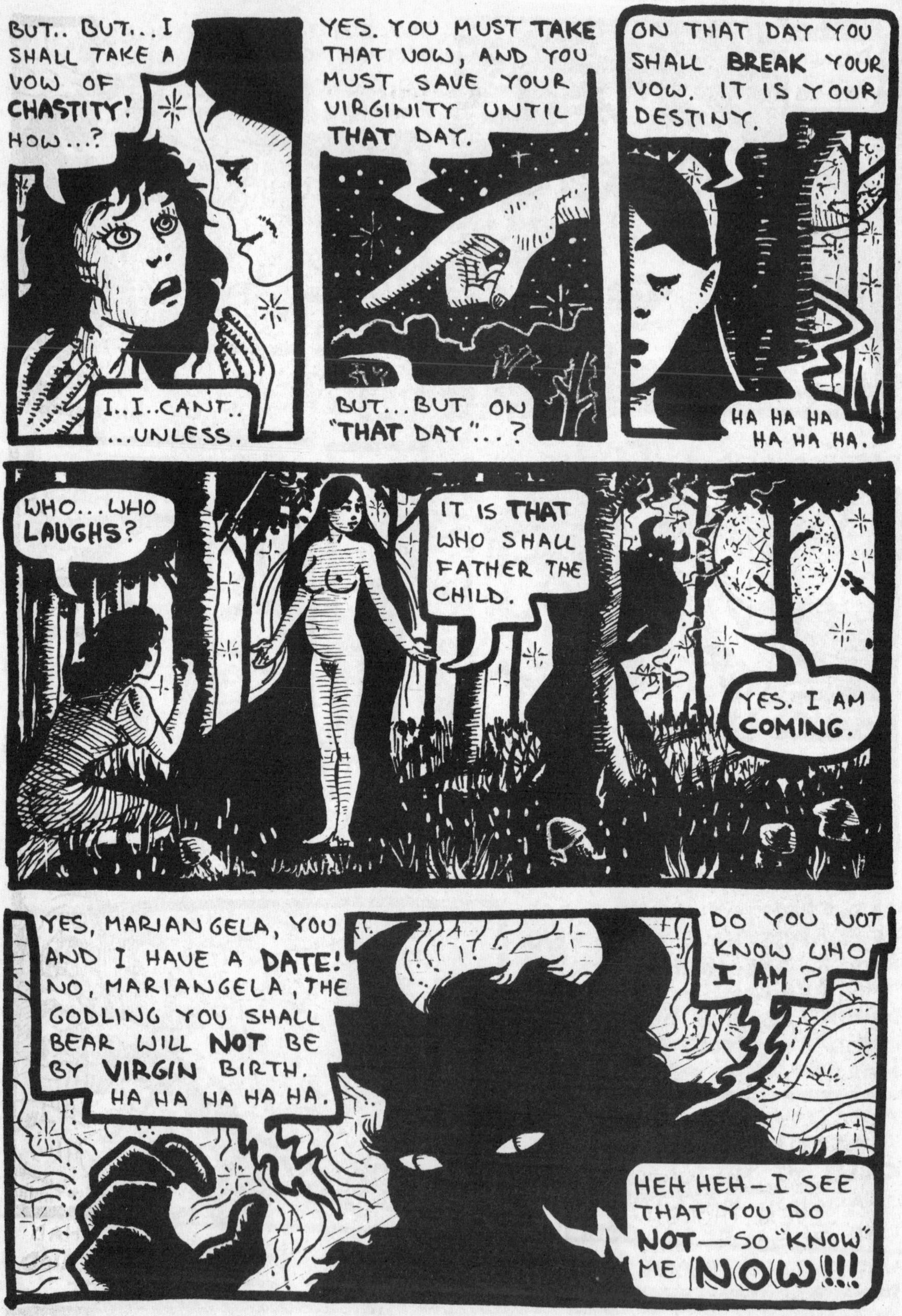

BUT.. BUT...I SHALL TAKE A VOW OF CHASTITY! HOW...?
I..I..CAN'T.. ...UNLESS.
YES. YOU MUST TAKE THAT VOW, AND YOU MUST SAVE YOUR VIRGINITY UNTIL THAT DAY.
BUT...BUT ON "THAT DAY"..?
ON THAT DAY YOU SHALL BREAK YOUR VOW. IT IS YOUR DESTINY.
HA HA HA HA HA HA.
WHO...WHO LAUGHS?
IT IS THAT WHO SHALL FATHER THE CHILD.
YES. I AM COMING.
YES, MARIANGELA, YOU AND I HAVE A DATE! NO, MARIANGELA, THE GODLING YOU SHALL BEAR WILL NOT BE BY VIRGIN BIRTH. HA HA HA HA HA.
DO YOU NOT KNOW WHO I AM?
HEH HEH—I SEE THAT YOU DO NOT—SO "KNOW" ME NOW!!!

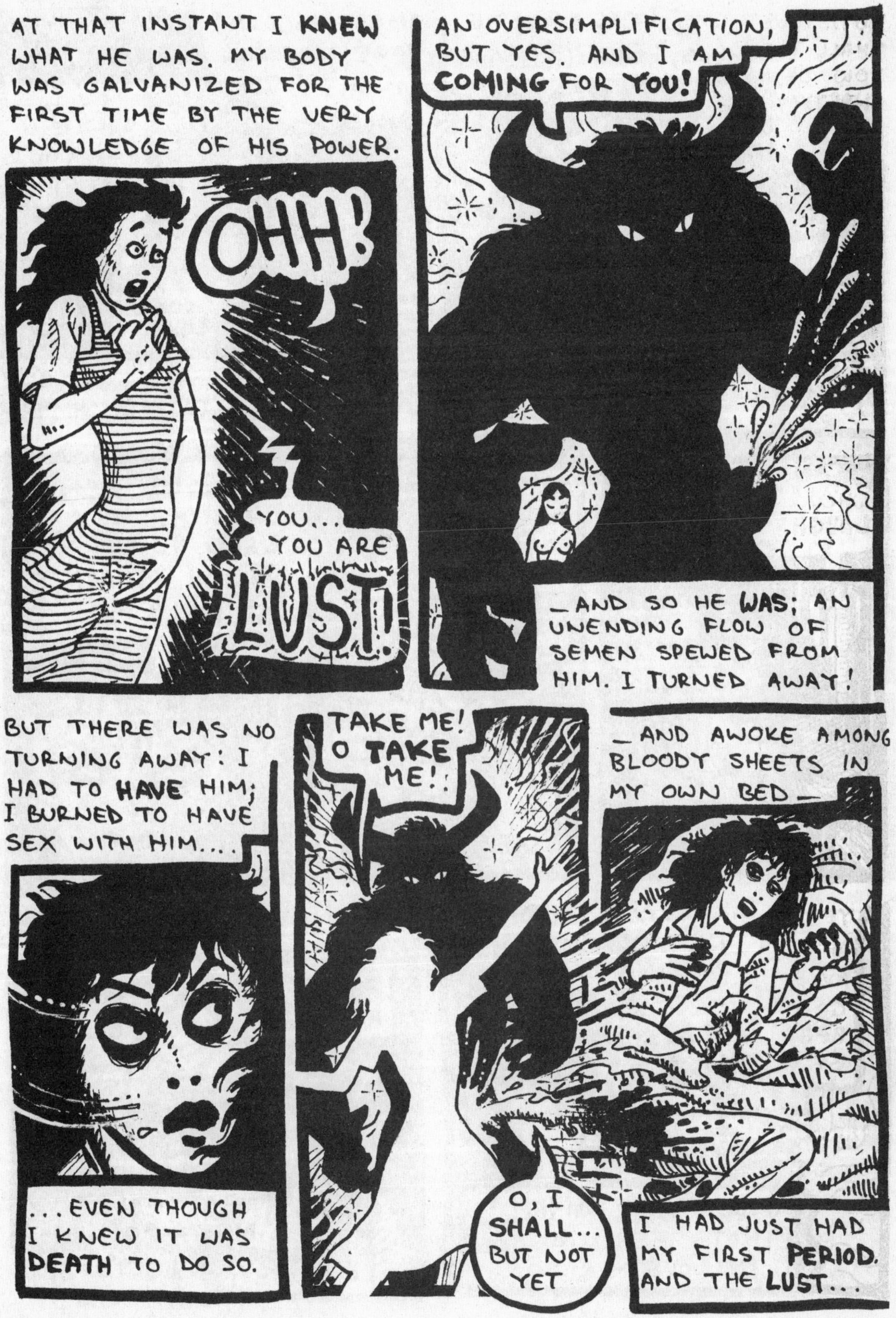
AT THAT INSTANT I KNEW WHAT HE WAS. MY BODY WAS GALVANIZED FOR THE FIRST TIME BY THE VERY KNOWLEDGE OF HIS POWER.
OHH!
YOU... YOU ARE LUST!
AN OVERSIMPLIFICATION, BUT YES. AND I AM COMING FOR YOU!
_AND SO HE WAS; AN UNENDING FLOW OF SEMEN SPEWED FROM HIM. I TURNED AWAY!
BUT THERE WAS NO TURNING AWAY: I HAD TO HAVE HIM; I BURNED TO HAVE SEX WITH HIM....
...EVEN THOUGH I KNEW IT WAS DEATH TO DO SO.
TAKE ME! O TAKE ME!
O, I SHALL... BUT NOT YET
_AND AWOKE AMONG BLOODY SHEETS IN MY OWN BED_
I HAD JUST HAD MY FIRST PERIOD. AND THE LUST...

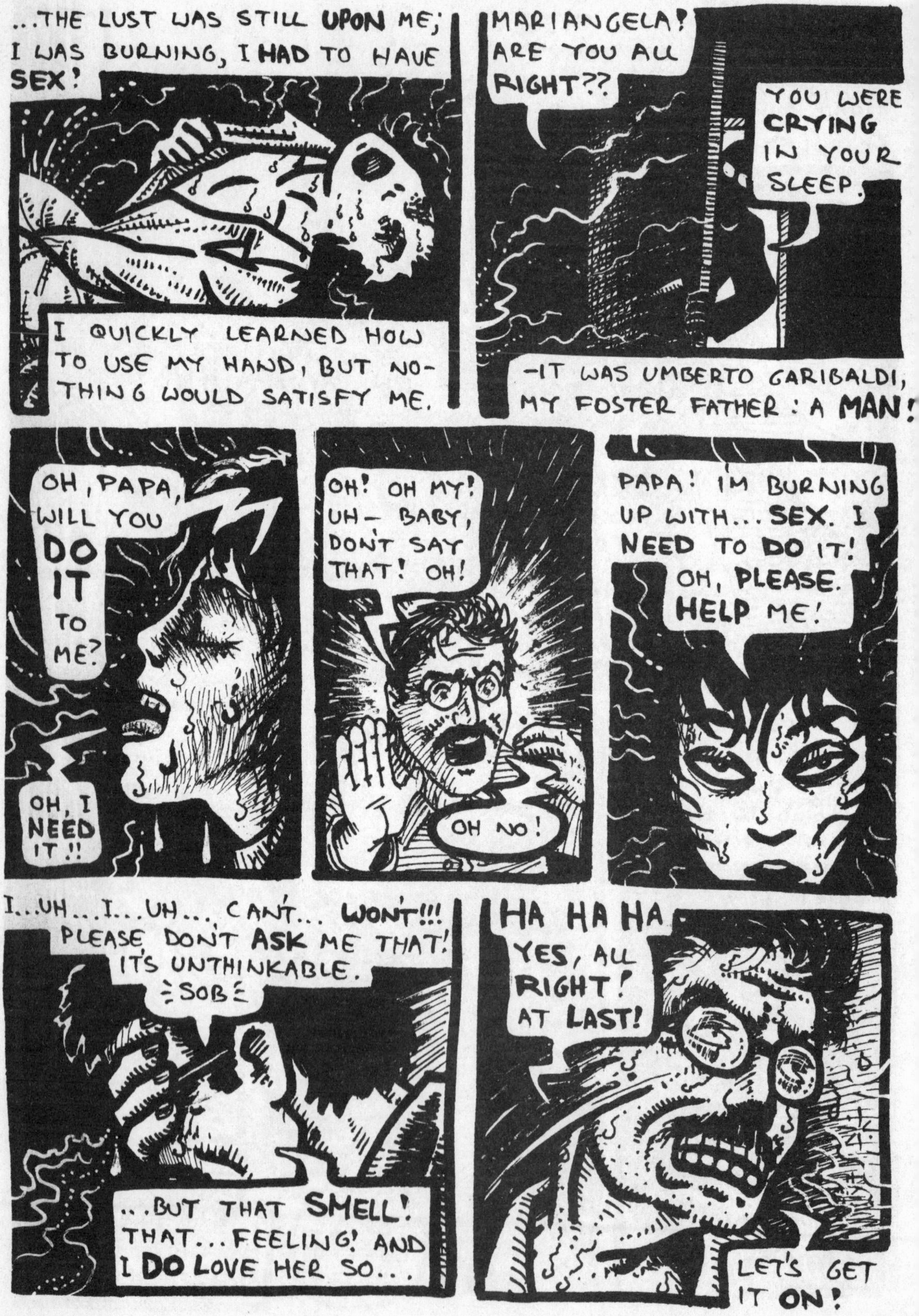

...THE LUST WAS STILL UPON ME; I WAS BURNING, I HAD TO HAVE SEX!
I QUICKLY LEARNED HOW TO USE MY HAND, BUT NOTHING WOULD SATISFY ME.
MARIANGELA! ARE YOU ALL RIGHT??
YOU WERE CRYING IN YOUR SLEEP.
-IT WAS UMBERTO GARIBALDI, MY FOSTER FATHER : A MAN!
OH, PAPA, WILL YOU DO IT TO ME?
OH, I NEED IT!!
OH! OH MY! UH- BABY, DON'T SAY THAT! OH!
OH NO!
PAPA! I'M BURNING UP WITH... SEX. I NEED TO DO IT!
OH, PLEASE. HELP ME!
I...UH...I...UH... CAN'T... WON'T!!! PLEASE DON'T ASK ME THAT! IT'S UNTHINKABLE.
SOB
...BUT THAT SMELL! THAT...FEELING! AND I DO LOVE HER SO...
HA HA HA
YES, ALL RIGHT! AT LAST!
LET'S GET IT ON!

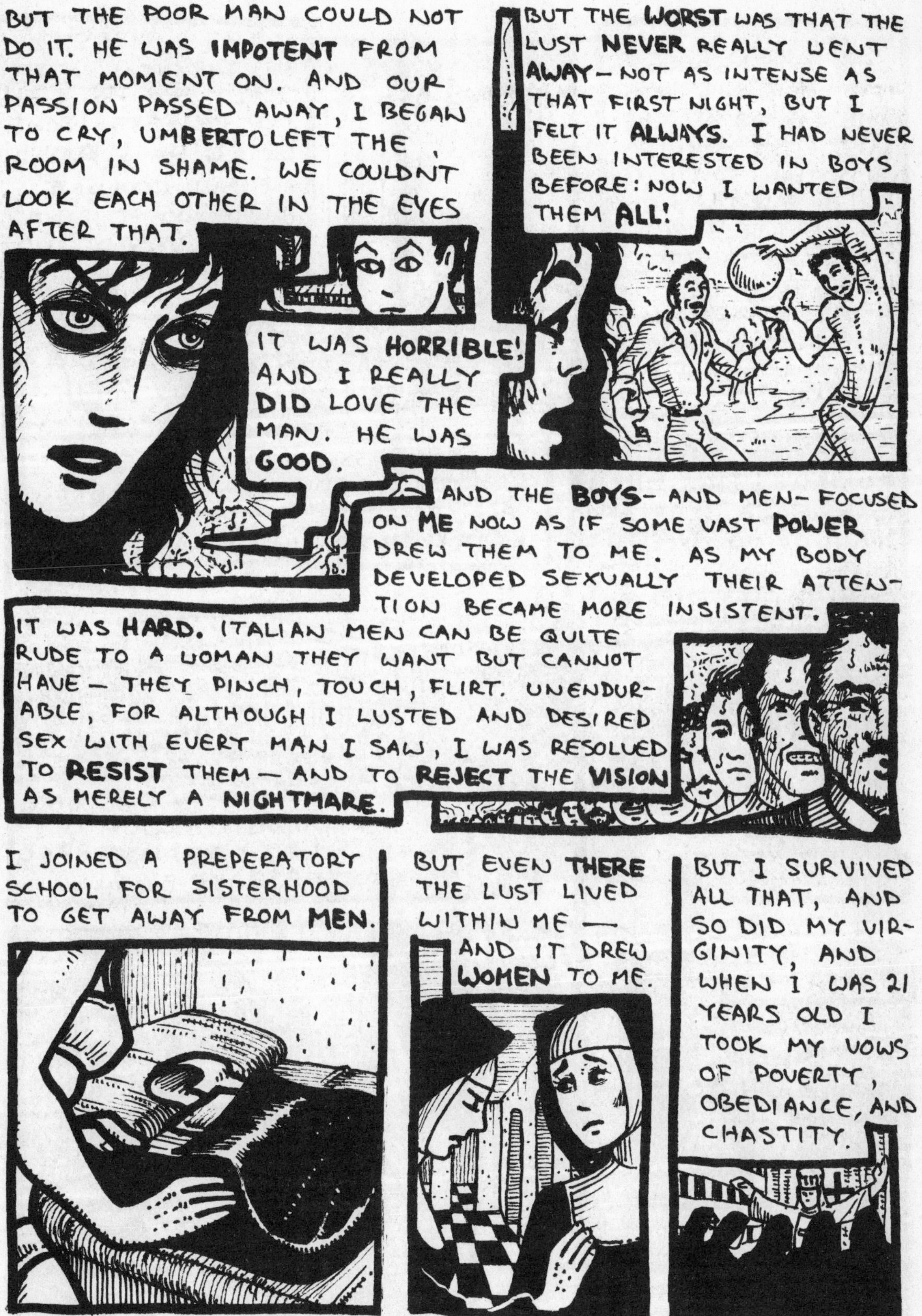
BUT THE POOR MAN COULD NOT DO IT. HE WAS IMPOTENT FROM THAT MOMENT ON. AND OUR PASSION PASSED AWAY, I BEGAN TO CRY, UMBERTO LEFT THE ROOM IN SHAME. WE COULDN'T LOOK EACH OTHER IN THE EYES AFTER THAT.
IT WAS HORRIBLE! AND I REALLY DID LOVE THE MAN. HE WAS GOOD.
BUT THE WORST WAS THAT THE LUST NEVER REALLY WENT AWAY—NOT AS INTENSE AS THAT FIRST NIGHT, BUT I FELT IT ALWAYS. I HAD NEVER BEEN INTERESTED IN BOYS BEFORE: NOW I WANTED THEM ALL!
AND THE BOYS—AND MEN—FOCUSED ON ME NOW AS IF SOME VAST POWER DREW THEM TO ME. AS MY BODY DEVELOPED SEXUALLY THEIR ATTENTION BECAME MORE INSISTENT.
IT WAS HARD. ITALIAN MEN CAN BE QUITE RUDE TO A WOMAN THEY WANT BUT CANNOT HAVE—THEY PINCH, TOUCH, FLIRT. UNENDURABLE, FOR ALTHOUGH I LUSTED AND DESIRED SEX WITH EVERY MAN I SAW, I WAS RESOLVED TO RESIST THEM—AND TO REJECT THE VISION AS MERELY A NIGHTMARE.
I JOINED A PREPERATORY SCHOOL FOR SISTERHOOD TO GET AWAY FROM MEN.
BUT EVEN THERE THE LUST LIVED WITHIN ME—
AND IT DREW WOMEN TO ME.
BUT I SURVIVED ALL THAT, AND SO DID MY VIRGINITY, AND WHEN I WAS 21 YEARS OLD I TOOK MY VOWS OF POVERTY, OBEDIANCE, AND CHASTITY.

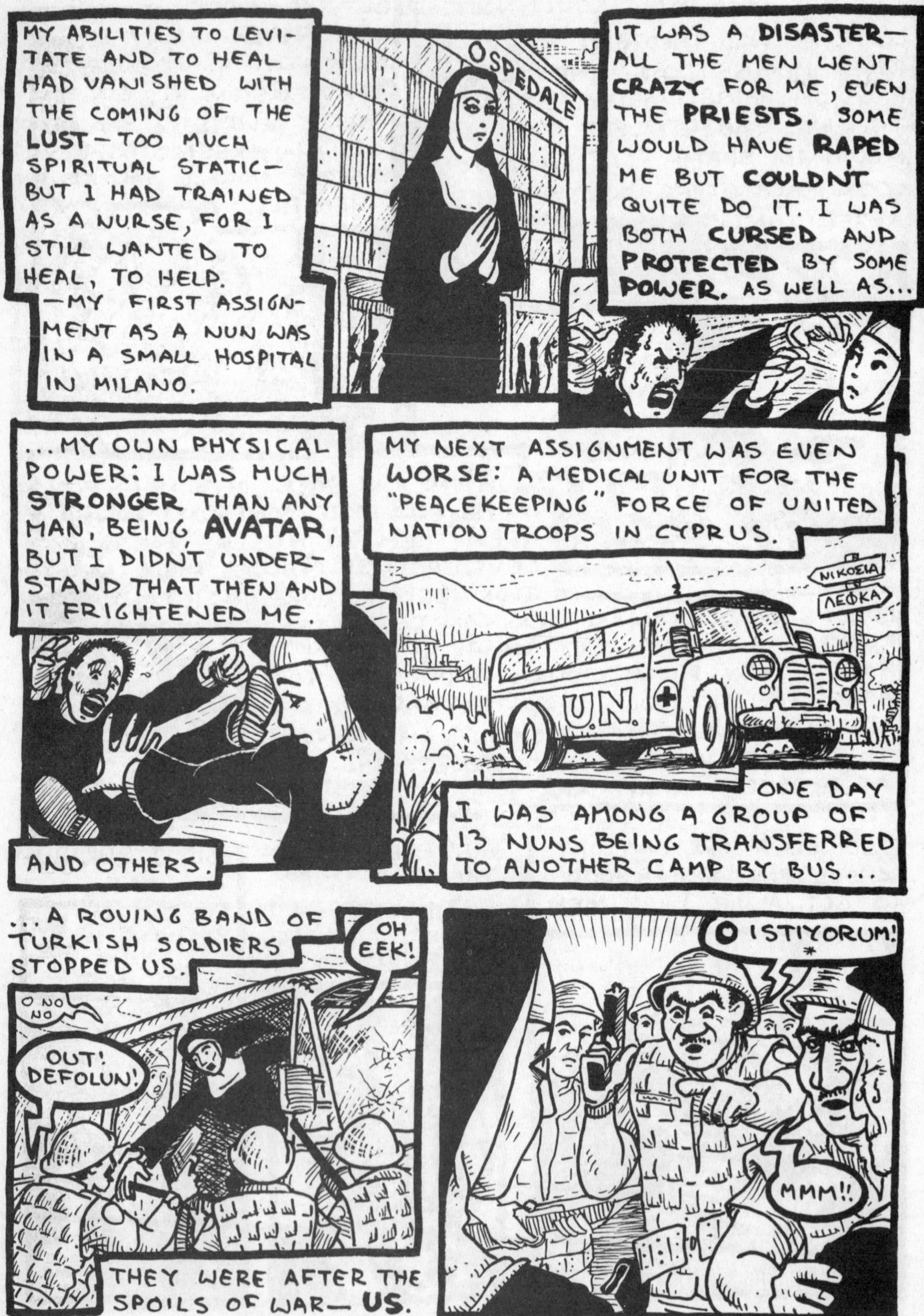
MY ABILITIES TO LEVITATE AND TO HEAL HAD VANISHED WITH THE COMING OF THE LUST—TOO MUCH SPIRITUAL STATIC—BUT I HAD TRAINED AS A NURSE, FOR I STILL WANTED TO HEAL, TO HELP.
—MY FIRST ASSIGNMENT AS A NUN WAS IN A SMALL HOSPITAL IN MILANO.
OSPEDALE
IT WAS A DISASTER—ALL THE MEN WENT CRAZY FOR ME, EVEN THE PRIESTS. SOME WOULD HAVE RAPED ME BUT COULDN'T QUITE DO IT. I WAS BOTH CURSED AND PROTECTED BY SOME POWER. AS WELL AS...
...MY OWN PHYSICAL POWER: I WAS MUCH STRONGER THAN ANY MAN, BEING AVATAR, BUT I DIDN'T UNDERSTAND THAT THEN AND IT FRIGHTENED ME.
AND OTHERS.
MY NEXT ASSIGNMENT WAS EVEN WORSE: A MEDICAL UNIT FOR THE "PEACEKEEPING" FORCE OF UNITED NATION TROOPS IN CYPRUS.
ΝΙΚΟΣΙΑ
ΛΕΦΚΑ
U.N.
ONE DAY I WAS AMONG A GROUP OF 13 NUNS BEING TRANSFERRED TO ANOTHER CAMP BY BUS...
...A ROVING BAND OF TURKISH SOLDIERS STOPPED US.
OH EEK!
O NO NO
OUT! DEFOLUN!
THEY WERE AFTER THE SPOILS OF WAR—US.
O ISTIYORUM! *
MMM!!
* I WANT THAT!

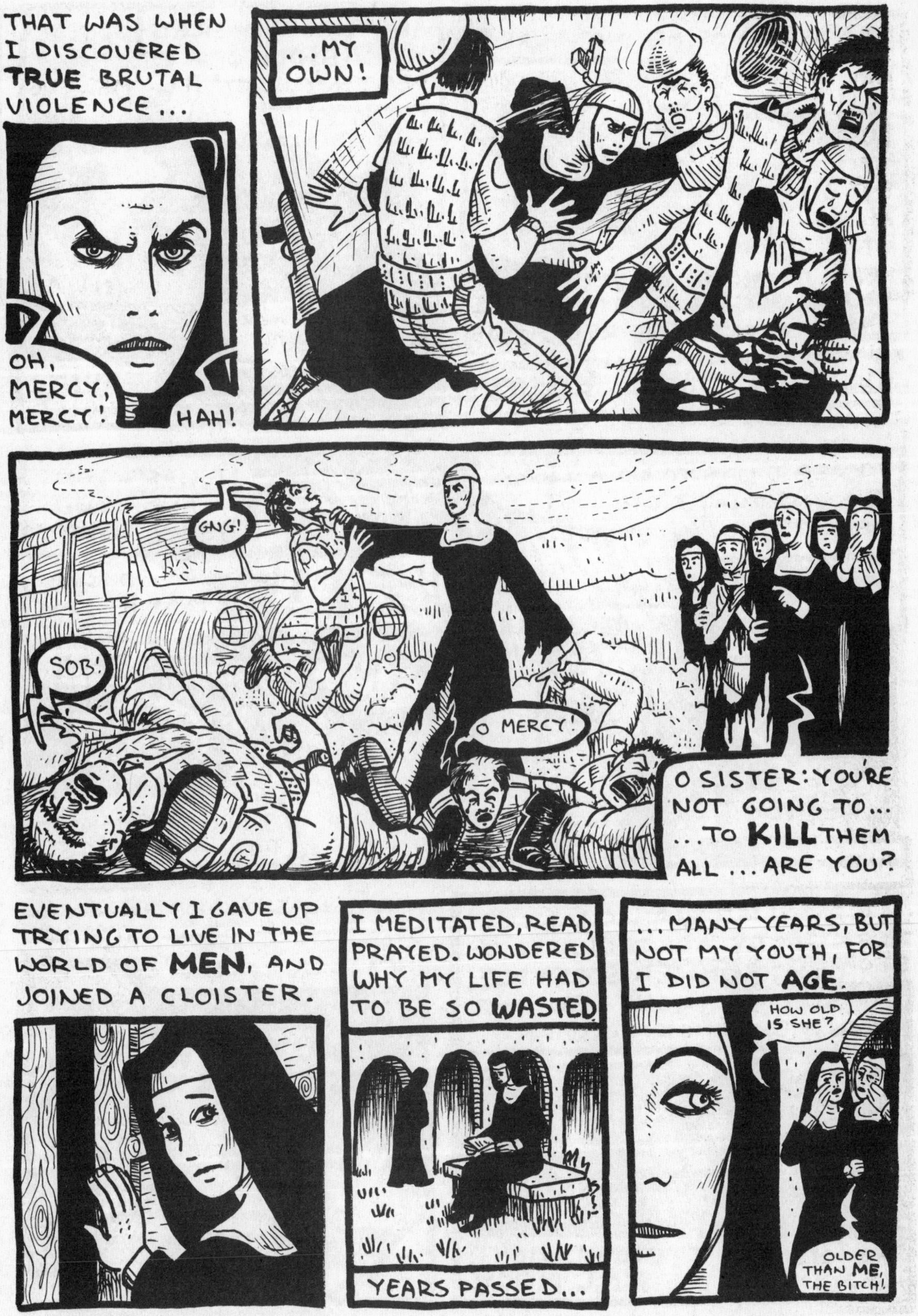
THAT WAS WHEN I DISCOVERED TRUE BRUTAL VIOLENCE...
OH, MERCY, MERCY!
HAH!
...MY OWN!
GNG!
SOB!
O MERCY!
O SISTER: YOU'RE NOT GOING TO... ...TO KILL THEM ALL... ARE YOU?
EVENTUALLY I GAVE UP TRYING TO LIVE IN THE WORLD OF MEN, AND JOINED A CLOISTER.
I MEDITATED, READ, PRAYED. WONDERED WHY MY LIFE HAD TO BE SO WASTED.
YEARS PASSED...
...MANY YEARS, BUT NOT MY YOUTH, FOR I DID NOT AGE.
HOW OLD IS SHE?
OLDER THAN ME, THE BITCH!

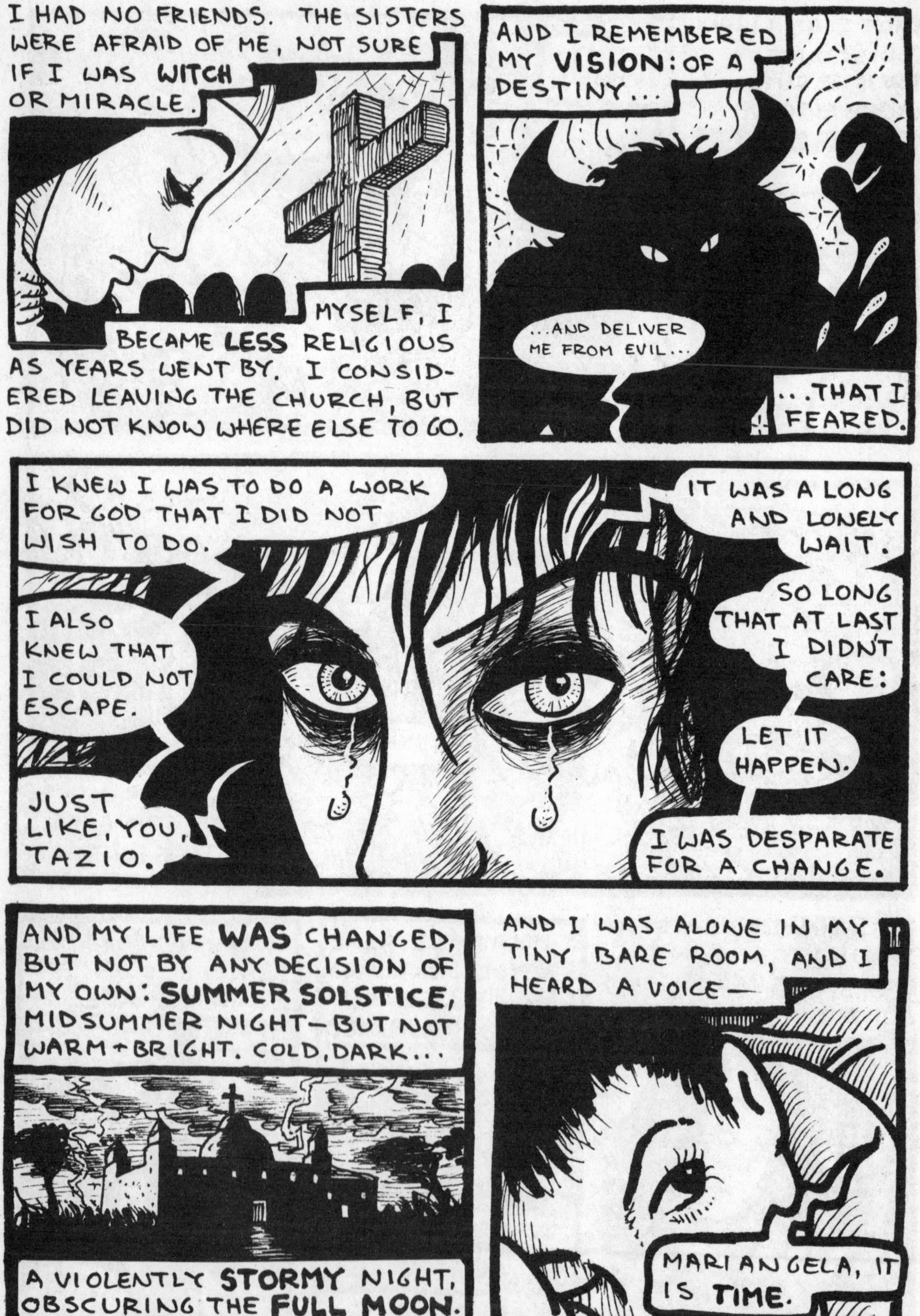
I HAD NO FRIENDS. THE SISTERS WERE AFRAID OF ME, NOT SURE IF I WAS WITCH OR MIRACLE.
MYSELF, I BECAME LESS RELIGIOUS AS YEARS WENT BY. I CONSIDERED LEAVING THE CHURCH, BUT DID NOT KNOW WHERE ELSE TO GO.
AND I REMEMBERED MY VISION: OF A DESTINY...
...AND DELIVER ME FROM EVIL...
...THAT I FEARED.
I KNEW I WAS TO DO A WORK FOR GOD THAT I DID NOT WISH TO DO.
I ALSO KNEW THAT I COULD NOT ESCAPE.
JUST LIKE, YOU, TAZIO.
IT WAS A LONG AND LONELY WAIT.
SO LONG THAT AT LAST I DIDN'T CARE:
LET IT HAPPEN.
I WAS DESPARATE FOR A CHANGE.
AND MY LIFE WAS CHANGED, BUT NOT BY ANY DECISION OF MY OWN: SUMMER SOLSTICE, MIDSUMMER NIGHT—BUT NOT WARM + BRIGHT. COLD, DARK...
A VIOLENTLY STORMY NIGHT, OBSCURING THE FULL MOON.
AND I WAS ALONE IN MY TINY BARE ROOM, AND I HEARD A VOICE—
MARIANGELA, IT IS TIME.

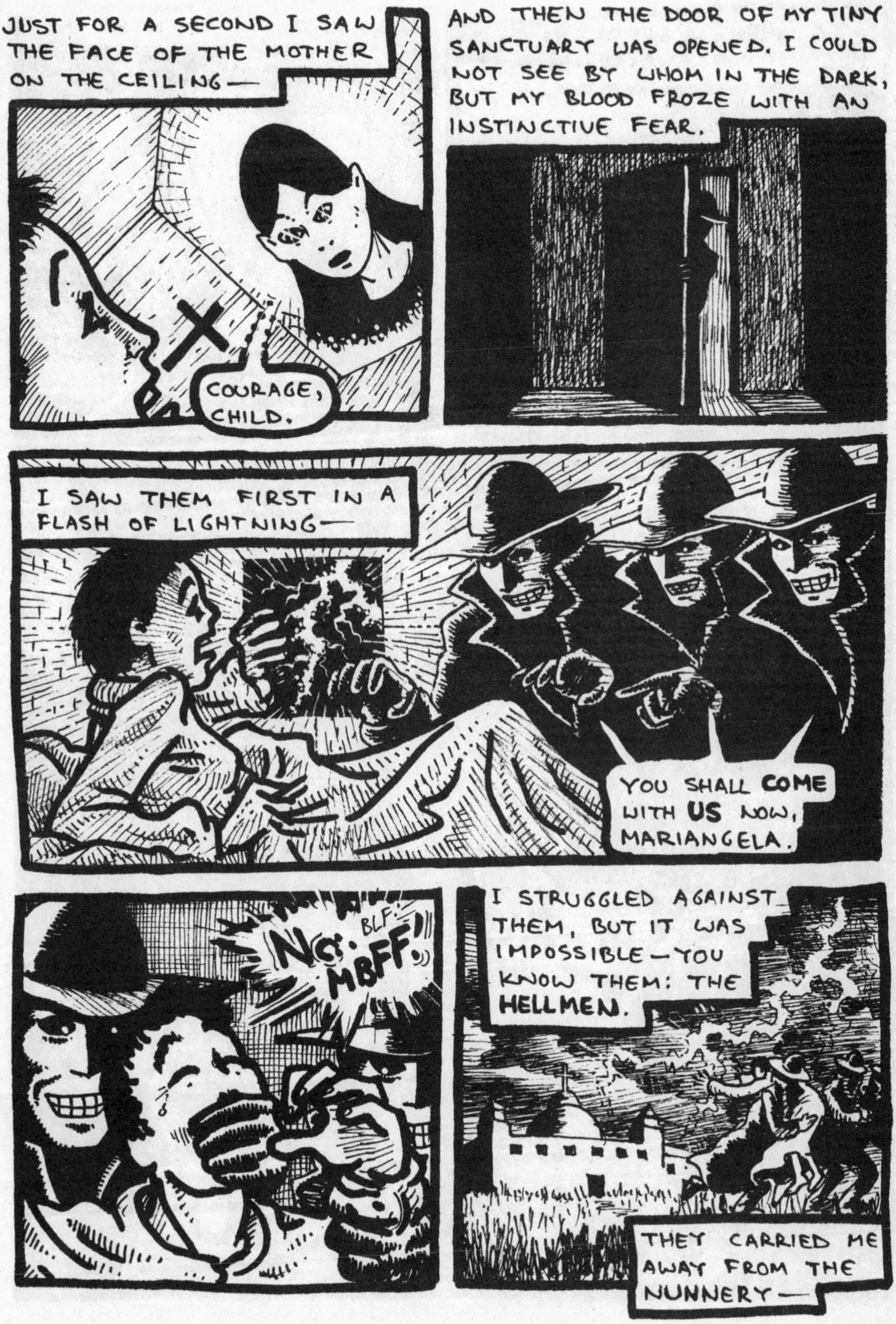

JUST FOR A SECOND I SAW THE FACE OF THE MOTHER ON THE CEILING—
COURAGE, CHILD.
AND THEN THE DOOR OF MY TINY SANCTUARY WAS OPENED. I COULD NOT SEE BY WHOM IN THE DARK, BUT MY BLOOD FROZE WITH AN INSTINCTIVE FEAR.
I SAW THEM FIRST IN A FLASH OF LIGHTNING—
YOU SHALL COME WITH US NOW, MARIANGELA.
NO! MBFF!
BLF!
I STRUGGLED AGAINST THEM, BUT IT WAS IMPOSSIBLE—YOU KNOW THEM: THE HELLMEN.
THEY CARRIED ME AWAY FROM THE NUNNERY—

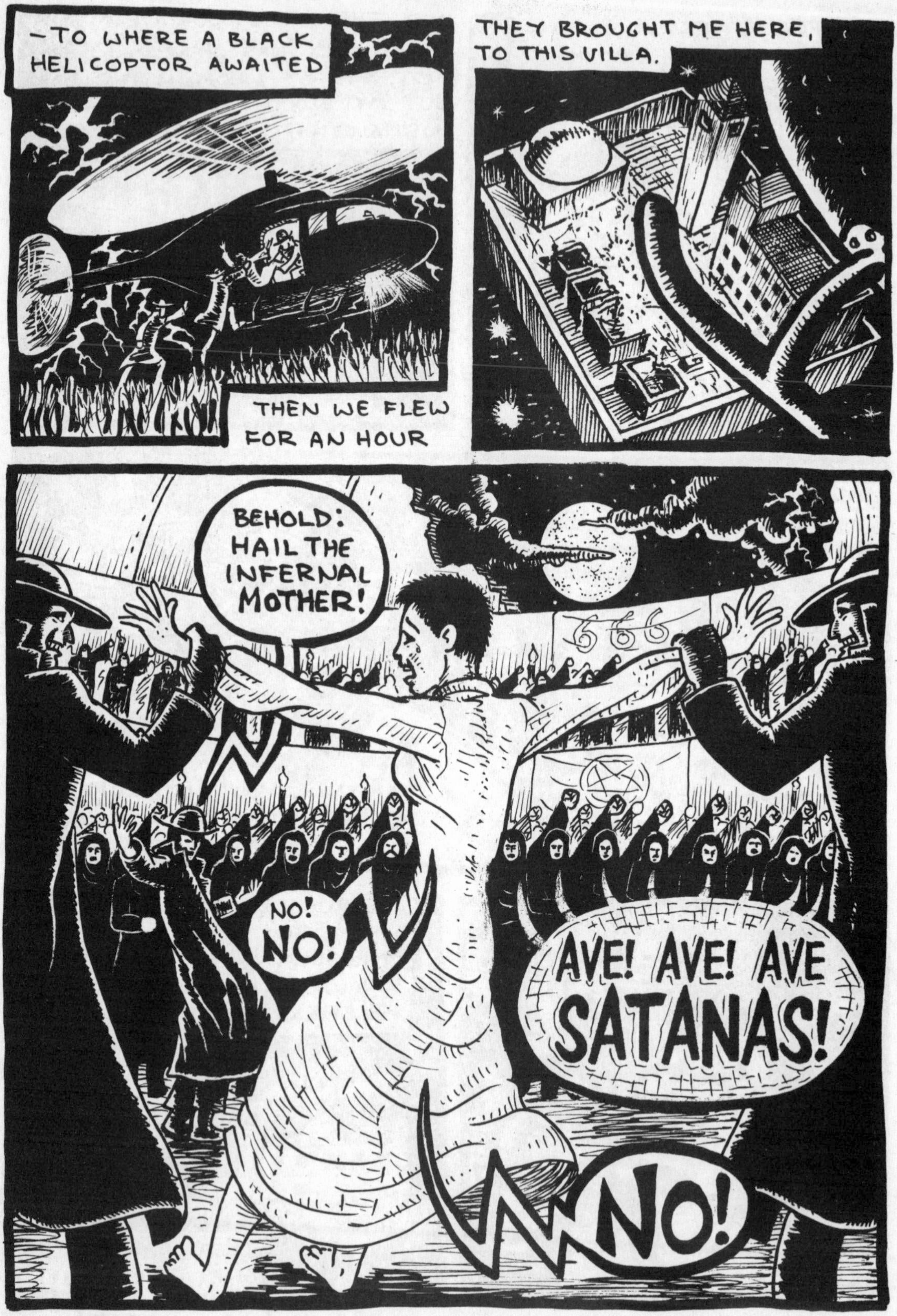

-TO WHERE A BLACK HELICOPTOR AWAITED
THEN WE FLEW FOR AN HOUR
THEY BROUGHT ME HERE, TO THIS VILLA.
666
BEHOLD: HAIL THE INFERNAL MOTHER!
NO! NO!
AVE! AVE! AVE SATANAS!
NO!

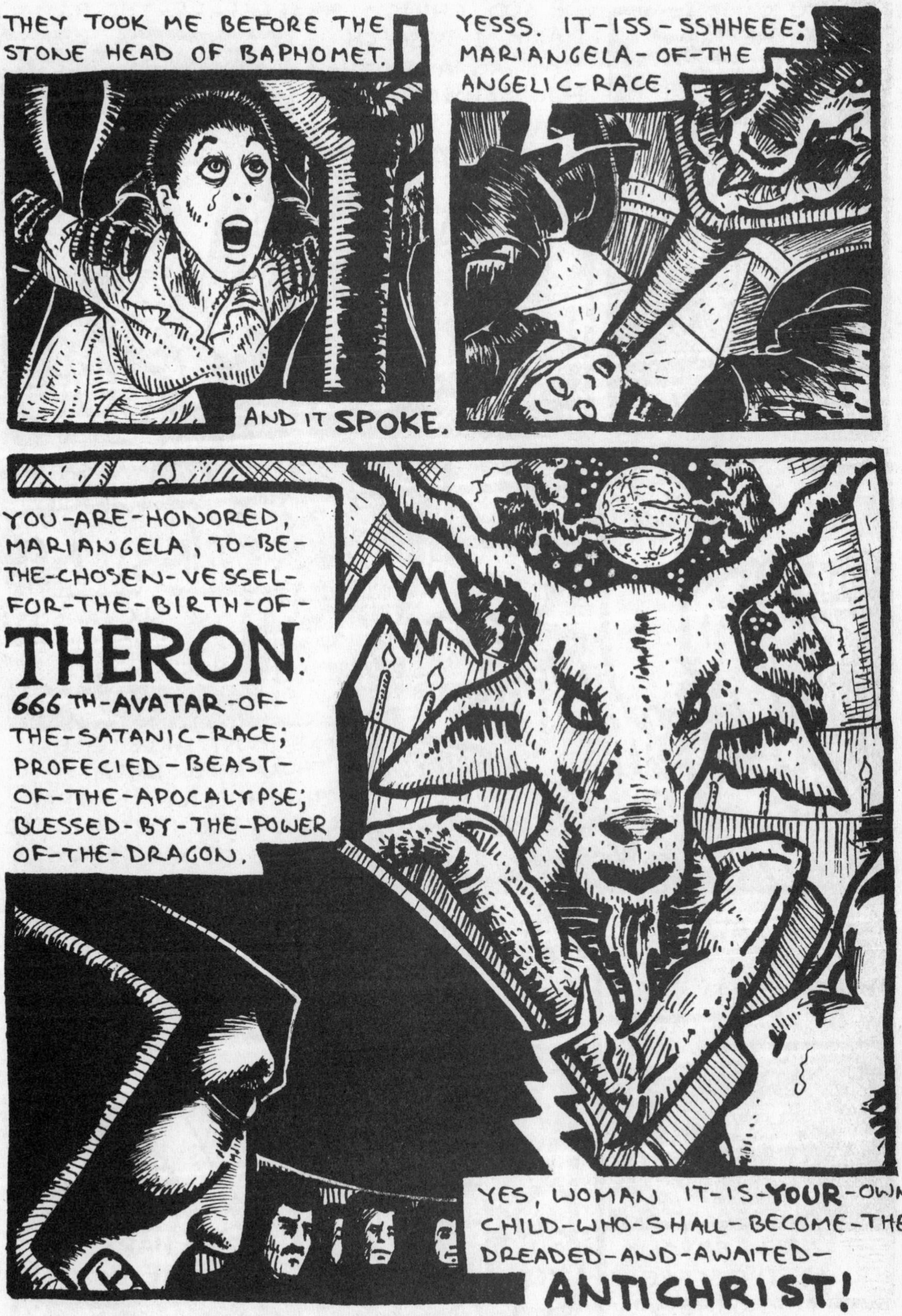

THEY TOOK ME BEFORE THE STONE HEAD OF BAPHOMET.
AND IT SPOKE.
YESSS. IT-ISS-SSHHEEE: MARIANGELA-OF-THE ANGELIC-RACE.
YOU-ARE-HONORED, MARIANGELA, TO-BE-THE-CHOSEN-VESSEL-FOR-THE-BIRTH-OF-
THERON:
666TH-AVATAR-OF-THE-SATANIC-RACE; PROFECIED-BEAST-OF-THE-APOCALYPSE; BLESSED-BY-THE-POWER OF-THE-DRAGON.
YES, WOMAN IT-IS-YOUR-OWN CHILD-WHO-SHALL-BECOME-THE DREADED-AND-AWAITED-
ANTICHRIST!

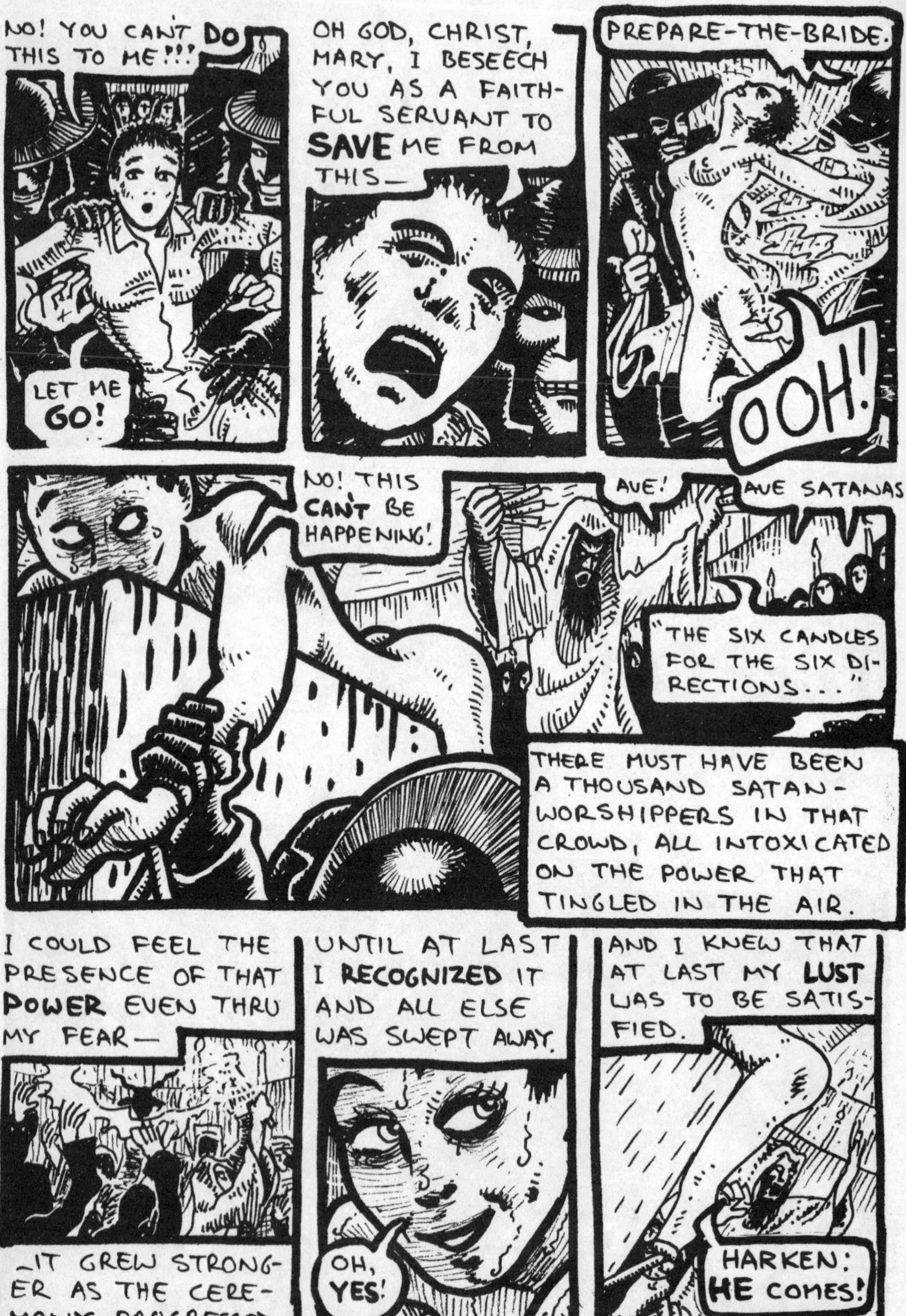

NO! YOU CAN'T DO THIS TO ME!?!
LET ME GO!
OH GOD, CHRIST, MARY, I BESEECH YOU AS A FAITHFUL SERVANT TO SAVE ME FROM THIS—
PREPARE-THE-BRIDE.
OOH!
NO! THIS CAN'T BE HAPPENING!
AVE!
AVE SATANAS
"THE SIX CANDLES FOR THE SIX DIRECTIONS..."
THERE MUST HAVE BEEN A THOUSAND SATAN-WORSHIPPERS IN THAT CROWD, ALL INTOXICATED ON THE POWER THAT TINGLED IN THE AIR.
I COULD FEEL THE PRESENCE OF THAT POWER EVEN THRU MY FEAR—
—IT GREW STRONGER AS THE CEREMONY PROGRESSED
UNTIL AT LAST I RECOGNIZED IT AND ALL ELSE WAS SWEPT AWAY.
OH, YES!
AND I KNEW THAT AT LAST MY LUST WAS TO BE SATISFIED.
HARKEN: HE COMES!

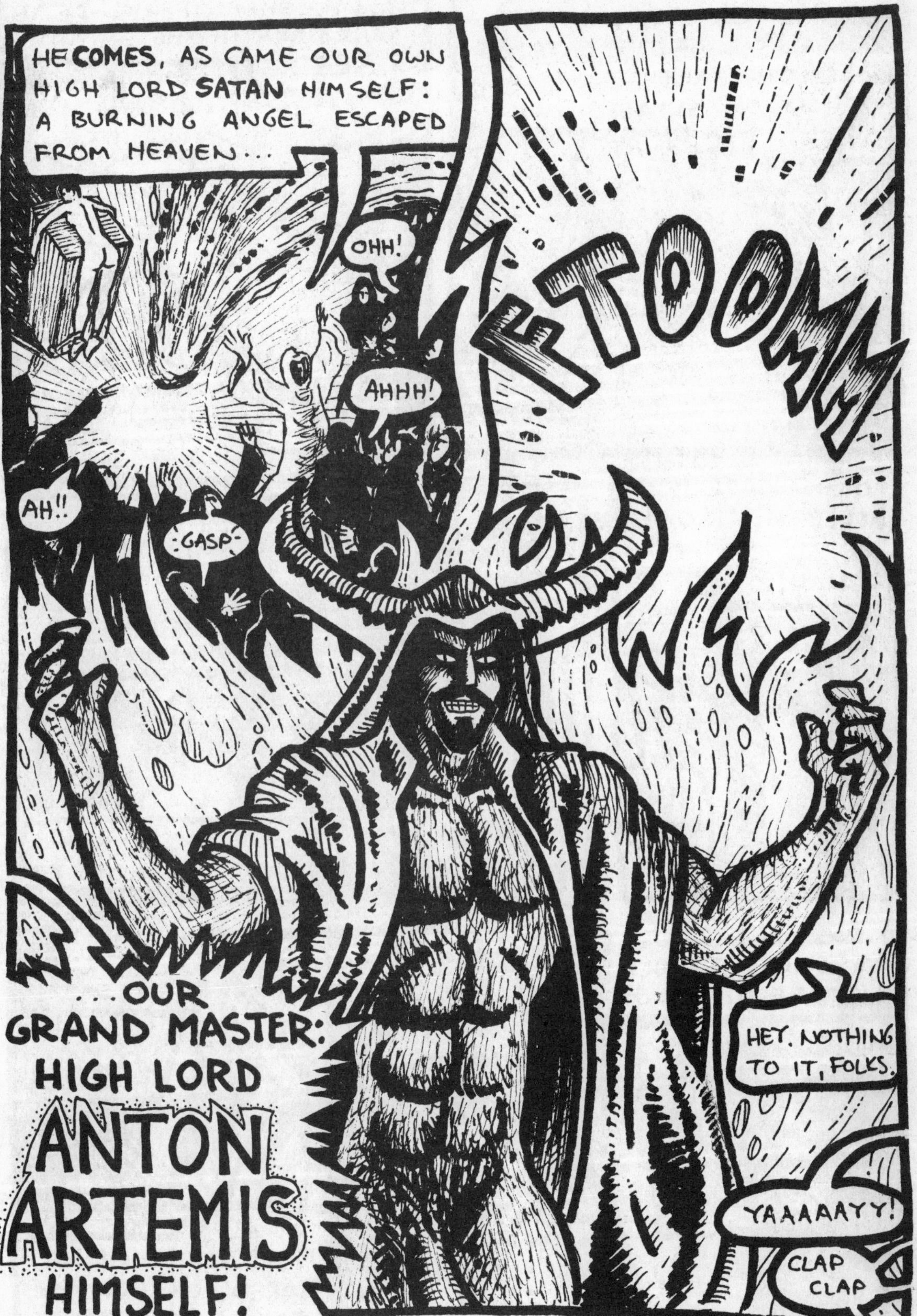
HE COMES, AS CAME OUR OWN HIGH LORD SATAN HIMSELF: A BURNING ANGEL ESCAPED FROM HEAVEN...
OHH!
AHHH!
AH!!
:GASP:
FTOOM
...OUR GRAND MASTER: HIGH LORD ANTON ARTEMIS HIMSELF!
HEY. NOTHING TO IT, FOLKS.
YAAAAAYY!
CLAP CLAP

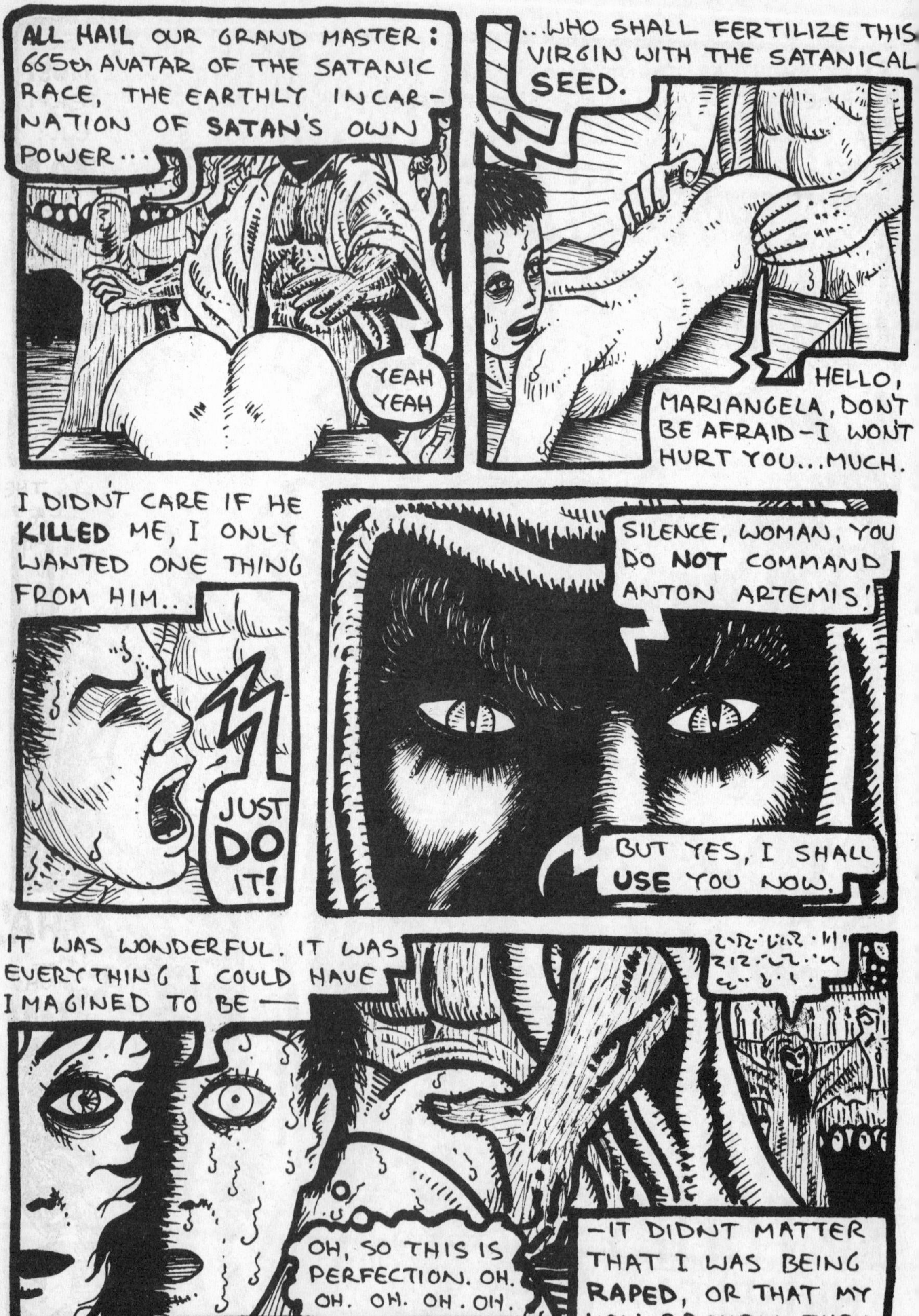
ALL HAIL OUR GRAND MASTER: 665th AVATAR OF THE SATANIC RACE, THE EARTHLY INCARNATION OF SATAN'S OWN POWER...
YEAH YEAH
...WHO SHALL FERTILIZE THIS VIRGIN WITH THE SATANICAL SEED.
HELLO, MARIANGELA, DON'T BE AFRAID - I WON'T HURT YOU... MUCH.
I DIDN'T CARE IF HE KILLED ME, I ONLY WANTED ONE THING FROM HIM...
JUST DO IT!
SILENCE, WOMAN, YOU DO NOT COMMAND ANTON ARTEMIS!
BUT YES, I SHALL USE YOU NOW.
IT WAS WONDERFUL. IT WAS EVERYTHING I COULD HAVE IMAGINED TO BE —
OH, SO THIS IS PERFECTION. OH. OH. OH. OH. OH.
-IT DIDN'T MATTER THAT I WAS BEING RAPED, OR THAT MY VOW BROKEN. THEN.

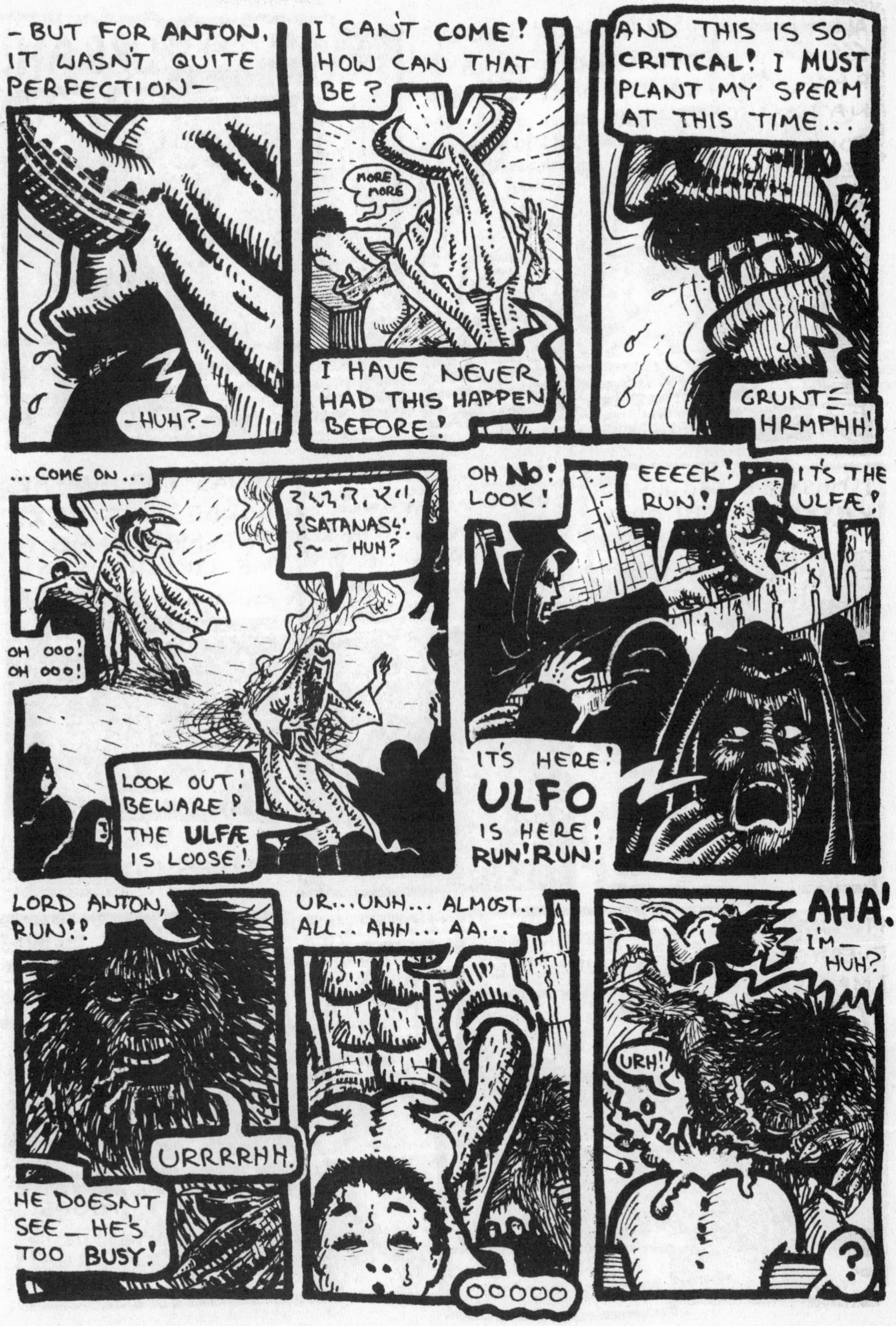
-BUT FOR ANTON, IT WASN'T QUITE PERFECTION-
-HUH?-
I CAN'T COME! HOW CAN THAT BE?
MORE MORE
I HAVE NEVER HAD THIS HAPPEN BEFORE!
AND THIS IS SO CRITICAL! I MUST PLANT MY SPERM AT THIS TIME...
GRUNT HRMPHH!
...COME ON...
SATANAS
OH OOO! OH OOO!
LOOK OUT! BEWARE! THE ULFÆ IS LOOSE!
OH NO! LOOK!
EEEEK! RUN!
IT'S THE ULFÆ!
IT'S HERE! ULFO IS HERE! RUN! RUN!
LORD ANTON, RUN!!
URRRRHH.
HE DOESNT SEE_HE'S TOO BUSY!
UR...UNH... ALMOST... ALL.. AHH... AA...
OOOOO
AHA! I'M_ HUH?
URH!
?

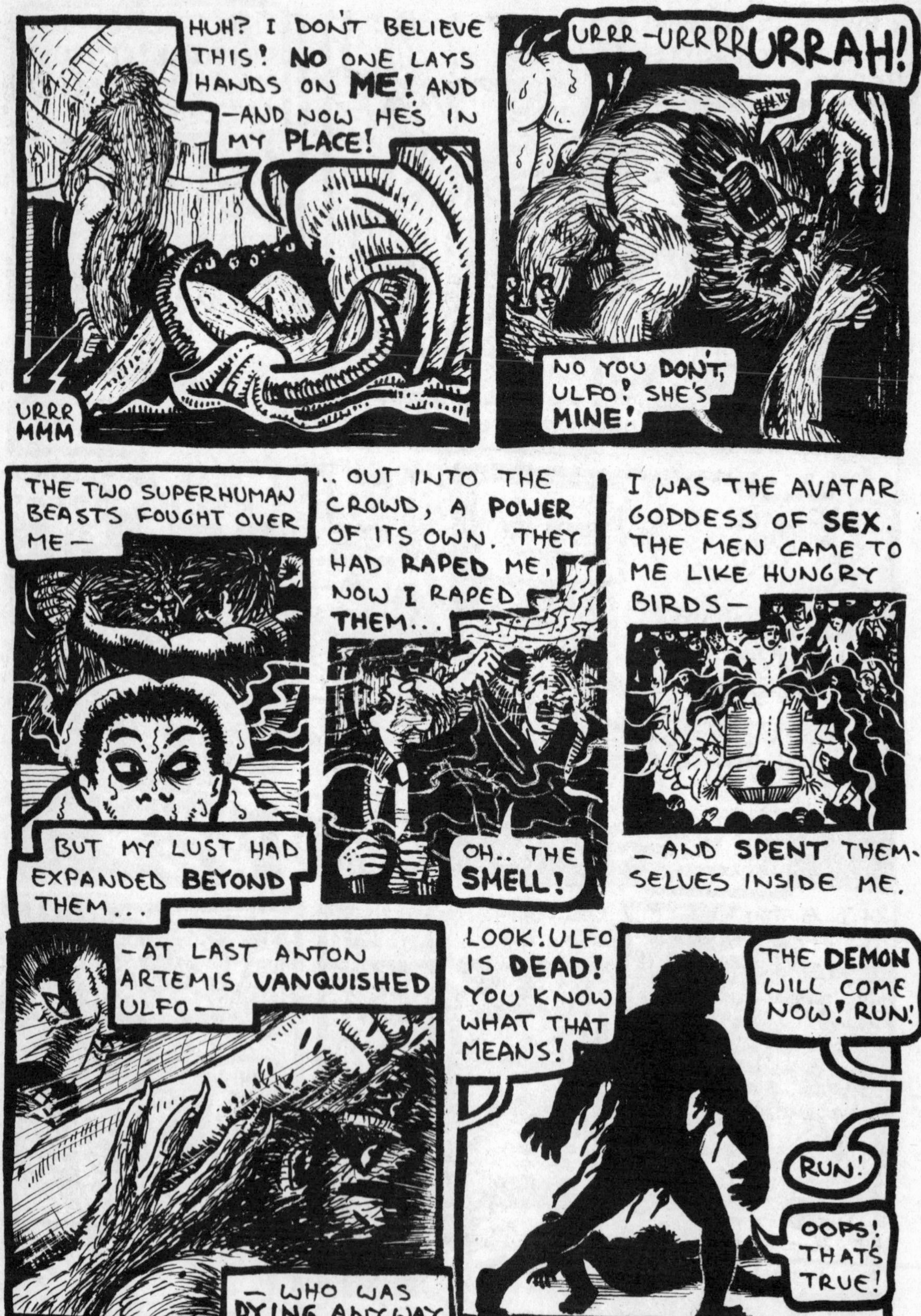
HUH? I DON'T BELIEVE THIS! NO ONE LAYS HANDS ON ME! AND —AND NOW HE'S IN MY PLACE!
URRR MMM
URRR-URRRRURRAH!
NO YOU DON'T, ULFO! SHE'S MINE!
THE TWO SUPERHUMAN BEASTS FOUGHT OVER ME—
BUT MY LUST HAD EXPANDED BEYOND THEM...
..OUT INTO THE CROWD, A POWER OF ITS OWN. THEY HAD RAPED ME, NOW I RAPED THEM...
OH.. THE SMELL!
I WAS THE AVATAR GODDESS OF SEX. THE MEN CAME TO ME LIKE HUNGRY BIRDS—
_AND SPENT THEMSELVES INSIDE ME.
—AT LAST ANTON ARTEMIS VANQUISHED ULFO—
—WHO WAS DYING ANYWAY.
LOOK! ULFO IS DEAD! YOU KNOW WHAT THAT MEANS!
THE DEMON WILL COME NOW! RUN!
RUN!
OOPS! THAT'S TRUE!

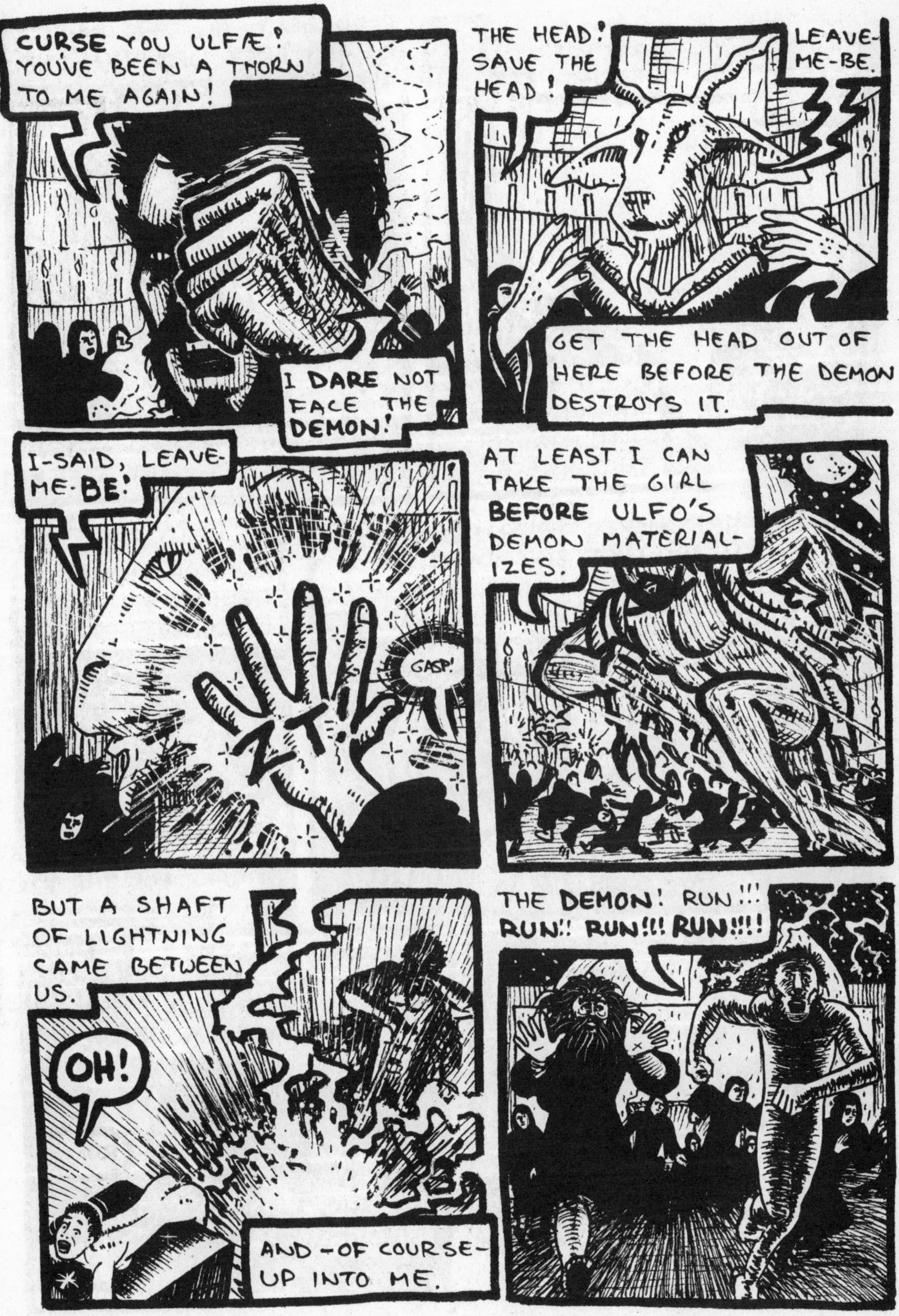
CURSE YOU ULFÆ! YOU'VE BEEN A THORN TO ME AGAIN!
I DARE NOT FACE THE DEMON!
THE HEAD! SAVE THE HEAD!
LEAVE-ME-BE.
GET THE HEAD OUT OF HERE BEFORE THE DEMON DESTROYS IT.
I-SAID, LEAVE-ME-BE!
GASP!
ZT!
AT LEAST I CAN TAKE THE GIRL BEFORE ULFO'S DEMON MATERIAL-IZES.
BUT A SHAFT OF LIGHTNING CAME BETWEEN US.
OH!
AND-OF COURSE-UP INTO ME.
THE DEMON! RUN!!! RUN!! RUN!!! RUN!!!!

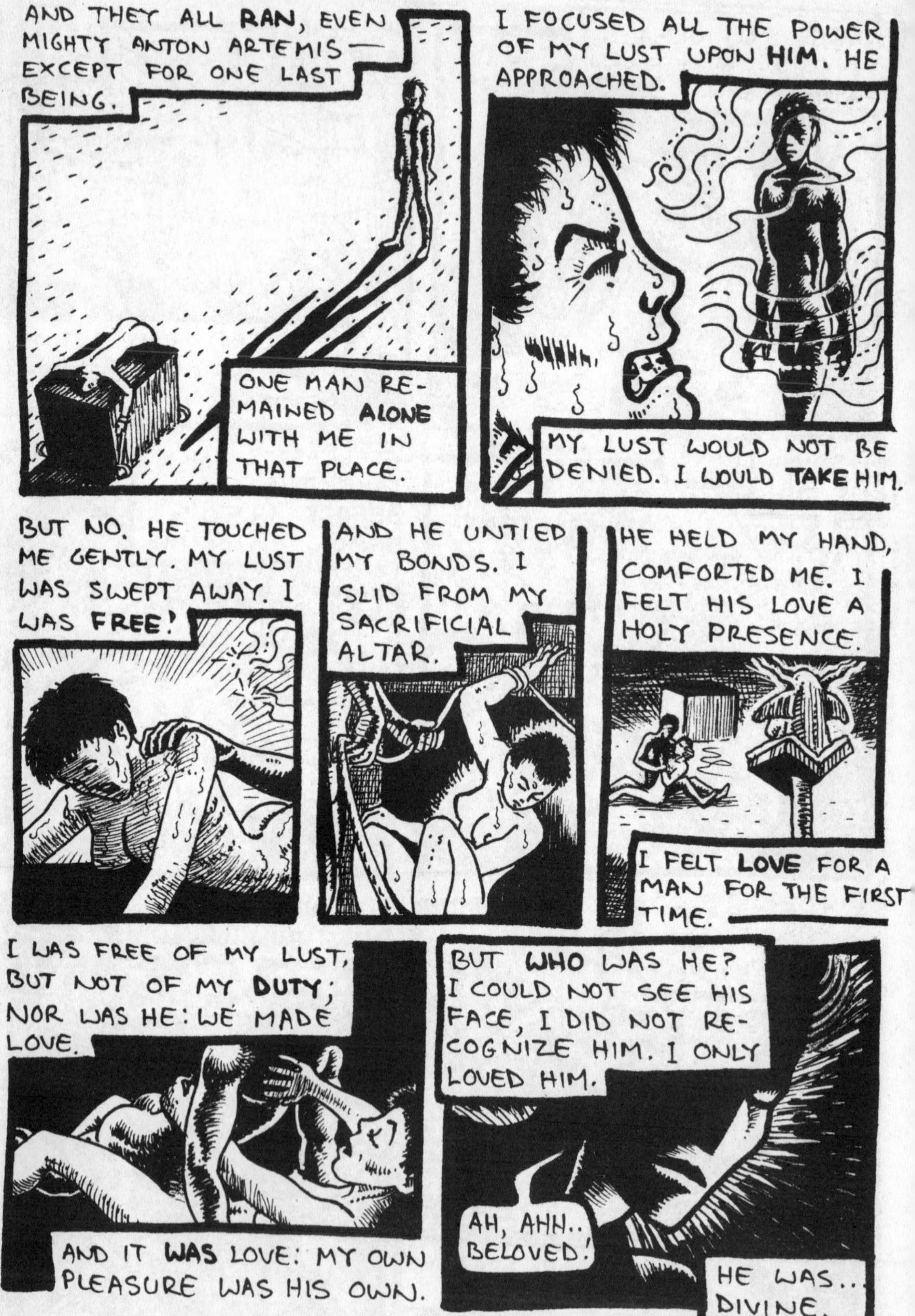
AND THEY ALL **RAN**, EVEN MIGHTY ANTON ARTEMIS— EXCEPT FOR ONE LAST BEING.
ONE MAN RE-MAINED **ALONE** WITH ME IN THAT PLACE.
I FOCUSED ALL THE POWER OF MY LUST UPON **HIM**. HE APPROACHED.
MY LUST WOULD NOT BE DENIED. I WOULD **TAKE** HIM.
BUT NO. HE TOUCHED ME GENTLY. MY LUST WAS SWEPT AWAY. I WAS **FREE**!
AND HE UNTIED MY BONDS. I SLID FROM MY SACRIFICIAL ALTAR.
HE HELD MY HAND, COMFORTED ME. I FELT HIS LOVE A HOLY PRESENCE.
I FELT **LOVE** FOR A MAN FOR THE FIRST TIME.
I WAS FREE OF MY LUST, BUT NOT OF MY **DUTY**; NOR WAS HE: WE MADE LOVE.
AND IT **WAS** LOVE: MY OWN PLEASURE WAS HIS OWN.
BUT **WHO** WAS HE? I COULD NOT SEE HIS FACE, I DID NOT RE-COGNIZE HIM. I ONLY LOVED HIM.
AH, AHH.. BELOVED!
HE WAS... DIVINE.

AND AS I ROCKED INTO ORGASM I FELT I KNEW THAT THIS WAS TO BE THE TRUE FATHER OF THE CHILD. SO I HAD TO SEE WHO HE WAS.

A **LIGHT** BEGAN TO GLOW NEARBY

AND I SAW WHAT HE WAS.

OH!

A HELLMAN.

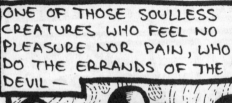

ONE OF THOSE SOULLESS CREATURES WHO FEEL NO PLEASURE NOR PAIN, WHO DO THE ERRANDS OF THE DEVIL—

A LESS-THAN NOTHING **THING**.

HE SAW THE LOATHING AND HORROR IN MY EYES. THE IMITATION OF LOVE IN HIS OWN EYES DIED AWAY—

—AND HE TURNED FROM ME AS THE **LIGHT** GREW—

—BRIGHTER AND BRIGHTER, LIKE **FIRE**.

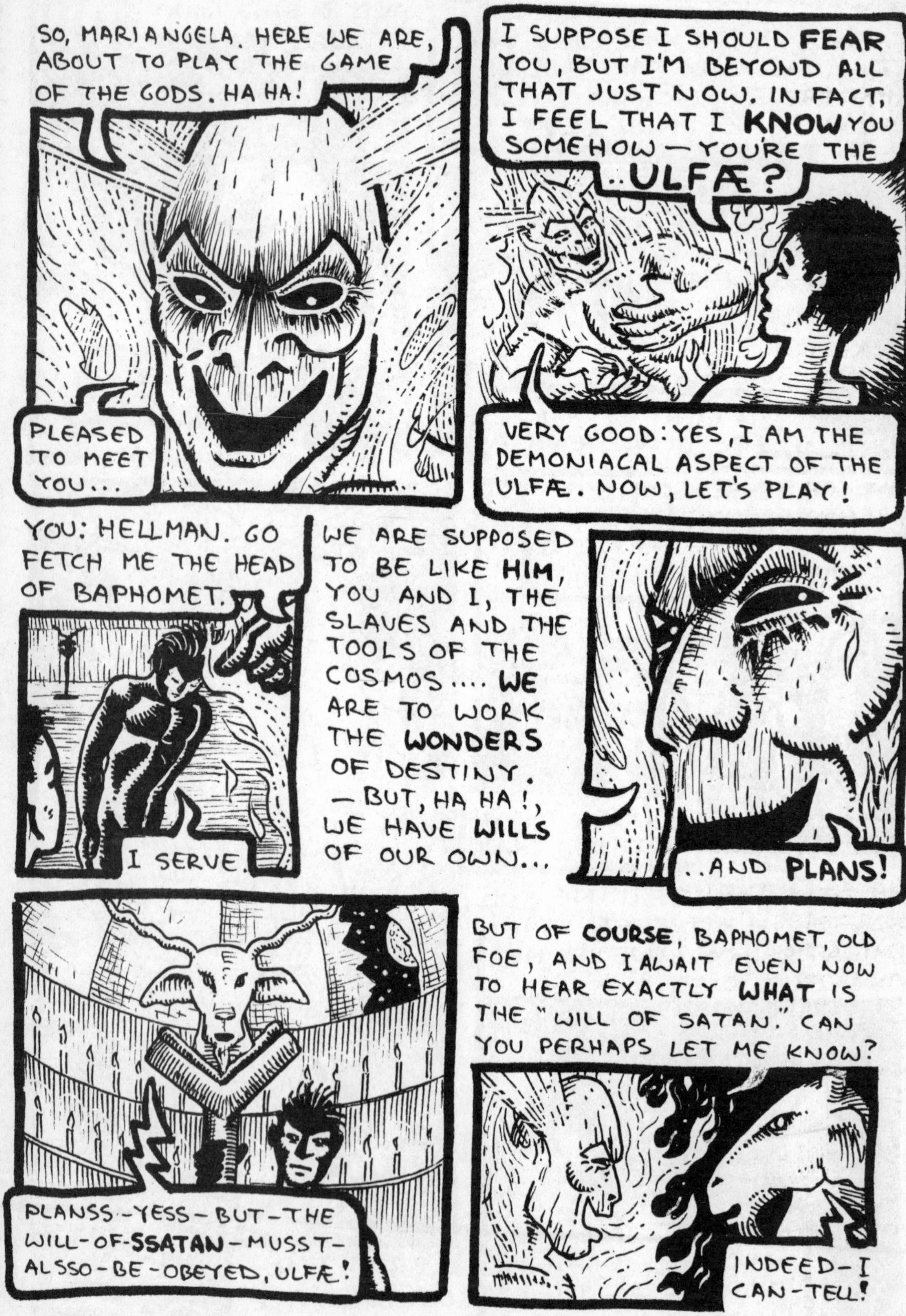
SO, MARIANGELA. HERE WE ARE, ABOUT TO PLAY THE GAME OF THE GODS. HA HA!
PLEASED TO MEET YOU...
I SUPPOSE I SHOULD FEAR YOU, BUT I'M BEYOND ALL THAT JUST NOW. IN FACT, I FEEL THAT I KNOW YOU SOMEHOW — YOU'RE THE ..ULFÆ?
VERY GOOD: YES, I AM THE DEMONIACAL ASPECT OF THE ULFÆ. NOW, LET'S PLAY!
YOU: HELLMAN. GO FETCH ME THE HEAD OF BAPHOMET.
I SERVE.
WE ARE SUPPOSED TO BE LIKE HIM, YOU AND I, THE SLAVES AND THE TOOLS OF THE COSMOS.... WE ARE TO WORK THE WONDERS OF DESTINY. — BUT, HA HA!, WE HAVE WILLS OF OUR OWN...
..AND PLANS!
PLANSS-YESS-BUT-THE WILL-OF-SSATAN-MUSST-ALSSO-BE-OBEYED, ULFÆ!
BUT OF COURSE, BAPHOMET, OLD FOE, AND I AWAIT EVEN NOW TO HEAR EXACTLY WHAT IS THE "WILL OF SATAN." CAN YOU PERHAPS LET ME KNOW?
INDEED-I CAN-TELL!

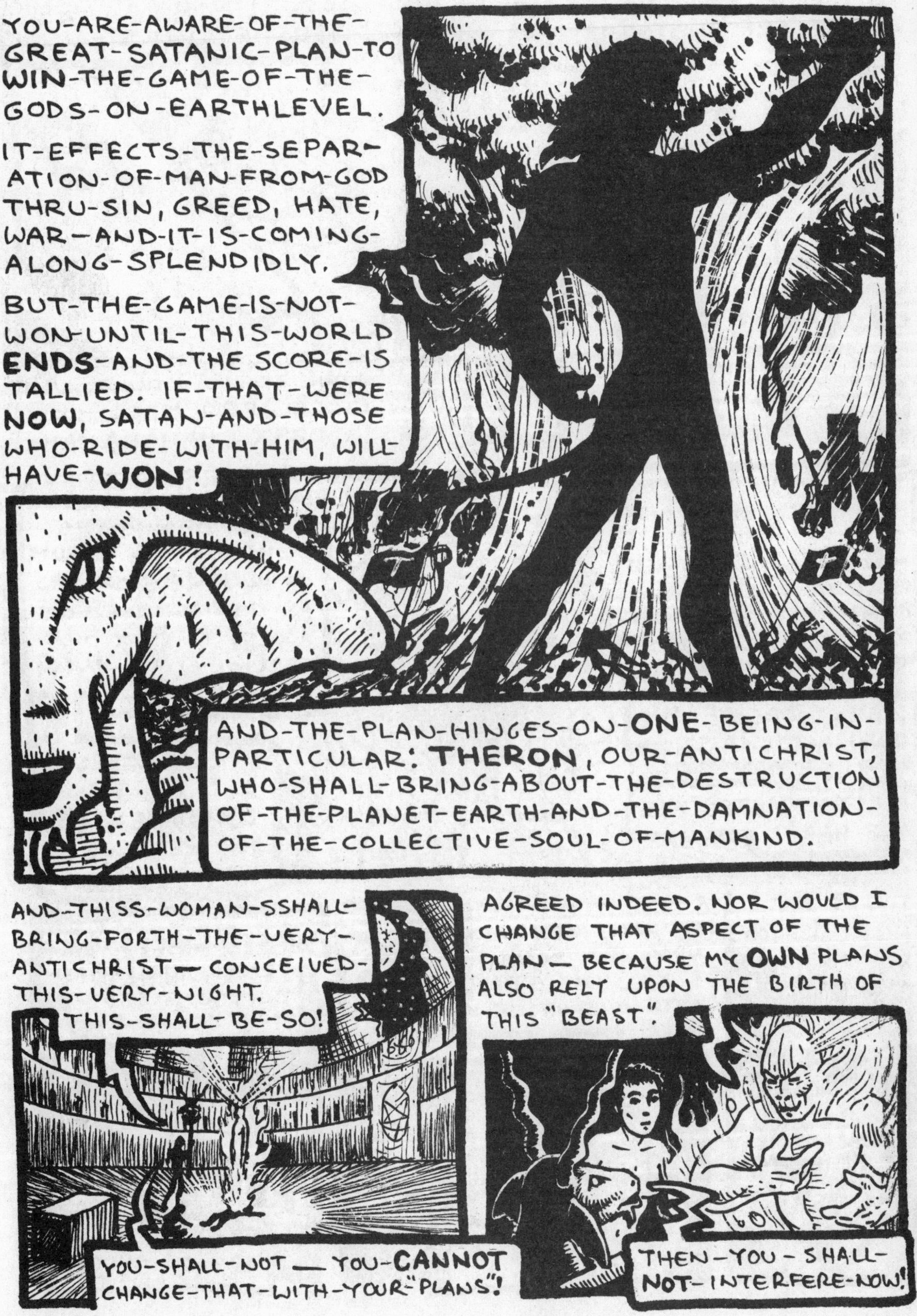

YOU-ARE-AWARE-OF-THE-GREAT-SATANIC-PLAN-TO **WIN**-THE-GAME-OF-THE-GODS-ON-EARTHLEVEL.
IT-EFFECTS-THE-SEPARATION-OF-MAN-FROM-GOD THRU-SIN, GREED, HATE, WAR—AND-IT-IS-COMING-ALONG-SPLENDIDLY.
BUT-THE-GAME-IS-NOT-WON-UNTIL-THIS-WORLD **ENDS**-AND-THE SCORE-IS TALLIED. IF-THAT-WERE **NOW**, SATAN-AND-THOSE WHO-RIDE-WITH-HIM, WILL HAVE-**WON**!
AND-THE-PLAN-HINGES-ON-**ONE**-BEING-IN-PARTICULAR: **THERON**, OUR-ANTICHRIST, WHO-SHALL-BRING-ABOUT-THE-DESTRUCTION OF-THE-PLANET-EARTH-AND-THE-DAMNATION-OF-THE-COLLECTIVE-SOUL-OF-MANKIND.
AND-THISS-WOMAN-SSHALL-BRING-FORTH-THE-VERY-ANTICHRIST—CONCEIVED-THIS-VERY-NIGHT.
THIS-SHALL-BE-SO!
YOU-SHALL-NOT — YOU-**CANNOT** CHANGE-THAT-WITH-YOUR-"PLANS"!
AGREED INDEED. NOR WOULD I CHANGE THAT ASPECT OF THE PLAN— BECAUSE MY **OWN** PLANS ALSO RELY UPON THE BIRTH OF THIS "BEAST".
THEN-YOU-SHALL-**NOT**-INTERFERE-NOW!

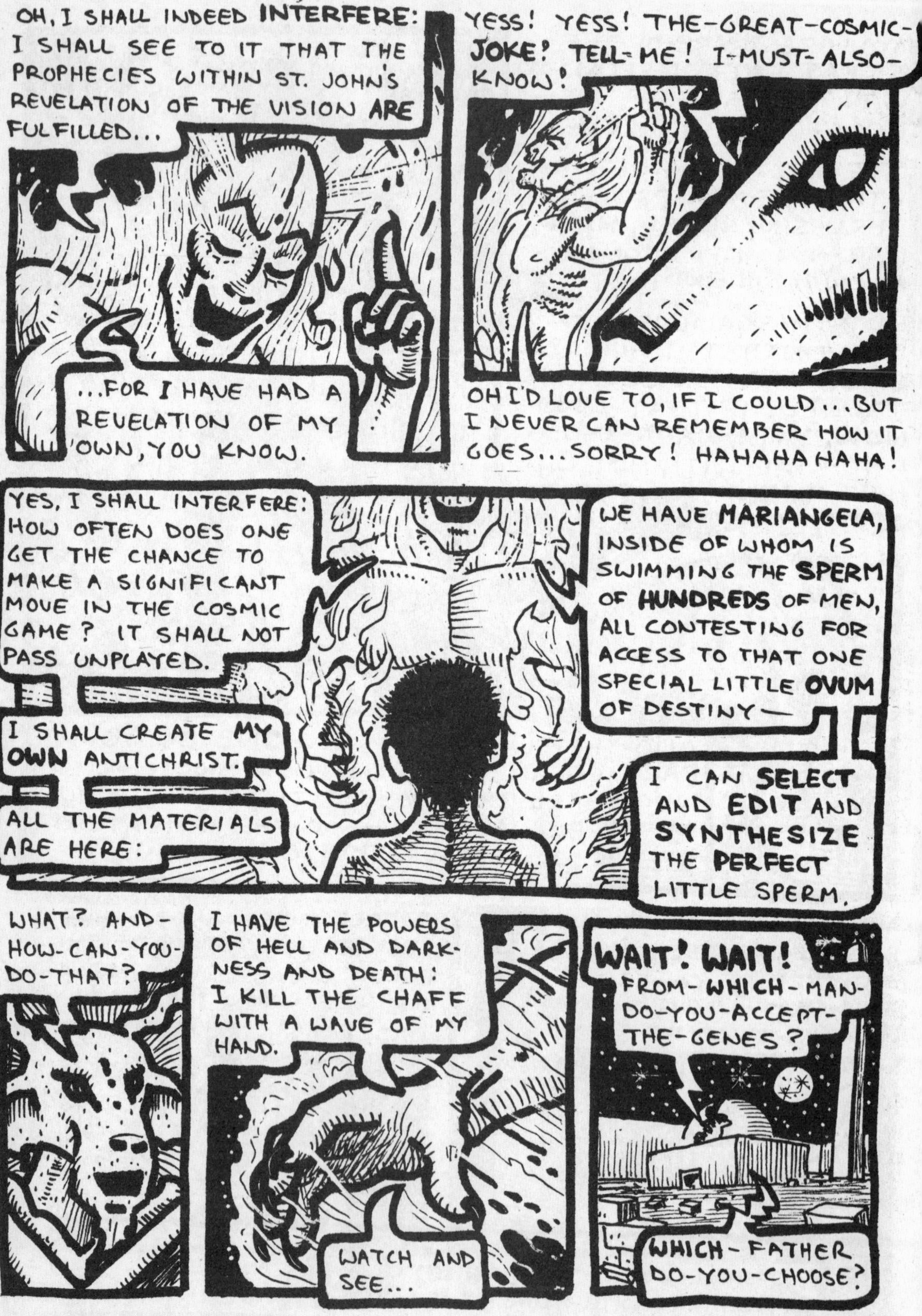
OH, I SHALL INDEED INTERFERE: I SHALL SEE TO IT THAT THE PROPHECIES WITHIN ST. JOHN'S REVELATION OF THE VISION ARE FULFILLED...
...FOR I HAVE HAD A REVELATION OF MY OWN, YOU KNOW.
YESS! YESS! THE-GREAT-COSMIC-JOKE! TELL-ME! I-MUST-ALSO-KNOW!
OH I'D LOVE TO, IF I COULD... BUT I NEVER CAN REMEMBER HOW IT GOES... SORRY! HAHAHAHAHA!
YES, I SHALL INTERFERE: HOW OFTEN DOES ONE GET THE CHANCE TO MAKE A SIGNIFICANT MOVE IN THE COSMIC GAME? IT SHALL NOT PASS UNPLAYED.
I SHALL CREATE MY OWN ANTICHRIST.
ALL THE MATERIALS ARE HERE:
WE HAVE MARIANGELA, INSIDE OF WHOM IS SWIMMING THE SPERM OF HUNDREDS OF MEN, ALL CONTESTING FOR ACCESS TO THAT ONE SPECIAL LITTLE OVUM OF DESTINY—
I CAN SELECT AND EDIT AND SYNTHESIZE THE PERFECT LITTLE SPERM.
WHAT? AND-HOW-CAN-YOU-DO-THAT?
I HAVE THE POWERS OF HELL AND DARKNESS AND DEATH: I KILL THE CHAFF WITH A WAVE OF MY HAND.
WATCH AND SEE...
WAIT! WAIT! FROM-WHICH-MAN-DO-YOU-ACCEPT-THE-GENES?
WHICH-FATHER DO-YOU-CHOOSE?

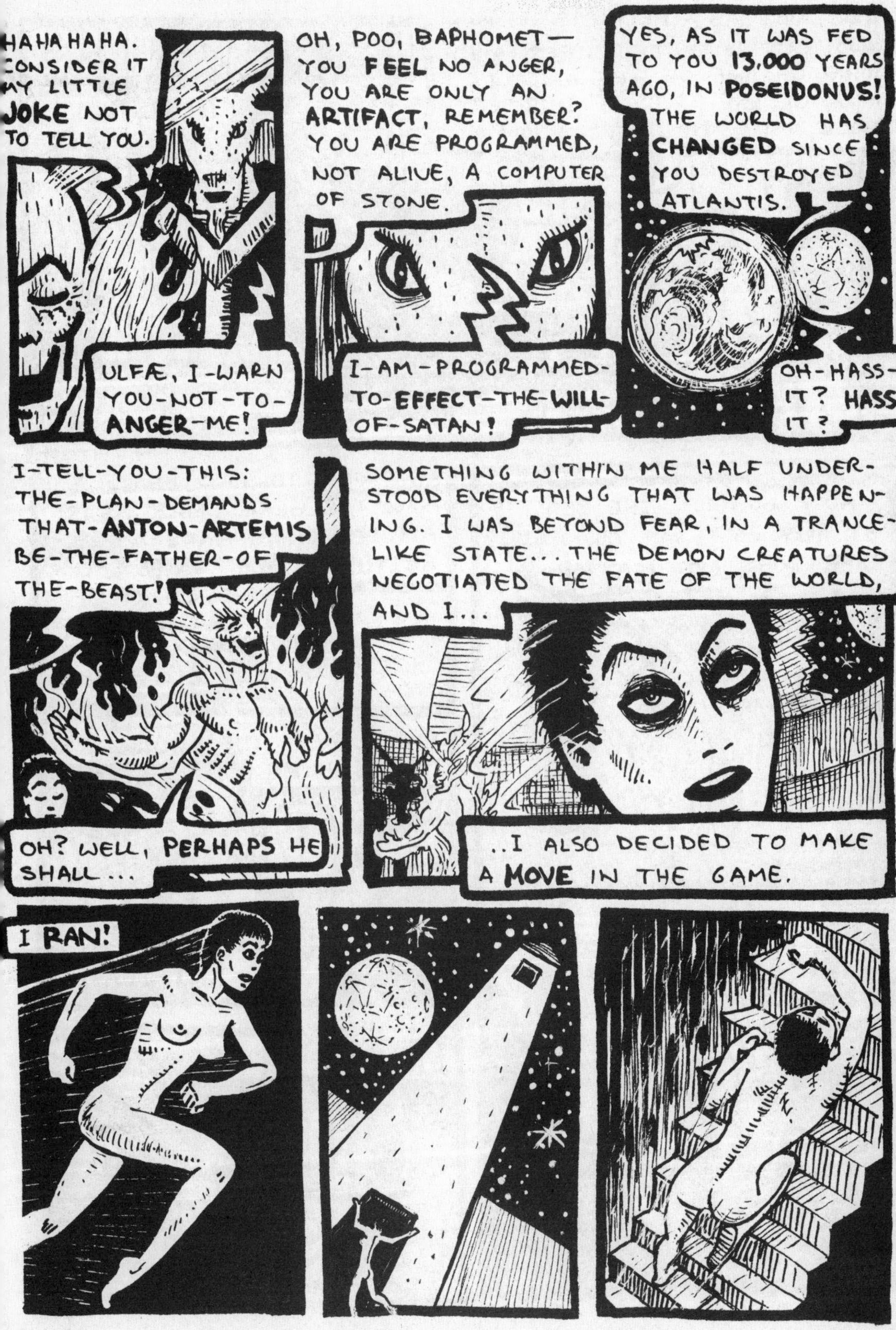

HAHAHAHA. CONSIDER IT MY LITTLE **JOKE** NOT TO TELL YOU.
ULFÆ, I-WARN YOU-NOT-TO-**ANGER**-ME!
OH, POO, BAPHOMET— YOU **FEEL** NO ANGER, YOU ARE ONLY AN **ARTIFACT**, REMEMBER? YOU ARE PROGRAMMED, NOT ALIVE, A COMPUTER OF STONE.
I-AM-PROGRAMMED-TO-**EFFECT**-THE-**WILL**-OF-SATAN!
YES, AS IT WAS FED TO YOU **13,000** YEARS AGO, IN **POSEIDONUS!** THE WORLD HAS **CHANGED** SINCE YOU DESTROYED ATLANTIS.
OH-HASS-IT? **HASS**-IT?
I-TELL-YOU-THIS: THE-PLAN-DEMANDS THAT-**ANTON-ARTEMIS** BE-THE-FATHER-OF THE-BEAST!
OH? WELL, **PERHAPS** HE SHALL...
SOMETHING WITHIN ME HALF UNDERSTOOD EVERYTHING THAT WAS HAPPENING. I WAS BEYOND FEAR, IN A TRANCE-LIKE STATE... THE DEMON CREATURES NEGOTIATED THE FATE OF THE WORLD, AND I...
..I ALSO DECIDED TO MAKE A **MOVE** IN THE GAME.
I **RAN!**

I RAN, NOT AS A HELPLESS WOMAN RUNS, BUT WITH THE SPEED AND POWER OF ONE OF THE ANGELIC RACE, UP THE STEPS OF THIS VERY TOWER, INTO THIS VERY ROOM...

...AND OUT THAT VERY WINDOW.

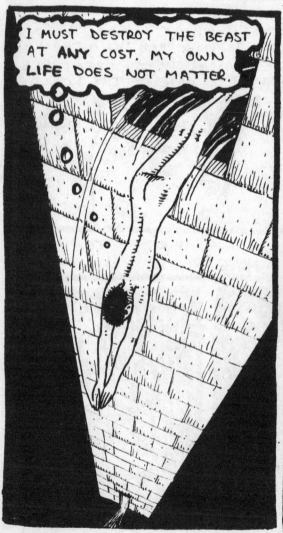

I MUST DESTROY THE BEAST AT ANY COST. MY OWN LIFE DOES NOT MATTER.

AS I FELL TOWARD DEATH I SAW THE ULFÆ SMILE AS IF AMUSED AND MAKE A GESTURE—

AND I FELT THE **SHOCK** GO THROUGH ME

TZT!

JUST BEFORE I HIT—

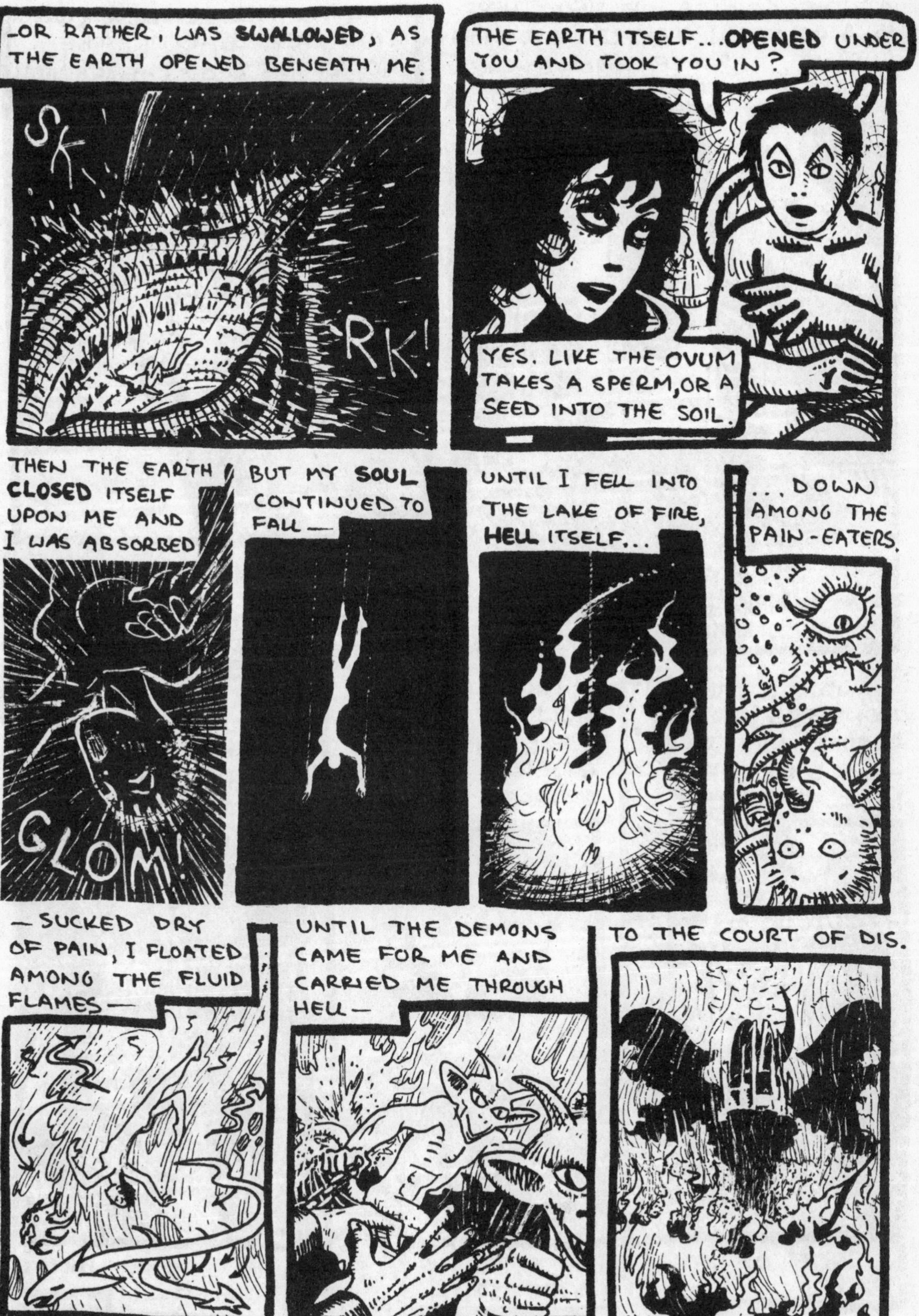
-OR RATHER, WAS SWALLOWED, AS THE EARTH OPENED BENEATH ME.
SK-
RK!
THE EARTH ITSELF... OPENED UNDER YOU AND TOOK YOU IN?
YES. LIKE THE OVUM TAKES A SPERM, OR A SEED INTO THE SOIL.
THEN THE EARTH CLOSED ITSELF UPON ME AND I WAS ABSORBED
GLOM!
BUT MY SOUL CONTINUED TO FALL—
UNTIL I FELL INTO THE LAKE OF FIRE, HELL ITSELF...
...DOWN AMONG THE PAIN-EATERS.
—SUCKED DRY OF PAIN, I FLOATED AMONG THE FLUID FLAMES—
UNTIL THE DEMONS CAME FOR ME AND CARRIED ME THROUGH HELL—
TO THE COURT OF DIS.

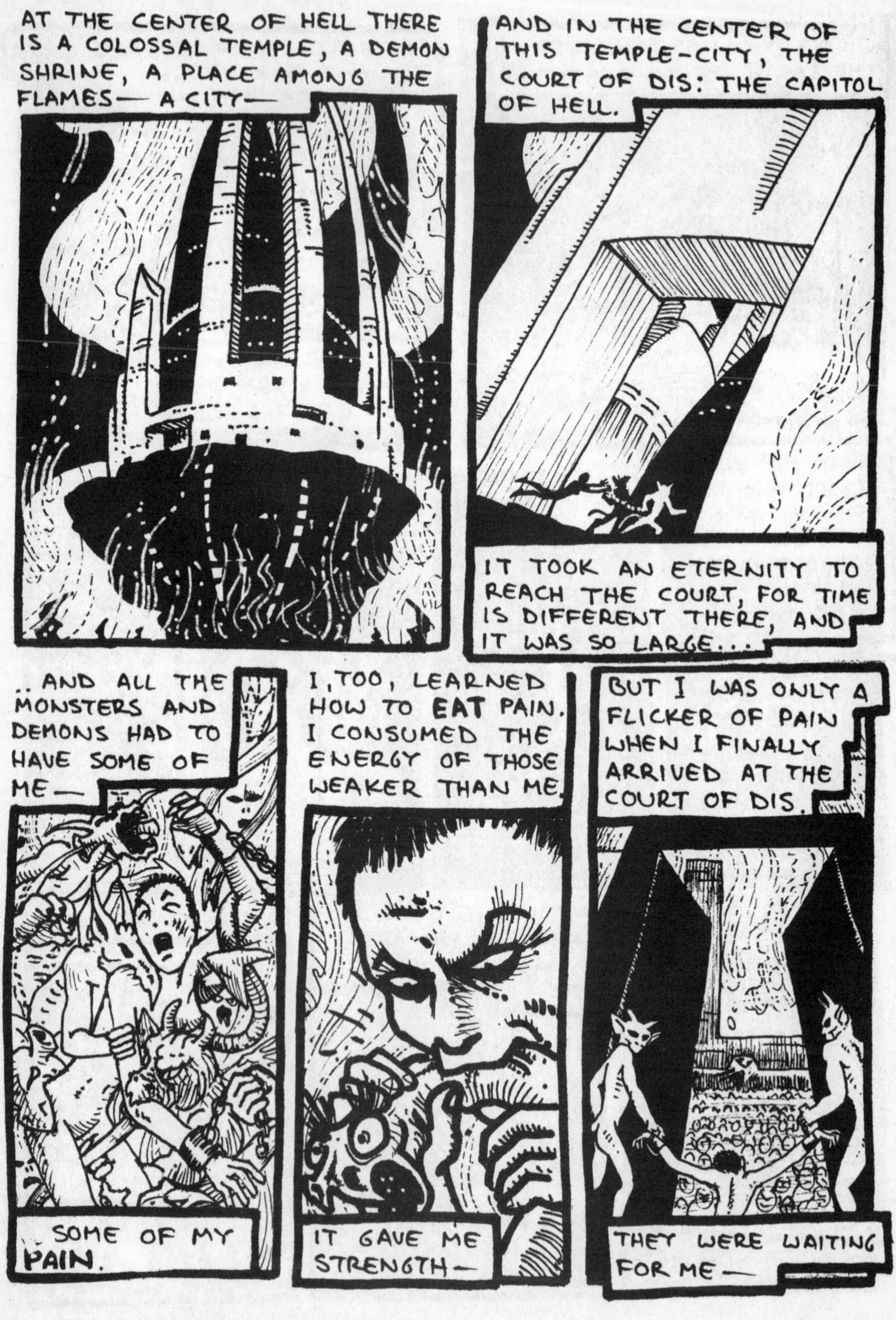
AT THE CENTER OF HELL THERE IS A COLOSSAL TEMPLE, A DEMON SHRINE, A PLACE AMONG THE FLAMES— A CITY—
AND IN THE CENTER OF THIS TEMPLE-CITY, THE COURT OF DIS: THE CAPITOL OF HELL.
IT TOOK AN ETERNITY TO REACH THE COURT, FOR TIME IS DIFFERENT THERE, AND IT WAS SO LARGE...
..AND ALL THE MONSTERS AND DEMONS HAD TO HAVE SOME OF ME—
..SOME OF MY PAIN.
I, TOO, LEARNED HOW TO EAT PAIN. I CONSUMED THE ENERGY OF THOSE WEAKER THAN ME.
IT GAVE ME STRENGTH—
BUT I WAS ONLY A FLICKER OF PAIN WHEN I FINALLY ARRIVED AT THE COURT OF DIS.
THEY WERE WAITING FOR ME—

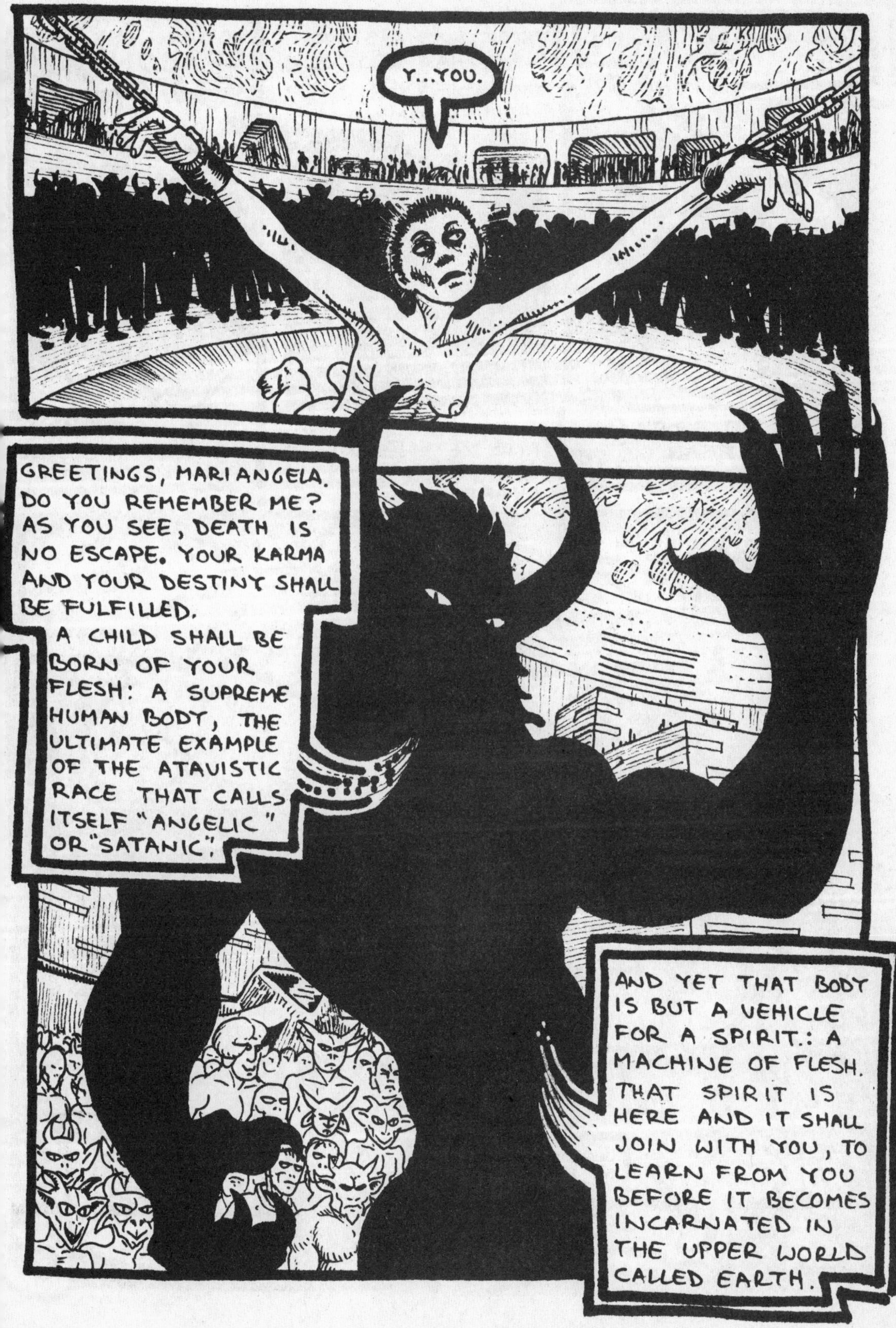
Y...YOU.
GREETINGS, MARIANGELA. DO YOU REMEMBER ME? AS YOU SEE, DEATH IS NO ESCAPE. YOUR KARMA AND YOUR DESTINY SHALL BE FULFILLED. A CHILD SHALL BE BORN OF YOUR FLESH: A SUPREME HUMAN BODY, THE ULTIMATE EXAMPLE OF THE ATAVISTIC RACE THAT CALLS ITSELF "ANGELIC" OR "SATANIC".
AND YET THAT BODY IS BUT A VEHICLE FOR A SPIRIT.: A MACHINE OF FLESH. THAT SPIRIT IS HERE AND IT SHALL JOIN WITH YOU, TO LEARN FROM YOU BEFORE IT BECOMES INCARNATED IN THE UPPER WORLD CALLED EARTH.

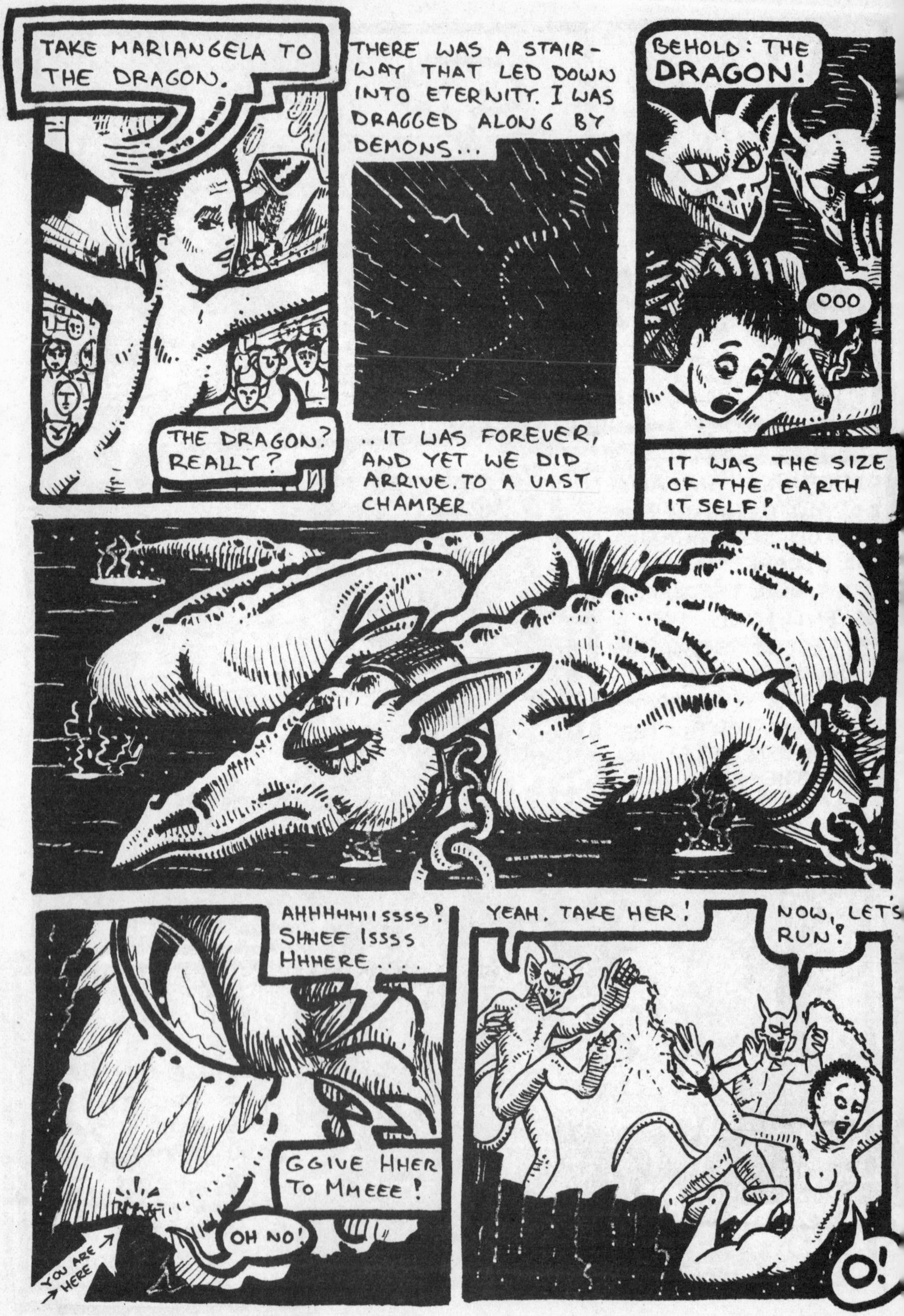

TAKE MARIANGELA TO THE DRAGON.
THE DRAGON? REALLY?
THERE WAS A STAIR-WAY THAT LED DOWN INTO ETERNITY. I WAS DRAGGED ALONG BY DEMONS...
..IT WAS FOREVER, AND YET WE DID ARRIVE. TO A VAST CHAMBER
BEHOLD: THE DRAGON!
OOO
IT WAS THE SIZE OF THE EARTH ITSELF!
AHHHHHIISSSS! SHHEE ISSSS HHHERE....
GGIVE HHER TO MMEEE!
OH NO!
YOU ARE HERE
YEAH. TAKE HER!
NOW, LETS RUN!
O!

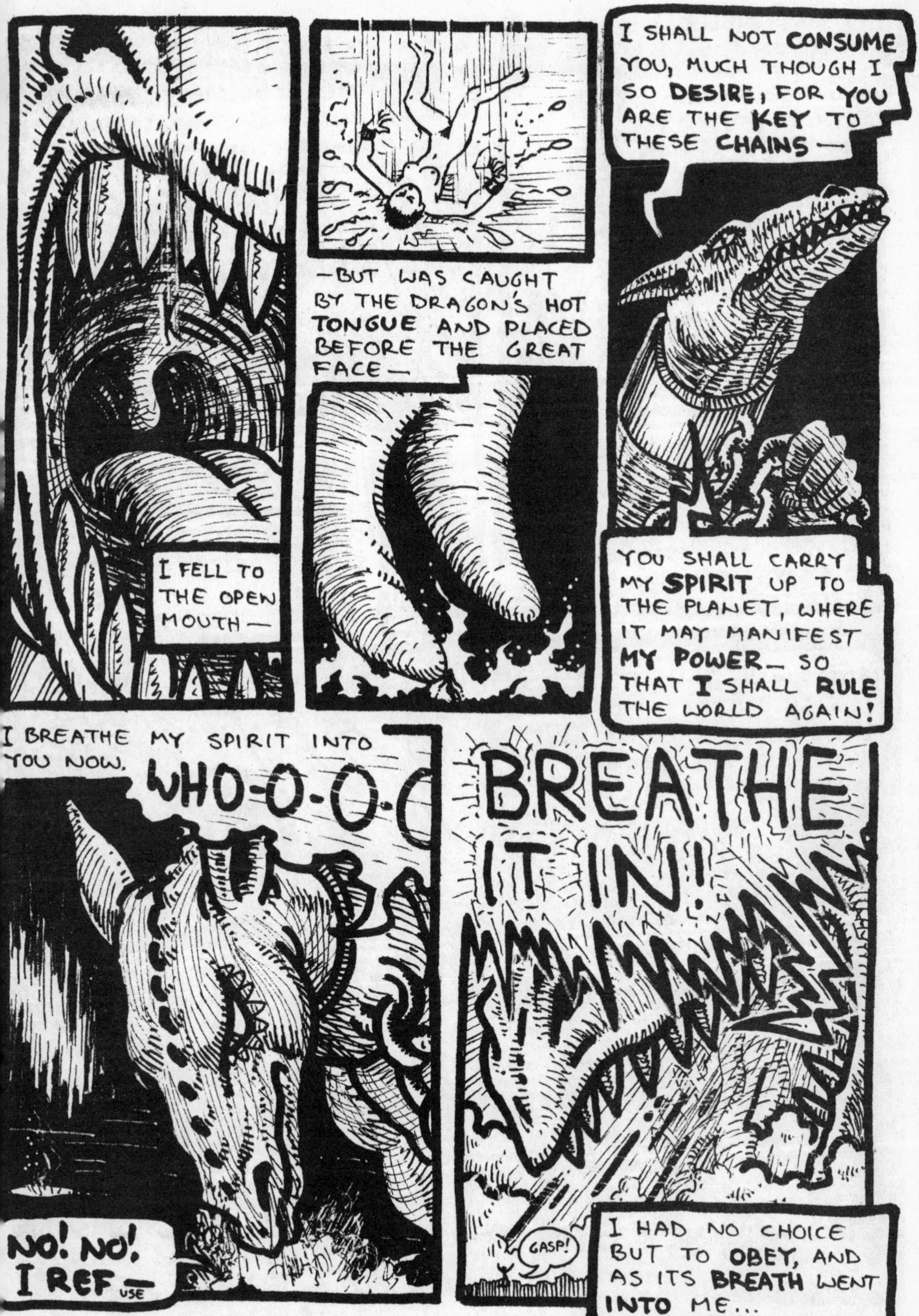
I FELL TO THE OPEN MOUTH —
—BUT WAS CAUGHT BY THE DRAGON'S HOT TONGUE AND PLACED BEFORE THE GREAT FACE—
I SHALL NOT CONSUME YOU, MUCH THOUGH I SO DESIRE, FOR YOU ARE THE KEY TO THESE CHAINS —
YOU SHALL CARRY MY SPIRIT UP TO THE PLANET, WHERE IT MAY MANIFEST MY POWER— SO THAT I SHALL RULE THE WORLD AGAIN!
I BREATHE MY SPIRIT INTO YOU NOW.
WHO-O-O-O
NO! NO! I REF—USE
BREATHE IT IN!
GASP!
I HAD NO CHOICE BUT TO OBEY, AND AS ITS BREATH WENT INTO ME...

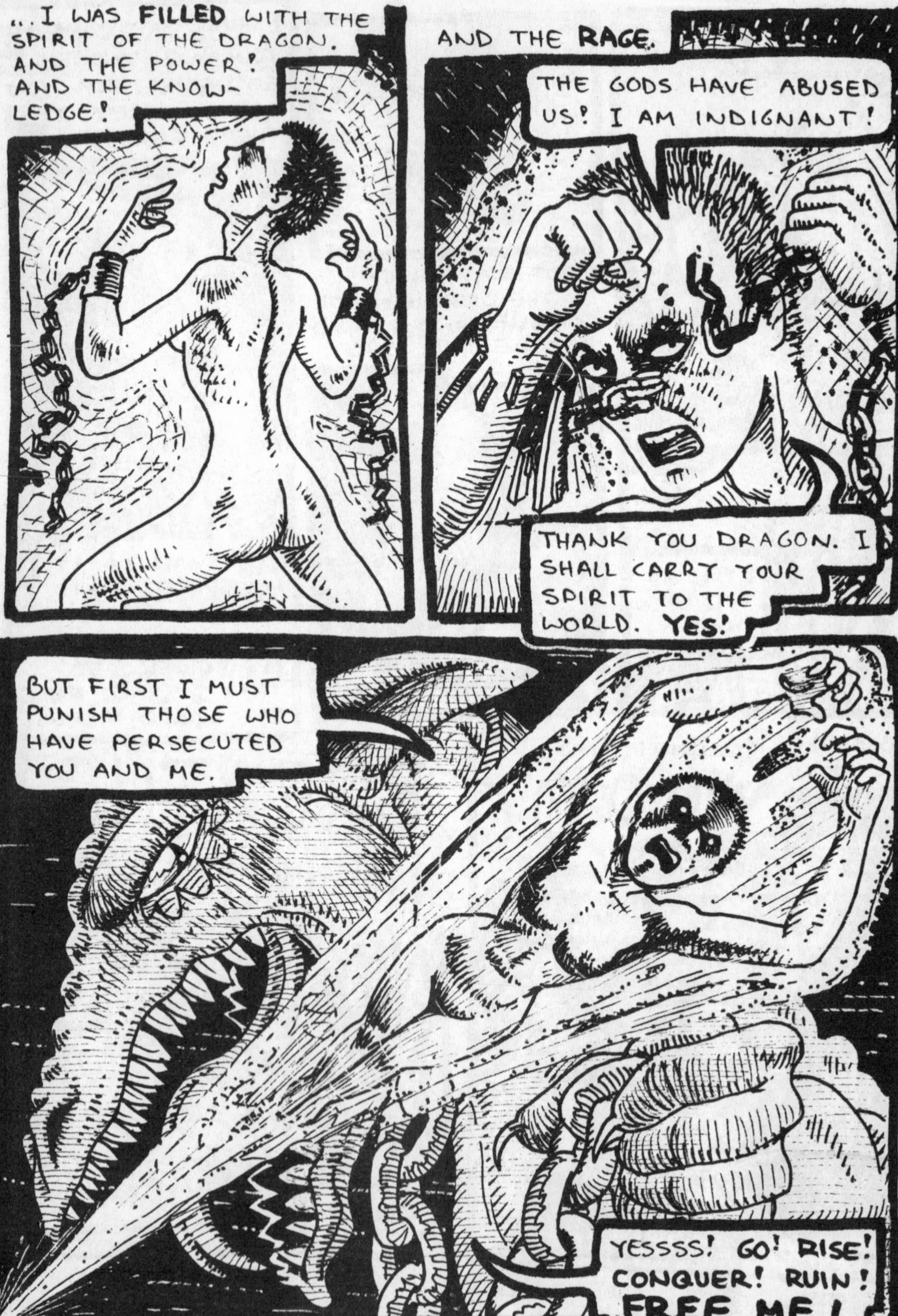
...I WAS FILLED WITH THE SPIRIT OF THE DRAGON. AND THE POWER! AND THE KNOW-LEDGE!
AND THE RAGE.
THE GODS HAVE ABUSED US! I AM INDIGNANT!
THANK YOU DRAGON. I SHALL CARRY YOUR SPIRIT TO THE WORLD. YES!
BUT FIRST I MUST PUNISH THOSE WHO HAVE PERSECUTED YOU AND ME.
YESSSS! GO! RISE! CONQUER! RUIN! FREE ME!

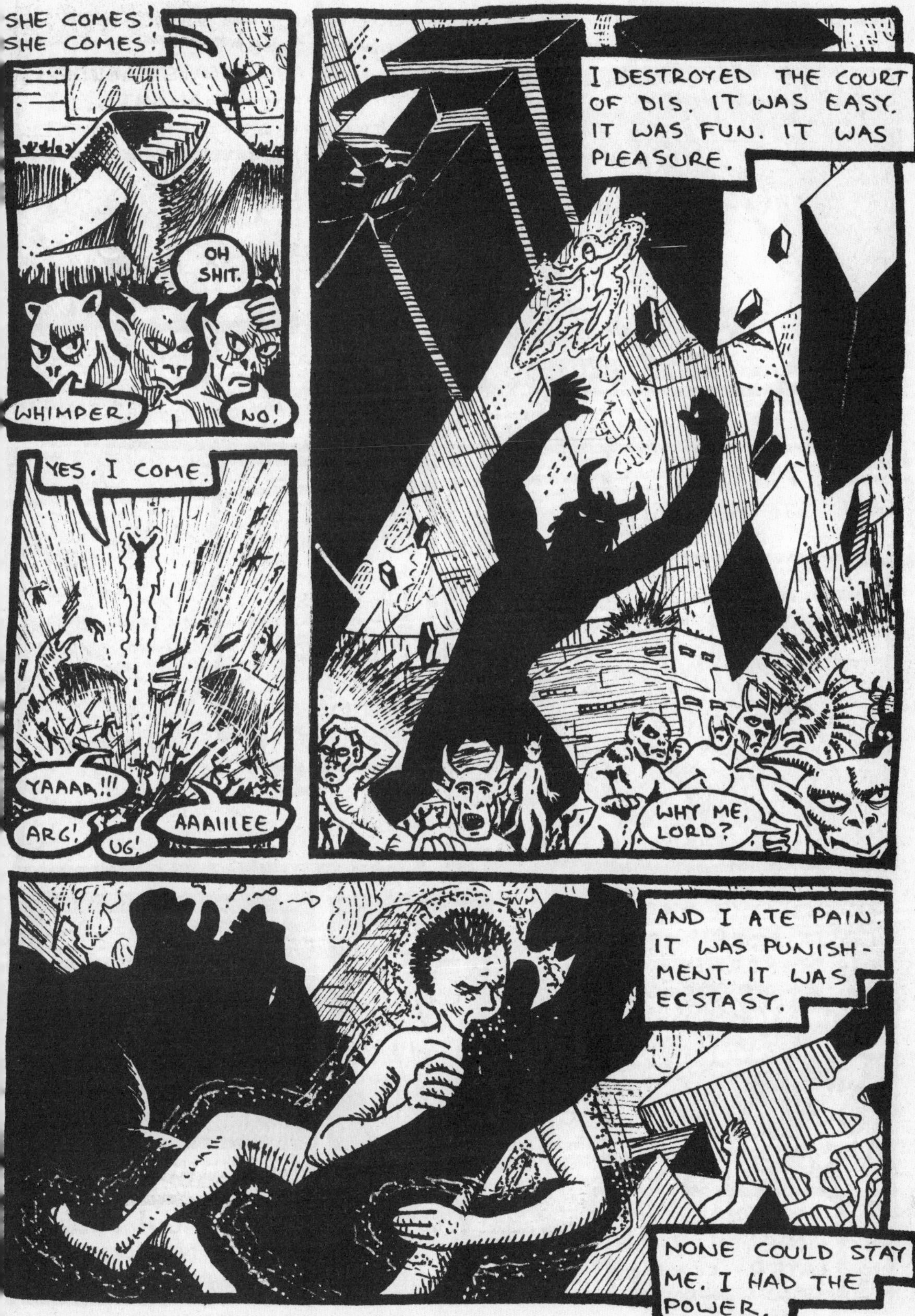
SHE COMES! SHE COMES!
OH SHIT.
WHIMPER!
NO!
YES. I COME.
YAAAA!!!
ARG!
UG!
AAAIIIEE!
I DESTROYED THE COURT OF DIS. IT WAS EASY. IT WAS FUN. IT WAS PLEASURE.
WHY ME, LORD?
AND I ATE PAIN. IT WAS PUNISHMENT. IT WAS ECSTASY.
NONE COULD STAY ME. I HAD THE POWER.

ALL OF HELL QUIVERED BEFORE MY WRATH.
I WAS CRUEL, I WAS MAD, I WAS...HAPPY.

IT WAS WONDERFUL
I FEARED NOTHING,
NO FRUSTRATIONS,
NO THOUGHTS — I
WAS A BEAST...

I WAS THE QUEEN OF HELL!

...ETERNITY WAS
THE PLEASURE OF
MY OWN MAGNIFI-
CENCE!

UNTIL MY ANGELIC
SELF STEPPED OUT
OF MY SPIRIT-SELF

HUH?

MARIANGELA:
ENOUGH OF
SYMBOLIC
FANTASIES!
WE MUST
ASCEND TO
THE EARTH
NOW AND
BECOME OUR
DESTINY.

NO! NO! NOT YET!
I WANT MORE OF
THIS! ARRRRHH!!

YOU SHALL HAVE
MORE OF THIS —
LATER. COME
NOW.

WE FELL UP OUT OF THE LAKE
OF FIRE, AT THE SPEED OF
THOUGHT, TOWARDS A DARK-
NESS —

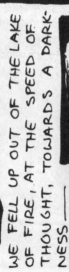

THERE WAS AN
INSTANT OF COLD
NOTHING NESS—

—THEN AN EXPLO-
SION OF SENSES;
PHYSICAL PAIN,
TASTE, FEAR, AS...

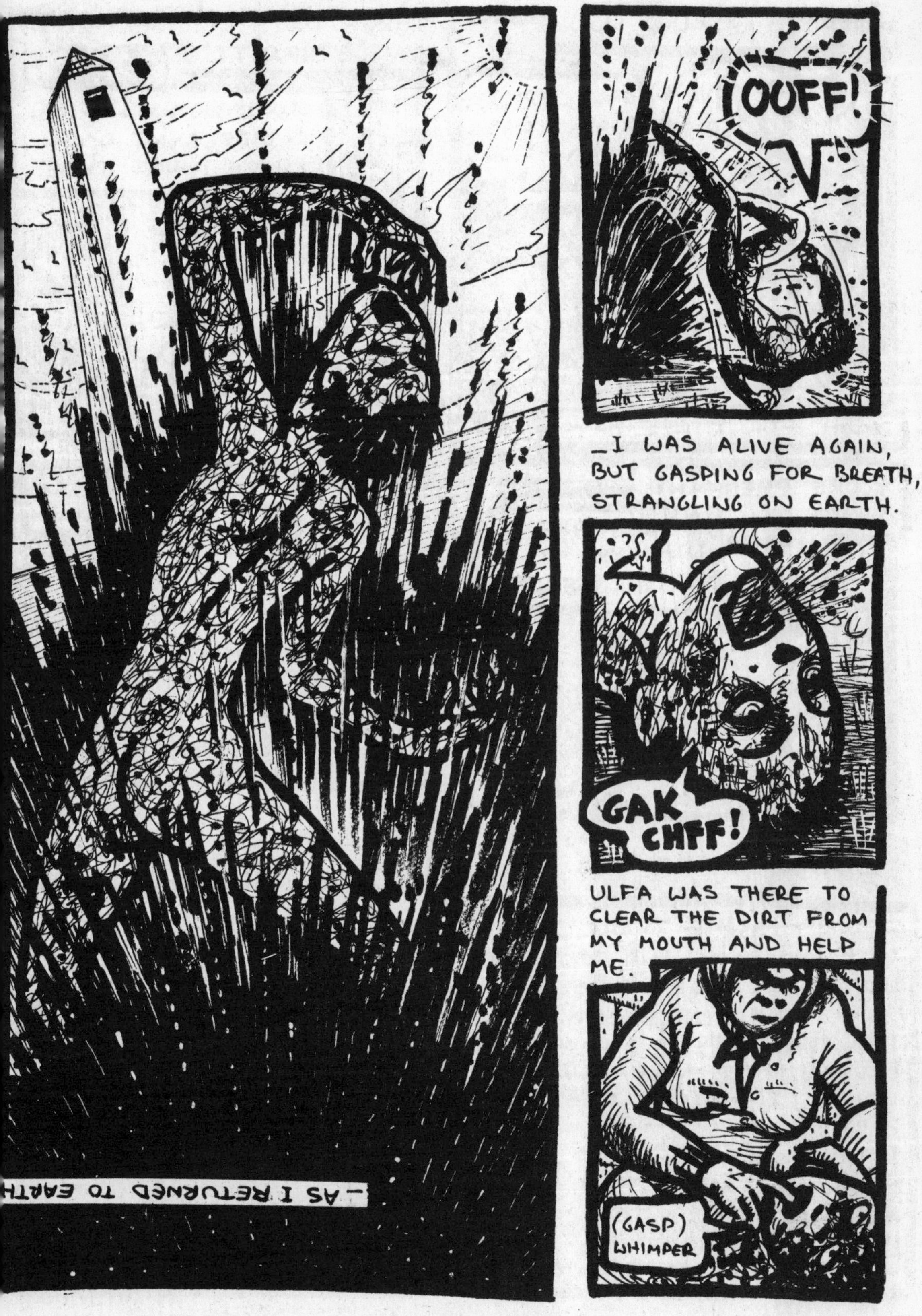
—AS I RETURNED TO EARTH
OUFF!
_I WAS ALIVE AGAIN, BUT GASPING FOR BREATH, STRANGLING ON EARTH.
GAK CHFF!
ULFA WAS THERE TO CLEAR THE DIRT FROM MY MOUTH AND HELP ME.
(GASP) WHIMPER

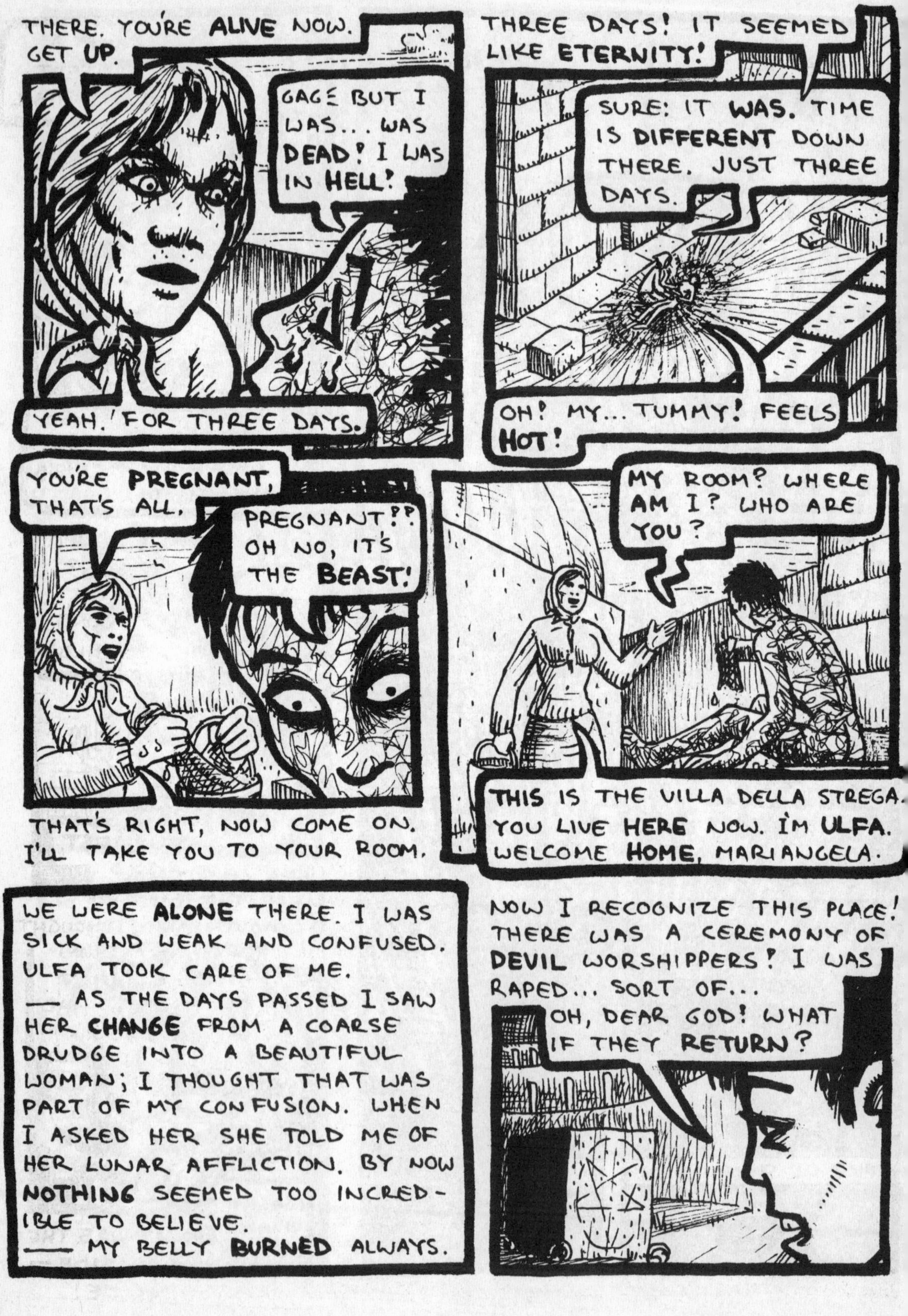
THERE. YOU'RE ALIVE NOW. GET UP.
GAGE BUT I WAS... WAS DEAD! I WAS IN HELL!
YEAH. FOR THREE DAYS.
THREE DAYS! IT SEEMED LIKE ETERNITY!
SURE: IT WAS. TIME IS DIFFERENT DOWN THERE. JUST THREE DAYS.
OH! MY... TUMMY! FEELS HOT!
YOU'RE PREGNANT, THAT'S ALL.
PREGNANT!? OH NO, IT'S THE BEAST!
THAT'S RIGHT, NOW COME ON. I'LL TAKE YOU TO YOUR ROOM.
MY ROOM? WHERE AM I? WHO ARE YOU?
THIS IS THE VILLA DELLA STREGA. YOU LIVE HERE NOW. I'M ULFA. WELCOME HOME, MARIANGELA.
WE WERE ALONE THERE. I WAS SICK AND WEAK AND CONFUSED. ULFA TOOK CARE OF ME.
— AS THE DAYS PASSED I SAW HER CHANGE FROM A COARSE DRUDGE INTO A BEAUTIFUL WOMAN; I THOUGHT THAT WAS PART OF MY CONFUSION. WHEN I ASKED HER SHE TOLD ME OF HER LUNAR AFFLICTION. BY NOW NOTHING SEEMED TOO INCREDIBLE TO BELIEVE.
— MY BELLY BURNED ALWAYS.
NOW I RECOGNIZE THIS PLACE! THERE WAS A CEREMONY OF DEVIL WORSHIPPERS! I WAS RAPED... SORT OF...
OH, DEAR GOD! WHAT IF THEY RETURN?

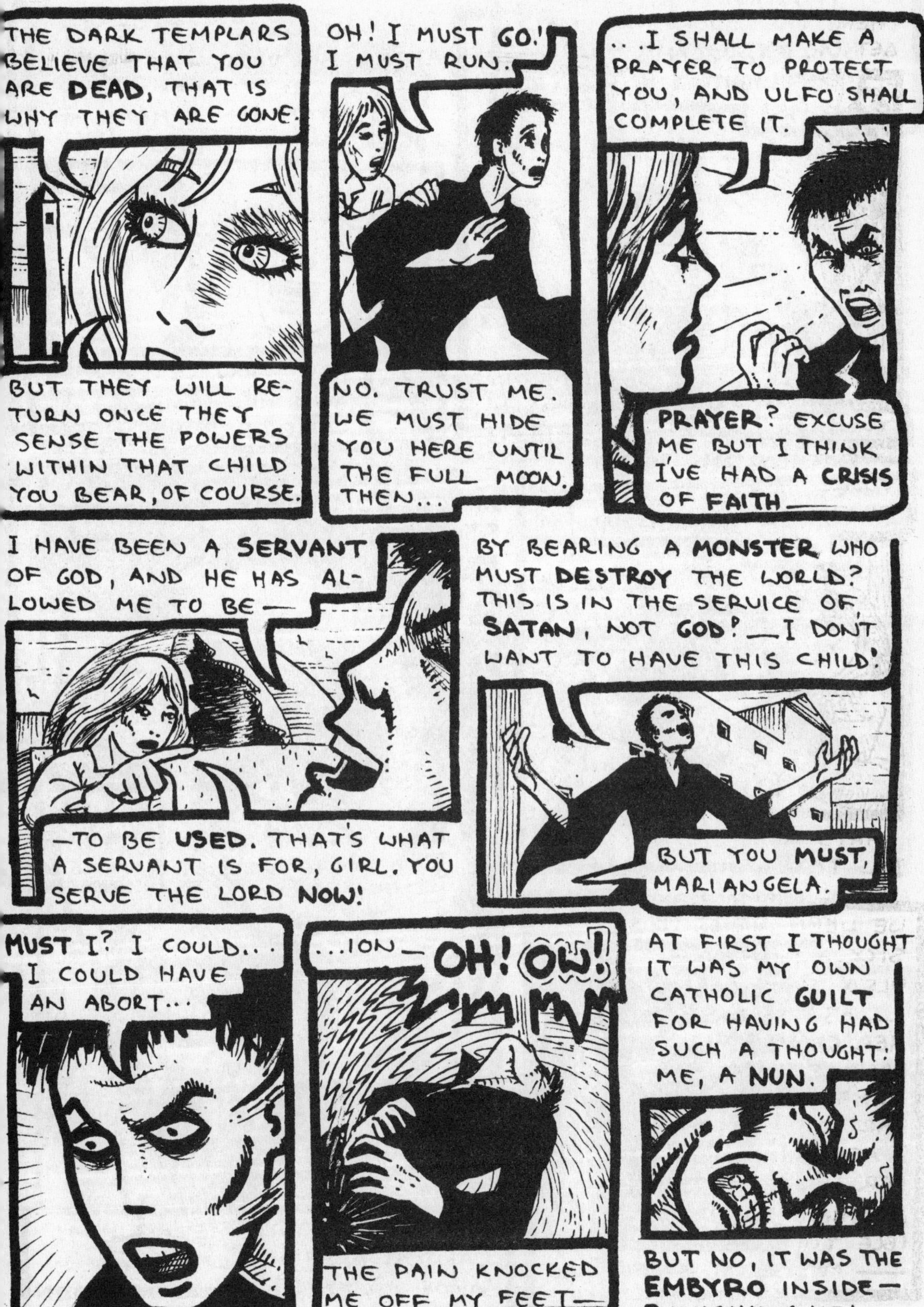
THE DARK TEMPLARS BELIEVE THAT YOU ARE DEAD, THAT IS WHY THEY ARE GONE.
BUT THEY WILL RETURN ONCE THEY SENSE THE POWERS WITHIN THAT CHILD YOU BEAR, OF COURSE.
OH! I MUST GO! I MUST RUN.
NO. TRUST ME. WE MUST HIDE YOU HERE UNTIL THE FULL MOON. THEN...
...I SHALL MAKE A PRAYER TO PROTECT YOU, AND ULFO SHALL COMPLETE IT.
PRAYER? EXCUSE ME BUT I THINK I'VE HAD A CRISIS OF FAITH—
I HAVE BEEN A SERVANT OF GOD, AND HE HAS ALLOWED ME TO BE—
—TO BE USED. THAT'S WHAT A SERVANT IS FOR, GIRL. YOU SERVE THE LORD NOW!
BY BEARING A MONSTER WHO MUST DESTROY THE WORLD? THIS IS IN THE SERVICE OF SATAN, NOT GOD!—I DON'T WANT TO HAVE THIS CHILD!
BUT YOU MUST, MARI ANGELA.
MUST I? I COULD... I COULD HAVE AN ABORT...
...ION—OH! OW!
THE PAIN KNOCKED ME OFF MY FEET—
AT FIRST I THOUGHT IT WAS MY OWN CATHOLIC GUILT FOR HAVING HAD SUCH A THOUGHT: ME, A NUN.
BUT NO, IT WAS THE EMBYRO INSIDE—PUNISHING ME!

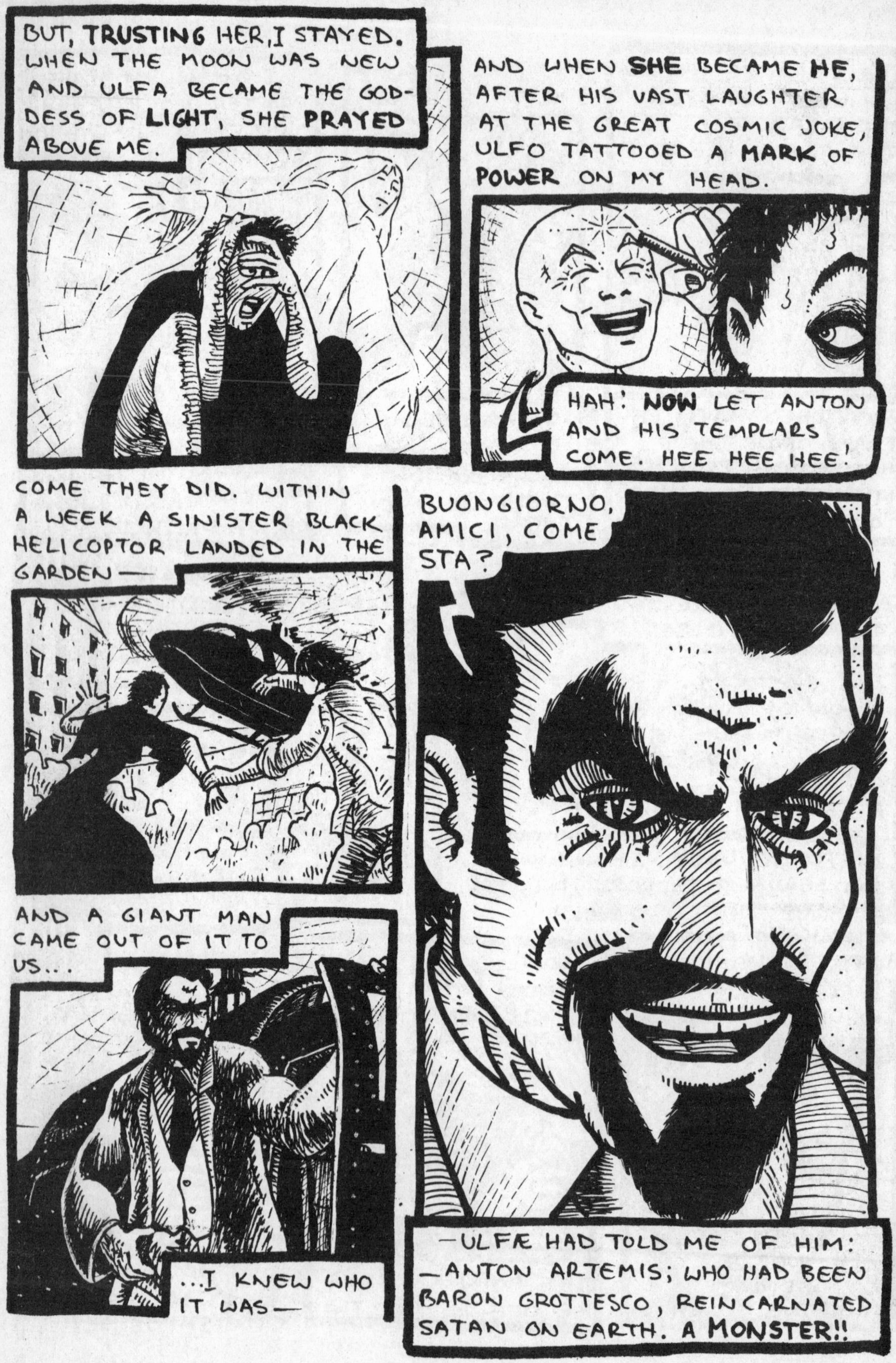
BUT, TRUSTING HER, I STAYED. WHEN THE MOON WAS NEW AND ULFA BECAME THE GODDESS OF LIGHT, SHE PRAYED ABOVE ME.
AND WHEN SHE BECAME HE, AFTER HIS VAST LAUGHTER AT THE GREAT COSMIC JOKE, ULFO TATTOOED A MARK OF POWER ON MY HEAD.
HAH! NOW LET ANTON AND HIS TEMPLARS COME. HEE HEE HEE!
COME THEY DID. WITHIN A WEEK A SINISTER BLACK HELICOPTOR LANDED IN THE GARDEN—
AND A GIANT MAN CAME OUT OF IT TO US...
...I KNEW WHO IT WAS—
BUONGIORNO, AMICI, COME STA?
—ULFÆ HAD TOLD ME OF HIM: —ANTON ARTEMIS; WHO HAD BEEN BARON GROTTESCO, REINCARNATED SATAN ON EARTH. A MONSTER!!

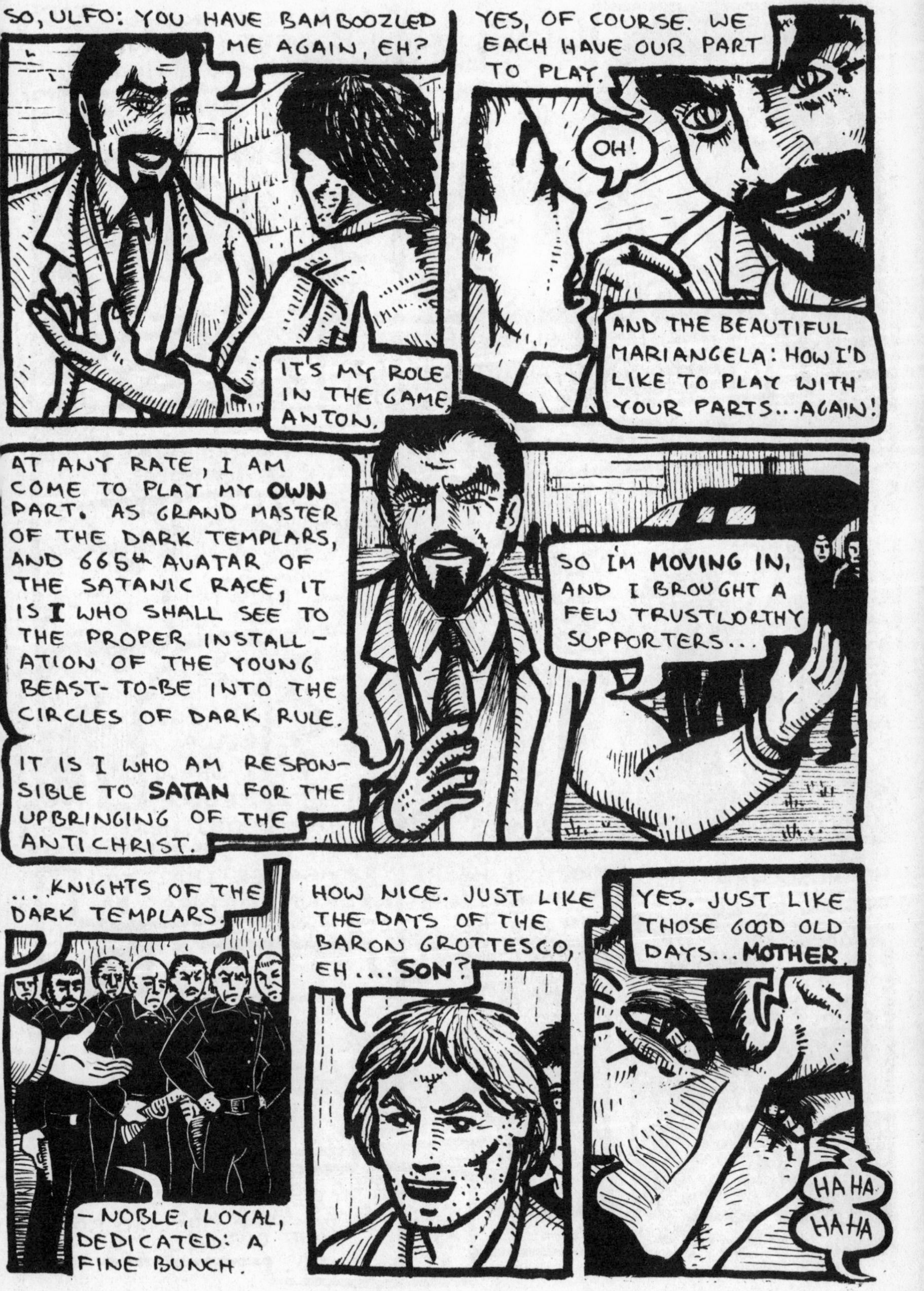
SO, ULFO: YOU HAVE BAMBOOZLED ME AGAIN, EH?
IT'S MY ROLE IN THE GAME, ANTON.
YES, OF COURSE. WE EACH HAVE OUR PART TO PLAY.
OH!
AND THE BEAUTIFUL MARIANGELA: HOW I'D LIKE TO PLAY WITH YOUR PARTS... AGAIN!
AT ANY RATE, I AM COME TO PLAY MY **OWN** PART. AS GRAND MASTER OF THE DARK TEMPLARS, AND 665th AVATAR OF THE SATANIC RACE, IT IS **I** WHO SHALL SEE TO THE PROPER INSTALL-ATION OF THE YOUNG BEAST-TO-BE INTO THE CIRCLES OF DARK RULE.
IT IS I WHO AM RESPON-SIBLE TO **SATAN** FOR THE UPBRINGING OF THE ANTICHRIST.
SO I'M **MOVING IN**, AND I BROUGHT A FEW TRUSTWORTHY SUPPORTERS...
....KNIGHTS OF THE DARK TEMPLARS.
—NOBLE, LOYAL, DEDICATED: A FINE BUNCH.
HOW NICE. JUST LIKE THE DAYS OF THE BARON GROTTESCO, EH.... **SON**?
YES. JUST LIKE THOSE GOOD OLD DAYS... **MOTHER**.
HA HA HA HA

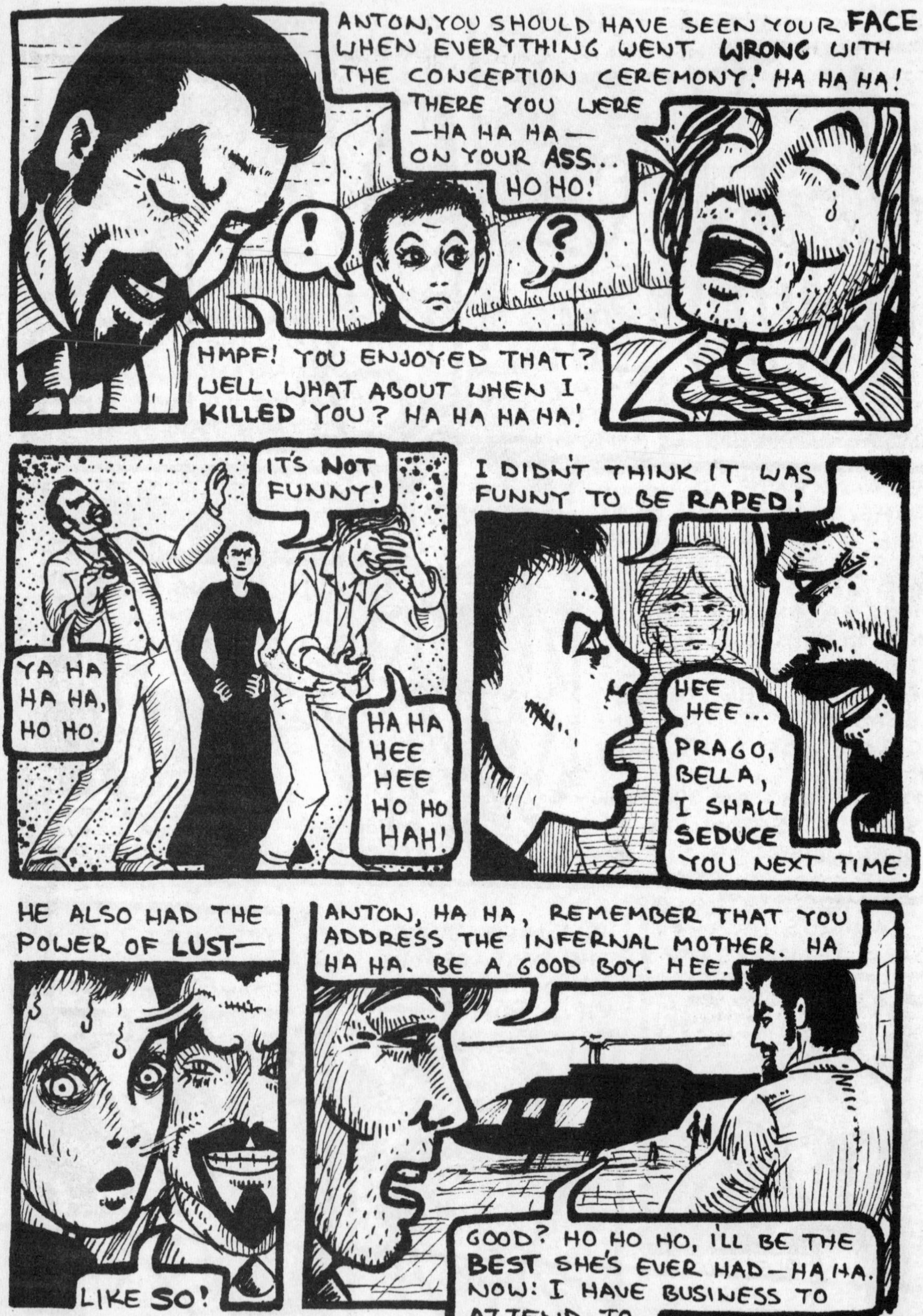
ANTON, YOU SHOULD HAVE SEEN YOUR FACE WHEN EVERYTHING WENT WRONG WITH THE CONCEPTION CEREMONY! HA HA HA!
THERE YOU WERE —HA HA HA— ON YOUR ASS... HO HO!
!
?
HMPF! YOU ENJOYED THAT? WELL, WHAT ABOUT WHEN I KILLED YOU? HA HA HA HA!
IT'S NOT FUNNY!
YA HA HA HA, HO HO.
HA HA HEE HEE HO HO HAH!
I DIDN'T THINK IT WAS FUNNY TO BE RAPED!
HEE HEE... PRAGO, BELLA, I SHALL SEDUCE YOU NEXT TIME.
HE ALSO HAD THE POWER OF LUST—
LIKE SO!
ANTON, HA HA, REMEMBER THAT YOU ADDRESS THE INFERNAL MOTHER. HA HA HA. BE A GOOD BOY. HEE.
GOOD? HO HO HO, I'LL BE THE BEST SHE'S EVER HAD—HA HA. NOW: I HAVE BUSINESS TO ATTEND TO.

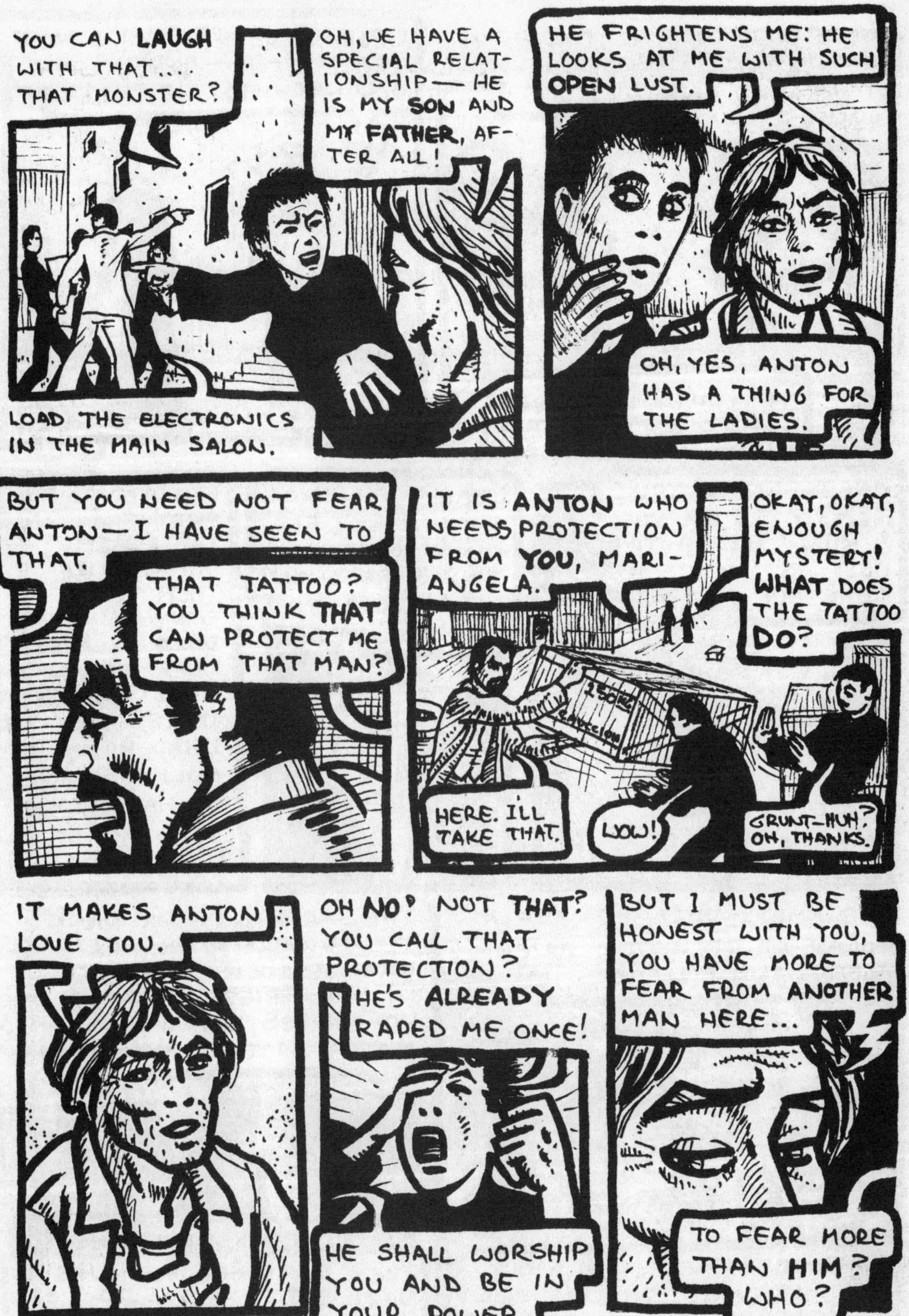
YOU CAN **LAUGH** WITH THAT.... THAT MONSTER?
OH, WE HAVE A SPECIAL RELATIONSHIP— HE IS MY **SON** AND MY **FATHER**, AFTER ALL!
LOAD THE ELECTRONICS IN THE MAIN SALON.
HE FRIGHTENS ME: HE LOOKS AT ME WITH SUCH **OPEN** LUST.
OH, YES, ANTON HAS A THING FOR THE LADIES.
BUT YOU NEED NOT FEAR ANTON— I HAVE SEEN TO THAT.
THAT TATTOO? YOU THINK **THAT** CAN PROTECT ME FROM THAT MAN?
IT IS **ANTON** WHO NEEDS PROTECTION FROM **YOU**, MARI-ANGELA.
OKAY, OKAY, ENOUGH MYSTERY! **WHAT** DOES THE TATTOO **DO**?
HERE. ILL TAKE THAT.
WOW!
GRUNT—HUH? OH, THANKS.
IT MAKES ANTON LOVE YOU.
OH **NO**! NOT **THAT**? YOU CALL THAT PROTECTION?
HE'S **ALREADY** RAPED ME ONCE!
HE SHALL WORSHIP YOU AND BE IN YOUR POWER.
BUT I MUST BE HONEST WITH YOU, YOU HAVE MORE TO FEAR FROM ANOTHER MAN HERE...
TO FEAR MORE THAN **HIM**? WHO?

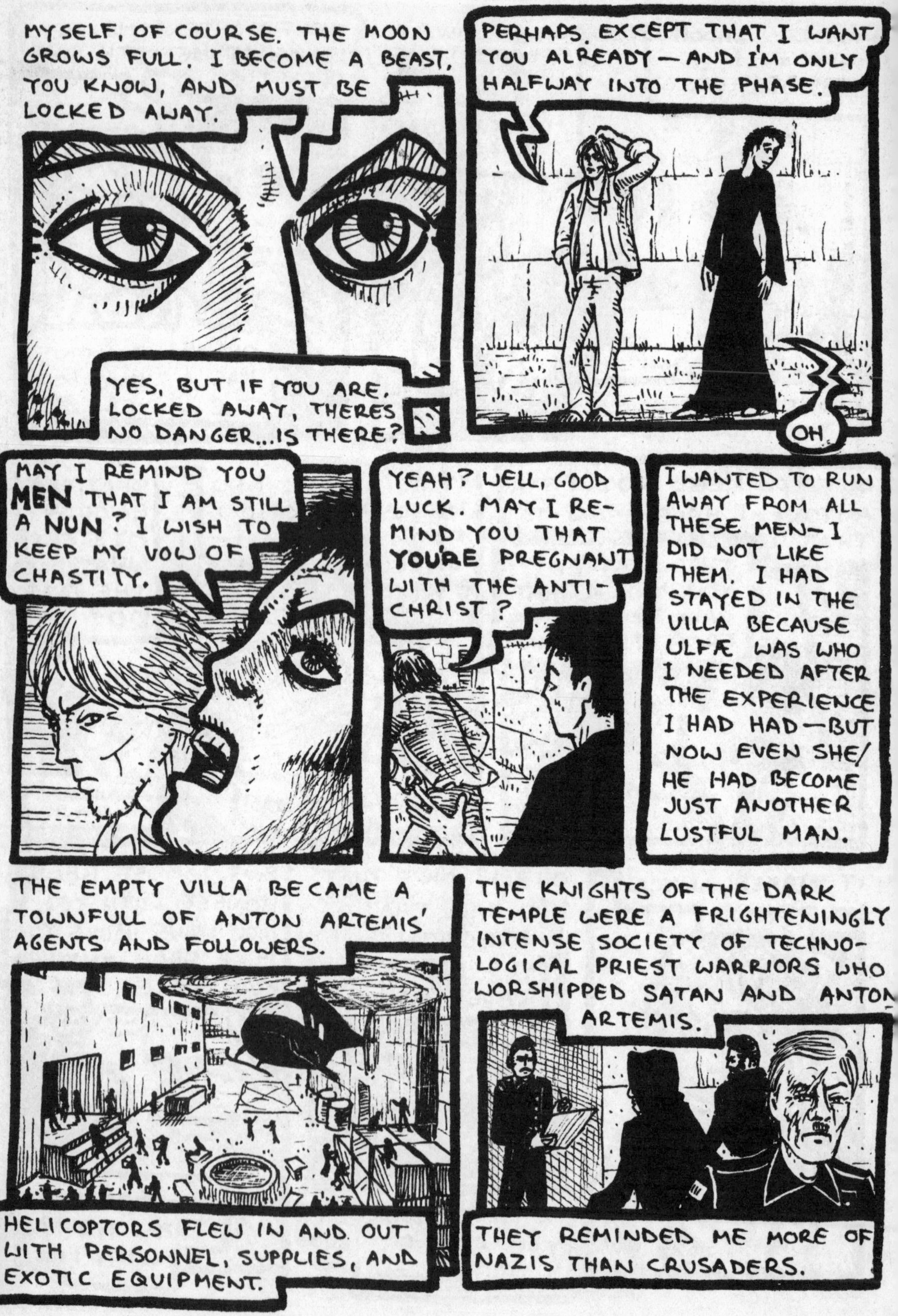
MYSELF, OF COURSE. THE MOON GROWS FULL. I BECOME A BEAST, YOU KNOW, AND MUST BE LOCKED AWAY.
YES, BUT IF YOU ARE. LOCKED AWAY, THERES NO DANGER...IS THERE?
PERHAPS. EXCEPT THAT I WANT YOU ALREADY—AND I'M ONLY HALFWAY INTO THE PHASE.
OH.
MAY I REMIND YOU MEN THAT I AM STILL A NUN? I WISH TO KEEP MY VOW OF CHASTITY.
YEAH? WELL, GOOD LUCK. MAY I REMIND YOU THAT YOU'RE PREGNANT WITH THE ANTI-CHRIST?
I WANTED TO RUN AWAY FROM ALL THESE MEN—I DID NOT LIKE THEM. I HAD STAYED IN THE VILLA BECAUSE ULFÆ WAS WHO I NEEDED AFTER THE EXPERIENCE I HAD HAD—BUT NOW EVEN SHE/HE HAD BECOME JUST ANOTHER LUSTFUL MAN.
THE EMPTY VILLA BECAME A TOWNFULL OF ANTON ARTEMIS' AGENTS AND FOLLOWERS.
HELICOPTORS FLEW IN AND OUT WITH PERSONNEL, SUPPLIES, AND EXOTIC EQUIPMENT.
THE KNIGHTS OF THE DARK TEMPLE WERE A FRIGHTENINGLY INTENSE SOCIETY OF TECHNOLOGICAL PRIEST WARRIORS WHO WORSHIPPED SATAN AND ANTON ARTEMIS.
THEY REMINDED ME MORE OF NAZIS THAN CRUSADERS.

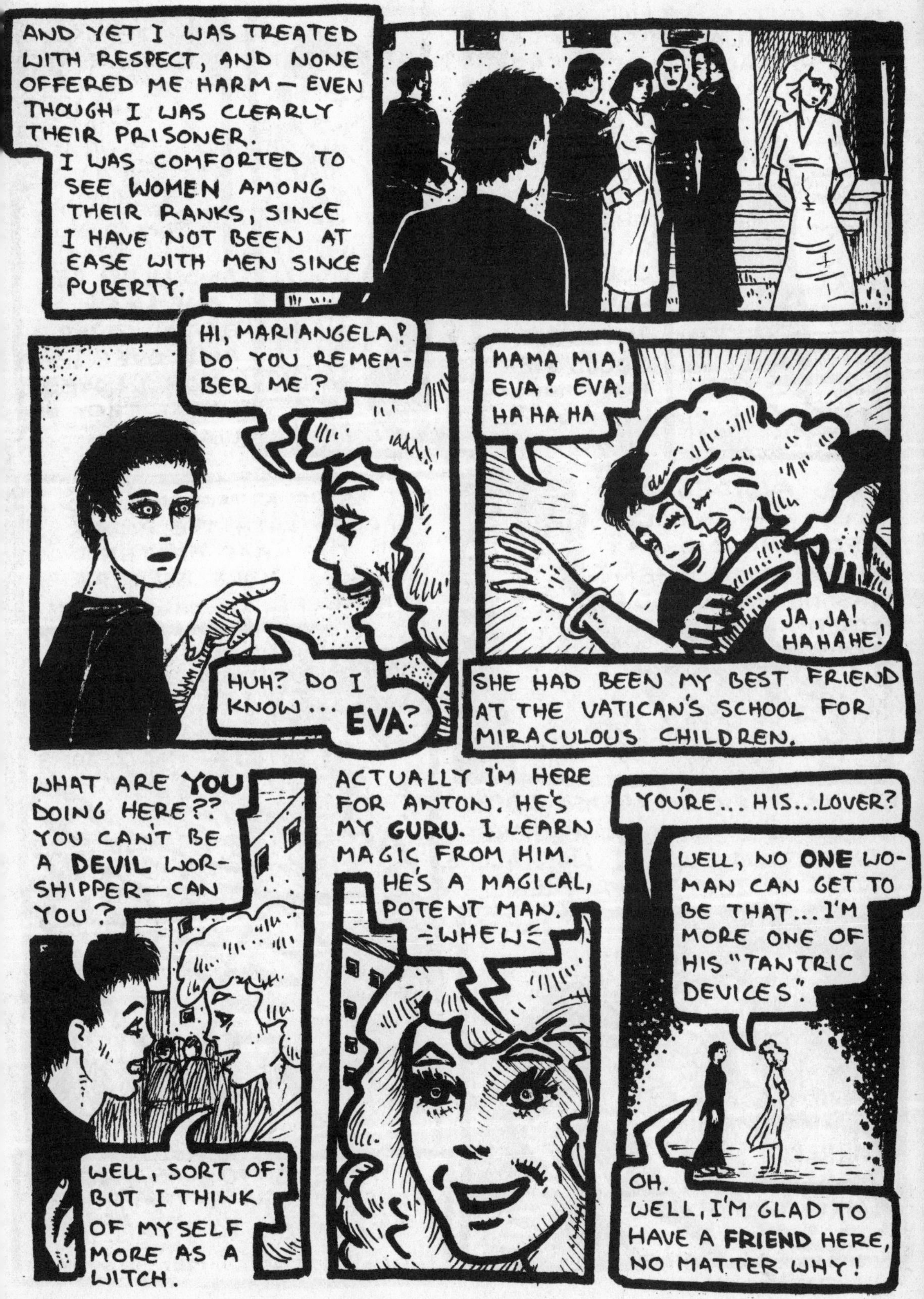

AND YET I WAS TREATED WITH RESPECT, AND NONE OFFERED ME HARM — EVEN THOUGH I WAS CLEARLY THEIR PRISONER.
I WAS COMFORTED TO SEE WOMEN AMONG THEIR RANKS, SINCE I HAVE NOT BEEN AT EASE WITH MEN SINCE PUBERTY.
HI, MARIANGELA! DO YOU REMEMBER ME?
HUH? DO I KNOW... EVA?
MAMA MIA! EVA! EVA! HA HA HA
JA, JA! HAHAHE!
SHE HAD BEEN MY BEST FRIEND AT THE VATICAN'S SCHOOL FOR MIRACULOUS CHILDREN.
WHAT ARE YOU DOING HERE?? YOU CAN'T BE A DEVIL WORSHIPPER—CAN YOU?
WELL, SORT OF: BUT I THINK OF MYSELF MORE AS A WITCH.
ACTUALLY I'M HERE FOR ANTON. HE'S MY GURU. I LEARN MAGIC FROM HIM.
HE'S A MAGICAL, POTENT MAN. =WHEW=
YOU'RE... HIS... LOVER?
WELL, NO ONE WOMAN CAN GET TO BE THAT... I'M MORE ONE OF HIS "TANTRIC DEVICES".
OH.
WELL, I'M GLAD TO HAVE A FRIEND HERE, NO MATTER WHY!

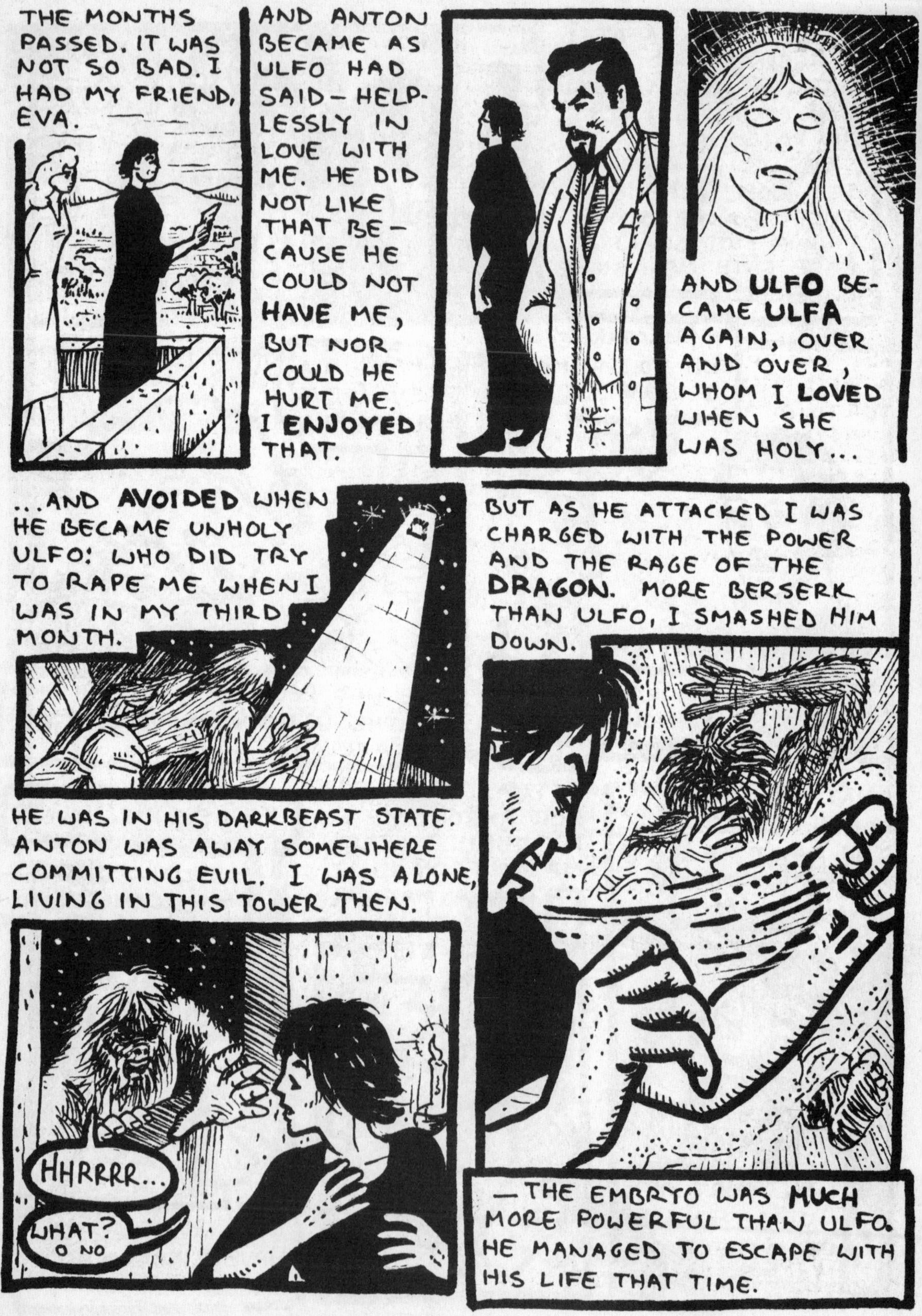
THE MONTHS PASSED. IT WAS NOT SO BAD. I HAD MY FRIEND, EVA.
AND ANTON BECAME AS ULFO HAD SAID—HELPLESSLY IN LOVE WITH ME. HE DID NOT LIKE THAT BECAUSE HE COULD NOT HAVE ME, BUT NOR COULD HE HURT ME. I ENJOYED THAT.
AND ULFO BECAME ULFA AGAIN, OVER AND OVER, WHOM I LOVED WHEN SHE WAS HOLY...
...AND AVOIDED WHEN HE BECAME UNHOLY ULFO: WHO DID TRY TO RAPE ME WHEN I WAS IN MY THIRD MONTH.
HE WAS IN HIS DARKBEAST STATE. ANTON WAS AWAY SOMEWHERE COMMITTING EVIL. I WAS ALONE, LIVING IN THIS TOWER THEN.
HHRRRR...
WHAT? O NO
BUT AS HE ATTACKED I WAS CHARGED WITH THE POWER AND THE RAGE OF THE DRAGON. MORE BERSERK THAN ULFO, I SMASHED HIM DOWN.
—THE EMBRYO WAS MUCH MORE POWERFUL THAN ULFO. HE MANAGED TO ESCAPE WITH HIS LIFE THAT TIME.

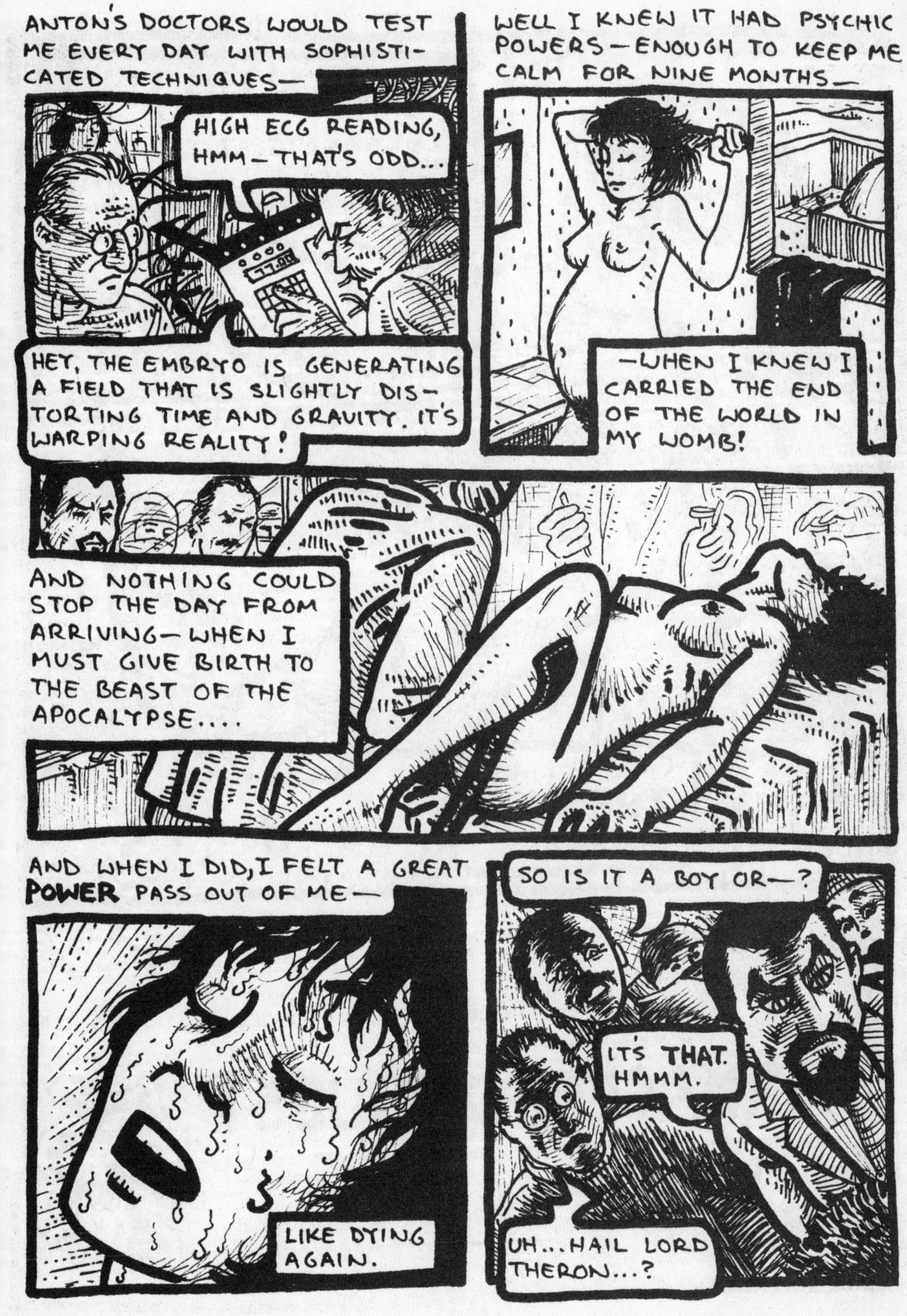
ANTON'S DOCTORS WOULD TEST ME EVERY DAY WITH SOPHISTICATED TECHNIQUES—
HIGH ECG READING, HMM—THAT'S ODD...
HEY, THE EMBRYO IS GENERATING A FIELD THAT IS SLIGHTLY DISTORTING TIME AND GRAVITY. IT'S WARPING REALITY!
WELL I KNEW IT HAD PSYCHIC POWERS—ENOUGH TO KEEP ME CALM FOR NINE MONTHS—
—WHEN I KNEW I CARRIED THE END OF THE WORLD IN MY WOMB!
AND NOTHING COULD STOP THE DAY FROM ARRIVING—WHEN I MUST GIVE BIRTH TO THE BEAST OF THE APOCALYPSE....
AND WHEN I DID, I FELT A GREAT **POWER** PASS OUT OF ME—
LIKE DYING AGAIN.
SO IS IT A BOY OR—?
IT'S **THAT.** HMMM.
UH...HAIL LORD THERON...?

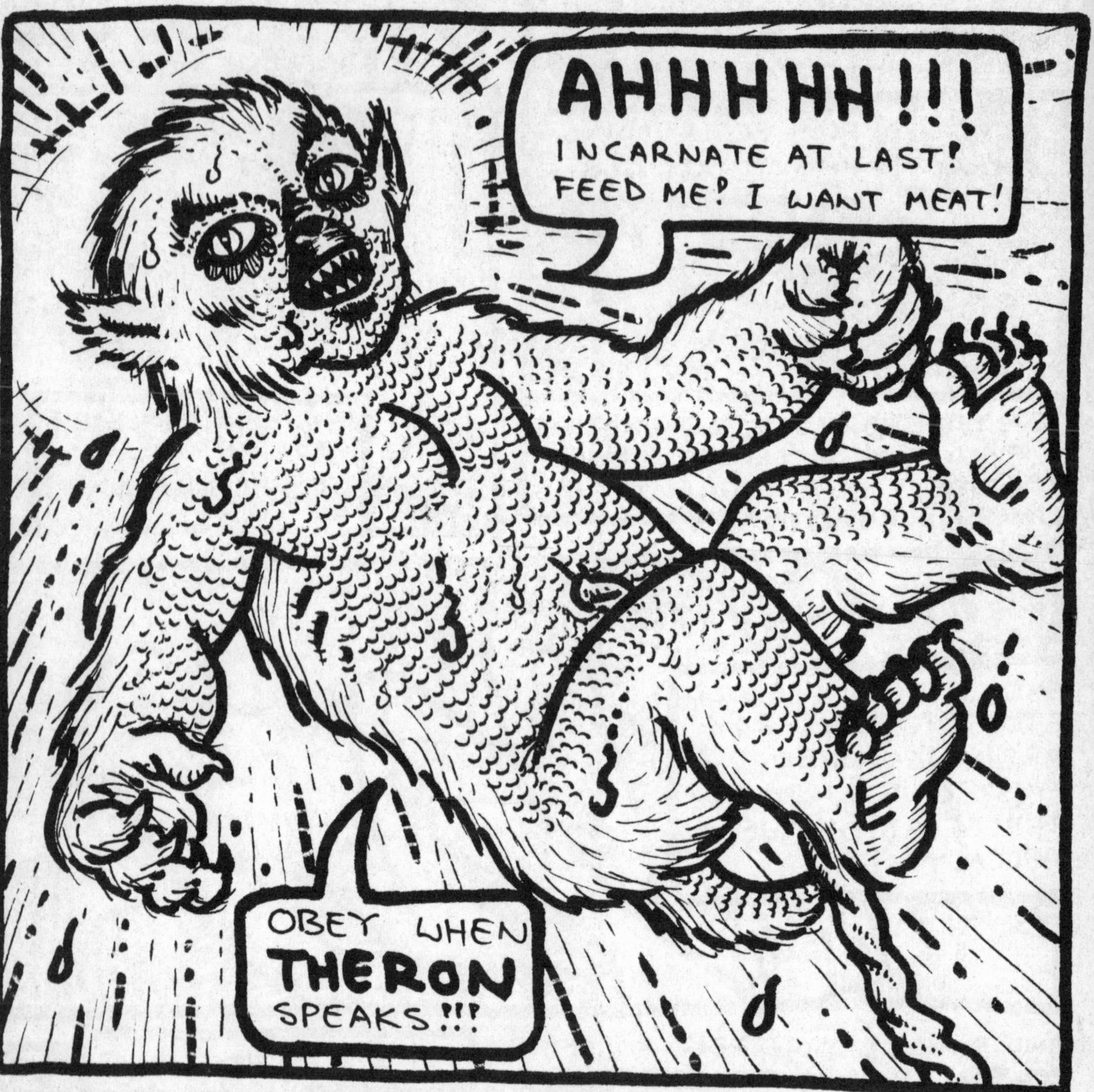
AHHHHH!!!
INCARNATE AT LAST! FEED ME! I WANT MEAT!
OBEY WHEN THERON SPEAKS!!!

ISN'T HE CUTE? BUT DO YOU SUPPOSE OUR LITTLE BABY BEAST MIGHT JUST BE A PROBLEM CHILD? AND IS THAT REALLY OUR HERO, TAZIO? HOWCUM?

THE ONLY WAY TO FIND OUT IS TO TUNE IN TO THE NEXT INSTALLMENT OF

# ARMAGEDDONQUEST

Ronald Russell Roach

January 30, 1985

R

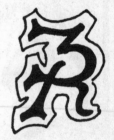

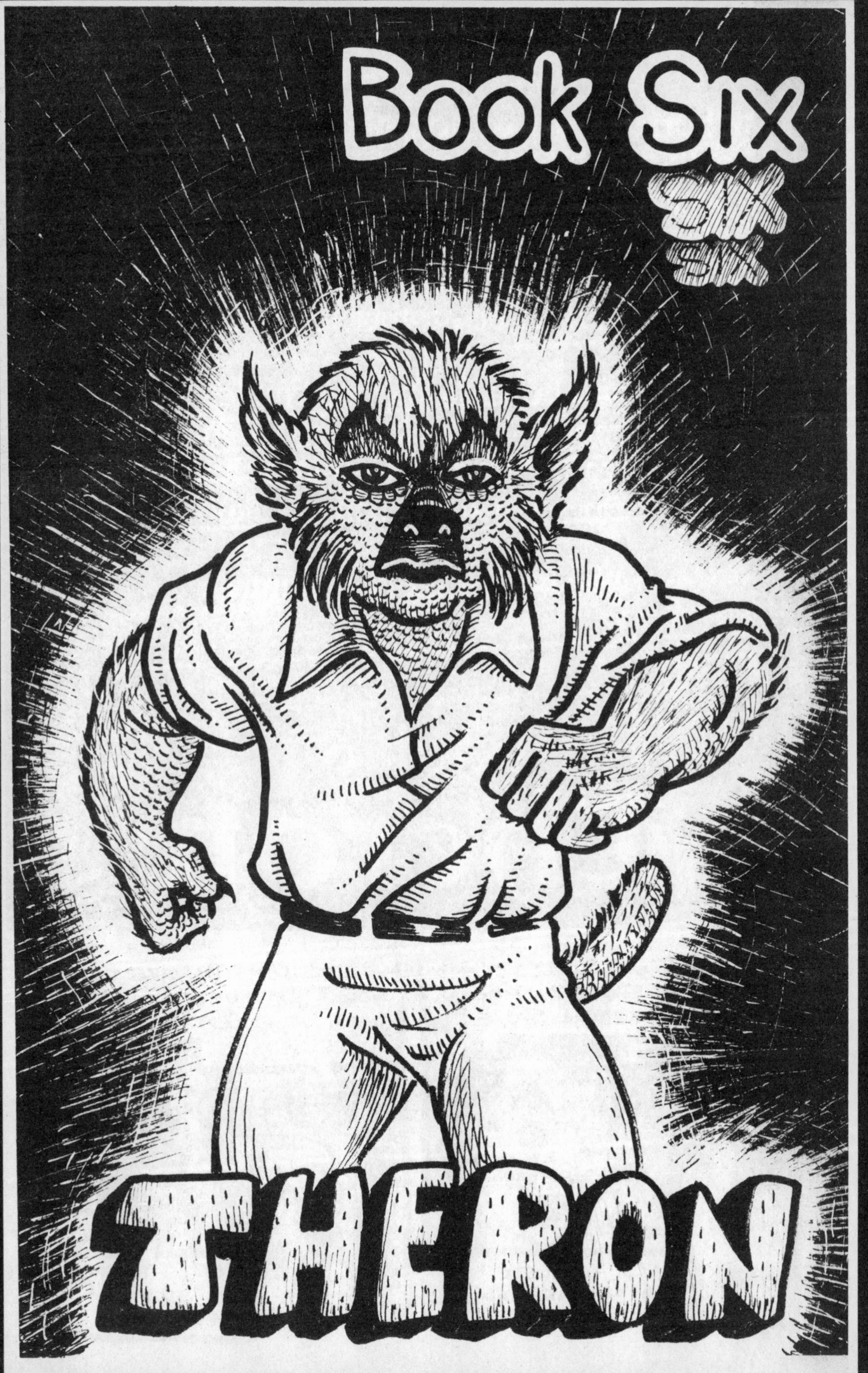
Book Six
SIX
SIX
THERON

Mariangela tells Tazio her tale:
a horror story of how she had been a child
with miraculous powers, then a nun in the
service of God, only to be misused by the
forces of good and evil, cursed with the
Lust and destined to suffer an unholy rape
ritual and thus be mother to the Antichrist.

But the child born did not resemble our Tazio,
it was a baby monster who commanded with
his first breath: "Incarnate at last! I want meat!
Obey when Theron speaks!"

The horror story continues.

# book 6
# Theron

FUR? SCALES? AND
I SPOKE?...I MEAN,
THERON SPOKE?

YES. YOU WERE BORN
A REPTILE-MAMMAL:
OF THE DRAGON.

SO HOW COME I'M LIKE THIS
NOW? I'M HUMAN... WELL,
SORT OF, EXCEPT FOR...UH,
LITTLE DETAILS.

THAT IS PART OF
THE STORY OF
THERON—

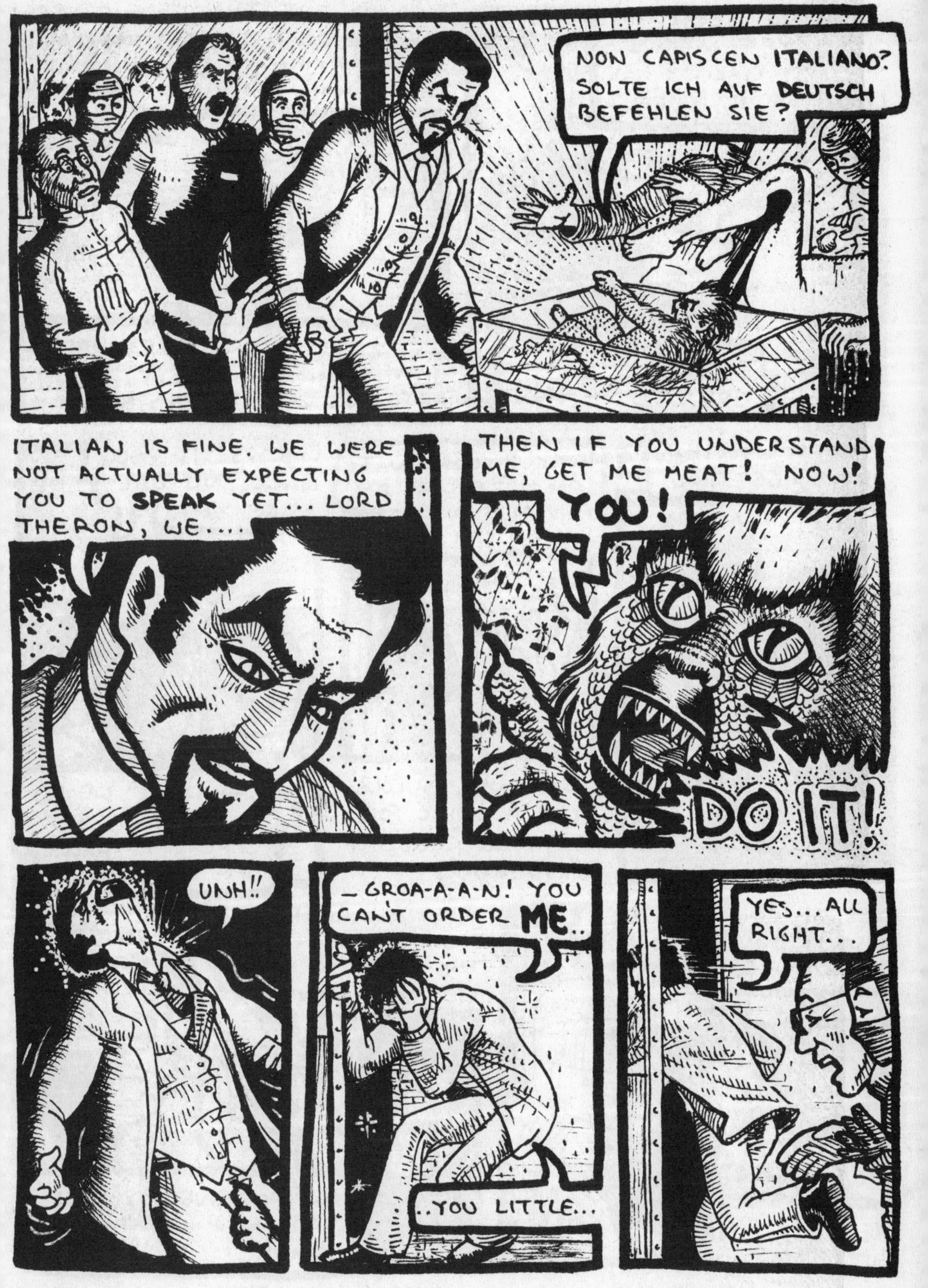
NON CAPISCEN ITALIANO? SOLTE ICH AUF DEUTSCH BEFEHLEN SIE?
ITALIAN IS FINE. WE WERE NOT ACTUALLY EXPECTING YOU TO SPEAK YET... LORD THERON, WE....
THEN IF YOU UNDERSTAND ME, GET ME MEAT! NOW!
YOU!
DO IT!
UNH!!
_GROA-A-A-N! YOU CAN'T ORDER ME..
..YOU LITTLE...
YES...ALL RIGHT...

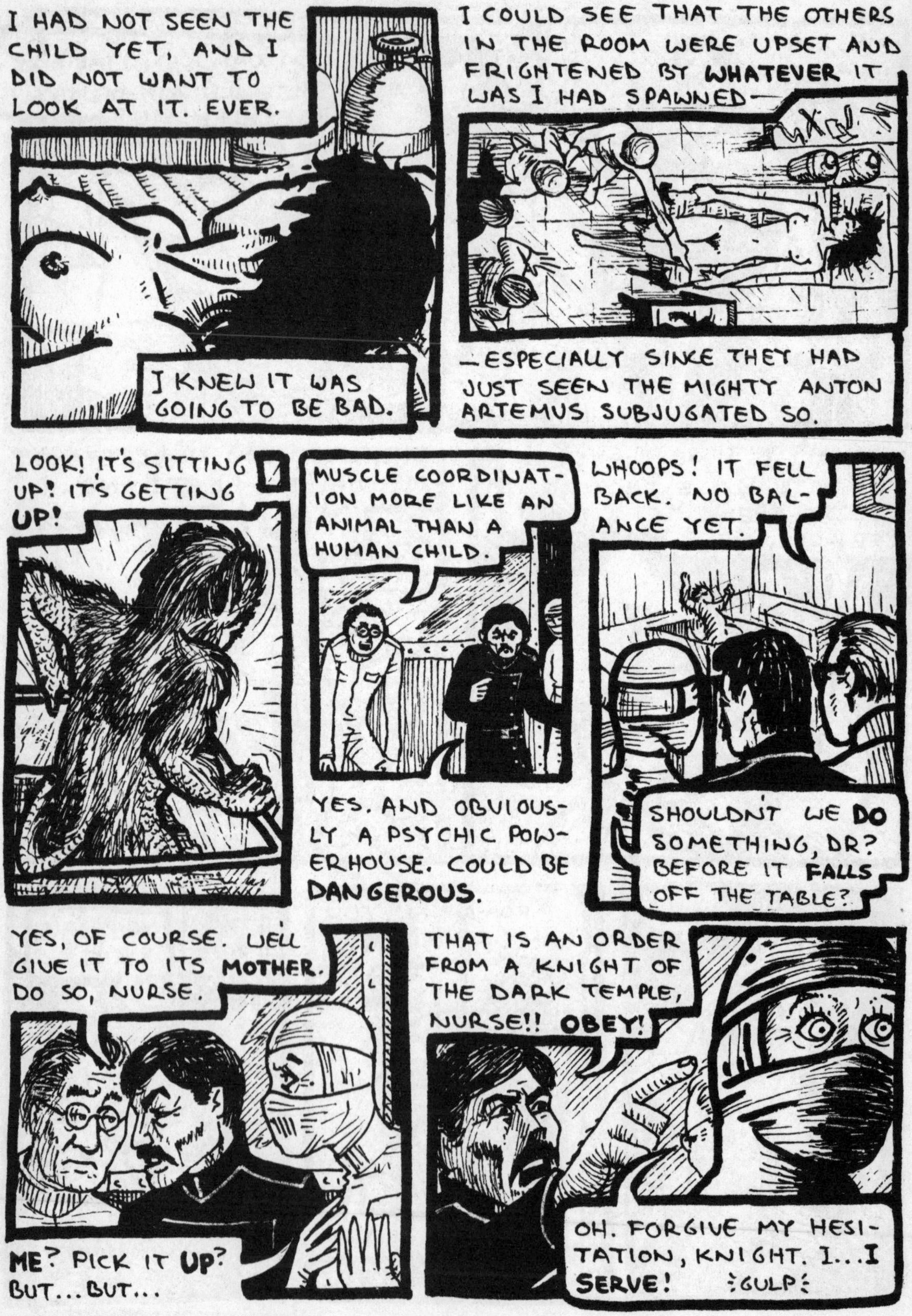

I HAD NOT SEEN THE CHILD YET, AND I DID NOT WANT TO LOOK AT IT. EVER.
I KNEW IT WAS GOING TO BE BAD.
I COULD SEE THAT THE OTHERS IN THE ROOM WERE UPSET AND FRIGHTENED BY WHATEVER IT WAS I HAD SPAWNED—
—ESPECIALLY SINCE THEY HAD JUST SEEN THE MIGHTY ANTON ARTEMUS SUBJUGATED SO.
LOOK! IT'S SITTING UP! IT'S GETTING UP!
MUSCLE COORDINATION MORE LIKE AN ANIMAL THAN A HUMAN CHILD.
YES. AND OBVIOUSLY A PSYCHIC POWERHOUSE. COULD BE DANGEROUS.
WHOOPS! IT FELL BACK. NO BALANCE YET.
SHOULDN'T WE DO SOMETHING, DR? BEFORE IT FALLS OFF THE TABLE?
YES, OF COURSE. WE'LL GIVE IT TO ITS MOTHER. DO SO, NURSE.
ME? PICK IT UP? BUT... BUT...
THAT IS AN ORDER FROM A KNIGHT OF THE DARK TEMPLE, NURSE!! OBEY!
OH. FORGIVE MY HESITATION, KNIGHT. I...I SERVE! :GULP:

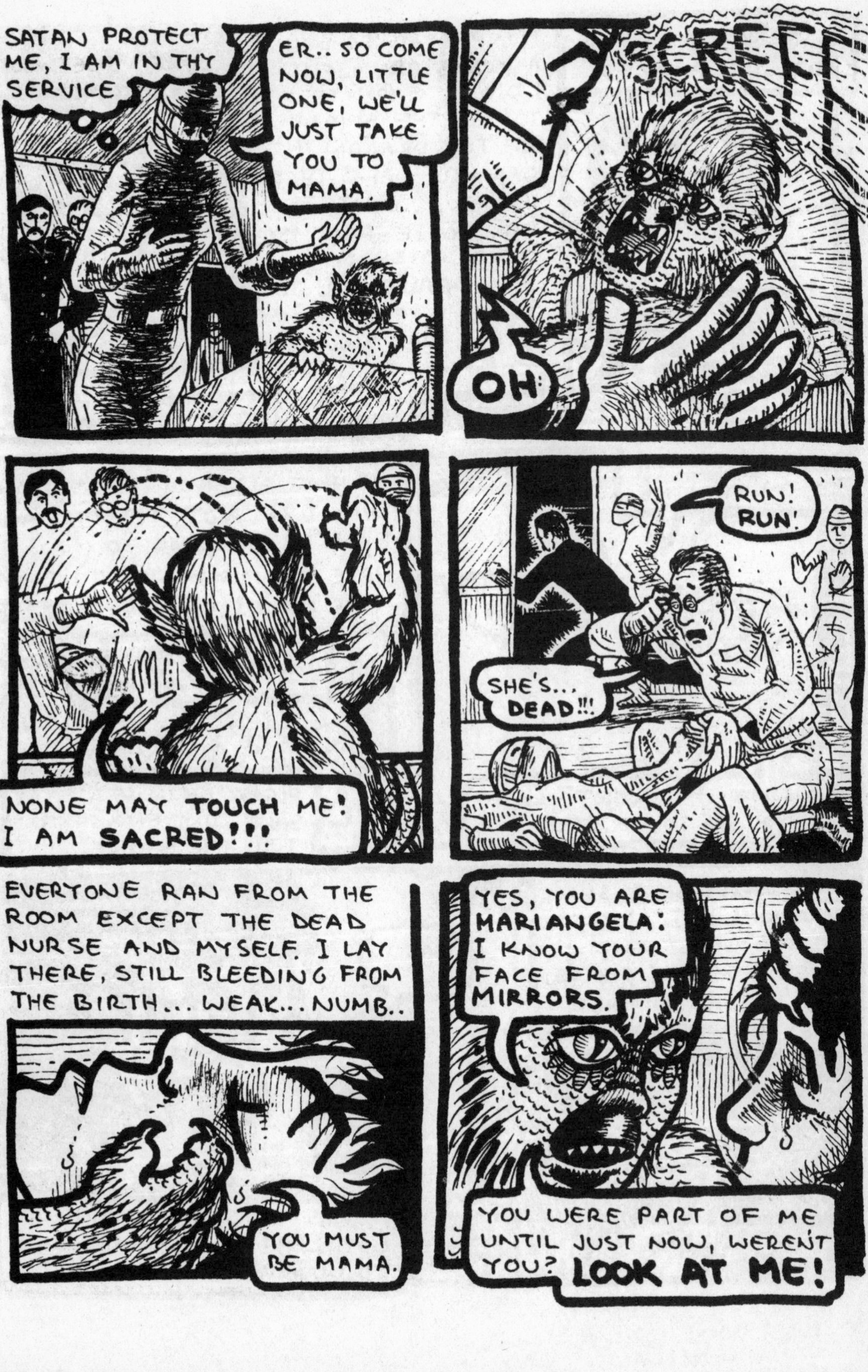
SATAN PROTECT ME, I AM IN THY SERVICE
ER.. SO COME NOW, LITTLE ONE, WE'LL JUST TAKE YOU TO MAMA.
SCREEE
OH
NONE MAY TOUCH ME! I AM SACRED!!!
RUN! RUN!
SHE'S... DEAD!!!
EVERYONE RAN FROM THE ROOM EXCEPT THE DEAD NURSE AND MYSELF. I LAY THERE, STILL BLEEDING FROM THE BIRTH... WEAK... NUMB..
YOU MUST BE MAMA.
YES, YOU ARE MARIANGELA: I KNOW YOUR FACE FROM MIRRORS.
YOU WERE PART OF ME UNTIL JUST NOW, WEREN'T YOU? LOOK AT ME!

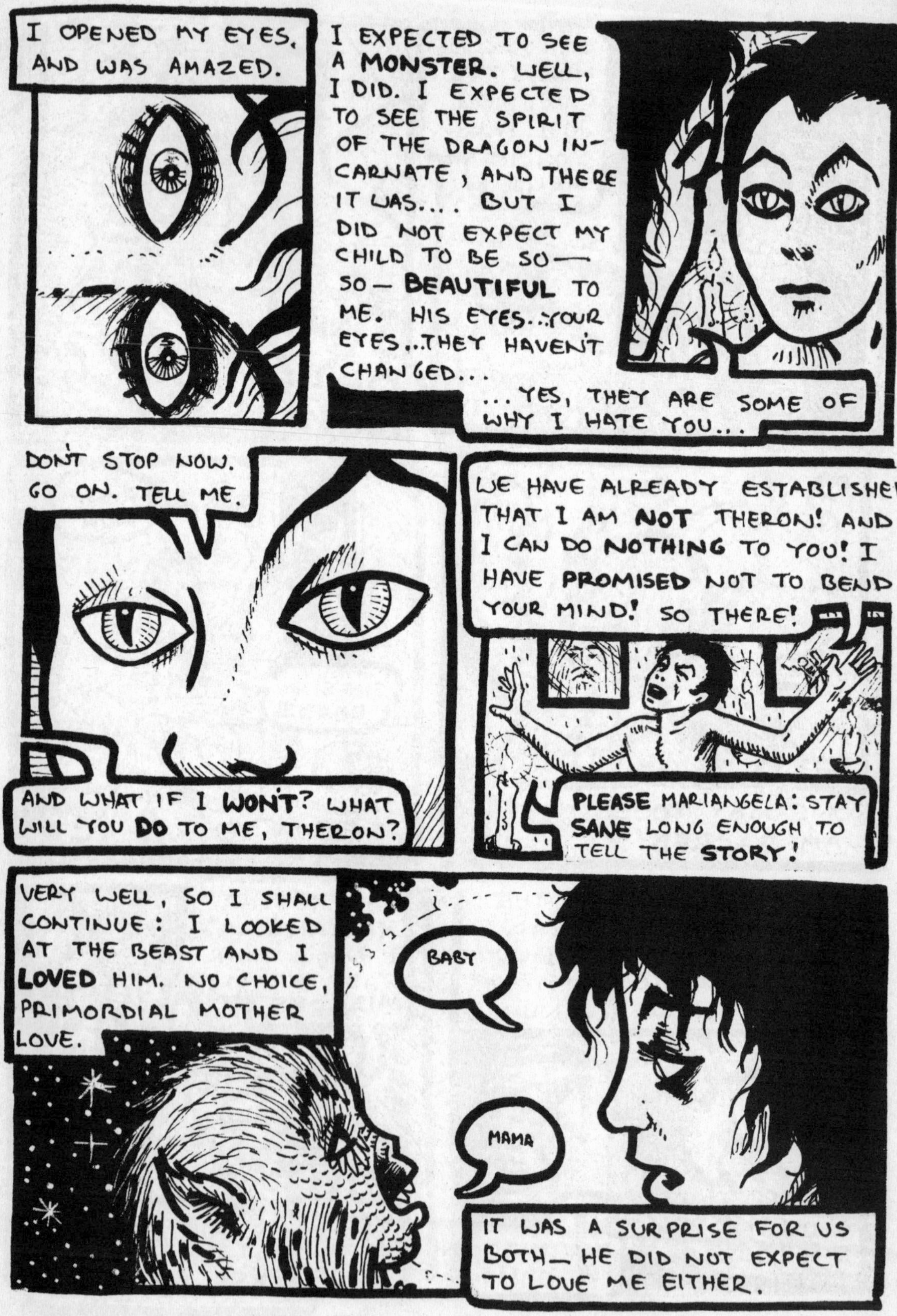
I OPENED MY EYES, AND WAS AMAZED.
I EXPECTED TO SEE A **MONSTER**. WELL, I DID. I EXPECTED TO SEE THE SPIRIT OF THE DRAGON INCARNATE, AND THERE IT WAS.... BUT I DID NOT EXPECT MY CHILD TO BE SO— SO— **BEAUTIFUL** TO ME. HIS EYES...YOUR EYES...THEY HAVEN'T CHANGED...
...YES, THEY ARE SOME OF WHY I HATE YOU...
DON'T STOP NOW. GO ON. TELL ME.
AND WHAT IF I **WON'T**? WHAT WILL YOU **DO** TO ME, THERON?
WE HAVE ALREADY ESTABLISHED THAT I AM **NOT** THERON! AND I CAN DO **NOTHING** TO YOU! I HAVE **PROMISED** NOT TO BEND YOUR MIND! SO THERE!
**PLEASE** MARIANGELA: STAY **SANE** LONG ENOUGH TO TELL THE **STORY**!
VERY WELL, SO I SHALL CONTINUE: I LOOKED AT THE BEAST AND I **LOVED** HIM. NO CHOICE, PRIMORDIAL MOTHER LOVE.
BABY
MAMA
IT WAS A SURPRISE FOR US BOTH— HE DID NOT EXPECT TO LOVE ME EITHER.

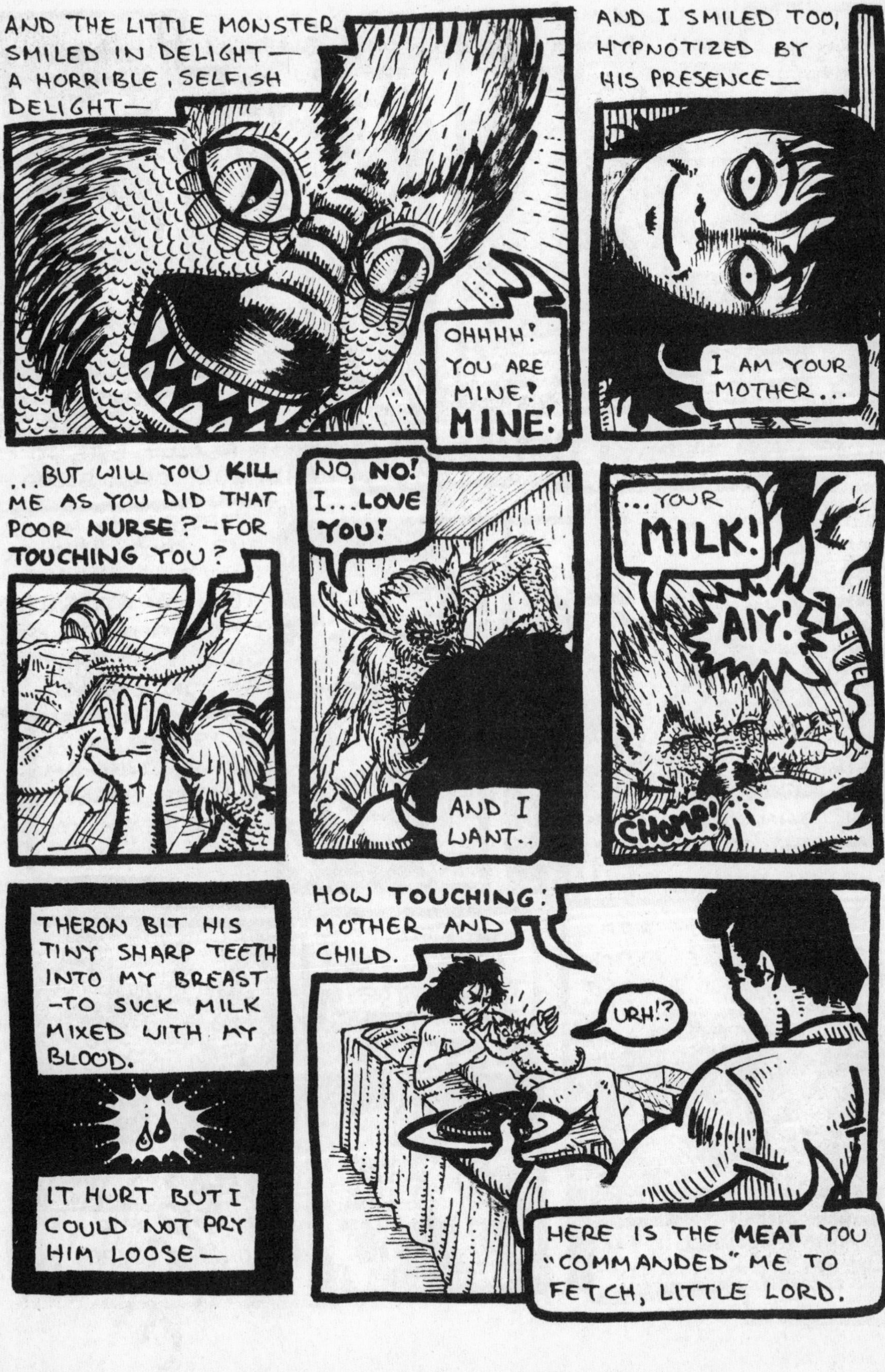

AND THE LITTLE MONSTER SMILED IN DELIGHT— A HORRIBLE, SELFISH DELIGHT—
OHHHH! YOU ARE MINE! MINE!
AND I SMILED TOO, HYPNOTIZED BY HIS PRESENCE—
I AM YOUR MOTHER...
...BUT WILL YOU KILL ME AS YOU DID THAT POOR NURSE?—FOR TOUCHING YOU?
NO, NO! I...LOVE YOU!
AND I WANT..
...YOUR MILK!
AIY!
CHOMP!
THERON BIT HIS TINY SHARP TEETH INTO MY BREAST —TO SUCK MILK MIXED WITH MY BLOOD.
IT HURT BUT I COULD NOT PRY HIM LOOSE—
HOW TOUCHING: MOTHER AND CHILD.
URH!?
HERE IS THE MEAT YOU "COMMANDED" ME TO FETCH, LITTLE LORD.

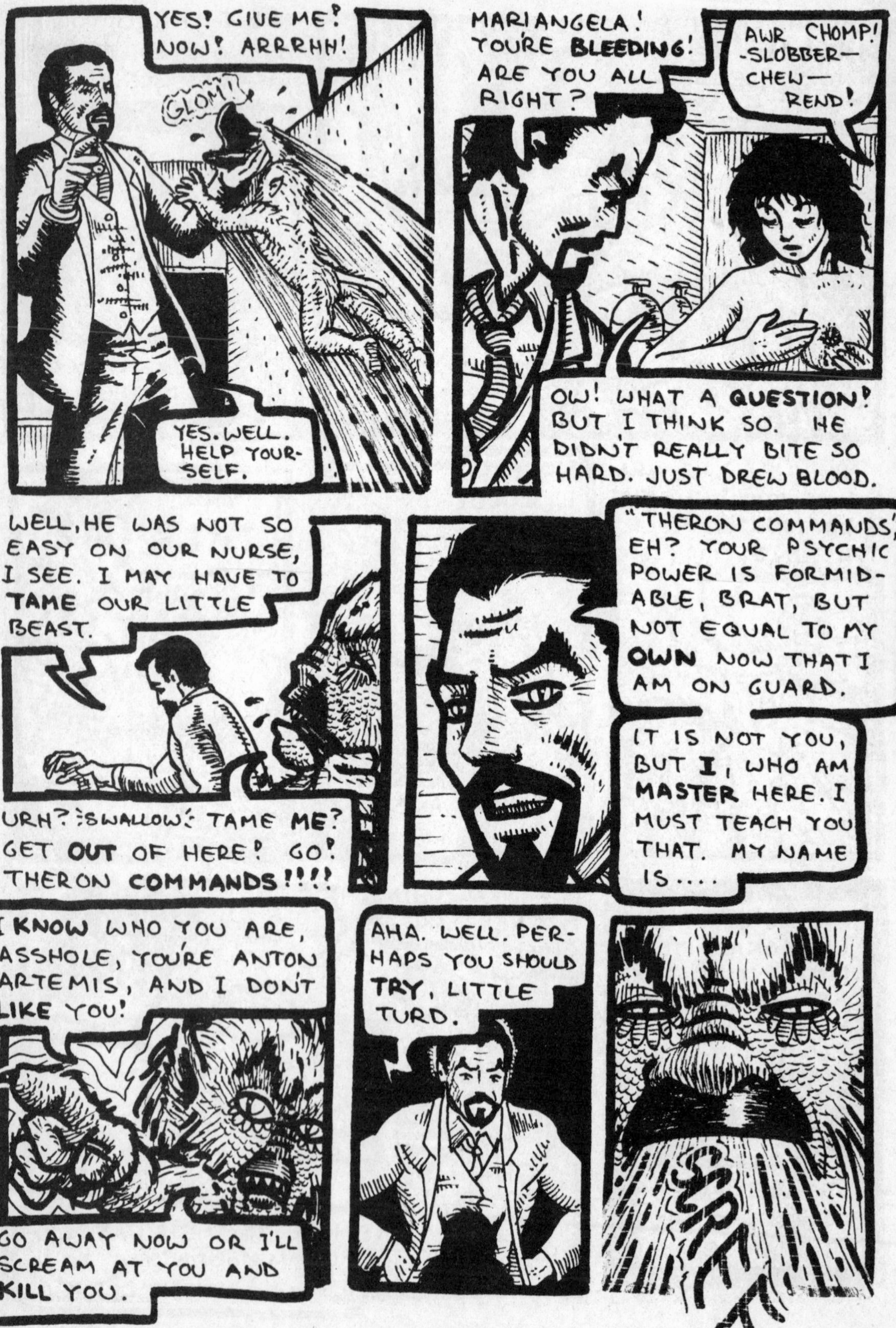
YES! GIVE ME! NOW! ARRRHH!
GLOM!
YES. WELL. HELP YOURSELF.
MARIANGELA! YOU'RE BLEEDING! ARE YOU ALL RIGHT?
AWR CHOMP! -SLOBBER- CHEW- REND!
OW! WHAT A QUESTION! BUT I THINK SO. HE DIDN'T REALLY BITE SO HARD. JUST DREW BLOOD.
WELL, HE WAS NOT SO EASY ON OUR NURSE, I SEE. I MAY HAVE TO TAME OUR LITTLE BEAST.
URH? :SWALLOW: TAME ME? GET OUT OF HERE! GO! THERON COMMANDS!!!!
"THERON COMMANDS", EH? YOUR PSYCHIC POWER IS FORMIDABLE, BRAT, BUT NOT EQUAL TO MY OWN NOW THAT I AM ON GUARD.
IT IS NOT YOU, BUT I, WHO AM MASTER HERE. I MUST TEACH YOU THAT. MY NAME IS....
I KNOW WHO YOU ARE, ASSHOLE, YOU'RE ANTON ARTEMIS, AND I DON'T LIKE YOU!
GO AWAY NOW OR I'LL SCREAM AT YOU AND KILL YOU.
AHA. WELL. PERHAPS YOU SHOULD TRY, LITTLE TURD.

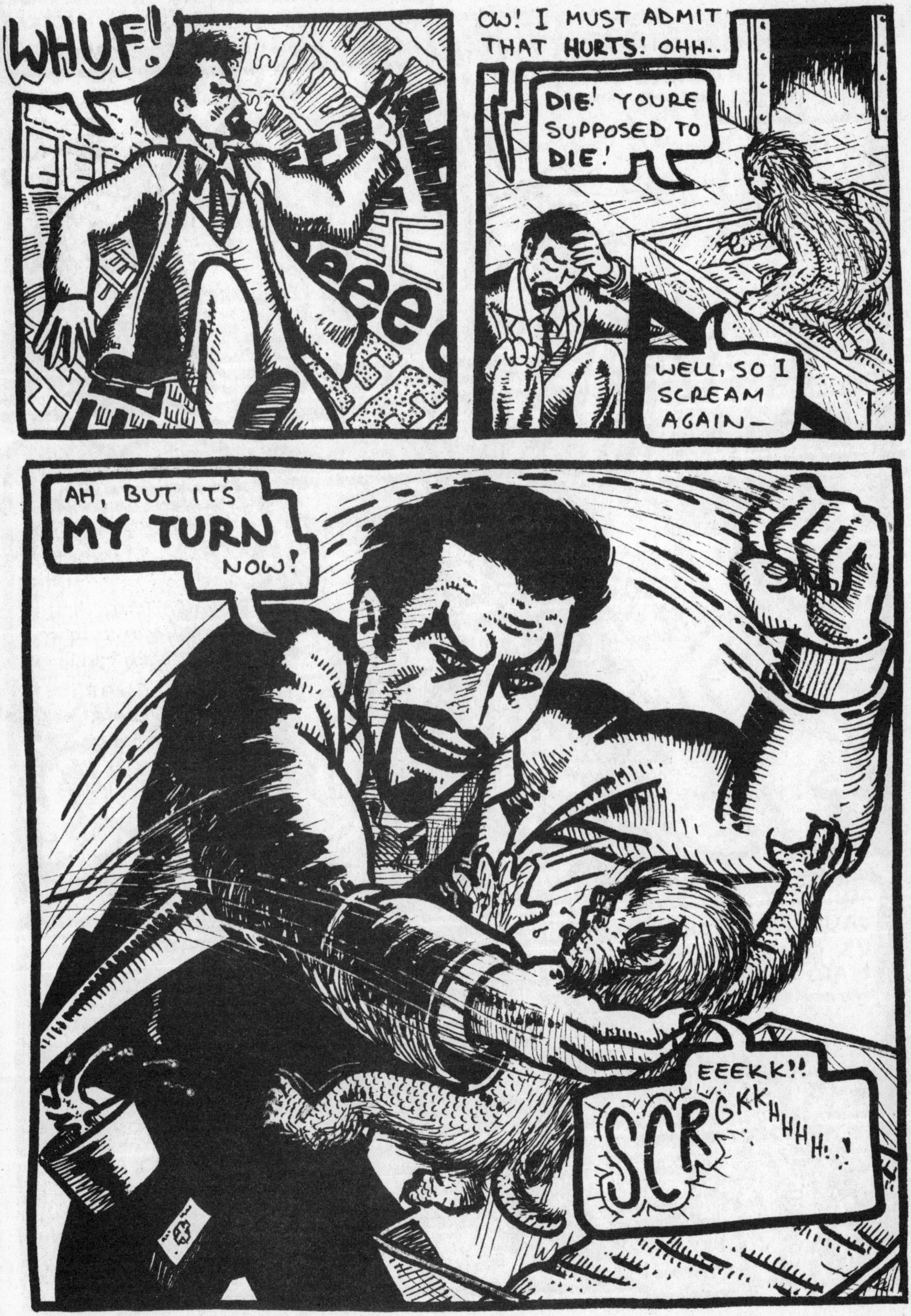
WHUF!
Eeeeeee
OW! I MUST ADMIT THAT HURTS! OHH..
DIE! YOU'RE SUPPOSED TO DIE!
WELL, SO I SCREAM AGAIN—
AH, BUT IT'S MY TURN NOW!
EEEKK!!
SCRGKKHHHH!..!

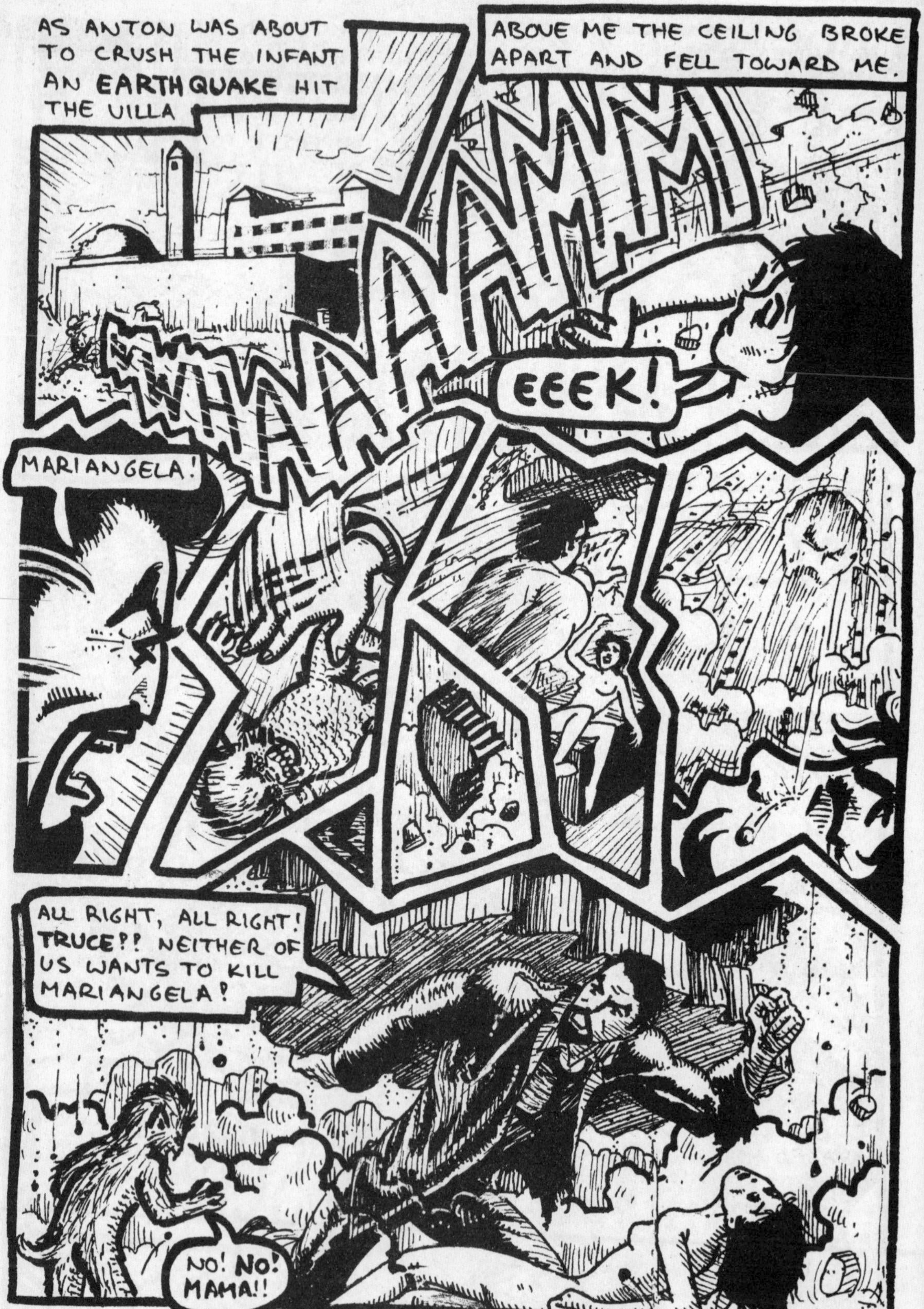
AS ANTON WAS ABOUT TO CRUSH THE INFANT AN **EARTHQUAKE** HIT THE VILLA
ABOVE ME THE CEILING BROKE APART AND FELL TOWARD ME.
WHAAAAMMM!
EEEK!
MARIANGELA!
ALL RIGHT, ALL RIGHT! **TRUCE?!** NEITHER OF US WANTS TO KILL MARIANGELA!
NO! **NO!** MAMA!!

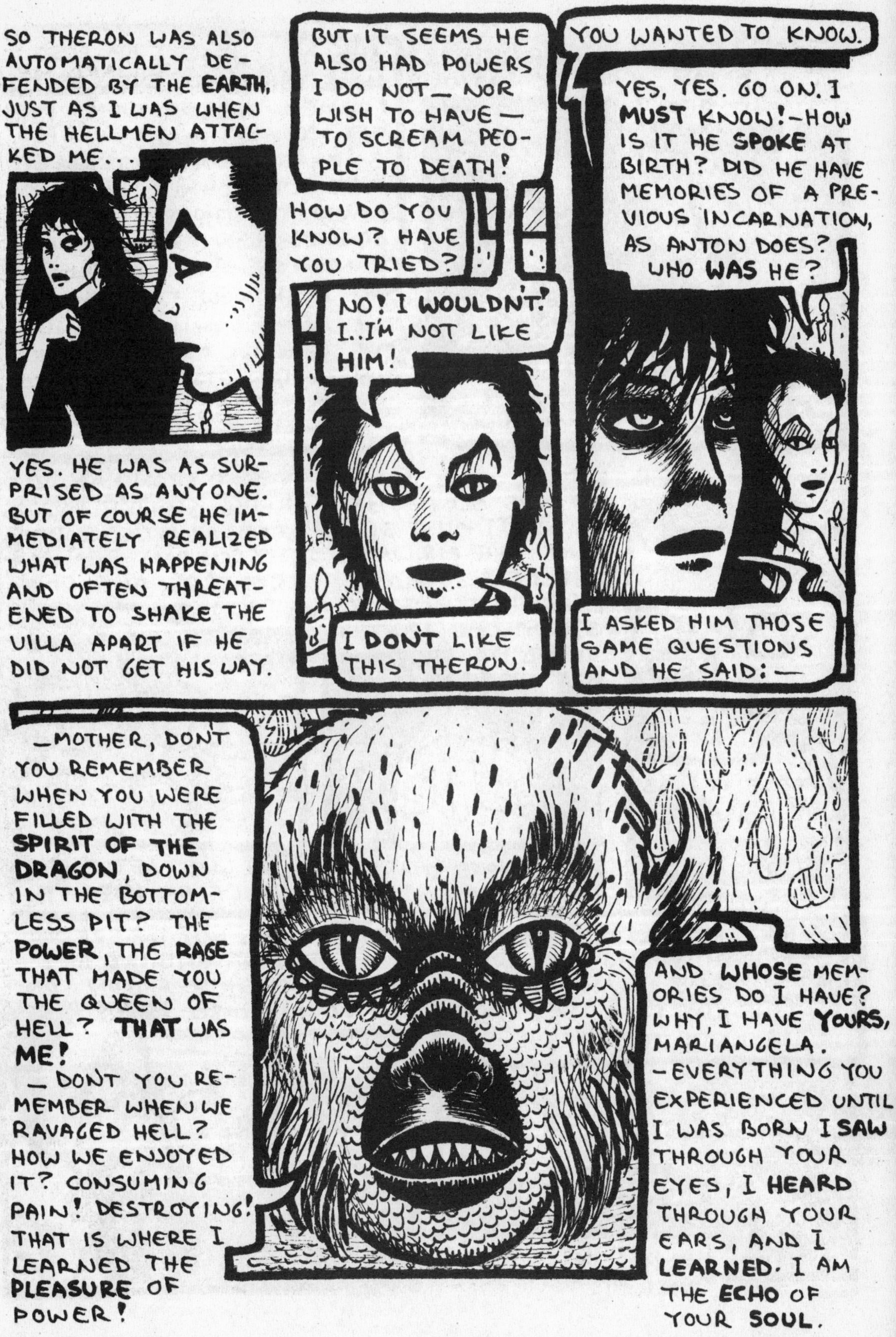

SO THERON WAS ALSO AUTOMATICALLY DEFENDED BY THE EARTH, JUST AS I WAS WHEN THE HELLMEN ATTACKED ME...
YES. HE WAS AS SURPRISED AS ANYONE. BUT OF COURSE HE IMMEDIATELY REALIZED WHAT WAS HAPPENING AND OFTEN THREATENED TO SHAKE THE VILLA APART IF HE DID NOT GET HIS WAY.
BUT IT SEEMS HE ALSO HAD POWERS I DO NOT— NOR WISH TO HAVE— TO SCREAM PEOPLE TO DEATH!
HOW DO YOU KNOW? HAVE YOU TRIED?
NO! I WOULDN'T! I..I'M NOT LIKE HIM!
I DON'T LIKE THIS THERON.
YOU WANTED TO KNOW.
YES, YES. GO ON. I MUST KNOW!—HOW IS IT HE SPOKE AT BIRTH? DID HE HAVE MEMORIES OF A PREVIOUS INCARNATION, AS ANTON DOES? WHO WAS HE?
I ASKED HIM THOSE SAME QUESTIONS AND HE SAID:—
—MOTHER, DONT YOU REMEMBER WHEN YOU WERE FILLED WITH THE SPIRIT OF THE DRAGON, DOWN IN THE BOTTOMLESS PIT? THE POWER, THE RAGE THAT MADE YOU THE QUEEN OF HELL? THAT WAS ME!
—DONT YOU REMEMBER WHEN WE RAVAGED HELL? HOW WE ENJOYED IT? CONSUMING PAIN! DESTROYING! THAT IS WHERE I LEARNED THE PLEASURE OF POWER!
AND WHOSE MEMORIES DO I HAVE? WHY, I HAVE YOURS, MARIANGELA. —EVERYTHING YOU EXPERIENCED UNTIL I WAS BORN I SAW THROUGH YOUR EYES, I HEARD THROUGH YOUR EARS, AND I LEARNED. I AM THE ECHO OF YOUR SOUL.

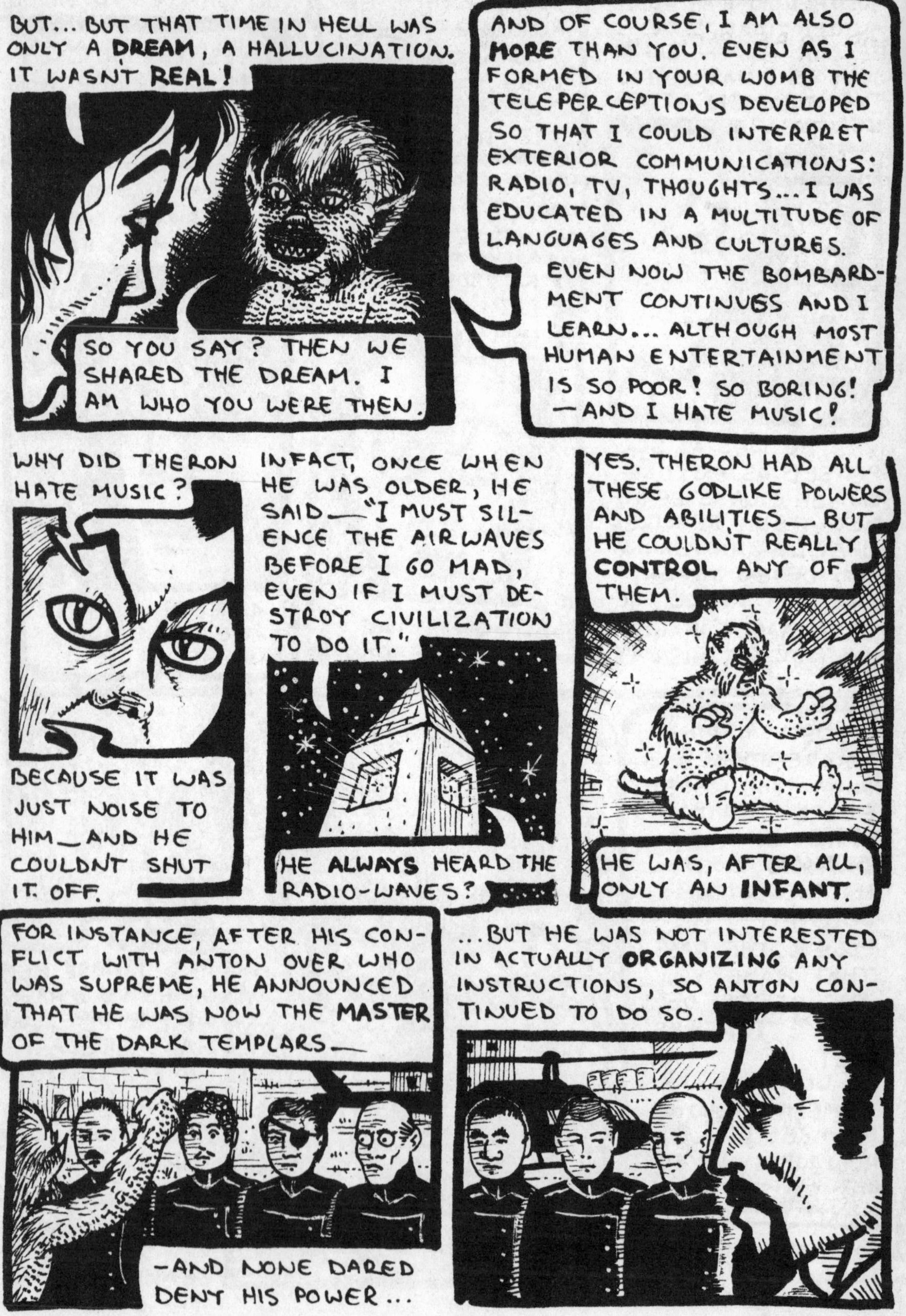
BUT... BUT THAT TIME IN HELL WAS ONLY A **DREAM**, A HALLUCINATION. IT WASN'T **REAL**!
SO YOU SAY? THEN WE SHARED THE DREAM. I AM WHO YOU WERE THEN.
AND OF COURSE, I AM ALSO **MORE** THAN YOU. EVEN AS I FORMED IN YOUR WOMB THE TELEPERCEPTIONS DEVELOPED SO THAT I COULD INTERPRET EXTERIOR COMMUNICATIONS: RADIO, TV, THOUGHTS... I WAS EDUCATED IN A MULTITUDE OF LANGUAGES AND CULTURES.
EVEN NOW THE BOMBARDMENT CONTINUES AND I LEARN... ALTHOUGH MOST HUMAN ENTERTAINMENT IS SO POOR! SO BORING! —AND I HATE MUSIC!
WHY DID THERON HATE MUSIC?
BECAUSE IT WAS JUST NOISE TO HIM_AND HE COULDNT SHUT IT OFF.
INFACT, ONCE WHEN HE WAS OLDER, HE SAID—"I MUST SILENCE THE AIRWAVES BEFORE I GO MAD, EVEN IF I MUST DESTROY CIVILIZATION TO DO IT."
HE **ALWAYS** HEARD THE RADIO-WAVES?
YES. THERON HAD ALL THESE GODLIKE POWERS AND ABILITIES_ BUT HE COULDN'T REALLY **CONTROL** ANY OF THEM.
HE WAS, AFTER ALL, ONLY AN **INFANT**.
FOR INSTANCE, AFTER HIS CONFLICT WITH ANTON OVER WHO WAS SUPREME, HE ANNOUNCED THAT HE WAS NOW THE **MASTER** OF THE DARK TEMPLARS—
—AND NONE DARED DENY HIS POWER...
...BUT HE WAS NOT INTERESTED IN ACTUALLY **ORGANIZING** ANY INSTRUCTIONS, SO ANTON CONTINUED TO DO SO.

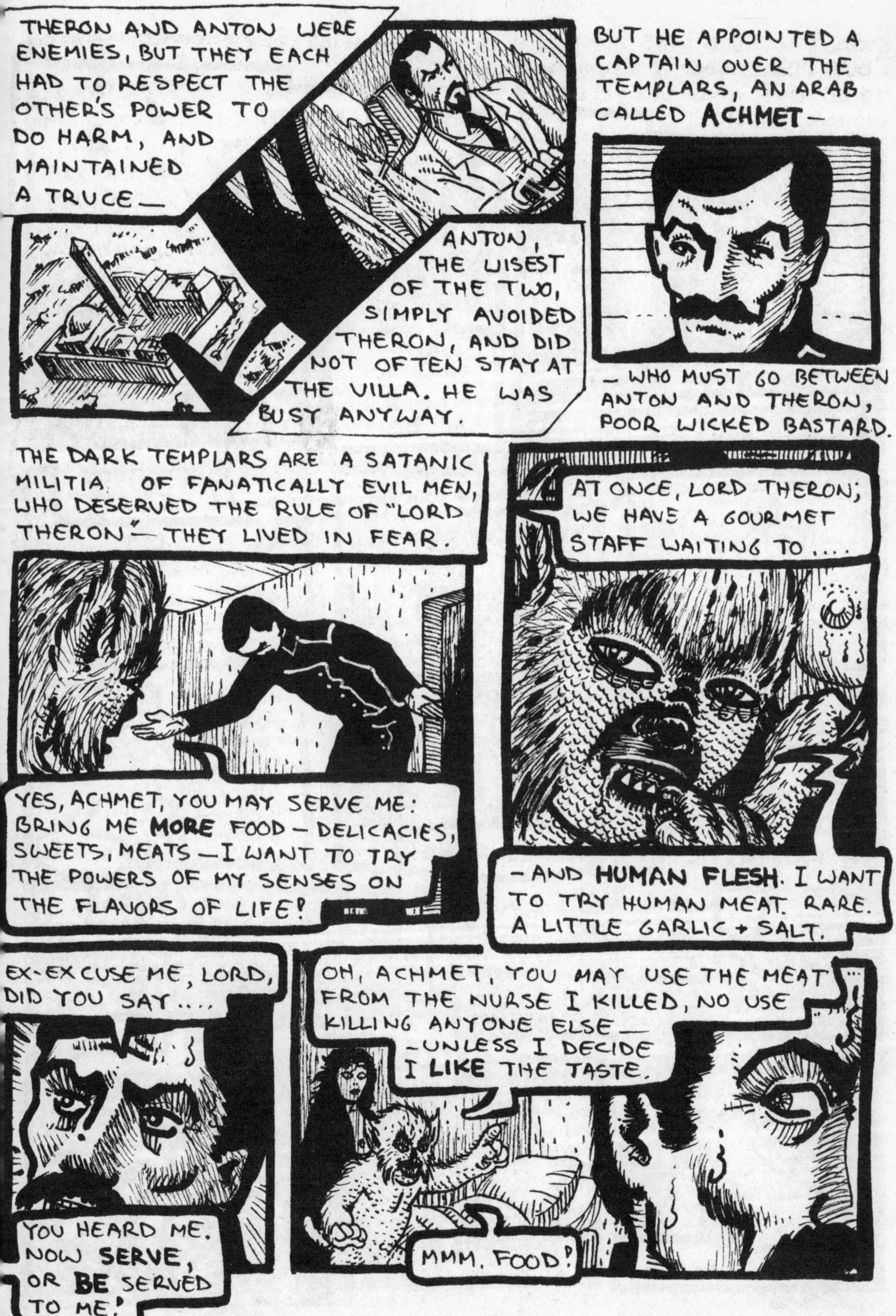
THERON AND ANTON WERE ENEMIES, BUT THEY EACH HAD TO RESPECT THE OTHER'S POWER TO DO HARM, AND MAINTAINED A TRUCE—
ANTON, THE WISEST OF THE TWO, SIMPLY AVOIDED THERON, AND DID NOT OFTEN STAY AT THE VILLA. HE WAS BUSY ANYWAY.
BUT HE APPOINTED A CAPTAIN OVER THE TEMPLARS, AN ARAB CALLED ACHMET—
—WHO MUST GO BETWEEN ANTON AND THERON, POOR WICKED BASTARD.
THE DARK TEMPLARS ARE A SATANIC MILITIA OF FANATICALLY EVIL MEN, WHO DESERVED THE RULE OF "LORD THERON"—THEY LIVED IN FEAR.
YES, ACHMET, YOU MAY SERVE ME: BRING ME MORE FOOD—DELICACIES, SWEETS, MEATS—I WANT TO TRY THE POWERS OF MY SENSES ON THE FLAVORS OF LIFE!
AT ONCE, LORD THERON; WE HAVE A GOURMET STAFF WAITING TO....
—AND HUMAN FLESH. I WANT TO TRY HUMAN MEAT. RARE. A LITTLE GARLIC + SALT.
EX-EXCUSE ME, LORD, DID YOU SAY....
YOU HEARD ME. NOW SERVE, OR BE SERVED TO ME!
OH, ACHMET, YOU MAY USE THE MEAT FROM THE NURSE I KILLED, NO USE KILLING ANYONE ELSE—
—UNLESS I DECIDE I LIKE THE TASTE.
MMM. FOOD!

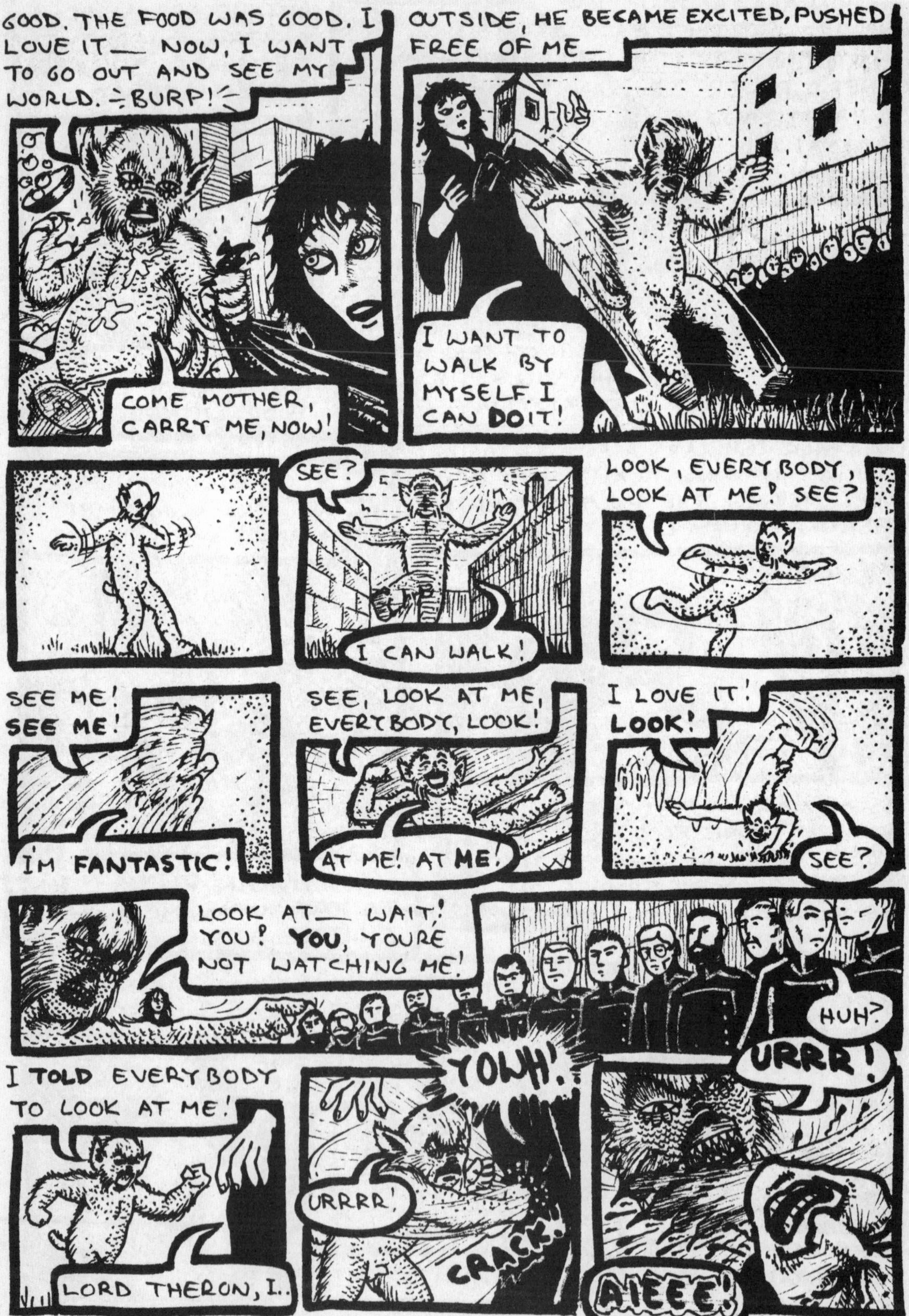
GOOD. THE FOOD WAS GOOD. I LOVE IT— NOW, I WANT TO GO OUT AND SEE MY WORLD. -BURP!
COME MOTHER, CARRY ME, NOW!
OUTSIDE, HE BECAME EXCITED, PUSHED FREE OF ME—
I WANT TO WALK BY MYSELF. I CAN DO IT!
SEE?
I CAN WALK!
LOOK, EVERYBODY, LOOK AT ME! SEE?
SEE ME! SEE ME!
I'M FANTASTIC!
SEE, LOOK AT ME, EVERYBODY, LOOK!
AT ME! AT ME!
I LOVE IT! LOOK!
SEE?
LOOK AT— WAIT! YOU! YOU, YOU'RE NOT WATCHING ME!
HUH?
I TOLD EVERYBODY TO LOOK AT ME!
LORD THERON, I..
YOWH!
URRRR!
CRACK!
URRR!
AIEEE!

NOW, EVERYBODY **WATCH ME!** SEE WHAT I CAN DO?

:GROAN: M..MERCY..

Y..YES, LORD!

OH! LOOK!

**SEE?**

HOW — GULP — CUTE!

AAIEE..

..URGKKGHHHHH..

THAT WAS FUN. I LOVE IT. I WANT TO DO SOME MORE.

WHO NEXT? HMMM??

NO. NOT NO MORE TODAY, THERON.

WHAT? WHO DARES?

YOU MUST LEARN SELF-CONTROL.

OH, IT'S YOU IS IT? GOOD. YOU ARE AN INTER-ESTING THING,

ULFA, UP FROM HER DUNGEON.

BUT STILL, YOU CAN'T SAY "NO" TO **ME!**

ULFA CAN. IT MY FUCKING DESTINY. TEACH YOU.

BUT IN YOUR PRESENT PHASE YOU ARE **STUPID,** A BEAST-WOMAN: WHAT CAN YOU TEACH ME?

THAT YOU, TOO, STUPID BEAST. RIGHT NOW.

I? STUPID? SHOWS WHAT **YOU** KNOW. I'M THE MOST INTELLI-GENT BEING EVER MADE MANIFEST ON THE PLANET...

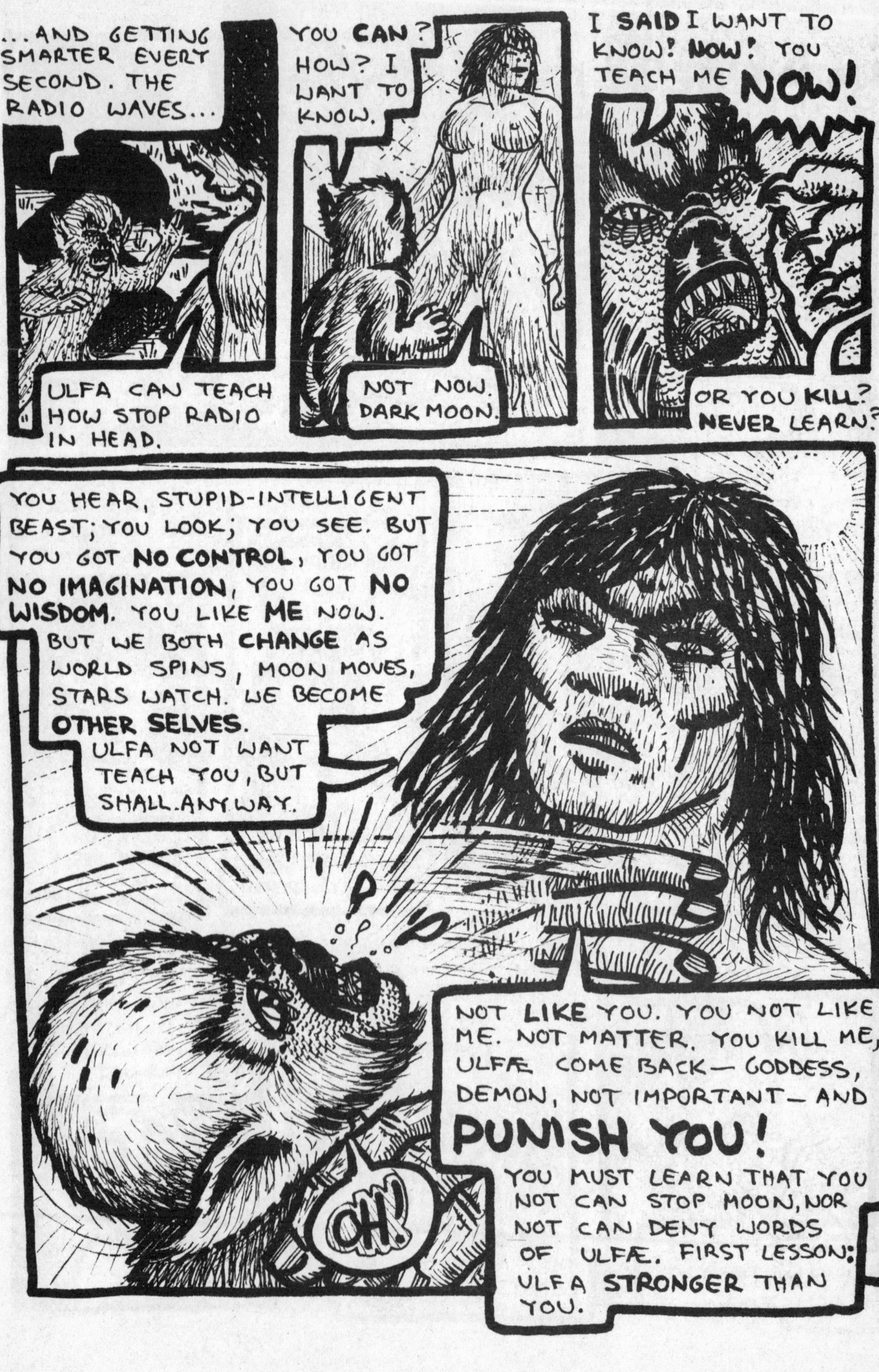

...AND GETTING SMARTER EVERY SECOND. THE RADIO WAVES...
ULFA CAN TEACH HOW STOP RADIO IN HEAD.
YOU **CAN**? HOW? I WANT TO KNOW.
NOT NOW. DARK MOON.
I **SAID** I WANT TO KNOW! **NOW**! YOU TEACH ME **NOW**!
OR YOU **KILL**? **NEVER** LEARN?
YOU HEAR, STUPID-INTELLIGENT BEAST; YOU LOOK; YOU SEE. BUT YOU GOT **NO CONTROL**, YOU GOT **NO IMAGINATION**, YOU GOT **NO WISDOM**. YOU LIKE **ME** NOW.
BUT WE BOTH **CHANGE** AS WORLD SPINS, MOON MOVES, STARS WATCH. WE BECOME **OTHER SELVES**.
ULFA NOT WANT TEACH YOU, BUT SHALL. ANYWAY.
?
??
NOT **LIKE** YOU. YOU NOT LIKE ME. NOT MATTER. YOU KILL ME, ULFÆ COME BACK— GODDESS, DEMON, NOT IMPORTANT— AND **PUNISH YOU**!
YOU MUST LEARN THAT YOU NOT CAN STOP MOON, NOR NOT CAN DENY WORDS OF ULFÆ. FIRST LESSON: ULFA **STRONGER** THAN YOU.
OH!

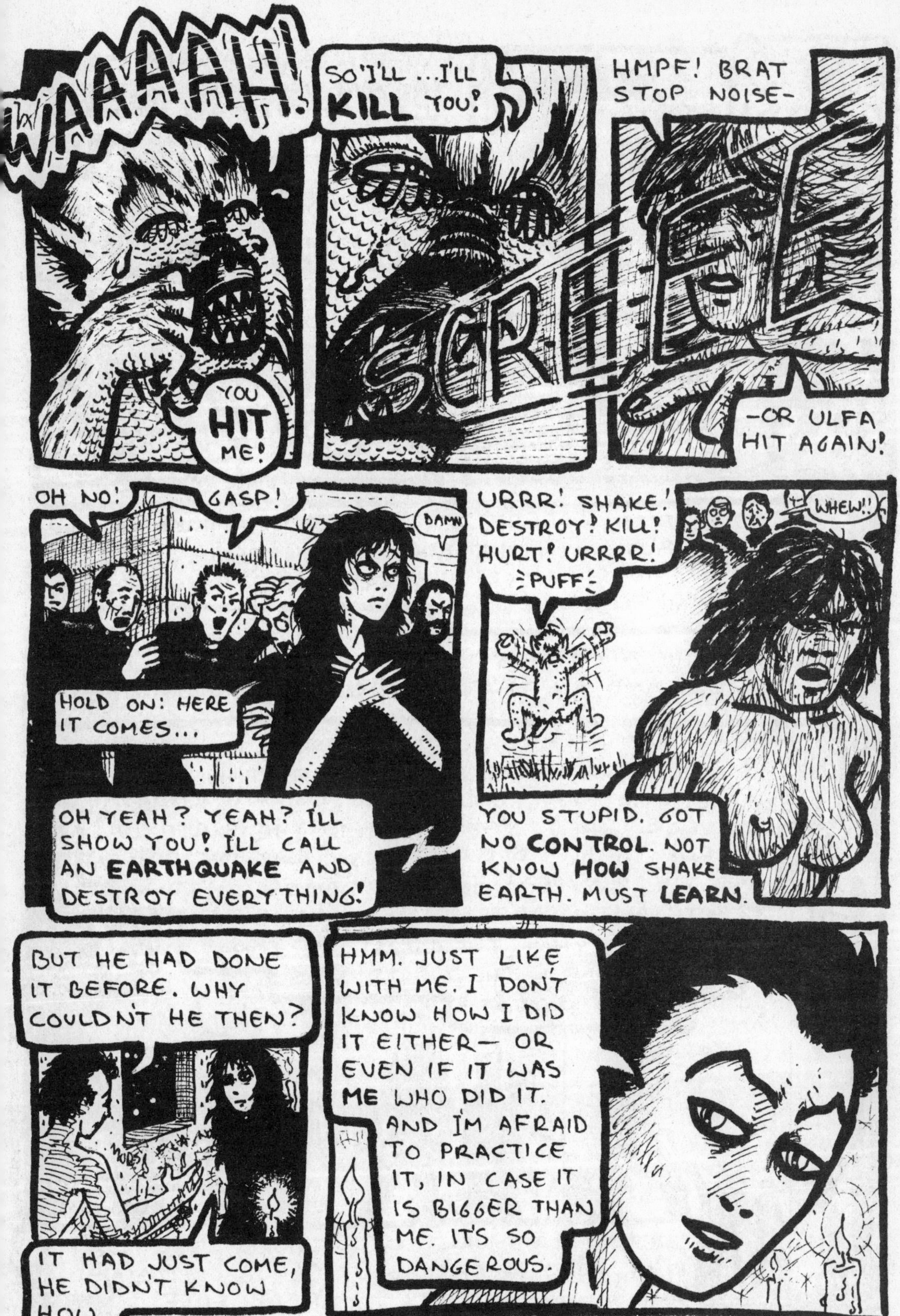
WAAAAH!
YOU HIT ME!
SO I'LL ...I'LL KILL YOU!
SCREE
HMPF! BRAT STOP NOISE-
-OR ULFA HIT AGAIN!
OH NO!
GASP!
DAMN
HOLD ON: HERE IT COMES...
OH YEAH? YEAH? I'LL SHOW YOU! I'LL CALL AN EARTHQUAKE AND DESTROY EVERYTHING!
URRR! SHAKE! DESTROY! KILL! HURT! URRRR!
PUFF
WHEW!!
YOU STUPID. GOT NO CONTROL. NOT KNOW HOW SHAKE EARTH. MUST LEARN.
BUT HE HAD DONE IT BEFORE. WHY COULDN'T HE THEN?
IT HAD JUST COME, HE DIDN'T KNOW HOW.
HMM. JUST LIKE WITH ME. I DON'T KNOW HOW I DID IT EITHER— OR EVEN IF IT WAS ME WHO DID IT.
AND I'M AFRAID TO PRACTICE IT, IN CASE IT IS BIGGER THAN ME. IT'S SO DANGEROUS.

OH, TAZIO, YOU'RE SO **GOOD!**

BUT FOR 3 AND A HALF YEARS YOU HAD NO COMPUNCTIONS ABOUT KILLING OR DESTROYING!! DEMON!

YEAH, OKAY, GO ON. TELL ME HOW BAD "I" WAS.

BAD? WELL, IN MANY WAYS THERON WAS A NORMAL CHILD:

**M:** HE WAS SELFISH, GREEDY, VIOLENT, CRUEL, LIKE ALL CHILDREN, BUT WITH THE FORCE AND POWER TO ACT OUT ANY WHIM, PANDER ANY PLEASURE. — POWERS HE DIDN'T EVEN KNOW HE HAD.

**T:** BUT WAS HE A CHILD AT ALL? HE HAD YOUR ADULT MEMORIES, AND ALL THAT "RADIO-WAVE" INPUT.

**M:** O, THERON WAS A CHILD, ALL RIGHT: NEW TO THE WORLD OF HIS OWN PERSONAL PLEASURES; SPONTANEOUS; EXCITEABLE; EMOTIONAL; UNINHIBITED; UNCONTROLLABLE. AND FOR THREE YEARS AFTER THE BIRTH OF THERON, LA VILLA DELLA STREGGA WAS THE PRISON AND THE PLAYPEN OF THAT DEMON CHILD— BOTH ANTON ARTEMIS AND THE ULFÆ INSISTED THAT THE BEAST BE CONTAINED UNTIL THE WORLD WAS READY FOR IT.

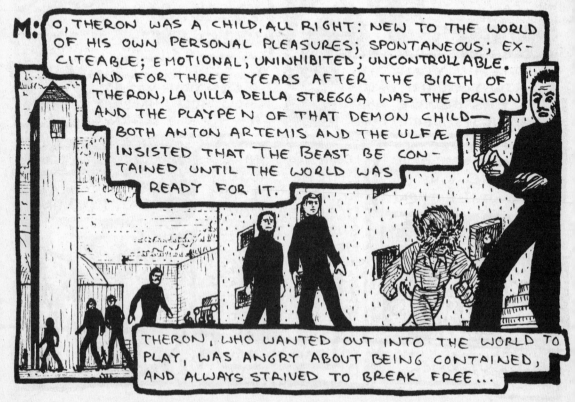

THERON, WHO WANTED OUT INTO THE WORLD TO PLAY, WAS ANGRY ABOUT BEING CONTAINED, AND ALWAYS STRIVED TO BREAK FREE...

WHY COULDN'T HE ESCAPE? I COULD. I DID.

AT THIS TIME HE WAS GUARDED BY A TROOP OF DARK TEMPLARS, UNDER PAIN OF DEATH. THEIR OWN.

AND ULFO, I SUPPOSE, CAST SOME "SPELL".

PERHAPS, THERON COULD NOT MANAGE TO GET FREE FOR 3 YEARS.

HE KNEW HE HAD SOME VAST POWERS, BUT NOT WHAT THEY WERE, NOR HOW TO CALL UPON THEM:

OKAY, FLY! COME ON, **FLY**! LIKE SUPERMAN! UP! UP!

HE RAGED AGAINST FAILURE:

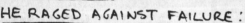

FLY, GODDAMNIT! WHY CAN'T I **FLY**?

IT'S NOT **FAIR**! WAAAAAHH!

AT THE SEALED PORT OF THE VILLA —

FALL! I SEND MY MIGHTY FORCE —

DOOR: **SMASH**! BREAK! **FOLD** BEFORE THE MIGHTY FORCE OF THERON! NOW!!

FUCKING **NOW**!

:SIGH: O WELL. IT'S HOPELESS! I'M FRUSTRATED! POOR ME!

AND FUCK YOU TOO, GARGOYLE.

BUT THE FORCES HE CALLED UPON WERE THERE, IT'S JUST THAT THEY MISSED THE PROPER TARGET:

LATER SOMETHING ELSE WOULD BREAK OR FOLD.

NO TELLING WHERE, WHEN OR WHAT—

OOPS!

POF:

SOMETIMES A DARK TEMPLAR OR TWO.

HEY, I'M ENCOURAGED BY THAT: I **DO** HAVE THE POWER!

I **LOVE** IT!

THE CHILD HAD COLOSSAL ENERGY, NEVER SLEPT— HE COULDN'T WITH ALL THE "RADIOS"— AND SO DEVOTED HIS TIME TO THE PURSUIT OF HIS SELFISH PLEASURES.

HE WAS A GLUTTON ON EVERY LEVEL; FOOD, DRINK, DRUGS, VIOLENCE, NOISE, PAIN, PLEASURE. AND THE DARK TEMPLARS SUPPLIED HIM WITH EVERYTHING BUT FREEDOM.

UNFORTUNATELY FOR THEM, HE WAS BORED ANYWAY. BORED AND MICHIEVIOUS, THAT LITTLE RASCAL—

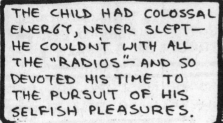

—FOR EXAMPLE, WHEN HE WENT THROUGH A MOVIE MONSTER PHASE: ALL THAT TELEVISION IN HIS HEAD...

YAARK!

SURPRISE! HEE HEE RRRH!

CHOMP

HE LOVED TO PRETEND HE WAS THE **WEREWOLF!**

A NORMAL CHILD'S GAME, EXCEPT THAT HE REALLY **KILLED.**

HOW-HOWOOOOU OO

IS IT HIM?

THIS MADE THE STAFF **UNEASY.**

MORALLY SPEAKING, THERON DID THE WORLD A FAVOR, THE DARK TEMPLARS WERE EACH AND EVERY ONE, GUILTY OF HUMAN SACRIFICE IN THEIR PURSUIT OF PERSONAL POWER— MANY WERE ALSO COWARDS AND WISHED TO QUIT OR ESCAPE, BUT DEATH WAS THE ONLY EXIT FROM THE TEMPLARS. ANTON REPLACED THEM AS THEY WERE KILLED OFF.

YES, I KILLED FOR SATAN. IT WAS **FUN.** THAT'S THE WAY TO POWER OVER OTHERS. —HUH? WHO'S **BEHIND** M....

LORD THERON, YOU **CAN'T** BE KILLING OFF ALL YOUR... SUBJECTS.

FUCK THAT SHIT, ACHMET, THEY'RE MY WARDENS AND WE ALL KNOW IT.

ONLY THE **ULFÆ** DARED COMMAND THE BEAST.

SELF CONTROL.

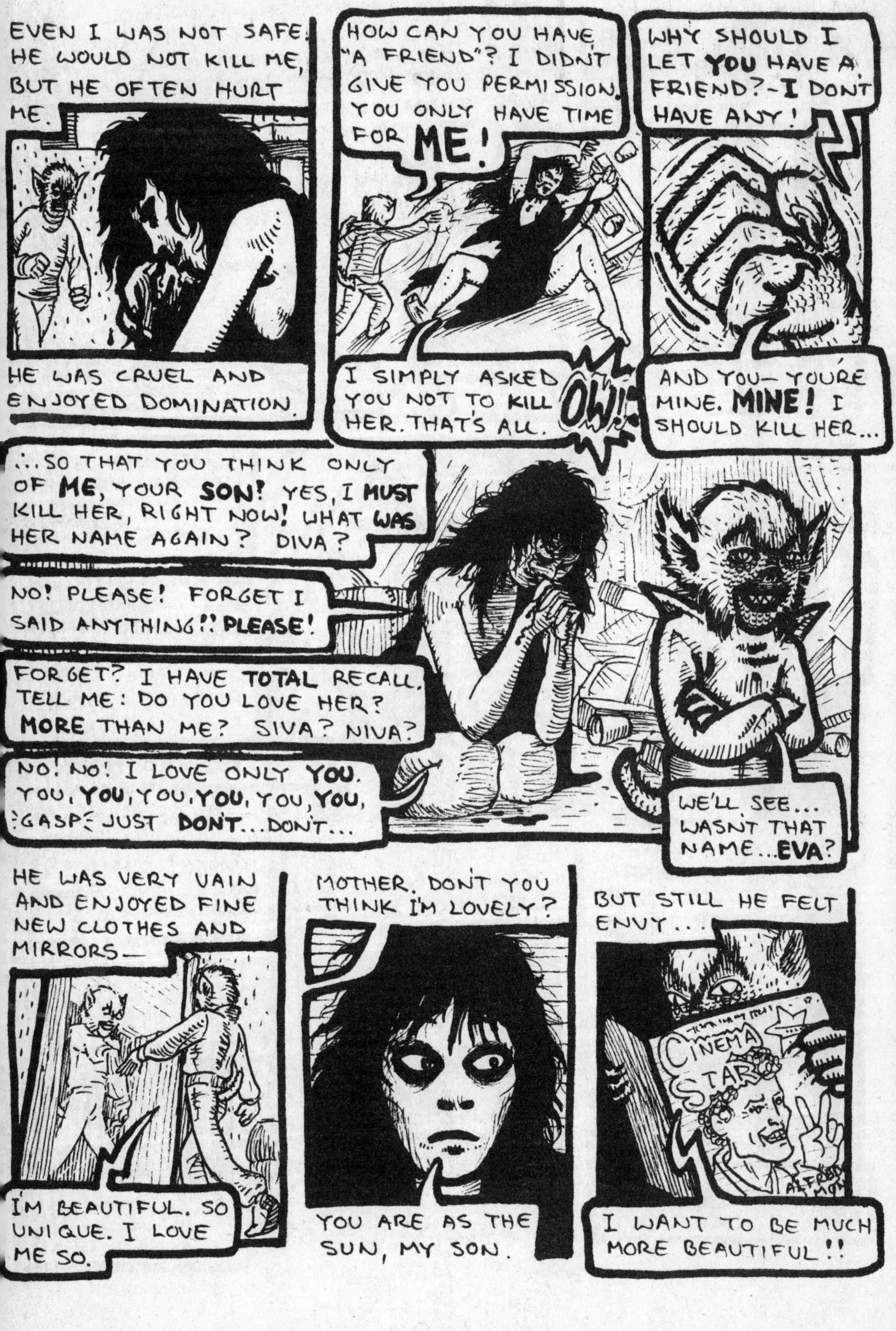
EVEN I WAS NOT SAFE. HE WOULD NOT KILL ME, BUT HE OFTEN HURT ME.
HE WAS CRUEL AND ENJOYED DOMINATION.
HOW CAN YOU HAVE "A FRIEND"? I DIDN'T GIVE YOU PERMISSION. YOU ONLY HAVE TIME FOR ME!
I SIMPLY ASKED YOU NOT TO KILL HER. THAT'S ALL.
OW!
WHY SHOULD I LET YOU HAVE A FRIEND? - I DON'T HAVE ANY!
AND YOU— YOU'RE MINE. MINE! I SHOULD KILL HER...
...SO THAT YOU THINK ONLY OF ME, YOUR SON! YES, I MUST KILL HER, RIGHT NOW! WHAT WAS HER NAME AGAIN? DIVA?
NO! PLEASE! FORGET I SAID ANYTHING!! PLEASE!
FORGET? I HAVE TOTAL RECALL. TELL ME: DO YOU LOVE HER? MORE THAN ME? SIVA? NIVA?
NO! NO! I LOVE ONLY YOU. YOU, YOU, YOU, YOU, YOU, YOU, :GASP: JUST DON'T...DON'T...
WE'LL SEE... WASN'T THAT NAME...EVA?
HE WAS VERY VAIN AND ENJOYED FINE NEW CLOTHES AND MIRRORS—
I'M BEAUTIFUL. SO UNIQUE. I LOVE ME SO.
MOTHER, DON'T YOU THINK I'M LOVELY?
YOU ARE AS THE SUN, MY SON.
BUT STILL HE FELT ENVY...
CINEMA STAR
I WANT TO BE MUCH MORE BEAUTIFUL!!

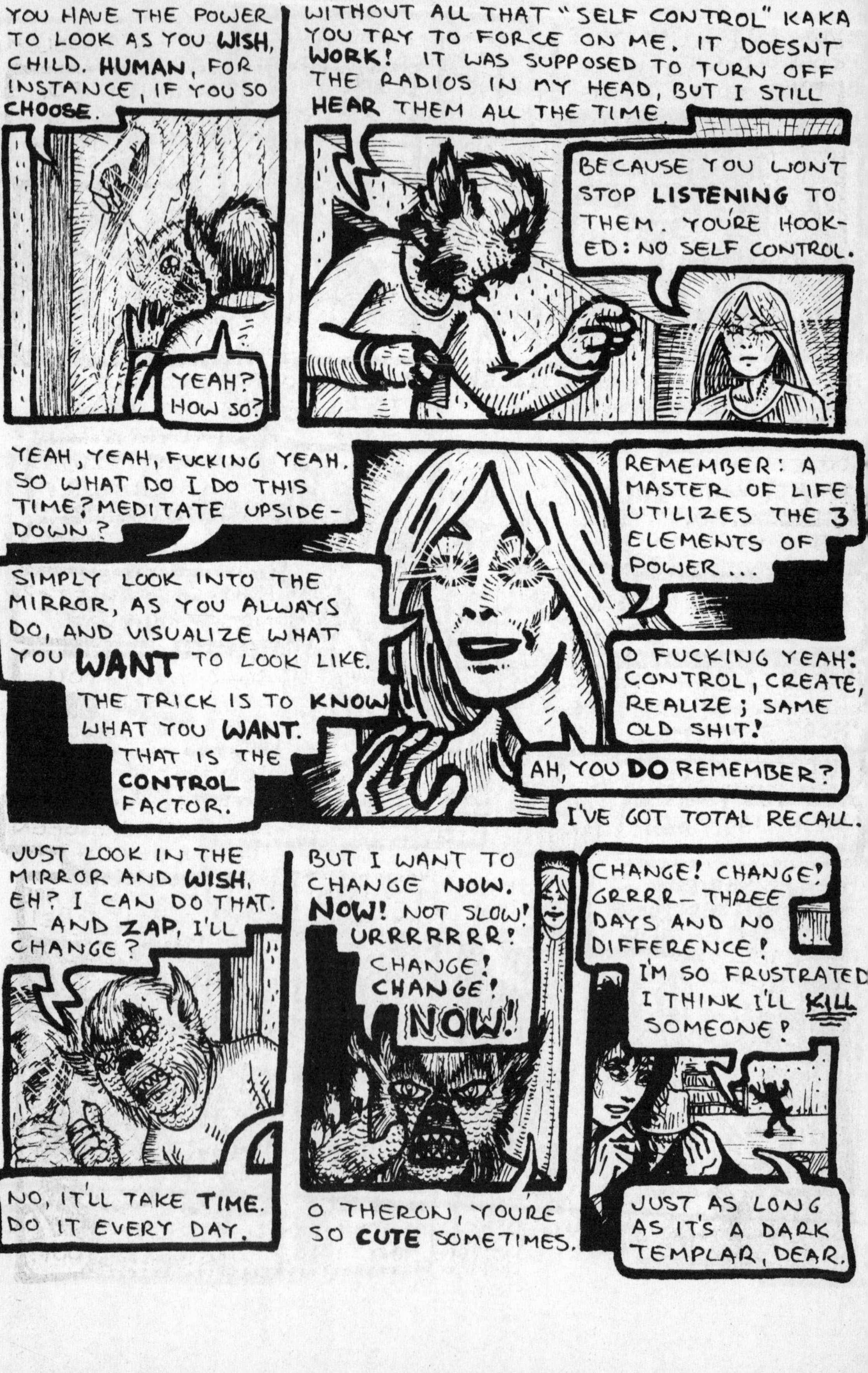

YOU HAVE THE POWER TO LOOK AS YOU WISH, CHILD. HUMAN, FOR INSTANCE, IF YOU SO CHOOSE.
YEAH? HOW SO?
WITHOUT ALL THAT "SELF CONTROL" KAKA YOU TRY TO FORCE ON ME. IT DOESN'T WORK! IT WAS SUPPOSED TO TURN OFF THE RADIOS IN MY HEAD, BUT I STILL HEAR THEM ALL THE TIME.
BECAUSE YOU WON'T STOP LISTENING TO THEM. YOU'RE HOOKED: NO SELF CONTROL.
YEAH, YEAH, FUCKING YEAH. SO WHAT DO I DO THIS TIME? MEDITATE UPSIDE-DOWN?
SIMPLY LOOK INTO THE MIRROR, AS YOU ALWAYS DO, AND VISUALIZE WHAT YOU WANT TO LOOK LIKE.
THE TRICK IS TO KNOW WHAT YOU WANT.
THAT IS THE CONTROL FACTOR.
REMEMBER: A MASTER OF LIFE UTILIZES THE 3 ELEMENTS OF POWER...
O FUCKING YEAH: CONTROL, CREATE, REALIZE; SAME OLD SHIT!
AH, YOU DO REMEMBER?
I'VE GOT TOTAL RECALL.
JUST LOOK IN THE MIRROR AND WISH, EH? I CAN DO THAT. — AND ZAP, I'LL CHANGE?
NO, IT'LL TAKE TIME. DO IT EVERY DAY.
BUT I WANT TO CHANGE NOW. NOW! NOT SLOW!
URRRRRRR!
CHANGE! CHANGE! NOW!
O THERON, YOU'RE SO CUTE SOMETIMES.
CHANGE! CHANGE! GRRRR— THREE DAYS AND NO DIFFERENCE!
I'M SO FRUSTRATED I THINK I'LL KILL SOMEONE!
JUST AS LONG AS IT'S A DARK TEMPLAR, DEAR.

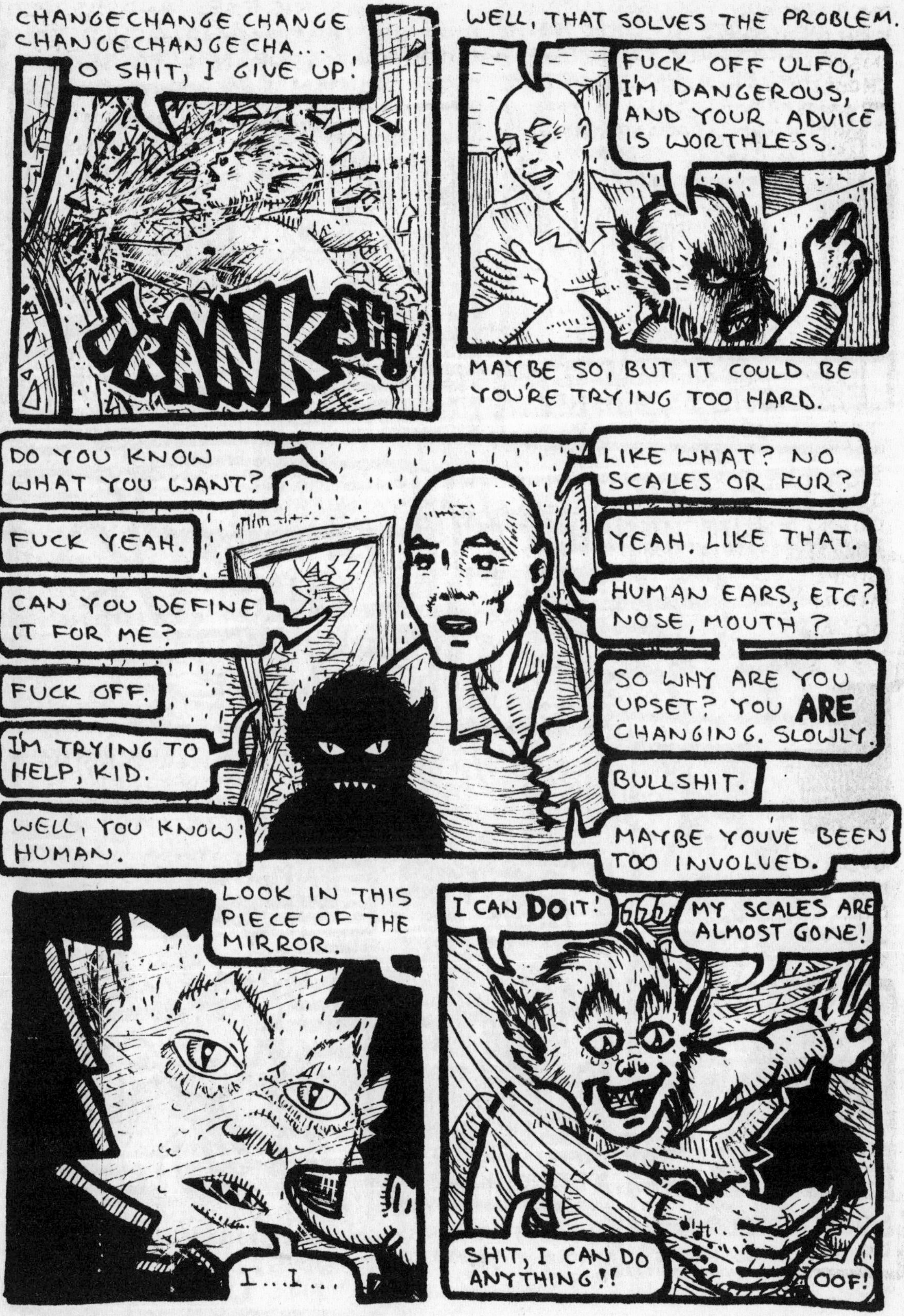
CHANGECHANGE CHANGE CHANGECHANGECHA... O SHIT, I GIVE UP!
CRANKSH!
WELL, THAT SOLVES THE PROBLEM.
FUCK OFF ULFO, I'M DANGEROUS, AND YOUR ADVICE IS WORTHLESS.
MAYBE SO, BUT IT COULD BE YOU'RE TRYING TOO HARD.
DO YOU KNOW WHAT YOU WANT?
FUCK YEAH.
CAN YOU DEFINE IT FOR ME?
FUCK OFF.
I'M TRYING TO HELP, KID.
WELL, YOU KNOW: HUMAN.
LIKE WHAT? NO SCALES OR FUR?
YEAH, LIKE THAT.
HUMAN EARS, ETC? NOSE, MOUTH?
SO WHY ARE YOU UPSET? YOU ARE CHANGING. SLOWLY.
BULLSHIT.
MAYBE YOU'VE BEEN TOO INVOLVED.
LOOK IN THIS PIECE OF THE MIRROR.
I...I...
I CAN DO IT!
MY SCALES ARE ALMOST GONE!
SHIT, I CAN DO ANYTHING!!
OOF!

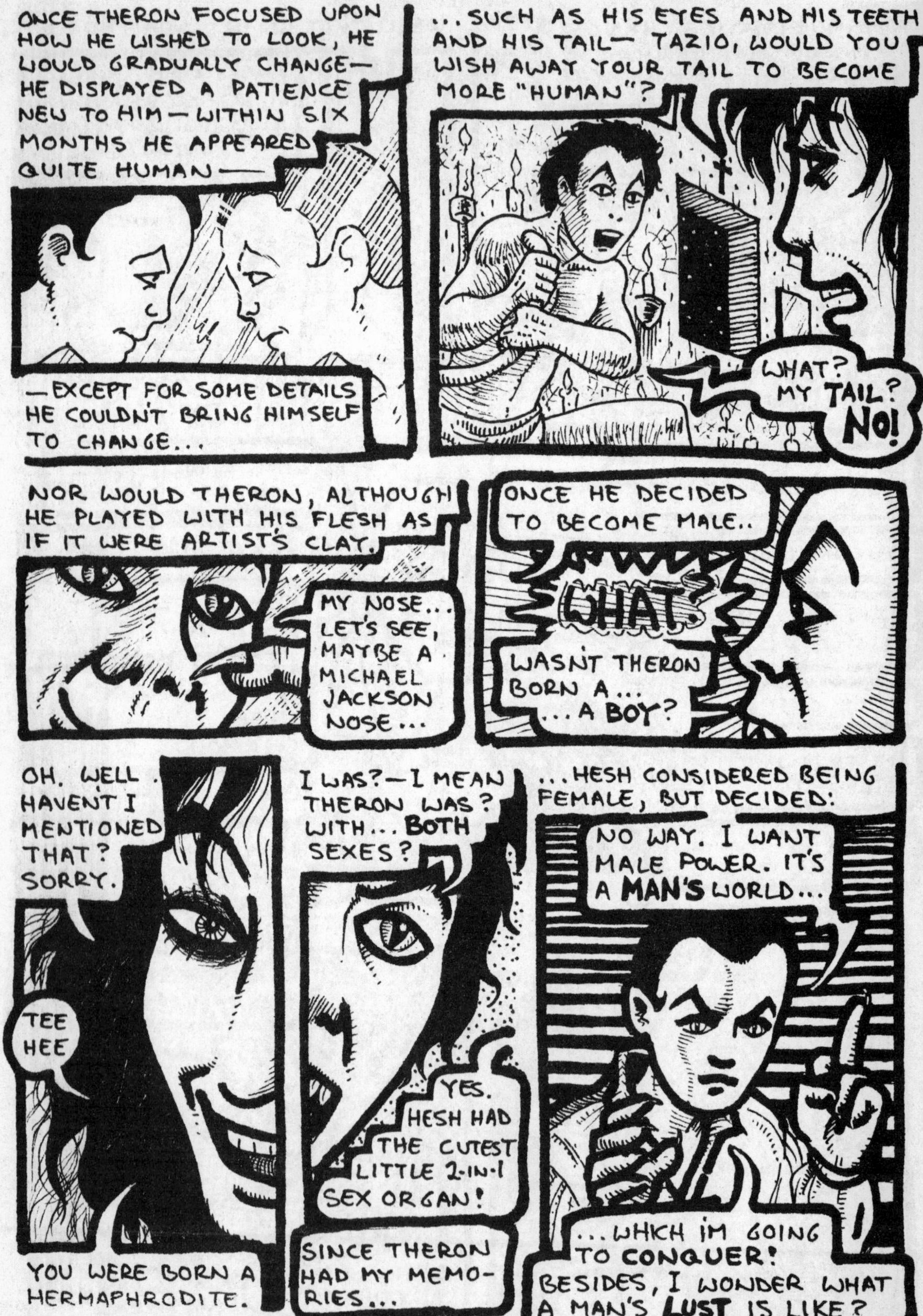

ONCE THERON FOCUSED UPON HOW HE WISHED TO LOOK, HE WOULD GRADUALLY CHANGE— HE DISPLAYED A PATIENCE NEW TO HIM—WITHIN SIX MONTHS HE APPEARED QUITE HUMAN—
—EXCEPT FOR SOME DETAILS HE COULDN'T BRING HIMSELF TO CHANGE...
...SUCH AS HIS EYES AND HIS TEETH AND HIS TAIL— TAZIO, WOULD YOU WISH AWAY YOUR TAIL TO BECOME MORE "HUMAN"?
WHAT? MY TAIL? NO!
NOR WOULD THERON, ALTHOUGH HE PLAYED WITH HIS FLESH AS IF IT WERE ARTIST'S CLAY.
MY NOSE... LET'S SEE, MAYBE A MICHAEL JACKSON NOSE...
ONCE HE DECIDED TO BECOME MALE..
WHAT?
WASN'T THERON BORN A... ...A BOY?
OH. WELL. HAVEN'T I MENTIONED THAT? SORRY.
TEE HEE
YOU WERE BORN A HERMAPHRODITE.
I WAS?—I MEAN THERON WAS? WITH... BOTH SEXES?
YES. HESH HAD THE CUTEST LITTLE 2-IN-1 SEX ORGAN!
SINCE THERON HAD MY MEMORIES...
...HESH CONSIDERED BEING FEMALE, BUT DECIDED:
NO WAY. I WANT MALE POWER. IT'S A MAN'S WORLD...
...WHICH I'M GOING TO CONQUER! BESIDES, I WONDER WHAT A MAN'S LUST IS LIKE?

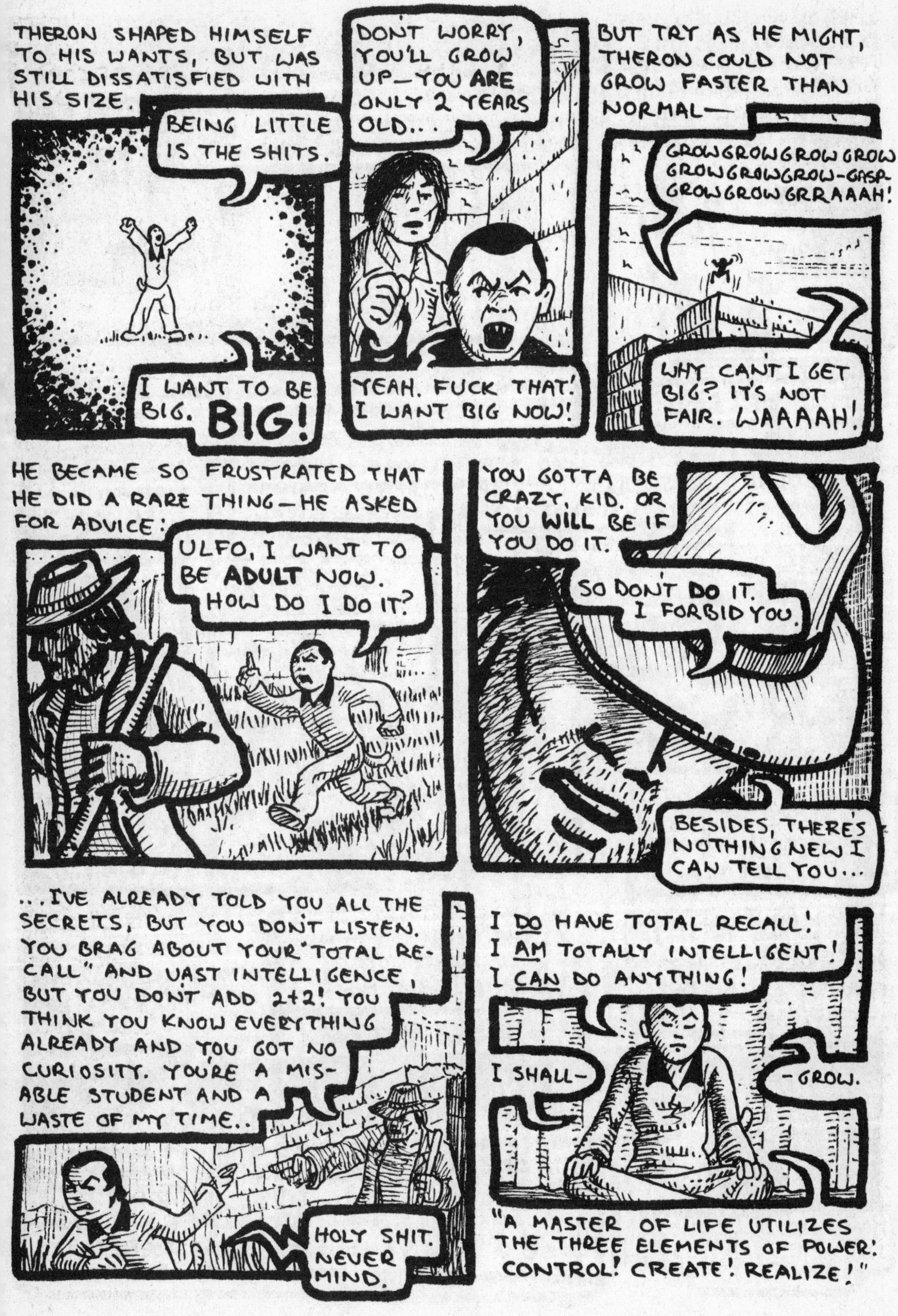
THERON SHAPED HIMSELF TO HIS WANTS, BUT WAS STILL DISSATISFIED WITH HIS SIZE.
BEING LITTLE IS THE SHITS.
I WANT TO BE BIG. BIG!
DONT WORRY, YOU'LL GROW UP—YOU ARE ONLY 2 YEARS OLD...
YEAH. FUCK THAT! I WANT BIG NOW!
BUT TRY AS HE MIGHT, THERON COULD NOT GROW FASTER THAN NORMAL—
GROWGROWGROWGROW GROWGROWGROW-GASP GROWGROWGRRAAAH!
WHY CANT I GET BIG? IT'S NOT FAIR. WAAAAH!
HE BECAME SO FRUSTRATED THAT HE DID A RARE THING—HE ASKED FOR ADVICE:
ULFO, I WANT TO BE ADULT NOW. HOW DO I DO IT?
YOU GOTTA BE CRAZY, KID, OR YOU WILL BE IF YOU DO IT.
SO DONT DO IT. I FORBID YOU.
BESIDES, THERE'S NOTHING NEW I CAN TELL YOU...
...IVE ALREADY TOLD YOU ALL THE SECRETS, BUT YOU DONT LISTEN. YOU BRAG ABOUT YOUR "TOTAL RE-CALL" AND VAST INTELLIGENCE, BUT YOU DONT ADD 2+2! YOU THINK YOU KNOW EVERYTHING ALREADY AND YOU GOT NO CURIOSITY. YOU'RE A MIS-ABLE STUDENT AND A WASTE OF MY TIME..
HOLY SHIT. NEVER MIND.
I DO HAVE TOTAL RECALL! I AM TOTALLY INTELLIGENT! I CAN DO ANYTHING!
I SHALL—
—GROW.
"A MASTER OF LIFE UTILIZES THE THREE ELEMENTS OF POWER: CONTROL! CREATE! REALIZE!"

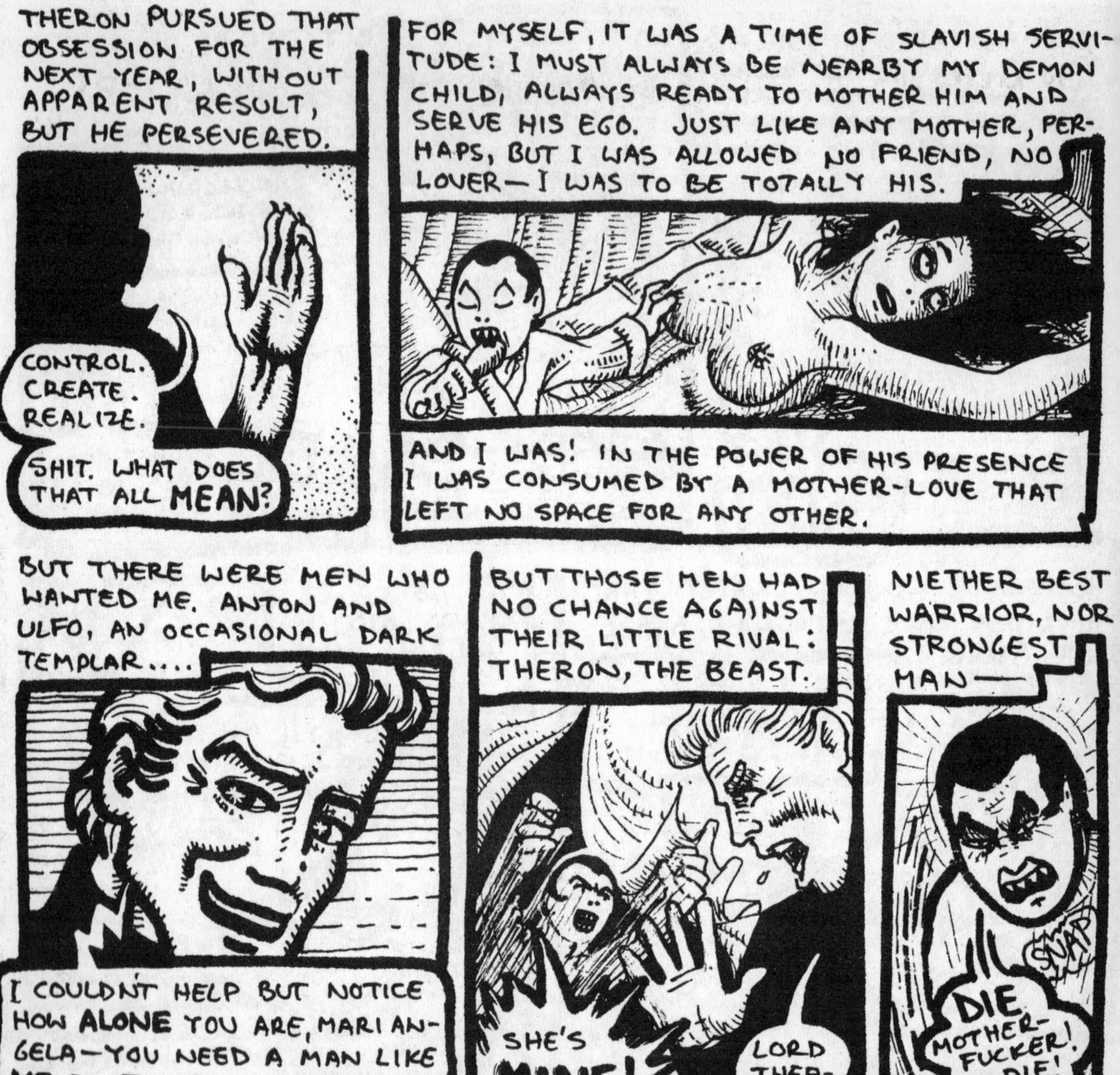

THERON PURSUED THAT OBSESSION FOR THE NEXT YEAR, WITHOUT APPARENT RESULT, BUT HE PERSEVERED.
CONTROL. CREATE. REALIZE.
SHIT. WHAT DOES THAT ALL MEAN?
FOR MYSELF, IT WAS A TIME OF SLAVISH SERVITUDE: I MUST ALWAYS BE NEARBY MY DEMON CHILD, ALWAYS READY TO MOTHER HIM AND SERVE HIS EGO. JUST LIKE ANY MOTHER, PERHAPS, BUT I WAS ALLOWED NO FRIEND, NO LOVER—I WAS TO BE TOTALLY HIS.
AND I WAS! IN THE POWER OF HIS PRESENCE I WAS CONSUMED BY A MOTHER-LOVE THAT LEFT NO SPACE FOR ANY OTHER.
BUT THERE WERE MEN WHO WANTED ME. ANTON AND ULFO, AN OCCASIONAL DARK TEMPLAR....
I COULDN'T HELP BUT NOTICE HOW ALONE YOU ARE, MARIANGELA—YOU NEED A MAN LIKE ME TO FULLFILL YOU.
BUT THOSE MEN HAD NO CHANCE AGAINST THEIR LITTLE RIVAL: THERON, THE BEAST.
SHE'S MINE!
LORD THER-
NIETHER BEST WARRIOR, NOR STRONGEST MAN—
SNAP
DIE MOTHER-FUCKER! DIE!
ULFO WAS SOMETHING ELSE AGAIN, OF COURSE, HE WOULD GET HORNY FOR ME AS THE MOON WAXED FULL—
MARIANGELA! COME WITH ME TONIGHT. I WANT YOU!
OH, NO, IT'S THAT TIME OF THE MONTH AGAIN—
NO, ULFO, I'M A NUN, REMEMBER?
NO, YOU ARENT A NUN ANY MORE, AND YOU NEED A MAN TO LOVE. ME! YOU NEED ME!
LEAVE MY MOTHER ALONE, ULFO. YOU KNOW MY RULES, NOBODY GETS HER BUT ME!
YOU?? HAH! SHE'S YOUR MOTHER, BRAT!!!

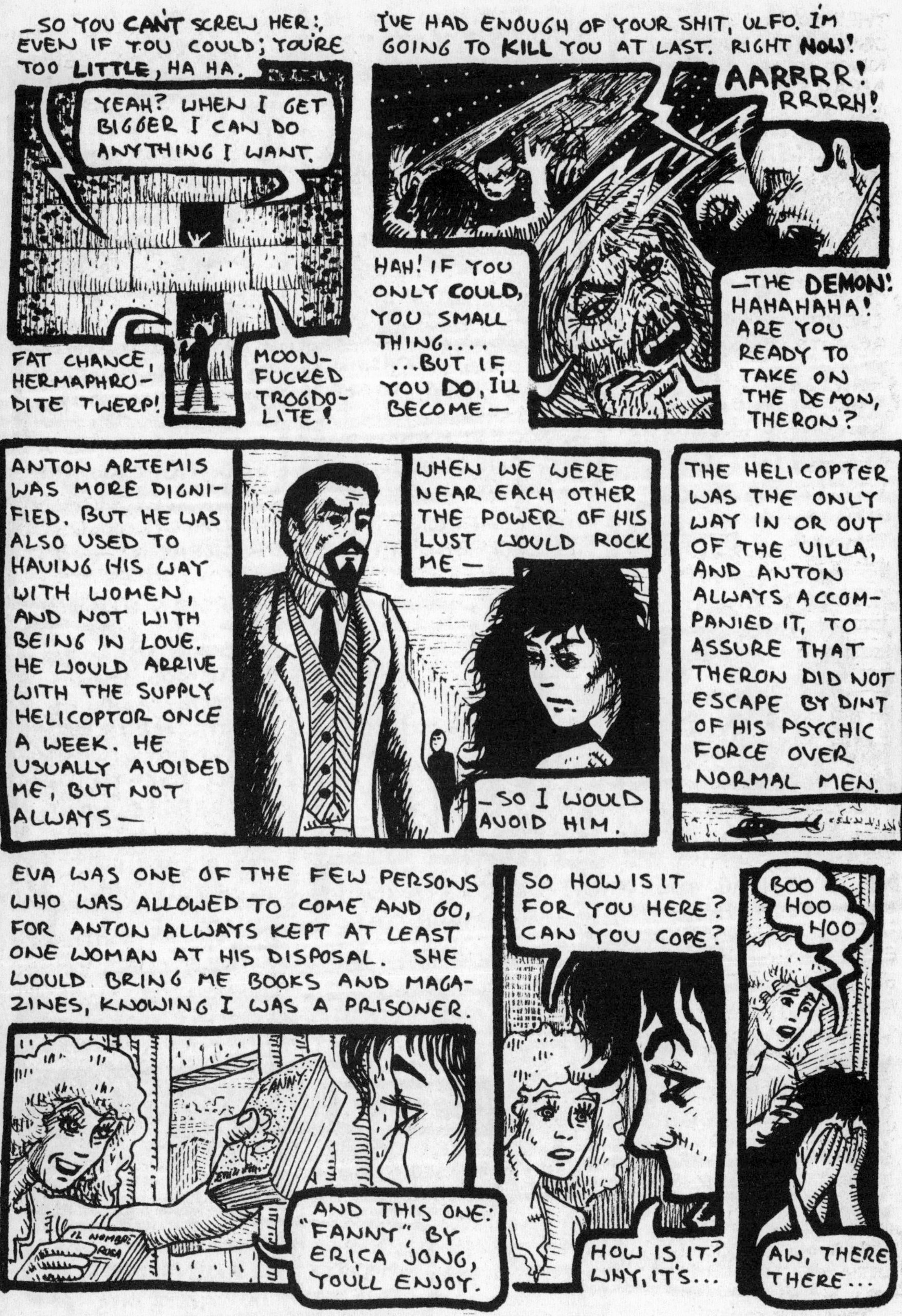

_SO YOU CAN'T SCREW HER:, EVEN IF YOU COULD; YOU'RE TOO LITTLE, HA HA.
YEAH? WHEN I GET BIGGER I CAN DO ANYTHING I WANT.
FAT CHANCE, HERMAPHRODITE TWERP!
MOON-FUCKED TROGDOLITE!
I'VE HAD ENOUGH OF YOUR SHIT, ULFO. I'M GOING TO KILL YOU AT LAST. RIGHT NOW!
AARRRR! RRRRH!
HAH! IF YOU ONLY COULD, YOU SMALL THING.... ...BUT IF YOU DO, I'LL BECOME—
—THE DEMON! HAHAHAHA! ARE YOU READY TO TAKE ON THE DEMON, THERON?
ANTON ARTEMIS WAS MORE DIGNIFIED. BUT HE WAS ALSO USED TO HAVING HIS WAY WITH WOMEN, AND NOT WITH BEING IN LOVE. HE WOULD ARRIVE WITH THE SUPPLY HELICOPTOR ONCE A WEEK. HE USUALLY AVOIDED ME, BUT NOT ALWAYS—
WHEN WE WERE NEAR EACH OTHER THE POWER OF HIS LUST WOULD ROCK ME—
_SO I WOULD AVOID HIM.
THE HELICOPTER WAS THE ONLY WAY IN OR OUT OF THE VILLA, AND ANTON ALWAYS ACCOMPANIED IT, TO ASSURE THAT THERON DID NOT ESCAPE BY DINT OF HIS PSYCHIC FORCE OVER NORMAL MEN.
EVA WAS ONE OF THE FEW PERSONS WHO WAS ALLOWED TO COME AND GO, FOR ANTON ALWAYS KEPT AT LEAST ONE WOMAN AT HIS DISPOSAL. SHE WOULD BRING ME BOOKS AND MAGAZINES, KNOWING I WAS A PRISONER.
FANNY
"AND THIS ONE: "FANNY", BY ERICA JONG, YOU'LL ENJOY.
SO HOW IS IT FOR YOU HERE? CAN YOU COPE?
HOW IS IT? WHY, IT'S...
BOO HOO HOO
AW, THERE THERE...

OH, EVA, I... NO! NO!! GET AWAY FROM ME! DON'T TOUCH ME! PLEASE!

MARIANGELA! WHAT? WHY? WHAT'S THE MATTER?

IT'S THERON! IF HE SAW US TOGETHER HE MIGHT JUST KILL YOU!? HE'S SO JEALOUS!

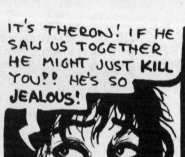

THE ONLY REASON I HAVE TIME TO SEE YOU NOW IS THAT HE'S OFF MEDITATING ON GROWING.

YES, WELL, ANTON WILL PROTECT ME. I BELIEVE.

IF HE CAN.

ANTON IS LIKE A GOD. HE CAN.

YOU DON'T KNOW THERON. HE TOO IS A GOD — BUT A SPOILED CHILD, A DEVIL GOD.

OH, POOR, MARIANGELA, YOU MUST HATE HIM, YOUR OWN SON.

HATE THERON? NO, I..I LOVE HIM. BUT I ALSO FEAR HIM.

I UNDERSTAND. I FEEL MUCH THE SAME ABOUT ANTON.

ACTUALLY... I SORT OF DREAD IT WHEN ANTON SEES YOU: IT UPSETS HIM.

SOMETIMES HE PRETENDS THAT I AM YOU. AND HE WANTS MORE SEX THAN USUAL—WHICH IS ALL RIGHT WHEN THERE'S SEVERAL OF US TO TAKE CARE OF HIM— BUT WHEN IT'S JUST ME... OW! TOO MUCH.

I THOUGHT YOU LIKED IT WITH ANTON

EVA SEZ: LOVE IT, BUT FLESH IS JUST FLESH—IT'S LIKE MAKING LOVE TO AN ARMY.

ISN'T HE EVER SATISFIED?

EVA SEZ: OH, HE COMES AND COMES, BUT THERE'S ALWAYS MORE.

AND YET, HE HAS THIS FANTASY THAT... THAT YOU COULD SATISFY HIM.

DOES HE?

YES. MAYBE YOU SHOULD DO US ALL A FAVOR...

I STILL HONOR MY VOW OF CHASTITY — AND I DO NOT LOVE ANTON ARTEMIS.

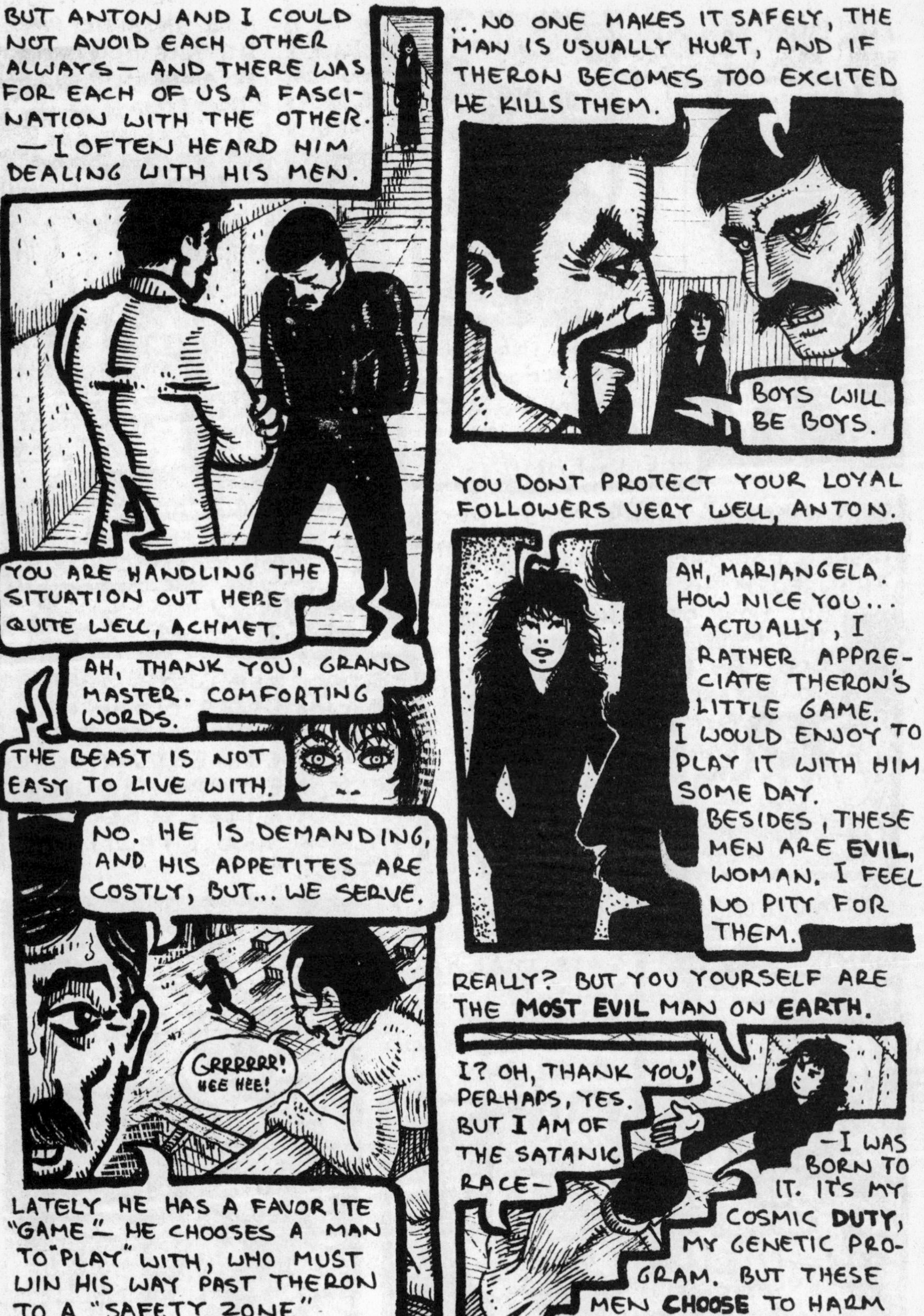
BUT ANTON AND I COULD NOT AVOID EACH OTHER ALWAYS— AND THERE WAS FOR EACH OF US A FASCINATION WITH THE OTHER. —I OFTEN HEARD HIM DEALING WITH HIS MEN.
YOU ARE HANDLING THE SITUATION OUT HERE QUITE WELL, ACHMET.
AH, THANK YOU, GRAND MASTER. COMFORTING WORDS.
THE BEAST IS NOT EASY TO LIVE WITH.
NO. HE IS DEMANDING, AND HIS APPETITES ARE COSTLY, BUT... WE SERVE.
GRRRRRR! HEE HEE!
LATELY HE HAS A FAVORITE "GAME"— HE CHOOSES A MAN TO "PLAY" WITH, WHO MUST WIN HIS WAY PAST THERON TO A "SAFETY ZONE"...
...NO ONE MAKES IT SAFELY, THE MAN IS USUALLY HURT, AND IF THERON BECOMES TOO EXCITED HE KILLS THEM.
BOYS WILL BE BOYS.
YOU DON'T PROTECT YOUR LOYAL FOLLOWERS VERY WELL, ANTON.
AH, MARIANGELA. HOW NICE YOU...
ACTUALLY, I RATHER APPRECIATE THERON'S LITTLE GAME. I WOULD ENJOY TO PLAY IT WITH HIM SOME DAY.
BESIDES, THESE MEN ARE EVIL, WOMAN. I FEEL NO PITY FOR THEM.
REALLY? BUT YOU YOURSELF ARE THE MOST EVIL MAN ON EARTH.
I? OH, THANK YOU! PERHAPS, YES. BUT I AM OF THE SATANIC RACE—
—I WAS BORN TO IT. IT'S MY COSMIC DUTY, MY GENETIC PROGRAM. BUT THESE MEN CHOOSE TO HARM THEIR OWN KIND. RATS!

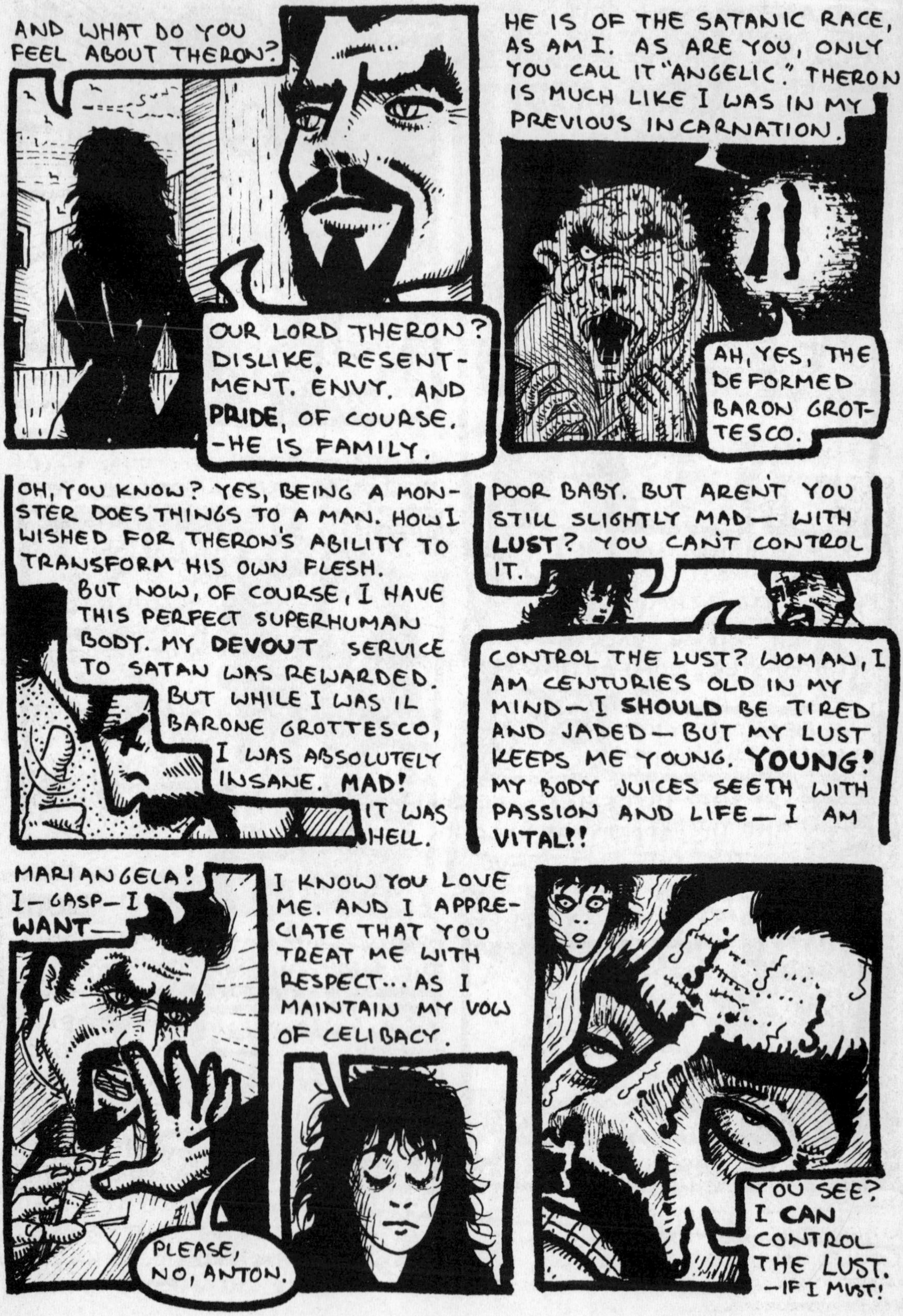
AND WHAT DO YOU FEEL ABOUT THERON?
OUR LORD THERON? DISLIKE, RESENTMENT. ENVY. AND PRIDE, OF COURSE. -HE IS FAMILY.
HE IS OF THE SATANIC RACE, AS AM I. AS ARE YOU, ONLY YOU CALL IT "ANGELIC." THERON IS MUCH LIKE I WAS IN MY PREVIOUS INCARNATION.
AH, YES, THE DEFORMED BARON GROTTESCO.
OH, YOU KNOW? YES, BEING A MONSTER DOES THINGS TO A MAN. HOW I WISHED FOR THERON'S ABILITY TO TRANSFORM HIS OWN FLESH.
BUT NOW, OF COURSE, I HAVE THIS PERFECT SUPERHUMAN BODY. MY DEVOUT SERVICE TO SATAN WAS REWARDED.
BUT WHILE I WAS IL BARONE GROTTESCO,
I WAS ABSOLUTELY INSANE. MAD!
IT WAS HELL.
POOR BABY. BUT AREN'T YOU STILL SLIGHTLY MAD— WITH LUST? YOU CAN'T CONTROL IT.
CONTROL THE LUST? WOMAN, I AM CENTURIES OLD IN MY MIND—I SHOULD BE TIRED AND JADED—BUT MY LUST KEEPS ME YOUNG. YOUNG! MY BODY JUICES SEETH WITH PASSION AND LIFE—I AM VITAL!!
MARIANGELA! I—GASP—I WANT—
I KNOW YOU LOVE ME. AND I APPRECIATE THAT YOU TREAT ME WITH RESPECT... AS I MAINTAIN MY VOW OF CELIBACY.
PLEASE, NO, ANTON.
YOU SEE? I CAN CONTROL THE LUST.
-IF I MUST!

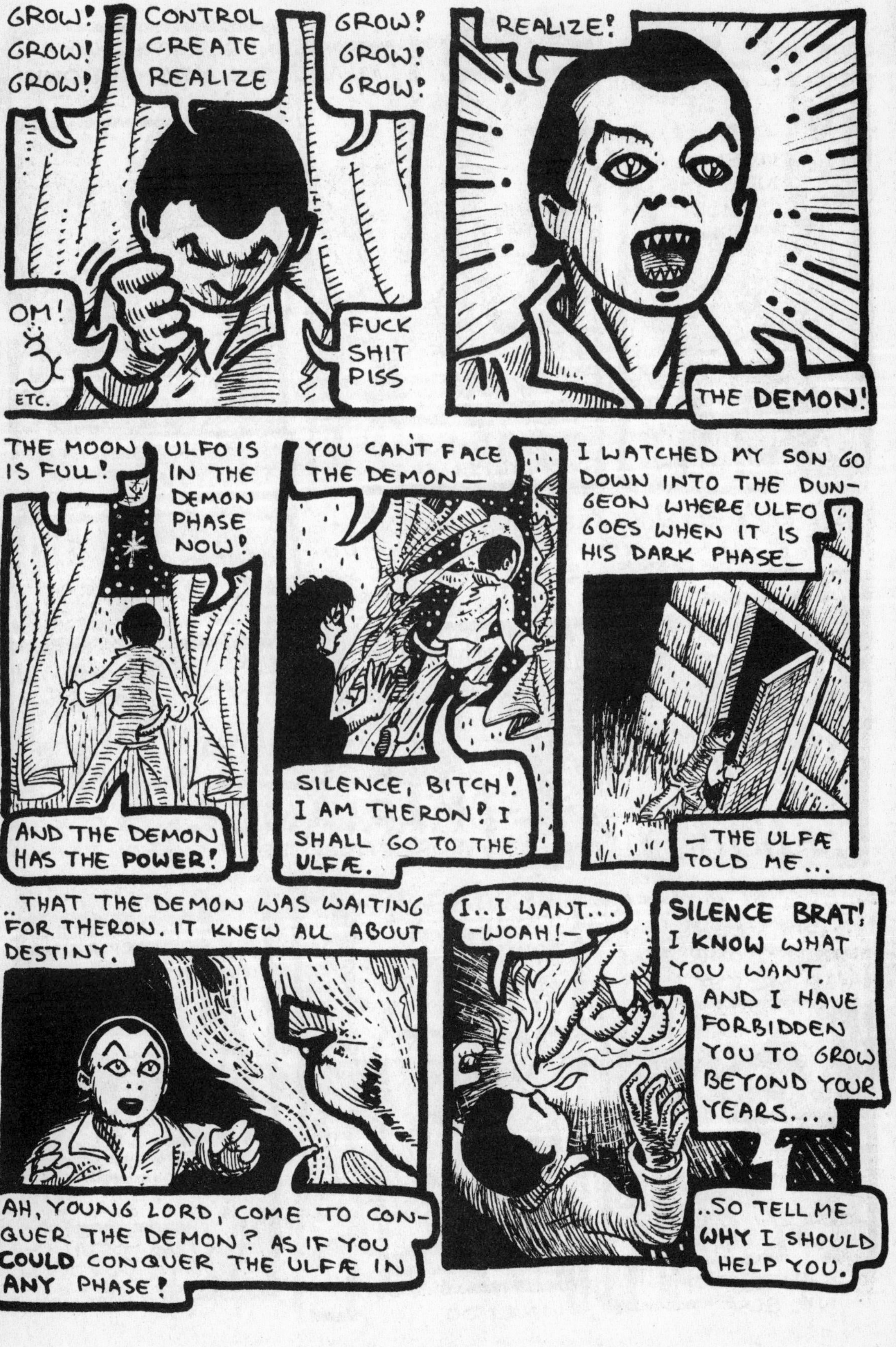
GROW! GROW! GROW!
CONTROL CREATE REALIZE
GROW! GROW! GROW!
OM! ETC.
FUCK SHIT PISS
REALIZE!
THE DEMON!
THE MOON IS FULL!
ULFO IS IN THE DEMON PHASE NOW!
AND THE DEMON HAS THE POWER!
YOU CAN'T FACE THE DEMON—
SILENCE, BITCH! I AM THERON! I SHALL GO TO THE ULFÆ.
I WATCHED MY SON GO DOWN INTO THE DUNGEON WHERE ULFO GOES WHEN IT IS HIS DARK PHASE_
—THE ULFÆ TOLD ME...
..THAT THE DEMON WAS WAITING FOR THERON. IT KNEW ALL ABOUT DESTINY.
AH, YOUNG LORD, COME TO CONQUER THE DEMON? AS IF YOU COULD CONQUER THE ULFÆ IN ANY PHASE!
I..I WANT... -WOAH!-
SILENCE BRAT! I KNOW WHAT YOU WANT. AND I HAVE FORBIDDEN YOU TO GROW BEYOND YOUR YEARS...
..SO TELL ME WHY I SHOULD HELP YOU.

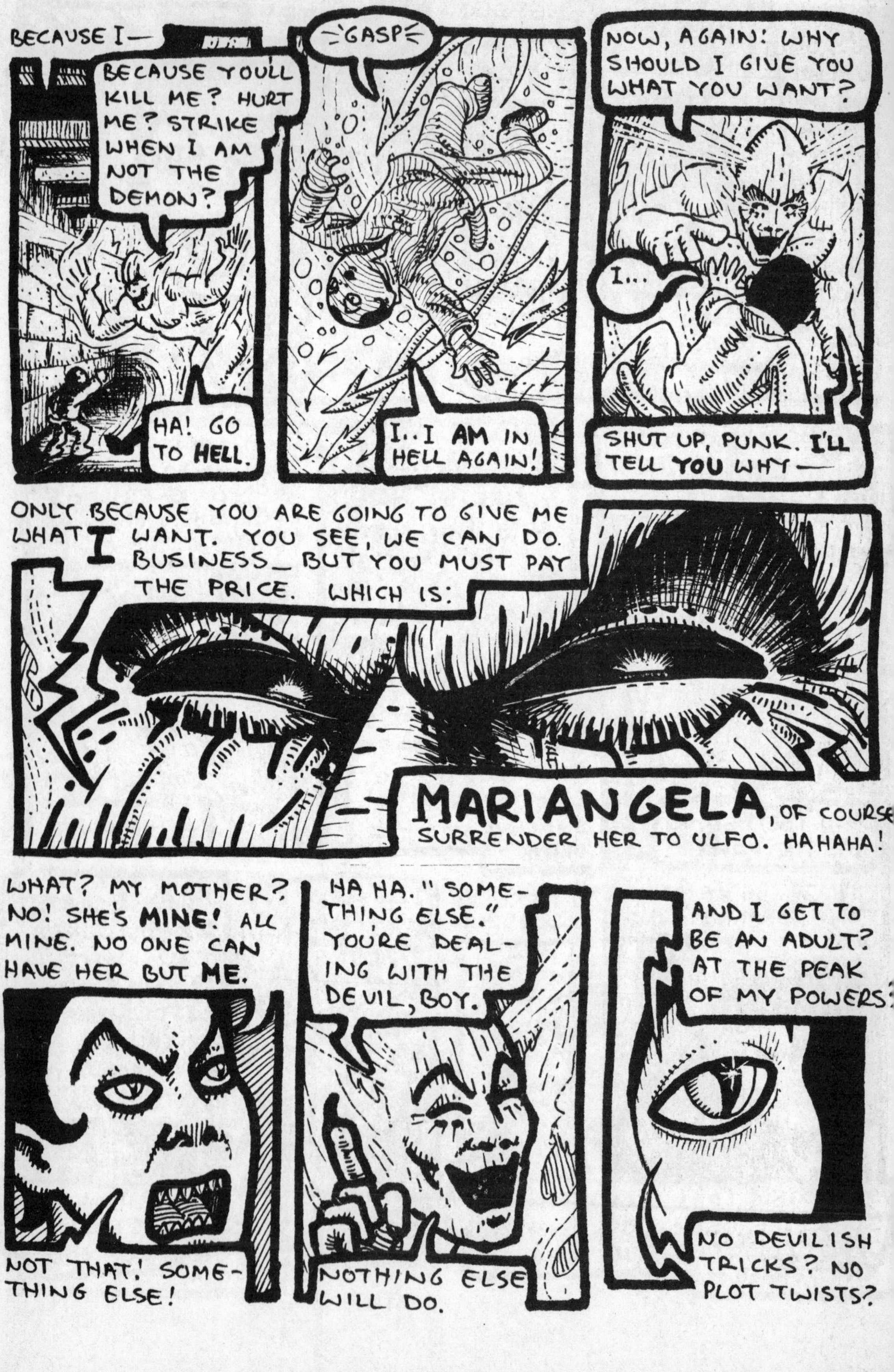
BECAUSE I—
BECAUSE YOU'LL KILL ME? HURT ME? STRIKE WHEN I AM NOT THE DEMON?
HA! GO TO HELL.
GASP
I..I AM IN HELL AGAIN!
NOW, AGAIN: WHY SHOULD I GIVE YOU WHAT YOU WANT?
I...
SHUT UP, PUNK. I'LL TELL YOU WHY—
ONLY BECAUSE YOU ARE GOING TO GIVE ME WHAT I WANT. YOU SEE, WE CAN DO. BUSINESS_ BUT YOU MUST PAY THE PRICE. WHICH IS:
MARIANGELA, OF COURSE SURRENDER HER TO ULFO. HAHAHA!
WHAT? MY MOTHER? NO! SHE'S MINE! ALL MINE. NO ONE CAN HAVE HER BUT ME.
NOT THAT! SOMETHING ELSE!
HA HA. "SOMETHING ELSE." YOU'RE DEALING WITH THE DEVIL, BOY.
NOTHING ELSE WILL DO.
AND I GET TO BE AN ADULT? AT THE PEAK OF MY POWERS?
NO DEVILISH TRICKS? NO PLOT TWISTS?

I CANNOT MAKE YOU AN ADULT, ONLY YOU DO THAT— I SHALL JUST SHOW YOU HOW TO GAIN ACCESS TO YOUR OWN POWER. — THEN YOU DO WITH IT WHAT YOU WILL, ANTICHRIST. CONQUER THE WORLD, FULFILL YOUR DESTINY NOW INSTEAD OF LATER.

IT COULD BE FUN.

BUT I CAN'T LET YOU HAVE MARIANGELA.

THEN DO WITHOUT MY HELP.

WAAAAHH. IT'S NO FAIR!! WAAAAAH!

ALL FUCKING RIGHT, YOU GOD DAMNED DEVIL— TAKE HER! SHE'S YOURS!

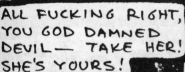

GIVE ME ALL MY POWER! NOW!

VERY WELL. BY THE WAY, IT IS MY DUTY AS YOUR PERSONAL MENTOR, TO WARN YOU THAT THIS MAY NOT BE THE VERY BEST THING FOR YOU. ALL THESE POWERS WOULD COME TO YOU IN TIME ANYWAY, IN SEVERAL YEARS, WHEN YOU ARE MATURE ENOUGH TO CONTROL...

CUT THE OLD SHIT!!! I WANT IT NOW! NOW! NOW!

AMEN. LET US CALL UP THE URRR.

THE EARTH TREMBLED ALL NIGHT UNDER THE FULL MOON.

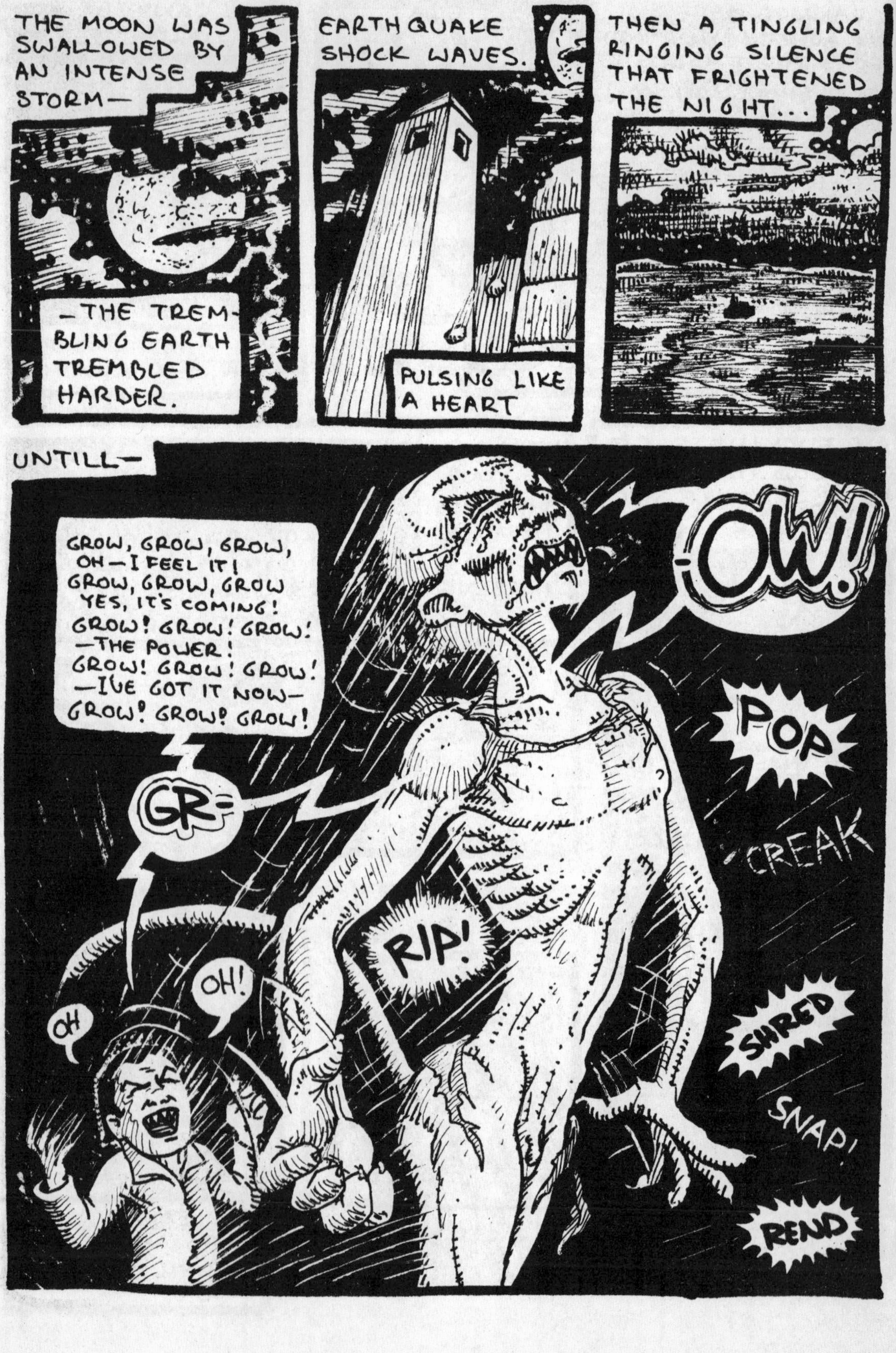
THE MOON WAS SWALLOWED BY AN INTENSE STORM—
—THE TREMBLING EARTH TREMBLED HARDER.
EARTHQUAKE SHOCK WAVES.
PULSING LIKE A HEART
THEN A TINGLING RINGING SILENCE THAT FRIGHTENED THE NIGHT...
UNTILL—
GROW, GROW, GROW, OH—I FEEL IT! GROW, GROW, GROW YES, IT'S COMING! GROW! GROW! GROW! —THE POWER! GROW! GROW! GROW! —I'VE GOT IT NOW— GROW! GROW! GROW!
GR-
-OW!
POP
CREAK
RIP!
OH!
OH
SHRED
SNAP!
REND

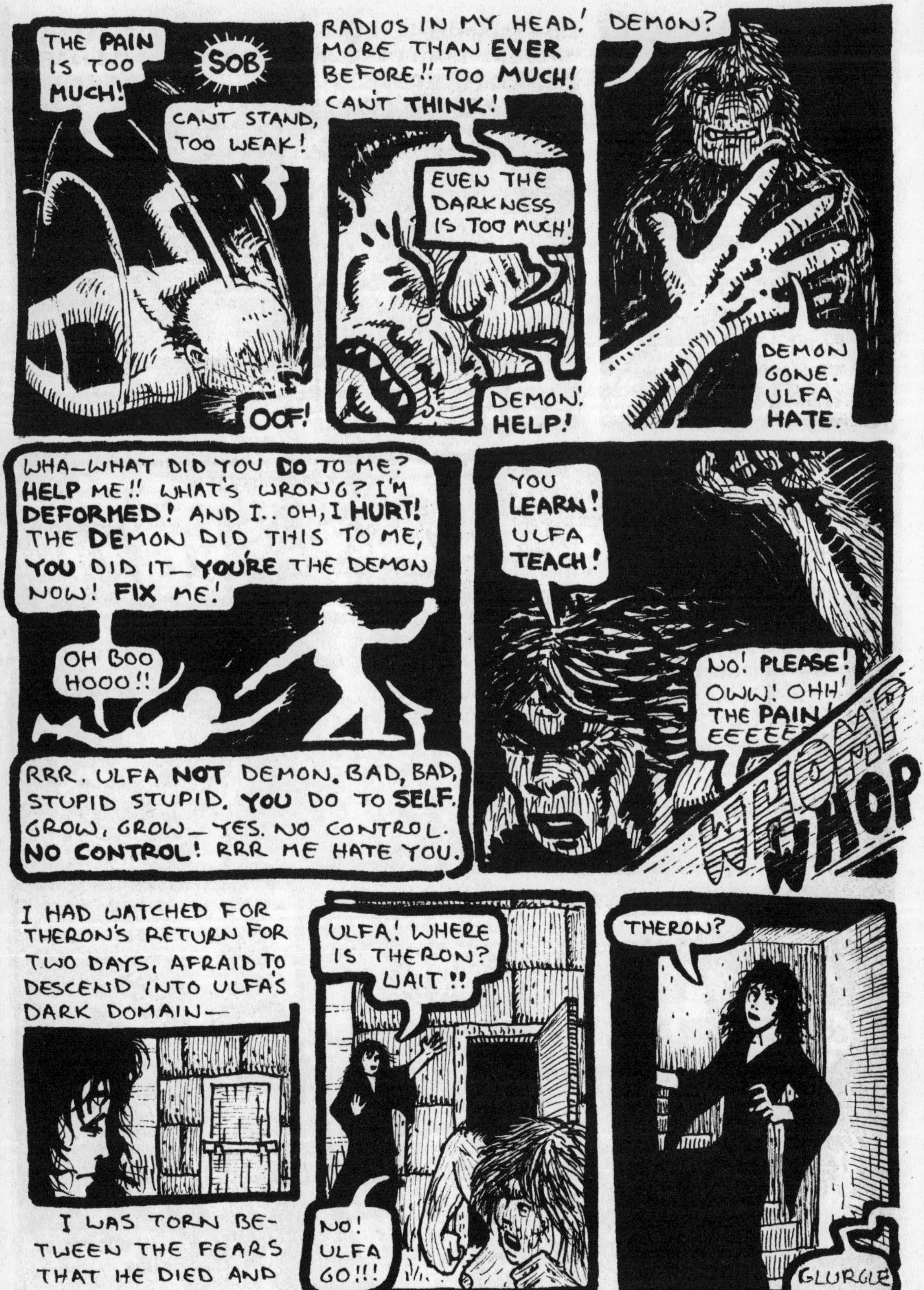
THE PAIN IS TOO MUCH!
SOB
CANT STAND, TOO WEAK!
OOF!
RADIOS IN MY HEAD! MORE THAN EVER BEFORE!! TOO MUCH! CAN'T THINK!
EVEN THE DARKNESS IS TOO MUCH!
DEMON! HELP!
DEMON?
DEMON GONE. ULFA HATE.
WHA—WHAT DID YOU DO TO ME? HELP ME!! WHAT'S WRONG? I'M DEFORMED! AND I.. OH, I HURT! THE DEMON DID THIS TO ME, YOU DID IT—YOU'RE THE DEMON NOW! FIX ME!
OH BOO HOOO!!
RRR. ULFA NOT DEMON. BAD, BAD, STUPID STUPID. YOU DO TO SELF. GROW, GROW—YES. NO CONTROL. NO CONTROL! RRR ME HATE YOU.
YOU LEARN! ULFA TEACH!
NO! PLEASE! OWW! OHH! THE PAIN! EEEEE
WHOMP
WHOP
I HAD WATCHED FOR THERON'S RETURN FOR TWO DAYS, AFRAID TO DESCEND INTO ULFA'S DARK DOMAIN—
I WAS TORN BETWEEN THE FEARS THAT HE DIED AND THAT HE LIVED.
ULFA! WHERE IS THERON? WAIT!!
NO! ULFA GO!!!
THERON?
GLURGLE

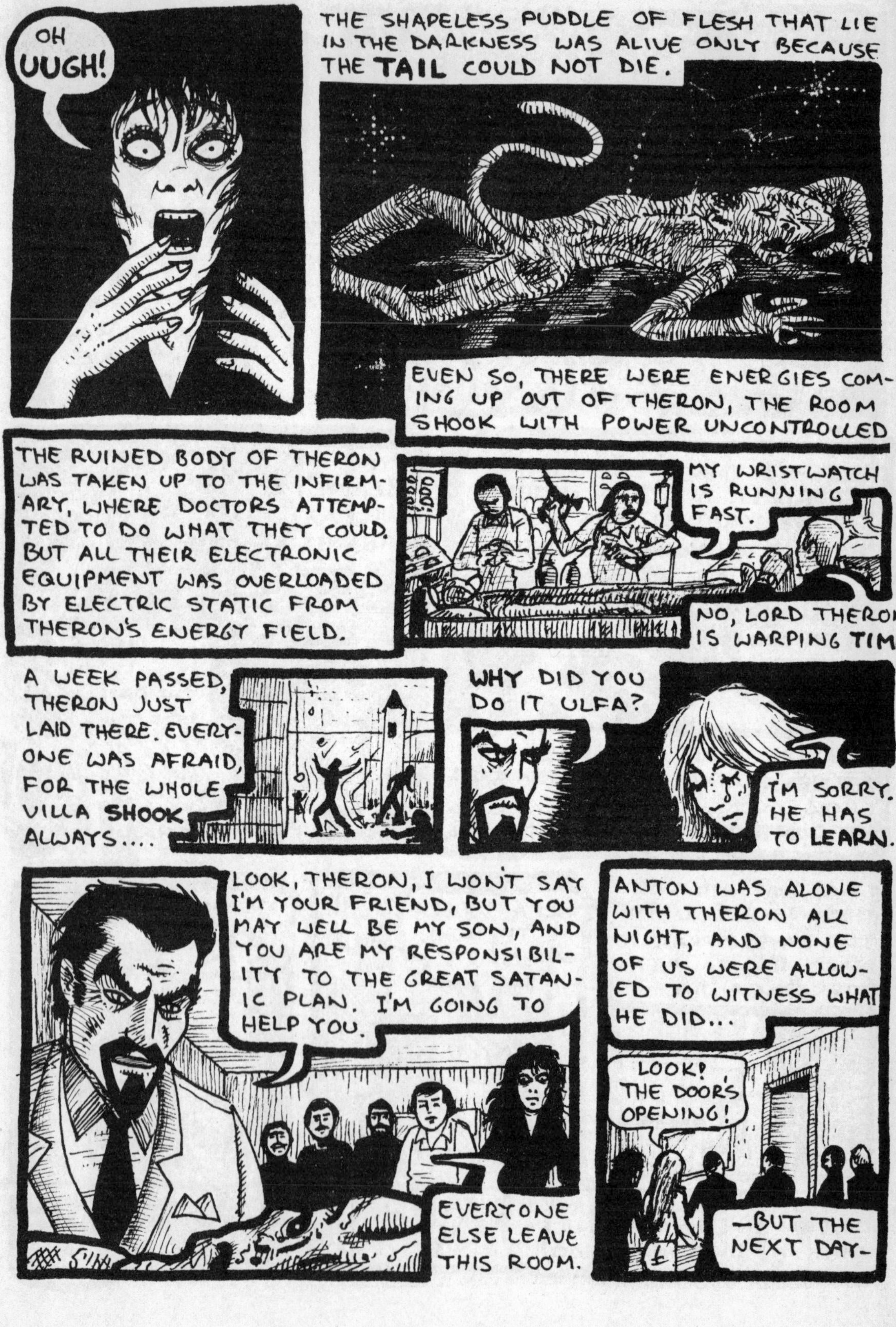
OH UUGH!
THE SHAPELESS PUDDLE OF FLESH THAT LIE IN THE DARKNESS WAS ALIVE ONLY BECAUSE THE TAIL COULD NOT DIE.
EVEN SO, THERE WERE ENERGIES COMING UP OUT OF THERON, THE ROOM SHOOK WITH POWER UNCONTROLLED
THE RUINED BODY OF THERON WAS TAKEN UP TO THE INFIRMARY, WHERE DOCTORS ATTEMPTED TO DO WHAT THEY COULD. BUT ALL THEIR ELECTRONIC EQUIPMENT WAS OVERLOADED BY ELECTRIC STATIC FROM THERON'S ENERGY FIELD.
MY WRISTWATCH IS RUNNING FAST.
NO, LORD THERON IS WARPING TIME
A WEEK PASSED, THERON JUST LAID THERE. EVERYONE WAS AFRAID, FOR THE WHOLE VILLA SHOOK ALWAYS....
WHY DID YOU DO IT ULFA?
I'M SORRY. HE HAS TO LEARN.
LOOK, THERON, I WON'T SAY I'M YOUR FRIEND, BUT YOU MAY WELL BE MY SON, AND YOU ARE MY RESPONSIBILITY TO THE GREAT SATANIC PLAN. I'M GOING TO HELP YOU.
EVERYONE ELSE LEAVE THIS ROOM.
ANTON WAS ALONE WITH THERON ALL NIGHT, AND NONE OF US WERE ALLOWED TO WITNESS WHAT HE DID...
LOOK! THE DOOR'S OPENING!
—BUT THE NEXT DAY-

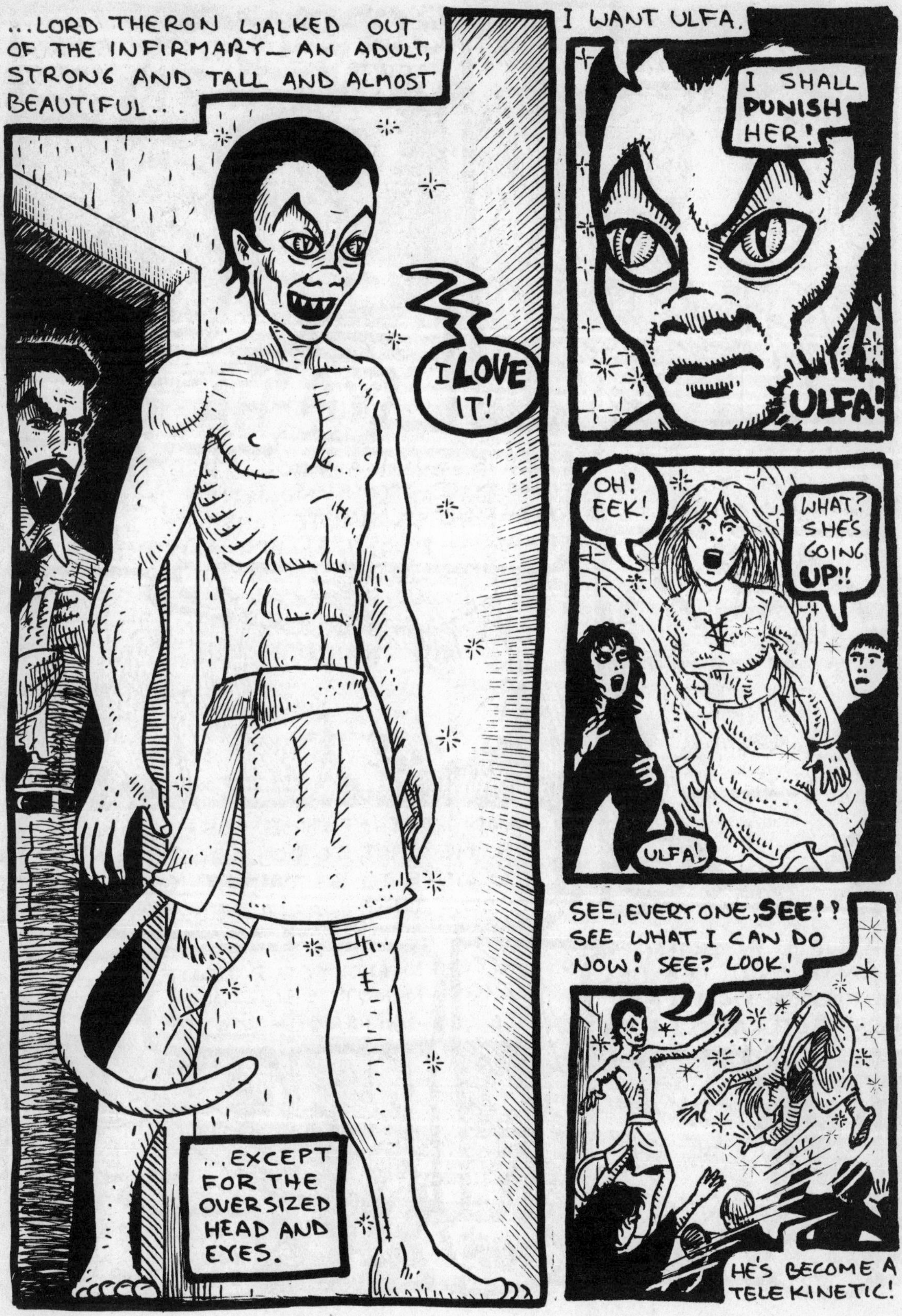
...LORD THERON WALKED OUT OF THE INFIRMARY—AN ADULT, STRONG AND TALL AND ALMOST BEAUTIFUL...
I LOVE IT!
...EXCEPT FOR THE OVERSIZED HEAD AND EYES.
I WANT ULFA.
I SHALL PUNISH HER!
ULFA!
OH! EEK!
WHAT? SHE'S GOING UP!!
ULFA!
SEE, EVERYONE, SEE!! SEE WHAT I CAN DO NOW! SEE? LOOK!
HE'S BECOME A TELEKINETIC!

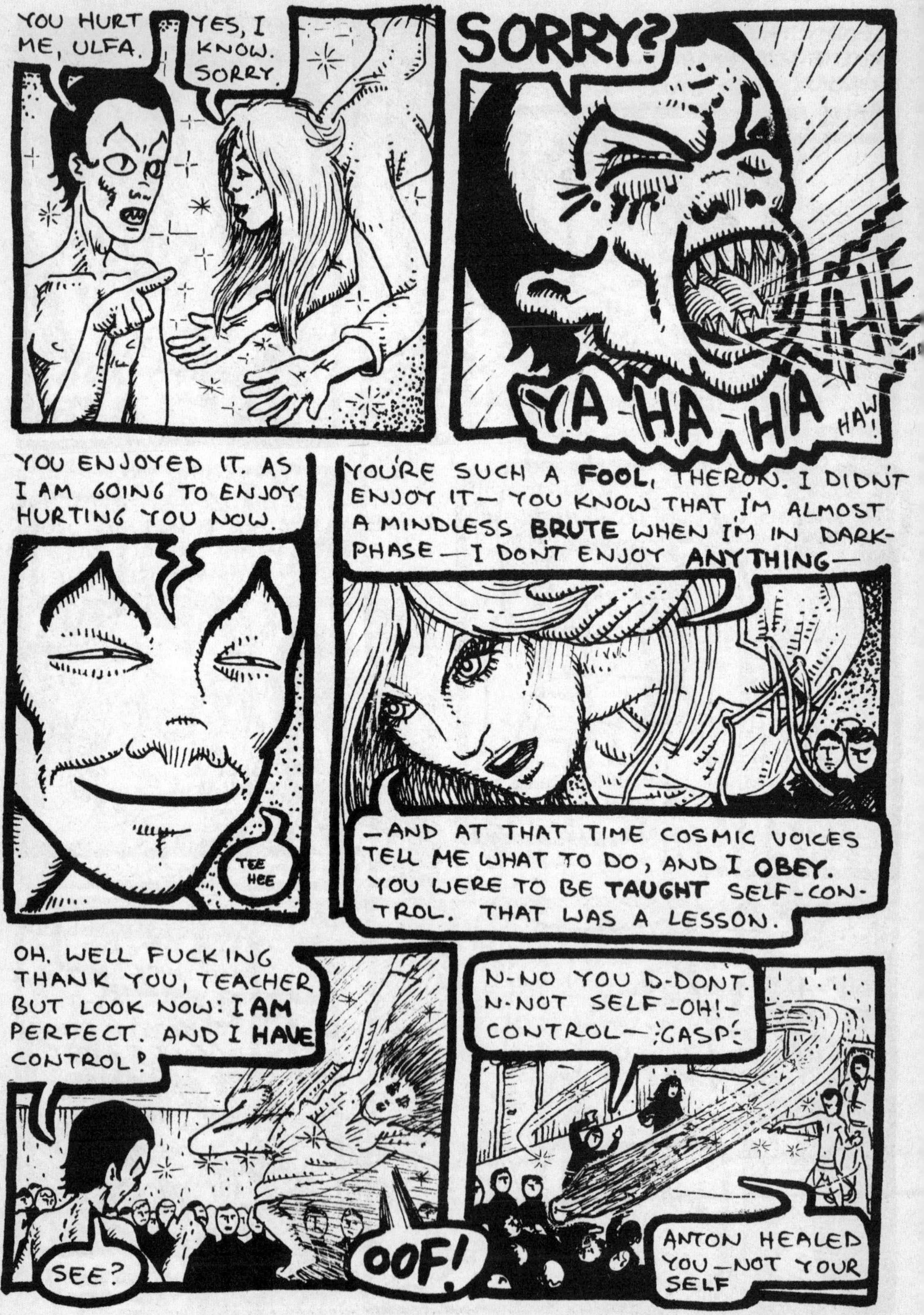
YOU HURT ME, ULFA.
YES, I KNOW. SORRY.
SORRY?
HEE
YA HA HA HA
HAW!
YOU ENJOYED IT. AS I AM GOING TO ENJOY HURTING YOU NOW.
TEE HEE
YOU'RE SUCH A FOOL, THERON. I DIDN'T ENJOY IT— YOU KNOW THAT I'M ALMOST A MINDLESS BRUTE WHEN I'M IN DARK-PHASE—I DON'T ENJOY ANYTHING—
—AND AT THAT TIME COSMIC VOICES TELL ME WHAT TO DO, AND I OBEY. YOU WERE TO BE TAUGHT SELF-CONTROL. THAT WAS A LESSON.
OH. WELL FUCKING THANK YOU, TEACHER BUT LOOK NOW: I AM PERFECT. AND I HAVE CONTROL!
SEE?
OOF!
N-NO YOU D-DON'T. N-NOT SELF-OH!- CONTROL— GASP
ANTON HEALED YOU—NOT YOUR SELF

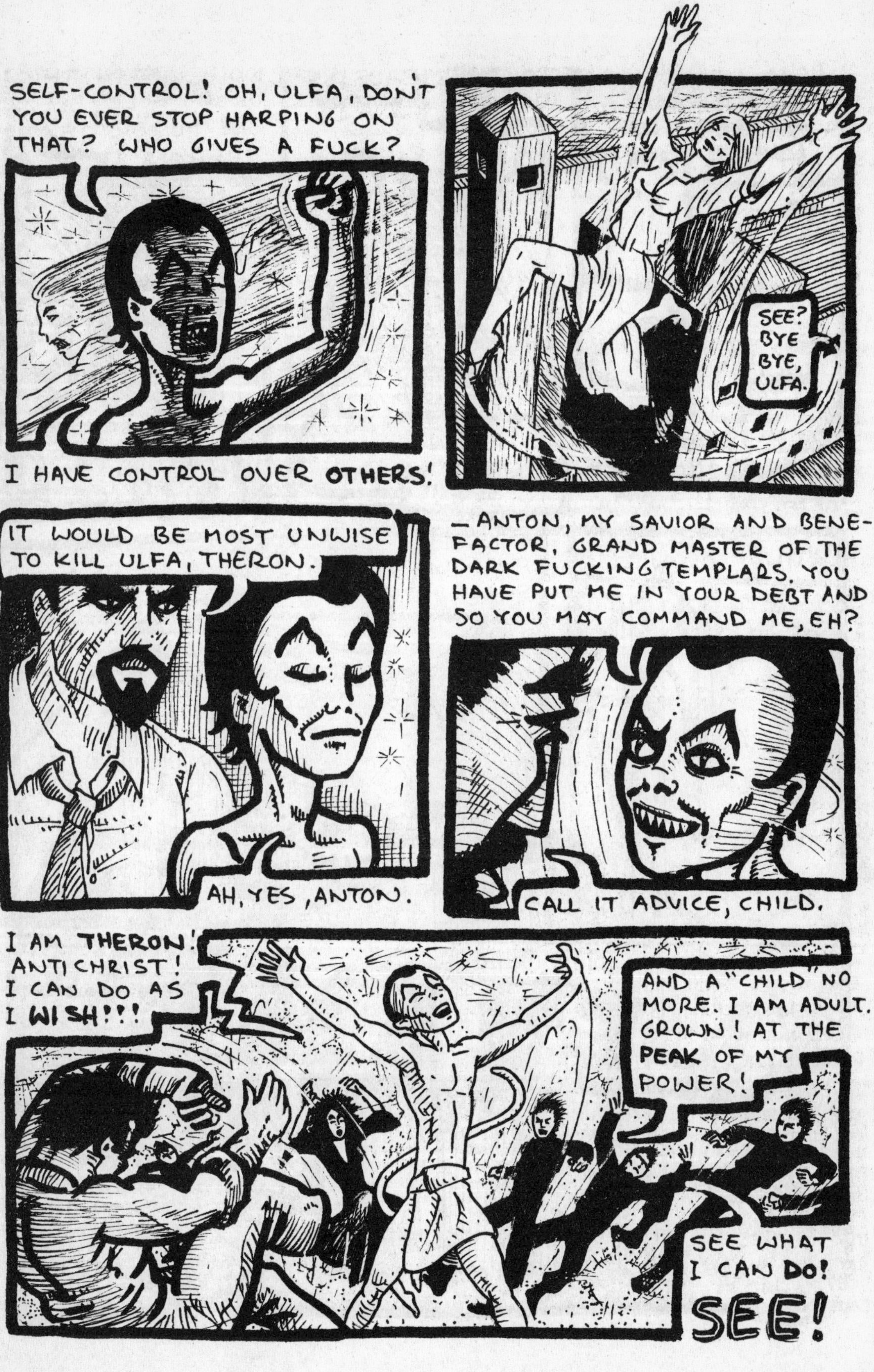
SELF-CONTROL! OH, ULFA, DON'T YOU EVER STOP HARPING ON THAT? WHO GIVES A FUCK?
I HAVE CONTROL OVER OTHERS!
SEE? BYE BYE, ULFA.
IT WOULD BE MOST UNWISE TO KILL ULFA, THERON.
AH, YES, ANTON.
-ANTON, MY SAVIOR AND BENEFACTOR, GRAND MASTER OF THE DARK FUCKING TEMPLARS. YOU HAVE PUT ME IN YOUR DEBT AND SO YOU MAY COMMAND ME, EH?
CALL IT ADVICE, CHILD.
I AM THERON! ANTICHRIST! I CAN DO AS I WISH!!!
AND A "CHILD" NO MORE. I AM ADULT. GROWN! AT THE PEAK OF MY POWER!
SEE WHAT I CAN DO!
SEE!

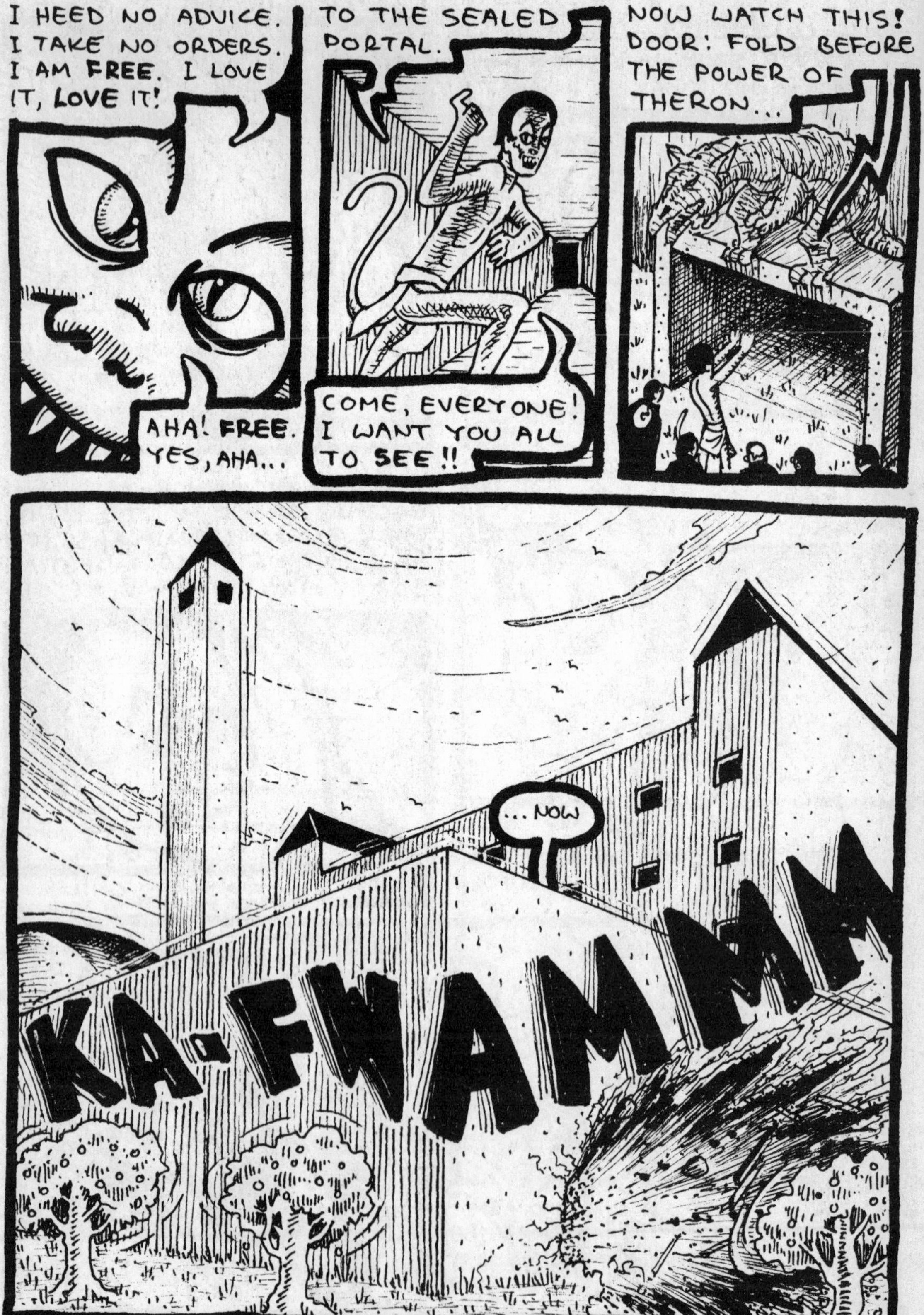

I HEED NO ADVICE. I TAKE NO ORDERS. I AM FREE. I LOVE IT, LOVE IT!
AHA! FREE. YES, AHA...
TO THE SEALED PORTAL.
COME, EVERYONE! I WANT YOU ALL TO SEE!!
NOW WATCH THIS! DOOR: FOLD BEFORE THE POWER OF THERON...
...NOW
KA-FWAMMM

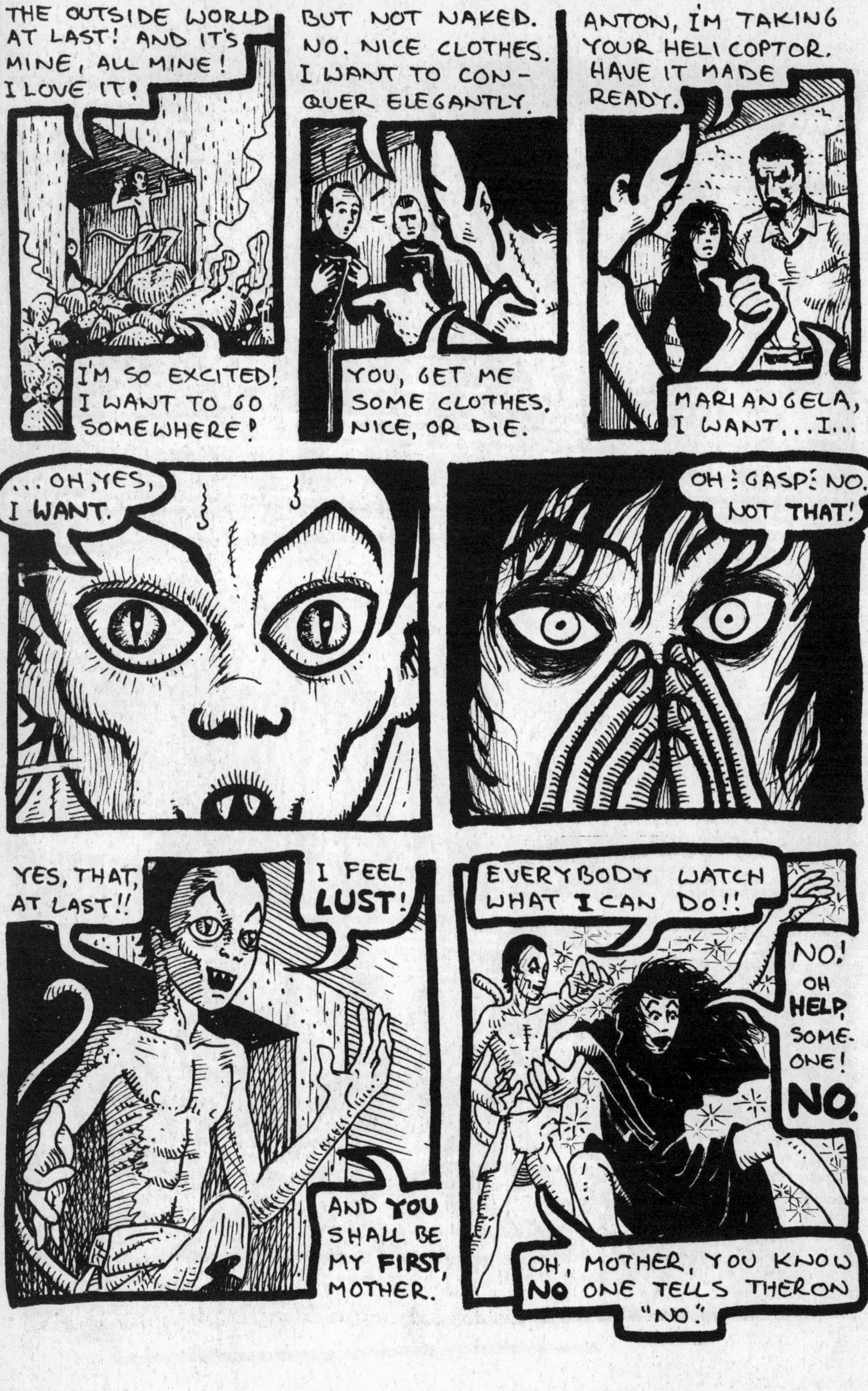
THE OUTSIDE WORLD AT LAST! AND IT'S MINE, ALL MINE! I LOVE IT!
I'M SO EXCITED! I WANT TO GO SOMEWHERE!
BUT NOT NAKED. NO. NICE CLOTHES. I WANT TO CON-QUER ELEGANTLY.
YOU, GET ME SOME CLOTHES. NICE, OR DIE.
ANTON, I'M TAKING YOUR HELICOPTOR. HAVE IT MADE READY.
MARIANGELA, I WANT...I...
...OH, YES, I WANT.
OH :GASP: NO. NOT THAT!
YES, THAT, AT LAST!!
I FEEL LUST!
AND YOU SHALL BE MY FIRST, MOTHER.
EVERYBODY WATCH WHAT I CAN DO!!
NO! OH HELP, SOME-ONE! NO.
OH, MOTHER, YOU KNOW NO ONE TELLS THERON "NO."

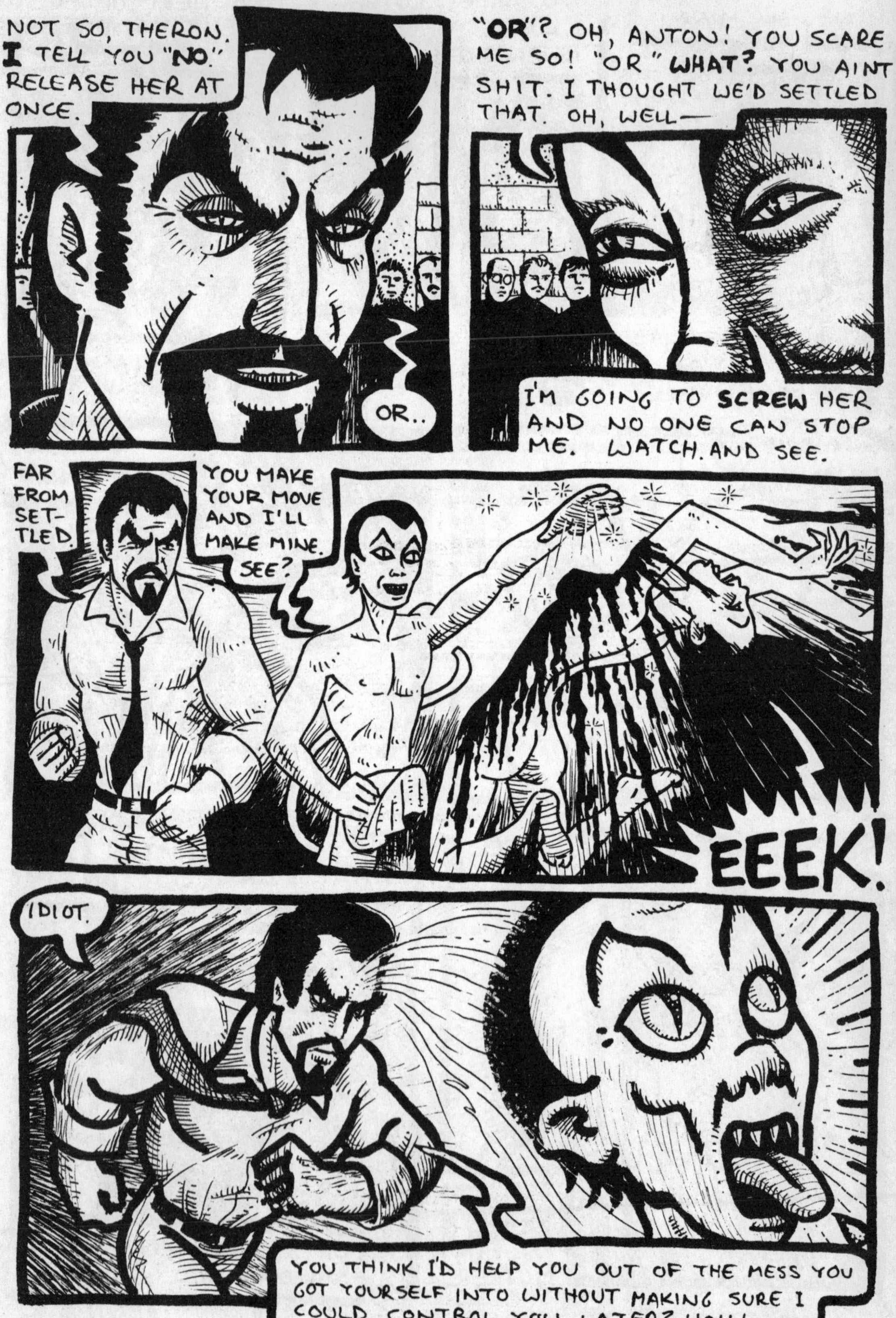
NOT SO, THERON. I TELL YOU "NO." RELEASE HER AT ONCE.
OR..
"OR"? OH, ANTON! YOU SCARE ME SO! "OR" WHAT? YOU AINT SHIT. I THOUGHT WE'D SETTLED THAT. OH, WELL—
I'M GOING TO SCREW HER AND NO ONE CAN STOP ME. WATCH. AND SEE.
FAR FROM SET-TLED.
YOU MAKE YOUR MOVE AND I'LL MAKE MINE. SEE?
EEEK!
IDIOT.
YOU THINK I'D HELP YOU OUT OF THE MESS YOU GOT YOURSELF INTO WITHOUT MAKING SURE I COULD CONTROL YOU LATER? HAH!

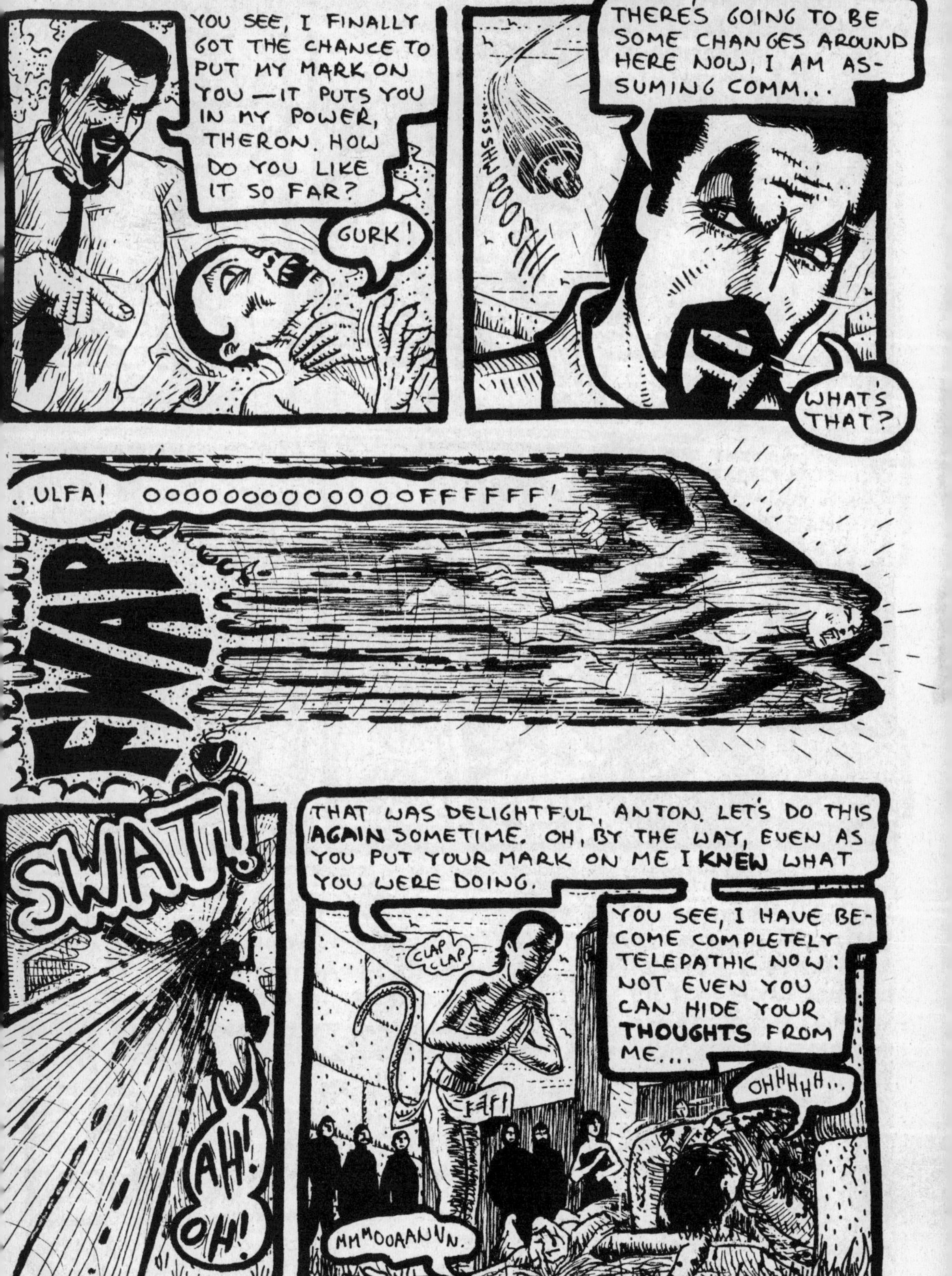
YOU SEE, I FINALLY GOT THE CHANCE TO PUT MY MARK ON YOU—IT PUTS YOU IN MY POWER, THERON. HOW DO YOU LIKE IT SO FAR?
GURK!
THERE'S GOING TO BE SOME CHANGES AROUND HERE NOW, I AM ASSUMING COMM...
SSSSHHWOOOSH!!
WHAT'S THAT?
...ULFA! OOOOOOOOOOOOOOFFFFFF!
FWAP
SWAT!
AH! OH!
THAT WAS DELIGHTFUL, ANTON. LET'S DO THIS **AGAIN** SOMETIME. OH, BY THE WAY, EVEN AS YOU PUT YOUR MARK ON ME I **KNEW** WHAT YOU WERE DOING.
CLAP CLAP
YOU SEE, I HAVE BECOME COMPLETELY TELEPATHIC NOW: NOT EVEN YOU CAN HIDE YOUR **THOUGHTS** FROM ME...
OHHHHH...
MMMOOAANNN.

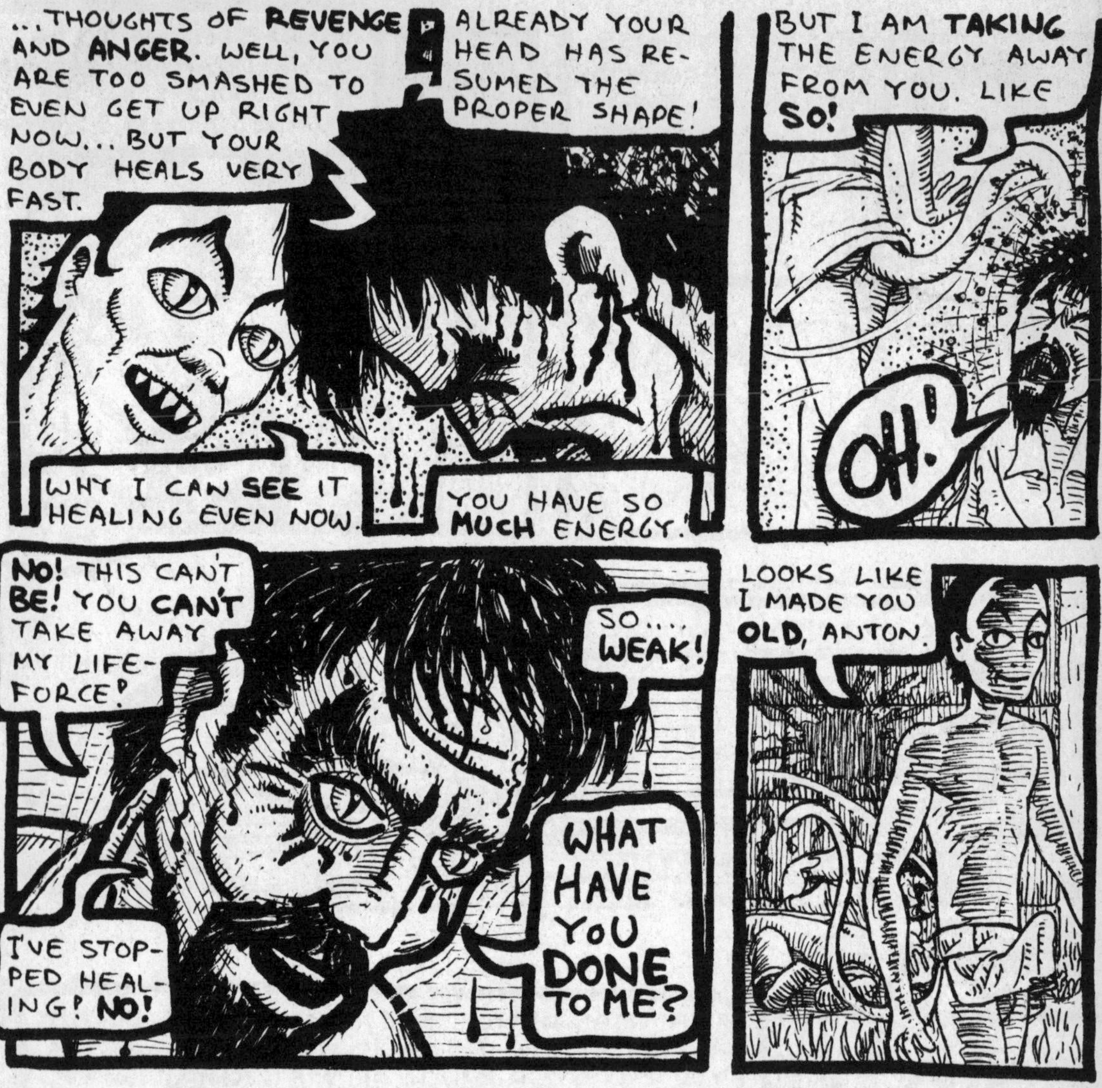
...THOUGHTS OF REVENGE AND ANGER. WELL, YOU ARE TOO SMASHED TO EVEN GET UP RIGHT NOW... BUT YOUR BODY HEALS VERY FAST.
ALREADY YOUR HEAD HAS RESUMED THE PROPER SHAPE!
WHY I CAN SEE IT HEALING EVEN NOW.
YOU HAVE SO MUCH ENERGY.
BUT I AM TAKING THE ENERGY AWAY FROM YOU. LIKE SO!
OH!
NO! THIS CAN'T BE! YOU CAN'T TAKE AWAY MY LIFE-FORCE!
SO.... WEAK!
WHAT HAVE YOU DONE TO ME?
I'VE STOPPED HEALING! NO!
LOOKS LIKE I MADE YOU OLD, ANTON.

WOW—"WHO IS LIKE UNTO THE BEAST? WHO IS ABLE TO MAKE WAR WITH HIM?" REV. 13:4 (THOUGHT I'D BETTER TOSS IN A BIBLICAL QUOTATION TO GIVE THIS COMIC BOOK A TOUCH OF LITERATE CREDIBILITY, SYMBOLIC MEANING, ETC.) ANYWAY, LOOKS LIKE ANTON AND ULFA LOSE THIS ROUND. AND WHAT ABOUT POOR MARIANGELA? HOW CAN THIS NASTY SUPERBRAT BECOME OUR GOOD-KID GOOD GUY TAZIO? —Y'KNOW, FOLX, I'M NOT SURE, I THOUGHT THIS THERON EPISODE WOULD JUST BE A LITTLE SIDE-STORY, BUT THAT'S NOT WHAT'S HAPPENING. WELL, LET'S RIDE IT OUT AND SEE WHAT IS THE TRUE STORY OF **ARMAGEDDONQUEST**

Ronald Russell Roach
August 15, 1985

# ronald russell roach timeline

• **6 Dec `41** • Ronald Russell Roach is born in Seattle, WA. Pearl Harbor is bombed the next day.

• **1952** • At the age of 10, 3R becomes an Edgar Rice Burroughs freak, and learns how to really tell stories.

• **1953** • 3R's father becomes deeply involved in religion.

• **1956 to 1959** • In high school, 3R becomes interested in Gustave Dore's Bible illustrations, an early influence on Armageddonquest. 3R writes and draws his first comic stories: a series of 2-page "to be continued" jokes concerning The Man With No Face.

• **1959** • 3R graduates from Shoreline High School in Seattle.

• **1961** • 3R begins at Western Washington State College in Bellingham, majoring in English literature. He becomes interested in the Book of Revelations. His Junior year he leaves for California.

• **1962** • 3R draws a series of "Son of Satan" pictures while living in Berkeley. These were the first incarnations of Tazio.

• **June, 1964** • 3R is drafted into the Army and stationed in Fulda, Germany. He is assigned to PIO and produces the base newspaper.

• **June, 1966** • 3R receives an overseas discharge from the Army and goes on the road. Spends time in several European cities (including Copenhagen), and travels around Africa for seven months.

• **1967** • 3R gets a summer job in Copenhagen, where he meets Marianne (his future wife). He then travels to India.

• **1968** • 3R travels to Katmandu, Ceylon, returns to Europe at a time of student revolution.

• **1969** • Completely broke, 3R returns to the States and gets a job, earning just enough to travel to Mexico and Central America for half a year.

• **1970** • 3R returns to the USA again, to a commune in Seattle, then back to college at Western Washington.

• **1971** • 3R writes a series of "Son of Satan" Tazio stories for creative writing classes, including one 12-page comic book on mimeograph paper.

• **1972** • 3R sends a copy of the "Son of Satan" comic book to Marvel Comics. Six months later Marvel Comics begins publishing a series also called Son of Satan, based on similar characters and situations. 3R is not involved.

• **1972** • 3R makes several mimeo comics for creative writing classes, since they were so well received the first time around. "Captain Psychic Phenomena," a funny series, and "Alex Comix," a continuation of Anthony Burgess' A Clockwork Orange.

• **1972** • 3R's first published comic story, "Space Bum," appears in Spaced Out, published by Print Mint.

• **1973** • 3R's second "Space Bum" story was a more professional production, but Print Mint never produced a second Spaced Out comic, so they sent it back to 3R's father's address. His father opens the package, is offended by 3R's "hippy humor," and burns the original pages. No copies remain.

• **1974** • 3R graduates from Western Washington with a bachelor's degree in English and art.

• **1974 to 1975** • 3R goes on the road again, spending nine months in Mexico and South America. He returns to the States with no money, "but at least I had a pretty good case of hepatitis."

• 1976 • 3R returns to Western Washington to get a Secondary Teaching Certificate.

• 1977 • Schools in a recession, providing no teaching jobs. 3R works as a carpenter, living in the woods outside Monroe, Washington.

• 1978 • 3R returns to Mexico and stays with friends in San Christobal, intending to write "*The Great Son of Satan novel,*" ends up writing a song a day instead.

• 1979 • 3R writes a first draft for "the great Sasquatch novel," *Adam Out of Eden.*

• 1980 • 3R writes and draws a Sasquatch comic series from the first draft, comprised of five stories and 200 pages.

• Sept, `80 to Jan, `81 • 3R writes and draws *Phæria* fairy tale series, consisting of 200 pages.

• March, `81 • 3R writes and draws *Heroes of Elveland*, a 75-page continuation of Phæria, while staying with friends in Mexico City.

• May to Dec, `81 • 3R writes and draws *Agents of the Chalice*, which chronicles the relationship between the angel Æthyr and the devil Malignan.

• 1981 • Carpentry in a recession, providing no jobs. 3R works as a prison guard at Washington State Reformatory. "Everybody in Monroe ends up working there."

• Jan, `82 • 3R writes and draws *Slammer Comix*, a tie-in to the Armageddonquest saga, which introduces Immanuel, the seventeenth incarnation of Christ.

• Nov to Dec, `82 • 3R writes and draws *Guard Comics*, introducing the super-human prison guard Officer Gargantua and the shamanistic Tattoo Master.

• 1983 to 1984 • 3R writes and draws *The Prison and the Planet*, a 200-page graphic novel tied directly into the *Armageddonquest* saga. It contains Gargantua, Immanuel, and the first appearance of Tazio as he was meant to be.

• March, `84 • 3R begins writing and drawing *Armageddonquest.*

• Sept, `84 • 3R quits his prison job to travel around the world. He arrives in Denmark to visit his old girlfriend Marianne and her 5-year-old son, Mads. He continues writing and drawing *Armageddonquest.*

• 1985 • 3R travels to Southeast Asia to visit his brother Owen, then returns to Copenhagen. He, Marianne and Mads hitchhike through Europe for several months.

• 1986 • 3R gets a job as a moving man. He and Marianne get married, and 3R continues to write and draw *Armageddonquest.*

• 1989 to 1992 • The *Armageddonquest* "crunch time." 3R works six months, then takes two months off to draw. When he runs out of money, he works another six months, then takes two months off to draw, etc.

• 9 Dec, `92 • 3R finishes *Armageddonquest.*

• Feb, `94 • Starhead Comix publishes *Armageddonquest #1.*

• Feb, `94 • Starhead Comix publishes *Armageddonquest #2.* Production halts. Sirius Publisher Robb Horan first reads the Starhead editions of *Armageddonquest.*

• June, `97 • Sirius publishes *Armageddonquest* Vol. 1.

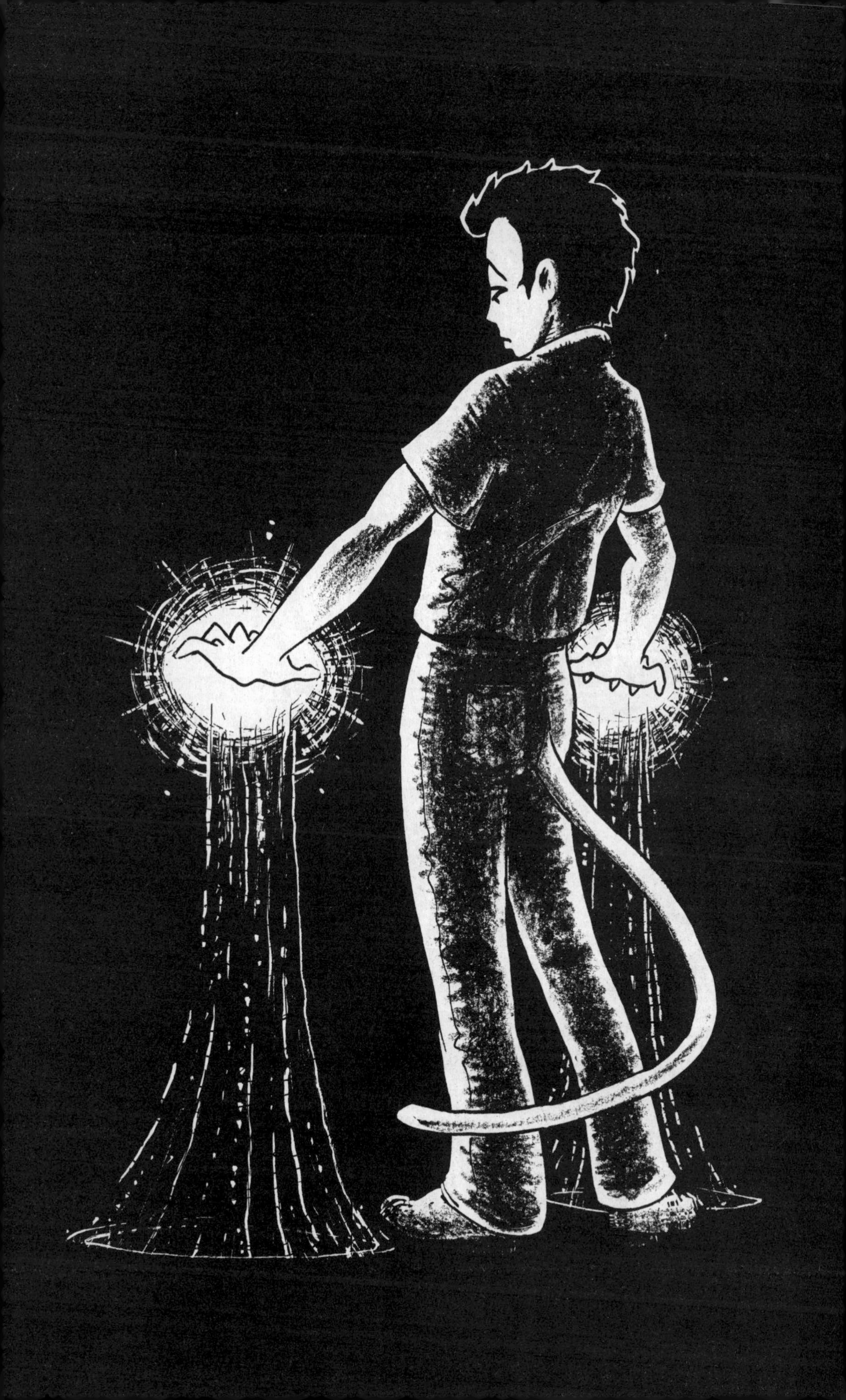

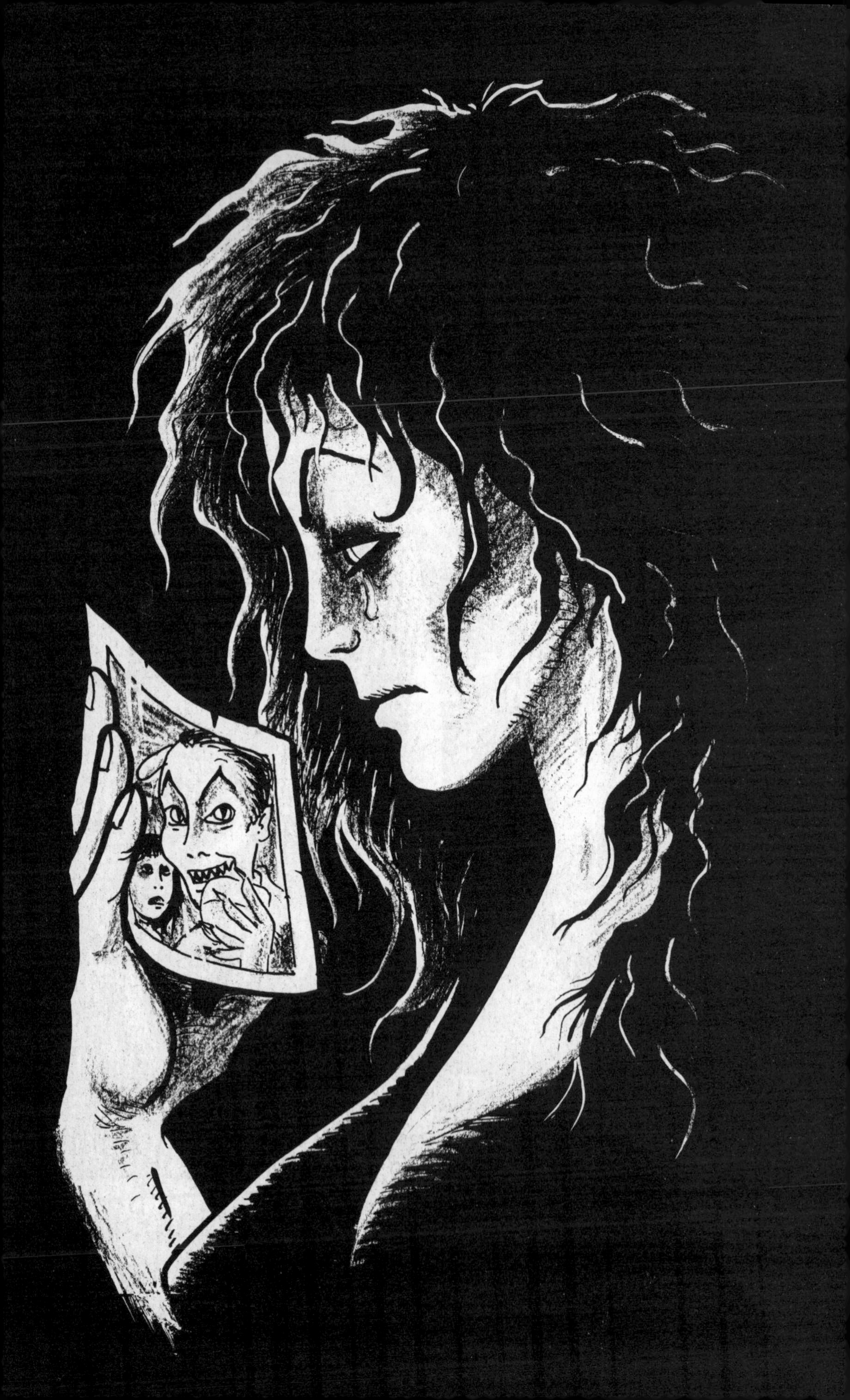

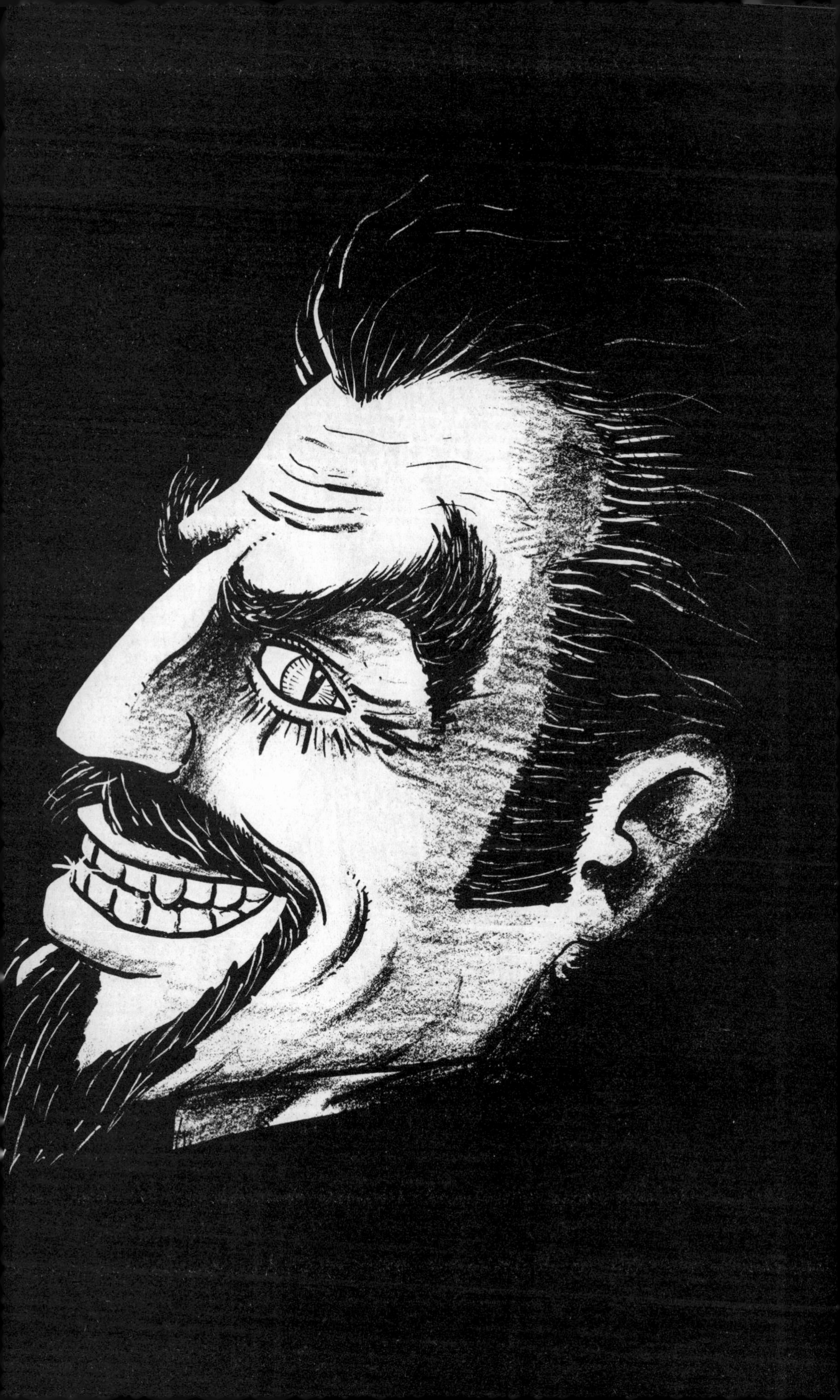

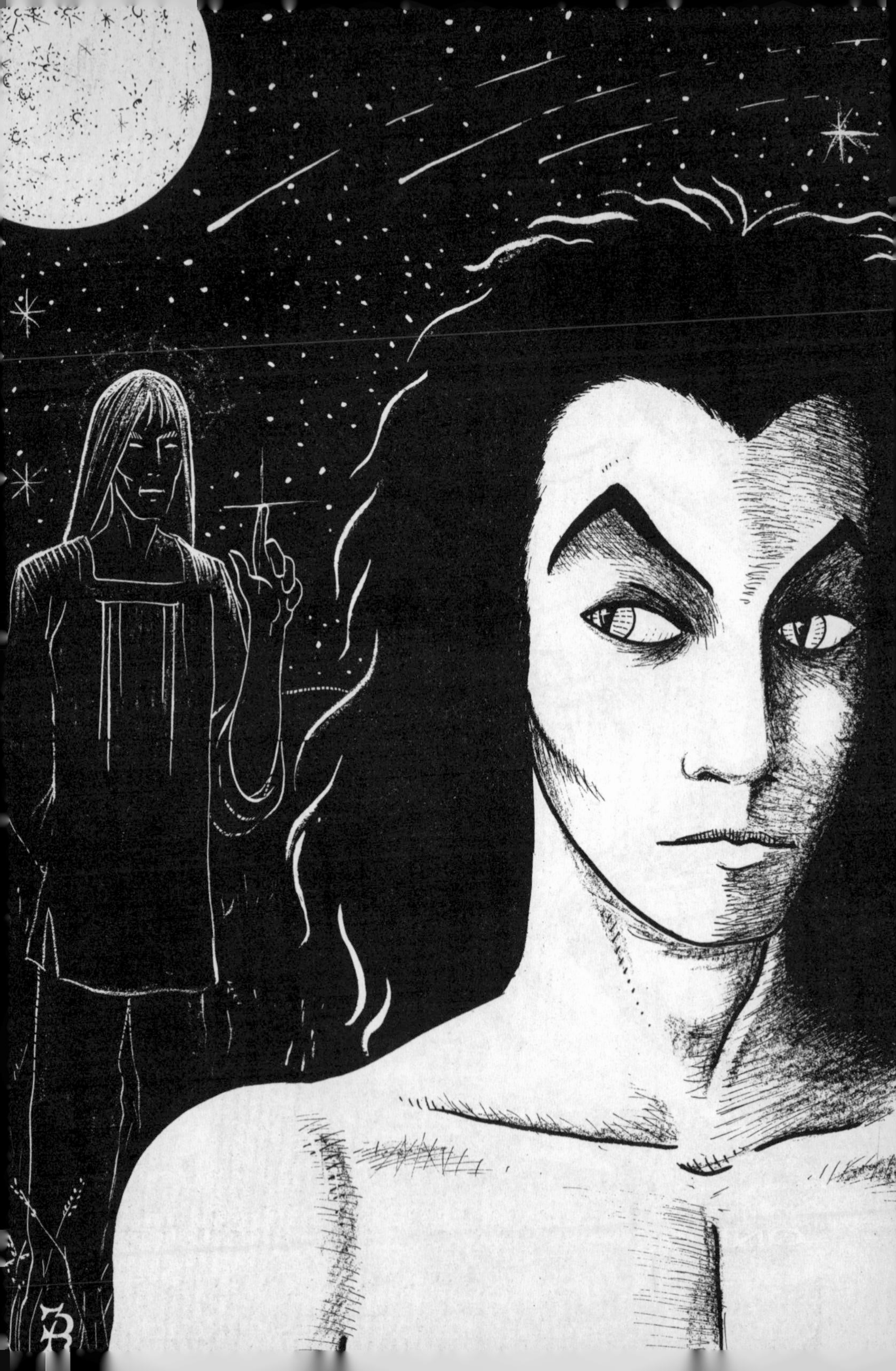

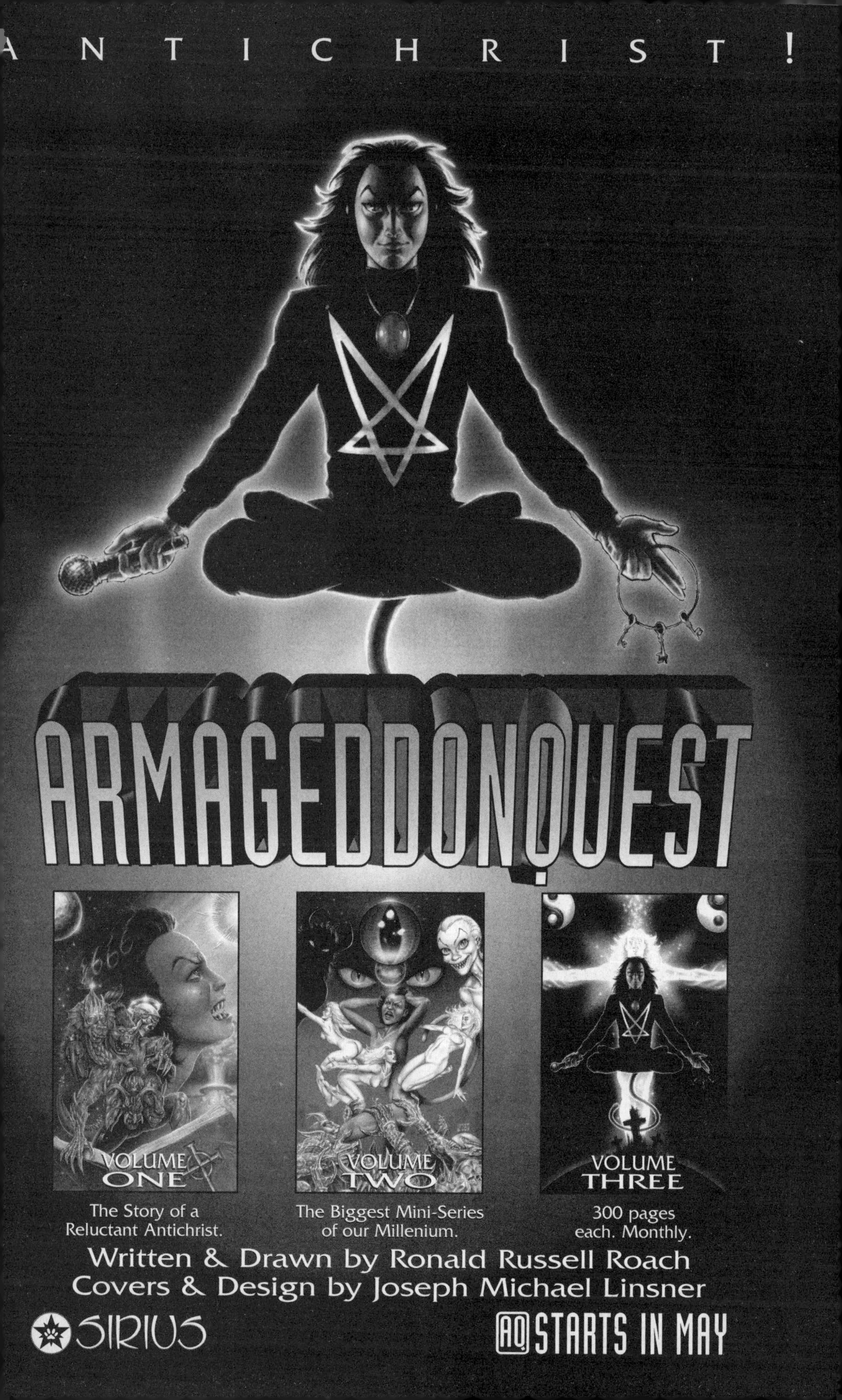

ANTICHRIST!
ARMAGEDDONQUEST
VOLUME ONE
VOLUME TWO
VOLUME THREE
The Story of a Reluctant Antichrist.
The Biggest Mini-Series of our Millenium.
300 pages each. Monthly.
Written & Drawn by Ronald Russell Roach
Covers & Design by Joseph Michael Linsner
SIRIUS
AQ STARTS IN MAY